Our Race against Time

This book puts all of Our clocks right,

it makes all of Our calendars look dated,

breaks all of Our rules, weights & measures

and puts Our World right - in one easy lesson.

Question Time

What is the age of Our Planet Earth?

What is the orbit of Our Planet Earth?

What is the spin of Our Planet Earth?

What is the girth of Our Planet Earth?

What are moonths, months and sunths?

Why are there 12 months in a year?

Why are there 12 signs in a zodiac?

Why are there 360 degrees in a circle?

Why are there 360 + 5 or 6 days in a year?

Why are there 24 hours, 60 minutes, 60 seconds?

Why are there 7 days in a week?

When does the year begin?

When does the moonth begin?

When does the week begin?

When does the day begin?

Why are there many ages, dates and times?

Why are there many time zones and summer times?

Why not use one chronology, calendar and clock?

Why are there many rules, weights & measures?

Why not use one global-digital-decimal system?

Why not use The Worldwide System?

The Worldwide System

Time, Space and Life on Earth

MICHAEL PINDER

 New Generation Publishing

A catalogue edition of this book is
available from the British Library

Dewey Decimal Classification: Time 529

General Classification: Utopias

Alternative Classifications:
History, Geography, Science, Technology, Philosophy,
Theology, Sociology, Economics, Ecology, Humanity,
Management, Politics, Current Affairs, Futurology

ISBN 978-1-78507-525-4

www.worldwidesystem.co.uk

Published by

New Generation Publishing
175-185 Gray's Inn Road
London
WC1X 8UE

www.newgeneration-publishing.com

Contents

Division

Half of this publication is all about the measurement of Time and Space. The other half is all about the enlightenment, management, government, enchantment and enactment of Time and Space on Our Planet Earth. It is written in a sequence of essays, which could be read in any order. Every essay exactly fits every page and every sentence fits every line. This may be the first book to be written, edited and typeset in this way.

Definition

It is necessary at the outset to define some new terms used in this book.
These do not fit into currently accepted standards because the author
is proposing a completely new system for measuring Time and Space.
He has also pioneered an innovative system of fully justified typescript.
Every sentence begins on a new line and ends at the right hand margin.
This new system makes this particular book clearer and easier to read.
When writing about ancient deities he usually names them in *italics*.
He also uses *italics* for book, film and programme titles, the names of
firms and products, foreign words and new ones that he has devised.
Whilst this book is written in English, he hopes that there will be many
translations but the words he has devised will be used in all languages.

The English language is still being developed and does not make enough
distinction between the larger word: Time and the smaller word: time,
which should be quite different words to avoid any verbal confusion.
Throughout this book: Time, means any age, date and time system.
For example: Chinese Time, Egyptian Time, Cosmic Time, Atomic Time.
Publishers have tended, over recent years, to use lower case letters for:
earth, sun and moon whereas the author prefers: Earth, Sun and Moon.
Some print: heaven and hell but the author prefers: Heaven and Hell.
These are all real or imaginary places and so they should have capitals.
We use a capital I for the first person singular; the author uses capitals
for: Us, We, Our, when referring to Mankind, because he is a Humanist.
He regards Pagans as equal to Christians so gives them a capital letter.

The term: day means: a mean Solar day, unless otherwise specified.
The term: year means: a mean Solar year, unless otherwise specified.
The term: sunth means: a Solar wind cycle of 28 mean Solar days.
The term: moonth means: a Lunar phase cycle of 29.5 mean Solar days.
The term: month means: a longer Man-made period used in a calendar.
The term: week means: a shorter Man-made period used in a calendar.
The term: millennium is any period of one thousand mean Solar years.
The term: Millennium is the beginning or the end of such a period.
The letters BC or AD are used to show ages in the *Anno Domini* system.
These ages are also considered by most secular states to be BCE or ACE
meaning: Before or After the Common Era - the latter is often omitted.
The author is proposing a new global chronological system based upon
the age of Our Planet Earth, the age of Our Civilization and Our Era.
This new age, date, time and zone system is identified by the suffix **WT**.
The term: **Worldwide Time** is used to describe the author's system for:
global age, digital date, decimal time and a single time zone.
The term: **Worldwide Space** is used to describe the author's system for:
distance, direction, angle, length, area, volume and weight.
The term: **Worldwide System** is used to describe the author's system for:
measuring, managing and governing everything upon Our Planet Earth.

Dedication

This hypothesis, in a series of essays, is dedicated to the many millions of citizens, upon Our Planet Earth, who have been, are still being or are soon destined to be: disadvantaged, displaced, injured, maimed or even killed because their leaders could not agree on the same system for measuring, managing and governing Time and Space.

Solution

Unemployment is a huge problem throughout Our Planet. Over a billion of its citizens are still too young to work. Over a billion of its citizens are now too old to work. Over a billion are caring for the young, the old, the sick. Over a billion are capable of working but have no jobs. Over two billion have jobs but are now working to death. We have the solution on Our hands and within Our grasp. We must share most jobs on a five day-on/five day-off basis. The Worldwide System could help Us build One Wide World.

Salvation

We can save Our Planet and Our Species
if We can share Our Time and Our Space.

Imagination

Imagine there's no Heaven
It's easy if you try
No Hell below Us
Above Us only Sky
Imagine all the people
Living for today...

Imagine there's no countries
It isn't hard to do
Nothing to kill or die for
And no religion too
Imagine all the people
Living Life in peace...

You may say I'm a dreamer
But I'm not the only one
I hope someday you'll join Us
And the World will be as One

Imagine no possessions
I wonder if you can
No need for greed or hunger
A brotherhood of Man
Imagine all the people
Sharing all the World...

You may say I'm a dreamer
But I'm not the only one
I hope someday you'll join Us
And the World will live as One

John Winston Lennon (1940-1980 AD)

One Brain

My birth certificate shows that I was born in London at the start of WW2.
My age, date, time of birth were based upon the Roman-Catholic system.
My popular forename means: I was named after a saint and archangel.
My vocational surname means: my ancestors impounded stray animals.
My passport number identifies me as: English, British and European.
My identity will soon change when the UK devolves and leaves the EU.
My birth sign was thought to be in Pisces but was really in Aquarius.
As the war ended I was sent to school and was soon being brainwashed.
They taught me this alphabet and about the place numbering system.
They taught me multiplication tables and to read and write English.
They taught me the Imperial System and pounds, shillings and pence.
They taught me the Anglican religion's chronology, calendar and clock.
Elsewhere: kids were given different names, taught different languages,
different scripts, different measurement systems, different currencies,
different religions with their different chronologies, calendars and clocks.
These make Us seem different when We all have ten digits to count on.

Our left cerebral hemispheres are for language, maths and reasoning.
Our right cerebral hemispheres are for emotion, recognition and music.
Our brains are not fully developed until We reach the age of twenty-one.
We were all brainwashed by our elders, teachers, preachers and leaders.
We had to trust them but as We grow older We learn to suspect them.
Our World is quite different from that of Our parents and grandparents.
We can phone anywhere and reach the opposite side of the globe in a day.
Many of Us have learned to use a new language, script, currency and
measurement system but We still use different ages, dates and times.
Memorising these systems is very hard but forgetting them is harder.
We must all try to use exactly the same system throughout Our Planet.
Otherwise, We will continue to fight, maim and kill each other - forever.

Digital computers have been rapidly developed during my own lifetime.
They all have memories that can be wiped clean and reprogrammed but
they are unable to think creative thoughts or to build better systems.
Their operating systems are based on a *BASIC* program with AD years,
Gregorian months, 7-day weeks, 24-hour, 60-minute, 60-second days.
The Internet and the Worldwide Web allow computers to communicate.
They no longer need their own memories, so they can be much simpler.
We could end-up with a gargantuan computer and billions of terminals.
We use billions of mobile phones incorporating ages, dates and times.
Our ultimate aim must be to use one language, one script, one system.
We will probably have to use this English language and this Latin script
but this does not mean that We have to use any other existing systems.
This comprehensive book suggests a more logical global-digital-decimal
measurement, management and government system for everyone to use.
Those who share their jobs must agree that two brains are better than one.

One Idea

All ideas start with one person, some spread quickly around the globe but others may take many years before they are adopted by everyone. Sadly, the cheapest, simplest and most obvious solutions are sometimes rejected for traditional reasons or because they are too early or too late. In order to make further progress We now need to reassess all of Our traditional practices and so it is now very timely, for numerous reasons, to reconsider and rebuild Time and Space: Our fundamental traditions.

When I was ten I had a Big Idea: Why not measure everything in tens? I did not know then that some ancient civilizations used the base of ten or that others had suggested that everything should be based on tens. All I wanted to do was to simplify the lists that We hang on Our walls and the gizmos that We strap on Our wrists, but I found that most people were extraordinarily sentimental about these everyday objects. In one day I devised my global-digital-decimal **Worldwide Time System**. Then I found that the Imperial and Metric systems were unsatisfactory and most people disliked one or the other, so I went back to basics. In one day I devised my global-digital-decimal **Worldwide Space System.** My Big Idea was also based upon the age, orbit, spin and girth of Earth. So, my rational but radical and revolutionary idea was based upon the number of digits on Our hands and the revolutions of Our Planet Earth.

The British revolution abolished the monarchy, aristocracy and theocracy but, after they were restored, science and technology began to flourish. Sir Christopher Wren suggested decimal coins and global-digital-decimal measurements, based upon the fixed length of a one second pendulum. Yet, it took the British over three centuries to adopt decimal coinage, the second is based upon a fraction and so it is not a decimal of a day and the period of a pendulum varies slightly with its global location. The industrial revolution started in Britain and led to the growth of the British Empire and the use of the Imperial System in all of its colonies. The French revolutionaries used a global-digital-decimal Metric System, based on an extrapolation of the surveyed length of the Paris Meridian, plus a revolutionary chronology, a digital calendar and a decimal clock. Yet, Napoleon Bonaparte soon abandoned this comprehensive system, after he crowned himself emperor and reverted to Roman-Catholicism. His solution to the political, social and economical problems in France was to conquer Europe and to make all citizens use the same system. Britain was a part of the European Union, which aimed to standardize everything from apples and pears to the same Time and Space system. However, it was run by faceless bureaucrats and useless politicians. The European Union adopted the Metric System and the decimal euro. Yet, Britain failed to fully metricate and to abandon the decimal pound. The electronic revolution started in Britain and has spread Worldwide. However, the Worldwide Web does not yet use: **The Worldwide System**.

One System

When I was at junior school I was always taught the Imperial System.
When I was at senior school I was always taught the International System.
When I was at college I was always taught the International System.
When I was at university I was always taught the Imperial System.
When I was an oil engineer I always worked in the American System.
When I was a designer I always worked in the International System.
When I was a navigator I always worked in the Navigational System.
When I was a lecturer I always taught in the International System.
But now I am an author and I have devised: **The Worldwide System.**

Every civilization and religion used a different Time and Space system.
This has caused inevitable bloody conflicts, wherever they overlapped.
French revolutionaries were free to use a decimal measurement system,
based upon logic not magic, maths not myths, physics not metaphysics.
Nevertheless, their revolutionary Time and Space System was not very
popular with the population, so Bonaparte reverted to the ancient regime.
Yet, he changed the territories he conquered to driving on the right side.
Napoleon III adopted their revolutionary Metric System in 1840 AD.
However, he failed to adopt their new age, digital date and decimal time.
Great Britain had not been conquered since 1066 AD and so it remained
independent of any new systems and is still very wary of any new ideas.
British politicians finally decided to metricate and they adopted most
of the International Metric System - although this is still far from perfect.
The ten-day week and ten-hour day have almost been forgotten now.
The seven-day week and the twenty-four hour day are taken for granted
and the second is the same size in every system - but they are all wrong!

Although length, area, volume and weight should have been metricated,
the UK is not fully converted, because it still uses the mile and the pint.
The population of the UK were taught to use the International System,
yet, due to political mismanagement, it took fifty years to become law.
The USA uses its own measurement system and its own paper sizes.
Its positive and negative electrical wires and port and starboard buoys
are oddly, perversely, dangerously, opposite from the rest of Our World.
It is supposed to be a secular federation of states and yet it still uses the
Roman-Catholic chronology, calendar and clock across eight time zones.
It readily adopts many complex systems such as: The Worldwide Web.
Will it ever adopt this simpler, secular system: **The Worldwide System?**

**The Worldwide Measurement System can be summarized as:
global age, digital date, decimal time with a single time zone;
plus global-digital-decimal angle, length, area, volume, mass,
substance, electrical current, light intensity and temperature;
plus navigational direction, distance, latitude and longitude.
It includes every other physical measurement - even wealth.**

One World

I can still remember the inauguration of The United Nations Organization, whose main aims were to stop further wars and to create One World. Yet, if We still want to unite all of Our nations and build One World, We must now dig very deep and begin again with its very foundations.

The bushman of the Kalahari knows his destiny better than most of Us. He follows in his father's footsteps, his few assets are all around him and the Sun and the Moon are his chronology, calendar and clock. He uses his body to measure everything and does not need any money. Whilst some people despise him for his simplicity and lack of property; he despises them for their complexity and dependence upon property. In Our efforts to civilize him We will probably destroy him (and her).

Civilization has brought Us to the point where We are grasping to find Our role in society: because We cannot follow in Our fathers' footsteps, We often have far too many possessions and Our ages, dates and times are incompatible with Our telephones, televisions, tablets and computers. We spend Our lives staring at their screens, which then ruin Our eyes, or slumped in stationary vehicles, breathing-in choking traffic fumes. We have polluted Our Planet by overpopulation, overproduction and waste. The rich are still getting richer; whilst the poor are still getting poorer. An increasing number of Us have no role in the post-modern World. The rate of failure is still increasing rapidly: with many oldsters thrown on the scrap-heap and many youngsters dropping-out of the system. We have not yet reached the point where robots will do everything and We will use all of Our Time for leisure but We have divided most of Our work into simple, repetitive jobs that often, literally, bore Us to death. We do not realize that the seven-day week is Man-made not *God*-given and that a ten-day working week would allow most jobs to be shared. The balance of work and leisure would lead to a redistribution of wealth. This simple, secular solution embodies both capitalism and socialism.

There are still some forty ages, dates and times in use around the globe. However, one global chronology, one digital calendar, one decimal clock, and one time zone may, sooner or later, help Us to build One World. The Atomic second is now the global standard, however the Civic second is still an eighty-six-thousand-four-hundredth part of a mean Solar day. The metre, litre and kilogram are used throughout most of the globe but they are arbitrary units that are not based upon anatomy nor geodesy. Land, sea and air distances are now based upon three different systems. A logical measurement system can be based on anatomy and geodesy. One millionth of a degree of longitude is the width of the average hand. **The Worldwide System** is based on the age, orbit, spin and girth of Earth, the linear number ten and the circular number three hundred and sixty. We can have Our Time, Our Space and Our World in and on Our hands.

One Book

One Time

One Time + One Space + One Script + One Language = One World

One Chronology + One Calendar + One Clock + One Zone = One Time

New Chronology + New Calendar + New Clock + New Zone = New Era

One Space

```
        •

      •   •

    •   •   •

  •   •   •   •
```

Pythagoras realized that Our Planet Earth is a sphere.
He thought that numbers controlled the Universe.
He considered this tetractys to be special.
Ten is the king of all the numbers.
The base of ten is Universal.
The ultimate solution is:
global-digital-decimal.

One Life

You only have one Life so do not spend all of it working.

One Job

One job needs two, four, six or eight workers.

One God

God = Space, Time and Life on Earth.

One Book

Everyone has one book in them.

Part One

Explanation

Time, Space, Life and the Solar System

"What then is Time? If no one asks me, I know.
If someone asks me to explain, I know not."

Augustine of Hippo (354-430 AD) *The City of God*

Clean Sheet

If We could begin again with a clean sheet of paper,
We could restart Our Human Race.

The Beginning of Time

Our World is rapidly becoming a global village but it may take another generation before We all use the same system and the best way to do this is to begin again, at square zero, with a clean sheet of paper or hard disc. Time can only flow in one direction, like a river, from beginning to end. The river of DNA flowing through Our generations ensures that We all have ten digits upon Our hands, several of Our ancient civilizations measured everything in tens and this global-digital-decimal number ten could solve many chronic problems throughout Our post-modern World. Many of these are caused by using different measurement, management and government systems, yet, We could use one comprehensive system.

We have devised ten different kinds of Time for many different purposes. Some of these are Natural, others are Man-made but none are *God*-given. Cosmic Time is based upon Natural cycles throughout the Universe. Atomic Time is based upon Natural cycles within every miniscule atom. Geotic Time is based upon Natural cycles within Our Planet Earth. Bionic Time is based upon Natural cycles within every form of Life. Humanic Time is based upon Man-made progress of Our Human Race. Mystic Time is based upon Man-made beliefs and liturgies of religion. Organic Time is based upon Man-made patterns and disciplines of work. Civic Time is based upon Man-made laws, by-laws, rules and regulations. Olympic Time is based upon Man-made times and speeds in most sports. Music Time is based upon Natural and Man-made sounds and rhythms. These ten kinds of Time are further explained in the following essays.

We now use four different Space systems, which need to be rationalized. Instead of the Imperial, American, International and Navigation systems, which have numerous faults, We need one global-digital-decimal system. Most of the earlier systems were based on non-standard Human anatomy. Most of the later systems were based upon the size of Our Planet Earth. The earlier ones were based upon fractions; the later ones on decimals. We have now arrived at an arbitrary system based upon light-waves. However, its base unit is not a handy size and it does not fit Our Planet. We now need one system based upon an accurate survey of the Equator, the approximate width of Our hands and a fixed number of light-waves.

We must all use one system of measurements around Our Planet Earth, based upon its age, orbit, spin, girth and the digital-decimal number ten. We must all use the same chronology, calendar, clock and time zone; the same directions, distances, angles, dimensions, volumes and weights; the same temperatures and all of the other physical measurements. We must globalize, digitalize and decimalize Our Time and Our Space. The Internet and Worldwide Web are reaching every corner of the globe. The electronic revolution needs one revolutionary Time and Space system. We all live in the same wide World so must use: **The Worldwide System**.

Cosmic Time

This Universe began with a Big Bang some 13,820,000,000 years ago. Clouds of dust and gas gradually coalesced into the Stars and Galaxies. Our Milky Way Galaxy slowly coalesced some 5,000,000,000 years ago. Our Sun or Star takes some 225,000,000 years to circuit Our Milky Way. There are probably billions of Stars with Planets like Our Solar System.

Cosmic Time can be based upon many cyclic periods in the Universe. It could be based upon the regular pulses of a distant pulsar or quasar but it is usually based upon irregular cycles within Our Solar System. The most useful ones are Our Planet's age, orbit and spin, which should be the basis for Our chronology, calendar and clock but there are also the phases of the Moon, which are the basis for some Lunar calendars. The lengths of the Solar day and year vary, so average values are used. There are approximately 365.242 mean Solar days per mean Solar year. There are approximately 29.531 mean Solar days to one Lunar moonth. So it is impossible to fit Solar days into Solar years or Lunar moonths. Mean Solar days are divided into 24 hours, 60 minutes and 60 seconds, for historical reasons, but they could be divided in various other ways. Clocks became far more accurate as the exploration of Space proceeded. Some are now more accurate than one second in the life of the Universe. Earth's orbit and spin are different when related to the Sun or the Stars. A Solar year is shorter and a Solar day is longer than the Sidereal ones. The Sun's equator revolves in about 24 days whilst its poles take about 38 days and its Sun-spot zone takes about 28 days, relative to Earth. The other Planets have different orbits (years) and different spins (days). The speed of light is now approximately 300,000 Kilometres per second. Cosmic distances can be measured in light-years, which are just under ten trillion Kilometres, and the next Star is over four light-years away.

Astronomers are slowly discovering some of the secrets of this Universe. Cosmologists use their imaginations and equations to postulate theories. Galileo proved that Earth is a Planet revolving around the Sun and the Moon revolves around the Earth, like other moons around other Planets. Newton showed that gravity is a powerful force that causes the Planets to revolve around the Sun and the Moon to revolve around the Earth. Planck's quantum theory showed that light is a particle and a wave. Quantum mechanics led to the development of electronics and computers. Einstein's theory that a small amount of mass could be converted into a huge amount of energy led to the science of nuclear power and bombs. Hawking predicted black holes that destroy matter and warp Space-Time These are now considered to be at the very centre of every galaxy. Most cosmologists believe that the ultimate barrier is the speed of light. However, this theory might now have been disproved by an experiment. Space once had three dimensions and Time was the fourth dimension. Space-Time is now considered to have about ten dimensions.

Atomic Time

The better Our telescopes or microscopes the smaller or larger We seem. Particle physics and cosmology were thought to be separate disciplines. They are now considered to be one science, however these scientists use different systems for measuring the largest and smallest parts of Time. Cosmologists think that Cosmic Time and Space began with a Big Bang, that most of the vast and finite Universe consists of invisible dark matter and that it is now expanding more rapidly due to invisible dark energy. Particle physicists claim Time and Space stretch into eternity and infinity. Both of these conflicting concepts are incomprehensible to most of Us.

Atomic Time is not used to determine the age, the date nor the time; but for timing many events of Atomic, Cosmic and Olympic proportions. It is part of the International Metric System, based on the Atomic second. This is now a fixed unit and it is accurately measured by Atomic clocks. It is multiplied or divided in a digital-decimal way like all of the SI units. It is currently defined as being 9,192,631,770 cycles during a particular oscillatory mode of the caesium 133 atom under very precise conditions. This arbitrary standard was agreed by a global convention in 1967 AD. The Atomic second was then the same as the Cosmic second but this is slowly becoming larger, as We can hear in the radio time signal pips. Cosmic Time and Space is measured in variable years and light-years. However, the speed of light is usually measured in fixed Atomic seconds. The metre, originally based upon the Paris Meridian, was redefined as the distance light travels in 1/299792458 Atomic second in 1983 AD. So the measurement of Space is based upon the measurement of Time. Since it is arbitrary, this fundamental unit could be larger or smaller. It could, ideally, be based upon one millionth of a degree of longitude. This new unit, the *han*, is about the width of the average Human hand. It is a handy unit for measuring everything from very large to very small.

We have probably made the ultimate timepiece already but it is the size of what is being measured that should now be seriously reconsidered. Earth's rotation is slowing down by about 0.000015 second per year. This change is mostly due to the tides, caused by the Sun and the Moon. It cannot be predicted and is constantly being monitored by instruments. The tiny difference between these Atomic and Cosmic seconds can cause huge problems in accounting computers and global positioning systems. Since the fixed Atomic second is arbitrary it could be larger or smaller. Its definition should, ideally, remain exactly the same for ever, so that precise comparisons can be made over many, many, many generations. Or, Atomic Time may be adjusted to be exactly the same as Cosmic Time at the beginning of every Solar year, decade, century or millennium. Our fixed Atomic time unit could be one millionth of a mean Solar day measured at midnight in Greenwich on the vernal equinox in 2000 AD. This tiny new unit, the *tik,* is less than one tenth of an Atomic second.

Geotic Time

Geotic Time is based upon the Natural cycles within Our Planet Earth.
It slowly coalesced from dust and gas about 4,550,000,000 years ago.
It is not a perfect sphere but an oblate one, which stops it from toppling.
It has a solid core, liquid outer core, mantle, thin crust and atmosphere.
The Moon was formed when the Earth was struck by another Planet.
Its orbit is the same as its spin and so only one hemisphere faces Earth.
Earth's water arrived when it was hit by frozen comets and asteroids.
Its crust is formed by tectonic plates that are moving around the globe.
Where they touch they cause volcanic eruptions or seismic earthquakes.

Our Planet Earth follows an elliptical orbit around the Sun, in a region
that is not too hot and not too cold, but it can be pulled by the other
Planets into hotter and colder regions, which causes Ice Ages and Thaws.
So the sea level rises and falls over 100m and it is now about half way.
The tropical year of the seasons, caused by its elliptical orbit and the
tilt of its axis, is divided into four parts by the solstices and equinoxes.
The summer and winter solstices, when the Sun is highest and lowest
in the Northern hemisphere, are reversed in the Southern hemisphere.
The vernal and autumnal equinoxes, when the day and night are equal,
are exactly the same throughout Northern and Southern hemispheres.
The tides are caused by the gravitational pull of the Sun and the Moon.
Spring tides occur at new and full Moons; neap tides at half Moons.
Tides are also higher at the solstices and equinoxes, because of the Sun.
The gravitational pull of the Sun and Moon is greatest at the Solar or
Lunar eclipses, when they are pulling together or in opposite directions.
This causes quakes and eruptions as well as higher and lower tides and
also effects the climate and the weather in various atmospheric layers.
Sun-spots and Solar winds also effect Earth's climate and weather.
They have a 28-day sunth cycle, due to the Sun's spin or rotation,
and an 11-12 year cycle, due to the pull of all the Planets on the Sun.

Our Planet Earth wobbles slightly so that its poles describe a circle in
the Sky and this cycle of precession takes 25,920 years to complete.
North and South polar circles lie 66.34 degrees N and S of the Equator.
Tropics of Cancer and Capricorn lie 23.5 degrees N and S of the Equator.
Earth's geographic polar axis is now tilted by 23.5 degrees but this
obliquity varies from 22.1 to 24.5 degrees over a 41,000 year cycle.
There are four seasons within the temperate zones between the tropical
and polar zones but fewer seasons in the tropics and more at the poles.
Earth's magnetic poles wander about each year in an unpredictable way.
They change places every 200,000 years or so and this flip is overdue.
Earth's core rotates at a faster rate than its crust in a 900 year cycle.
This causes a dynamo effect forming a magnetic field around the globe.
This magnetosphere protects all Life forms from harmful Cosmic rays.
Earth may be the only Planet in the Universe to support intelligent Life.

Bionic Time

Bionic Time upon Planet Earth began at least 3,850,000,000 years ago. Every Life-form has a chronology, calendar, clock, compass and ruler. They are embodied in every gene and they motivate every living thing. They are controlled by the cycles of the Sun, the Moon and the Earth. The enormous range of species is usually referred to as biodiversity. Some are active by day; others by night: some like it hot; others cold. Some live on the highest mountains; others live in the deepest oceans. We are still finding many new species; whilst destroying many others. We have not found any other Life forms elsewhere in the Solar System. There may be Life on other planets with other suns and other moons. More and more Earth-like exoplanets are being discovered every year.

The trees live longer than Us and their annual rings are their chronology. The flowers know what season it is and when to open their petals. The caterpillar/butterfly knows that its life-cycle lasts exactly one year. The birds know when to migrate, when to breed and where to go next. They trust their leader and their formation flying is better than Ours. The birds and the fish know exactly where and precisely when to mate. The nautilus and the horseshoe crab lived long before the dinosaurs. The dolphins have two brains and yet We still cannot understand them. Our cities are not only inhabited by Us but many other species as well. The foxes, cats and rats are waiting to take-over as soon as We leave. The insects feed on Us, so We are part of their food chain, not *vice versa*. The ants and termites know how to cooperate and built huge colonies. The bees, wasps and hornets know how to protect themselves from Us. We have no divine right to inhabit this Planet, which some of Us call: Earth.

We can learn a great deal from the other species about how to navigate, fly, swim, run, hide, fight, build, cooperate, communicate and copulate. Their main objective is to ensure the survival of their species and they can adapt to their surroundings and specialize over many generations. We have learned how to breed or modify other species for Our own needs. Our species has evolved in many different forms over the millennia but We are now beginning to interbreed and exchange ideas around the globe. We have explored most of the land, most of the sea and most of the air. We have been to the Moon and explored much of the Solar system. We can see the edge of the Universe and are now probing Outer Space. Our species is the only one to think about the past, present and future. We are the only species to count and measure everything about Us. Yet, We use different systems for counting or measuring Time and Space. We will only become one species when We agree to use the same system. Many attempts have been made to achieve this before but all have failed. The International Metric Time and Space System is arbitrary and wrong. This book explains a new global-digital-decimal Time and Space System. **The Worldwide System** could be used by all *Homo Sapiens* forever.

Humanic Time

We Humans evolved from tiny mammals that seized their chance when the dinosaurs were wiped-out by an asteroid about 65,000,000 years ago. The history of Ape-Man started in Africa about 6,000,000 years ago. The history of Man began when We stood-up about 2,000,000 years ago. Our own species very nearly became extinct about 1,000,000 years ago. The history of civilization goes back to the last Ice Age 12,000 years ago. This was when We started to settle down, communicate and cooperate. Many civilizations have risen and fallen, all over the globe, and each had a different way of measuring, managing and governing Time and Space. We will only have one civilization when We pool Our resources and use one chronology, one calendar, one clock, one rule, one script, one tongue. This will be the ultimate technological achievement of Our Human Race. We already count the years in tens, hundreds, thousands and millions. We should count or divide days in the same global-digital-decimal way.

Our bodies incorporate clocks, in Our brains and in Our other organs, which control rhythms of sleeping, eating, resting, playing and working. We are all programmed to rise at dawn and retire at dusk, as We all did before artificial light and artificial calendars and clocks were invented. We all need regular rest days and occasional holidays but these need not be based upon seven-day weeks nor holy days in annual liturgical cycles. In the tropics 6 AM and 6 PM roughly coincide with dawn and dusk, so it is Natural to base Our working times upon this diurnal rhythm. In temperate zones daylight varies with the seasons, so work should too. In the polar regions We must hibernate or use artificial light in winter. Our Natural body clocks are otherwise in conflict with artificial ones. We are liable to suffer heart attacks or strokes due to stress and strain. Time zones and daylight saving measures do nothing to alleviate this. Women have about ten menstruation periods to one gestation period. Our hearts beat at the rate of approximately 100,000 pulses per day. Most of Us have ten digits with which to count, multiply and divide. We Human beings are already globalized, digitized and decimalized.

We regard *Mother Earth* as Ours and yet We are *Her* youngest children. Nevertheless, We think We have the right to change *Her* to Our needs. We are beginning to question whether Our Human Race is big enough. Wars, floods, droughts, wildfires or epidemics can break out anywhere, causing great migrations, yet there is not enough land or food to share. We are beginning to question the wisdom of building more roads and destroying the green belts around Our cities by building more homes. We are beginning to predict the end of fossil fuels and cheap energy. We are beginning to talk about living on the Moon or another Planet. We can do a great deal to save this Planet by reorganizing Ourselves and using its resources in a much more efficient and sustainable way. We can save Our Planet and Our Species if We share Time and Space.

Mystic Time

Every religion has its own chronology, calendar and clock for regulating millennial, centennial, annual, monthly, weekly, daily and hourly rituals. Some religions have their own distances and dimensions as well as their own directions or orientations for architecture, prayer and funeral rites.

Every religion and sect has a different method for numbering its years. Jewish chronology was based on mean Solar years since the Creation. Orthodox chronology was based on mean Solar years since the Flood. Catholic chronology was based on mean Solar years since the Nativity. Coptic chronology was based on mean Solar years since the Martyrum. Shiite chronology was based on mean Solar years since the *Hejira*. Sunni chronology was based on mean Lunar years since the *Hejira*. Hindu chronology was based on mean Solar years since the Recreation. Buddhist chronology was based on mean Solar years since the Incarnation. These totally different chronological beliefs still divide Our Human Race.

Most religions were based on worship of the Sun, Moon, Stars or Planets. Consequently, their calendars are either Solar, Lunar, Stellar or Planar. Every religious calendar year has completely different feasts and fasts. Jewish calendars are based upon the cycles of the Sun and the Moon. Christian years are based on the Sun, but Easter is based on the Moon. The Sunnis fast during daylight during their holy moonth of Ramadan. The Shiite men flagellate themselves during their annual festival of Ali. The three monotheist Western religions use the Mystic seven-day week. This was based upon the Pagan worship of the *Seven Heavenly Bodies*. Each religion has a different week-day off work to honour its founder: Jews on Saturdays, Christians on Sundays, Muslims on Fridays and each has a different way of naming or numbering the days in the week. The Eastern religions do not have a Mystic week nor a Sabbath day. These totally different calendrical beliefs still divide Our Human Race.

Pagan religions involved the dawn and dusk worship of their Sun-god. The variable period between them was divided in many different ways. Each variable division became another time to worship their Sun-god. The development of mechanical clocks fixed these variable divisions. Whilst the twenty-four hour day is now used throughout the globe there are now twenty-five different time zones at sea and some forty on land. These totally different horological beliefs still divide Our Human Race.

Mother Earth was the primordial deity, long before written history began. We can now measure how old *She* is and the length of *Her* year and day. We can now measure how big *She* is, in different measurement systems. However, We still have not found one measurement system for use by all. The solution is to use one system throughout *Our Mother Earth* based upon *Her* age, orbit, spin and girth plus the global-digital-decimal number ten.

Organic Time

Organic Time manages Our rhythms of working, resting and playing.
We all count years in digital tens, hundreds, thousands and millions.
Yet, We, incompatibly, count month-days and week-days not year-days.
These days would drop into handy groups of ten, twenty, thirty or forty.
We peculiarly divide days by twenty-fours, sixties, sixties then decimals.
We should divide Our days in the same decimal way as everything else.

Our Pagan weekly cycle was based upon the *Seven Heavenly Bodies*:
the Sun, the Moon and the five Planets that are visible to the naked eye.
The seven week-days are still named after them in several languages.
There are three more Planets, visible through telescopes, plus this one.
It could be argued, for this reason, that We should use a ten-day week.
There are more logical reasons to use a 5 day-on/5 day-off bi-cycle.
Not only is this Planet becoming more crowded, due to the population
explosion, but usable land area is also being eroded by the deserts and
swamped by the sea, so We must find new ways of using working Space.
A ten-day week would allow half of Us to work whilst the other half
were resting and this would greatly improve productivity and life-style.
We are now using-up Our non-renewable resources at an alarming rate.
We need to recycle Our paper, plastic, glass, metal and Organic Time.

Every organization has its own routines, rosters and working patterns.
These are continually being changed in response to new global trends.
Our World is becoming a global village with a 7-day/24-hour economy.
Most service tills, service stations and some shops open-all-day every day.
Many organizations are finding it more efficient to operate continuously.
So We could now use a continuous ten-day week and a ten-hour day.
Yet, it is better to use 36 discontinuous ten-day weeks during 360 days.
The remaining five or six days should then be reserved for elections.

The electronic revolution is rapidly changing Our view of Organic Time.
Computers can translate many different languages but they find great
difficulty in transposing different chronologies, calendars and clocks.
There are many different ways of writing the same age, date and time.
Operating systems and programs could all be simplified if they only had
one chronology, calendar and clock based upon one age, date and time.
Computers did not understand abbreviated two-digit year numbers so
some failed at the Millennium and the rest cost a $trillion to put right.
A three-digit system could be used for the age, the date or the time.
A row or square of nine numbers could be used in a digital timepiece
to indicate the age, date and time during the rest of this millennium.
Time zones are anachronisms that divide and confuse Our Human Race.
The Internet has no divisive time zones nor daylight saving measures.
The Worldwide Web already incorporates digital date and decimal time.
Google Earth and *Satnav* are already based upon decimals of a degree.

Civic Time

The Civic Time, now used in Britain and many other parts of the globe, is a political concoction of Cosmic Time, Atomic Time and Mystic Time. It consists of: backwards and forwards millennia, centuries and decades; Solar years with 12 months, about 52 x 7-day weeks and 365/6 days; 2 x 12 or 24 hours; 60 minutes; 60 seconds and, finally, decimals. Some of these Man-made divisions of Civic Time are different in other nations and this causes a great deal of friction throughout Our World. Even when nations using this same system become united by a treaty, such as: The Commonwealth or: The European Union, there are different holidays, time zones and days for changing to and from summer time.

Britain is now a multicultural community and all religion is dying out. The silent majority are now atheists, agnostics, secularists or Humanists. Some 40% say that they are Christians, yet they never read *The Bible*. Christmas and Easter are public holy days, yet only 1% go to church, less than 25% are baptized, more than 40% are born out of wedlock, 50% of marriages are dissolved but 75% of funerals are still religious. The current government admit that Britain is now a secular state but they have only recommended changing its chronology to: Common Era. This is the same as *Anno Domini* but instead of BC/AD are BCE/ACE. Britain still uses the Gregorian calendar with higgledy-piggledy months and month-days together with the continuous seven-day working week. Although most British laws and by-laws making Sunday a special day have now been repealed, a handful of them remain in the statute book.

We now know the age of Our Planet as well as the age of Our civilization, and so Our chronology should be based upon these chronological facts. All days were created equal and 360 of them should be equal once more. There should then be 36 ten-day weeks and most jobs should be shared. The 5 or 6 days at the end of the year should be devoted to democracy: for holding local, regional, national, international and global elections. The higgledy-piggledy Roman-Catholic calendar months and month-days are now being superseded by week numbers and by week-day numbers. The next step is to use ordinal year-day numbers with ten-day weeks. These are perfectly legal and they are already printed in most diaries. There is no need for the market week to be seven days long when most people can shop at supermarkets or hypermarkets every ten days or so. Britain now changes to summer time and back to winter time on the same day as the European Union but sets its clocks to an hour behind. This is one of the many factors that separate Little Britain from Europe. However, all the clocks around the globe could read exactly the same. This would demolish the invisible barriers that divide Our Planet Earth. No politicians, yet, advocate a global-digital-decimal system based upon the age, orbit, spin and girth of Our Planet Earth with no time zones, no daylight saving measures and a return to the global gold standard.

Olympic Time

The Greeks were the first civilization to encourage sport in gymnasiums. The annual Panhellenic Games began at the full-Moon after the summer solstice in a four-year Olympian, Pythian, Nemian and Isthmian cycle and each year was chronologically named after the victor of the games. The first was Choroebus in 776 BC so, from then on, ages are known. The Olympic Games are still organized on a four-year cycle but as well as trying to beat all the others, competitors also try to beat the record book. So the measurement of Time and Space has become very important in most sports and both of these are needed for the measurement of speed. The battle of Marathon, where the Athenian army miraculously defeated the Persian army in 490 BC, is still commemorated by the modern race. The distance run, to tell of this victory, by the Greek soldier Pheidippides is still disputed but it is now standardized to be 25.4 miles or 40.8 Km. Whether this is based upon miles, stadia, cubits, yards, feet or metres and hours, minutes or seconds (units of time devised in ancient Greece) or some other measurement system, it is still exactly the same record.

Most sports are now based upon Kilometres, metres and millimetres. Horse racing is still based upon furlongs and odds are still in fractions. Cricket pitches are still based upon the old Imperial unit of one chain. Football pitches may vary in size and shape, depending upon location. However, all football goalposts still measure 24 feet wide by 8 feet high. Tennis courts are still measured in feet but they are converted to metres. Motor racing is now based upon decimals, but not fractions, of a second. Athletics was based upon tracks of 440 yards but now on 500 metres. Swimming and diving are now usually based upon Metric-sized pools. Olympic ice hockey rinks now measure 30 metres wide by 200 feet long. Whole numbers such as the four minute mile or ten second Hectometre seemed to be extremely important, when they were really quite arbitrary. Speeds were measured in miles per hour but now in Kilometres per hour. If both time and distance were based upon the spin and girth of Earth, the global-digital-decimal number ten and the round number 360 then all speed records would need to be converted to this **Worldwide System**.

Most amateur sports are run at weekends, when workers are resting. Most professional sports are run on any day during the seven-day week. If the week was ten days, divided into five left-days and five right-days, then workers could play or watch sport during the five days that they were not working but there would have to be two teams and two leagues. This would allow stadiums, tracks, courses, courts, rinks, pools, pitches to be used more often and it would encourage amateurs to take-up sport. Professional sportsmen and sportswomen are now paid far too much. The Greeks were probably the first civilization to share their jobs, so that they could spend half of their days in improving their sporting prowess. The Olympic Games could coincide with the leap year, every four years.

Music Time

The nine Greek *Muses* engendered music, museums and amusements. Greek musicians played upon flutes, pan-pipes, lyres, harps and drums. We can devise many musical instruments, all tuned to different scales. The most impressive type of musical instrument is the concert organ. The most coordinated kind of organization is the symphony orchestra. There is nothing more pleasing to the ear than the sound of a choir.

Music: note, pitch, frequency, melody, harmony, timbre and rhythm, has numerous uses: to inspire congregations, to entertain generations, to stir-up or to calm-down conflagrations, to make shoppers buy more, to encourage workers to work harder or relax after a hard day's work. Would it sound different if it was globalized, digitalized and decimalized?

Different civilizations developed completely different musical instruments and different musical scales and there is still no global Music standard. Music of the East sounds completely different from Music of the West. However, both hemispheres have begun to appreciate each other's tunes. European and Russian concert pianos are tuned slightly differently. The musical scale across a piano keyboard is not linear but logarithmic. The volume of sound is now measured by the logarithmic decibel system. Vibrations and rhythms are used to create music but vibrations are measured in cycles per second and rhythms are in beats per minute. Our hearts pound at the rate of between 60 to 180 beats per minute. Most of the popular dance rhythms have around 130 beats per minute. If the fractional second and minute were replaced by new decimal units, the cycle per second and the beat per minute would become obsolete and the musical scale on a metronome would have to be recalibrated. Music is already recorded on digital rather than analogue equipment. Would global-digital-decimal Music sound any better or worse?

The musical notation or score is written from left to right across the page. It can be read by anybody, anywhere - whatever language they speak. The members of any symphony orchestra may not be able to converse. The eight-note musical scale was used because a flute has eight holes, halving the length of a taught string raises its musical note by an octave, the female singing voice is usually an octave higher than the male voice, but together they sing in harmony, so Music is based upon number eight. Would a ten-note musical scale sound any sweeter?

The author cannot answer these musical questions and they may be a matter of opinion, culture and taste but there is much food for thought. This hypothesis is written like a symphony of words that fit every page. We can now download thousands of tunes, from ballads to symphonies, carry them in Our pockets and listen to them anywhere and anytime. We may soon be listening to **Worldwide Music** on Our iPods and iPads.

Our Time

Our Time is one of transition but few understand Our place in history. This Millennium is a mile-stone and a kilometre-stone, for We have not forgotten the Imperial System nor fully changed to the Metric System. We still use old measurement, management and government systems, which have gradually become cobbled together in the most illogical way. They have become so familiar that some of Us think of them as friendly. Yet, they are so unfriendly that they may cause Our civilization to fail. It is already failing but the politicians are so interested in themselves that they will not listen and they turn a blind eye to all of the omens.

Our global civilization is failing because a third of its workforce lies idle. Those who have jobs are now insecure, overstressed and overstretched. Inexperienced youngsters and experienced oldsters are all out of work. The poor are becoming much poorer; the rich are becoming much richer. The moral values of Our leaders do not set any example to the rest of Us. We cannot trust them with Our money when many fiddle their expenses. We used to trust Our bankers but they are running away with Our cash. We can no longer trust Our children to the care of priests and nuns. Most crimes go undetected, yet all the prisons are full and overflowing. The welfare system is overloaded and the taxation system is in a mess. Many family values are breaking down but there is no alternative society. Drug abuse is way out of control and the suicide rate is higher than ever. We are using up all Our resources and We keep printing more money. We are poisoning Our own food and ruining Our own environment. We are slaughtering endangered species and culling the species We eat. Doctors and hospitals are overloaded and yet their equipment lies idle. Schools and colleges are all under-funded, universities are not universal. However, most of their expensive facilities are unused for half of the year. Our great cities are congested and all of Our transports are overloaded. We overspend on weapons but research and development is underfunded. Wars are breaking out everywhere but no one can discover the cause. Democracy is breaking down when a large sector are not able to vote. Few new ideas are reaching the top and most books lay unpublished. Many of Our leaders become corrupt and there are uprisings everywhere. There are even riots and strikes in Little Britain, the cradle of democracy.

Our civilization has so many weaknesses that the politicians are running around like headless chickens trying to solve one problem after another. Their manifestos are a joke and they readily steal each other's slogans. They have no new ideas or ideals but still use their worn-out paradigms, dogmas and rules, without thinking anything out from first principles. They set-up new departments with new offices, equipment and staff but they still use the same old ages, dates, times, zones and rules. This book could be the basis of a new philosophy, which could unite all nations into a global civilization, which will go from strength to strength.

Our Space

The Sun never set on the British Empire with forty divisive time zones.
Only a century later Little Britain lost its empire and was part of the EU.
However, it still has its own sovereign, currency, language and time zone.
Some politicians say that the whole of Europe should use one time zone.
Others say, in 22 official languages, it is impossible to build a Eutopia.
China has one script, one common language and one official language.
It has only one time zone and so it has survived as one economic state.
India invented the positional number and zero system including decimals.
However, the Indian sub-continent is now divided into four time zones.
The USSR was too big, with eleven time zones, so inevitably fell apart.
The USA is too big for its boots, with eight time zones, so may collapse.
The Internet has rapidly become far bigger than any state or federation.
Many surfers already use **digital date, decimal time** and **one time zone**.

Our Space is changing as Britain adopts the International Metric System.
However, the metre is an awkward rule that does not fit into your pocket.
Despite being part of the European Union, Britain did not intend to
drive on the same side, use the same distances or the same currency.
The Irish use euros, their distances are in Km and their speeds in Km/h.
However, most Irish motorists still drive down the left side of the road.
All British speedometers already read in Km/h as well as in m.p.h.
Yet, British odometers still read in miles and so do British road signs.
If Kilometres and hours were replaced then speed limits would change,
but they are arbitrary and most people would drive safely without them.
Speed over land is still measured in statute miles or Kilometres per hour.
Speed at sea or in the air is measured in knots (nautical miles per hour).

The Worldwide System can be used over land, at sea or up in the air.
It divides the circle into 360 degrees and these are divided by decimals.
Its standard unit of measure is one millionth of one degree of longitude,
measured around the Equator, which is roughly the width of your hand.
This handy new rule can be marked along the bottom of a protractor.
This is a very handy size for measuring many things around the home.
It is squared for measuring areas and cubed for measuring volumes.
The Imperial, American and International standards all have different
sized units for volume and/or capacity and this can be very confusing.
Imperial and American cubic feet are the same but gallons are different.
A standard oil barrel holds 42 American gallons or 35 Imperial gallons,
which are approximately 159 International litres or 0.159 cubic metres.
The Worldwide System has the same units for volume and capacity.
It has handy size increments for all of the commonly used measures.
The oil barrel remains the same size and so does the pint beer tankard.
Weight is related to capacity or volume in the same way that the pound is
related to the gallon, or the kilogram to the litre, by using fresh water.
Wealth can be measured by using this standard weight in pure gold.

Time and Space

The study of Time and Space was believed to be a Mystical experience. Some believed *Yahweh/God/Allah* commanded Us to use a 7-day week. Some believed that everything was created in 6 days, plus one for rest. Some believed the 7 days in the Mystic week were guarded by angels. Some believed there were *7 Heavenly Bodies*: Sun, Moon and 5 Planets. This was disproved when Uranus was found by Herschel in 1781 AD, Neptune by Galle in 1846 AD and then Pluto by Tombaugh in 1930 AD. The California Institute of Technology (CIT) has recently discovered five other objects in the Kuiper belt, at the very edge of Our Solar System. The International Astronomical Union said these were minor Planets. Consequently, there were only eight major Planets in Our Solar System. However, in 2016 AD the CIT discovered another Planet way out in Space. So there are now *Ten Heavenly Bodies*: the Sun and nine Planets.

The ancient civilizations developed their own Time and Space systems. These were usually taught by rote before children could read or write. This took a great deal of learning time and turned many off education. Many of Us found it difficult to learn how to count years back and forth. Most of Us found it difficult to learn which months have 30 or 31 days. Some of Us found it difficult to learn how to read a clock or a watch. All of Us found it difficult to learn how to measure distances, directions, angles, lengths, areas, volumes and weights with many fractional units. So, three centuries ago, a simpler base-ten Metric System was devised. Some said it should be based on the length of a one second pendulum. Then, a century ago, it was agreed, at an Earth Summit in Washington, that both Time and Space should be decimalized throughout Our Planet. Some say that the International Metric System embodies this intention but it is not a coherent global-digital-decimal Time and Space system. This hypothesis presents the case for a coherent global-digital-decimal Time and Space system that can be used throughout Our Planet forever.

As soon as We could measure Time and Space We began to advance. We can now save a great deal of Space by dividing Our Time in half. Our Race multiplied and divided many times; now it is time to integrate. We must stop differentiating between many ethnic or cultural variations and devise an ethos based upon the same global-digital-decimal system. Otherwise, We will have to keep dividing up Our Planet and building more barriers until We each inhabit the footprint upon which We stand. Our Human Race is still expanding, using up all the resources on its only Planet and running out of energy, water, food, Space and Time. In another generation there may be twice as many to feed, water, clothe, house, medicate, educate, employ, pension, entertain, police and transport. **Full-time-job-sharing-as-the-norm** would allow all of Our infrastructure, Our transportation and Our manpower to be used evenly on every day. This redistribution of work would lead to a redistribution of wealth.

Time and Life

We made many Earth-shattering discoveries during the last century. We now know when this Planet coalesced, how and when Life began, how different species evolved and even how Our own species developed. We are now beginning to understand how Our Human brains work, what memory is and how Our body clocks control the rhythms of Life. We have managed to unravel the hidden secrets of Our genetic codebook. We are starting to correct Our genetic disorders, such as cystic fibrosis. We can clone mice, rats, sheep, pigs, horses, dogs, monkeys and Us. We have now even learned how to create a simple form of synthetic Life. We know a great deal about how tools, weapons and systems evolved. We alone, of all the countless species, have sufficient brain power and dexterity to invent, develop and produce better ones, as the need arises. We take Time for granted but We should take a closer look at the way We measure, manage, govern, embody, perceive, mystify and define it.

Habits are personal traits, which We generally pick-up from Our parents. To learn any language takes more brainpower than writing a thesis. We may learn to tell the age, date and time before We go to school and so We may never be formally taught about how they all evolved. Few teachers or lecturers can explain why Time is in such a muddle. Most people are so used to the habits of a lifetime associated with the year, the month, the week, the weekend, the day, the hour, the minute and the second that they never consider that they could be different. Some are so punctilious that they are forever checking their calendars, diaries, timetables and watches, without ever thinking about Time itself.

Our success or failure depends on the way We measure Time and Space. Most of Us use the backward and forward *Anno Domini* chronology and the higgledy-piggledy Gregorian calendar but they are chronically sick. Some use a twenty-four-hour clock; whilst others use a twelve-hour one. We still use the ancient Sumerian hexadecimal system of sixty minutes and sixty seconds, which still divide-up Our Space as well as Our Time. Our Human Race is still divided-up by some forty different time zones and by many different dates for changing to and from summer time. With a new age-scale We could put Our history into chronological order. With a new date-scale We could put Our society into calendrical order. With a new time-scale We could put Our industry into horological order. With a new rule-scale We could put Our World into geographical order. If We do not change Time and Space in step with Our Era, We could be heading for conflict as We run out of Time, Space and everything else. We have already started Our long slide down that fatal slippery slope. Some prophets of doom are already predicting the end of civilization. The end of **Time** may well be nigh but Our World and Our Human Race might last a little while longer, if We are prepared to change Our minds. We can and should change to **The Worldwide Time and Space System**.

Making Time

The electronic revolution is already changing Our Planet in exactly the same way that the agricultural revolution and industrial revolution did. We are all living through an Age of great social and economic change. A few are working around-the-clock and some shops are open-all-hours. Some are working so hard and so long that they never have any fun. Many are working in part-time jobs, where they forego all their benefits. However, a large cross-section of the community have no jobs to go to. Single parents and their children are all suffering from the new regime. Entire families, unemployed for many years, are now turning to crime. The courts and prisons are overflowing and many crimes go unsolved. Law and order is breaking down, the state itself is now under pressure. Governments cannot govern if less than 50% can be bothered to vote. Whenever the rich get richer and the poor get poorer revolution ensues. This book presents a simple solution to this complex problem.

The revolutionary **Worldwide System** is based upon Earth's revolutions, together with the number of digits that We have on both of Our hands. It involves scrapping all the working patterns based upon the seven-day week and all the religious and trade union dogmas associated with it. Governments, all over the globe, consult so-called experts about how to tackle their socio-economic problems, but they all use calculations that are out-of-date because they consider the working week to be a fixed period of seven days; not a variable period, which could be ten days. A ten-day week would allow most jobs to be shared and this simple change to working patterns could solve many socio-economic problems. Our calculators and computers are already familiar with counting in tens. Politicians have not yet woken-up to the social advantages that IT can bring by allowing most jobs to be shared and wealth to be redistributed. Regrettably, those with power are still influenced by Sabbatarians who think that every seventh day should be devoted to *Yahweh/God/Allah*. They say that the seven-day week was *God*-given; yet it was Man-made.

They try to restrict shop and public house opening to certain hours. Yet, there are signs that days and hours are all becoming equal again. In Britain the week is getting weaker and so the economy is stronger. In Europe the week is getting stronger and so the economy is weaker. The International Standards Organization now permits Us to number the days in the year and to forget about unequal months and odd weeks. The seven-day week only needs a push and it will vanish into oblivion. Britain should take a more active part in running Europe and in showing the World how to manage its economy by changing to a ten-day week. The key to the door marked progress is education but not brainwashing. We must learn how to think for Ourselves and take nothing for granted. Our children already know how to count everything else on their digits. They could count **Worldwide Time and Space** in exactly the same way.

Making Space

We already count years in tens, hundreds and thousands, so think that a new decade, century or millennium will bring changes to Our lives. We measure Life-spans in years, decades and scores but the old target of three score years and ten has been passed and many live for a century. Perhaps, in another century, most of Us will be living for over a century. Yet, many people now retire early, when their jobs become redundant. The birth rate is booming again, so there are not enough school places. The youth of today have no incentive to learn the skills of their elders. They do not save money for their old age and live beyond their means. These are opposing demographic trends, which cannot be reconciled with Our current pattern of working, so something must be done to change it. Yet, nothing is being done and Our pensions are being frittered away. In another generation there may be twice as many to feed and to house. It is no good closing Our minds, doors and borders to this dilemma. We should make more money in less Space by sharing most of Our jobs. We should be prepared to retrain several times during Our lifetimes. We should work until We are older but for less time in the working day.

Successive governments failed to solve the crucial unemployment problem. They fudge all of the figures and create more and more civil servants. The higher education and youth employment schemes do not create jobs. Many are unable to claim benefits, so they do not show up in the figures. Life goes on and We have neither had a bloody nor bloodless revolution. Yet, there have been strikes and riots and there is still much discontent. Politicians now say that a high level of unemployment is unavoidable, even necessary, in an increasingly mechanized and computerized World. However, this malady is neither economically nor socially desirable and statistical analysis shows that We are heading for a Man-made calamity. When any government tries to cure unemployment, inflation goes up. When any government tries to cure inflation, unemployment goes up. **Job-sharing-as-the-norm** could cure both inflation and unemployment. Poverty, sickness and crime are related to unemployment and inflation. There are numerous other, good and bad, trends in Our modern society, directly or indirectly, related to the way that We use Time and Space.

We still remember decades like the roaring twenties or the swinging sixties, and the last decade was sometimes described as the naughty noughties. Changes do not occur in convenient age-spans, date-spans, time-spans. They usually occur so slowly that We barely notice them happening. Then We suddenly wake-up to the fact that many of Us are out of work. Or the pound, dollar or euro in Our pocket is not worth nearly so much. We can shrug Our shoulders and say: nothing can be done, or We can analyze the situation and make changes to the way that We run Our lives. This book attempts to analyze the situation and suggests changes to the way that We run Our lives, which have never been considered before.

Bad Time

Secularity, rationality and humanity are slowly replacing every religion. Yet they cling to their different chronologies, calendars, clocks and rules. These make believers think differently and some are even prepared to kill themselves or others because of different dogmas about Time and Space. Most religions were based on beliefs that the Earth, the Sun, the Moon, the Planets and the Stars were deities who could control the weather, the seasons and tides plus: floods, famines, earthquakes and volcanoes. We now know how the Sun and the Moon control the seasons and tides. We have yet to understand how the *Heavenly Bodies* cause catastrophes.

In the West all the deities became merged into one *God* of Space-Time. *He* is supposed to have created the Universe in six days plus one for rest. Abraham the patriarch of Judaism, Christianity and Islam, is said to have used a seven-day week, yet he spent years in Egypt using a ten-day one. Joseph, in his multi-coloured dream coat, lived in Egypt with the ten-day week but had dreams about the seven good years and seven bad years. Moses came from Egypt, where they used a ten-day week, but according to the Judeo-Christian-Islamic tradition, he talked to *Yahweh/God/Allah* who commanded the Children of Israel to observe the seven-day week. Jesus was raised in Egypt with a ten-day week but said that the Jewish Sabbath day and seven-day week was made for Man and not *vice-versa*. The Gnostic Christians, who lived in Egypt, also used the ten-day week. The Roman Empire adopted Christianity and the Jewish seven-day week. Then, after the fall of Rome, Mohammed adopted the seven-day week. It is now used throughout Our Planet and most of Us take it for granted. However, it is dividing Our Human Race rather than uniting Us because: Jews pray on Saturdays, Christians on Sundays, Muslims on Fridays. The seven-day week and its Sabbaths are not part of Eastern religions. The East readily accepts change and so it is rapidly overtaking the West.

The astrologers had great power over the king and the country and used chronologies, calendars and clocks for divining ages, dates and times. Some hours, days, months and years were good but others were bad. Astrology has now replaced religion for many weak-minded people today. They consult the horoscopes printed in every newspaper before losing their shirts on the dogs, the horses, the pools, the cards or the lottery. If only the media would publish logical temporal arguments, instead of illogical spiritual rubbish, We might be able to rebuild a better Planet. The Second Millennium in *Anno Domini* chronology was two thousand years after Christ was supposed to have been born and one thousand years after Christianity became established in many parts of the globe. It was celebrated by Christians throughout the globe but was marked with senseless destruction by fanatics and weird sects of other religions. **The Worldwide System** is the answer to many mathematical problems, as well as to theological, political, social, ecological and economical ones.

Good Time

Decimals have been used for a millennium but We have missed the point.
Zeros have also been used for a millennium but We have learned nothing.
We count years in millennia, centuries and decades, so We could count
days in tens and then divide them into *decidays, centidays, millidays...*
French revolutionary Time began at the autumnal equinox and had
digital weeks and decimal days but they started at year one, not zero,
their ten-day week had no zero day, their ten-hour day had no zero hour.
Napoleon I abandoned the metre and their age, date and time system.
Napoleon III reinstated the metre but he retained Roman-Catholic Time.
Most of the World has now adopted this as: The International System.
Yet, the second and metre are arbitrary and not based on Planet Earth.
The French are not always right and they never listen to the British.
They want to limit working hours and extend the weekend to three days.
It would be better to extend the week to ten days and to share jobs.
For business would be kept busier; whilst We would have more leisure.
This simple remedy for socio-economic ills of the twenty-first century,
since the start of Christianity, is still being suppressed by the Church.
The Catholics still use Roman numerals with no zeros and no decimals.

The mechanical clock was introduced during the first Elizabethan reign.
Its twelve hour, half-day dial became a standard, which never changed.
It became the means by which navigators could find their way around
the globe and they helped the missionaries to spread its use Worldwide.
Throughout history, conquerors have imposed their cultures on others,
who have resisted it, and even in the last century the Victorians were
imposing laws about age, date and time throughout the British Empire.
It is difficult for Us, neo-Elizabethans, to explain that they were wrong.
The ability to trot around the globe has come within reach of many of Us.
If We cannot afford it, We can now see it on TV, video or *Google Earth*.
Our Planet is shrinking, for We can experience other cultures as well as
Our own and some of Us choose to live and work in another country.
We have already realized that We must use the same nuts and bolts,
cut Our paper to the same sizes, use decimal currency and count in,
multiply or divide by digital tens, hundreds, thousands and millions.
However, We omitted to standardize driving on the right side of the road
and a logical, secular, global-digital-decimal Time and Space system.

The politicians promise Us good Times ahead if We will vote for them.
Yet, none of them understand how to govern Our Time nor Our Space.
Some say there are no quick fixes for the fine mess they got Us into.
A ten-day *wek* and **full-time-job-sharing-as-the-norm** is a quick fix.
It could be an instant remedy for many of Our socio-economic problems.
It could even be an instant remedy for many of Our political problems.
You are having a very bad Time if you are wasting your opportunities.
You are having a very good Time if you are using all of it efficiently.

Wrong Time

The history of Time is a chronicle of attempts to find order in the Universe. There have been numerous different chronologies, calendars and clocks but none of these measurement systems have withstood the test of Time. If We want to advance, We must be critical of everything around Us and be prepared to make changes to any of the systems that We use. Technological changes in Our life-times mean that We must change Our habits or be left behind by the March of Progress or the Steps in Time. To stand-still is, in relative terms, to go backwards, yet, many of those in power still seem to believe in the stand-still doctrine of the *status quo.*

We have no global leaders and The United Nations is not uniting nations. Hence businessmen, clergymen and politicians try to control Our World. Some businesses are more powerful than any state so pull many strings. Some religions are more powerful than any state so pull other strings. Some politicians are still under the influence of big business or religion. Most of them simply reiterate ancient dogmas, without thinking at all. There are very few independent politicians who do not toe a party line. Religion is still in control of the state in various parts of the globe. Whilst in many other places it is the state that is in control of religion. Religious dogmas are now seriously holding-up the progress of Mankind. Muslims use dogmas of a millennium ago - Our World was very different. Christians use dogmas of two millennia ago - it was very, very different. Jews use dogmas of three millennia ago - it was very, very, very different. The East always accepts inevitable changes more readily than the West. This is, fundamentally, why the East is now rapidly overtaking the West.

Although mathematicians could devise all manner of complex systems; the simplest system is the best one for the lowest common denominator. Mathematics is a universal language mostly based upon the number ten. Mankind is always multiplying, dividing, differentiating and integrating. If We could count the same way; We may be able to think the same way. Then We might be able to ignore the summation of all Our differences. We have known about zeros, numbers and decimals for a millennium. Yet, We have not yet applied this mathematical knowledge to all of Time. Different ages, dates, times and zones lead to inevitable conflicts and so do many different rules, measures, weights, currencies and languages. By replacing calendars, diaries and timetables - which We do annually; watches and clocks - which We do regularly; maps and charts - which We do occasionally; rulers, measures and weights - which We do rarely; currencies - which We all have to do every time that We travel abroad; languages - which We all have to do if We want to be understood; We Humans could then build a new kind of global civilization in which Our differences could be minimized, Our resources could be shared and then many of Our Man-made barriers would, rapidly, become obsolete. It is never too late to put Our Time, Our Space and Our World right.

Right Time

Study the age, date and time and you will feel the pulse of Our Planet.
Mother Earth has a dicky ticker, a dodgy dater and is chronically sick.
An urgent transplant is needed for her chronology, calendar and clock.
They beat: backwards and forwards, sometimes in 28s, 29s, 30s or 31s
sometimes in 7s, sometimes in 12s or 24s, sometimes in 60s and 10s.
We are taught the current, irrational and complex hotchpotch before
We have the experience to question it, We then take it for granted,
We regard it as divine or We dejectedly say: it's too late to change now.
Yet, any Man-made system can be changed, if the majority desire it.

The British Imperial System had a mile of 1,760 yards, a yard of 3 feet,
a fathom of 6 feet, a foot of 12 inches divided by 8ths, 10ths or 12ths.
Or 22 yards to a chain, 10 chains to a furlong and 8 furlongs to a mile.
Then there were 144 square inches to a square foot, 9 square feet to a
square yard, 4,840 square yards to an acre, 640 acres to a square mile.
Then 1,728 cubic inches to a cubic foot and 27 cubic feet to a cubic yard.
Nevertheless, cubic capacity was considered to be different from volume.
So there were 20 fluid ounces to a pint (which was 34.68 cubic inches);
there were also 2 pints to a quart and 4 quarts or 8 pints to a gallon,
2 gallons to a peck, 4 pecks to a bushel and 8 bushels to a quarter.
Then 16 drams to an ounce, 16 ounces to a pound, 14 pounds to a stone,
8 stones to a hundredweight and then 20 hundredweights to a ton.
The Avoirdupois System had a pound of 16 ounces or 7,000 grains.
The Troy System was based on a pound of 12 ounces or 3,760 grains.
The grain was the smallest unit of weight and was equal to 0.0648 grams.
Britain has abandoned this nonsense - except for the mile and the pint.

Worldwide Time & **Worldwide Space** are the bases for **The Worldwide System.**
Worldwide Time = **global age + digital date + decimal time + single zone.**
It is always best to start at square zero, so 2000 CE becomes 000 **WT**.
Civilization began 12,000 years ago, so 2000 CE should be 12,000 **WT**.
We know the **global age** of Earth, so this is really 4,550,012,000 **WT**.
The **digital date** divides into 36 ten-day weeks + 5 or 6 remainder days.
The days are numbered, beginning with day 000 on the vernal equinox.
We are now using two different time systems with either 12 or 24 hours.
It would be less confusing to use one **decimal time** starting with 000.
The start of **global age : digital date . decimal time** was **000:000.000.**
We should scrap all of the divisive time zones and use one **single zone.**
Daylight saving measures make no difference to the amount of daylight.
We must abandon the habit of rigid working hours and be more flexible.
Worldwide Space is, simply, based upon the girth of Our Planet Earth.
The length of the Equator is then divided by the round number 360 and
sub-divided in a decimal way by tens, hundreds, thousands and millions.
One millionth of a degree of longitude is the width of an average hand and
this handy new unit is the basis for area, volume, weight and wealth.

Real Time

There are now *Ten Heavenly Bodies*: the Sun and the nine major Planets; instead of *Seven Heavenly Bodies*, which were visible to the naked eye when the Mystic seven-day week was originally devised in Mesopotamia. The Gregorian calendar months are irregular, illogical and misaligned. All of the ancient day and month names are now quite meaningless. Some people now use week-day and month numbers instead of names. Many organizations currently use 52 week numbers rather than months. Most bankers now use ordinal year-day numbers for calculating interest. These are printed in most diaries, they are more useful than month-days or week-days and they drop into handy groups of ten.

We use the same seven-day week but We do not take the same days off and the unproductive weekend is gradually getting longer and longer. A seven-day week was found to be the best interval between market days. Yet, We do not need to go to market or hypermarket every seven days. We now have many different methods of storing and preserving food. Most of Us now have cars and most supermarkets now have big trolleys. Consequently, We now only need to shop for food, vacuum the carpets, mow the lawn and do many other household chores every ten days or so.

In industrial countries We work on about half of the days in the year. In developing countries there is only work for about half of Us to do. If the week-end was equal to the work-end, most jobs could be shared. The whole of society could be divided equally into two separate teams. Many are already sharing jobs but by doing this on a five + five basis all equipment could be used much more intensively and productively. This would be more economical and work could be completed sooner. Any organization using a ten-day week would become more competitive. Any country using it would make faster progress, it would experience lower inflation or even deflation and then be able to balance its books. The globe would deflate and become a much more civilized community. Global warming would be reduced and congestion would be minimized. During free-days We could look after Our families, maintain Our property, do voluntary work for the community, help to raise funds for charities, participate in sports and pastimes, visit cinemas, theatres and museums, follow politics, philosophy or religion, develop new ideas, take vacations, rest, shop, read, learn, play, listen and watch, electronically or for real. We could equalize what the sociologists now call: Our work/life balance.

The main snag with this simple idea is religious and trade union dogma. It denies people their Human Rights and is still holding back progress. Would anyone be any less good if they only went to synagogue, chapel, church, cathedral, temple, mosque or shrine once in every ten days? Why does progress have to stop dead because a few people want to pray? Has individual, group or mass prayer ever been proven to be effective?

False Time

We have only been able to determine the circumference of the Equator, or girth of the Earth, since the Global Positioning System was launched. We now have all of the data needed to create **The Worldwide System**. The Metrical System was meant to be based upon the girth of the Earth, however, it was inaccurately based on the length of the Paris Meridian. The Navigation System is based upon the Greenwich Meridian and the girth of the Earth divided by 360 degrees, 60 minutes and then decimals. So navigators use a mixture of hexadecimal and decimal systems when calculating their position by latitude, longitude and compass directions. The Imperial and American Systems are irrational and incompatible with most of the International Metrical System, now used by most countries. Nevertheless, this system is false, because the metre is now based upon the second, which was a 60th of a 60th of a 24th of a mean Solar day, but this is now an arbitrary number of intangible Atomic vibrations. So the metre, the litre, the Kilogram and the second are all arbitrary. Time and Space are now based on intangible, arbitrary, false measures. They should be based on the true age, orbit, spin and girth of the Earth.

We still speak in many different languages, write many different scripts and use many different chronologies, calendars, clocks, zones and rules. Any new system should use the minimum of words and it should be capable of being easily and quickly understood by anyone, anywhere. There is no reason for Us all to work, rest, play and pray simultaneously. Indeed, every time zone has a different working and resting schedule and every state has its own laws or by-laws about working and resting times. These are based upon artificial clock time instead of Natural daylight. This is what Our body clocks have been used to since time immemorial. There is no reason why all days cannot be considered to be equal, why all working times cannot be varied to suit the length of daylight, why all clock times cannot be based upon the same Prime Meridian. Indeed, the International System now permits the days of the year to be ordinally numbered and they then drop into very handy groups of ten. It is possible to use a ten-day week and job-sharing-as-the-norm today. Nevertheless, it would be very much better to start again at square zero. Or, indeed, at square zero-zero-zero, for Time is a scalar measurement.

The crisis We face today is the minor problem We neglected yesterday. Our Planet desperately needs help to cope with its population explosion. **Full-time-job-sharing-as-the-norm** would reduce waste and pollution, minimize congestion, encourage democracy and even promote humanity. This would be a long-term solution but not an expedient compromise. Nevertheless, it could also be a quick fix, because We could use it now. Our descendants might still be using it in another thousand generations. Yet, no one with any kind of authority, on this very disorganized Planet, will even listen to these arguments, let alone take any sort of action.

Old Time

Chronologies, chronicles and chronometers are parts of a chronic system, supposed to have been decreed by the Roman-Pagan Time-god: *Chronos*. Our working, playing, praying and resting patterns are all based upon chronologies, calendars and clocks and every nation has its own system. In many cases the nation-state is under the control of a single religion, whilst those who live there may have many different beliefs - or none. This is, largely, what makes a nation-state different and autonomous. If We were to use the same age, date, time and zone this might signal the end of the nation-state, yet We are all *Homo sapiens* and should all be able to live and work wherever We want to, on this crowded Planet Earth.

Some ancient Greeks used ten-day weeks and shared some of their jobs. Their empire grew much larger than the territory called: Greece, today. However, every city-state in their great empire used a different calendar. Athenians started to adopt philosophy instead of their traditional religions. However, they were over-run by the Roman-Pagan Empire and were lost. The Roman Empire used the Julian *kalendar* devised for Julius Caesar. This originally started at the vernal equinox with alternate months of 30 and 31 days but Octavian or Augustus gave it higgledy-piggledy months and instead of starting with March it eventually started with January. So their tenth month, named: December, then became the twelfth month. Each *kalendar* month was sub-divided into *kalends, ides* and *nones*. The Roman Emperor Constantine made Christianity the state religion. He adopted the Mystic seven-day week and made Sunday a day of rest. The Orthodox Church became established in the Eastern Roman Empire. It still uses the Julian calendar, which has slipped behind the seasons. The Catholic Church became established in the Western Roman Empire. It uses the Roman calendar months and seven-day weeks but it is now thirteen days ahead due to a correction made by Pope Gregory XIII. He updated the date but failed to restart the year on the vernal equinox. Roman-Catholics devised AD chronology, based upon the birth of Christ, but this is also wrong and it is unsuitable for use by the whole Planet. Our clocks were based upon the original twelve hours of daylight and twelve hours of darkness, which were used by the ancient Egyptians. However, We now have 24 equal hours, which were used by the Greeks. They divided their hours into sixty first units and sixty second units. Dividing by sixties goes back to the ancient Sumerians and Babylonians.

The one thing that We all have in common today is the seven-day week. This Mystic week originated in Mesopotamia and Persia and it was used by the Jews before being adopted by some of the earliest Christians. In Mesopotamia it was bad Saturn's day that became their day of rest. In Persia it was good Sun's day that was their religious day of rest. The Jews chose Saturday as their Sabbath, the Christians chose Sunday and, just to be different, the Muslims chose Friday for their day of rest.

New Time

The Greek philosophers were the founders of the arts and the sciences.
They were the first to establish formal education at centres of learning.
They invented democracy and were the first to visualize an ideal state.
Nevertheless, their mythical Elysian Fields still seem as elusive as ever.
The modern, independent state of Greece was reformed in 1832 AD.
But many of those idyllic islands have only been ceded to it since then.
Greece has used the Roman-Catholic Gregorian calendar since 1923 AD.
Yet, it still celebrates Easter based on the old Orthodox Julian calendar.
The Greek Orthodox Church continued to use Sun-dials until 1900 AD.
Greece has been an isolated part of the European Union since 1981 AD.
Yet, despite many handouts, its economy is now the weakest in Europe.
It may soon have to drop out of the eurozone and the European Union.
Perhaps **full-time-job-sharing-as-the-norm** would help it to catch-up.

The Greek islands all have different histories, geographies and societies.
Some of the smaller islands, which are off the beaten track, still uphold
their traditions: the Sabbath is sacrosanct and women know their place.
Most of the larger islands have sold their souls to tourism so, in summer,
Sunday is no longer a rest day but the same as any other working day.
The best months are May, June, September, October, when it is warm;
yet most visitors go there in July and August, when it is usually stifling.
This is entirely because of school holidays and factory shutdowns in
places where July and August were reserved for gathering in the harvest.
If 5+5 job-sharing became the norm then families would be able to take
a short or long break at any time of the year, so the annual pattern of
tourism would change and become much more enjoyable and profitable.

The key to the door of the New World Order lies in public education.
The academic year and its terms are under the control of the state.
However, most educational buildings are now empty for half of the year.
If the academic year started on the vernal equinox and then ran for 36
ten-day weeks, two teams of teachers and students could work on
alternate five-day periods and the buildings would be used every day.
This would halve the overhead costs at all levels of education and allow
teachers and students to prepare or to do their assignments at home.
Formal education could be based upon ten core subjects but informal
education would take place, on an optional basis, during the rest days.
Higher education could be based upon the same system and vocational
training or retraining courses could be held during workers' rest days.
Thus the quality of education at all levels could be greatly improved.
The whole of society would quickly adjust to the same working pattern.
The traditional working pattern based on the seven-day week is rapidly
being eroded and laws enforcing it are now being repealed, yet We still
have many dogmas associated with it, which keep this rhythm going.
All days and hours were once equal and they should be equal again.

Working Time

Working is a reason for living and many of those who are deprived of it, even if they are financially secure, can gradually lose their will to live. Civilization is all about the organization of labour for the common good. We once built pyramids, obelisks, spires and minarets for the Sky-gods. We now build Sky-scrapers, Sky-rides, Sky-rockets and Sky-stations. It is difficult to justify these projects on economic grounds but they are starting to take over from the complete waste of Time, Space and Life that is represented by the manufacture and use of all kinds of weapons.

Working is an essential part of Our lives but We have been so successful in making labour-saving devices that an ever-increasing proportion of Our population have no work to do and so civilization is breaking-down. Women used to stay at home to do the housework and look after the kids. They now make up half of the labour force and many men stay at home. Sexual equality has had a huge effect on the unemployment statistics. We used to spend about half of Our lives working but now the average worker in Britain works for about half their lives, on about half of the days in the year, for about a third of a day, or about 7.5% of their lives. Many people work extremely long hours and do not get enough sleep; whilst a third of Us are out of work and the Welfare State cannot cope. Capitalism is based upon the law of the jungle and survival of the fittest. Socialism was a forlorn attempt that failed to reorganize all the workers. We must find a third way of reorganizing work for the benefit of Us all. Yet, there is absolutely no point in creating work in order to create jobs. The British Civil Service created a million new jobs after New Labour came into power and a quarter of these leeches were tax inspectors. The taxation and benefit system needs redesigning from top to bottom. There is no point in taxing workers to pay for shirkers to do nothing. We must share Our wealth by sharing Our work in a ten-day week.

Automation is still improving productivity and reducing manpower but manufacturers of fast moving consumer goods are finding that it pays to move production lines to countries where overheads and labour costs are lower, even though their main markets may be in richer countries. The Organization for Economic Co-operation and Development reported that in 2003 AD the South Koreans, Czechs, Slovakians and Greeks worked for around 2,000 hours/year, USA 1,800, UK, NZ and Aus 1,600, French and Germans 1,400 but the Norwegians only worked for 1,300. South Korea works 6 days/week; France wants to work 4 days/week. Futurologists predict that mechanization and automation will continue until there is no work left, and reach this conclusion by extrapolating graphs of the decline of manpower in every field of Human activity. They now predict that **full-time-job-sharing** with **flextime** and **flexdate** will become the most civilized way to work in any industrial country. So, the **digital week** and the **decimal day** could soon become the norm.

Shirking Time

It is very hard to distinguish what is paid-time and what is unpaid-time, because unions insisted that workers were sometimes paid for nothing. So they were paid on their annual holidays, having lunch or tea breaks, when they were sick and, sometimes, when they were travelling to work. Overtime was paid at a higher rate than normal time, which encouraged workers to work more slowly and so spend less time with their families. Mothers were paid on maternity leave and fathers on paternity leave. Absenteeism is estimated to cost the UK economy some £12G per year. Many people do voluntary work in their spare time or when they retire. The Bank of England say this adds £100G per year to the UK economy. On the other hand, employers sometimes treated employees like slaves. Some companies still consider that they have the right to completely take-over Our lives if they pay Us highly enough and then throw Us on the scrap-heap as soon as We burn-out from overwork and exhaustion. Whilst the official working hours have diminished over recent decades, many work harder than ever and some are not getting enough sleep.

Many now work from or at home, which reduces wasteful travelling time. The Internet and Worldwide Web allow Us to work or rest at any time. E-mail, voice-mail and text save money and time but also shift time. We can now watch or listen to Our favorite programmes at any time. However, the law still says that some days are different from others. By making 360 days equal, adopting a ten-day week and sharing jobs; We would have 180 work days per annum but working time could vary; We would have 180 spare days per annum to do what We want, not what the boss wants Us to do, but We could use some of this time to improve Our knowledge and skills by taking courses, either at college or at home. Instead to going to evening classes after a long and tiring day's work; We could take day classes, short courses or distance learning degrees. We would only be remunerated for the time We actually spent working. The unions would have to negotiate a new deal with the employers and the government would be able to reorganize its social security benefits.

Spare or unpaid time would include all holidays, meals or tea breaks and sickness so it would be up to Us to save and take out health insurance. With five days-off in every ten We would be able to take a break away from work and home whenever We chose, so the tourism industry would have fewer peaks and troughs caused by holy days and bank holidays. If We needed a longer break We could swap with the person with whom We shared Our job so that each of Us could take ten or fifteen days-off. We need time with Our families to do the household chores, maintain and improve Our property, pursue a hobby or interest, meet friends, help the community, take exercise, have a rest or even go to church. The 5 or 6 remainder days would not be worked, paid nor taxed but only used for local, regional, national, international and global elections.

Buying Time

When We were hunter-gatherers We worked for about two days in seven. Agriculture tied Us down and made Us work harder but We could then afford to divide Our workforce into specialists under a central hierarchy. The artisans who built the pyramids were not slaves but paid workers and most public and private structures were built by cooperative effort. The craftsmen who decorated the royal tombs in the Valley of the Kings, four millennia ago, were paid for the work and took two days rest in ten. Life was very different a millennium ago - before clocks were invented. Time was thought of as a gift from *God* so it could not be bought or sold. The invention of mechanical clocks changed Our whole concept of work. Labour was then divided and different skills received different rewards. The very best craftsmen were employed to make the clocks and watches. In the last millennium We lost Our independence and self-sufficiency. Employers now tend to think of employees, contractors or consultants as man-hours that can be bought just like Kilowatt-hours and they are starting to realize that part-time-job-sharing can be more cost effective. It is a small step forward for **full-time-job-sharing** to become the norm.

During the last millennium there have been many changes to **Time**. We have changed from using the reigns of Kings in Our chronicles to the supposed date of birth of Our savior from the Pagan gods in the Sky. We do not use Roman *kalends, ides* and *nones* but month-day numbers. We have changed the beginning of Our year several times but, whilst We all use a seven-day week, the Sabbath has grown into a weekend. We have moved the start of Our day several times, over the centuries. Our clocks have changed from being a measure of the length of daylight into a measure of the whole diurnal cycle and Our working hours are the same the whole year round, irrespective of Natural lightness or darkness. Our time zones were adopted by every state, yet We do not need them. Our so-called daylight saving measures are a complete waste of time. It is now time to rationalize the whole Time system and to incorporate the zero and the decimal point, which reached Europe a millennium ago.

Our Planet's economy depends upon international communications and so We needed a global standard for Our chronology, calendar and clock; but instead of starting again We used the Roman-Catholic Time 'system'. There are still many different ages, dates and times in use around the globe but this Roman-Catholic 'system' was adopted for commercial use. No one understands what *God* is all about and so they carry on faithfully with ceremonies and celebrations without knowing what they all mean. No one understands what Time is all about so they carry on faithfully using ancient divisions, which are totally incompatible with modern Life. No one understands how the global economy works and why the stock markets peak and trough as incompetent politicians forever buy Time. So *God* = Time + Space + Life and the World revolves about its measures.

Selling Time

Time has gradually become the basis for a multi-billion dollar industry. About a billion clocks and half a billion watches are now sold annually. All calendars, planners, diaries and timetables are replaced annually. Vested interests want to keep this established industry exactly the same. Nevertheless, there are many valid reasons to begin again at square zero. Clock and watch making used to be a great British industry but it was frittered away as management and unions fought over the cost of time. The Swiss took over the quality end of the market for accurate watches. The Americans found that their mass-produced ones were just as good. The Japanese led the way when they mass-produced cheap digital ones. Today's fashion is to wear analogue watches with electronic movements; whilst digital clocks are now built into state-of-the-art electronic gizmos. The next step is analogue dials or digital windows with **decimal time**. Although production of new watches and clocks could be set-up quickly, several years would be needed for huge global stocks to be built-up. The tax on them could pay for public clocks and signs to be changed. Many of Us have only recently changed from Imperial to International and so We would be reluctant to change again but that system is faulty. Planned replacement need not involve significant extra expenditure.

Many electronic gizmos have **Time** built into their operating systems. They rapidly become obsolete when something much better is developed. In a few years some of the basic computer languages became obsolete. Yet, they contained basic programs for the age, the date and the time. In **Y2K** the papers were full of special offers on home or office computers. They said they were **Y2K** compliant, yet some failed at the Millennium. This was because of a single digit in the age used in a program language. The **Y2K** problem has still not been solved but it was merely postponed. Some claim that English will be superseded by Internet or text jargon. The next innovation could be the language of: **The Worldwide System**.

The Worldwide System would create a new global industry and market. **Worldwide Time and Space** need not necessarily be replaced together. **Global age** would replace all the existing chronologies at very little cost. What could be simpler than to globalize the Solar year, starting at 000? **Digital date** calendars, planners, diaries, timetables would be perpetual. What could be simpler than to digitalize the Solar day, starting at 000? **Decimal time** clocks or watches would be simpler and cheaper to make. What could be simpler than to decimalize the Solar day, starting at 000? **Single zone** would make all time zones and daylight saving obsolete. What could be simpler than to make clocks and watches read the same? **World Space** would make Imperial, American, International and Nautical measures obsolete but the global savings would soon cover the costs. **The Worldwide System** would cost a great deal of money to implement. However, the global savings would be very, very, very much greater.

Wasting Time

The Time and Space wasted in industry, commerce and other workplaces, is probably far more than that used to achieve something worthwhile. Most factories, offices, universities, colleges, schools and their expensive facilities are totally unused for almost half of the days in every year. If they were to be used every day their overhead costs could be halved. All We need to do is adopt a ten-day working week and share most jobs. This would reduce the cost of goods and services, save expensive energy, ease congestion, reduce pollution and it would minimize unemployment. The greatest obstacles to this are the Judaeo/Christian/Muslim Sabbaths and the belief that the seven-day week was carved upon tablets of stone. We now know that the Universe was not created in seven days and that We evolved over millions of years after the dinosaurs were annihilated. Most Britons now realize that all religion is a complete waste of Time but they have not yet realized that it should be replaced by Humanism.

We take penny-pinching measures; whilst Our leaders waste £trillions upon useless defence equipments and quite unnecessary civil services. Our taxation system has become so complex that it needs millions of collectors and inspectors, who waste a great deal of Time and Space. We should have one standard rate of VAT on everything and stop firms from claiming it back on the precious fossil fuels that they have wasted. Much of Our expensive food is wasted when it passes its sell-by-date. We also waste a great deal of free daylight and expensive fuel because We have not yet learned how to use Our calendars and clocks efficiently. Daylight saving time or summer time is really a complete waste of time. For We spend many hours changing Our many timepieces forwards and backwards when all We need to do is start and stop work earlier or later. Our leaders are still under the impression that noon and midday are the same thing, that 12:00 must fall in the middle of the working day and that this must always be the same length throughout the entire year. They pass laws which perpetuate these anachronisms instead of letting employers and employees decide their own optimum working patterns. Spare time should not be wasted, for there are many worthwhile things to do for the good of the local community without any remuneration.

Much of Our very expensive time spent using telephones is wasted as We grapple with the problems caused by the incompatibility of months with weeks, date lines, time zones, so-called daylight saving measures and the mental arithmetic needed to convert from 12 to 24 hour clocks. The abbreviation 01/02/03 could mean: year one/month two/day three or day one/month two/year three or month one/day two/year three. Computers need one age, date and time built into them but they have many different systems and options in the way that they are presented. The Internet does not care what year, month, week, day or time it is. The Worldwide Web should incorporate **The Worldwide System**.

Saving Time

We never get to the end of the learning curve for, no matter how good any product is, there is always a better one that could save more time. The vacuum cleaner is a classic example of such a time-saving device. A new product may have taken many years of research and development before reaching its market but can sweep its competitors off the floor. A woman's place used to be in the home but they now have many time saving devices, many of them go out to work and there are now as many of them in employment as men, which has had a big effect on the labour market and is part of the reason why many more of Us are out of work. However, the end of the learning curve will come soon enough when We run out of cheap energy and have to return to the dustpan & brush.

Most of what We do in the developed World today is about saving Time. Many enterprises could be twice as productive for a fixed investment in buildings and equipment if they used **full-time-job-sharing-as-the-norm**. Money is still the foremost reason why We must work but time-off is becoming just as significant to Our life-styles and must also be earned. We will have reached social equilibrium when workdays equal free-days. Yet, only two-thirds of all Our workers are now being gainfully employed. The main cause of this is the Mystic seven-day week, its Sabbath day and its unproductive weekend, which could soon grow to three days. We all need to take regular rest days, like the working beasts of burden, but We do not have to take them together, like a grazing herd of sheep.

It takes a Natural catastrophe or a Man-made calamity to make Us think. New York is the global centre of capitalism and the World Trade Center, was destroyed at 8:46 am EST on Tuesday 11 September 2001 AD. The time, zone, week-day, moonth-day, moonth and year were all different at the opposite side of the globe where lunatic assassins called the shots. Had the pilots chosen Sunday to commit their suicides then Wall Street would have been closed and most workers would have been at home. On that fateful day almost 3,000 workers and rescuers lost their lives. The USA used weapons of mass destruction to kill, some say, 1M Iraqis, who had no weapons of mass destruction and nothing to do with 9/11. This date was probably chosen because it was on the Coptic New Year. Almost 4,500 American service men and women lost their lives in the hunt for Saddam Hussein, whose secular regime was replaced by Islam. Afghanistan was destroyed in the hunt to annihilate Osama bin Laden, but instead of hiding in a cave there he was living in luxury in Pakistan. New York was brought to a halt again at the end of October in 2012 AD by the Natural disaster called: Sandy, the largest hurricane in history, which, some say, was due to global warming, caused by waste heat. Some of Us never, ever stop to think what We are doing to Our Planet. Our Human population is already far more than Our Planet can sustain. We can save Our Planet and Our Species if We share Time and Space.

51

Finding Time

It is only now that Our quest for the cycles, ratios and sizes of Time and Space can finally be rationalized and programmed into digital computers. The Metric System was merely an interim measure; not the ultimate one. The metre and second were based upon the size and spin of this Planet, but are now based upon a completely arbitrary number of vibrations. The second and the meter (metre) are now under the control of the USA. However, the USA has not yet adopted the International Metric System. The Worldwide Web has become the communication system that pulls Our World together and IT now works tirelessly all day and every day. Many offices, factories and shops now need to be manned day and night. The best way to achieve efficient new working patterns is by adopting a ten-day week and **full-time-job-sharing-as-the-norm** but, although this can soon be achieved in any organization, it needs to be implemented in a community, a country, a continent and throughout this entire Planet.

We now know that there is nothing special about this Planet, this Solar System nor this Galaxy but We can, for the moment, assume that Our species is as advanced as any other intelligent Life-form in the Universe. There is nothing special about Sundays, Christians or the Human Race. This is contrary to the teaching of the Catholic Church, which holds that its chronology, calendar and clock were divinely inspired, its seven-day week is sacrosanct and the hands on its clocks must point up at noon. Unfortunately, many Americans still believe that this Planet was created in seven days and that *God* commanded Us to use the seven-day week. The American constitution says it is a secular federation and the Bill of Rights says that it should not discriminate against any race nor religion. Yet, it does favour the Roman-Catholic chronology, calendar and clock. John Paul II wanted the EU constitution to include a preference for *God;* but this was strongly resisted by the other religions and by Humanists.

Humanists are the silent majority in Britain and much of Our World. They should all use the same, simple, secular Time and Space system. What could be simpler than a system of units based upon the age, orbit, spin and girth of the Earth and the global-digital-decimal number ten? This rational but radical idea is the basis for: **The Worldwide System.** It may soon become the global standard system, like the Worldwide Web. All of the national and international standards organizations should be replaced by **One Worldwide Standards Organization** under the UN. Yet, the UN has fallen short of expectations and although it considered a global calendar, when it was first formed, this was vetoed by the USA. The USA also vetoed the proposal that all the clocks in Our World should be set to the same time, based upon midnight along the Prime Meridian. This baseline of Time and Space passes through Greenwich in London. The cross-wires in the eyepiece of a telescope at the Royal Observatory could soon become the focus of **Worldwide Time** and **Worldwide Space**.

THE WORLDWIDE SYSTEM

Part Two

Standardization

Time, Space, Life and the Metric System

"Man is the measure of all things."

Protagoras (c.485-c.410 BC)

Diversity

The past was of no interest to prehistoric Man, who lived for the present, but the future slowly became more important as agriculture developed. Observing the motions of the Sun, the Moon, the Planets and the Stars not only helped to predict the seasons and the tides but may also have helped to predict floods, storms, droughts, earthquakes and eruptions. This was the beginning of astronomy, astrology, science and religion. Many temples were observatories built to study the celestial clockwork. Some of them housed great libraries of observations and calculations, which had to be kept up-to-date by a select group of astronomer-priests. Each civilization, each culture, each religion and each sect developed its own way of measuring, managing and governing Time and Space.

The Stone Age troglodytes devised a Lunar/Solar calendar based upon the quarter phases of the Moon and the solstices and equinoxes of the Sun. Egyptians needed to know: when Sirius, the brightest Star, would rise at dawn as the Nile flooded to irrigate their crops; in which season and month to plant seeds under the best conditions; how to divide months into weeks to fix market days and festivals; how to divide day and night into hours so that they could honour their many gods and pay skilled workers to construct, decorate and furnish their great stone monuments. They measured the height of the floods and the sizes of their fields to collect taxes; they measured buildings, furniture, chariots and boats; they measured water, beer and milk; they weighed materials and produce. Babylonians needed to know when the Moon would be full so that they could travel at night and when the Sun would be at its vernal equinox, so they could irrigate their crops when the Tigris and Euphrates flooded. They thought that the Stars and Planets could predict their own future. Greeks gave names to many of the sciences of Space, Time and Life. They developed their arts and their crafts to a very high standard. Their stadiums were dedicated to the measurement of Human prowess. Their temples embodied sacred proportions, dimensions and directions. Romans were not scientists but they were technologists who developed the skills to conquer other civilizations and construct their great empire. They standardized everything from weights and measures to language. Their temples were not only for gods but were the sign of law and order. The Latin words: temple, tempo and tempus mean the division of Time. The Chinese, Japanese, Indian, Persian, Minoan, Egyptian, Maya, Inca, French and British empires all standardized their Time and their Space.

Different civilizations with their tools, weapons, superstitions, religions, beliefs, traditions, cultures, laws, languages, numerals, scripts, signs, rules, weights, measures, chronologies, calendars, clocks and zones evolved in different ways and these ancient differences divide Us today. Sometimes We need to replace several tools with a single improved one: a panacea, that can be used by anyone, everywhere on every occasion.

Uniformity

Many different beliefs about Time, Space and Life still prevail, around the globe but they are fading as We discover more about the Universe. Time was thought to be cyclic because it was measured by the apparent, but variable, cycles of the Sun, the Moon, the Planets and the Stars. Space was once thought to revolve around Our insignificant little Planet but it was also measured by many different methods, all over the globe. Distances, directions, angles, lengths, areas, volumes, and weights were all measured by different methods with no logical basis for any of them. Life was also thought to be cyclic and so many different beliefs about immortality were imagined in many different superstitions and religions. These beliefs divide Our Human Race and still cause millions of deaths. We will be reunited when We use one global-digital-decimal system for measuring, managing and governing Our Time, Our Space and Our Life.

Although it seems Natural to count everything in tens on Our digits, there are not an exact number of days in a moonth nor a year, nor an exact number of moonths in a year, nor weeks in a moonth or a year. So many kinds of calendar were devised and then many kinds of clock. Every society, culture, civilization or religion had a very different way of counting years, months and weeks, so this divided Our Human Race. The use of hours, minutes and seconds in clocks and watches united Us. Yet, they are counted and divided by 12 or 24, 60, 60 and then decimals. The imposition of standard time zones divided Us with invisible barriers. There are 24 sea time zones but about 40 on land and some states still do not accept that Time and Space should be based upon Greenwich.

The French revolutionaries were strongly influenced by scientists and mathematicians, who had rejected religion and then become enlightened. They started again with a clean sheet of paper and devised a new system, which, they hoped, would eventually be adopted by the entire Planet. However, their idea that lengths, areas, volumes and weights should be based on the size of the Earth and that ages, dates and times should be based on years, ten-day weeks and decimals of a day was abandoned. Politicians and civil servants turned a logical temporal and spatial idea, which could have united Our Human Race, into a fiasco that divided Us. There were different ways of measuring temperature and other scales. The International Metric System is now based upon an Atomic second, and this arbitrary unit is also in the Imperial and American systems. The metre is used by most of the World, except for the USA who still insist on writing: meter, instead of: metre, and: center, instead of: centre. What Our World needs now is a United Nations Organization which does what it says and is totally free to suggest the best way of doing things. It should be free from all political and religious pressures and it should be given the power to resolve all kinds of humanitarian issues such as: one global-digital-decimal system for all kinds of measurements.

Digits

The Egyptians, Persians and Chinese used their digits to count in tens.
However, other ancient civilizations adopted a variety of counting systems.
The Sumerians counted up to 24 on their finger joints with their thumbs.
The Etruscans counted in eights upon their fingers with their thumbs.
The Romans did too but changed to counting in Vs, Xs, Ls, Cs and Ms.
The Mayans and Celts counted up to twenty on their fingers and toes.
The Celts counted in scores and so the British say: eleven, not: ten-one,
and the French say: *onze*, not: *dix-une*, and they also say: *quatre-vingt*
or *quatre-vingt-dix* instead of: *octante* or *nonante* for eighty or ninety.
The British count up to twelve before counting in teens up to twenty.
The Japanese say one-one instead of eleven - and so they count faster.

The Indians and Arabs developed the positional numbering system.
The largest numbers are on the left and the smallest are on the right.
The abacus, developed by the Babylonians, Greeks, Romans and Arabs
is still used in the Far East but was superseded by the pocket calculator.
This usually has ten windows, each showing the digital numbers 0-9.
The binary system was devised by Gottfried Leibniz in about 1700 AD.
He also devised the calculus at about the same time as Sir Isaac Newton.
Computers use a binary system but they usually perform calculations to
the base of ten, whilst other bases can be used for special purposes.
Programs often use a two-digit system to indicate: time, date and age.
Each digital group has a different base, which is mathematically wrong.
After showing: 23:59 on 31-12-99 some went to: 00:00 on 01-01-00.
This caused uncorrected computers to go haywire at the Millennium.
Some failed on 09-09-99 due to an obsolete program language code.
Others failed on 01-03-00 which should have been 29-02-00, a leap day.
The cost of putting them right was estimated to be $1,000,000,000,000.
This was only a fudge and so they will all go wrong again on 19-01-38.
The Americans count in hundreds whilst the British count in thousands.
So 2100 AD will be twenty-one-hundred or two thousand one hundred.
Some write the monthday number before the month number; some after.
This difference (9/11 or 11/9) causes confusion and catastrophic mistakes.
So a global-digital-decimal system is needed to avoid all of these issues.

This book advocates an age, date and time system based on three-digits.
e.g. 012:345.678 meaning simply: year : year-day . thousandths of a day.
Each group has the same base, fewer digits are needed, the largest units
are on the left and this system does not repeat itself for a millennium.
A calculator can easily incorporate a chronology, a calendar and a clock.
A mobile phone can have a calculator, chronology, calendar and clock.
A computer can be programmed for any counting or numbering system.
The only mathematical problem with this system is that there are not one
thousand days in a year but the colon indicates this and the decimal
point shows that the day is divided into a thousand units and so on.

Units

Counting with pebbles led to written numbers, probably before written languages, then addition and subtraction and then, step by step, on to multiplication, division and, eventually, the entire logic of mathematics. The old Latin and new English word: calculus, literally means: pebbles.

The Sumerians were the first to use numbers in the third millennium BC as attested by clay tablets found at Susa, Uruk and Tell Beydar. Shapes were made with reeds: units were strokes and tens were holes. They found that 60 is the smallest number divisible by 10 and 12 so used this for their fractions and they divided circles into 360 degrees.

The Egyptian system, first written down in fifth dynasty pyramid texts, used strokes for 1 to 9 and hieroglyphs for 10, 100, 1,000 and 1,000,000. They also used unique hieroglyphs for the numbers from one to twenty. Many of the pyramids were based upon a square of one hundred cubits. Parts of the sacred eye indicate fractions based on halving down to 1/64.

The Greek system was based upon a series of dots in 6s, 12s and 24s. They changed to strokes and letters for 5s, 10s and 100s after Alexander the Great invaded Egypt and saw that their base-ten system was better. They used the Sumerian system for fractions and circular measure.

The Romans inherited many Etruscan ideas and so used their base-eight before adopting the base-ten system, introduced to them by the Greeks. I = 1   V = 5   X = 10   L = 50   C = 100   D = 500   M = 1,000   MM= 2,000 At the first AD Millennium the year changed from DCCCCLXXXXIX to M. Oxbridge taught maths in Roman numerals until the XVII century AD.

The Mayans used a simple system of dots for digits and dashes for fives (thus ... means 8) and they incorporated these symbols into mythical glyph figures who carried burdens or parcels of Time on their backs.

The Vedic Hindus developed their positional counting and numbering system in the fifth century AD and this was later adopted by the Arabs. The Arabic numbering symbols were devised after the fall of the Roman Empire when Baghdad became the greatest centre of Western learning. This logical Islamic counting and numbering system was eventually adopted by the Protestant Church and is now used throughout the globe. Nevertheless, the Catholic Church continues to use Roman numerals.

Some people prefer to number the seven days in the working week. Others object to this but are happy to number the days in the month. Some people number the years, the months, the weeks and the days. Why not use numbers to identify the year since this Planet was formed, the day in the year and the smaller and smaller parts of a day?

Zeros

The use of zeros is a vital part of Our counting and numbering system. Nevertheless, this is a comparatively recent addition to Our mathematics. Missing units were denoted by a space until 300 BC but zeros were not used in Chinese, Sumerian, Persian, Egyptian, Greek nor Roman maths. The zero is of Indian origin, like the numbers 1 to 9 still in use today. Indian maths was translated into Arabic and the Persian mathematician Al-Kwarizimi used these ten numbers in his book: *Arithmetic* of 830 AD. This was introduced to the West by the Moors when they invaded Spain. A French monk called Gerbert became interested in Arabic arithmetic when he visited Cordoba in 980 AD and was able to spread the use of these numbers and zeros when he became Pope Sylvester II in 999 AD. However, he was considered to be a heretic and was soon bumped-off. The word: zero comes from: *sunya*, which means: nothing, in Sanskrit; it became: *sifr* in Arabic, it was Latinized into: *zephirum* by Leonardo Fibonacci in his *Liber Abaci* of 1202 AD and it finally became: zero in 1491 AD in a Florentine treatise - but some prefer: nought or naught.

There is still confusion about whether to start at number zero or one. It depends on whether you are measuring a scalar quantity like weight, length or time or counting an integer quantity like coins, cars or sheep. During Our first year of Life Our age is zero years and months or weeks. The origin on a graph, where the axes intersect, is usually marked zero. The navel of Earth's navigation system is 000 latitude; 000 longitude. The 24-hour digital day starts with 00:00 however the 12-hour half-day, which is usually shown on an analogue dial, always starts with 12:00. This is because a chiming clock must ring 12 times but zero is silent. The *Anno Domini* system was devised before zero arrived in the West. This chronic chronological system should have had both 0 BC and 0 AD. It counts backwards and forwards from an arbitrary year, however, We no longer need to do this for We now know the age of Our Planet. The French revolutionaries included the age, date and time in their new Metric System but this was wrong because their new chronology started with *An* I instead of *An* 0 ; their digital calendar started with *jour 1, premiere decade* and *primidi* instead of *jour 0, zero decade* and *zerodi* and their decimal clock usually had 10 at the top of the dial but not 0.

Placing zeros before whole numbers, e.g. 007, is a recent innovation due to digital counters: each window has ten digits numbered from 0 to 9. Some still say that zero is not a number because it behaves differently. In the last century decades were given names like the Swinging Sixties. The first decade in this century was often called the Naughty Naughties.

Some cosmologists believe that at the very origin of this Universe there was absolutely nothing, because all of the positive and negative forces, all matter and anti-matter, cancelled each other out - no matter!

Decimals

The Chinese astronomers and mathematicians invented decimals and merchants used a base-ten system for weights & measures in 1450 BC. The Sumerians utilized the base of sixty for most of their fractions and this hexadecimal system was used by most Mesopotamian civilizations. The Egyptians divided weights & measures by 2, 4, 8, 16, 32 or 64. The Romans used base-ten for counting but base-twelve for fractions. The Hindu Gupta dynasty developed decimals in the fifth century AD. Abul Hassan al-Uqlidisi was probably the first Arab astronomer to use decimals to calculate the length of the mean Solar year during 925 AD. The Persian mathematician and astronomer al-Kashi used them in his treatise The Key to Arithmetic in Samarkand in the 15th century AD. In Europe, however, small parts of numbers were expressed as fractions with the Sumerian hexadecimal base until the end of 16th century AD. Francois Viete, a French mathematician, suggested that these sixtieths should be replaced by thousandths, hundredths and tenths in 1579 AD. Simon Stevin, a Flemish mathematician and physicist, suggested using decimal numbers in all calculations and measurements in 1582 AD. John Napier, a Scottish mathematician, devised logarithms in 1600 AD. He was the first person to use decimal points in his book of tables. Christopher Wren suggested decimal coins and a decimal measurement system, based upon the length of a one second pendulum, in 1664 AD.

A Metric (Greek for measure) System, based upon the size of the Earth, was proposed by Gabriel Mouton, a Roman-Catholic priest, in 1670 AD. This was introduced by the French Academy of Sciences in 1799 AD. However, Napoleon Bonaparte reverted to the *ancien regime* in 1805 AD. So the Metric System was not finally adopted in France until 1840 AD. Parliament voted, unanimously, to adopt the Metric System in 1862 AD. Britain adopted the CGS (centimetre, gram, second) System in 1947 AD. This became the MKS (metre, kilogram, second) System in 1952 AD. It was modified to the SI (*Systeme Internationale*) System in 1960 AD. This was adopted in 1965 with the aim of complete change by 1975 AD. It did not replace the FPS (foot, pound, second) system until 1995 AD. The final stage (except for the pint and the mile) arrived in 2000 AD. The EU may, eventually, force Britain to abandon the mile and the pint. However, some traders continue to use the fractional Imperial System. Conservative Britain was the last to adopt decimal coinage in 1971 AD. Cheap pocket calculators made it easier for everyone to use decimals. Whereas numbers can be reckoned by any base; the base of ten is now used for all the common units - except for the hour, minute and second.

Thomas Jefferson (1743-1826 AD) was keen on decimals and metres but the USA only adopted decimals of an inch and the digital-decimal dollar. The USA is now the only country in the World without the Metric System. Although many American scientists, engineers and athletes use it.

Cosmology

Cosmology is the science of the origin and development of the Universe. The Greeks attempted to rationalize the Solar System and the Universe. Anaximander (7th century BC) thought that Earth was floating in Space and that the Sun, Moon, Planets and Stars revolved around it in circles. Pythagoras (6th century BC) thought Earth was the centre of the Universe. Plato (5th century BC) thought the Sun was the centre of the Universe. Aristotle (4th century BC) thought Earth was the centre of the Universe. Aristarchus (2nd century BC) suggested that the Earth orbits the Sun. Ptolemy (2nd century AD) thought Earth was the centre of the Universe. Augustine of Hippo (5th century AD) in his *City of God* accepted this as proof that *God* created the Universe and He was in control of everything. Thomas Aquinas (13th Century AD) in his *Summa Theologiae* adopted this geocentric theory, without any question, as the fundamental truth and the Church said that those who proposed alternative theories were heretics.

In 1514 AD Pope Leo X asked astronomer-priest Nicolaus Copernicus (1473-1543 AD) to devise a better calendar and after three decades of calculation he suggested in his *Revolutionibus* or Planetary Tables that: the Earth spins and orbits the Sun whilst the Moon orbits the Earth. In 1609 AD Johannes Kepler of Prague, using the measurements of the Danish nobleman: Tycho Braye, said that Planets have elliptical orbits. The Italian astronomer Galileo Galilei (1564-1642 AD) proved all these theories with his telescope by observing the phases of Venus, the four moons of Jupiter and the 28 day rotation of Sun-spots relative to Earth. The Vatican put him under house arrest to keep this news a secret. When it became public knowledge John Donne (1572-1631 AD) wrote that it changed everything, so he gave up Catholicism for Protestantism. Many thinkers began to question whether *God* had created the Universe in six days and then taken a rest day, as stated in the *Bible*, but nobody seems to have questioned whether there should be seven days in a week. Sir Isaac Newton (1642-1727 AD) invented the larger reflecting telescope, discovered gravity and postulated that the Earth was an oblate sphere. However, he still believed that *God* wrote all of the laws of the Universe.

The current Big Bang theory was developed between 1927 and 1933 AD by Henri Le Maitre, a Belgian astronomer and priest, who suggested that the Universe was once very small, then exploded with the speed of light. His Big Bang theory is now accepted by most cosmologists, who agree that the Universe is still expanding but has unknown forces and matter. The Hubble Space Telescope sees nearby Stars expiring and distant ones being created at the edge of Space and the beginning of Cosmic Time. We now know that there are other Planets orbiting other Stars, however, We have yet to discover whether there is Life elsewhere in the Universe. We will probably never know if Space and Time are finite or infinite, if there have been previous Universes or if there are now more than one.

Geology

Geology is the science of the composition, structure and history of Earth. During the last century We have learned a great deal about Our Planet. The first clues that it was much older than the six millennia in the Bible came to light when the strata within the Grand Canyon were studied. Further evidence came from deep coal mines and from oil drilling rigs. Geophysicists can now see beneath the surface using magnetometers and gravitometers, which measure the variations of these two forces. Seismologists detect quakes on a scale used by C. F. Richter in 1935 AD. They use the shock waves from explosions to find oil, gas and water. Volcanologists attempt to predict volcanic and super-volcanic eruptions, which have already changed and could still change the course of history.

Earth is not quite spherical because centrifugal forces make its equatorial diameter greater than its polar diameter and this keeps it from toppling. A super-continent, which was much thicker on land than under the sea, broke into smaller continents that gradually moved about the globe. Antarctica was once a tropical continent sitting astride the Equator. In some places tectonic plates are still being formed whilst in other places they are forced under each other, so Earth's girth stays the same. The Atlantic grows or the Pacific shrinks at the rate of fingernail growth. Earth's magnetic polarity can be measured from the magma emerging at the bottom of the mid-Atlantic ridge and reverses every 200,000 years. Its iron core rotates faster than its crust, this generates a magnetic field, which protects Us from cosmic rays and the plasma from Solar flares. The temperature of Earth's core is greater than the surface of the Sun. Earth's climate is affected by Sun-spots and flares in an 11-12 year cycle, which may be due to the pull of Jupiter and other Planets on the Sun. Ice Ages and Thaws are caused by the pull of the other Planets on Earth, which perturb its orbit so that it draws nearer to or farther from the Sun. There have been ten major Ice Ages during the past million years. As the ice melts and freezes the sea level rises and falls by over 100m. Earth's climate is forever changing and it is overdue for another Ice Age. However, there is little doubt that it is also changing due to Mankind.

Our Planet Earth is made up of almost one hundred Natural elements and more of them are being created synthetically in the laboratory. The alchemists failed to turn base metal into gold but some elements can metamorphose into others over very long periods of geological Time. The age of the Universe is 13.82 Gy and the age of the Earth is 4.55 Gy. The figure of 4.55 Gy was determined by Clair Patterson in 1956 AD by measuring the metamorphosis from uranium to lead in meteorites. Similar methods help geologists to determine the ages of most rocks. They divide Earth's past into geological eras, periods, epochs and ages. These are tabulated in the next essay and there is now a new geological epoch called the Anthropocene, because We are changing Our Planet.

Paleontology

Paleontology is the science of Life forms on Earth in the geological past. There is a great deal of debate about how and when Life began on Earth. The theory that it was caused by a flash of lightning in the primordial soup has recently been questioned by oceanographers who found living organisms at the bottom of the ocean where there is no Natural light. Simple cells gradually evolved into complex species like you and me. By following the fossil sequence and changes in rock strata the eras, periods and epochs of geological chronology were slowly pieced together during the eighteenth and nineteenth centuries AD but it was not until the discovery of radioactivity during the twentieth century AD that it was possible to determine how long ago these changes occurred.

Geological and Biological Ages in Megayears Before Present				
Era	**Period**	**Epoch**	**Age**	**Species**
		Anthropocene	0.0	Post-modern Man
		Holocene	0.01	Civilized Man
	Quaternary	Pleistocene	6	Man
Cenozoic		Pilocene	11	Mastodons
		Milocene	26	Sabre-toothed tigers
	Tertiary	Oligocene	37	
		Eocene	54	Whales
		Paleocene	65	Horses
	Cretaceous		135	Birds
Mezazoic	Jurassic		210	Mammals
	Triassic		250	Dinosaurs
	Permian		280	Reptiles
	Carboniferous		345	Amphibians
Paleozoic	Devonian		400	Insects
	Silurian		435	Land plants
	Ordovician		500	Fish
	Cambrian		570	Sea plants, shellfish

Evolution was proven when Charles Darwin (1809 - 1882 AD) discovered how the finches and many other species adapted to the environments on different islands in the Galapagos group and it is possible to explain how every part of every living or dead species slowly developed over the ages. Built into every living species is the incredible ability to tell the Time. There have been at least five mass extinctions of different Life forms. An asteroid caused the demise of the dinosaurs but some evolved into birds and We are descended from mammals, then the size of a shrew. We are now living in the Anthropocene Epoch and as well as causing the demise of many other species We may be causing the demise of Our own.

Archaeology

Archaeology is the study of civilizations through their material remains. Some 6My ago Our progenitors roamed about on the plains of Africa. They gradually discovered how to make tools, how to make fire, how to stand upright, walk and run, how to communicate and how to cooperate. We evolved larger brains when We learned to cook food about 200Ky ago. We only started to explore and populate Our World some 100Ky ago. We walked along the global coastline until We finally reached Australia. We followed great Natural water courses - upstream and downstream. The Nile, the longest river in Our World, has two main tributaries: the Blue Nile rises in Ethiopia and the White Nile Rises in Uganda. Both places are where the earliest Human remains have been found. The Nile finally reached the Mediterranean about twelve millennia ago. We discovered Our origins and the sources of the Nile only a century ago.

The earliest form of civilization began with the agricultural revolution. Crops were planted and animals domesticated from about 10,000 BC. There may have been a Garden of Eden near the sources of the great Tigris, Euphrates and two other rivers that flow into the Caspian Sea. The earliest civilizations flourished around these Mesopotamian rivers. Some scholars think the pre-dynastic pharaohs came from Mesopotamia and that the Phoenicians spread civilization around the ancient World. However, others think that civilization began in several parts of the globe at approximately the same age and there was no intercommunication. The earliest stone dwellings, in Europe, age back to about 10,000 BC. The earliest stone settlements, in Jericho, age back to about 9,000 BC. The earliest limestone temples, in Malta, age back to about 4,000 BC. History only began with the development of writing in about 3,000 BC. However, historians can only be sure of exact ages since about 1,000 BC. Every civilization developed a unique counting and numbering system, a unique language and script, a unique chronology, calendar and clock.

Our prehistoric development can be traced through tools and weapons. Prehistory is roughly divided into Stone, Copper, Bronze and Iron Ages. The Paleolithic (Old Stone Age) primitive stone tools, before 10,000 BC. The Mesolithic (Middle Stone Age) is the variable intermediate period. The Neolithic (New Stone Age) polished stone tools, after 10,000 BC. The Copper Age began in about 1850 BC and it ended in about 1650 BC. The Bronze Age began in about 1650 BC and it ended in about 550 BC. The Iron Age coincided with the Roman Empire from 550 BC to 540 AD. The Dark Age began in 540 AD, ended with the renaissance in 1500 AD. The Steel Age began in 1750 AD and led to the industrial revolution. The Petroleum Age began in 1860 AD and led to the transport revolution. The Aluminium Age began in 1900 AD and led to the aviation revolution. The Silicon Age began in 1950 AD and led to the electronic revolution. The Information Age began in 1990 AD and IT may lead to One World.

Anthropology

Anthropology is the study of Mankind through societies and customs. We gradually became more civilized by hunting or gathering in groups, then by forming tribes and eventually by building ancient civilizations. Each one developed a different language, a different method of counting, a different system for measuring things and a different pantheon of gods. Some tribes became isolated and so they did not develop any new ideas, although they were able to survive by living, simply, from day to day. They shared their work and their wealth and they had fine moral values, but never developed a love or fear of gods nor a sense of Time and Space.

When Robert Fitzroy surveyed Tierra del Fuego in *The Beagle* in 1828 AD he encountered a tribe of naked cannibals who could withstand the cold and had developed a vocabulary with more words than in basic English. They shared their workload and all their possessions but were extremely hostile to all attempts to communicate with them and understand them. Attempts to civilize some of them, by transporting them to England and educating them, came to nothing when they returned to their homeland. They cut-up their new clothes and shared the pieces around the tribe. They died out when they were given unclean clothing by missionaries, who probably killed more 'savages' than they converted to Christianity.

On 17 July 1998 AD a disastrous tsunami washed away the northern coastline of Papua New Guinea and thousands of natives who lived there. We have no way of knowing whether this has happened before, because this region is very remote and there are no written records, but fear of Natural disasters or joy at Natural providence must have created gods. During WW2 the Japanese threatened to invade unexplored New Guinea. So the Allies had to defend the tribes who had never seen a white man. Allied troops established bases around the coast, which were re-supplied by parachute and this led to the natives believing that great silver birds were sent by their Sky-gods to drop crates of corned beef and *Spam*. This is known as the Cargo Cult and is just as valid as other religions. The Umeda tribe in central New Guinea can only count up to seven, on one hand, wrist and elbow, their seven-day week is: the day before the day before yesterday, the day before yesterday, yesterday, today, tomorrow, the day after tomorrow, the day after the day after tomorrow. They only have seven rivers and never need to count to more than this. These hunter-gatherers have no need for agriculture, animal husbandry nor any kind of measurement, management or government system.

A native of one the isolated Amazon tribes was recently flown to England. He saw modern civilization and was given a watch and other things that We cannot live without, but when he returned he gave them all away. We must not assume that civilization, as We know it, is the final answer. There is a much better way of living - by sharing work and possessions.

Geography

We Humans came out of Africa and inhabited most of Our Planet Earth.
As We progressed from tribes of nomadic hunters and gatherers into
agricultural groups, rooted to the spot or into industrial communities,
who needed to be near their raw materials, the need to mark and defend
political, social and economic boundaries became much more important.
Great empires were built and destroyed by others or by *Mother Nature*.
She was mistaken for malicious, destructive Earth-gods and Sky-gods.
They had to be worshipped or venerated at certain ages, dates and times.
Different religions fought each other for possession of hearts and minds.
They all tried to outbreed each other and so expanded Our Human Race.
During the last twelve millennia We have changed the face of Our Planet.
Some 75% of the land area between the polar regions has been utilized.
Our rape of *Mother Nature* and the burning of fossil fuels has changed
the balance of gases in the atmosphere and the climate of Planet Earth.
We have used-up half of *Her* fossil fuels during the last two centuries.
We will probably use-up all the rest before the end of this century.
The lack of energy, food and water may soon prove to be Our downfall.
Unless We discover a better way of sharing Our Time and Our Space.

Our World is divided by politics and religions as much as by geography.
Natural borders such as: mountain ranges, deserts, rivers or shorelines,
marked many territories but the lack of these led to many conflicts.
Some arbitrary border lines are now based upon latitude or longitude.
The division of each state into smaller and smaller administrative units
causes a great deal of debate but Our World is slowly being divided-up
into new local, regional, national and international administrative units.
As transport systems become faster and more reliable it becomes easier
to administer a larger area but some islands are still divided by political
or religious factions and this includes the islands of Britain and Ireland.
Catholic Ireland is still part of the EU but Protestant Britain has left.
Northern Ireland now has to decide whether to rejoin the Republic.
Some Europeans would like it to become a Roman-Catholic enclave;
others believe that religion is fading as its citizens become enlightened.
All of Europe uses the Roman-Catholic chronology, calendar and clock.
If it became a secular federation what age, date and time would it use?

The spherical globe can be represented by land maps and sea charts.
The blue, red, brown, yellow and white lines are usually drivable by car.
The black lines are usually passable by electric trams or railway trains.
The dark blue lines are usually navigable by amphibious hovercraft.
The black dotted lines cannot be crossed without a passport and visa.
The invisible lines are called: time zones, which divide Our Human Race
but they are totally unnecessary - We should all use the same clock time.
This may help Us to communicate more easily and perhaps realize that
We are all travelling in the same tiny Space-ship called: Our Planet Earth.

Geometry

Every civilization independently developed its own set of standards for: lengths, distances, directions, areas, volumes, weights and wealth.

Ying Zheng united China and standardized its measurements in 221 BC. Their weight: *shih*, was about 60 kg, measure: *sheng*, was about 1 litre, length: *chih*, was about 250 mm, distance: *chang*, was about 3 metres. All of these units were multiplied or divided in a digital or decimal way.

The Sumerians based their lengths on the size of a barleycorn = 1 *she*. 6 *she* = 1 *shu-she* (finger), 30 *shu-she* = 1 *kush* (about 500 mm), 6 *kush* = 1 *gi* (reed), 12 *kush* = *nindan* (rod), 10 *nindan* = 1 *eshe* (rope), 60 *nindan* = 1 *ush* (about 360m), 30 *ush* = 1 *beru* (about 10.8 Km). A standard clay pot of barleycorns was also used as a form of currency.

The Egyptians used a system of digital measurements: 4 digits = 1 palm, 20 digits = 1 remen cubit, 24 digits = 1 cubit, 28 digits = 1 royal cubit (1 remen cubit = 370mm, 1 cubit = 449mm and 1 royal cubit = 524mm) The royal cubit is the diagonal of a square with sides of one remen cubit. Their standard distance: 20,000 royal cubits = 1 iteru (about 10.5 Km)

The Greeks learned their geometry from the Sumerians and Egyptians. Pythagoras's theorem and Euclid's treatise were mostly about triangles. The Parthenon was built upon the sacred Acropolis hilltop in Athens. The original one was named the *Hekatompedon* = Hundred Foot Temple. A *stylobate* was 100 Greek feet. (One Greek foot = 1.014 ft or 309 mm) This sacred distance equates to one second of longitude at this latitude.

The Roman mile was derived from a mille meaning: one thousand paces. The legions usually marched for a distance of L (50) mille in one day. A pace was two steps or five feet and so a Roman mile was 5,000 feet. Some mileposts still stand. (One Roman foot = 0.973 ft or 296 mm) There were 75 Roman miles to one degree of longitude at this latitude. Vitruvius related proportions of the Human body to a circle and a square.

The British Imperial System evolved from the Roman Imperial System. The yard, chain, furlong and mile were used for measuring distances. The foot, hand, inch and fractions were used for measuring lengths. The ounce, pound, hundredweight and ton were for measuring weights. The pint, quart, gallon and barrel were used for measuring capacities.

The metre, with its digital multiples and decimal divisions, is now used for measuring lengths and distances, however, it is a cumbersome rule. Whilst the gram was the basic unit for weight, this is now the Kilogram. It is confusing to use litres for capacity but cubic metres for volumes. These fundamental problems are solved by **The Worldwide System**.

Geodesy

Geodesy is the scientific study of the size and shape of Our Planet Earth. Every civilization developed a system of land surveying based upon a navel from which distances, directions and elevations were measured. The Babylonians probably used the huge Tower of Babel as their navel. The Egyptians probably used the Great Pyramid as their dead centre. They had to re-measure their fields for taxation after every inundation. Their taxes were based upon the, carefully recorded, height of the flood. The Greeks used a carved *omphalos* stone, near to the oracle at Delphi. The Romans used obelisks in Rome and Byzantium as their references. These Navels became political, administrative and religious centres.

In 200 BC Erastosthenes estimated the size of the Earth by using a well in Aswan, an obelisk in Alexandria and the measured distance between. However, it was not until the Enlightenment that the size and the shape of Our Planet Earth could be measured with much greater accuracy. Sir Isaac Newton considered that the Earth must be an oblate sphere, otherwise it would not turn regularly upon its axis, like a spinning top. This was proven when an Academy of Sciences expedition to the Andes in 1735 AD discovered that lines of latitude were closer nearer the poles.

The English yard was based upon the length of the standardized arrow. The English, Scottish, Irish, German and French miles were all different. A Statute mile is defined as 5,280 feet or eight furlongs (long furrows). The English yard = 3 feet, furlong = 220 yards and mile =1760 yards. The surveyor's chain, which is divided into 100 links, was invented by the English mathematician Edmund Gunter during the 17th century AD. It is 22 yards long and an area of ten square chains equals one acre. The chain was the only Imperial measure to be based on the number ten. The surveyor's rod, pole or perch was defined as five and a half yards. Christopher Wren (1632-1723 AD) suggested to the new Royal Society in 1660 AD that all measurements should be based upon the number ten. His fundamental ruler was to be the length of a one second pendulum. The Academy of Sciences suggested a digital-decimal geodetic system. Their metre was based upon one 10,000,000th of the surveyed length of the Paris Meridian from Dunkirk to Barcelona extrapolated to give the distance from the North Pole to the Equator, nevertheless, it was wrong. It should have been based upon the length of the Equator, so that all land and sea distances could be measured by the same system.

Every state established its own national geodetic grid reference system as well as its own datums for measuring heights of hills and mountains. However, these were incompatible and so a global standard was needed. The Worldwide Geodetic System was standardized in 1984 AD and it is now the basis for Google Earth and new digital-decimal maps and charts. These are drawn to a scale of 1:1,000,000 in **The Worldwide System**.

Cartography and Hydrography

Cartography and hydrography are the Earth sciences of maps and charts. It has been deduced that Stone Age Britons used a circle of 366 units. The Chinese invented the compass and decided that its rose should have North pointing down with 24 points and divided circles into 365 1/4 *pu*. However, the Sumerians decided that their compass rose should have North pointing up with 32 points and divided circles into 360 degrees. A Greek astronomer-mathematician Hipparchus of Samos (190-120 BC) is credited with being the first to propose a grid of latitude and longitude. His system could not be used until the globe was navigated and charted. Most maps and charts drawn up to the 16th century AD embodied the portolan system of nodes and radial lines crisscrossing the land and sea. Directions were in points and distances in leagues (about three miles). In 1569 AD, the Flemish globe maker and cartographer Gerard Mercator published the first atlas with the meridians of longitude represented by equally spaced vertical lines and the parallels of latitude represented by horizontal lines, which were drawn closer together towards the Equator. These imaginary lines of latitude and longitude, became real barriers when America, Australia, Arabia and Korea were divided by these lines.

Chronography is the cartographic division of the globe into time zones. Every state had its own Time and Space until it was agreed in 1884 AD that the crosshairs of a telescope at the Royal Observatory in Greenwich should define the Prime Meridian dividing the globe into East and West. The Earth's Navel lies where the Prime Meridian crosses the Equator. Most navies were already using this 000 000 Navel on their sea charts. However, it is not a landmark, like ancient Navels, but lies in the sea. A minute of longitude at the Equator is a nautical mile, so the Equator is: 360 x 60 = 21,600 nautical miles and a knot is a nautical mile/hour. The nautical mile was also defined by the First International Extraordinary Hydrographic Conference in Monaco in 1929 AD as exactly 1,852 metres. The USSR, USA and UK did not immediately accept this international unit, because each country was still using its own measurement system.

The chronometer, sextant, compass and log helped the British to build an empire but they are now superseded by global positioning satellites. Cartographers use these with satellite images and aerial photographs. The British Ordnance Survey draw Metric maps to an accuracy of 25mm. The Hydrographer to the Navy produces Admiralty charts of the globe. Depths and heights are now shown in metres on all new British charts. The Civil Aviation Authority produces charts with altitudes in feet but distances in nautical miles, because aircraft speed is measured in knots. Navigators divide direction, latitude and longitude into 360 degrees then 60 minutes, but 60 seconds have recently been replaced by decimals. However, most global positioning systems now use decimals of a degree. These are also part of the global-digital-decimal **Worldwide System**.

Metrology

Metrology is the science of measurement for every physical quantity. Every civilization had its own measurement system, which was usually based upon Human anatomy, although We are not of a standard size. The fractional measurement system used throughout the Roman empire was based on the *uncia*, the origin of the English words: inch and ounce. There were twelve *uncia* to a foot and twelve *uncia* to an *as* of weight. After the fall of Rome there were many different yards, feet and inches. Imperial weights and measures were used around the British Empire. The French Avoirdupois pound weighs 16oz but the Troy pound is 14oz. An Avoirdupois pound of feathers weighs more than a Troy pound of gold. Pierre-Simon Laplace (1749 - 1827 AD) the physicist and mathematician, who extended Newton's work, was the champion of this Metric System. This was based upon the surveyed distance of the Paris Meridian from Dunkirk to Barcelona and agreed by a global conference in 1799 AD.

The Metric System was based upon three fundamental measurements: mass, length and time, from which other mechanical quantities such as: area, volume, pressure, acceleration, work and power could be derived. Since 1887 AD many national standards laboratories have been founded to set-up and maintain standards of measurement for the basic units. The eleventh General Conference on Weights and Measures in 1960 AD established the International System of units and this is now used throughout the globe, except for the USA, Liberia and Myanmar (Burma). The second became 9,192,631,770 vibrations of caesium in 1972 AD. The metre became the distance light spans in 1/299792458s in 1983 AD. The International Metric System now includes standards for physical quantities such as temperature, electrical current and light intensity, as well as standards for the measurement of plane and solid angles.

The British Imperial System will soon be a fond memory in Little Britain, which once ruled the greatest empire that Our World has ever known. Furlongs, chains, rods, poles, perches, cables, fathoms, yards, hands, feet and inches; acres; gills, quarts, gallons and bushels; pounds, stones, hundredweights and tons are superseded but pints and miles remain. Since inches, feet and yards are obsolete, the mile is 1609.344 metres. The centimetre should not be used with the International Metric System, which prefers primary units separated by increments of three digits. To measure a length by this system We choose a suitable linear scale: say Gigametres, Megametres, kilometres, metres, millimetres or microns. (It is called a micron because a micrometer is a measuring instrument.) If the length is less than one We can go to a smaller scale or We can use a decimal of the larger unit, so it might be say: 217mm or 0.217m. The same prefixes and suffixes are used for most physical quantities. The metre, kilogram and second are arbitrary but this book proposes a rational system based upon the age, orbit, spin and girth of the Earth.

Chronology

Chronologies were based on good or bad happenings to the community.
Chinese chronology was based upon the dynasties of their emperors.
Hindu chronologies were based upon Eras in different parts of India.
Babylonian chronology was based upon the positions of their Sky-gods.
Egyptian chronology was based upon the dynasties of their pharaohs.
Greek chronology was based upon on the four-year Olympiad cycle.
Roman chronology was based upon the founding of Rome in 753 BC.
Jewish chronology was based upon the year of the Creation in 3761 BC.
Christian chronology was based upon the year of the Flood in 5500 BC.
Muslim chronology was based upon the year of the *Hejira* in 622 AD.
Buddhist chronology was based upon the Buddha's death in 543 BC.
Japanese chronology was based upon the start of the empire in 660 BC.
However, most of these counting systems were chronologically wrong.

The *Anno Domini* chronological system was devised by a Scythian monk,
Dionysus Exiguus, in the fifth century AD but is proven to be inaccurate.
Jesus must have been born before 4 BC because Herod died in that year.
Some say he was born in 7 BC when there was a Planetary conjunction.
Others say he was born in 7 AD but he may never have been born at all.
Many consider that he was a collection of ancient myths and legends.
Showing the *Anno Domini* age, the Gregorian date and seven-day week
on the same calendar is an accident of history, which means that users
have to throw their calendars, diaries and timetables away every year.
They then have to purchase new ones, which look almost the same.
Roman-Catholics have spread this chronic 'system' around the globe and
it is now used by most Christian and many non-Christian countries.
Humanists use the term: Common Era but this is still the same 'system'.

Sir Isaac Newton tried to put historical events into chronological order.
The chronicles of all the ancient civilizations are still being corrected.
Historic events such as battles or catastrophes allow them to be aligned.
Science came to the aid of history with archaeology, genealogy, geology,
radiology, magnetrometry, seismology, thermoluminescence, coredrills,
dendrochronology, philology, astronomy and astral computer programs.
So most of the history books will soon have to be revised or rewritten.
Some historians now use the backward chronological term: BP meaning:
Before the Present and this is now usually taken to mean 2000 AD or CE.

We no longer need to count forwards and backwards from year one.
We need a new system, based on the ages of Our Planet, Our Civilization
and Our Era, so that We can put all the ages into chronological order.
We know, approximately, that Our Planet is 4,550,000,000 years old,
Our Civilization is 12,000 years old and Our Era is 2,000 years old.
So year 2000 AD or CE becomes 4,550,012,000 WT or 000 for short.
I call this more logical, chronological system: **global age**.

70

Calendrology

Notches on bones, scratches on rocks or groups of pebbles helped early
Man to count the Natural days, moonths, years and Man-made weeks.
Some used Lunar phase moonths that are not an exact number of days.
Others devised and used alternate calendar months of 29 and 30 days.
Yet, neither of these Lunar calendars would fit into the mean Solar year.
Some used 12 equal months of 30 days plus a variable remainder.
Others devised months of different sizes, so that they fitted the year.
Some used 13 sunths of 28 days (4 seven-day weeks) making 364 days.
Others found a Lunar/Solar cycle in which 235 moonths equal 19 years.
An alternative to using the Sun or the Moon was the zodiac of the Stars.
The Sky at night could be measured by the equatorial Constellations.
However, the Solar year of the seasons was found to be slowly moving
relative to this Stellar or Sidereal year of the Stars, due to precession.
Some simply numbered the days in the year.

Different sizes of market weeks were used in different parts of the globe.
They were usually of equal size and they normally ran continuously.
The seven-day week is roughly equal to a Lunar phase, four are roughly
equal to a Lunar moonth and 52 are roughly equal to a Solar year.
The seven days of the week were venerated by Pagans and named after
the *Seven Heavenly Bodies* (Sun, Moon and the five visible Planets).
They are still named in this way in several languages although it is now
believed that there are *Ten* (the Sun and nine major Solar Planets).
Mystics said the Universe was created in six days plus one day of rest.
This became one of *God's Ten Commandments* in the *Old Testament*.
So the continuous seven-day week and Sabbath day became sacrosanct.
This is now used throughout the globe but with different Sabbath days.
Some simply numbered the weeks in the year.

Calendars, planners, timetables and diaries are annual documents that
help Us to record important events as they occur and to plan ahead.
They remind Us when to do routine things, such as: planting crops,
breeding animals, paying taxes, taking holidays or praising the Lord.
Writing helped Us to devise measuring or counting systems for recording
and predicting events but most of Us cannot measure, read nor write.
We should all be able to count up to ten upon Our digits and most of
Us are able to count up to thirty, forty or even three hundred and sixty.
This book advocates a perpetual Solar calendar whereby ten-day *weks*
and thirty-day *mons* or forty-day *anks* exactly fit into a 360-day *yer*.
There is also a five-day remainder plus a leap-day every fourth year.
After studying many old calendars Otto Neugebauer (1899-1990 AD)
the Austrian science historian, concluded that this calendrical system,
as used by the ancient Egyptians and the French revolutionaries, was:
The only intelligent calendar that ever existed in Human history.
I call this intelligent calendar: **digital date**.

Horology

Horology is the science of measuring time and making clocks or watches. Simple devices that tracked and measured the position of the Sun; developed into complex timepieces that were independent of daylight. These inventions represent the gradual progress of Our Human Race. From something which cost almost nothing, but was not very important, the measurement of time became an expensive and precise necessity. Owning an expensive mechanical clock or watch was a status symbol. Nevertheless, clocks and watches are now cheap, because of automated production lines controlled by accurate timepieces built into computers. The development of the hardware has continued to show great progress; the development of the software has stopped well short of perfection.

Sun clocks divided daylight into units that varied throughout the year. This variation depended on the latitude from the Equator to the Poles. Mechanical clocks allowed the whole day to be divided into fixed units. Fixed working times made it necessary for workers to use artificial light. A day can be divided in many different ways but, for historical reasons, We now use 24 hours, 60 minutes, 60 seconds and decimals of a second. Life would be simpler if We divided the entire day in a decimal way. I call this rational horological system: **decimal time**.

The English word: clock is derived from the Latin: *clocca* meaning: bell. St. Benedict (480-543 AD) was the founder of Western monasticism. His monasteries were strictly ruled by the sound of an hourly bell. The monks could not eat their lunch until the midday bell had sounded. After chiming clocks were invented 12 bells were sounded at midday. The hands of all clocks then had to point upwards at midday or noon, so that sundials and clocks were in agreement about *God's* own time. Each monastery and then every town had its own time but with the coming of railways and telegraphs it became necessary for each state to have the same time, until time zones were standardized in 1884 AD.

Most of Us have five main senses: sound, sight, touch, smell and taste. A light sensitive body clock is built into Our brains but usually takes several days to adjust to changes in working patterns or time zones. These are further complicated by various 'daylight saving' measures. The average household now has well over ten timepieces which all have to be changed, every spring and autumn, to and from summer time. All time zones and 'daylight saving' measures are totally unnecessary. They are Mankind's greatest mistakes but they could soon be corrected. It would cost nothing to alter all of the clocks to Greenwich Mean Time. We must forget the dogma that midday and noon are the same thing. We should go back to the old routine of mostly working in daylight. This simple remedy would save energy and demolish invisible barriers. I call this global chronographical system: **single zone**.

Futurology

This is the study of postulating possible, probable and preferable futures. Some universities have futurology departments, where all kinds of trends are studied and extrapolated to try and predict what may happen in future. Nevertheless, every futurological thesis and hypothesis is inevitably wrong. Universities were established to study the Universe and all it contains. Yet, there is no university where Time and Space are studied together. No museum tells the story of Time and Space as this book attempts to do. The National Maritime Museum and The Royal Observatory at Greenwich now houses a permanent exhibition on Time and Space measurement, throughout history, but this does not include chronologies nor calendars. There are no exhibits on future Time and Space measurement systems. There seem to be no other books about the measurement, management and government of Time and Space in the past, present and future.

There are science-fiction books, programmes and films about the future, yet they usually perpetuate traditional Time and Space measurements. The first line in George Orwell's *1984* (Eric Blair 1903-1950 AD) reads: 'It was a bright cold day in April and the clocks were striking thirteen'. We have not yet arrived at his dystopian society nor met *Big Brother*. Arthur C. Clarke (1917-2008 AD) predicted journeys through Space. His book and film *2001 A Space Odyssey* warned about bad computers. He used some of my ideas in his last book *3001 The Final Odyssey*. Isaac Asimov's (1920-1992 AD) science fiction book and film: *I Robot*, predicting a battle to take over the globe by robots, was set in 2200 AD. There have been many books, programmes and films about Time travel. I once took part in a *Doctor Who* chase scene dressed as the Time Lord. I chased the villain in my own *Skima* hovercraft but he dematerialized. You can watch this episode: *Planet of the Spiders* on your smart watch. You can *Google* some of the hovercraft made by my company *Pindair*. The movie: *Back to the Future* only got one thing right about 2015 AD. We are not yet using flying cars nor hoverboards but We are still using the *Anno Domini* chronology, Gregorian calendar and Benedictine clock. In his first *Star Wars* film George Lucas based his *landspeeder* upon my hovercraft and in his latest one there were no wheels on any vehicles. The Empire was using Imperial 24 hours, 60 minutes and 60 seconds. The latest census states: *Jediism* is now Britain's fifth largest religion. Captain Kirk was still using the Mystic seven-day week in *Star Trek*. Mr. Spock would comprehend the logicality of **The Worldwide System**. Even though the age, orbit, spin and girth of Planet Vulcan are different and intelligent alien life-forms may have more or less digits than Us.

Many different years, months, weeks, days, hours, minutes and seconds are still in use around Our Planet Earth but in future they could all be based upon its age, orbit and spin as well as the digital number ten. These traditional units of Time are summarised in the next few essays.

Years

We came from Africa, where animal migrations follow the annual rains. When We moved down the White Nile and the Blue Nile into Egypt, and began to cultivate the land, an annual event became of great importance. Every year, after the summer solstice, the Nile would swell to many times its usual flow and bring irrigation, silt and nutrients to the desert. On this day the brightest Star would appear on the horizon at dawn. Thus the beginning and length of the Solar and Stellar years were known and a calendar could be devised to record events and to plan ahead. They could forecast when to plant their crops and when to harvest them. They even had spare Time to imagine a family of gods, to plan for the after-life and build their tombs and temples at the edge of the desert. As Egyptians developed their great civilization their kings became gods, the hierarchy grew more powerful and years were counted in dynasties.

The Mesopotamians also studied Stars but they had different seasons. The Tigris and Euphrates flood in the spring after the vernal equinox. They used twelve Constellations to divide their year into equal sectors, identified by signs of the zodiac, which started at the vernal equinox. Each zodiac sign marks the, very gradual, precession of the equinoxes. The Solar year begins a little earlier relative to the Stars of the zodiac. The Stellar year begins a little later relative to solstices and equinoxes. We are now leaving the Age of Pisces, which is linked with Christianity. We are now entering the Age of Aquarius, which is linked with Humanity. The Chinese used another zodiac, which started at the autumn equinox.

Many of the early calendars were based on twelve Lunar phase moonths. The problem with this Lunar year is that it is shorter than the Solar one, so wanders through the seasons and does not have an obvious start. Nevertheless, this unwritten Lunar year is still used by Sunni Muslims; whereas the Shiite Muslims now use the Solar year, which is written. This is the fundamental reason why Sunnis and Shiites hate each other.

Several of the ancient civilizations devised a vague year of 360 days. This round number allowed an exact number of months and/or weeks. Astronomers made estimates of the seasonal year until they found it to be 365 days - but the last quarter day took a long time to discover. The Egyptians knew about it much earlier than others but kept it secret. Julius Caesar learned from them and incorporated it into his calendar. The Orthodox Julian calendar has since been used for over two millennia. It was not quite right and so ten days were deleted four centuries ago and most centennial leap days are missing from the Gregorian calendar. This is based upon a year of 365 days, 5 hours, 48 minutes, 45 seconds. We also have several different religious, legal, tax and academic years. These start on different dates from the mean Solar year, which begins on the spring or vernal equinox when day and night are of equal length.

Months

At the Equator there are clear skies, no seasons and high temperatures. So hunting and fishing were usually done during the cool of the night. Therefore, moonlight and tides were more important than the seasons. Solar years and seasons were more important in the temperate zones. The cold winter nights restricted farming and hunting to Sun light but the phases of the Moon and their tides were still important for fishing. Lunar moonths were also used for predicting menstruation and gestation, however this appears to be governed by the 28-day Solar wind sunth. There are about ten menstrual sunths to one Human gestation period. Perhaps it is best to forget about moonths and sunths, simply number the Solar days in the Solar year and then they would drop into tens. Some calendars, planners and diaries now show year-day numbers, starting with 001 on New Year's Day in the Gregorian calendar.

Every civilization tried, in vain, to find some mathematical relationship between the cycles of the Moon and the Sun, which had a great social and mystical influence upon the earliest civilizations - and still do today. Most Pagan religions had a Sun-god and a Moon-god, and the three great monotheistic religions of today incorporate both Solar and Lunar rituals. The Moon's cycle of phases provided a perpetual and Natural calendar. Yet, even those who used simple Lunar calendars had many arguments about whether a moonth should begin at a new-Moon or at a full-Moon. Some civilizations chose the full-Moon but others chose the new-Moon. The Babylonians used a Lunar-Solar calendar by adding a moonth every three years and the Jewish calendar is a development of this system. The Chinese also used a Lunar-Solar calendar and the extra moonth was added at the discretion of the emperor, who controlled everything. The Greek astronomer Meton discovered that 235 moonths are equal to 19 Solar years and his Metonic cycle was used in Lunar-Solar calendars. Whilst Christians use Solar calendars for most of their fixed feasts the movable fast of Easter is still determined in the Jewish Lunar-Solar way.

Any calendar month must have a whole number of mean Solar days. Some used alternate 29 and 30 day months but they did not fit the year. The Egyptians used twelve months of thirty days plus 5 or 6 dog days. The higgledy-piggledy months, which most of Our World now uses in the Orthodox Julian and Roman-Catholic Gregorian calendars were decreed by the Caesars but were originally based upon alternate 30 and 31 days. These higgledy-piggledy months are now used in most parts of the globe. They are regarded as imperial by Sunnis, who use the Lunar moonths. These are also used by Buddhists, who gather at every quarter phase. There are either seven or eight Solar days between each Buddha day. Hindu sects use a variety of Lunar, Solar and Lunar-Solar calendars. Sikhs once used Lunar-Solar calendars but they now use Solar ones. Different calendars cause a great deal of friction throughout Our World.

Weeks

In the beginning all days were equal in importance to hunter/gatherers.
Weeks were needed when Our ancestors turned to farming and herding.
They soon found that they had produce, livestock or goods to spare,
which they bartered or sold on a regular special day in a weekly cycle.
Another day in the week gradually became reserved for religious rituals.

The Sumerians seem to have used sixty six-day weeks in a 360 day year.
The Babylonians seem to have rested on moonth-days: 7, 14, 21 and 28.
The Persians honoured their Sun-god on month-days: 1, 8, 15 and 22.
The Buddhists divided the Lunar moonths into four 7 or 8-day periods.
The Greeks divided the Lunar moonths into three 9 or 10-day periods.
The Etruscans had continuous 8-day weeks with staggered market days.
The Romans divided their months into 8-day *kalends, ides* and *nones*.
The Celts divided the Lunar moonths into two 14 or 15-day fortnights.
The Maya had eighteen 20-day *uinals* plus 5 to 6 days at a year's end.
The Saxons and also the Indo-Chinese used 73 five-day market weeks.
The Icelanders use continuous 7-day weeks with no moonths or months.
The Chinese used continuous ten-day weeks for thousands of years.
The Hindus and the Inca also grouped their days in handy units of ten.
The Egyptians used 36 ten-day weeks per Solar year plus a remainder of
5 days in their Civic calendar or 5 to 6 days in their Pharaonic one.
A continuous seven-day week was first used by the Sabaeans of Harran
who worshipped at seven temples dedicated to *Seven Heavenly Bodies*.
The Hebrews adopted this week and they later introduced their *shabbat*
on bad Saturn's day, when they stopped work for rest and for prayer.
Judaea was a Roman province so would have used their 8-day week.
Galilee was a free state so would have used the Jewish 7-day week.
The Essenes used discontinuous 7-day weeks, aligned with their year.
These many different weeks were pivotal in the conflict which divided
Christians from Jews and also caused the Jewish revolt against Rome.
The Gnostic Christians in Egypt used a discontinuous 10-day week.
The Mithraists used continuous 7-day weeks with reverence to Sun-day.
This influenced the legions who eventually persuaded Rome to adopt it.
Tertullian of Carthage (155-222 AD) the founding father of the Church,
decreed that Christians must use 7-day weeks and meet on Sundays.
The Eastern and Western Roman Empires were reunited and forcibly
converted to Christianity under the Emperor Constantine in 325 AD.
The continuous 7-day week was imposed throughout the Roman Empire.
However, subsequent emperors reverted to *kalends, ides* and *nones*.

Although the 7-day week is now global, Jews, Christians and Muslims
have different days for working, shopping, resting, playing and praying.
A post-modern secular society has no need for a market or religious week
but it does need a regular working rhythm and most jobs can be shared.
The best size of job-sharing week has five left-days and five right-days.

Days

The day is both the smallest unit of date and the largest unit of time. The length of a day can be measured by an accurate clock but it varies throughout the year and so We use an average: the mean Solar day. This is not quite constant because the Earth is gradually slowing down, due to the gravitational effects of the Sun, the Moon and other Planets.

Should the Solar day begin at dawn, at dusk, at midlight or at midnight? If you are using a Sun-clock the moment to start the day is either: at dawn, dusk, Sun-rise, Sun-set or when the Sun is highest in the Sky. If you are using a 24-hour mechanical clock the obvious place to start the day is at midlight when all the hands are at the top of the dial. If you are using a 12-hour half-day clock the hands go around twice so you have a choice of using midlight or midnight for the start of the day. Jews, Muslims, Orthodox and Catholic Churches start their day at dusk. The Protestant Church says that all days start and stop at midnight. In England it was decided by the Romans, that the day should start and stop at midnight, by the Saxons at dawn, by the Normans at midlight. The start of the day was put back to midnight throughout every state during the nineteenth century AD and it has stayed there ever since. There is also a better solution, and this is for the age, date and time, everywhere, to be based upon midnight all along the Prime Meridian. This would be much more convenient for international communications, which allow all clocks to be synchronized, throughout the globe.

There have been many different answers to the question of how the day should be divided, in different parts of the globe, throughout the ages, and there are many different ways of measuring or indicating the time. As the technology of time measurement improved, smaller and smaller units could be devised and then several different divisors were tried. Western civilizations were using sundials, which divided daylight into twelve variable hours, until long after mechanical clocks were invented. The Egyptians divided sunlight into ten hours plus two hours of twilight. They also divided the night into twelve hours by observing the Stars. There were several other divisions of the day and the night as well. Jews used three 4-hour night watches; Romans used four 3-hour ones. The Romans also divided daylight into *ante meridiem* and *post meridiem*. The Saxons at first used 4 daylight *tides*, which give us the word: time, and later used 8 divisions, but Alfred the Great is said to have divided his day into three equal parts, with candles marked in 8 inches/hours. Other civilizations divided the day in different ways, for it was by no means obvious which way to do it and few realized then that it would eventually be necessary to divide it up into smaller and smaller parts. Our day is divided into 24 hours, 60 minutes, 60 seconds then decimals. Dividing the mean Solar day into a thousand parts is a much more logical solution and it could be further divided by decimals *ad infinitum*.

Hours

When the need arose to divide up the day, We noticed that shadows changed in both length and angle so could be marked on the ground. Shadow clocks were used where and when the Sun shone but when time measurement spread to dark or cloudy places, We needed other clocks. Water clocks came first, then sand glasses, then graduated candles and even different incense powders burnt so that one could smell the time. The force of gravity or the energy in a spring power mechanical clocks. The pulse of electricity is now at the heart of most timekeepers.

The Egyptians divided up their scale of daylight using their ten digits. Morning and evening twilight threw long shadows, which were not at first measured but extra divisions were later added to include them. Another twelve hours divided up the night by using the *Decan* Stars. The day and night hours varied according to the location and the season. The Egyptians considered it important to divide the year and the day, for this was part of their religious rituals, thus *Hours* became deities. The Mesopotamians used this 24-hour system for civic purposes but astronomers divided days into 12 double-hours and 60 double-minutes. The Greek astronomers used 24 fixed hours, 60 minutes, 60 seconds. They considered 24 to be a Natural number because we have 24 finger joints and 24 finger widths (*uncia*) from fingertips to elbows (*cubits*). The Chinese also divided their civic day into twelve equal double-hours. They developed water clocks with escapement mechanisms in 723 AD. A Chinese clock of 1190 AD divided the imperial day into 96 equal parts. The imperial day was later decimalized into 100 equal parts called *k'e*. The Japanese used six variable hours for daylight and six for night, which they displayed in mechanical clocks during the 17th century AD.

The Roman-Catholics developed several different timekeeping devices. The Latin word *horogium* was used for any timekeeping device and this makes it impossible to discover which kind of clock was being used. The Roman-Catholics originally adopted the Egyptian canonical system, with the twelve variable night hours and the twelve variable day hours. The temporary or canonical 12 hours of daylight and 12 hours of night became fixed at 12 hours a.m. and 12 hours p.m. when gravity powered bell-ringing clocks were invented in late 13th century AD monasteries. The first of these only rang bells, to call the faithful to prayer, but by the end of the 14th century AD some were fitted with 24 hour dials. These were hard to read and so half-day 12-hour ones replaced them. The quarter hour could also be displayed, however this was the limit of accuracy of these mechanical clocks, which needed frequent adjustment. It was not until the pendulum was invented in the 17th century AD that clocks became more accurate, reliable and useful but in some parts of the globe canonical hours were still used until the 19th century AD. Some still use 12 analogue hours; others now use 24 digital hours.

Minutes

The Sumerians used the number 60 as the base for all their fractions. The Greek astronomers were the first to use 24 hours of fixed length. They divided both hours and degrees into 60 'firsts' then 60 'seconds' before it was possible to measure these smaller units very accurately. The word 'minute' comes from the mediaeval Latin *minutia* 'small part'.

Sun-clocks forever divided daylight into variable hours and minutes. Water-clocks could show either variable or fixed hours and minutes. Sand-clocks or hour-glasses were used for periods of one hour or less. Candle-clocks were normally used for longer periods of several hours. Sand, water and candle clocks need Human intervention to start them. They were for measuring elapsed time; rather than the time of day. Gravity clocks rang or showed the time of day in hours and quarters. Minutes were added when mechanical clocks became more accurate. They continued to be based on 60 because it was simplest to divide-up the 12-hour half-day dial into 5 sub-divisions and add another hand.

Reliable mechanical and electrical clocks helped to unify time and to start the engineering industry, which led to the industrial revolution. They did not become vital until the 19th century AD when the factory workers were paid by the hour, rather than by the day or the week. They had to start and stop work at the same time, lateness was a reason for dismissal and timing work to the minute became more and more important as clocks were developed and they became less expensive. Stage coaches left on the hour but trains had to be based on the minute. Every town had its own time, based on noon, until Greenwich Mean Time became the British Standard, whilst other countries had their own times. In 1884 AD it was decided that there should be international time zones, in which all clocks would be synchronized to Greenwich Mean Time. There would be 24 hourly sea time zones with an international date line. The land time zones would be decided by governments in every country. Clocks and watches soon became necessities rather than luxuries.

Now that most of Us own clocks and watches they are of no use unless they all read the same, however, they are all set to different time zones. We do not really need these divisive, invisible, artificial time zones at all. We should all use the same time but rise at dawn and retire at dusk. As We all did before artificial light and artificial time were invented. Despite 'daylight saving measures', which complicate the issue greatly, We waste much of Our free daylight and resort to expensive alternatives. The 24-hour full-day clock is back again but this time in digital form. It is the norm for airline timetables but still causes much confusion. Airlines hate it and all of the time zones and daylight saving measures. They work to Coordinated Universal Time, which is known as Zulu time. However, one global time zone has not been properly considered before.

Seconds

Although seconds had been defined for over two millennia, it was not possible to measure them accurately until mechanical clocks arrived. The earliest ones were not accurate and needed frequent adjustments. The invention and application of the pendulum was a huge step forward. However, clocks were immobile until spring-driven ones were developed. These, eventually, allowed timekeeping to be independent of Sun-dials. Better escapements, fusees, foliots, hairsprings and compensators for temperature and pressure were progressively added to precision clocks until it was possible for a marine chronometer to be moved around the globe without gaining or losing more than a tenth of a second per day. Navigation then became much safer, because the only other method for determining longitude was by very careful astronomical observations. These needed accurate measuring instruments, clear skies, calm seas and complex calculations or interpolations of printed ephemeris tables. World trade was expanded considerably by these inventions, especially by the French, Dutch and English, who made the first chronometers. Clocks shrank until they could fit in a pocket or be strapped to a wrist. Mass production methods made it possible for everyone to own one.

The second was of little practical use until chronometers and reliable stop watches were developed, then many events could be timed - from races and records to biological rhythms - such as the beating of a heart. The variable Cosmic second became the standard scientific unit of time. When it became possible and desirable, only a century ago, to measure smaller divisions of time the hexadecimal base was discarded in favour of decimals, which were by then coming into common use, everywhere. Unfortunately, the opportunity was not taken to decimalize all of time.

Variable Cosmic time only needs to be divided by a thousand *millidays*. Fixed Atomic time needs to be sub-divided by decimals *ad infinitum*. Accurate and reliable timepieces can now be used by everyone on Earth. These can all be all be synchronized electronically via the Internet. Clocks are now so accurate that it is no longer acceptable to think of a second as an eighty-six-thousand-four-hundredth of a mean Solar day. The motion of Our Planet, the Solar System or any body in the Universe is not regular enough to be the basis for scientific measurements so the vibration of a caesium atom is now the standard upon which it is based. Leap units are used to keep Atomic time in accord with Cosmic time. The constant Atomic second is not equal to the variable Cosmic second. It is based on arbitrary vibrations not astronomical observations and can be multiplied or divided like other SI units, whereas the Cosmic second is multiplied in the hexadecimal way but divided in the decimal way. Atomic Time now has to be divided into billions and billions and billions. Ever more accurate Atomic timepieces are progressively being developed. Some are now accurate to one second in the Life of the Universe.

THE WORLDWIDE SYSTEM

Part Three

Diversification

Chronology and Calendrology

"Had I been present at the Creation, I would have given some useful hints on the better ordering of the Universe."

Alfonso the Wise (1221-1284 AD)

Stone Time

Civilization began with the Holocene period, some twelve millennia ago. Hunter-gatherers began to grow crops, breed animals and share work. This voluntary cooperation established their community and hierarchy. They were just as intelligent as Us but they did not have Our technology. As they developed their flint tools and weapons they standardized them and developed their chronologies, calendars, clocks, rules and measures. They built boats that were capable of navigating the rough seas and they were prepared to spend a great deal of time in constructing monuments. These often pointed towards midsummer Sunrise and midwinter Sunset. They worshipped *The Great Goddess* alias *Mother Earth* or *Mother Nature*. And, later, the Sky-gods of the Sun, the Moon, the Stars and the Planets. Astronomer-priests used wooden posts or monoliths to measure the Sky over many generations and left a legacy for future generations to follow. The solstices and equinoxes were extremely important for agriculture. Since the hottest or coldest days occur after solstices they had quarter days on the (Gregorian) 9 May, 8 August, 7 November and 7 February. New Year and Spring were both marked by a fertility festival on 9 May. Another important festival was the harvest full-Moon after 8 August.

The Stone Age civilization left monuments throughout Western Europe. There are many theories on the shapes, sizes, positions and orientations of megalithic monuments and the reasons why they were constructed. The author has included some of these theories and a few of his own. Lines were chronologies, circles were calendars and obelisks were clocks. Some circles may have been compasses and global positioning systems. They may even have been accurate scale models of Our Planet Earth. One theory is that Time and Space were based upon the number six. They rounded the year up to 366 days and used a six-day market week. A circle of 366 megalithic degrees divided by 60 minutes and 6 seconds gives an arc at the Equator of 366 megalithic yards, 6 of these units equal one megalithic mile and so the standard megalithic yard is 829mm. This theory has been proven by surveys of many prehistoric monuments.

Although they had no form of writing they were excellent communicators. Their leaders were cremated and their remains placed in passage graves. Near the river Boyne in Ireland lie the six millennia old passage graves of Newgrange, Knowth and Dowth, which were accurate observatories. Newgrange was aligned with the winter solstice Sun-rise and the eight year cycle of Venus, whilst Knowth contained a stone map of the Moon. The five millennia old observatory at Stanton Drew had nine concentric rings of oaken posts plus a tenth ring with about fifty standing stones. This probably means that they measured or counted everything in tens. At Carnac in Brittany a 300 tonne stone obelisk was erected in 3600 BC. Thousands of mounds, cairns, barrows and monoliths in the form of menhirs, dolmens, rings and lines were built there until about 2500 BC.

Stone Time

Solar and Lunar observatories were erected in Scotland 5,000 years ago.
On Stornoway in the Outer Hebrides a stone circle lies at Callenish,
where the Moon is directly overhead when it is at its highest latitude.
On Orkney the fishing village of Scara Brae was buried in a sand dune.
It had grooved pots, stone axes, flint knives, antler picks, bone shovels.
The Ring of Brodgar had either 60 or 61 megaliths about six paces apart.
It was astronomically aligned with the rising Sun at the summer solstice,
the setting Sun at the winter solstice and the four cardinal directions.
At nearby Stenness were twelve huge megaliths with Lunar orientations.
The Maes Howe passage grave is oriented to Sun-set at the winter solstice.
A newly discovered stone temple enclosure on the narrow isthmus of the
Ness of Brodgar lies in between these Solar and Lunar observatories.

Avebury, at the highest point in southern England, is the World's largest
stone henge within a massive outer mound and very deep inner ditch.
It lies near the Ridgeway, an ancient roadway, which runs for 140 Km.
Its entrances represent Earth's Axis and Equator angled at 23 degrees.
The size of the circle relates to the size of the Earth in the ratio 1:36524.
Its 100 stone ring in 1000 megalithic yards shows they counted in tens.
The avenues leading up to the henge were also marked with 100 stones.
It contained two inner rings of 27 and 29 standing stones and these
were used to count both the sidereal and the phasal cycles of the Moon.
At the centre of one ring there was an obelisk to measure daytime.
Nearby lies Silbury Hill, the greatest Man-made mound in all of Europe.
It was probably an observatory used to watch the horizon on which were
placed stones to mark the stations of the Sun and the paths of the Moon.
A 50 megalithic yard high chalk cone with seven steps was surrounded
by a reflecting lake in the shape of the pregnant goddess *Mother Earth.*
It was fed by the Swallowhead spring, source of the Kennet and Thames.

Stonehenge is the most famous megalithic observatory in all of Europe.
It may have served as a healing centre and as a monument to the dead.
It was built on Salisbury Plain in three stages from 3000 to 2000 BC.
This is where the directions of midsummer Sun-rise, midwinter Sun-set,
Moon-rise standstill and Moon-set standstill crossover at right-angles.
It lies near the 3 Km Cursus and 3 Km Avenue leading to the river Avon.
The 2 Km Palisade of wooden posts may have been their year counter.
The dressed sarsen stones were rolled from Avebury over 30 Km away.
The smaller blue stones were shipped over 300 Km from west Wales.
The outer ring of 56 blue stones allowed them to predict Solar eclipses.
The inner ring of 30 megaliths had lintels that made a complete circle.
This may have been their calendar month and an artificial horizon for
marking the positions of the Sun, the Moon, the Planets and the Stars.
The five larger trilithons at the centre marked solstices and equinoxes.
The inner ring of 40 blue stones was probably added in the Bronze Age.

Bronze Time

The discovery of copper and tin and the invention of their alloy: bronze, had a profound effect upon ancient civilizations, throughout the globe. Stone and wood could then be cut and joined more accurately and this enabled larger, faster and safer ships and wheeled vehicles to be made. It was the start of a money economy, based upon weights and measures, the division of labour into working organizations, a hierarchy based upon wealth and heredity but also the beginning of warfare and fortifications. During the Bronze Age a number of observatories were built in stone throughout NE Scotland and they were all oriented towards the SSW. They were used to observe the setting position of the full-Moon nearest to the summer solstice, which has a Lunar/Solar cycle of 18.6 years. The complex patterns embossed in conical golden crowns found in royal tombs in France, Germany and Switzerland are Lunar/Solar calendars.

Whilst the Bronze Age settlements throughout Europe were primitive; those on the largest Aegean island of Crete were much more advanced. The Minoan civilization flourished from about 3000 to about 1450 BC. Sir Arthur Evans named it after the legendary king Minos in 1900 AD. Minoans worshipped a Sun-goddess who protected them from snakes. They built multi-storey palaces with running water and even flush toilets. They painted very colourful frescoes and made fine pottery and jewellery. Their advanced culture was peaceful, so they did not build fortifications. They had Natural sheltered harbours, so built fishing and trading boats. They reached Britain, India and even America in search of copper and tin and traded bronze, glass and ceramics for gold, silver, amber and jewels. An Aegean form of writing, known as linear A, has not been deciphered. Another form, linear B, was deciphered by Michael Ventris in 1952 AD. They used a base-ten counting and numbering system for their accounts. An embossed clay disc found at the palace of Phaestos is probably a calendar and map of the Sky with the Constellations shown as symbols. They used a compass of 366 degrees and a 366 day Sidereal year with 30 or 31 day months, which helped them to navigate as well as to farm. Forty Sidereal years less 31 days is about the same as forty Solar years. They may have also used a six-day week, which fitted their 366-day year. Scholars have proposed a theory that they knew the girth of the Earth: One degree = 60 miles = 360,000 feet = 1/366 of Earth's circumference. They seem to have used twelve zodiac Constellations based upon their twelve months as well as twelve double-hours during a complete day. The half-man/half-bull minotaur myth and their practice of bull leaping shows that they worshipped bulls during the zodiac Age of Taurus. The Minoan foot (or hand span) was approximately 204 mm or 8 inches. Their civilization was devastated in about 1450 BC when the Minoan island of Thera (Santorini) erupted in the Old World's greatest explosion. It caused great tsunamis, ash deposits, acid rain and climate changes. This is probably the origin of Plato's legend of the lost empire of Atlantis.

Bronze Time

Bronze not only made much better tools but also much better weapons. The fortified citadel of Mycene with its lion gateway and its legendary King Agamemnon was far from the sea on the Peloponese peninsula. So it escaped the disastrous Theran tsunami and was able to expand. The warlike Myceneans conquered the eastern Mediterranean and the legend that Menelaus's wife Helen was abducted to Troy may be true. Archaeologists have found a mound in Turkey with 46 strata and using carbon dating they can show that the city was sacked in about 1210 BC. Like so many other legends the Trojan horse may be based upon truth. The horse became more important after the bronze bit was developed. We do not know what age, date, time and rule the Myceneans used.

Twelve kingdoms between the Tiber, the Arno and the Tyrrhenian Sea loosely formed Etruria, between the eighth and second centuries BC. They developed an alphabet, which was very similar to that of the Latins. However, the Etruscan script and language has not yet been deciphered. The kings met on the vernal equinox at the temple of Fanum Voltumnae. Etruscan entertainment, discussion and sport was held at full-Moons. Their twelve city-states were laid-out on grids in the cardinal directions, incorporating complex underground irrigation and drainage systems. Soothsayers believed in a link between Heaven and Earth, so they could forecast future events such as: storms, eruptions and earthquakes. Their vegetarian deity *Voltuma* became their protector or tutelary god. The Sun was associated with gold and the Moon was linked with silver. Their greatest Sky-god *Tinius* (Jupiter) was named after the metal: tin. Perhaps Mars = zinc, Saturn = copper, Venus = lead, Mercury = mercury. The measurement of Time and Space was fundamental to their religion. They counted everything in eights and invented eight-note octave scales. Their 360-day year was divided into 45 eight-day weeks plus 5 or 6 days. The days in their week were alphabetically named from A through to H. Markets were staggered so that traders could travel from one to the next. King Tarquinius Priscus founded the Etruscan city of Rumlua (Rome). The Romans attempted to obliterate all of the prehistoric civilizations. So they devised the myth about Romulus, Remus and the she-wolf Lupa.

Southern Italy and Sicily were part of the Greek federation of states who developed warfare and athletics as well as the arts and the sciences. Each city-state had its own ruler and way of doing things because the land We now call Greece was divided by the mountains and by the sea. Eventually, it was united by the Spartans and using the power of bronze the Greek empire was to spread to Anatolia, southern Italy and beyond. Bronze tools allowed their architects to build some very fine temples, aligned to astronomical marks and dedicated to their mythical Sky-gods. The Greeks developed philosophy, democracy, geometry and job-sharing, before being overrun by the Romans at the beginning of the Iron Age.

Iron Time

The discovery that wrought iron can be produced from iron ore, charcoal and a blast of air from a pair of bellows led to a metallurgical revolution. Iron was known in Egypt in about 3000 BC, the Hittites were using it in 1400 BC but it did not reach Europe until about 1000 BC when it was developed by the Greeks and was then manufactured by the Etruscans. Although it led to better plough shares; it also led to sharper swords. There was less time for astronomy and the meaning of ancient henges was forgotten as Britons took to the hills and built earthen enclosures. One of these great hill forts: Maiden Castle in Dorset, had three rings of fortifications, yet this was not strong enough to repel the Romans.

The Galatians were tribes who inhabited much of north-west Europe by 1000 BC and many of their Pagan beliefs lasted until about 500 AD. In France they were called: Gauls but in Britain they were called: Celts. They lived in villages, yet developed advanced forms of arts and crafts and were united by a calendrical culture based upon regular festivals. They had no form of writing, so their ancient knowledge was passed on by oral tradition through myths and legends in their Gaelic language. They worshipped gods associated with mountains, caves, springs, trees plus many weather-gods, warrior-gods a Sun-god and a Moon-goddess. They were ethnically cleansed by the Romans who pushed them out of mainland Europe into Brittany and the British Isles, then out of England. Some became hermits in the first century AD and their remote oratories and monasteries are the first signs of Christianity in western Ireland.

The Teutons defended most of northern Europe from the Roman armies. They counted nights not days: 7 were a senight and 14 were a fortnight. I use the word: sunth, to mean the 28 day rotational period of Sun-spots, relative to the Earth, and this is the duration of the Solar wind cycle. 'A year and a day' is a Teutonic term for 13 sunths + one day = 365. Rather than being based upon astronomical observations this calendar needed a continuous day-count but restarted at the autumnal equinox. After becoming Christian the Teutonic Knights took part in the Crusades together with the Knights Templar and the Knights Hospitalier.

Human menstruation takes one sunth and gestation takes ten sunths. So the Human life-cycle may be controlled by the Sun's Solar wind cycle rather than the Moon's position or its phases, as is usually supposed. Some still believe in the ancient Wicca or witchcraft religion which uses a calendar based upon the menstrual cycle with thirteen 28 day sunths, or 52 seven-day weeks in a 364 day vague year, plus one extra day. Since their seven-day week is discontinuous their Black Sabbath day does not fall on any particular day of the Judeo/Christian/Muslim week. Many witches and heretics were burnt at the stake by the Inquisition, during the Dark and Middle Ages, because they used different calendars.

Iron Time

The Roman Empire grew rapidly with the strength of its new iron fist.
It encompassed the Mediterranean and then many ancient civilizations
including: Greece, Egypt, Libya, Carthage, Iberia, Gaul and England.
However, it was repelled in Scotland, Ireland, Germany and Scandinavia
and by the Parthian Empire, which included both Persia and Babylonia.
Many millions were slain or enslaved in the quest to enlarge their coffers.
Whilst later Romans relinquished Paganism and adopted Christianity;
they did not give up their great compulsion to conquer the entire globe.
Their successors, the Roman-Catholics, continued this global conquest.
Their chronology, calendar and clock have conquered most of Our World.

During the Dark Ages in Europe, after the fall of the Roman Empire,
the development of metallurgy from wrought iron to cast iron and steel
took place in China and India - but took a millennium to reach Europe.
The development of cast iron in northern Italy, in the 15th century AD,
may be linked to the visit of Chinese fleets during the 14th century AD.
The development of steel in Great Britain, during the 18th century AD,
may be linked to the invasion of Spain by Moors in the 9th century AD.
The Victorians developed many industries with these new materials.
Their steam engines, steam ships and steam trains led to the Steam Age.
The discovery of petroleum and the invention of the internal combustion
engine led to the reshaping of the globe during the 20th century AD.
A simple steel invention that united Our World was the clock spring.
It enabled time to be transported by land or sea and used for navigation.
Another simple steel invention that divided Our World was barbed wire.
Iron curtains were built across the globe to keep warring factions apart.
Many of these were built along invisible barriers marking time zones.

Each religion or cult had its own deity, chronology, calendar and clock.
Some chose the Sun for counting years, sunths, days and parts of days.
Some chose the Moon for counting years, moonths and moonth–days.
Some chose the Stars for counting years, parts of years or parts of days.
Some chose the Planets for counting auspicious periods or waging wars.
The Sun's seasons change from place to place and so the Solar year
has no obvious starting point, other than at an equinox or at a solstice.
The Moon's moonthly cycle of phases is the same from any viewpoint but
it cannot be seen in cloudy places and it is hard to see whether it is full.
The Stars appear to revolve daily and they annually move up and down.
The equatorial Constellations, which represent the signs of the zodiac,
may appear to represent different familiar forms in different locations.
Ursa Minor, The Plough, Great Bear or Big Dipper points to due North.
Its seven Stars are said by some to be the origin of the seven-day week.
Yet, this is not visible in the Southern Hemisphere, where due South is
indicated by five Stars in the Constellation of the Southern Cross.

Western Time

A zodiac is a Stellar or Sidereal calendar that divides the year and Sky. This was probably devised in Mesopotamia, well over six millennia ago. Navigators and astronomers allotted symbols to the 88 Constellations. The twelve Constellations with their symbols lying along the ecliptic are: *Aries* the ram, *Taurus* the bull, *Gemini* the twins, *Cancer* the crab, *Leo* the lion, *Virgo* the virgin, *Libra* the balance, *Scorpio* the scorpion, *Sagittarius* the archer, *Capricorn* the goat-fish, *Aquarius* the water-bearer and *Pisces* the two fishes.

There are two different Western zodiacs: the Sidereal and the tropical. The tropical year is based upon the equinoxes and solstices of the Sun. It was divided according to the number of Lunar moonths per Solar year. There are 91 1/4 days in each quarter, so the number of days in each sign were rounded up or down and astronomers gave these twelve divisions the same symbols as the Constellations in the Sidereal or Stellar zodiac. Stylized versions of the twelve tropical zodiac signs are called: sigils.

Zodiac comes from the Greek ζοδιαχ which means: a circle of animals. The Greeks imagined the divine river *Oceanis* flowed around the Earth, like a snake swallowing its own tail and carrying a zodiac on its back. The most ancient Greek Time-god was *Aion*, the power controlling all of the changes in the World and the mystical circular element of eternity. Greek myths describe the characteristics, motions and conjunctions of the Planets and their moons - so they may have invented telescopes. Conventional wisdom has it that there were always twelve signs in the zodiac but there is growing evidence that in Greece there were thirteen. The thirteenth sign was *Asklipios* with *Serpens* the Sky-gods of healing.

Precession causes the Poles to, very slowly, describe a circle in the Sky. Hipparchus, discovered that the equinoxes were precessing in 130 BC. The vernal equinox was considered to be the start of the tropical year. It retrogrades through the Sidereal zodiac in a cycle of 25,920 years. An Age during which it retrogrades through each sign lasts 2,160 years. Christianity is linked to the Age of Pisces - two fishes and a silver string. Before the Age of *Pisces* was the Age of *Aries*, the Egyptian ram-god. Before this came their Age of *Taurus*, when bulls were worshipped. Before this was their Age of *Gemini* when twin deities were venerated. Some say that the Great Sphinx was a lion carved during the Age of *Leo*. Orion is associated with the ancient Egyptian Star-god cult of *Osiris* and Sirius or Sothis is associated with their Star-goddess cult of *Isis*. The Constellation of Orion is currently at its highest point in the Sky. Their First Time was when it was at its lowest point 13,000 years ago. This was before the first civilizations emerged at the end of last Ice Age. The North Pole Star is currently Polaris but when the Great Pyramid was completed it was Alfa Draconis and so the air shafts that pointed to it, the Constellation of Orion and the brightest Star Sirius, no longer do so.

Western Time

The Babylonians were totally entranced by the *Seven Heavenly Bodies*. The Sun, the Moon and the five visible Planets were represented by gods and these, eventually, named the seven days of the continuous week. They believed in astrology and destiny - so an eclipse was a conjunction to be dreaded, especially if it occurred near a solstice or an equinox. A conjunction of two visible Planets was considered to be auspicious and could coincide with good happenings such as the coming of a new leader. Many legends in the *Old Testament* may be myths based upon astrology. The twelve tribes of Israel were each allotted a sign of the tropical zodiac. There were many astrological predictions that a messiah would come. The Bright Star described in the *New Testament* might have been: a comet, a meteor, a nova, a supernova or a conjunction of Planets. Whether a messiah did come is still open to question and the legend of twelve disciples and a last supper may be a myth based upon astrology.

During the Modern or Christian Age, Jesus the Christ became regarded as the *Sol Salutis* (Sun of Salvation) or the *Sol Justitae* (Sun of Justice). He ruled over the tropical zodiac and its imaginary influences on man. They were incorporated into horogiums in or nearby many cathedrals. e.g. *St. Petra's* Rome, *St. Marco's* Venice, *San Miniato al Monte* Florence. Seven French cathedrals represent a map of the Constellation of *Virgo*: *Notre Dame*, Paris, Chartres, Evreux, Bayeux, Rouen, Amiens and Reims. They were constructed to celebrate the first Millennium of Christianity. Yet, they were built upon Pagan Roman and Druidic temple foundations.

Horoscopes were devised during the fifth century BC, however there is no proof that the position of Stars or Planets has any influence upon Us. A conjunction or group of Planets may have a gravitational or magnetic influence upon the Sun or the Earth and variations of Cosmic rays may affect Our fertility or personality but there is, so far, no proof of this.

The signs used by most astrologers today do not correspond with the true positions of the Constellations in the Sky, because of precession. Astrology now includes the invisible outer Planets: Neptune and Uranus and could include all the planetoids, asteroids, meteorites and comets. Another Solar Planet has recently been discovered, way out in Space. So there are now *Ten Heavenly Bodies*: the Sun and nine Planets.

We are now moving from the modern Age of Pisces, the Christian Era, into the post-modern Age of Aquarius, which is linked with Humanity. The Dead Sea Scrolls show that many Christian ideas began in 160 BC. So the Christian Age ended and the New Humanist Age began at MM. This Millennium was predicted to start an Age of fundamental change. Could this be a new measurement, management and government system based upon the age, orbit, spin and girth of Our Planet Earth?

Eastern Time

In an ancient Chinese myth the god *Pan Ku* grew inside a cosmic egg. This egg contained all the elements of the Universe and as *Pan Ku* grew he separated the Earth from the Sky, male from female, wet from dry... As the egg hatched *Pan Ku* died and his eyes became the Sun and Moon, his tears became rain and his voice became thunder.

The Eastern tropical zodiac also has twelve signs for equal divisions of the year and was mentioned in Chinese astronomical texts of 2,857 BC. It once started at the autumnal equinox but the Eastern and Western zodiacs have been realigned and both now start at the vernal equinox. The signs for Taurus the Bull and their Ox are the only similarities. All their zodiac signs are animals, the dragon is the only mythical beast. It is the Taoist symbol for the creative, dynamic force in the Universe. Since it was a link with Heaven the emperors adopted it as their emblem. The dragon came first in a mythical hierarchy of 360 scaly creatures. The same signs were used to name the years in a twelve-year cycle. Each sign was halved to make 24 Solar seasons, each named after an astronomical or Natural observation e.g. winter solstice or grain in ear. The same signs were used for twelve fixed-length *shi* (double-hours). The complete Solar day was also subdivided into either 96 or 100 *k'e*.

Western	Eastern	double-hours
Aries	Rat	11 p.m - 1 a.m.
Taurus	Ox	1 a.m. - 3 a.m.
Gemini	Tiger	3 a.m. - 5 a.m.
Cancer	Hare	5 a.m. - 7 a.m.
Leo	Dragon	7 a.m. - 9 a.m.
Virgo	Serpent	9 a.m. - 11 a.m.
Libra	Horse	11 a.m. - 1 p.m.
Scorpio	Sheep	1 p.m. - 3 p.m.
Sagittarius	Monkey	3 p.m. - 5 p.m.
Capricorn	Cock	5 p.m. - 7 p.m.
Aquarius	Dog	7 p.m. - 9 p.m.
Pisces	Boar	9 p.m. - 11 p.m.

Their Great Cycle of sixty years is linked with Jupiter, which completes five cycles, and Saturn, which completes two cycles during this period. The five Jovian cycles are named: wood, fire, earth, metal and water. These five elements were then sub-divided to make ten terrestrial roots: growing wood, cut timber, Natural fire, artificial fire, earth, earthenware, raw or cast metal, wrought metal, running water and standing water. These ten terrestrial elemental roots combined with the twelve celestial animal branches in a continuous hexadecimal cycle to name their years. A Great Cycle starts at a year of the wood rat and ends at the water pig. The Chinese used these duodecimal and decimal systems in parallel. The mathematical argument about the use of base-twelve or base-ten has been raging around the globe for millennia.

Eastern Time

Chinese Taoism is a mystical philosophy, rather than being a religion. No statement is accepted as being entirely true nor absolutely false. It was based upon the ideas of Lao Tzu, a contemporary of Confucius. Lao wrote the *Tao Te Ching* or *I Ching* meaning: *The Book of Change*. Some zodiacs incorporate eight Taoist *Kua* or trigrams which are like binary bar codes and are based upon the opposites of *Yang* and *Yin*. Time and Spirit belong to the masculine *Yang* principle: ▬▬▬▬▬
Space and Matter belong to the feminine *Yin* principle: ▬▬ ▬▬
Together they manifest the *Tao,* the secret law that governs the Cosmos. These opposing symbols are used in 64 hexagrams which have specific meanings about Life and they also appear on the South Korean flag. The various signs for sub-divisions of the year have been preserved on the back of bronze mirrors, which represent both Space and Time. These usually show the eight *I Ching* signs or *Yang* and *Yin* principles. They also show the twelve equatorial Constellations and their animals. Animals of eternal life represent the cardinal points and the seasons:

Phoenix = South = Summer

Kilin (Unicorn) = East = Autumn   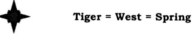   **Tiger = West = Spring**

Tortoise = North = Winter

The Eastern convention is South at the top and North at the bottom. The Eastern compass rose had 24 points; the Western had 16 points. The Chinese discovered magnetism and invented the magnetic compass. They divided the great circle of their horizon into exactly 365¼ *pu.* So that the Sun moved around the ecliptic approximately one *pu* per day. They recorded the Stars, Constellations and Planets in the night Sky. They could predict the Solar and Lunar eclipses extremely accurately. Chinese astronomers also discovered the precession of the equinoxes. The Nine Roads of the Moon is a complex Lunar diagram which shows the progressive forward motion of the major axis of the Moon's orbit. These nine roads were traditionally assigned different symbolic colours.

During the Ming dynasty (1368-1644 AD) they built huge fleets of junks. Some of these had six masts and were larger than any Western vessel. They followed the ocean currents and prevailing winds all over the globe. They discovered and charted the Americas, before Columbus, as well as Australia, New Zealand, Antarctica, Greenland, Iceland and the Arctic. They used the Pole Stars to determine their true heading, the Sun to determine their latitude and the Stars to determine their longitude. Most of their junks, charts, logs, instruments and ephemeris tables were destroyed when China closed its borders but a few were saved. We are discovering more about their fantastic voyages from the wrecks, animals, plants, artifacts, DNA, buildings and diseases they left behind.

Chinese Time

The Chinese began to cultivate rice and cereals some 12,000 years ago.
The Lang Shan culture of 3500 BC developed the first written symbols.
These ancient symbols are still used today by all of the Chinese people.
North and South China eventually divided into separate warring states.
Both used the same written symbols but they spoke different languages.
The North grew cereals and used continuous celestial twelve-day weeks.
The South grew rice and used continuous terrestrial ten-day weeks.
China (*Qin*) was reunified by the first emperor Ying Zheng in 221 BC.
China then used both ten-day and twelve-day weeks simultaneously.
His rule, by terror, was so supreme that his pyramid-shaped mausoleum
has never been excavated but his terracotta army has been uncovered.
Zheng erected the 2,400 Km Great Wall to keep out nomadic invaders.
He organized a vast hierarchy of bureaucrats to standardize all of the
laws, rules, weights, measures, coins, chronologies, calendars and clocks.
He even standardized axles so that all of the wheels ran in the same ruts.

Chinese chronology with its sixty-year cycle is traditionally based upon
the year 2637 BC when their Great Flood is believed to have occurred.
The Moon was always considered to be just as important as the Sun.
Hence they used a Lunar/Solar calendar as well as the tropical zodiac.
Alternate 29 and 30-day months occasionally had a thirteenth month
intercalated at the discretion of the emperor to align with the Solar year.
As well as the year names the Chinese also used dynasties according
to the family names of their emperors e.g. *Han* = 202 BC to 220 AD.
Each dynasty was celebrated by the introduction of a new calendar.
About a hundred calendars were issued between the first unification of
the empire and the end of the *Ch'ing* or Manchu dynasty in 1911 AD.

Keeping the track of Time died out after China was invaded in 1215 AD
by the brutal Mongolian, Genghis Khan (Ruler of All 1162-1227 AD) and
soon became part of the greatest empire that the World had ever known.
His grandson, Kublai Khan (1216-1294 AD) conquered the rest of China.
He built an enormous pleasure dome at Xanadu but then his empire fell.
Mongolians still use the twelve heavenly branches and ten earthly roots
for their chronology, calendar and clock e.g. year of the timber tiger,
zodiac sign of the horse, day of the metal ox, double-hour of the rat.
The Mongolians were expelled during the Ming dynasty (1368-1644 AD)
Ming emperors extended the Great Wall, widened the Grand Canal and
moved their capital, with its Forbidden City, from Nanjing to Beijing.
Their huge fleet of treasure ships reached the far corners of Our Planet.
Their eunuch admirals divided each day at sea into ten equal watches.
The emperor forbade anyone to learn about astronomy, except for those
who had an hereditary right, in order to prevent innovation and change.
The only observatory he allowed was inside the walled Forbidden City.
The Solar year was progressively measured down to six decimal places.

Chinese Time

Imperial China encouraged several spiritual and philosophical beliefs, which were mutually compatible and appealed to different age groups. These included Taoism and, later on, the more pragmatic Confucianism. The Chinese philosopher K'ung Fu-tzu, (Confucius 551-479 BC) had many sayings and most of these still have a great deal of meaning today. The continuous ten-day *xun* became the working and resting pattern with some job-sharing and compulsory community bathing every *xun*. The *xun* is still used in formal documents, instead of the seven-day week. The 6,000 km Silk Road between China and Rome was opened during the first century AD allowing Western and Eastern ideas to cross-fertilize. Paper was invented in China in the second century AD and this helped ideas and ideals to spread all around the globe, however the Chinese script was not so easy to print as the Latin one, which held China back. The Chinese were the first to issue paper money during the Ming dynasty.

Christianity reached China when Father Matteo Ricci (1552-1610 AD), a Jesuit missionary, gained access to the Forbidden City in Beijing by presenting the emperor with a mechanical clock that chimed the hour. China adopted the 24-hour 60-minute 60-second day and 7-day week. It still uses the Gregorian calendar in parallel with the traditional one.

China became a republic in 1911 AD, after a period of female misrule. It removed the power of Manchu Emperor Pu Yi, Lord of 10,000 years. The Min Kuo dynasty began in 1912 AD but became even more corrupt. The Peoples Republic began in 1949 AD and adopted the Metric System. Mao Zedong decided that time zones were divisive, so they have just one spanning 60 degrees of the globe without any daylight saving measures. He forbade religion and philosophy and put many intellectuals to death.

The Gregorian and Chinese New Year celebrations are not always happy occasions for they highlight the conflict between the old and the new. New Year now falls on the second new-Moon after the winter solstice. A month is intercalated to keep the Lunar and Solar years in alignment. A thirteenth or leap month, considered unlucky, occurred in 1976 AD when a huge earthquake struck in Tangshan killing 240,000 people. Chairman Mao, Premier Zhou En-Lai and Marshal Zhu De died that year. In 1995 AD a leap month coincided with a powerful earthquake on the same day as an eclipse and many feared that Chairman Deng would die. The Communist Party leadership changes by secret ballot every decade. President Hu Jintao allowed more capitalism, so the economy flourished but this led to corruption and a greater disparity between rich and poor. President Xi Jinping replaced him, on the vernal equinox in 2013 AD. However, a great earthquake in Sichuan coincided with a Lunar eclipse. An estimated 85% of Chinese people have now given-up Communism for Humanism, Christianity, Buddhism, Islam, Taoism or Confucianism.

Japanese Time

Japan was once a group of separate island-states, which are now united. The imperial family in Yamato claimed direct descent from the ancient Sun-goddess: *Amaritsu Omikami,* hence: The Land of the Rising Sun. The emperors were thought to possess the ability to call on her powers. Japanese legend has it that their first emperor, Jimmu, ascended the throne on 11 February, the first day of their spring, in 660 BC, however, historians argue that Japan did not become one state until 601 AD. The difference of 1260 years is regarded as an auspicious Japanese Era. The year 1940 AD corresponded with their very auspicious year 2600. These two zeros named their Zero fighter aircraft which flew into WW2.

The Japanese have always feared earthquakes, tsunamis and volcanoes. The cone-shaped Mount Fuji is still considered to be a sacred mountain. Most Japanese today believe in both Zen Buddhism and Shintoism. Buddhism reached Japan via China; Shintoism gradually developed from Buddhism, it has been in existence for 1,500 years and literally means: 'teaching of the gods' but has no recognized founder nor written dogma. Whilst ancestors are honored in Buddhist temples, the Sun, the Moon and other forces of Nature are worshipped in Shinto shrines at solstices, equinoxes and full-Moons, but neither of the beliefs incorporate a week. Their working day was much longer in the summer than in the winter. So their day was divided into 6 variable hours of daylight and 6 for night.

From 1600 AD Japan was ruled by shoguns, whose policy was isolation, until 1853 AD when Commodore Perry secured a US Consulate there. They now use the Metric System, the Gregorian calendar, the 7-day week and 24-hour clock with one time zone but no daylight saving measures. Their education is still run on a military basis, which is heavily biased towards science but does not give very much scope for original thought. In 1868 AD Emperor Meiji took over and since then their chronology has been based upon the reigns and names of their divine emperors.

Japan tried to dominate the Pacific in WW2 which ended when Hiroshima and Nagasaki were annihilated - the holy city of Kyoto was spared but Emperor Hirohito was forced to abdicate his divine powers in 1947 AD. General Douglas MacArthur helped the emperor to rewrite the Japanese constitution and replaced the ancient feudal system with democracy. Emperor Akihito now has the same status as a constitutional monarch. Despite their connections with the USA, they still drive on the left. Despite their booming car industry they have not invested in roads. Cars that are older than three years must now be sold and exported. Public transport is grossly overloaded but they have regular fast trains. The Kobe earthquake on 17 January 1995 AD killed 5,000 people and the earthquake and tsunami on 11 March 2011 AD killed 10,000 people, sending shockwaves through the insurance and banking industries.

Japanese Time

The Japanese language is now spoken by virtually the whole population.
It has no genders, no article and no number in either nouns or verbs.
It is written vertically in a partly ideographic and partly syllabic system.
The ideographs were adopted from the Chinese some two millennia ago.
The traditional Japanese calendar was Lunar based with no work week.
This has been replaced by their version of the Solar Gregorian calendar.
Their months are numbered but the seven days in their week are:

Nichiyobi	Sun-day	Sunday
Getsuyobi	Moon-day	Monday
Kayobi	Fire-day	Tuesday
Suiyobi	Water-day	Wednesday
Mokuyobi	Wood-day	Thursday
Kinyobi	Metal-day	Friday
Doiyobi	Earth-day	Saturday

Although the Japanese have recently adopted the seven-day week, and
Doiyobi is their main market day, *Nichiyobi* is not regarded as a rest day.
It is often used for doing another job, such as tending the paddy fields.
Apart from weekends there are 13 Lunar days which are normally used
for honoring ancestors at Buddhist temples and visiting Shinto shrines.
The spring and autumnal equinoxes are celebrated by national holidays.

Zen has different ethics to orthodox Buddhism and so they work harder.
Perhaps it is the feudal influence of Shinto and Bushido, their form of
chivalry, and the loss of face caused by failure which makes them work.
It was traditional to work during daylight and many workers still do this.
Some 10,000 Japanese die every year from sheer fatigue and overwork.
Although most Japanese workers are now entitled to up to 23 days paid
leave each year, very few take vacations and 3 or 4 days is the norm.
It is usual for men to stay at work beyond the normal working hours,
even if there is no work to do and most children do extra study at night.
It is traditional in Japan to have a job for life but many are now sharing
their jobs due to the rising value of the yen and the global recession.
As well as banking their money some Japanese also bank their Time.
The Time spent caring for the aged can be drawn on in their own old age.

By using their meager Natural resources and learning from Americans,
they failed to expand in WW2, recovered rapidly after it and developed
technological products with high quality and low price without being
encumbered by the need to maintain an expensive defensive policy.
The population saved their money and invested it in their own industry.
This had the effect of raising the value of the yen on foreign markets.
Many Japanese companies are now investing in other countries such as
Korea, Thailand, Australia, USA or Britain where both labour and money
are cheaper and there are fewer language, trade and tariff restrictions.

Indian Time

The Harrapins built stone cities by the river Indus from about 10000 BC. They are thought to have begun worshipping Hindu gods in about 5000 BC. Their civilization collapsed when the Indus changed course in 3000 BC.

Dark-skinned Dravidians colonized India between 3250 and 2750 BC. They worshipped Sky-gods and Nature-gods including those linked with the Sun: *Surya*, the Moon: *Soma*, Fire: *Agni*, Rain: *Indra* and Time: *Siva*. This male or female god of destruction is black since he or she is pitiless. *Prajapati* the god of Creation and the Universe was honored by sacrifice. They feared eclipses when *Rahu* might swallow the Sun and the Moon. During one day *Vishnu*, the protector of the World, winks 1,000 times. The life of *Brahma* (reality) is 100 great years, each having 360 *kalpas*. A *kalpa* is 12,000 divine years x 360,000 Solar years = 4,320,000,000. The Lord *Krishna* was born in about 1700 BC of a virgin mother, under a Bright Star and was thought to be the eighth reincarnation of *Vishnu*. *Krishna* or *Krista* is worshipped as the god of the calendar and the clock.

Light-skinned Nordic or Aryan people invaded the North from Asia between 1400 and 500 BC and their god of cosmic order was *Varuna*. Their language was Vedic, which eventually led to the development of Sanskrit in which the ancient religious literature: *The Vedas* was written. The *Mahabharata* tells a very similar legend to Moses in the bull-rushes. The *Aryabhatiya*, a very ancient mathematical and astronomical treatise, says that a year had 12 months of 30 days and a week had 10 days. There were four Universes in cycles called: *yugas* and We are now in the dying fourth one: the *Kaliyuga* since *Kali* is the goddess of destruction. This *Kaliyuga* Era, used from the fourth century AD, began in 3102 BC. In the hills the *Saptarshi* Era started at the moment their saints became the Seven Stars of the Great Bear in 3076 BC, but in the north-west they use Lunar moonths in the *Vikrama Samvat* Era which began in 57 BC. The new Moon after the autumnal equinox *is* the Hindu New Year: *Diwali*. This Lunar/Solar festival of lights celebrates the victory of good over evil. There are normally twelve moonths but an extra one may be inserted. The *Saka* Era was used in the south from 78 AD and was based upon a Solar calendar starting at the vernal equinox with 5 months of 31 days, then 7 months of 30 days in ordinary years, but 6 of each in leap years.

Hindu astronomers used an accurate hexadecimal system with the day divided into 60 *ghatikas;* subdivided into 60 *palas;* then 60 *vipalas*. A Star in the Constellation of Pisces was used to mark the start of their Sidereal year and they knew all about the precession of the equinoxes. The Gupta dynasty (320-550 AD) began north India's classical age when their Sanskrit literature, mathematics and architecture were developed. Aryabhata thought Earth was a sphere spinning on its own axis and revolving around the Sun and its shadow on the Moon caused eclipses.

Indian Time

Millions of Hindus bathe in the Ganges every 12 years when astrologers divine that Jupiter has entered Aquarius and the Sun has entered Aries. Their Kumbh Mela festival attracts the holy men in the belief that *Ganga* will cleanse their sins and free them from the cycle of death and rebirth.

Sikhism was originally a Hindu sect and was founded by the guru Nanak (1469-1538 AD) who condemned the formalism of Hinduism and Islam. Emphasizing the fundamental moral values in all religions, his mission was to end all religious conflicts and to promote universal toleration. All gods were exactly the same, whether called: *Vishnu, Allah* or *God*. His progressive ideas were welcomed by the great Mogul Emperor Akbar. He built the Golden Temple at Amritsar and abolished caste distinctions. The hair is not cut and the name: Singh (Lion) is used by every follower. There have, so far, been ten gurus and the number ten is venerated. *Nanakshaki* chronology is based upon the birth of the guru Nanak. Sikhs once used the Hindu Lunar-Solar calendar with movable festivals. On 14 March 1999 AD or 1 *Chet* 531 *Nan* they adopted a Solar calendar. This has five months of 31 days, six months of 30 then one of 30 or 31.

Jainism offers an austere path to enlightenment and it is different from Hinduism because it is not based upon The Creation but Cycles of Time. Jain ascetics attempt to conduct their lives following these five vows: to injure no living thing; to speak the truth; to take only what is given; to be chaste; and to achieve detachment from places, people and things. Their examples in following this discipline are the 24 spiritual teachers called: *tirthankaras* who have appeared during the present Cycle of Time. A *tirtha* enables believers to escape from the endless round of rebirth. Their *Veer Nirvan Samat* year 2527 corresponded with 2000 AD and their feasts and fasts are based upon the Hindu Lunar-Solar calendar.

Islam came via Afghanistan and the Kyber Pass in the form of bandits. The Sultans of Delhi controlled the Ganges and used Lunar calendars. They were overcome by the Moguls, who used Sidereal zodiac calendars. They ruled from 1527 AD until defeated by the British in 1757 AD.

The British Raj arrived by steam ship to Bombay, Madras and Calcutta. The ability to travel on steam railways, mixed-up the races and religions. Gandhi tried to keep India in one piece but failed to keep the peace. The sub-continent was divided and Hindus segregated from Muslims. India and Pakistan gained their independence from Britain in 1947 AD. The Sikh territory of Punjab, was divided between India and Pakistan. The New *Saka* Era was declared the national age on 22 March 1957 AD. It is now used with Roman-Catholic months, 7-day weeks and 24-hours. East Pakistan became the separate country of Bangladesh in 1972 AD. Hindus and Muslims are still trying to dominate Kashmir.

Buddhist Time

Buddhism is considered to be a philosophy rather than a religious belief. A Hindu prince, Siddharta Gautama, is known as: The Enlightened One. After leaving his palace and family for six years of study, with hermits and self-torturing recluses, he sat down for 49 days under the sacred botree in Buddh Gaya, to understand the cause and cure of suffering. He accepted the Hindu doctrine of a cycle of lives but not the existence of any deity and he did not accept the caste system nor animal sacrifice. He became the Buddha and the results of his meditations were written, three centuries later, in the *Pali Canon* containing the *Four Noble Truths*:

> Existence is unhappiness.
> Unhappiness is caused by selfish desire.
> Desire can be destroyed by following the *Noble Eightfold Path*:
> Right views;
> Right desires;
> Right speech, plain and truthful;
> Right conduct, including abstinence from immorality and taking life;
> Right livelihood, harming no one;
> Right effort, always pushing on;
> Right awareness of the past, the present and the future;
> Right contemplation or meditation.

If this path is followed the soul may reach *Nirvana* - The Timeless State. The Buddha taught about liberation through discipline and ethics, such as sharing work and possessions, but he did not claim any divine right. Nevertheless, many gilded images of the Buddha are honored in temples. Buddhists honour the Sun and Moon but do not worship them as gods.

Buddhist chronology is based on the death of the Buddha, which they reckoned to be in 543 BC, however, the year was actually about 483 BC. He predicted that his teaching and wisdom might last a thousand years. Yet, this would be only 500 years if women were admitted to the faith. There have been other Buddhas and there will probably be many more. Buddhaghosa, 500 years later, changed this prediction to 5,000 years. So some now believe that the end of Buddhism will occur in 4456 AD. Buddhists regard Time as cyclic but they do not have a written calendar. Their Lunar/Solar year starts at a new-Moon before the vernal equinox. They ritually celebrate 49 Lunar Buddha days during each Solar year. These festival days are based upon the Moon's quarter phases but they can be either 7 or 8 days apart and the full-Moon is the most important. Buddhists rise at dawn, retire at dusk and so have no need for clocks. Nevertheless, their prayer wheels must be turned to make Time pass by.

Buddhism enjoyed a spectacular growth in India after Emperor Ashoka embraced it in 262 BC but faded as Hinduism revived from 200-800 AD. It spread to Tibet, Ceylon (Sri Lanka), Nepal, Mongolia, Vietnam, Laos, Cambodia, Java, Burma (Myanmar), Siam (Thailand), China and Japan. In Tibet it developed into Lamaism, in China: Ch'an and in Japan: Zen.

Buddhist Time

Although most Himalayas have now been climbed, some are still sacred. Mount Kailas is pyramid-shaped and is the source of four great rivers. It was venerated by the ancient religion of Bon-po and is still considered to be sacred by Hindus, Buddhists and Jains who circumambulate it.

The vast Cambodian city of Angkor, with its roads, canals and reservoirs, was constructed by the Kymer rice emperors from around 1000 AD. Its great Hindu and Buddhist temples of Angkor Wat and Angkor Thom vanished into the jungle when the climate changed in about 1500 AD. When Pol Pot and his Communist Kymer Rouge seized power in 1975 AD he killed a million Buddhists and restarted their chronology at year zero.

Burma had no roads nor railways before WW2 when the Japanese built their infamous railways, roads and bridges using POWs as slave labour. Now called Myanmar it is a Communist-Buddhist military dictatorship. It has a unique alphabet consisting of circles but with no straight lines, it has a non-decimal currency and it has yet to adopt the Metric System.

The Thais now use the Western Gregorian months and the 7-day week. Each has a colour: Monday = yellow, Tuesday = pink, Wednesday = green, Thursday = orange, Friday = blue, Saturday = purple, Sunday = red. The present King was born on a Monday, so his royal ensign is yellow. The *Songkran* water festival is when the Sun transits Aries (13-15 April).

Buddhists on the Indonesian island of Java still use the Waku calendar. Each day in their 210-day *odalan* cycle is named in nine different ways in 2,3,4,5,6,7,8,9 and 10-day weekly cycles or in seven 30-day months. Being near the Equator there are no seasons but a rice cycle is 210 days. Java's Sailendra dynasty used this calendar to control their rice empire. Their huge pyramid-temple mandala of Borobadur was built in 850 AD. It has 7 steps (4 square, 3 circular) 1460 relief panels in ten chapters depicting the life of Siddharta Gautama and 504 statues of the Buddha. Some Javanese, Madurese or Sundanese still use a calendar inaugurated by Sultan Agung of Mataram in 1633 AD, which has both a 5-day week and a 7-day week as well as Lunar moonths and an 8-year Solar cycle. The five weekday names also represent colours and cardinal directions: *Legi*/white/E, *Pahing*/red/S, *Pon*/yellow/W, *Wage*/black/N, *Kliwon*/blue/Centre.

The original botree is now dead and gone but a seed from it was taken to Kandy, Sri Lanka (Ceylon) and is now a botree some 2,500 years old. Whilst Buddhism is a peaceful belief, there have recently been riots in Sri Lanka between rival sects as well as the guerrilla war with Hindu Tamil Tigers, who were brought in to work in the many tea plantations. The government recently moved clocks forward an hour, to save energy, without telling anyone in advance, and so they caused total chaos.

African Time

Although Our origins are known to be in Africa We know less about the dark continent and its civilizations than many other parts of the globe. The great variety of climate, terrain, flora and fauna throughout Africa led, over the millennia, to the evolution of men with different physical characteristics, tools, weapons, beliefs and cultures, who formed tribes. The 1m Pygmy were a quite different tribe from the 2m Watusi because the former evolved in the forests and the latter evolved on the plains. The annual migration of the great herds of wildebeest, zebra and many other species led to the belief that Life is cyclic and We are born again. Animism imparted spirits to the trees, rocks, mountains and volcanoes. So there were no stone temples or other permanent religious structures. Nevertheless, there are still traces of lost civilizations throughout Africa. Egypt had the greatest civilization but there are more pyramids in Nubia.

Sub-Saharan culture was, and still is, quite different from the North. The Sun and the Moon represented their chronology, calendar and clock. The number of moonths in a year was usually considered to be thirteen and an intercalary correction made by occasionally deleting a moonth. The quarter phases often marked religious festivals as well as markets. However, the continuous market week varied between four and ten days. The seasonal pattern was dominated by annual rains and one of the shamans' jobs was to predict their arrival by astronomical observation. They gave animal names to Stars, Constellations, Planets and Comets. However, their Constellations were different from the ones used today. For example: the three Stars in Orion's belt were considered to be zebras. The rising of the Pleiades at dawn was an annual indication that crops should be sown, whilst the number of seasons varied from two to five. Equatorial tribes still divide both day and night into twelve hours each and their day starts at dawn, even though they use clocks and watches.

David Livingstone (1813-1873 AD) was the first European to cross the dark continent in 1855 AD and to witness the spectacular Victoria Falls. He thought that most of the rivers would eventually be made navigable. His Victorian mission was to convert all of the natives to Christianity. He was only partially successful and they still remember ancient ways. Voodoo is a bizarre combination of Roman-Catholicism with Animism. Since there are many different languages with no written records, most traditions and beliefs have been lost, before they could be understood. Yet, anthropologists have discovered ancient knowledge which remained secret and was preserved in the memories of shamans and tribal elders. The imposition of white man's culture, in just one century, has made a huge impact on African society but there is still a long way to go before the democratic system of government is seen to be working properly. In another century the black man may have adopted the white man's ways but, conversely, they may be able to survive; whilst whites may not.

African Time

Early civilizations developed in Egypt, Libya, Nubia, Sudan and Ethiopia. The Carthaginians were related to the Phoenicians in Syria and Lebanon. They traded British copper, tin and gold with the produce of the Nile. They certainly reached Zanzibar and probably circumnavigated Africa but were eventually defeated in the Punic wars by the Roman Empire. The Romans built many stone cities along the North African coast but after the collapse of the Roman Empire most of this region fell to Islam and this religion is still gradually expanding into Sub-Saharan Africa. Nevertheless, the Muslim Brotherhood is now being challenged by a new democratic movement and may soon become a chain of secular states.

The Dondo near Timbuktu on the river Niger in Mali measure the age in sixty-year cycles and the date by four calendars based upon cycles of the Sun, the Moon, the Planet Venus and the brightest dog-Star Sirius. They say Saturn has a ring around it, Jupiter has four moons and Earth rotates and goes round the Sun with the other Planets in elliptical orbits. They say Sirius is actually a group of three Stars, which orbit each other. These beliefs go back well beyond their first contact with white men. Nevertheless, they may have had contact with yellow men during their great junk voyages around the globe during the fifteenth century AD. Sirius A is like the Sun, Sirius B a white dwarf, discovered in 1862 AD, with a 50-year orbit and Sirius C is a red dwarf, discovered in 1993 AD.

The stone-built township of Zimbabwe, lying between the Zambezi and Limpopo rivers, is another remnant of civilization South of the Sahara. It was abandoned for no apparent reason in the fifteenth century AD. However, this was the era when white men first began the slave trade. Perhaps a nomadic life-style is better for survival in these circumstances. Most tribes had a nomadic existence, within a well-defined territory. Crossing a sacred boundary, such as a river, could lead to a tribal war. Measurement of Time and Space has no importance to nomadic people.

By the end of the nineteenth century AD the whole African continent (except Ethiopia and Liberia) had been annexed by the European states. Ethiopia (Abyssinia) was later annexed by the Italians during 1935 AD. Christian Ethiopia continues to use the ancient Egyptian Solar calendar but its Jewish origins are thought to go back to the Queen of Sheba. Liberia was established by the American Colonization Society in 1822 AD. This colony of freed slaves became an independent republic in 1884 AD. Liberians freely chose to work within a continuous five-day week and were the last to sign the standard time zone convention in 1972 AD. They still use the American system of lengths, weights and measures. Many ocean going vessels choose to fly the Liberian flag of convenience. Like many other African states, they have recently had a civil war and still cannot find the right socio-economic, political or religious system.

Egyptian Time

The Nile finally reached the Mediterranean about twelve millennia ago. Before then much of the Sahara was swamps, marshes and fertile plains. This great change created a desert, a fertile valley and a new civilization. The ancient Egyptians worshipped Time and religiously followed rituals based upon the cycles of the Sun, Moon, Planets, Stars and the Nile. Not only were all of their chronologies, calendars and clocks based upon Heavenly and Earthly cycles of Time but also their pantheon of gods. *Maat* (law and order) was based upon their remarkable understanding of the measurement, management and government of Time and Space. Their temples and monuments were astronomically orientated and their tombs were filled with multifarious inscriptions related to timekeeping. *The Book of the Dead*, the oldest religious text on Earth, was inscribed upon the walls of the inner sanctum of several of the largest pyramids. The beginning of their hieroglyphic script can be traced back to 3200 BC.

Natural catastrophes plus the Roman occupation, Christian usurpation and Islamic destruction wiped-out much of their archaeological records. Nevertheless, many of their massive stone monuments have survived. In 1798 AD Napoleon invaded Egypt and this was the start of Egyptology. His 136 scholars made very detailed records of the ancient monuments; until Nelson destroyed the French fleet and sent Napoleon into retreat. The trilingual Rosetta stone was found in the Nile delta by the French but captured by the British and it is now kept in the British Museum. It was not until 1822 AD that Jean François Champollion deciphered it. We can now read their hieroglyphs and understand more of their history.

The Sphinx at Giza, where Upper and Lower Egypt meet, was an outcrop of rock, which is thought to have been carved over five millennia ago. This enormous sculpture faces toward the Sun rising at the equinoxes. The Sphinx's temple has twelve massive pillars, representing the twelve hours of the day or the night and twelve Lunar moonths in a Solar year. The Great Pyramid was a tomb, compass, chronology, calendar, clock, observatory and landmark, constructed at the apex of the Nile delta. When it was completed, facing the cardinal points, in the 4th dynasty, c2600 BC, the North Pole Star was Alpha Draconis but it is now Polaris. It was believed to be the launching pad for the *ka* or spirit of Pharaoh and his Queen on their journey to eternal after-life as Stars in the Sky. Passages and air shafts pointed at the Pole Star, Orion's belt and Sirius. The Great Pyramid may represent the tombs of the gods of these Stars. The other pyramids at Giza may represent the Sun-god and Moon-god. Despite all the efforts of their architects all of these tombs were robbed. At the head of the Valley of the Kings in Upper Egypt, where many of the later pharaohs were entombed, there is a pyramid-shaped mountain. In some of these well-hidden rock tombs there were brightly coloured chronologies, calendars and clocks for Pharaoh to use in the after-life.

Egyptian Time

The Egyptian civilization nearly collapsed three times due to Natural causes.
Egyptologists have named, numbered and aged the dynasties as follows:

Pre-Dynastic Period	0	3900 - 3100 BC
Early Dynastic Period	1-2	3100 - 2686 BC
Old Kingdom	3-6	2686 - 2160 BC
First Intermediate Period	7-10	2160 - 2061 BC
Middle Kingdom	11-12	2061 - 1786 BC
Second Intermediate Period	13-17	1786 - 1567 BC
New Kingdom	18-20	1567 - 1086 BC
Third Intermediate Period	21-25	1085 - 656 BC
Late Period	26-31	656 - 332 BC
Greek or Ptolemaic Period		332 - 30 BC
Roman Period		30BC - 540 AD

However, some pharaohs were omitted and so these dates may be wrong.
The *Apis* bull-cult provided a different kind of chronology: a single bull
was worshipped for thousands of years, when he died he was replaced
by another, mummified, named, dated and then entombed in a catacomb.

They used three calendars: a Lunar one for Mystic festivals, a Solar one
for most Civic purposes and a Stellar one for astronomy and agriculture.
The wandering Civic calendar had 12 months of 30 days plus five days.
Month-days were numbered and divided into 10-day weeks or *decades*.
The last day, devoted to rest and religion, was called their Sun-day.
Star-groups called *Decans* were used to measure the time at night and
the days in the Stellar year, which moved through their three seasons.
The agricultural seasons were: flood-time, growth-time and harvest-time.
The Stellar, Pharaonic or Siriac calendar had a leap day every four years.
The wandering, vague Civic one and the Stellar, Pharaonic, Siriac one
coincided in 2773 BC during the reign of Djoser in the third dynasty.
It may have been devised by Imhotep, the father of Egyptian science.
The Stellar year began with the heliacal rising of the brightest Star,
Sirius the Dog, which coincided with the annual inundation of the Nile.
These calendars coincided every 1461 Civic years or 1460 Siriac years.
A *decade* was chosen in the Civic year to predict the start of the flood.
In 238 BC Eudoxus of Cnidus calculated the year to be 365 1/4 days.
Ptolemy Euergetes failed to introduce leap days to the Civic calendar.
In 26 BC the first Roman Emperor: Octavian, who became: Augustus,
introduced Civic leap days throughout his personal estate of Egypt.
The heliacal rising of Sirius fell on 29 August in the Julian calendar.
The twelve month-gods of the Civic and Siriac calendars were named during
the Ptolemaic Period as follows: (with Coptic names in brackets)

Thoth (Tut), Paophi (Babah), Athyr (Hatur), Choiak, (Kiyahk)
Tobi (Tubah), Mechir (Amshir), Phamenoth (Baramhat), Pharmuthi (Baramundah)
Pacons (Bashans), Payni (Ba'unah), Epiphi (Abib), Mesore (Misra).
Plus a little month of 5/6 days named: *Henu-renpet (Hepagomene)*

Egyptian Time

During the Old Kingdom they worshipped a Great Ennead of nine gods.
The Sun-god: *Atum* created himself upon a mound in the watery chaos.
He engendered the twin deities of the air: *Shu* and moisture: *Tefnut*.
They engendered the Earth-god: *Geb* and the Milky Way-goddess: *Nut*.
They bore: *Osiris*, his sister: *Isis,* their brother: *Seth* and sister: *Nephthys*.
Osiris and Isis bore one son: *Horus* who fought *Seth* to become Pharaoh.
These five gods named the last five dog-days in the Solar calendar year.
The god of embalming and funery rites: *Anubis* had the head of a jackal.
The grand vizier: *Thoth,* the god of writing, measurement and learning,
was shown as an ibis-headed man or as a sacred ibis or as a baboon.
This lord of order, wisdom, astronomy, chronologies, calendars, clocks
was sometimes shown with the Moon's crescent and disk on his head.
Osiris = Orion, *Isis* = Sirius, *Seth* = Venus, *Nephthys* = Pleides,
Horus = Mars or Jupiter or Saturn, *Anubis* = Comets, *Thoth* = Mercury.
Heh = Time and he always had an *ankh*, the symbol of Life, on his arm.

During the New Kingdom the Sun and the Moon became more dominant.
The ram-headed *Amen* or *Amun,* god of air and wind, was omnipresent.
He measured Time when he sailed his Solar or Lunar ark through Space.
During twelve daylight hours he had the body of a different creature,
rising as a scarab beetle, descending into the underworld as a crocodile.
His ithyphallic idol was worshipped at the temple of Karnak in Thebes.
This was accurately aligned with the Sun-rise at the winter solstice.
Amen was considered to be the Creator and the king of all the gods.
He eventually became linked with the falcon-headed Sun-god *Ra*, as
Amen-Ra and he was often shown with the Sun's disc on his head.
His wife was the goddess *Mut* and their son was the Moon-god *Khonsu*.

During the reign of Akhenaten, the only Sky-god was the Sun-disc: *Aten*.
This god-king built a capital at Amarna with his goddess-queen Nefertiti.
His first temple had hundreds of mud-brick offering tables or altars.
This was destroyed when Thera erupted and sent a tsunami up the Nile.
His second temple had many stone altars arranged in sevens and 28s.
So they probably used 52 seven-day weeks and thirteen 28-day sunths.
This totals 364 so they probably had an extra day, named after the Aten.
Akhenaten's successor Tut-ankh-amen was his son by his sister Kiya.
Tut's young queen Ankh-esen-amen was one of Nefertiti's six daughters.
They had two stillborn daughters and Tut died at the age of nineteen.
He restored all the traditional gods, chronologies, calendars and clocks.
Tut's successors Ay and Horemheb tried to destroy all traces of Atenism.

The *ankh* was usurped by the Gnostic monks and the Coptic priests.
This symbol of Life has morphed into the symbol of Death: the crucifix.
The Coptic calendar still has twelve 30-day months and 5 or 6 dog days.
Coptic New Year now falls on 11 September in the Gregorian calendar.

Egyptian Time

Evidence of the Egyptian obsession with the measurement, management and government of Time and Space can be found in tombs and temples. Some of the tombs contained 365 *shabti* figurines depicting their owners. A diagonal Star-chart from a Middle Kingdom coffin lid shows 36 *Decans* which were used to divide the night Sky into twelve variable hours and were also used as ten-day *decades* to divide the Siriac and vague years. Like Sirius or Sothis each *Decan* group of Stars disappeared from the night Sky for seventy days and was reborn upon the horizon at dawn. The mummification process also took seventy days to complete.

The tomb of the young pharaoh Tut-ankh-Amen was discovered by Howard Carter and the Earl of Carnarvon on 22 November 1922 AD. The west wall illustrates the importance of Time in Egyptian religion. *Amen-Ra*, in the form of a scarab at Sun-rise, rides in a spaceship. *Osiris, Seth, Horus, Isis* and *Nephys* mark the last five days of the year. *Osiris*, the dead pharaoh, is the god of the dead; *Horus*, his living son, represents order in the Nile valley; *Seth*, the brother/enemy of *Osiris*, represents chaos in the desert; *Isis* is the sister and wife of *Osiris* and mother of *Horus*; and *Nephys* is her sister, the consort of *Seth*. *Amen-Ra* has twelve daughters called: *Hours* who act in concert against his adversaries and they also control the destinies of Human beings. *Thoth*, in the guise of twelve baboons, measures the twelve night *Hours*. Baboons hold out their hands at dawn, like praying, to warm their blood. They represent Time because their dawn chorus would awaken the dead. There may be more hidden chambers entombing Akhenaten and Nefertiti.

The ceiling inside the mortuary temple of Ramesses II in Western Thebes portrays twelve moonths of the Lunar religious calendar as demi-gods. A monument from the reign of Ramesses III at Medinet Habu lists the Lunar dates of the annual religious celebrations and animal sacrifices. A wall of this temple is devoted to inscriptions about Time and Space. The ceiling of Ramesses VI's tomb represents his age, date and time. A procession of pharaohs represents their dynasties with their years. A procession of gods represent the twelve months and five dog days. A series of inscriptions marks the thirty-six *Decans* or ten-day *decades*. The Sky-goddess *Nut* daily swallows and gives birth to the Sun-god *Ra*. During the night *Ra* passes through twelve Star-gates, which mark *Hours*. *Nut's* arched body represents the Milky Way and *Ra* was considered to have been conceived at the vernal equinox and born at the winter solstice.

The Naos of the Decades, recently discovered near Alexandria, indicates that the Egyptian religion, with its chronologies, calendars and clocks, was still in use when a large area of the Nile delta suddenly sank below the sea during a Natural catastrophe at the end of the Roman Empire. They eventually devised a new system in which 25 years = 309 moonths.

Greek Time

Greece was formed from many city-states, each with a different calendar. They fought each other for supremacy until Athens became dominant. The Athenian year began at the full-Moon after the summer solstice and was chronologically named after the victor of the Panhellenic Games. This Lunar calendar was based upon twelve moonths of 29 or 30 days plus an intercalary moonth, after the sixth moonth every two years. Twelve moonth-gods were: *Dios, Apellaios, Audynaios, Peritios, Dystros, Xanthikos, Artemisios, Daisios, Panemos, Loios, Gorpiaios, Hyerberetaios.* Each moonth was divided into three weeks of 10, 10 and 9 or 10 days. The Lunar year was also divided into 10 *prytanies* by the ruling council with four delegates serving for 36 days then six for 35 days = 354 days.

The Titanic Sky-gods lived on Mount Olympus and they created Mankind. They were responsible for everything that happened to Man on Earth. Yet, the philosophers held that Man was in control of his own destiny. Homer (c 850 BC) wrote about ancient gods, heros, myths and legends. Hesiod (c 700 BC) related agricultural activities to solstices or equinoxes and the movements of the Constellations in his book: *Works and Days.* Pythagoras (582-500 BC) developed the basic new science of geometry. Socrates (470-399 BC) passed his ideas, verbally, to Plato (429 -347 BC) who wrote them down and passed them on to Aristotle (384-322 BC). Alexander the Great (356-323 BC) the eldest son of Philip of Macedonia, was taught by Aristotle but his ideas about the Universe were wrong. The Macedonians used the Lunar/Solar cycle discovered by the Athenian astronomer Meton (c 1500 BC) in which 235 moonths equalled 19 years. Alexander invaded Babylonia, Persia, Judaea and Egypt from 332 BC. The Egyptians considered Alexander to be a god, because he was their liberator from Persian domination, and so they made him the son of *Ra.* Alexander founded Alexandria, the cultural capital of the ancient World, where Euclid (c300 BC) taught logic, numbers and geometry.

After Alexander's death in Babylon, General Seleucus Nicator founded the Seleucid dynasty which ruled western Asia from Antioch until 65 BC. The first Greek pharaoh was Alexander's friend, General Ptolemy Soter. Soter founded the Graeco-Egyptian or Ptolemaic dynasty of pharaohs. Many ancient Egyptian traditions were allowed to continue, including the use of the ten-day *decades* and thirty-day months but Ptolemy III issued a decree in 238 BC that one day should be added to every fourth year. The Sky-cult of *Osiris, Isis* and *Horus* and the bull-cult of *Apis* became merged into a new cult of *Serapis* and *Isis,* which became very popular. The *Serapeum* temple housed thousands of books in many languages after the library was accidentally burned to the ground by Julius Caesar. Greece was finally conquered and unified by the Romans in 87-84 BC. Egypt finally became a Roman province in 30 BC, after Cleopatra VII and Mark Antony were defeated by Octavian's fleet off Actium in Greece.

Greek Time

The Greeks were the first of the western nations to use their script to record the present and the past and to speculate about the future. The αβ alphabet named itself. Omega Ω means Time. We use μ for micro. They turned writing into an art form, they wrote many books and plays and wrote down ancient myths about gods and legends about heroes. Pindar of Thebes wrote many odes about gods, heroes and athletes. Their marble statues, temples, theatres, forums, markets, academies and gymnasiums are timeless relics of their advanced civilization.

The Romans usurped many Greek ideas and worshipped similar deities. The Latin weekday names developed into the ones now used in French:

Greek	Latin	Origin	French	English
Helios	Dies Solis	Sun	*Dimanche*	Sunday
Selene or Mene	Dies Lunae	Moon	*Lundi*	Monday
Ares	Dies Martis	Mars	*Mardi*	Tuesday
Hermes	Dies Mercredi	Mercury	*Mecredi*	Wednesday
Zeus	Dies Jovis	Jupiter	*Jeudi*	Thursday
Aphrodite	Dies Veneris	Venus	*Vendredi*	Friday
Kronus	Dies Saturni	Saturn	*Samedi*	Saturday

This seven-day *Heavenly Body* week gradually became established with the first day dedicated to *Helios* who was worshipped throughout Greece. The colossal statue of *Helios* on Rhodes was one of the Seven Wonders. *Selene* was a sister of *Helios* and another was *Eos,* the goddess of dawn. The Time-god was *Kronus* whose name was given to the hill at Olympia. His Titanic parents were: *Uranus* (Heavenly Father) *Gaia* (Mother Earth). He castrated his father with a sickle and ate all of his children but one. He ruled the idyllic Golden Age, his son was *Zeus*, whose son was *Apollo.* The ivory statue of *Zeus* at Olympia was another of the Seven Wonders. *Apollo* was the god of Sunlight to both the *Greeks* and the Romans. The two invisible outer Planets were named after *Uranus* and Neptune. The International Astronomical Union has named four minor Planets *Pluto*, Charon, Ceres and *Eris* and there may prove to be many others. All of the moons in the Solar System have been given the names of gods as well as most of the Stars and Constellations named in ancient times. What name will be given to the recently discovered ninth Solar Planet? Chronos, the Roman god of Time, gave Us chronology, chronometers...

Greece was part of the Eastern Roman Empire and so became Orthodox. It then became part of the Venetian and Ottoman Empires before finally becoming an independent state in 1832 AD when Otto became the King. Greece adopted BC/AD chronology, the Gregorian calendar and 24 hour clock in 1923 AD but the Greek Orthodox Church still uses the Julian calendar when determining Easter and other movable feasts and fasts. It is much stricter about Sunday observance than the Catholic Church.

Roman Time

Rome was a kingdom, a republic, a dictatorship, then finally an empire. Roman *Ab Urbe Condita* chronology was devised by Varro (116 - 27 BC) based upon the myth of the founding of Rome by Romulus in 753 BC. The Romulus year began at the new-Moon after the vernal equinox and had ten alternate 29 or 30 day months plus an intercalary remainder. These were named and numbered from I to X and two extra months were added in 713 BC by the second king Numa Pompilius to make 355 days. March, the original first month, was named after *Mars* the god of war. The ten days between Lunar and Solar years were known as *Mercedonius*. New Year was moved to the winter solstice during the republic when a pair of elected consuls took office and shared their jobs month by month. The early Romans continued to use the Etruscan eight-day market week.

Dictator Julius Caesar consulted Sosigenes, an Egyptian astronomer, who devised 12 months of alternate 30 or 31 days in a 365 1/4 day year. January, the first month, was named after *Janus*, the god of the portal. February was given the remaining 29 days, or 30 in every fourth year. The year 47 BC was 445 days long and this caused great confusion. The months were sub-divided into eight-day *kalends, ides* and *nones*. These Pagan festival days were counted down or numbered backwards. Gaius Julius Caesar was assassinated on the *ides* of March in 44 BC. The 7th month was renamed July by Mark Antony in Julius' honour. Julius' great nephew Octavian became Augustus, the first emperor. He made the Julian calendar illogical in 7 BC when he renamed Sextilis, the 8th month, after himself and added an extra day to it, which he took from February, so that his month of August could be equal to Julius'. To avoid three 31-day months together, September and November were reduced to 30 days, October and December were increased to 31 days. In 190 AD megalomaniac emperor Commodus renamed the twelve months after the titles he had given himself - but no one took any notice.

The Eastern empire split from the Western when it became too large. The legions incorporated images of their Pagan gods on their standards. They also painted Babylonian/Persian zodiac symbols on their shields. They worshipped the Persian or Parthian Time-god or Sun-god *Mithras*. The Mithraist continuous seven-day market week was adopted in 302 AD. Constantine the Great founded Constantinople at Byzantium in 312 AD. He reunited the empire and converted it from Mithraism to Christianity. His legions then painted the early Christian monograms on their shields. Sun-day became the Christian Sabbath and Saturn-day was for markets. The Western part of the empire fell to the Pagan Visigoths in 510 AD. But the Eastern emperor Justinian (527-565 AD) introduced a unified administration system, a revised code of law and an Orthodox creed. Justinian built the huge basilica of Hagia Sophia in Constantinople, as well as churches and monasteries throughout his Byzantine Empire.

Roman Time

The Roman *kalendar* could not be easily memorized, because it was so complicated, and so it had to be written down and announced publicly.

	March, May, July, October	August, December, January	April, June, September, November	February
I	kalendis	kalendis	kalendis	kalendis
II	VI ↑	IV ↑ ante	IV ↑ ante	IV ↑ ante
III	V ante	III ↕ nonas	III ↕ nonas	III ↕ nonas
IV	IV nonas	pridie nonas	pridie nonas	pridie nonas
V	III ↓	nonas	nonas	nonas
VI	pridie nonas	VIII ↑	VIII ↑	VIII ↑
VII	nona	VII	VII	VII
VIII	VIII ↑	VI ante	VI ante	VI ante
IX	VII	V idus	V idus	V idus
X	VI ante	IV	IV	IV
XI	V idus	III ↓	III ↓	III ↓
XII	IV ↓	pridie idus	pridie idus	pridie idus
XIII	III	Idibus	Idibus	Idibus
XIV	pridie idus	XIX ↑	XVIII ↑	XVII ↑
XV	Idibu	XVIII	XVII	XVI
XVI	XVII ↑	XVII	XVI	XV
XVII	XVI	XVI	XV	XIV
XVIII	XV	XV	XIV	XIII
XIX	XIV	XIV	XIII	XII
XX	XIII	XIII	XII	XI
XXI	XII	XII ante	XI ante	X ante
XXII	XI ante	XI kalendas	X kalendas	IX kalendas
XXIII	X kalendus	X	IX	VIII
XXIV	IX	IX	VIII	VII
XXV	VIII	VIII	VII	VI*
XXVI	VII	VII	VI	V
XXVII	VI	VI	V	IV
XXVIII	V	V	IV	III ↓
XXIX	IV ↓	IV	III ↓	Pridie kalendus
XXX	III ↓	III ↓	Pridie kalendus	
XXXI	Pridie kalendus	Pridie kalendus		

* repeated in leap years which were called *bisextillus annus*

Backward *kalends*, *ides* and *nones* were replaced with Roman month-day numerals by Charlemagne the Catholic King of the Franks (742-814 AD). He was the first to adopt *Anno Domini* chronology and became the first Holy Roman Emperor on Christmas Day XXV December in DCCC AD. The month-day numerals were eventually replaced by Arabic numbers. Yet, an Arabic zero has never been used in the Catholic age, date or time. Arabs regard the higgledy-piggledy Roman *kalendar* months as imperial. They have never been very popular and yet they have never been changed.

Persian Time

The Persians were part of the Aryan race, who believed in immortality. Their omnipotent Creator-god *Zurvan* can be traced back to 1700 BC. He was honored in temples with eternal fires on the mountain of Shiz.

The prophet Zoroaster or Zarathustra was believed to have been born of a virgin mother and the Time-god *Ahura Mazda* in the sixth century BC. At the Beginning of Time *Ahura Mazdah* created two spirits: *Spenista Mainyu* or *Ohrmazad,* the good; and *Angara Mainyu* or *Ahriman,* the bad. Man was compelled to follow one or other of these spirits by his conduct. *Ohrmazad,* The King of Light, was supported by these six archangels: Wisdom, Righteousness, Dominion, Devotion, Totality and Salvation. *Ahriman,* The Prince of Darkness, was supported by six archdemons: Anarchy, Apostacy, Presumption, Destruction, Decay and Fury. Zoroastrianism involved a teleological, predictive interpretation of Time. The positions of Constellations and Planets were predicted or divined. Astrologers eventually believed that they could foretell their own future. Civilization was predicted to last for a finite period of twelve millennia. When Zarathustra died, his beliefs were taken up by a priestly class known as the Magi and became the faith of the Achaemenid dynasty. Under Cyrus the Great their empire soon became the greatest on Earth. It was built with the innovation of chariots, wagons and straight roads. Darius founded the capital city of Perseopolis and extended the empire. It had huge square tributary halls and the first formal water gardens. Nomadic subjects travelled to Perseopolis to pay tribute to their King. Cambyses conquered Egypt in 525 BC and found their Solar calendar was better than his Lunar one, so he introduced one, with 11 months of 30 days and the 8th month of 35 days, on the vernal equinox in 503 AD. An additional month of 30 days was intercalated after every 120 years. The month-days 1, 8, 15 and 23 were devoted to honoring *Ahura Mazda.* Xerxes attacked Greece in 480 BC but his navy was defeated at Salamis. Zoroastrianism grew more and more mystical until Alexander the Great defeated the twelfth King Darius III and destroyed Persepolis in 331 BC.

Mithraism continued these ideas but its origins go back to the Hindus. This was the greatest competitor to Christianity in the Roman Empire. It was very popular with the legions, however, it did not admit women. A Mithraist temple has been discovered in the Roman city of London. *Mithras,* the Time-god, is depicted as a lion-headed monster or as a bull. This is often constricted by a snake marked with the signs of the zodiac. He was born of a virgin mortal in a stable near to the winter solstice, and his conception/resurrection was celebrated at the vernal equinox. Time was thought to be cyclic, like the Sky, and this lead to the belief that history repeats itself, man can be born again and has many lives. Mithraists adopted a continuous seven-day week, which was based upon the *Seven Heavenly Bodies*, with special reverence to the Sun's day.

Persian Time

The nomadic Parni tribe established the Parthian dynasty in 238 BC.
Parthia was expanded largely under Mithradates the Great (171-138 BC).
It repelled Roman invasions led by Crassus, Mark Antony and others.
Nevertheless, Mithraism with its seven-day week and Sun-day temples
was adopted by the legions and then by most of the Roman Empire.
This is why Sunday is special and why Christ's halo is the Sun's corona.
The Adoration of the Magi was a symbol of submission of the Persians
and Babylonians to Jesus Christ, yet they have never been Christians.
Maybe the Magi noticed the conjunction of Saturn and Jupiter on 29th
July 7 BC and warned Herod that the predicted Messiah had been born.
Prompting him to order the death of all infants under the age of two.
The Roman taxes were collected every 15 years and were due in 8 BC.
Octavian/Augustus introduced his modified Julian *kalendar* in 7 BC.
If Jesus was a man, not a myth, he may have been born in the same year.

Zoroastrianism was revived by the Sassian dynasty from 226 to 651 AD,
when it was overwhelmed by Islam, and its chronology was based upon
11 June 632 AD when the last King, Yazdgard III, ascended the throne.
This is still used, with the Zoroastrian calendar, by the Parsees in India.
The Shiite Muslim sect known as the Twelvers believe that the spiritual
heirs of Mohammed were the twelve imams who were his descendants.
They use a Solar calendar which starts at *Nowruz* on the vernal equinox.
This has six months of 31, then five of 30, then one of 29 or 30 days.
This calendrical reform was originated by the Seljuq sultan Malik-Shah.
It was later named the Gelalian calendar after the sultan: Jalali al-Dawla.
The poet, astronomer and mathematician Omar Khayyam (1048-1131 AD)
measured the true length of the mean Solar year to within 16 seconds.
Shah Abbas became ruler in 1587 AD and moved the capital to Isfahan.
He repelled an invasion by the Ottoman Turks and reestablished Persia.
Abbas set up a shrine to Imam Reza, the only Shiite imam buried in Iran.
This alternative to Mecca is visited by 3 million pilgrims every New Year.

After the fall of the Muslim Ottoman Empire in WW1 the Peacock Dynasty
ruled over a secular state, which was created by the Western powers.
Reza Shah Pahlavi attempted to reintroduce Zoroastrianism and to move
the holy day from Friday to Sunday but Shiite Muslims objected to this.
He was replaced by his son Mohammad after he sided with Adolf Hitler.
There was a period of liberal democracy when Mohammed Mossadegh
came to power and nationalized the oil industry but he was overthrown,
with the help of the CIA, and the Shah was then reinstalled as a despot.
Mohammad crowned himself emperor whilst sitting on a jewel encrusted
golden peacock throne inside the ancient ruins of Persepolis in 1970 AD.
He was deposed by Shiite Muslim leader Ayatolla Khomeni in 1979 AD.
Spiritual and temporal matters are now combined under the same laws.
It is now compulsory for all men to attend a mosque every Friday.

Mesopotamian Time

The Garden of Eden was near the sources of the Tigris and Euphrates. On the flood plains around these two great rivers the earliest civilizations measured, managed, governed and enchanted both Time and Space. The first signs of permanent settlements go back some twelve millennia. A Great Flood of about 6000 BC wiped-out much of the evidence of these earliest civilizations but antediluvian legends remained in their memory. The successive civilizations, who gained dominance over the area, each worshipped a different set of Sky-gods who, they believed, caused great floods and droughts and so the positions of the Sun, Moon and Planets, relative to the Stars, were carefully monitored, recorded and analyzed. Some juxtapositions were thought to be good omens but others were bad. Solar and Lunar eclipses were particularly ominous and conjunctions of the Planets with each other or with the Moon all had special meanings.

Mesopotamian cylinder-seals show the origins of Western religious belief. One seal shows a man, a woman, a serpent and a seven-branched tree. Another seal shows the Sun surrounded by the Moon and ten Planets. A cuneiform Sumerian king-list provides some clues to their chronology. It was believed that kings were divinely appointed and that temples were holy places giving direct access to the gods, who must be appeased. The Sky-gods were represented by large statues or idols in temples and small, portable talismans such as: a golden calf or crescent representing the horns of the Moon, an equal-armed cross and/or circle representing the four rays of the Sun or an eight-pointed star representing Venus. The Sky was divided into three concentric circles: *Ea, Anu* and *Enlil* and these were divided into twelve segments, giving a total of 36 domains. The twelve segments were the origins of the Western Stellar zodiac, with each Constellation or sign represented by a different Sky-god. The Sun and the Moon represented the most powerful deities in the Sky. The Moon's halo (ice crystals) and the Sun's corona (seen at an eclipse) crowned the graven images of these Sky-gods in their Human forms.

The city of Babel slowly grew in importance until it dominated the area. Civilization flourished there for two millennia, yet it finally collapsed when they poisoned their soil with salt, due to too much irrigation. This disaster is remembered in the *Bible* story of Sodom and Gomorrah. The ancient city of Babylon now lies below the water table in Iraq. Its Tower of Babel, Hanging Gardens and Royal Palace are only ruins. Saddam Hussein tried to restore it and its dominance of the World. He asserted that Iraq, Iran and Kuwait were once parts of Mesopotamia. Iraq was a secular state using the Roman-Catholic age, date and time. Yet, Sunnis still use a Lunar calendar, Shiites still use a Solar calendar, Kurds still use a Lunar/Solar calendar and so they are at loggerheads. America and Britain invaded Iraq on the vernal equinox in 2003 AD. The Seventh Wonder of the World became an American military base.

112

Sumerian Time

Sumeria was a loose federation of thirteen Mesopotamian city/states. Each city/state honored a Sky-god, who was represented by their King. Due to floods, earthquakes and the shortage of stone many cities were rebuilt several times on the same spot, which created a mound or tell. They seem to have known that the Sun is the centre of the Solar System. They used astronomy, astrology, chronology, calendrology and horology. They invented metallurgy, money, boats, wheels and cuneiform writing. Their maths was based upon 10, the sacred number 12 and the base 60. Their circle was divided into 360 degrees, 60 minutes and 60 seconds. They named each year after the most important event of the one before. They also named and numbered years after the kings ruling at that age. The oldest calendar so far discovered came from their city of Nippur. It began at the vernal equinox and had 12 Lunar moonths plus 11 or 12 intercalary days to make it fit the Solar year in a 19-year golden cycle. The oldest temple to Creator-god *Enki* has been aged to about 3800 BC. Their capital became Ur where they built a pyramid/temple or ziggurat. It was aligned with the cardinal points and the solstices and equinoxes. It had seven steps of different colours representing the *Heavenly Bodies*.

The World's oldest astrological text: *Enuma Anu Enlil* found in the library of the kings at Nineveh, on the Tigris, is now in the British Museum. It is a baked clay tablet inscribed with their miniature cuneform script. *Anu* was the Sumerian god of Heaven and *Enlil* was their god of Earth. It describes the 584 day synodic cycle of Venus as it becomes visible in the East, moves to the centre of the ecliptic, disappears for two moonths, reappears in the West for about eight moonths, then disappears again. They used 12 double-hours, 60 double-minutes and 60 double-seconds. Their standard length unit: the *kush,* was equal to 180 barley seeds. Their standard volume unit may have been a number of barley seeds. They seem to have developed a timekeeping and navigational system based upon the beat and length of a pendulum and the girth of Earth. Their practice of linking historic and astronomical events, such as the start of a reign, with the position of Venus, the phase of the Moon, the rising point of the Sun or an eclipse, on clay tablets or stone stelae permits astronomical computer programs to calculate ages and dates.

The Babylonians were of Sumerian origin and their capital city, Babylon, stood upon the plain of Shinar near to the west bank of the Euphrates. In 2600 BC the Sumerians were pushed out by the Semites, who came from Arabia, and their Empire grew until they were pushed out by another Sumerian Empire, which was then overtaken by the Akkadians. Led by Sargon, who arrived in about 2340 BC, they built the largest empire known by that era, they developed a phonetic script and they worshipped three Sky-gods: Moon = *Sin,* Sun = *Shamash,* Venus = *Ishtar.* They were pushed out by barbaric Gutians from the Zagros mountains.

Babylonian Time

Babylon continued to expand in both strategic and religious importance. The **El**amites took over in 2025 BC, their Tower of Bab**el** was a seven stepped ziggurat, which helped them to escape from the annual floods. It was built so that the astronomer/priests could get nearer to their great god **El** (Lord) who, they believed, created the flat Earth in seven days. Venus, was represented by a lion and **El** put it to death in the morning. His winged messenger was called *Michaiel* who became an archang**el**. There were seven archang**els** who guarded the seven days of the week. They captured the land of Canaan and so **El** became the Canaanite god. The Kurdish religion was based on the worship of the seven archang**els**.

The Babylonians extended astrology beyond the concept of omens for the King and the state to personal horoscopes, based upon the positions of the Planets and the Stars, especially their twelve signs of the zodiac. The pantheon of gods, linked with their *Seven Heavenly Bodies*, were:
Sin = Moon - Father of Time - lord of the calendar and clock - crescent.
Shamash = Sun - Judge of Heaven and Earth - the watcher - equal cross.
Ishtar = Venus - Queen of Heaven - goddess of love - eight pointed star.
Nergal = Mars - Lord of the dead - wager of wars - axes and/or swords.
Ninurta = Saturn - Brother of Mars - sun of the night - two headed eagle.
Marduk = Jupiter - King of the gods - savior of Babylon - golden man.
Nabu = Mercury - Son of Jupiter - herald and scribe to the gods - desk.
There are many parallels between *Ishtar* and the Egyptian goddess *Isis*. Her brother or consort or son *Tammuz* equates with *Osaris* and *Horus*. Their herald and scribe *Nabu* equates with the vizier and scribe *Thoth*. The statues or idols of these gods, and the temples where they resided, were considered to be sacred manifestations of the gods themselves. The priests took meals to them twice a day and the population honoured them on special feast days connected with their different cycles of Time. Hammurabi (d 1750 BC) sixth king of the first dynasty is remembered for his code of laws inscribed on a stele in the temple of *Marduk* in Babylon. He was the first to state the importance of equality for all of his subjects.

The Babylonians used a 12-moonth calendar with a 354-day Lunar year beginning with a feast at the new-Moon preceding the vernal equinox. Beacons were lit upon every hilltop to signal the start of the New Year. Their twelve moonth-gods were named: *Nisanu, Ayaru, Simanu, Du'uza, Abu, Ululu, Tashritu, Arahsamnu, Kislimu, Tebetu, Shabatu, Addaru.* An extra moonth was intercalated by the King at irregular intervals. Each moonth was divided into four by the 7th, 14th, 21st, 28th days. On these special days the King, the court and all the population rested. This eventually became the Hebrew: *Shabbat* and in English: Sabbath. The Moon was stronger than the Sun because it controlled the calendar. Babylonia continued to be a great power until it was captured by the Persians, the Greeks and the Romans, who called its people: Chaldeans.

114

Assyrian Time

The Semitic Assyrian empire emerged in 2000 BC but fell in 605 BC.
Its capital city Nineveh housed a great library of cuneiform clay tablets.
Their chronology was based on the founding of their temple in 4750 BC.
Their Lunar/Solar calendar had months of alternate 29 or 30 days plus
an additional 30-day month, which was intercalated every third year.
The Assyrian city-state of Haran lay near a crossing of the Euphrates.
Haranians used a continuous week based on the *Seven Heavenly Bodies.*
Each Sky-god had a differently shaped temple and a gate dedicated to it.
The Moon-god *Sin* was the greatest of these ancient celestial deities.
His wife *Ningal* can be compared with the Egyptian Sky-goddess *Nut.*
The followers of this cult, who believed in rebirth, were called Sabaeans.
They may have been the first congregation to meet regularly for prayer.
They made many pilgrimages to Egypt, where they visited the pyramids.
Greek philosophers escaped to Haran when Athens fell to the Romans.
The Sabaean cult persisted until long after the beginning of the Christian
and Islamic eras and was mentioned in both *The Bible* and *The Koran.*
Haran was sacked by the Christians during the crusades and the last
centre of Sabaean worship and astronomy was razed by the Mongols.

According to *The Bible* Abraham was born at Ur of the Chaldees [Edessa].
He passed through the city-state of Haran during his great migration.
This is reckoned by some scholars to have been in about 1800 BC.
It was at Haran that Jacob, fleeing Esau, tended the flocks of Laban.
The Sabaean Lunar/Solar years, months and seven-day weeks became
Hebrew ones and are still used by the Jews, in a slightly modified form.
Abraham continued his journey to Egypt, so would have encountered
Lunar, Solar and Stellar calendars and their shadow or water clocks.
According to tradition, which is accepted by both the Arabs and Jews,
these two peoples sprung from Ishmael and Isaac, the sons of Abraham.
According to *The Bible*, Abraham offered to sacrifice Isaac, whose
mother was Sarah, on an outcrop of rock at a place called Jerusalem.
According to *The Koran*, Abraham offered to sacrifice Ishmael, whose
mother was Hagar, his Egyptian servant, at a place called Mecca.
Ishmael became an exile in the wilderness and was the progenitor of the
twelve Bedouin tribes, from whom the Arab nations claim descent.
Isaac was the ancestor of the twelve tribes of the Jews - but ten were lost.
The rivalry of Jew and Arab is that of brothers from the Semitic race.
Their languages are similar and they both claim Canaan as their home.
According to *The Bible* Moses led the Israelites through the wilderness of
Sinai (the land of *Sin*) to Canaan, which Abraham had promised them.
In Sinai *God* commanded them to adopt the continuous seven-day week.
Under the leadership of Joshua they defeated the Egyptian garrison at
Jericho and conquered, then subdued, the many tribes who lived there.
Aged to about 8000 BC, Jericho is probably the oldest citadel on Earth
and granaries near to the Dead Sea have been carbon-dated to 9000 BC.

Hebrew Time

The Hebrews were Semitic shepherds and goatherds who lived in tribal communities in the land between Mesopotamia, Egypt and Mediterranea. The Hebrews worshipped the Canaanite god *El* and the goddess *Aserah*. An outcrop of rock overlooking the Dead Sea is known as Mount Moriah. Abraham was said to have offered to sacrifice his son Isaac on the Rock. The legend that Abraham's first wife Sarah also married a pharaoh links the bloodline of the Hebrews with that of the ancient Egyptians. Some scholars say that Thothmosis III was Isaac's father, not Abraham. Thothmosis III built an empire which stretched as far as the Euphrates and is thought to have built the fortress of Jerusalem upon the Rock. The first Solar temple on the Rock was built underground by Enoch.

The story of Joseph becoming a vizier now seems to be based upon fact. Joseph really built canals, reservoirs and silos for the seven lean years. Moses may have lived during the reign of the pharaoh Amenhotep IV who changed his name to Akhenaten in honour of his one Sun-god: *Aten*. He abandoned the old Sky-gods with their temples, astronomer-priests and calendars and replaced them all with a new capital, a new temple and a new Solar calendar with 7-day weeks and thirteen 28-day sunths. We can deduce this because his great open-air temple had hundreds of altars on both sides of an aisle set in rows of seven or in lines of 28. However, following a great Natural catastrophe, his heretic regime fell. The legend of the Exodus of the Hebrews from Egypt was not written down until a thousand years after it was supposed to have happened. It is probable that they fled across the Sea of Reeds in the Nile delta following a great volcanic eruption upon the Minoan island of Thera. There is no trace of their wandering in the wilderness for forty years. We do not know where Mount Sinai was and there is no evidence that the original *Ten Commandments* and Ark of the Covenant ever existed. The Hebrews settled down in Judah and Israel, their promised lands. King David is reputed to have united the tribes against the Philistines and his son Solomon is reputed to have founded the city of Jerusalem. There is no trace of King David nor the Temple built by King Solomon as a permanent tabernacle to house *Jehovah* in the Ark of the Covenant.

Babylon grew great under Hammurabi and it was at its peak in the sixth century BC under Nebuchadnezzar II, who sacked Jerusalem twice in 597 and 586 BC and enslaved many Hebrew leaders in Babylon. This was the start of Rabbinical Judaism, when Hebrews became Jews who rested 7 times per day, on every 7th day and in every 7th year. Jerusalem also fell to the Persians in 539 BC and it was still under their control when Alexander the Great and Hellenism took over in 332 BC. Sumerian, Akkadian, Elamite, Babylonian, Sabaean, Hittite, Assyrian, Caananite, Egyptian, Persian, Phoenician, Hellene, Roman and Hebrew myths, legends, ages, dates and times fought each other for supremacy.

Phoenician Time

The seafaring Phoenicians were based around Byblos and Tyre (Lebanon.) They were shipwrights and used cedar wood to build ocean going vessels. They learned to navigate at night by measuring the angle of the Pole Star. They built many cities with stone temples around the Mediterranean. Their Sun-god of health and healing was *Eshmun*, their Venus-goddess of love and war was *Astarte* and their Man-god, who always died at every autumn equinox and was born again every spring equinox, was *Adonis*. *Astarte* was linked with the heliacal rising of Venus as the Morning Star. The first phonetic alphabet and then the first *Bible* came from Byblos. They devised a calendar with nine forty-day *quadrigesima plus 5/6 days*. The Phoenician city of Carthage became so powerful that it rivaled Rome. Hannibal (247-183 BC) the great Carthaginian commander fought in the Punic wars and used forty elephants against Rome but was defeated. After a long siege Carthage fell and eventually became a Roman outpost. Tertullian of Carthage was later to become the first father of the Church. He devised the liturgical cycle of forty-day feasts and fasts and adopted the continuous seven-day week with communal prayers every Sunday.

The Phoenician King Hiram is reputed to have helped the Jewish King Solomon to build his Solar Temple on the Rock in the city of Jerusalem. Two great bronze pillars named: *Boaz* and *Jachin*, guarded its entrance. The Holy of Holies, where the Ark of the Covenant was supposed to have been kept, was illuminated by a shaft of Sun-light at every equinox. All the dimensions were in holy cubits and all the angles were in degrees. In Jerusalem the summer and winter solstices are at 60^0 to each other. The Hebrew year began at the autumnal equinox, and the Jewish civil year continues this tradition but, after the Exodus, New Year was moved to the vernal equinox and so their ecclesiastical year starts on that date. The dawn conjunction of Venus with Mercury occurs every forty years. Solomon's Temple is thought to have been aligned with this rare event. They called this the *Shekinah* and it occurred near the winter solstice in 7 BC and again in 33 AD, the Messiah's predicted birth and death years.

The Temple was stripped of all its treasures by the pharaoh Ramesses II and razed by the Babylonians when the leaders were taken into captivity. This is probably when the Jewish *Old Testament* and *Torah* were written. On their return from exile in the 6th century BC the Persian King Cyrus authorized Prince Zerubabbel of Judea to build his Temple on the Rock. Greek King Antiochus Epiphanes set up a statue of *Zeus* in this Temple. This led to the revolt of the Maccabees in 168 BC and to the Essene sect. Roman Legions invaded Israel and took control of Jerusalem in 37 BC. Herod the Great then built his enormous Temple on the Rock in 10 BC. The Jewish revolt against Rome was quashed between 66 and 70 AD. The razing of Herod's Temple by Titus and the construction of a Pagan temple to Jupiter marked the diaspora of the Jews around the globe.

Jewish Time

There is little archaeological evidence of the states of Israel and Judah, supposed to have been united by King David some three millennia ago. The modern state of Israel was created in 1947 AD by the United Nations for the Zionists, who originally wanted to create an exclusive faith zone. The Jews had not lived in their promised land for almost two millennia. There are currently about twelve million Orthodox Jews living Worldwide. Whilst some religions are increasing by population growth or persuasion, the Jewish faith remains static and they no longer have large families. Except for those who still live inside the Jewish quarter of Jerusalem. Whilst the *Torah* is still strictly observed by the Orthodox Jews in Israel, this is more difficult in other places and so the Jewish community in North London have created an *Eruv* zone, where it is strictly observed.

King Herod and Pontius Pilate were historical figures but there is no record of Joshua or Jesus, a common Jewish name, two millennia ago. The Christian faith in the *New Testament* is based upon the Jewish faith in the *Old Testament* and the seven-day week is fundamental to both. The Muslim faith is also based upon the seven-day week but all three religions have different days set aside for rest, recreation and religion. Anti-Semitism is based on a Catholic belief that the Jews were expelled from Israel because they did not recognize Jesus as their Messiah. However, they were expelled by Roman-Pagans when they refused to work on their Sabbath day, so revolted in 66-70 AD and again in 132-135 AD.

Time is fundamental to the Jewish faith and is governed by a holy law. This law can only be altered by a special council: The Great Sanhedrin. *Anno Mundi* chronology is based upon Monday 7th October 3761 BC. The Universe is believed to have been created by *Yahweh* on that day. The Roman-Catholic 2000 AD converts to the Jewish *Anno Mundi* 5761. The Jews believed that their Messiah would be born after a Great Year, under a Bright Star and the archangel Gabriel would introduce him. Their Great Year was a Sumerian *sar* of 3600 (60x60) years and so they expected their Messiah in 161 BC - when the Essene sect was formed.

The seven-day week and seven-part day were fundamental to Judaism. They used seven week-day numbers, not the Heavenly Body day names, because Pagan Sun, Moon, Planet or Star worship was strictly forbidden. Orthodox Jews now pray three times per day: at dawn, noon and dusk. Their seventh or Sabbath day begins at dusk on their sixth week-day. Doing any form of work, even gathering sticks, is strictly forbidden. They may not draw water, prepare food nor kindle fires on the Sabbath. Sacred geometry is a fundamental part of the Orthodox Jewish religion. Noah's Ark was 300 x 50 x 30, Moses' Ark was 2 x 1.25 x 1.25 cubits. Solomon's Temple was 50 x 25 x 25 cubits (A Jewish cubit = 555 mm). Orthodox Jews may not walk more than 1,000 cubits on their Sabbath.

Jewish Time

Orthodox timekeeping is very accurate and controlled by the Sanhedrin. They use 24 fixed-length hours each divided into 1080 (12x90) *minims*. The start of the Jewish day is sometime between Sunset and nightfall. The exact time of this is decided and announced by the chief rabbi. The Jerusalem Meridian is 2 hours 21 *minims* in advance of Greenwich. A phasal moonth is reckoned to be 29 days 12 hours 793 *minims* long. Twelve of these comprise 354 days and so a thirteenth moonth is now intercalated every 3rd, 6th, 8th, 11th, 14th, 17th and 19th year to keep their Lunar/Solar calendar accurately aligned with the tropical year.

The Orthodox calendar was devised by rabbi Hillel II in 358 AD because the Jews lost track of Time after they were dispersed by the Romans. Their twelve months are: *Tishri, Marcheshvan, Kislev, Tebet, Shebet, Adar (Adar Rishon* in leap years*), Ve-Adar, Nisan, Iyar, Sivan, Tammuz, Ab, Elul.* There are six kinds of years which all have alternate 29 and 30 day calendar months except for the following variations:

Minimal Common	353 days	third month has 29 days
Regular Common	354 days	
Full Common	355 days	second month has 30 days
Minimal Leap	383 days	third month has 29 days
Regular Leap	384 days	
Full Leap	385 days	second month has 30 days

In leap years a 30-day month is intercalated before *Adar* and usurps its name whilst its festivals (named below) are kept in *Ve-Adar*.

Tishri 1-2	Rosh Hashanah (New Year)	Tebet	10	Fast of Tebet
Tishri 3	Gedaliah (Fast)	Adar	10	Fast of Esther
Tishri 10	Yom Kippur (Day of Atonement)	Adar	14	Purim
Tishri 15-21	Succoth (Feast of Tabernacles)	Adar	15	Sushan Purim
Tishri 21	Hoshana Rabba	Nisan	15-22	Psach (Passover)
Tishri 22	Shemini Atseret (Assembly)	Sivan	6-7	Shavuot (Feast of weeks)
Tishri 23	Simchat Torah (Rejoicing Law)	Tammuz	17	Fast of Tammuz
Kislev 25	Hanukkah (Temple Dedication)	Ab	9	Fast of Ab

This Solar calendar is further complicated by the position of the Moon at midday and rules that apply when a feast or fast falls upon a *Shabbat*. There are several other religious cycles, which all have Mystic meanings. Some Jewish scholars believed that when their sacred *Shemitah* cycle ended in the year 2000 AD the very strict laws of the *Torah* ended with it.

The rabbis are still in control of Jewish Time and Space and by this means they are in control of the whole Jewish nation, around the globe. The holy city of Jerusalem has been in Jewish hands since 1967 AD, although Jews, Christians and Muslims are all permitted to pray there. Many medieval maps showed it to be at the centre of the Western World. The Holy Land is still the centre of many bloody conflicts, which are all, fundamentally, caused by different chronologies, calendars and clocks.

Essene Time

Alexander invaded Jerusalem, whilst it was at prayer on the Sabbath day. Greek religious influence continued through the cult of the Sadducees. The calendar shown below is believed to have been introduced in about 160 BC, after the Greek Seleucid dynasty eventually came to an end. This was devised by a visionary, using the antediluvian name of Enoch. The ruling Maccabeans were a zealous sect of Judaism who insisted on adherence to the letter of the laws of Moses' Covenant with *Jehovah*. The Essenes were their rivals who lived in a small monastery at Qumran. Excavations at this site by the Dead Sea show that families lived there. The Zealots, who rebelled against the Romans in 70 AD and committed suicide at Masada by the Dead Sea, were more militant than the Essenes.

The Dead Sea Scrolls were discovered in caves near Qumran in 1947 AD. Some were written in Hebrew, some in Greek and some in Aramaic. The publication of any translations or interpretations was suppressed, because they could shake the foundations of Judaism and Christianity. However, in October 1992 AD, the first translations and interpretations of the most important fifty Essene Time scrolls were finally published. The eighteen calendrical texts from Qumran are central to any attempt to understand the full significance of these crucial religious documents.

The continuous Essene week was based on the *Seven Heavenly Bodies*. It was also based on the Elamite belief of the Creation in seven days. The year always started on a Wednesday (to use the English word for it). The Universe was thought to have been created on this weekday by: *El* or *Bel* or *Baal* or *YHWH* or *Yahweh* or *Jehovah* so it was placed at the start of the year, the week and every third month as follows:

Months >	I, IV, VII, X	II, V, VIII, XI	III, VI, IX, XII
Wednesday	1, 8, 15, 22, 29	6, 13, 20, 27	4, 11, 18, 25
Thursday	2, 9, 16, 23, 30	7, 14, 21, 28	5, 12, 19, 26
Friday	3, 10, 17, 24	1, 8, 15, 22, 29	6, 13, 20, 27
Saturday	4, 11, 18, 25	2, 9, 6, 23, 30	7, 14, 21, 28
Sunday	5, 12, 19, 26	3, 10, 17, 24	1, 8, 15, 22, 29
Monday	6, 13, 20, 27	4, 11, 18, 25	2, 9, 16, 23, 30
Tuesday	7, 14, 21, 28	5, 12, 19, 26	3, 10, 17, 24, 31

This perpetual Solar calendar started on the vernal equinox and was probably used for many years by the monastic Essene community. Days numbered 31, falling before a solstice or an equinox, were ominous. The great advantage of this dating system is that all festivals, such as the Passover or the Pentecost, fall on the same week-day every year. However, the Essene Sabbath day usually fell on a different day from the Pharisee and Sadducee one, because their week was not continuous.

Essene Time

The Scrolls also explain the Priestly Course cycle, which amounts to job sharing by the priests in the Temple on a 7 days-on/7 days-off basis. During their 7 days-off the priests returned to more temporal duties. The Essene Solar calendar coincided every 3 years with the Lunar one used by the Pharisees and every 6 years with the Priestly Course cycle. The Jewish calendar has now lost its regularity, because an extra 30-day month is sometimes intercalated after two years rather than after three. This is so that it aligns more closely with the seasonal or tropical year.

A Heavenly Concordance is when an equinox coincides with an eclipse. One of these rare events may have caused the parting of the Reed Sea and the Exodus from Egypt, which is still remembered at the Passover. The Essenes believed this was the basis for all regular Cosmic events, festivals and sabbatical years (the priests took a holiday every 7th year). The Jews became obsessed by number 7: an *otot* cycle of 49 years (7x7), a Jubilee of 294 years (6x49) and a World-week of 490 (10x49) years were considered to be extremely ominous and so the Last Judgment would occur exactly 4,900 (100x49) years after the Creation [1139 AD]. Attempts were made to fit, past and future, good and bad, events like the Creation, the Flood, the Exodus, Babylonian and Greek conquests, the construction and the destruction of Solomon's and Herod's temples, the coming of the Messiah and the Apocalypse into a regular sequence. They tried to prove that all events on Earth are regularly willed by *God*.

The Essene calendar was rejected for use in the Temple because it was anti-Pharisee (forerunners of Rabbinical Judaism) and so anti-Herod. There was a most unholy row when it was rejected by the Pharisees, who preferred their Hebrew calendar, the Sadducees, who preferred their Metonic cycle and the Romans who imposed their Julian/Augustine one. Qumran was razed and the scrolls were not seen again for 2,000 years.

The Essene calendar was better than the ones which Jews and Romans (Pagan, Orthodox and Catholic) have been using for over 2,000 years. There would have been none of the divisive and bloody arguments over which day was the Sabbath and the dates of the Passover and Easter. Indeed, it is hard to devise a better perpetual calendar incorporating a Mystic seven-day week, unless there are thirteen sunths of 28 days. Although their logical calendar months and weeks were soon obliterated; many of the other Essene beliefs including: monasticism, love, marriage, baptism, burial rites and resurrection have developed into Christianity. There are now many books on the interpretation of the Dead Sea Scrolls. One theory is that Jesus the Christ was a blood relative of King David. He survived crucifixion at Qumran then lived there with his wife Mary Magdalene and their three children for many years, then died of old age. Some say that they sailed to France and started the Carolingian dynasty.

Christian Time

The Gnostic Christians in Egypt continued to follow the Siriac calendar. They believed that Jesus Christ was born at the heliacal rising of Sirius. The annual liturgical cycle of Christian feasts and fasts was based upon the Egyptian ten-day week, by Demetrius during the second century AD. However, Tertullian of Carthage decreed that Christians should use a seven-day week and should meet on Sundays, in the third century AD. The Coptic Church was formed at the Council of Chalcedon in 451 AD as a reaction to the Catholic belief that Christ was mortal and divine. Coptic Time began at the helical rising on 29 August (Julian) 284 AD, the first year of Emperor Diocletian, who killed thousands of Christians. The Coptic New Year currently falls upon 11 September (Gregorian). The Siriac months are used by Coptic, Ethiopic and Armenian Churches. Coptic months are named in the Greco-Egyptian way, starting with *Tut*. Ethiopic chronology began in 7 AD and their months have other names. Armenian chronology began in 551 AD when they began their New Era.

The Roman Empire was reunited by Constantine the Great (274-338 AD). He was proclaimed emperor by the Western legions at York in 306 AD. He believed that *God* helped him to win the Battle of the Milvian Bridge. He saw a bright cross in the Sky (now thought to be a meteorite impact). He proclaimed total religious freedom in the Edict of Milan in 313 AD. Byzantium became his new capital, renamed in Greek: Constantinople. The Byzantine Church was founded at the Council of Nicea in 325 AD. The *Nicean Creed* established a formal summary of Orthodox doctrine. *The New Testament* was added to *The Old Testament* to make *The Bible*. Byzantine chronology was based upon the year of the Flood in 5509 BC. The Julian calendar continued but New Year was moved to I September. It included the continuous seven-day week and made Sunday special. Rome became the capital of the Catholic Church because Saint Peter was believed to have founded the Church there, to become its first bishop. Rome fell to the Visigoths, led by Alaric, in 410 AD and the whole of the central and western regions had been ravaged by Barbarians by 478 AD. However, over the next two centuries, the Barbarians became Christians.

Christmas was not at the start of the calendar year but on 25 December, because Jesus was immaculately conceived on the vernal equinox, which then fell on 25 March, and so he was born nine calendar months later. The last supper was on the eve of the Passover, celebrating the Exodus from Egypt, which was determined by the Jewish Lunar/Solar calendar. Roman-Catholic Easter was decided at the Synod of Whitby in 664 AD. Before that the Celtic and Saxon Churches observed it on different dates. The Great Schism of 1054 AD divided Eastern and Western Churches. They excommunicated each other due to a row over the date of Easter. It now falls on the first Sunday after the full-Moon after the 21 March. Sometimes, due to leap days, the vernal equinox falls on 20 not 21 March.

Christian Time

In the second millennium AD the Catholic Church almost dominated Western Europe and enthroned its popes in the eternal city of Rome. They ruled until now, apart for a period when rivals ruled from Avignon. The Church gradually changed from simple poverty to complex richness and always kept a very firm grip on its chronology, calendar and clock. Only clerics were permitted to calculate the date of Easter and this was traditionally announced from the pulpit on Epiphany (6 January). Laws and by-laws enforced the measurement and management of Time. It became an offence to meet on Saturdays and to work on Sundays. Those who did not regularly attend church, and pay taxes to support its property and hierarchy, were ostracized and the belief in any other astronomy, astrology, superstition, religion or Time was a grave offence.

Roman-Catholics used *Ab Urbe Condita* until the sixth century AD when the Sythian monk Dionysus Exiguus devised *Anno Domini* chronology. Although AD was used by the venerable Bede in the 8th century AD, and then by Charlemagne, the first Holy Roman Emperor, in 800 AD, and it was eventually adopted by the Council of Chelsea in 816 AD, it has only been used for Civic purposes since the 17th century AD. The usual practice was to number regnal years after the kings or popes.

Bede Christianized the Julian calendar by allotting days to the saints, but pointed out that the calendar year was slightly too long when he wrote: *De Temporum Rational - On the Reckoning of Time* in 725 AD. Successive popes took over eight centuries to put their calendar right. Other curious monks who noticed that the tropical and calendar years were moving apart were: Notker the Stammerer in 896 AD, Hermann the Lame in 1042 AD and Reiner of Paderborn during the 12th century AD. Roger Bacon was a Franciscan monk who invented magnifying glasses and predicted telescopes, engines and aircraft in the 13th century AD. He was ostracized by his fellows in Oxford and Paris and made to do penance for his heresy but stuck to his ideas on science and technology. He may have convinced Pope Clement IV that the date was out of date. However, they both died of bubonic plague along with 30M Europeans. The error was 11 minutes 14 seconds per year or 1 day in 128 years.

Pope Gregory XIII, with his astronomical adviser Christopher Clavius, realigned and corrected the length of the calendar year by deleting ten days and some centennial leap-days at the Council of Trent in 1582 AD. These corrections caused a riot in Frankfurt, because landlords did not pay rent rebates and were not used in Protestant England until 1752 AD. However, there was then a riot in Bristol due to the lack of tax rebates and so the British tax year still starts on the old Julian date, now 5 April. The Gregorian calendar is currently thirteen days ahead of the Julian. It is accurate to 1 day in 4,442 years - but it is far from being perfect.

Christian Time

The Christian liturgical year is a complicated cycle of feasts and fasts, which were carefully designed to obliterate the earlier Pagan festivals. This cycle starts with Advent: 24 days of penitence before Christmas, followed by 11 days of feasting, ending on Epiphany (January 6th) when decorations, such as holly, ivy and mistletoe, must be removed. Jesus was circumcised on New Year's Day and baptized on Epiphany. These 12 days of Christmas were originally the Roman-Pagan Saturnalia. This was the festival when the masters and the slaves exchanged places. After Epiphany comes Carnival which is the variable period before Lent. Carnival starts on Candlemas (February 2nd) and is a period of freedom, release and transgression that ends on Shrove Tuesday or *Mardi Gras*. Ash Wednesday is the start of the forty days penitence of Lent, which ends on Easter Sunday and also marks the start of the agricultural year. The two months after Easter are now marked by the Rogation Days: Ascension Day (forty days after Easter) and Pentecost (ten days later). To these the feast of *Corpus Christi* (ten days later) was added in the thirteenth century AD as part of the Catholic cult of the Virgin Mary. The Pagan return of fair weather was celebrated when poles were erected and maidens danced at their fertility festival on Mayday (May 1st). The Church tried to obliterate this by instituting a feast for the finding of the true cross on May 3rd and for three days before Ascension Day the priests and villagers paraded through the fields to ensure good crops.

The Church also established an annual cycle of many angels and saints. From the beginning of Christianity the apostles, martyrs and confessors had inspired their own individual devotions and the Church was careful to fix these holy days on dates that had formerly been Pagan festivals. Jesus the Christ was immaculately conceived on the vernal equinox. The archangel Saint Michael slew the Devil on the autumnal equinox. John the Baptist's Day, on June 24th, once fell on the summer solstice. Christmas Day, on December 25th, once fell on the winter solstice. The feast of the first martyr Saint Stephen falls on December 26th. The feast of the first evangelist Saint John falls on December 27th. The feast of choirboys, The Holy Innocents, falls on December 28th. Advent was broken by feasts such as Saint Nicholas on December 6th. This was popular in Central Europe and led to the myth of Santa Claus. In Britain there were forty saints' days when everyone stopped work. These included the Patron Saints: George, Andrew, David and Patrick. St. Valentine's Day is still celebrated by sweethearts on February 14th. All Saints Day or Allhallows Day always falls on November 1st, however, Allhallows Eve or Halloween now seems to have greater importance.

Christianity usurped 7 **Ela**mite angels, who guard the days of the week: *Michaiel, Raphaiel, Uriel, Ragiel, Remiel, Sariel, Gabriel* - all end in **el**. *Michaiel*'s first day was Sunday and *Gabriel*'s last day was Saturday.

Christian Time

The Roman-Catholic Church's chronology, calendar, clock and zodiac represented its control over every social, economic and spiritual activity. Astrology was widely practiced as part of the Roman-Catholic religion. The dawn of the Age of Pisces coincided with the start of Christianity. So Christianity would probably end at the dawn of the Age of Aquarius. A major part of the work of monasteries was to design and publish the calendar for the following year, which kept the monks and scribes busy. The *kalends, nones* and *ides* continued in some places and month-day numerals or numbers took many centuries to become the Civic system. Holy days were usually announced from the pulpit on a weekly basis. Every aspect of family life was controlled from the cradle to the grave. The Church prohibited all kinds of work on the holy days and Sundays. Catholics were not permitted to have any sexual relations on Sundays, nor during Lent and Advent, nor holy days, nor the days preceding them, nor at the beginning of each season - these were known as Ember Days. Contraception was banned and they were urged to go forth and multiply. Baptism not only captured defenceless babes but labelled them for life. Marriage was not only monogamous but it was also strictly indissoluble. Death was not an escape from the system because of strict burial rites. Astronomy, medicine and science were suppressed for a thousand years.

Part of the protest throughout Northern Europe, leading to the formation of the Protestant Church, was the use of Latin instead of a local language. *The Holy Bible, The Creed, The Book of Prayer, The Catechism,* the *Anno Domini* chronology, Gregorian calendar and Benedictine clock were ecclesiastical implements that did not come into general use until the end of the second millennium as printing and production flourished. The use of calendars, almanacs, diaries and clocks for commerce and industry has slowly reduced the power of the Roman-Catholic Church. Its strict rules have never been relaxed and yet they are usually ignored. The priesthood has often ignored its own rules of celibacy and decency.

The only biblical reference to a Millennium is in the *Book of Revelations.* Saint John the Devine predicted that an Apocalypse would occur at one. If Time had a beginning, when *God* created the World or the Universe, then it would also have an ending, when everything would be destroyed. According to James Ussher (1581-1656 AD) C of I Archbishop of Armagh, who counted backwards from the death of Herod, the Beginning of Time was at the entrance to night [where?] on 22 October [Julian] 4004 BC. Some said that the End of Time would be exactly six millennia later. The first Millennium was passed with a sad feeling of impending doom. Many Christians expected: The Apocalypse or The Day of Judgement. The second Millennium was celebrated and feared by many Christians. Some expected a Messiah to be born again but others expected the End. MM did bring many Man-made calamities and Natural catastrophes.

Muslim Time

The Arabs worshipped a different local deity for every tribe in Arabia. *Allah*, the local deity for Mecca, was worshipped at their great *Kaabah*. A meteorite, sent by *Allah*, was built into this black cubic monolith, which was said to have been built by Adam and modified by Abraham. It was carved with demons, djinn, demigods and other mythical figures. Tales of flying carpets, magic lamps, genies in bottles and evil eyes were described in ancient Arabic texts, now known as: *The Arabian Nights*. The prophet Mohammed (570-632 AD) was born in Mecca but he was expelled, because he was an orphan, and so he went to live in Medina. He came into contact with Jews and Christians with their *Testaments*. Mohammed considered that Abraham, Moses and Jesus were prophets. He prescribed a new Way of Life, from cradle to grave, known as Islam. These beliefs were taught to him in dreams by the archangel *Gabriel*, then dictated to the scribes of the *Koran* over a period of twenty years. In a dream Mohammed flew on his winged horse to the ancient site of the Temple in Jerusalem, where the Dome of the Rock now stands. When he died he is believed to have risen to Heaven from that very spot.

Islamic, Mohammedan or Muslim ages are based upon the *Hejira* on 16 July 622 AD (Julian) when Mohammed fled from Mecca to Medina. Islam split after his death because of an argument over his succession. Sunnis are organized on a local basis but Shiites have national leaders. The seven-day week had become established by Mohammed's lifetime. The Muslim holy day is Friday because *Allah* created Man on that day. Muslims divide light and dark into five, so already have a ten-part day. A stick in the ground is their Sun-clock, which tells them when to pray. They must pray, facing Mecca at the appointed time, wherever they are. In towns, *muezzins* proclaim the hours of prayer from mosque minarets. During the Dark Ages, after the fall of the Persian and Roman empires, now thought to caused by global climate changes and urban epidemics, the nomadic Arabs survived and were then able to build a new empire. Islamic armies captured the Near & Middle East, North Africa and Iberia. Islam was once an exclusive Arab religion but it was spread, by the sword, around the globe and so Arabs now account for only 20% of its followers. Muslims advanced astronomy, mathematics, physics, chemistry, medicine at universities in Baghdad, Damascus, Istanbul, Seville, Cordoba...

Although the *Koran* was written and copied it was not permitted to be printed and so it was taught by word of mouth, until recent times. This is why Sunnis prefer a calendar based upon the Moon's phases to one based upon the Sun's seasons, which must be written or printed. The start of the day, the moonth and the year was decreed by the *mullah*. So it was impossible to print calendars, planners, diaries and timetables. All images of Mohammed or any other person were strictly forbidden. Mohammed had twelve wives and Muslims are permitted to wed four. The consumption of alcohol is still prohibited in most Islamic countries.

Muslim Time

The Shiites and Sunnis use different Solar or Lunar ages and dates. Shiite chronology uses Arabic numbering beginning at Solar year 0 AH. Sunni chronology uses Arabic numbering beginning at Lunar year 1 AH. The Sunni moonths of alternate 29 and 30 days are only approximate, because new moonths are visually linked by *mullahs* to the new Moon. The Sunni Lunar calendar year is 354 days 8 hours 48 minutes long. The calendar cycle is based upon 360 moonths being equal to 30 years. An extra day is added to the twelfth moonth of Lunar years numbered: 2, 5, 7, 10, 13, 16, 18, 21, 24, 26 & 29, these are called *kabishah* years. The twelve moonths are:

Moonth	Days
Muharram	30
Safar	29
Rabia l	30
Rabia ll	29
Jumada l	30
Jumada ll	29
Rajab	30
Shaaban	29
Ramadan	30
Shawwal	29
Dhu'l-Qu'da	30
Dhu'l-Hijja	29 or 30 days

The ninth moonth: *Ramadan* is one of the *Five Pillars of Wisdom* when all Sunnis are forbidden to eat or to drink whilst the Sun is still visible. They must learn the *Koran* by heart, pray five times per day whilst facing Mecca and visit it once in their lifetime during the *Hajj*, the second week of *Dhu'l-Hijja*, and they must then walk seven times around the *Kaabah*. Abraham offered to sacrifice his son Ishmail on Mount Arafat at Mecca. The archangel *Gabriel* told him to sacrifice a goat instead, so thousands of goats, sheep and camels are still sacrificed during their *Hajj* festival. Every Lunar year 2 to 3 million supplicants become known as *hajji*.

Muslims should visit their mosque on Fridays, with the men at the front and the women at the back of the congregation, who must kneel upon mats and must remove their shoes and wash their feet before entering. Women must wear the veil and clothes which cover the body in public. Although public holidays are now printed in diaries and on calendars, they may only be taken when the Sunni *mullah* has seen the new Moon. Although all Muslims should attend their local mosques every Friday this is not considered to be a Sabbath day and so it is also a market day. This day of rest and religion has now grown to be a two-day weekend. This was once Thursdays and Fridays but is now Fridays and Saturdays. All of the five prayer times were proclaimed every day by the local *imam*. However, they may now be broadcast automatically according to clocks. Some old prayer mats had a *quiblah* (compass) marked with 400 *grads*. Nevertheless, new ones are now marked with conventional 360 degrees. The Arabic Measurement System was based upon digits, hands and feet. The Arabic hand unit is still used to measure horses and camels.

Celtic Time

The cyclical passage of Time was fundamental to the Celtic belief system.
Their festivals were held on special days in their Lunar/Solar calendar.
This was not written down but based upon the Sky and its Sky-gods.
Lug, the Sun-god, was their chief deity and there were many others.
The primary annual divisions were the solstices or equinoxes of the Sun.
The secondary annual divisions were the full or new phases of the Moon.
Samain the second full-Moon after the autumnal equinox, started winter.
Imbolc the second full-Moon after the winter solstice, started spring.
Belteine the second full-Moon after the vernal equinox, started summer.
Lugnasad the second full-Moon after the summer solstice, started autumn.
Barriers between the dead and the living were broken-down on *Samain.*
The Celtic New Year lives-on through the ghoulish tradition of Halloween.
They built huge fires and this flaming tradition lives-on as Bonfire Night.
Some Celtic traditions are perpetuated by Mummers and Morris Men.

The Druids were astronomer-priests who were in charge of the calendar
and various religious festivals held throughout their Lunar/Solar years.
A bronze tablet calendar was found at Coligny near Lyons in 1897 AD.
It reveals a different Lunar/Solar system from the one described above.
This calendar lists 62 Lunar moonths over a five Solar year period.
To reconcile the Lunar and Solar years two extra moonths were added,
and then, after a thirty Solar year period, one moonth was subtracted.
This system kept the 12 moonth Lunar year in line with the Solar year.
Each moonth was divided into two periods of fifteen or fourteen days.
These astronomer/priests united the Celts against the Romans and built
forty temples, throughout Britain, honoring the *Seven Heavenly Bodies.*
The Galatians, Gauls and Celts were ethnically cleansed by the Romans,
who destroyed much of their culture by imposing their own systems.
However, they adopted *Janus,* the Celtic Time-god of the past and future,
as their god of the portal and his name lives on in the month of January.
Queen Boudicca of the Iceni tribe fought against the Roman invaders
and burnt down their main towns at Colchester, London and St. Albans.
However, she was defeated in 61 AD and then committed suicide.

Those who remained in Scotland, Wales, Cornwall and Ireland after the
Roman invasion, finally became Christian in the fifth century AD after
St. Patrick told the legend of a man-god who had arisen from the dead.
Through Christianity and monasticism they learned to read and write.
This was the only part of Europe where scholarship persisted and their
calendrical knowledge in the 8-9th century AD has come down to us in
illuminated manuscripts: *The Book of Kells* and *The Lindisfarne Gospels.*
The Celtic Church remained independent from Roman-Catholicism until
the Synod of Whitby in 664 AD but was more monastic than evangelistic.
The Lunar/Solar position of Easter was the subject of a heated debate,
which still divides the Church and causes Christians to kill each other.

Romano-English Time

Julius Caesar tried to invade England in 55 and 54 BC but was repelled. It took an army of twenty thousand men to finally capture England for Emperor Claudius in 43 AD and the invaders stayed for four centuries. England became one of the forty-five provinces of the Roman Empire. Yet, the Roman conquerors failed to invade Scotland, Wales and Ireland. Emperor Hadrian came to Britain in 122 AD and ordered the building of a great wall which still, to this day, divides this disunited kingdom. The English month names came from the Roman-Pagan Solar *kalendar.*

January	Named after *Janus,*	two-faced Celtic/Roman god of the portal.
February	Named after *Februa,*	Roman festival of purification.
March	Named after *Martis,*	Mars the Roman Sky-god of war.
April	Named after *Aprilis,*	*aperire* to open - when buds open
May	Named after *Maia,*	Etruscan/Roman goddess of growth.
June	Named after *Juno,*	Etruscan/Roman god of the family.
July	Named after Julius Caesar,	who introduced this *kalendar.*
August	Named after Augustus,	Caesar's adopted son Octavian.
September	Named after *Septem*	original 7th Roman month.
October	Named after *Octo*	original 8th Roman month.
November	Named after *Novem*	original 9th Roman month.
December	Named after *Decem*	original 10th Roman month.

Emperor Constantine, ended the persecution of Christians and others. His mother St. Helena became a Christian and founded many churches. She discovered the holy places where Jesus Christ was born and died. A Roman Basilica is said to lie under the Saxon Church at Bosham. Yet, this in turn may have been built upon the site of a Celtic temple. There is other evidence of Christianity but We cannot assume that this was widespread nor that the Christian seven-day week was adopted. A temple in London shows that the Mithraist cult reached these shores. So the Romano-English may have used the Mithraist seven-day week. Every working day was divided into *ante-meridian* and *post-meridian.* We still use the terms: a.m. and p.m. and high noon is at any Meridian. Britons still use the Roman years, months, weeks, hours and miles.

The Romans built a series of fortifications and a network of straight, well-paved roads that interconnected their ports, forts, towns and cities. Milestones were placed along the roads and some survive to this day. Whilst they brought law and order to this province they did not bring science or technology, so the productivity of the land remained the same. Their towns were designed to expand but the population did not grow. The Roman Empire fell in 536 AD due the volcanic eruption of Krakatoa, which caused crop failures and plagues throughout the entire globe. This chaotic period in World history is usually called: The Dark Ages. St. George, the patron saint of England, was a Roman-Catholic soldier and his mortal remains were brought to England during the Crusades.

Anglo-Saxon Time

After the Romans had departed much of Britain became a wasteland.
Angles, Saxons and Jutes settled in much of it by the 7th century AD.
The warlike Angles and Saxons came from what is now north Germany.
The more peaceful Jutes came from Jutland in what is now Denmark.
The Angles settled in the north and the east (Anglia became England).
The Saxons settled in the midlands and the south (but not Cornwall).
The Jutes settled in what is now Kent, Hampshire and the Isle of Wight.
The kingdom of Scotland and principality of Wales stayed independent.
England was ruled by seven kings, who claimed descent from gods.
Each kingdom was divided-up into parcels of land known as hundreds.
Their chronology was reckoned by counting the summers of their reigns.
They used five-day weeks and 12 or 13 Lunar moonths in a Solar year.

A mission was established by St. Augustine at Canterbury in 597 AD.
He reintroduced written and spoken Latin but English was not written.
Penda, the last Pagan King of Mercia, was slain in battle during 655 AD.
The venerable Bede (672-735 AD) studied at Jarrow in Northumberland
and learned from the Celtic Church on the holy island of Lindisfarne.
He adopted the Celtic year of *Samhain, Imbolc, Beltane* and *Lugasad*.
He wrote *The Ecclesiastic History of England, The Theory of Timekeeping*,
invented the word: *calculator* but he alone used *Anno Domini* chronology.
He described the life of St. Cuthbert and is buried in Durham Cathedral.
Bede used the word *computas* for the calculation of Time and Space.
The Anglo-Saxons adopted the Roman-Catholic months and the Mystic
seven-day week but they gave some of the months different names:

January	became their *Wolf* month.
March	became their *Hlyd* (storm) month.
June	became their *Sear* (dry) month.
July	became their *Maed* (mead) month.

Alfred the Great (849-899 AD) the Christian King of Wessex studied in
Rome, met Pope Leo IV but was almost defeated by the Vikings or Danes.
He fought many battles and united the Anglo-Saxons against the Danes.
Alfred translated many Latin texts into what was to become Old English.
He commissioned *The Anglo-Saxon Chronicles,* which inform Us about
the trials and tribulations of their daily life over one thousand years ago.

The seven Anglo-Saxon kingdoms were united by Aethelstan in 927 AD.
This was mainly due to the increasing number of raids by the Danes.
At the Millennium, Ethelred the Unread sat upon the throne of England.
In Rome: Gerbert of Aurillac became Pope Sylvester II and introduced
new zeros, numbers, mathematics, abacuses, astrolabes and astronomy.
He was thought to be the Antichrist and soon went to meet his maker.
The last Anglo-Saxon king Harold II beat the Danes at Stamford Bridge
but was defeated by the Normans at the battle of Hastings in 1066 AD.

Viking Time

The Vikings were Teutonic folk who lived in the 8th to 11th centuries AD.
The forests and mountains of Scandinavia did not encourage agriculture
and so their culture was based upon trade in fur, amber and slaves.
Their light and fast clinker-built boats represented the state-of-the-art.
They settled in many parts of northern England, Scotland and Ireland.
They colonized Iceland and Greenland and even reached Newfoundland.
They rowed and sailed up many rivers from the Baltic to the Black Sea.
They had no magnetic compass so used a wooden Sun-compass instead.
They used Iceland spar crystals to find the Sun in an overcast Sky.
At first they made raiding expeditions, seizing plunder and slaves who
they sold to the wealthy Muslim Kingdoms in Spain and North Africa.
Later they befriended, coexisted and interbred with the Anglo-Saxons.
Their most famous settlement was Jorvik, which became the city of York.
They became Christian, yet still remembered their myths and legends.
They finally became known as the North men, Norse men or Normans.

They developed a form of writing known as runes, which was scratched
upon stones, bones, swords and boats and has now been deciphered.
The Norse mythology of the Vikings was based upon the Teutonic gods.
It involved numerous Earth-gods, giants, dwarfs, valkeries and heroes.
Before the beginning of Creation there was a vast emptiness called:
Ginnungagap and an invisible god called *Allfather* who existed for ever.
Asgard, the home of the gods, was totally invisible to mortals and it was
situated on the plain of *Idavoll* which floated high above the Earth.
Valhalla was the hall where warriors went to after being slain in battle.
Woden or *Odin* was the war-god who was liable to impregnate virgins.
Frigga or *Freya,* his third wife, was the principal goddess of fertility.
Thor his son was the god of thunder and he was liable to kill anything.
English week-day names came from the Saxons and the Vikings who,
like their close relatives the Teutons, all used a five-day market week:

Monday	**called by the Saxons *Monandaeg* (Moonday)**
Tuesday	**named after *Tuesco* the Saxon god of war.**
Wednesday	**named after *Woden* the Viking god of war.**
Thursday	**named after *Thor*, the Viking god of thunder.**
Friday	**named after *Frigga*, the third wife of *Woden*.**

There were no gods of the Sun, the Moon nor Time and the Vikings do
not seem to have developed their own chronology, calendar nor clock.
However, there were gods of day and night and of summer and winter.
Odin was raised from the dead in a legend like Christ's resurrection.
The Norse equivalent of the Christian Apocalypse or Jewish Armagedden
was *Ragnorok,* the final battle between good and evil when the old gods
would die and be replaced by a new pantheon and a renewal of all Life.
The German equivalent of *Raganorok* was *Gotterdammerung* and the
Nazis adopted the symbolism of the Sun and Cross as their *swastika*.

Norman Time

Catholic Normans conquered Catholic Anglo-Saxon England in 1066 AD. This year is memorized by every pupil in Britain but would have meant nothing to the Normans nor the Saxons who lost their lives in that year, because their chronologies were based upon the reigns of their kings. After the death of Edward the Confessor, Duke Guilliem of Normandy claimed the crown and beat King Harold II at the Battle of Hastings. King William I reorganized much of English life and built many stone castles, abbeys, cathedrals and churches throughout both his Kingdoms, in appreciation that the first Millennium AD was not the End of Time. *The Domesday Book* was the very first census and included all of the boundaries, churches, dwellings, people, livestock and trees in the land. The Normans became the ruling classes and the Saxons were their serfs. Under this feudal system the population gradually expanded as they learned new methods of tilling their soil and breeding their livestock.

The English language became a mixture of several different cultures. The Normans brought their early French week-day names with them. They were based upon the *Seven Heavenly Bodies* in Latin and so the English have ended-up with a mixture of languages for their week-days.

English	Latin	French	Italian	Spanish	Origin
Sunday	*Dies Solas*	*dimanche*	*domenica*	*domingo*	Sun
Monday	*Dies Lunae*	*lundi*	*lunedi*	*lunes*	Moon
Tuesday	*Dies Martis*	*mardi*	*martedi*	*martes*	Mars
Wednesday	*Dies Mercurii*	*mecredi*	*mercoledi*	*miercoles*	Mercury
Thursday	*Dies Jovis*	*jeudi*	*giovedi*	*jueves*	Jupiter
Friday	*Dies Veneris*	*vendredi*	*venerdi*	*viernes*	Venus
Saturday	*Dies Saturni*	*samedi*	*sabato*	*sabado*	Saturn

The Church grabbed England and held onto it by the scruff of its neck. The Divine Right of its Kings has only been challenged a very few times. The *Magna Carta* was the charter of English liberties granted on the fifteenth day of June in the seventeenth year of the reign of King John. This standardized weights and measures but it was not a constitution. King Henry VIII protested at the Pope's power to deny him a divorce so he became the Supreme Governor of the Church of England in 1532 AD. The monarchy was abolished, then restored with no power in 1660 AD.

The Kings and Queens of England conquered Britain and an Empire. They adopted the *Anno Domini* chronology, the Gregorian calendar and the Benedictine clock and then imposed them throughout their World. The basis of their chronology, calendar and clock have not changed for a millennium, yet, over the centuries, there have been many additions and alterations to the system by which they measured the age, date and time. The *Magna Carta* is 800 years old but some of its weights and measures have only recently been changed and England still has no constitution.

British Time

Queen Elizabeth founded the Protestant Church of England in 1573 AD. During her very long reign both the arts and the sciences flourished. There were several failed attempts to establish a Protestant calendar by replacing saints with martyrs, since many Protestants had been executed by Catholics and statues of saints had been removed from cathedrals. The court astrologer Dr. John Dee (1527-1608 AD) very nearly persuaded the excommunicated queen to accept the papal bull on calendar reform. His friend Thomas Diggs (1546 –1595 AD) said the Universe was infinite and predicted that the Cosmos would yield a global cosmopolitan order. In 1583 AD Dee predicted the conjunction of Saturn with Jupiter and warned that this would probably produce an *annus horribilis* in 1588 AD. Pope Sixtus V supported Spanish King Philip II's plan to invade Britain. When their armada was defeated in the English Channel in 1588 AD, by good seamanship and exceptionally bad weather, the papal bull was killed and John Dee's warning was rubbished, because it was a victory. It was during the reign of Good Queen Bess that the zero and infinity finally entered Western mathematics, despite Roman-Catholic objections. Britain finally accepted all of the Gregorian calendar reforms in 1752 AD.

The British Empire and Colonies covered a quarter of the globe by the 19th century AD and so Anglican versions of the Gregorian calendar, with fewer saints' days, are used throughout the British Commonwealth. Public holidays were once holy days and there were some forty of them. The industrial revolution brought major change to the British calendar. All but three days: Good Friday, Easter Saturday and Christmas Day, were replaced by a one week holiday plus all Saturday afternoons off. This encouraged the new British habits of playing or watching sport and going away on a steam train to a boarding house by the seaside. Four Bank Holidays: Easter Monday, Whit Monday, August Monday and Boxing Day were introduced in 1871 AD, Mayday was added in 1975 AD. There is also now a Spring Bank Holiday, which is different in Europe. Since 1950 AD the weekend has grown to two days and is often more. Annual paid holidays are now usually 25 working days or 5 weeks.

There are different public holidays in England, Scotland, Wales and Northern Ireland - all but Easter are based upon the Gregorian months. The Irish and Northern Irish take their patron saint St. Patrick's Day off but there are no patron saint's holidays in England, Scotland nor Wales. The English and Welsh Sunday trade laws, passed in 1950 AD, were the legal enforcement of Christian ethics and dogmas, related to **Time**. The Scots do not celebrate Christmas, which they consider to be Pagan. When the Scottish Presbyterian trade laws were passed, the Church elders were very much stricter about the proper observance of Sunday. Ferries did not sail, service stations were all closed, trains did not run. In Scotland today there is more freedom, so shops may open on Sundays.

French Time

France was established by the Franks from the remains of Celtic Gaul. The Roman-Pagan then Roman-Catholic chronology, calendar and clock gradually became established throughout the whole of mainland Europe. French Kings and Cardinals continued to gain more power and riches, frequently fighting each other to gain control of the state and the people. However, a succession of plagues and famines devastated the population and the ruling classes became pitiless and disinterested in their plight. By the end of the eighteenth century AD many poor citizens were being imprisoned, tortured and publicly executed in sadistic ways and this led to the storming of the Bastille prison and then to the French revolution.

The revolutionaries wanted to enact the thinking of the Enlightenment, so they introduced a Metric System to supersede all ancient measures. This included a new chronology, a digital calendar and a decimal clock. Their metre was based upon a seven year survey of the Paris Meridian from Dunkirk to Barcelona, led by Jean-Dominique de Cassini of the Paris Observatory and surveyed by Jean Delambre and Pierre Mechain. Their chronology was based upon the age and date of the revolution. However, it marked years using Roman numerals, not Arabic numbers. Consequently, it started with the year one instead of with the year zero. They burned the Gregorian calendar and adopted the ancient Egyptian Siriac one with twelve thirty-day *mois* and thirty-six ten-day *decades*. The Roman-Catholic calendar was by then completely full of saints' days. The revolutionaries replaced some of them with names of their heroes, but, since there were not enough of these symbols of nationality for all the days in the year, they named the remainder after foods and tools. The ten-day *decades* used number-names for the days - but not *Zerodi*. This ten-day week was not popular because there was only one day off. The five or six feast days at the end of their revolutionary year were named and dedicated to: virtue, talent, labour, opinion and rewards. Leap day was *Françiade* for celebrating: *liberte´, egalite´ et fraternite´*. Leap year was the occasion when the Olympic Games should be held. They questioned the 24-hour full-day dial and the 12-hour half-day dial and they tried to introduce a ten 'revolutionary hour' full-day clock dial. Each 'hour' divided into a hundred 'minutes' and a hundred 'seconds'. However, their clock dials were marked with 10 at the top but not 0. Most of these also showed conventional time with a 24-hour full-day dial. They were very expensive and so were never adopted throughout France.

Their revolutionary ideals were forgotten as their regime soon turned into a reign of terror when Maximilien Robespierre (1758-1794 AD) became a virtual dictator, who put 17,000 citizens to the guillotine. When Robespierre was ousted by a military *coup d'etat* an ambitious young general from Corsica, named Napoleon Bonaparte, came to power. He was more interested in global domination than global decimalization.

French Time

Napoleon invaded Egypt in 1798 AD whilst it was devastated by plagues. His fleet was destroyed by Nelson at the Battle of the Nile but he escaped. Bonaparte captured Lombardy then France in a *coup d'etat* in 1799 AD. On *11 Frimaire An XIII* (2 December 1804 AD) he crowned himself as emperor after snatching the crown out of the hands of Pope Pius VII. Later, to improve relations with the Pope and to restore Catholicism, he decreed a return to the *pied* (12.79 inches) the *Anno Domini* years, the Gregorian months, the seven-day weeks and twenty-four hour days. The combined French and Spanish fleets were soundly defeated by the British fleet under Vice-Admiral Horatio Nelson at Trafalgar in 1805 AD. Napoleon Bonaparte's armies occupied Rome from 1808 to 1814 AD. He made his son the King of Rome and his brothers the Kings of Naples, Holland and Westphalia but in Spain he provoked the Peninsular War. He was defeated by the Russians and their freezing weather in 1812 AD and exiled to the Mediterranean island of Elba in 1814 AD but escaped and was defeated by the Duke of Wellington at Waterloo in 1815 AD. He was exiled on the island of St. Helena where he wrote in his memoirs:

> The scientists had another idea which was completely at odds with the benefits to be derived from standardization of weights and measures; they imposed the decimal system, taking the metre as a unit, and suppressed all complicated numbers. Nothing is more contrary to the organization of the mind, the memory and the imagination...
> The new system of weights and measures will be a stumbling block and a source of difficulties for several generations to come...

The French people destroyed their monarchy, aristocracy and theocracy, restored them, and then destroyed their monarchy and aristocracy again. The 300m Eiffel Tower was built to commemorate the revolution but also symbolized the pinnacle of the industrial revolution and the start of the electronic revolution for it was one of the first radio and TV masts. The first radio time signal was transmitted from it on 1 July 1913 AD. The French Metric System has become an international standard but their digital ten-day week and decimal ten-hour day have been forgotten.

France is shut on Saturday afternoons, Sundays and Monday mornings. All commercial vehicles are forbidden to use the roads on Sundays. President Mitterand suggested to the first European Summit after the ratification of the Maastricht Treaty on All Saint's Day, 1 Nov. 1993 AD, that, in order to solve increasing unemployment throughout Europe, it should adopt a four-day working week with a three-day weekend. By the year 2000 AD France was working to a maximum 35-hour week, but instead of creating more employment this had the opposite effect. President Sarkozy wanted to allow Sunday trading to boost the economy. His campaign in the year 2009 AD to *abolir le Dimanch* (abolish Sunday) was supported by the unemployed but opposed by the Catholic Church.

French Time

Their digital, secular calendar was suggested by the anti-religious poet, mathematician, propagandist and philosopher Pierre Sylvain Marechal in his *Almanach des Honnetes Gens* (Almanac of Honest Folk, 1788 AD). He was imprisoned for this heresy, yet, after the revolution in 1792 AD his ideas were accepted by the mathematician and astronomer Laplace. The revolutionary government agreed about the numerous faults in the *Anno Domini* chronology, Gregorian calendar and Benedictine clock. Their chronology was restarted because it was no longer a Christian age. Their years were in Roman numerals, beginning with *An I* in 1792 AD and started at the autumnal equinox when the republic was declared. Their calendar had twelve 30-*jour mois* plus a 5 or 6 *jour* remainder. The *mois* were named after a climatic condition or agricultural activity by Phillipe Francoise Nazaire Fabre, known as: *Fabre´ d'Eglantine*:

Vendemiare (vintage)   **Brumaire** (fog)   **Friaire** (sleet)   **Nivose** (snow)
Pluviose (rain)   **Ventose** (wind)   **Germinal** (seed)   **Floreal** (blossom)
Prairial (pasture)   **Messidor** (harvest)   **Thermidor** (heat)   **Fructidor** (fruit)

There was much debate about which names should replace the saints. Marechal suggested the names of celebrities, arranged by their date of birth or death and his birthday, the former 15th August, was included. This was also the birthday of, then unknown, Napoleon Bonaparte. Many of the days were named after foods but there was much debate about the proper use of the remainder days or *jours complementaires,* described as *Fetes des Sans-Culottides* (holidays without breeches). These 5 or 6 special days were set aside for family or civic occasions. The revolutionary calendar was imposed on the French colonies but the day and month names did not match their crops nor their seasons. The digital ten-day week or *decade* did not prove to be very popular. The shops and banks were shut on *Decadi* and on *Quintidi* afternoons. Devout Catholics insisted on working on *Decadi* and taking Sunday off. Fabre was guillotined on *16 Germinal An II* - for being too moderate.

The Metric System was proposed by Abbe Gabriel Mouton, in 1670 AD. He suggested that a metre should be based upon the girth of the Earth. Bishop Charles Maurice de Tallyrand-Perigord suggested, in 1790 AD, that a metre should be the length of a pendulum with a period of 1 sec. However, the periodicity of any pendulum depends upon its latitude. Tallyrand said it should be measured at latitude 45⁰ N (Paris, France). Thomas Jefferson said it should be measured at 33⁰ N (Washington DC). However, since the French Academy of Sciences proposed changing to decimal time it was decided to base the metre on a ten millionth part of the distance from the North Pole to the Equator, so in 1791 AD Louis XVI was asked for his approval to measure an arc of the Paris Meridian. This inaccurate geophysical survey proved to be a hazardous expedition. The first Metric System was introduced throughout France in 1799 AD.

French Time

Calendrier Republicain (first three months, without accents)

decade	jour	mois > nom	1er Vendemaire	2me Brumaire	3me Frimaire
premier	1	Primidi	Raisin	Pomme	Raiponse
	2	Duodi	Safran	Celeri	Terneps
	3	Tridi	Chataines	Poire	Chicoree
	4	Quartidi	Colchique	Betterave	Nestle
	5	Quintidi	**Cheval**	**Oye**	**Cochon**
	6	Sextidy	Balsamine	Heliotrope	Mache
	7	Septidi	Carottes	Figue	Chou-fleur
	8	Octidi	Amaranthe	Scorsonniere	Miel
	9	Nonidi	Panais	Alisier	Genievre
	10	Decadi	**Cuve**	**Charrue**	**Pioche**
deuxieme	11	Primidi	Pome de terre	Sasifis	Cire
	12	Duodi	Immertele	Macre	Raifort
	13	Tridi	Potiron	Topin unbeurs	Cedre
	14	Quartidi	Reseda	Endive	Sapin
	15	Quintidi	**Ane**	**Dindon**	**Chevreuil**
	16	Sextidi	Belle-de-nuit	Cheroi	Ajone
	17	Septidi	Citrouille	Cresson	Cypress
	18	Octidi	Sarracin	Dentalaire	Lierre
	19	Nonidi	Touresol	Greade	Sabine
	20	Decadi	**Pressoir**	**Herse**	**Hoyau**
troisieme	21	Primidi	Chanore	Bacchante	Erable sucre
	22	Duodi	Peche	Acerole	Brinjere
	23	Tridi	Navet	Garence	Roseau
	24	Quartidi	Amarillis	Orange	Oseille
	25	Quintidi	**Boeuf**	**Faisan**	**Grillon**
	26	Sextidi	Aubergine	Pistace	Pignon
	27	Septidi	Piment	Macjone	Liege
	28	Octidi	Tomate	Coing	Truffle
	29	Nonidi	Orge	Cormieer	Olive
	30	Decadi	**Tonneau**	**Rouleau**	**Pelle**

Russian Time

Slavonic years were reckoned in summers, so their Solar year started at the summer solstice, yet the people of the steppes used Lunar calendars. Mongol and Chinese migrants in the east; Anatolians, Mesopotamians and Persians in the south and then the Jews, Christians and Muslims, each introduced their different chronologies, calendars, clocks and zones. With few Natural barriers across a vast tract of land, spanning half the globe, these many different and quite independent ethnic, religious and cultural groups have fought each other for supremacy - to this very day.

Christianity took a millennium to reach Russia - Grand Prince Vladimir (980-1015 AD) abandoned Paganism, he set up the Russian Orthodox Church in the principality of Kiev and he adopted the Julian calendar. He also controlled the geographically independent republic of Novgorod. For two centuries after 1240 AD the Mongols controlled most of Asia. The Khans used the Eastern zodiac as a calendar but they allowed the Russian states to run their own affairs as they wished, including the Eastern Orthodox religion and its continued use of the Julian calendar.

The dynasty of the Tsars (Caesars) began when Constantinople fell to the Turks in 1453 AD and Ivan III married the daughter of the last Eastern Holy Roman Emperor, he then brutally annexed all of the surrounding, mostly Muslim, territories and soon became known as Ivan the Terrible. His son's coronation in 1547 AD was the beginning of the Russian state. The Tsars were holy intermediaries between the people and their *God*. Moscow became the first religious and political capital of all Russia.

With the election of Michael Romanov as the Tsar in 1613 AD a new Russian dynasty was begun, which was to last for three hundred years. The first Romanovs were sickly youths but Peter the Great was a giant. His accession in 1682 AD began an era in which strength grew rapidly. Peter fought to the Baltic and so made contact with the modern World. He sailed to England and he then learned how to build seagoing ships. He modernized his army and navy, and to pay for this he debased the currency and taxed beehives, hats, beards, smokestacks and bathrooms. Towards the end of his long reign he introduced an annual poll tax. He built-up many industries, especially those with military importance. St. Petersburg was founded in 1703 AD and became Russia's capital. As its importance grew it collected many of the World's finest treasures. By Peter's death in 1725 AD Russia had grown to be the dominant state in northern and eastern Europe, but it still used the Julian calendar. The Tsarina Catherine the Great (1762-1796 AD) further extended the Russian territory and she put down the Cossack rebellion in 1773 AD. The Romanov dynasty ended when the Tsar Nicholas was assassinated, with all of his family, 16 months after the 1917 AD revolution, because his cousin, King George V, would not give them asylum in Great Britain.

Russian Time

Soon after the October revolution in 1917 AD the Russian state, then the whole of the USSR adopted the Roman-Catholic Gregorian calendar. So the anniversary of their October revolution now falls in November. The USSR scrapped Imperial measures and adopted the Metric System. Like French revolutionaries they did not like the 7-day week, with its different days for rest and religion, nor the traditional public holidays. Although the USSR continued to use the Gregorian New Year it changed to twelve 30-day months including five-day weeks from 1929-1932 AD. Workers were divided into five groups who worked for four days then took one day off in a staggered roster, so that the factories kept working. They changed to a six-day week with one day-off and five holidays during the global economic slump from 1932-1940 AD before reverting to the seven-day week with one day-off and seven public holidays in 1940 AD.

Lenin and his successors failed to keep to Marx's *Communist Manifesto* and did not use their scientific knowledge for the benefit of the people. Stalin achieved full employment by sending 25M comrades to *Gulags*. The Catholic Church was driven underground; the Orthodox Church was allowed to continue and was instrumental in overthrowing Communism. The Soviet Union finally collapsed in 1991 AD when President Gorbechov allowed more freedom, however, he was replaced by President Yeltsin who put down bloody revolts in states that wanted to return to Islam. Yet, Yeltsin's military might rusted away and his troops were not paid. Capitalism had a very difficult rebirth and its unacceptable face led to a few people becoming very rich and then taking their new wealth away, whilst the ruble dropped in value and by 2000 AD was almost worthless. Yeltsin chose the eve of the second Roman-Catholic Millennium to resign.

The Commonwealth of Independent States is a misleading designation for the former Soviet Union states are still very dependent upon Russia. Russia now gains much of its foreign currency by selling its oil and gas. Many former Soviet states and much of Europe now depend on Russia for their energy but President Putin has cut their pipelines and lifelines. It remains to be seen whether post-modern Russia will revert to the Orthodox calendar but Christmas is celebrated on Gregorian 7 January. The CIS has 11 time zones but railway timetables are based on Moscow. President Medvedev considered that time zones were anachronisms but he did not realize that they divide his people with invisible barriers and that if they were abolished there would be much less strife in the CIS. Russia desperately needs a new way of working and sharing its assets. However, they have already tried the old spiritual and temporal ideas. A ten-day week and job-sharing-as-the-norm might be a socio-economic miracle helping old comrades to share their hammers and sickles as well as diaries, timetables, calendars, clocks, rules, weights and measures. This might lead to a new philosophy combining capitalism and socialism.

German Time

The Saxon, Aryan and Gothic races held meetings at a new or full-Moon. Nevertheless, their new year began at the autumnal equinox of the Sun. Goths invaded the Western Roman Empire from 3rd to 5th centuries AD. Their Barbarian Kings of the 6th and 7th centuries AD: the Visigoths in Spain and Ostrogoths in Italy, adopted Roman titles, laws and methods of government as well as the Roman chronology, calendar and clock.

The Holy Roman Empire was formed when Pope Leo III crowned the great Frankish King Charlemagne as its Emperor on 25 December in 800 AD. Otto the Great restored some of the Western Roman Empire in 962 AD and built many Gothic churches and cathedrals throughout Germany. Frederick I (1122-1190 AD), known as Barbarossa, fought a holy war against the papacy and was excommunicated by Pope Alexander III. Frederick II (1192-1250 AD) fought crusades but was excommunicated because he did not believe in the virgin birth nor in the resurrection. Frederick III (1415-1493 AD) allowed war to rage around him whilst he extended the Habsburg power through the marriages of his relatives. During this period three million witches and heretics were put to death. Martin Luther (1483-1586 AD) was brought up with this cruel tradition. After being sent to Rome for rigorous schooling, Luther questioned the meaning of the word: righteousness, when he found that Pope Leo X was selling indulgences to finance the building of St Peter's Basilica. Luther's 95 essays, nailed to a church door, were meant to start an academic debate but lead instead to the start of a new Christian sect. Luther subsequently translated The Bible from Latin into German. Yet, it would not have reached the masses had Johann Gutenberg not invented moveable type and introduced his printing press in 1440 AD.

The state took part of Austria and Poland and was known as Prussia. A notable ruler was Frederick the Great (1712-1786 AD) who was a Humanist, soldier, writer, architect, composer and a patron of the arts. His association with Voltaire resulted in him renouncing his religion. He also believed in the French proposal to decimalize all measurements. The Napoleonic Wars finally marked the end of the Holy Roman Empire. Napoleon was defeated at Waterloo by the British and the Prussians. The German Empire was created in 1871 AD by the merger of 27 states. Most of these territories had formerly been ruled by royal families.

The Gothic style was used for many cathedrals and churches in Europe. The neo-Gothic style was popular in the 18th and 19th centuries AD for buildings such as the Houses of Parliament and Osborne House. Prince Albert of Saxe-Coburg-Gotha had a hand in both of their designs. The British Royal Family has German lineage which caused problems and led the Battenbergs to change their family name to Mountbatten and the Hanover-Saxe-Coburg-Gothas to change their name to Windsor.

German Time

The Kaisers began their short dynasty in 1861 AD with the coronation of
Wilhelm I after Germany was united by the Prussians against the French.
Wilhelm II had an inferiority complex which made him very aggressive.
Count Otto von Bismark became the Prime Minister and Alfred Krupp
was responsible for building Germany's industrial and military strength.
World War I started at Sarajevo, then in the Austro-Hungarian Empire,
but the Germans soon used this as an excuse to expand their fatherland.
They abolished all time zones throughout their territories and put their
clocks forward one hour on 1 May 1916 AD - the British followed suit.

The 1st *Reich* was the Holy Roman Empire, which lasted 1,000 years.
The 2nd *Reich* was the much shorter dynasty of the Kaisers (Caesars).
The 3rd *Reich* was predicted by Adolph Hitler to last for 1,000 years.
Nazi ideas were based on a mixture of Nordic Paganism and Christianity.
The *swastika* was both the Christian cross and the circle of the Sun-god.
Christian dates were cut from the calendar and replaced by Pagan ones.
Hitler was keen on decimal time but never put his ideas into practice.
However, he insisted that his global war machine fought to Berlin Time.
Both of the World Wars had devout Christians fighting on both sides.
This violation eventually caused many millions to abandon their faith.
Christianity is thought of as a peaceful religion but six million Jews and
ten million Christians died in Christ's name - they forgot that Christ was
a Jew and they used ethnic cleansing to create an Aryan master race.
Pope Pius XII and the Vatican did nothing to stop this fascist holocaust.

Germany was divided by the Capitalist and Communist allies after WW2.
Capitalist West Germany recovered from the war and became richer.
Communist East Germany was relatively poorer, yet everyone had a job.
Germany was eventually reunited in 1989 AD and whilst most of the
East Germans are now better-off; many are now worse-off and jobless.
The vast majority of the former East German Communists are atheist.
The united Germans still have an extremely regimented kind of society.
They are very strict about Time and even have laws about mowing lawns.
It is *verboten* on a Sunday and on other days between 12:00 and 14:00.
Chancellor Kohl wanted the EU to have one currency called: the euro.
He wanted the EU to merge into one Christian state by the Millennium.
He was keen for Europe to have one time zone spanning 45⁰ of the globe.
He wanted to impose a 48-hour working week throughout all of Europe.
He wanted Europe to be stricter about Sunday trading and all kinds of
weekend working, so many companies now work for four days in seven.
However, Chancellor Merkel considers all days and hours are the same.
Europe is expanding to include former Communist states in the East.
Large numbers of migrant workers are free to work anywhere in the EU.
Some Western manufacturers are now establishing factories in the East,
because there are fewer restrictions on working days and hours.

Italian Time

The Etruscans lived in Etruria, the region between the Arno and Tiber. Their sophisticated city-states were at their height in about 500 BC. But they were completely obliterated by the Romans by about 200 BC. When central Italy was under Etruscan control, southern Italy and Sicily were influenced by the religious, philosophical, political and scientific teachings of Pythagoras and so they were known as the Pythagoreans. They believed in reincarnation, vegetarianism and a geocentric Universe. The Romans created Italy by conquest and ruled it for a millennium. Their successors, the Roman-Catholics, divided-up Italy into city-states. During the 5th century AD the ports of Genoa, Pisa, Venice and Amalfi flourished and the city-states of Turin, Milan, Verona, Bologna, Florence, Siena and Rome became rich on the profits from trading and banking. The Rule of Saint Benedict, written in the 5th century AD, told monks what to do and when, so Benedictine monasteries were ruled by the bell. By the 10th century AD *The Julius Work Calendar* and *The Book of Hours* showed what must be done every hour of the day and month of the year. This religious ritual eventually spread throughout the whole community. Most schools, colleges and universities are still ruled by the hourly bell.

Francesco Petrarch (1304-1374 AD) rediscovered classical literature and became the father of modern Humanism, which led to the Renaissance. In Florence, the Medici family became very rich by lending money to the crown heads of Europe and became patrons of the arts and sciences. They were Hermeticists and Humanists who questioned many doctrines of the Church but they were very careful not to annoy the Inquisition. Fillipo Brunelleschi (1377-1446 AD) a goldsmith and also a clockmaker, designed and constructed Europe's largest dome on Florence Cathedral. Its great lantern was the most accurate observatory, calendar and clock. He was the first artist to fully understand and demonstrate perspective. Leonardo da Vinci (1452-1519 AD) was probably the very first polymath. He invented the aeroplane, helicopter, parachute, tank and alarm clock. He wrote notes in mirror code and his paintings had hidden meanings. Was the *Last Supper* really the wedding of Jesus to Mary Magdalene? Was the *Mona Lisa* really the portrait of the wife of his benefactor? Does the *Salvato Mundi* depict his male muse holding a crystal ball? Michelangelo Buonarroti (1475-1564 AD) spent five years decorating the ceiling of the Sistine Chapel - does it show *God* creating Man or vice-versa? Does the *Pieta*, his sculptural masterpiece at the centre of St. Peter's, depict the body of Jesus Christ being held by his wife Mary Magdalene? Niccolo Machiavelli (1467-1527 AD) demonstrated how to retain power. He helped the powerful but corrupt Borgia family to produce two popes.

Italians Christopher Columbus (1446-1506 AD) and Amerigo Vespucci (1451-1512 AD) discovered the Americas, with the help of the Spanish. Yet, these two vast continents were named after Amerigo by mistake.

Italian Time

Galileo Galiei (1564-1642 AD) found that all objects fall with the same acceleration and all pendulums of the same length have the same period. So the accuracy and repeatability of stationary clocks could be improved. He was probably the first to use a telescope to explore the Solar System. By observing the four moons of Jupiter he found an astronomical clock, which was sometimes used to find longitude before the chronometer. He observed the Sun-spots and the Solar flares and discovered that they rotate, relative to the Earth, every 28 days (I call this period: a sunth). He proved that the Earth orbits the Sun, which was directly in conflict with the Church, who continued to hold the Pythagorean view that the Earth and the Human Race were at the very centre of the Universe. The Inquisition put him under house arrest and made him recant his heretical statements but Our World has not been the same since then. Pope John Paul II apologized to Galileo in 1992 AD, then spent £5M on telescopes to search for the hands of *God* somewhere in the Universe.

Guiseppe Garibaldi (1807-1882 AD) fought the Austro-Hungarian empire and united Italy into one kingdom under Victor Emmannuel in 1860 AD. The whole country then used the same chronology, calendar and clock. Italy became one time zone, which became synchronized when Gugliemo Marconi (1874-1937 AD) invented radio and broadcast time signals. He came to Britain where he sent radio messages across the Atlantic and his company invented the television system that superseded Baird's.

Fillippo Marinetti (1876-1944 AD) founded Futurism, an artistic and social movement that aimed to liberate Italy from the weight of its past. He encouraged youths to take violent action against the establishment. They loved technology and industry making fast cars, boats and planes. The movement ended in WW2 but Italians are still infatuated by speed.

Benito Mussolini (1883-1945 AD) came to power as a Fascist dictator, during a reaction to Communism, annexed Abyssinia and supported the civil war in Spain before entering WW2 in 1940 AD, as part of the Axis with Hitler, but was deposed after the North African campaign and the invasion of Sicily and was killed by partisans when he tried to escape. He instituted a new chronology based upon his rise to power in 1922 AD. He thought that Fascism and Catholicism would last another millennium and would be the final solution to all of the problems in Our World. Since WW2 governments have been very unstable and often undermined by the Mafia or the Church, consequently there is still great inequality between the richer industrial north and the poorer agricultural south. Whilst most Italians are Catholics, the birth rate is the lowest in the EU and there is currently a campaign to remove all crucifixes from schools. The last two popes were not Italian and the Argentinean Pope Francis I is currently the first non-European pontiff for over a millennium.

Spanish Time

The Iberian peninsula was successively inhabited by the Carthaginians, Celts, Romans, Visigoths, Muslims and Catholics but the division between Mediterranean Spain and Atlantic Portugal is political, not geographical. Muslims taught Catholics about reading, writing and arithmetic as well as navigation by drawing maps, measuring angles and using almanacs. They may have taught them how to make rudimentary gravity clocks. Spain was re-conquered in the 11th century AD and split into kingdoms. It was reunited in the 15th century AD by the marriage of Ferdinand of Aragon and Isabella of Castille, who financed Columbus's expeditions. They were succeeded by Charles V (1500-1558 AD) the Habsburg King and Holy Roman Emperor, who eventually abdicated both these crowns. The Spanish Inquisition (1479-1820 AD) was infamous for the torture and execution of millions of Jews, Muslims, Protestants and heretics. Philip II (1527-1598 AD) married Mary Queen of Scots and built an armada to restore Catholicism in England after Henry VIII dissolved the monasteries. But it was chased-up the Channel by Sir Francis Drake (1540-1596 AD) and tried to sail round Scotland when half the fleet were lost in a storm. This ruined Spain and it opened the seas to the English and Dutch. The Rock of Gibraltar has been in British hands since 1704 AD and it still has strategic command over the gateway to the Mediterranean.

During the industrial revolution most of western Europe adopted new working patterns and practices, ruled by the calendar and the clock. Most workers were glad to swap holy days for holidays and weekends, because it gave them more income and greater freedom to travel. Spain stuck to its *fiestas* and *siestas* and so remained a farming and fishing community ruled by its monarchy, aristocracy and theocracy. This inequality led to an uprising of the have-nots against the haves. Communists were beaten by Fascists during the Civil War in 1939 AD. General Francisco Franco (1892-1975 AD) was helped by the Nazis and became a dictator, restoring democracy and the monarchy when he died. Long after the rest of Europe had modernized its industry and transport Spain and Portugal were still using beasts of burden over dirt tracks. They are now democracies within the EU and have many new industries. Their agriculture is mechanized and their fishing fleets are up-to-date. Their roads and railways are excellent and most people live in city flats. Their greatest industry is tourism but most shops still close on Sundays. Some 25% of the population are unemployed, the economy is in a mess, crime is on the increase and many ex-pat residents are returning home.

Although Latin Spain and Portugal are united by the Catholic Church they are still separated by different time zones and modern languages. Roman gladiators fought wild animals in arenas throughout the Empire. Spanish bullfights became their entertainment on a Saturday afternoon. Football has now taken its place as the national blood sport.

Portuguese Time

In the Roman Era the south-west corner of the Iberian peninsula was the province of Lusitania but Portugal's border is not quite the same. Alfonso the Wise (1221-1284 AD) King of Leon and Castille was known for his planetary tables, for his code of law and for his history of Iberia. Portugal became independent of Spain during the 12th century AD and has remained so, largely due to its longstanding alliance with England. The Portuguese language gradually became different from the Spanish.

Prince Henry the Navigator (1394-1460 AD) established a navigation school on Cape St. Vincent, his captains explored as far as Cape Verde and laid foundations of imperial expansion in Africa and the Far East. Stars were used for navigation at night and the phases of the Moon indicated the state of tide from high and low springs to lesser neaps. Tidal currents were carefully measured and drawn on special charts. Latitude was found using an astrolabe, quadrant or sextant to measure the angle of the Sun at noon related to the age and date in an almanac. The position of the Moon relative to the Sun was used to find longitude. These navigation systems were kept secret and allowed the Portuguese to discover parts of the globe that were inaccessible to the other seafarers. Vasco da Gama (1469-1524 AD) led the first expedition around the Cape of Good Hope and crossed the Indian Ocean to Calicut where he was welcomed by the Raja - but the settlers he left behind were massacred. Ferdinand Magellan (1480-1521 AD) was the first to pass Cape Horn by finding a passage through the straits that now bear his name and the remaining ship from his fleet completed the first circumnavigation of the globe after he was killed during a native war in the Philippines.

Portugal colonized all of its overseas territories on behalf of the Pope. Jesuit missionaries conducted a reign of terror whilst spreading the word. Believers would be granted eternal salvation; non-believers put to death. Catholicism did more than any other religion to spread the concept of one chronology, one calendar and one clock but not one time zone. They taught the Chinese about clocks and learnt about compasses. The compass was one of the most important navigational inventions. Portugal became one of Europe's greatest colonial powers but lost a golden opportunity to expand when it shunned Christopher Columbus. Independence was lost to Spain in 1580 AD but regained in 1688 AD. Brazil was colonized in the 16th century AD and is the largest country speaking Portuguese but independence was granted later than to others.

Portugal became a democratic republic in 1910 AD then lapsed into a military dictatorship in 1933 AD under Antonio Salazar (1889-1970 AD). Now a democratic republic it was one of the poorest states to join the EU. The Portuguese were not very keen to adopt Central European Time. They tried it and then abandoned it, so are in the same zone as Britain.

Dutch Time

William I, Prince of Orange, (1533-1584 AD) founded The Netherlands.
The Low Countries of the Scheldt-Rhine Delta were once ruled by Spain,
but in 1568 AD the Dutch, who were mostly Protestant, rebelled against
their Roman–Catholic overlords and, during the next eighty years, they
took over control of the high seas and built the richest state in Europe.
They used wind pumps and dykes with drainage and navigation canals
to turn the marshes into lakes and polders of fertile agricultural land.
Rich merchants used their money to pay mercenary armies and navies,
to finance agriculture and industry and to support the arts and sciences.
This was achieved by borrowing money and paying it back with interest.
It was the beginning of Capitalism, upon which their global empire was built.

The formation of the Protestant Church caused the schism from Rome.
Desiderius Erasmus of Rotterdam (1466-1536 AD) was a Catholic priest.
He edited the *New Testament* in Latin and Greek, which led to reform.
Erasmus wrote many influential works extolling the virtues of: *Free Will*.
Amongst his followers he enjoyed the sobriquet: *Prince of Humanists*.
Erasmus's portrait was painted by Hans Holbein the Younger, who also
painted King Henry VIII and his six wives, when he became a Protestant.
Square rigged ships from Holland, France, Spain, Portugal and Britain
fought each other for centuries, even though they were all Christians.
The Protestant alliance was strengthened after The Glorious Revolution,
when the Dutch army invaded Britain and deposed James II in 1688 AD.
William of Orange (1650-1702 AD) wed cousin Mary Stuart (1663-1694 AD).
They shared the job of ruling over England, Wales, Scotland and Ireland.
However, the Roman-Catholic Irish resented their new Protestant rulers.
This led to the battle of the Boyne, won by William and Mary in 1690 AD.

The Dutch East and West Indies provided great wealth for a small state.
Amsterdam and Rotterdam became great ports and they still are today.
The Dutch traded with China, Japan and other states in the Far East.
They gradually took over the spice islands to form the state of Indonesia.
Yet, they had no regard to the suffering in Java, Sumatra and Malacca.
They captured South Africa and used slaves to mine gold and diamonds.
They still control the gold and diamond industry, based in Amsterdam.
Fortunes were made out of the slave trade between Africa and America.
They gained a foothold on Manhattan Island named: New Amsterdam,
and built a small town with a defensive wall to keep the 'red' men out.
This is now New York and Wall Street lies where that wall once stood.
The reordering of the Dutch calendar led to the Protestant work ethic.
They used their own month names, based upon seasonal indications.
However, these made little sense to those living in the Dutch colonies.
The Dutch no longer have an empire but they maintain their work ethic.
Many of them now share their jobs and they also work for shorter hours.
They have discovered that this new system leads to greater productivity.

Swiss Time

Switzerland is a federation of autonomous cantons with a long history stretching back to the Roman Empire and then the Holy Roman Empire. Some of these cantons formed republican alliances over 700 years ago. Some are Catholic others Protestant, speaking German, French or Italian. Swiss Catholics have provided the guard at the Vatican for 500 years. The majority of Swiss Protestants still refer to themselves as Calvinists. Jean Calvin (1509-1564 AD) was born in France and trained as a lawyer. He then broke away from the Roman-Catholic Church in about 1530 AD. But following a violent uprising against Protestants, he fled to Geneva where he published his seminal work: *Institutes of the Christian Religion*. He subsequently wrote commentaries on most of the books in the *Bible* as well as numerous theological treatises and confessional documents. At first he was called a heretic but his new ideas were eventually adopted and he was later accepted as the spiritual leader of the reformed church. As church leader he introduced new forms of government and liturgy. The Reformed Congregational and Presbyterian Churches follow his lead.

Switzerland has remained independent ever since the French revolution. Most of its important political decisions are now made by referendums. It remained politically independent and neutral in both the World Wars. It closed all of its borders and turned itself into a mountain fortress. It is surrounded by: The European Union, but it still uses Swiss francs and became a global banking hub with secret accounts as tax havens. It became the founder of the Geneva Conventions and the host nation of: The International Red Cross and later: The World Health Organization. Switzerland annually hosts the Worldwide Economic Forum at Davos. They should debate the benefits of **full-time-job-sharing-as-the-norm**. After World War I it hosted: The League of Nations, who proposed a global calendar but this was forgotten in the turmoil of World War II. The United Nations again tried but failed to introduce a global calendar. Switzerland is the home of the International Standards Organization. The ISO standardized many things including the metre and second. They have tried to standardize the Roman-Catholic age, date and time. The first day in their standard seven-day week is Monday, not Sunday.

Switzerland became the home of the clock and watch making industry. This led to their punctuality and their prowess in precision engineering. A Swiss patent clerk in Berne worked on the synchronization of clocks. Albert Einstein (1879-1955 AD) dreamed up some relatively new ideas. His ideas on relativity soon led to nuclear power and to nuclear bombs. He claimed that if had realized this he would have become a clockmaker. The Swiss still manufacture most expensive mechanical and electronic analogue clocks and watches, which are regarded as status symbols. *Swatch* tried to to sell global-digital-decimal watches at the Millennium but failed to recognize that they are part of **The Worldwide System**.

North American Time

Tribes from Europe reached North-East America by kayak in 15,000 BC.
Tribes from Asia reached North-West America by ice-bridge in 10,000 BC.
Some tribes remained hunter-gatherers; others built great civilizations.
Most tribes developed some form of chronology, calendar and clock as
well as myths and legends based upon the worship of their Sky-gods.

The Kutenai from British Colombia, Alberta, Washington, Idaho and
Montana were given their name meaning: 'white men' by the Blackfoot.
The Kutenai have a myth about an island called *Samah-tumi-whoo-lah*
which means: 'white man's island' - where they came from long ago.
Their mythology identifies four Rocky Mountains: Mt. Baker, Mt Rainier,
Mt. Jefferson and Mt. Shasta where they sheltered during the Flood.
They still watch the North Star every night in case it changes position.

The Utes of Utah worshipped a Sun-god: *Ta-vi* and a hare-god: *Ta-wats*.
Ta-vi singed the fur of *Ta-wats* so he shot arrows at him until a magical
arrow hit its mark and caused the Sun to explode in a thousand pieces.
The fiery destruction that ensued was then quenched by a Great Flood.
The Sun-god was conquered and then forced to travel across the Sky
by the same trail every day creating days and nights, seasons and years.

In the Appellations, a Cherokee named Sequoia created an alphabet and
transcribed many myths and legends from his people's oral traditions.
In one of these legends a Great Flood was caused by the tears of the
Sun-goddess following the death of her daughter, the Moon-goddess.

Mississippians grew maize on the flood plains and built wooden henges.
Every village had a totem pole, used as a navel, calendar and clock.
Their mound at Cahokia near St. Louis was as big as the Great Pyramid.
They aligned this temple with the cardinal points and honored the Sun.
Their civilization began in about 700 AD and ended in about 1400 AD.

The Anasazi of Pueblo Bonito, Chaco Canyon, New Mexico built circular
stone *kivas* that were not only dwellings but also Solar observatories.
They built long straight roads, although they did not discover the wheel.
Their advanced civilization disappeared when all of their crops failed.

The Hopi of Arizona used a Solar calendar based upon landmarks on the
horizon to determine the appropriate dates for planting and harvesting.
These were observed by astronomer-priests who gave the landmarks
names and organized ceremonies on the solstices and equinoxes.

The Sioux used a series of picture charts to keep track of passing years.
1762 AD was remembered by a prairie fire which destroyed their camp.
1800 AD was the fateful year in which nine 'white' men came to trade.

North American Time

'White' men brought horses, cattle, sheep, seeds, crops, ploughs, tools, wheels, cabins, concrete, railroads, ships, money, laws, democracy, Christian morals, ages, dates, times, zones and many other innovations. 'White' men also brought 'black' slaves, disease, pestilence, deprivation, dust, dogma, greed, guns, whisky, crime, prison, barbed wire and war. Apart from the National Parks and the Indian Reserves, the 'white' men have completely changed the landscape that the 'red' men once knew.

The native North Americans were forced to become Christian at gunpoint. Some Protestant settlers in the New World were poisoned by Catholics. The Mormons allowed polygamy to expand their population, whilst the single men were riding the range, tilling the soil or panning for gold. The Seventh Day Adventists hold that Saturday is the true Sabbath. Others believe that Sunday is special but there are no laws about it. Many Americans are Jewish and they bankrolled the new state of Israel. The Muslim religion and its sects now appeal to some of the 'blacks'. The Eastern religions were brought in by 'yellow' immigrants who won most of the gold then lost it again when they were expelled by 'whites'.

Gold and the get-rich-quick philosophy drew many poor people to USA. Oil and gas were first found in Titusville, Pennsylvania during 1859 AD. This discovery changed the whole Planet and made USA a super-state. The railroads opened up the country and unified timetables in 1880 AD. The artificial barriers between Canada, USA and Mexico are becoming less pronounced but their main languages: English, Spanish and French still divide people living in exclusive zones based upon their language, their skin or their bankroll, which prevent them becoming one nation.

The whole of North America uses the Christian *Anno Domini* chronology, the Gregorian calendar, the 7-day week, the 24-hour clock and has eight time zones stretching from Hawaii and Alaska across to Newfoundland. Some states have so-called: daylight saving measures but others do not. The USA public holidays are: New Year, Martin Luther King, Presidents, Memorial, Independence, Labor, Columbus, Veteran's and Thanksgiving. Christmas and Easter, however, are not considered to be public holidays. Their work week is getting shorter; their work hours are getting longer. Most of the North Americans only take a two-week annual vacation.

Mexico lost much of its territory to USA but uses the Metric System. Canada has used both Imperial and Metric but the latter is taking over. The USA uses its own system, based on the Imperial one, its yards, feet and inches are the same but its gallons, quarts and pints are smaller. The USA still uses different paper sizes from the rest of Our World. American scientists and technologists normally use the Metric System and they are urging Congress to be the same as the rest of Our World.

South American Time

Great civilizations were built by collective endeavor and mutual support.
Huge lines across the Nazca desert were made some two millennia ago.
Symbols, like spiders and monkeys, that can only be seen from the Sky,
represent the Nazca zodiac and also represented the names of the tribes.
Straight lines marked the precession of equinoxes over many centuries.
Solar and Lunar eclipses were carefully recorded by groups of stones.
Tiwanaku, now in Bolivia, was high in the Andes near salt lake Titicaca.
It has a huge pyramid and temple aligned to the solstices and equinoxes.
They tamed and used llamas to carry loads along their mountain roads.
They developed agriculture and they made fishing boats from the reeds.
Their civilization grew from 500-1100 AD but collapsed due to droughts.
The Moche built mud-brick pyramids and were expert jewellers but their
desert kingdom was devastated by climatic changes in around 750 AD.
The Kingdom of Chimor grew from 1000 to 1500 AD and united the
western desert by irrigating the land and their capital of Chan Chan, in
Moche valley, had mud-brick pyramids housing gold-encrusted tombs.
The stone pyramids at Caral were as large as those in ancient Egypt.
They knew about astronomy and navigation and they counted in tens.
Hundreds of mud-brick pyramids in the Lambayeque valley had palaces
on top and a temple where human sacrifices were made to the Sky-gods.
Wari, now in Peru, was a city with paved roads and irrigation canals.
However, all of these civilizations died out or were absorbed by the Inca.

Inca, means: son of the Sun, and referred to their emperor: Sapa Inca.
The Inca god *Viracocha* created the Earth, the Sky and then the people.
He created the Sun-god *Inti*, Moon-god *Coniraya* and mountain-god *Apu*.
Incas prayed at the solstices of the Sun and the new and full Moons.
They watched the Milky Way and venerated the dark shapes within it.
They tracked the Planets and feared conjunctions, when they believed
that a Great Flood would destroy the western desert and eastern forest.
They built quakeproof stone cities, terraced fields and food storage silos.
Their massive masonry was so accurate that it did not need any mortar.
Their network of mountain tracks ran the entire length of the Andes.
They constructed rope bridges across the mountain rivers and ravines.
They did not use any system of writing but used knotted string *quipus*
for counting and measuring with a base-ten place numbering system.
Landmarks on the horizon around the temple in Cuzco were calendars.
This began with the first sighting of the Pleiades before dawn (June 8-9).
Their Lunar year was divided into 12 moonths or 13 in every third year.
Their Solar year was divided into 12 *quilla* of 30 days plus 5 or 6 days.
They also used a working week of ten days including one day for resting.
The Inca empire was the largest in the Americas with some 8M people.
A handful of the Spanish *conquistadores* killed 5M Incas in 1532 AD.
Their emperor had recently died and his successors began a civil war.
Some of the refugees fled to Machu Picchu, hidden high-up in the Andes.

South American Time

The *conquistadores* searched in vain for the legendary city of *El Dorado* but they discovered an extensive agricultural civilization in Amazonia. The ancient tribes were very well organized and could work together in harmony to build bridges, roads, canals, fields, dwellings and temples. They were skilled potters and many funeral urns have been discovered. They turned their water and infertile soil into a sustainable ecosystem. Their advanced civilization was annihilated by a virus and so was lost. The primitive tribes that remain in Amazonia are very wary of outsiders.

The Vatican divided most of this continent between Portugal and Spain. So Brazilians speak Portuguese whilst most other states speak Spanish. Uruguay was originally Portuguese but it was captured by the Spanish. Chile resisted the conquest for many years until it finally succumbed. Argentina is temperate and was mostly colonized by North Europeans. Venezuela was named by Italians, who thought it looked like Venice. Columbia was named after the Italian explorer Christopher Columbus. Bolivia was named after the liberator Simon Bolivar (1783-1830 AD). Pope Francis, the first non-European pontiff, came from Latin America.

As they became independent, many new republics were run by dictators and so an educated democracy took a long time to become established. Massive debts to North American and European banks have caused the destruction of the rain forests for hardwoods and short-lived cash crops. Gold is excavated, panned and smelted in very hazardous conditions. The South American coffee trade has gradually come under US control. Many of the World's pharmaceuticals and drugs come from Colombia. Ecuador has large deposits of lithium, which is used in many batteries. Venezuela has crude oil but the rest of South America has little or none. An increasing proportion of cars run on alcohol, the road system is less developed because of the difficult terrain and the shortage of bitumen. Their railways have fallen into disuse and most rivers are un-navigable. Argentina's economy was based on cattle, whose meat became fast food. Now it is bankrupt and global fast food empires are starting to collapse.

It is estimated that only about 50% of South Americans now have jobs. Many of them have abandoned their villages and have moved to shanty towns near cities and orphaned children wander the streets then vanish. Murder, prostitution, drug dependence and alcoholism are commonplace. Almost all of the South American republics are now devout Christians and so they use the Roman-Catholic chronology, calendar and clock. They have many holy days but their economies are in an unholy mess. The exception is secular Uruguay, the smallest but wealthiest republic. It has high literacy, an extensive welfare system, a balanced economy, low unemployment and is the most democratic state on the continent. It could be the first to adopt **full-time-job-sharing-as-the-norm**.

Central American Time

Several Stone Age civilizations flourished in Mesoamerica, then vanished. The Olmec civilization began in 1150 BC but disappeared after 800 BC. They built the first pyramid-temples and played games with rubber balls. Without metal tools they carved huge basalt heads, which were probably images of their leaders and these were transported over long distances. Their pottery and jade carvings showed a hybrid human/jaguar god. They used a form of glyph writing, an anatomical system of measures, and a calendar based upon the 260 day cycle of their staple maize crop. Their stone inscriptions linked great terrestrial and celestial events.

Another lost civilization built a gigantic metropolis some 2,000 years ago. The Aztecs later named this: Teotihuacan - The Place where Time began. It was oriented at 15.5 degrees E, in line with the Pleiades Constellation. It housed 100,000 people in stone dwellings with running water and sewers in wide pedestrian streets laid out in a square grid pattern. This great empire advanced with the power of volcanic glass or obsidian and developed a form of writing and a standard measurement of 83 cm. The enormous pyramid-temple of the Sun was 260 of these units square whilst the smaller pyramid-temple of the Moon was 105 units square. These represented their sacred calendar rounds of 260+105 = 365 days. There was also another great temple dedicated to the feathered serpent. A meteorite or asteroid leaves a feathered trail across the Sky like a jet plane and may be the origin of their fear of a Sky-god of destruction. Teotihuacan expanded by force but became established with civic pride. It collapsed in 536 AD after Ilopango erupted and blotted out the Sun.

The Toltecs lived in central Mexico from the 10th to 12th centuries AD. Their Pyramid of the Morning Star is thought to honor Planet Venus. Their Pyramid of the Niches has seven tiers with 365 square niches. Their Lord of the calendar round was *Quetzalcotl* (feathered serpent). They carved many strange altar/statues known as *Chac-Mool* figures.

The Mayan civilization lasted two millennia, reached its peak between the 7th and 10th centuries AD but died out over the next two centuries. The main reason for the failure of their civilization was overpopulation. They cut down the rainforest and planted crops everywhere, including the sides of hills, without letting the soil recover its Natural fertility. Eventually, there was a period of extraordinary rainfall that produced landslides and floods, which washed away the soil and their maize crops. Their temples were lost in the forests of Mexico's Yucatan Peninsular. Many have also been rediscovered in Belize, Honduras and Guatemala.

The Aztecs took over from the Maya and they used the same calendars. The successors of these ancient civilizations are Mixtecs and Zapotecs. These Mexicans still believe in Sun and Moon worship, as well as Christ.

Central American Time

The Maya developed a theory of the Universe which accords with recent Big Bang and Big Crunch thinking, rather than the Steady State theory. They believed there were four other Suns and this one will end soon. They predicted the annual arrival of thirteen equatorial Constellations. These do not correspond with either the Eastern nor the Western zodiacs. They were particularly interested in the Pleiades and Orion star groups. They measured the exact cycles of Venus, Mars, Mercury and Jupiter and could predict Solar and Lunar eclipses with very great accuracy. They feared that earthquakes and eruptions would coincide with eclipses. Time was symbolized by a jade serpent which sometimes has two heads. They developed a cult based on the rattlesnake, which has 13 rattles, renews its fangs every 20 days and sheds its skin every midsummer. The square pattern on its back is used in their architecture and the head of a snake appears in their system of counting and writing in glyphs.

Their astronomer-priests could predict many cosmic events and so they had control of the state and everything was ruled by their calendars. The Mayan Lord Pacal (703-743 AD) was ruler of the city of Palenque. His tomb was discovered in 1952 AD hidden inside a pyramid-temple. His head was covered by a jade mask and his body by a suit of jade. The decorated lid of his sarcophagus has recently been deciphered. They appear to have discovered the Solar wind and Sun-spot cycles. The 28-day Solar wind or sunth cycle seems to control menstruation and gestation in the ratio of ten to one and the 11-12 year Sun-spot cycle seems to be related to the pull of Jupiter and all the smaller Planets. They seem to control the *El Nino* (Spanish for Christ Child) phenomenon, which effects the equatorial currents and winds in the South Pacific and, in turn, the weather patterns in the Americas and the rest of Our World. There is also a 206 year Sun-spot cycle and this may have caused the catastrophic drought and flood, which ended the Mayan civilization.

The Maya made Human sacrifices atop their stepped pyramid-temples to honor the Sun and the Moon, ensuring that they rose every day. One at Chichen Itza has four flights of 91 steps to a square making 365. On both the equinoxes a snake-like shadow appears beside these steps. The eyes of a jaguar statue-throne light-up when the Sun is overhead. Chichen Itza was built near Natural cisterns on the Yucatan peninsular. These form an underground cave complex which was created when an asteroid collided with Earth and caused the extinction of the dinosaurs. Their architects had a remarkable understanding of Time and Space. They were able to construct huge monuments by mutual cooperation. Yet, none of these civilizations developed a clock, a wheel nor a coin. Most believed that climate changes were caused by supernatural gods but there are many Natural causes for global warming and cooling, as well as the effects of greenhouse gases caused by too many of Us.

Central American Time

The Maya were totally obsessed with the measurement of age and date. Their base 20 number system starts with a shell symbol meaning: zero. Their numbers are in a series of dots and dashes, rather like Morse code. One dash = 5. Four dots + three dashes = 19. One dot + one shell = 20.

Their first calendar, the sacred *tzolkin* cycle, was like a combination of two intermeshing gears, one with the numbers 1 to 13 and the other with twenty glyphs, which named the days and the people born on them. Those born on the same day had the same name, so could not marry. The cycle repeats every 260 days and this number may be based on the rattlesnake cult and/or the appearance of Venus and/or the maize crop. The 20 glyphs are named in Mayan and English as follows:

Imix	**Alligator**	*Cheun*	**Monkey**
Ik	**Air/Wind**	*Eb*	**Broom/Grass**
Akbal	**Night/House**	*Ben*	**Reed**
Kan	**Corn/Lizard**	*Ix*	**Jaguar**
Chiccan	**Serpent**	*Men*	**Eagle/Wise One**
Cimi	**Death**	*Cib*	**Owl/Vulture**
Manik	**Deer**	*Caban*	**Force/Earthquake**
Lamut	**Rabbit**	*Eznab*	**Flint/Knife**
Muluc	**Water**	*Cauac*	**Storm/Rain**
Oc	**Dog**	*Ahau*	**Lord/Flower**

Their second calendar was the *Haab* or vague year which had a 360 day *tun* plus 5 bad days when they feared that their World would end. The *tun* was divided into 18 *uinals* and each *uinal* had 20 *kins* (days). The *kins* were numbered from zero to nineteen and each *uinal* was given a special glyph, plus an extra glyph for the 5 bad or remainder days. These nineteen *uinal* glyphs are called by the following Mayan names:

Pop, Uo, Zip, Zotz, Tzec, Xul, Yaxkin, Mol, Chen,

Yax, Zac, Ceh, Mac, Kankin, Muan, Pax, Kayub, Cumhu, Ayeb

Their third calendar was the Long Count which repeats every 52 years. It is based upon the following counting system:

20 *kins* (days)	=	1 *uinal*	**20 day period**
18 *uinals*	=	1 *tun*	**360 day vague year**
20 *tuns*	=	1 *katun*	**7,200 days**
20 *katuns*	=	1 *baktun*	**144,000 days**

The age and date on a building might use all three systems and read say: Introduction: 5 *baktuns* :12 *katuns* :7 *tuns* :4 *uinals* :12 *kins* :1 *ben* : 0 *mol* A New Fire ceremony was held at the beginning of every Long Count. This may represent rebirth, since a lifetime was less than 52 years.

Their fourth calendar was Solar based and consequently the agricultural year began on Gregorian 16 July when the Sun was directly overhead. Their chronology was based upon a cosmic event which they called: The Birth of Venus, and this started their Great Cycle of 13 *baktuns*. It began on 13 August 3114 BC and ended on 21 December 2012 AD.

Central American Time

The Maya built many temples, but the people all lived in the countryside. The Aztecs built many great cities, where thousands of people resided. They used the same calendars as the Maya, also worshipped the Sun and the Moon and practiced Human sacrifice on top of their pyramids. Their supreme god *Tonacatecutli* or *Omoteotl* was Lord of Time and Fire. Through the mediation of the four *Tetzcatlipocas*, which represent the four cardinal points of the compass, he created both Time and Space. There were also many other gods representing different aspects of Life. A huge calendar stone was carved in 1479 AD for Emperor Axayacatyl. In the centre is the Sun-god who sets the measures of Time, to his left and right are claws holding Human hearts to sustain him on his journey. In the four panels are the ages when the previous Suns were destroyed. On the top of the outer ring is the age when the present Sun was born. The inner ring names all of the twenty days in the *uinal,* the next ring incorporates eight Solar rays, the outer ring consists of two fire serpents. This is now displayed at the Anthropological Museum in Mexico City.

The Aztecs were so-called from Aztlan (White Land) and they were also known as the Tenochca from an eponymous ancestor Tenoch, or Mexica from Metzliapan (Moon Lake) their mystical name for Lake Texcoco. Their ninth elected ruler Moctezuma II lived in their capital Tenochtitlan. This was in Lake Texcoco, now Mexico City, the largest city on Earth. The Aztecs used their calendar to foretell events and predicted that the god-king *Quetzalcotl* would return in the year One Reed = 1519 AD. When Hernan Cortez arrived in this year they thought he was their god. He saw the Pacific for the first time, slaughtered the natives, conquered Mexico and burnt most of the relics of Aztec and earlier civilizations. However, some were saved and they are helping to unravel the past. An Aztec codex calendar showing numbers, gods and burdens of Time, was written on fig-bark paper, probably during the 13th Century AD. It was sent to Charles V, the King of Spain and Holy Roman Emperor. Known as the Dresden Codex it is now kept at the Dresden Museum but was damaged in WW2 when the city was destroyed by a firestorm. Other codices have been found and they are now in museums but their ancient religious text the *Popol Vuh* has probably been lost forever.

The Spanish Conquistadors eventually captured most of Mesoamerica. Mexico, Guatemala, El Salvador, Honduras, Belize, Nicaragua, Costa Rica and Panama now use Roman-Catholic Time and the same time zone. Mexico recently adopted 'daylight saving' although it is in the tropics. The seven-day week is established and the churches are full on Sundays but unemployment and crime are increasing and some yearn for the days when everyone had a role in society and the gods were happier. Mesoamericans are still making exactly the same mistakes as the Maya. Overpopulation will be their downfall - if this Sun does not expire soon.

Australasian Time

Ptolemy of Alexandria considered there must be a landmass in the South to balance the one in the North and called this territory *terra australis*. Captain James Cook (1728-1779 AD) claimed Australia and New Zealand for Great Britain but failed to reach the continent of Antarctica.

Aboriginal hunter/gatherer tribes reached Australia in prehistoric times. They forgot how to build boats and never developed agriculture, animal husbandry, wheels, writing nor any form of age, date and time system. In their secret Dreamtime beliefs the past, present and future coexist. Their ancestors named features after body parts (e.g. eye = waterhole). *Uluru* or Ayer's Rock is the geographic and spiritual centre of their land. Their rock paintings, in a series of dots, often show the Constellations and the Milky Way, for they used the night Sky as a map of their land. With the naked eye and no instruments they charted the shapes and colours of the Constellations, which appeared to them like kangaroos, crocodiles or snakes, and noted the positions of the five visible Planets. The Sun was a woman who carried a fire from east to west in daylight and she then traveled underground during the night, back to the east. The Moon was a man, with changing moods or phases, who was linked to fertility, since young girls who gazed upon him often became pregnant. Rock paintings of a mythical being called the Rainbow Serpent in north Australia date back some 6,000 years and are based upon a sea horse. However, the paintings are several hundred Km inland and it is known that some 6,000 years ago the sea flooded a fifth of northern Australia.

The Maoris discovered their 'Land of the Long White Cloud' by canoe about 1,000 years ago and had many cultural links with the peoples of South Pacific islands, who were excellent astronomers and navigators. They had no form of writing and so their history and mythology has been passed down by oral tradition and has only recently been written down. The warring tribes built villages with ornate huts and meeting houses. They constructed ornate war canoes, which were paddled by many men. They liked to eat their foes but considered it disgusting to eat women. Their art turned the Constellations into familiar objects such as a canoe. Their Universe consisted of twelve heavens, the closest one to Earth's surface being called: *Rangi* across whose body celestial objects moved. The Sun called: *Ra* speeded across the Sky for most of the day until he was persuaded to slow down and give some more night-time for sleeping. The Moon called: *Hina* had different names when she was new, full, waxing or waning and was associated with menstruation and childbirth. Their tribal chronology was based upon the reigns of their chiefs. Seasonal names were given to ten Lunar moonths in the Stellar year that began at the new Moon after the Pleides appeared in the dawn sky. The days in a moonth were each given a name but they had no weeks. They had no need to divide their days with any form of clock.

Badi Time

Baha'i is an all-embracing peaceful religion founded in Persia in 1844 AD when Mirza Hasayan Ali, (1817-1892 AD) now known as: Bahaullah, declared himself a 'gate' or prophet, foretold by the founder of the Babi movement: Ali Mohammed Shirazi, (1819-1850 AD) known as: the Bab. The Bab's followers believe in the *Old and New Testaments* and *Koran*. They also have their own texts based upon the writings of Bahaullah as interpreted by his successors: Abdul-Baha and Shogi Effendi and these relate to Life as We live it today, with equality for all men and women. They regard Abraham, Moses, Zoroaster, Buddha, Isaiah, John, Jesus, Mohammed and Bahaullah as the prophets of the one omnipotent *God*. The purpose of Human Life is to know and worship *God* the Creator. All gods, all religions and all Humans are, fundamentally, the same. They assert that science and religion are not in opposition and that, eventually, there will be one language and one system of government. They believe that global peace is not only possible but inevitable.

The Bab was martyred as a heretic by the Shiite Muslims in Persia and his followers are still being ostracized and victimized by them in Iran. Baha'i is not evangelistic in any way, so was dying out with its founders, but has had a revival in the developing World during recent decades. There are five million followers and houses of worship have been set-up on every continent, centred upon a school, hospital or orphanage. The Universal House of Justice, their supreme governing body, consisting of nine democratically elected members, was established in 1963 AD. They meet every five years in Hiafa, Israel where there is a shrine to the Bab upon Mount Carmel, built in stages between 1899 and 1953 AD. There are no initiation rites, ministers nor sacraments in Baha'ism but followers pray every day and consider that working is part of worship.

Every religion and every sect has its own chronology, calendar and clock. The Badi system, based upon nineteen squared, was devised by the Bab. Number nineteen is significant because 19 Solar years = 235 moonths. The year starts on the vernal equinox and the day starts at local Sun-set. In Badi chronology: day 1 in year 1 BE fell upon 21 March 1844 AD. The Badi calendar has 19 'months' of 19 days = 361 plus 4 or 5 days. These remainder days are intercalated before the nineteenth 'month'. Each Badi 'month' begins with a feast day and ends with a fast day, when scriptures are read, and the last 'month' is a fast during daylight. Leapday follows exactly the same rules as in the Gregorian calendar. Their seven-day week begins on Saturday and their Sabbath is on Friday. However, the days in the week have different Persian names meaning: Glory, Beauty, Perfection, Grace, Justice, Majesty and Independence. The Badi day has the usual 24 hours, 60 minutes and 60 seconds but since it starts at local Sun-set on the previous day they do not recognize any time zones nor daylight saving measures.

Global Time

Whilst some secular states now use BCE and ACE instead of BC and AD it is still the same chronology and it is certainly not used by everyone. Whilst most states use the Gregorian calendar, its idiosyncrasies make it difficult to build into timepieces and it is different in every language. Whilst everyone now uses the 12 or 24 hour, 60 minute, 60 second then decimal clock or watch, this hotchpotch causes a great deal of confusion. Whilst all states have their own time zones there is now a strong lobby for each continent to use the same one - so why not the whole globe?

In 1583 AD the French historian Joseph Scaliger suggested a continuous day-count with decimals of a day, starting at midday in Greenwich on 1 January 4713 BC, assuming the Julian calendar had been in use then. **Modified Julian Date** is used by many astronomers and historians but, since it has no years, months nor weeks, it has no Civic applications. It was modified by deleting 2,400,000 days and now starts at midnight. e.g. Gregorian 20 February 1996 AD at 1:30 pm GMT = 2,450,134.563

In 1834 AD Abbe Marco Mastrofini, a Roman-Catholic priest, proposed a **World Calendar** similar to the Essene one, which had been forgotten. It had four equal quarters containing three months of 31, 30 & 30 days plus an intercalary *Worldsday* at the end and a leap-day in the middle. The months kept their Gregorian names and the seven-day week was retained but it was interrupted, so that the first month in each quarter began on a Sunday, the second on a Wednesday, the third on a Friday. The League of Nations and the United Nations both considered adopting it but the USA were against any changes and so the idea was scrapped.

In 1850 AD the sociologist Auguste Compte suggested a perpetual Solar calendar with thirteen 28-day sunths plus one extra day and a leap-day. Now known as the **International Fixed Calendar** it retains the month names of the Gregorian calendar and it starts upon the same day but intercalates an extra 28-day sunth called: *Sol* between June and July. An extra day falls at the end of the year and leap-day at the end of June. The seven-day week is discontinuous so every sunth starts on a Sunday. The British government now uses a continuous sunth for pensions.

The author proposed **Worldwide Time** in the *New Scientist* in 1996 AD. He later proposed **Worldwide Space** in a worldwidewebsite in 1999 AD. **Worldwide Time and Space** are both parts of **The Worldwide System**. This is not only a rational global-digital-decimal measurement system, but also a rational management, government and environment system. The Internet is a global system and so it does not recognize time zones. Some Internet surfers now use year-day numbers and decimals of a day. Some watches now show **global age, digital date** and **decimal time.** (Surf: new scientist/time for a change)   (Surf: worldwidesystem.co.uk)

Part Four

Unification

Horology and Chronography

"Work is necessary for Man.
Man invented the alarm clock."

Pablo Picasso (1881-1973 AD)

Sky Clocks

The first clock was the shadow of a man, a stone or a stick in the ground. These developed into much more accurate Sky-clocks for measuring the positions of the Sun, Moon, Planets and Stars and this study of the Sky gradually led to the science of astronomy and quasi-science of astrology.

The Egyptians worshipped time and inscriptions in some of their tombs describe the rituals to be performed at every hour of the day or the night. The first Egyptian obelisk was the pillar of *Amen,* the father of the gods. This was a phallic symbol for creative power, regeneration and sacrifice. It was erected in about 3000 BC at the centre of a temple at Anu or On. The stone pillar was capped by a pyramid-shaped meteorite: the *benben.* The *bennu* was the bird of rebirth, regeneration and calendrical cycles. The Greeks called it the *pheonix* and it was said to rise out of its ashes. During the Ptolemaic period On was known as Heliopolis: city of the Sun.

The sandstone pyramids at Giza were once faced with white limestone. They were capped by gilded pyramidions to catch the first and last rays. They were aligned with, so represented, the Stars, the Sun and the Moon. Reflections and shadows of the pyramids could be seen from far away. They not only gave the time of day but they also marked the equinoxes. The Great Pyramid was built precisely in line with the cardinal points. It was built, by well-paid craftsmen, where the Kingdoms of Upper and Lower Egypt met and so symbolized the power of their United Kingdom. It has no inscriptions inside but its builders were able to read and write, tell the age, the date and the time and measure its geographic position.

The points of the obelisks were also pyramidian shaped and gilded. They were erected after the pyramid era in the 18th and 19th dynasties when the centre of Egyptian civilization moved up the Nile to Thebes. Obelisks were quarried as single stones weighing hundreds of tonnes. Usually carved from granite at Aswan, then shipped down the Nile, they were often erected in pairs at the entrance to a Sun-god temple. An inscription on one dedicated to Pharaoh Seti I at Karnak in about 1300 BC shows that there were ten variable daylight hours between Sunrise and Sunset, when the Sun's disc was visible upon the horizon, plus another two variable twilight hours in the morning and evening. The twelve night hours were measured by observing the *decan* Stars. They also divided the whole day into 1,000 parts by feeling their pulse and they probably discovered the regular period of a free pendulum.

The Greek astronomer and philosopher Anaximander (610-545 BC) who is believed to have introduced Sun-clocks to Ionia, suggested that We are descended from fish and that the Earth is the centre of the Universe. Greek Sun-clocks were divided into six hours before and six after noon. A pin that casts a shadow is a gnomon, from γνωμων 'one who knows'.

Sky Clocks

Obelisks evolved into symbols of religious, political and economic power. Many were taken as trophies of war and erected in some distant land. Some were used as war memorials, battle monuments or ornaments at stately homes and a few of them are still used as Sun-clock gnomons. Augustus took one, dedicated to Seti I, from Heliopolis to Rome in 10 BC to prove that Anthony and Cleopatra were dead and Egypt was Roman. The one now at the centre of St. Peter's Square was brought to Rome in 40 AD by Caligula, erected at the centre of the Vatican Circus and then crowned with a bronze ball, said to contain the ashes of Julius Caesar. St. Peter was believed to have been crucified by Nero near this obelisk. It was moved to its present site in 1588 AD by Pope Sixtus V who exorcised it, consecrated it and then crowned it with a golden crucifix. The ball was empty but is now said to hold a fragment of the true cross. Hence, a Pagan Sun-clock lies at the very centre of Roman-Catholicism.

The Dikilitas obelisk was commissioned in 1500 BC by Thothmosis III. This 800 tonne Sun-clock was erected in Thebes and commemorated his expedition to Syria and his army's crossing of the River Euphrates. It was removed by Constantine the Great in the fourth century AD and was later erected in his honour in the hippodrome of Constantinople by Theodosius the Great (346 -395 AD) who banned all forms of Pagan cult. The Laterno obelisk, also made for Thothmosis III, was given to Rome in 357 AD by Constantine to signify that the centre of Christendom had moved from Alexandria to Rome and it still acts as a Sun-clock gnomon. Napoleon Bonaparte invaded Egypt in 1798 AD and took many trophies. One of a pair of obelisks to Ramesses II from the temple of Luxor now stands in the *Place de la Concorde* at the very centre of Paris. 'Cleopatra's Needles' were really made for Thothmosis III in 1475 BC, they stood in Heliopolis, were moved by Augustus to Alexandria in 12 BC and to London's Embankment and New York's Central Park in 1878 AD. London, Portsmouth, Glasgow and Dublin built obelisks and columns to Nelson's victories over Bonaparte at the Battles of the Nile and Trafalgar. Adolf Hitler planned to move Nelson's Column from London to Berlin.

The largest granite obelisk ever to be quarried weighed about 1200 tonne but cracked before it was finished and can still be seen at Aswan today. An obelisk at Axum in Ethiopia weighing 900 tonne it is said to have been quarried and erected using the power of the Ark of the Covenant. Another was captured by Mussolini in 1935 AD and erected in Rome. An obelisk at Mecca is believed by Sunni Muslims to represent *Satan.* Millions of pilgrims each throw 49 pebbles at it during the *Haj* festival. The Washington Monument is the World's largest stone obelisk at 555 ft. The CNTV Tower in Toronto is the World's tallest steel structure at 555 m. The World Trade Center is 1776 ft high to commemorate independence from Britain in 1776 AD and from the International Metric System.

Sun Clocks

Whilst the pyramids and obelisks were Sun-clocks, for astronomers to use and all to see, the Egyptians also used more portable Sun-clocks. Some were made from blocks of soapstone with notches in them and others were made from bronze with a horizontal scale and gnomon bar. They were turned, at midday, from facing the East to facing the West. The divisions were 1:2:3:4:5 digits wide to keep all the hours the same. The Egyptians worked ten variable hours between Sunrise and Sunset.

Late Roman Sun-clocks had a marble quarter sphere divided by thirteen vertical lines into the twelve daylight hours and three horizontal lines indicating the summer and winter solstices and both of the equinoxes. The shadow of the tip of the horizontal gnomon showed time and date. It was invented by the Babylonian astronomer Berosus in about 300 AD.

The Jews used staffs to tell them when to pray, seven times per day: 1 at first light, 2 when the Sun was on the horizon, 3 when the shadow was the same length as the staff, 4 when the Sun was overhead, 5 as number 3, 6 when the Sun was on the horizon, 7 at last light.

The Christians adopted the Jewish system at first but there were several different ways in which they divided-up daylight and said their prayers. A seventh century AD Celtic Sun-clock on Bewcastle Cross in Cumbria shows that there were then only four segments, which they called *tides*. This is probably the origin of both the English words: 'time' and 'tide'. An eleventh century AD Sun-clock on the Saxon church at Kirkdale in Yorkshire shows that daylight was by then divided into eight segments. The twelve-hour sundial did not come into common use in England until the arrival of the Normans, who considered that it measured holy time. Some churches use shafts of daylight to indicate the time and the date. Their East-West orientation captures and venerates light from the Sun.

The Muslims pray five times per day at dawn, dusk, noon and when the length of a shadow is the same length as the vertical staff casting it. Or, if they are near a mosque, they listen out for their muezzin's voice, now with an amplifier, praising *Allah* and calling them to prayer.

The Hindus only pray twice every day, before Sunrise and after Sunset. They were very accurate timekeepers, mathematicians and astronomers. Maharajah Jai Singh erected a 30m gnomon at Jaipur in 1728 AD. He used this to discover how the day varied during the tropical year.

The Tibetan Buddhists also used an accurate but portable Sun-clock. An octagonal time stick with eight scales was marked according to the location and month, then the shadow of a peg gave the time after dawn. Chinese Sun-clocks were used by the emperors but not by the people.

Sun Clocks

Yahweh, God or Allah is thought to be omnipotent and to live in Heaven. *He, She or It* was quintessentially a Sky-god, or a Sun-god or a Time-god. The Sun was considered to be a god in most religions and the ritual use of a Sun-clock to organize working was both spiritual and temporal. Although mechanical and electronic timepieces are now commonplace, some worshippers still use Sun-clocks to determine their times of prayer. Dawn, dusk, Sunrise, Sunset and midday are all auspicious moments. However, they depend upon the geographical position of the supplicant. Although the silent Sun-clock had less affect upon Our psyches than the noisy mechanical clock, Our body clocks are more affected by Natural light and darkness than by artificial light, hours, minutes and seconds. Sunrise and Sunset are still important times of the day for some of Us. Yet, artificial time and artificial light dominate the lives of the rest of Us. We have gradually become slaves to the little gizmos that We invented.

The English word: dial comes from the Latin word: *dias* meaning: day. Sun-dials could be considered to be more accurate than any modern clock because the lengths of the day and daylight vary during the year. Some later Sun-dials were designed to allow for seasonal variations. When used at higher latitudes the gnomon should be positioned at an angle to the scale and set tangentially to the Sun at noon or parallel with the Earth's axis, so the angle of each hour is then the same every day. If the timescale is marked on a metal band encircling the gnomon the divisions are equal and this style was popular in the sixteenth century AD. These were often made from bronze and are still sold at garden centres. Yet, they are usually imported and may have the wrong angle of gnomon.

Although Sun-clocks have not been discovered in the ruins of ancient cities in the Americas, the totem pole was probably a Sun-clock gnomon, as well as having many other mystic, esoteric or shamanistic meanings.

The depiction of the passage of time in paintings is a subject on its own. Hans Holbein the Younger was very interested in timekeeping and his masterpiece *The Ambassadors* is exhibited at London's National Gallery. Two French ambassadors to the court of Henry VIII are depicted with Sun-dials, calendars, celestial and terrestrial spheres and instruments. A skull can only be seen properly from an angle of 27 degrees and a partially hidden crucifix aligns with the same angle and viewpoint. This has been decoded to read 4 pm in London on Good Friday 1533 AD. The Sun was at the angle of 27 degrees above the horizon at that time. This was reckoned to be exactly 1500 years after the death of Christ. Some thought that this would herald The Apocalypse or The End of Time.

To celebrate the second Millennium AD the town of Gosport erected a Sun-dial, at great expense, a year late, in the shadow of a block of flats.

Water Clocks

Water-clocks were independent of daylight but had to be calibrated by Sun-clocks, so needed different scales for various parts of the Solar year. They were mostly used to time events, rather than the time of day. The earliest water-clocks were graduated pots made for water to run in. The later out-flowing type were tapered like a bucket so that the rate of flow remained constant when the pressure at the outlet hole changed. The Chinese used a floating bowl with a hole in it that sank on time.

The Egyptians were using water clocks by about 1400 BC and divided day or night into twelve variable hours, adjusted to their twelve months. A water-clock made for Amenhotep III is now in the Cairo Museum. On the outside it shows many celestial deities with their hieroglyphics. The Sun is shown as the god *Amen-Ra* and the Moon as the god *Thoth*. Venus is depicted as a *bennu* bird perched upon the hand of Orion-*Osiris*. He is standing in a Spaceship and so are Sirius-*Isis* and Jupiter-*Zeus*. Then come the celestial timekeepers: the thirty-six *Decan* Constellations. Next come the seven celestial genii, the gods of the four cardinal points, images of the circumpolar Constellations and gods of the ten-day *decade*. Finally, there are twelve demigods representing the calendar months.

The Babylonians were using water-clocks in 600 BC and they divided the complete day into twelve double-hours and sixty double-minutes. According to a baked clay tablet, which is now in the British Museum, their night and day double-hours were variable and were calibrated by measuring the amount of water that they poured into their *dibdibbu*. This allowed them to divide the night into three equal watches.

The Greeks called them: χλεπσψδραε, *clepsydrae* (water thief) and they used half-hour ones for timing speeches (attendants were often bribed). They regarded Time as a judge and their word for justice was: *themis*. They experimented with fixed-hour clocks and divided 24 hours into 60 firsts and 60 seconds, although they could not measure them accurately. The famous Greaco-Egyptian astronomer Ptolemy (90-168 AD) divided a complete day into four equal parts, or 24 equal hours or 360 *chronoi*. Thus one *chronus* was the equivalent of four of Our Cosmic minutes. He also divided each hour into 40 *momenta* equal to 90 Cosmic seconds. A type invented by Ctesibius of Alexandria in the third century BC had a tank with an overflow to give a constant flow through an orifice into a vessel with a float attached by a cord via a revolving dial to a weight. The first public *clepsydra* used in Rome was made in about 158 BC. Private ones were tended by slaves who called-out the time or rang bells. The Muslims developed some sophisticated water-clocks associated with fountains, where they washed their feet before entering their mosques. Two of them survive, in the courtyards of mosques, at Fez in Morocco. We still think of time flowing - but sometimes it seems to flow faster.

Sand Clocks

Sand has the advantage over water of not freezing in colder climates. Powdered eggshell was discovered to be very much better than any sand. Sandglasses were probably invented in China three thousand years ago. This is how the Chinese measured their twelve fixed-length double-hours or their ten watches when navigating their huge junks around the globe. They were used in Roman Times for timing the watches of the legions and they may also have been used to calculate their marching speeds. They were re-invented by a monk who revived the art of glass blowing at Chartres in the eighth century AD and were used for timing sermons. Charlemagne (742-814 AD) the first Holy Roman Emperor, constructed an enormous sand clock that ran for twelve hours.

Sand clocks came into prominence in the 14th Century AD and they were then used for timing bouts or jousts during the Age of Chivalry. King Henry VIII is known to have used them in his various palaces. His flagship *Mary Rose* sank in the waters of Spithead and was recently raised and displayed in Portsmouth Dockyard with many of its artifacts. These include an hourglass that was probably used for timing watches. They were hung so that they would not be effected by the ship's motion. They became highly treasured objects in the court of Queen Elizabeth I. Mary Queen of Scots used one with four glasses showing quarter hours. She lost her head for plotting to restore Roman-Catholicism.

Used with logs of wood attached to twine, they indicated water speed. Knots at seven fathom intervals were timed by a 28 second sandglass. Hence the nautical terms: 'log' and 'knot' for water distance and speed. Navigators used these logs with magnetic compasses for dead reckoning. Dr William Gilbert (1544-1603 AD) royal physician to Queen Elizabeth I devised the term 'electricity' and also discovered bipolar geomagnetism. His study of its direction, variation and declination improved navigation. Sir Francis Drake (1540-1596 AD) circumnavigated the globe in his ship *The Golden Hind,* sunk many Spanish ships in Cadiz harbor and under Lord Howard led the British fleet against the Spanish Armada in 1588 AD. Sir Walter Raleigh (1552-1618 AD) founded a colony he called: Virginia. He imported tobacco and potatoes but lost favour under James I and was sent to the Tower of London where he wrote his *History of the World.* He was released to lead an expedition but was beheaded after it failed.

Sandglasses are still sold for timing boiled eggs but are now rarely used. They became a symbol for Time and are used as icons in computers. However, they are also used in religious art as the symbol for death. The Egyptian Time-god *Heh,* alias the Babylonian Time-god *Anu,* alias the Greek Time-god *Kronos,* alias the Roman Time-god *Chronos,* alias *Old Father Time,* alias *The Grim Reaper,* alias *The Angel of Death* is often shown with an hourglass in one hand and a sickle in the other.

Combustion Clocks

Just as natural Sunlight or Moonlight formed the basis of religious belief so artificial light also became venerated and was sometimes worshipped. The Persians worshipped Natural gas fires, which still burn there today. This may be the origin of the biblical story of the burning bush.

The Egyptian artists who decorated the tombs in the Valley of the Kings used oil lamps in the pitch blackness with wicks lasting for five hours; and then another team would take over and work for another five hours. The Chinese used combustion clocks in which their twelve double-hours were roughly measured by the time taken to burn a stick of incense or through parts of a maze of grooves containing the powdered kind. The type of incense was varied so that the time could even be smelled. The sense of hearing was also used to tell the time with gongs and bells. Metal balls threaded onto a smoldering fuse would drop onto a metal plate at fixed intervals and thus its length and the time were related. The Romans used candles made of beeswax, with wicks made from flax. Roman candles of about one inch diameter were marked with iron nails, inserted every inch, which dropped onto a metal plate to sound the hour.

A seven-branched candlestick, the *menorah,* is the symbol of Judaism. It symbolizes the Mystic seven-day week and the Mystic seven-part day. The golden *menorah* was kept in the Holy of Holies inside the Temple. This was also the resting place the Ark of the Covenant, which was illuminated by the Sun at dawn on the vernal and autumnal equinoxes. On these important Solar dates the temporal and spiritual years began. King Solomon was believed to have added another ten candlesticks, which were stolen when the leaders were taken as captives to Babylon. Candlesticks found in synagogues do not have seven candles but some other number because the Temple was considered to be holy and unique. The *hanukkah* has eight candles and is used to celebrate an eight-day light festival which commemorates Judas Maccabea's re-consecration of the Temple after its desecration by the Greek dynasty of the Seleucids. This festival usually runs from 15-23 December, so precedes Christmas. The Roman occupation of the Temple led to the beginning of Christianity. Although Romans fought against it for three centuries they eventually used it to subjugate the masses, who were then forced to attend Mass. They thought that group worship was stronger than individual prayer. The Rule of St. Benedict (5th century AD) told monks what to do when. They prayed together seven times during daylight at the canonical hours, when the monastery bell was rung, and once during the night for vigil. The ritual of lighting candles is still part of the Roman-Catholic religion.

It was customary to fire a cannon at noon from every castle in Britain. This could be accomplished, automatically, by using a magnifying glass. The by-laws said that no food or drink could be served until after noon.

Combustion Clocks

The Gnostic Christians usurped many of the ancient Egyptian temples. However, the soot from their oil lamps still blackens the temple ceilings. Waking during the night to say prayers became part of monastic life. Evensong only became a Christian tradition because of candle light and a striking feature of Eastern Orthodox churches is the hanging oil lamps. Islam is still spreading by the use of brightly coloured fluorescent lights that attract nocturnal worshippers to mosques - like moths to flames.

According to legend, Alfred the Great, King of Wessex, who united the Anglo-Saxons, vowed, when a fugitive from the Danes in 878 AD, that he would spend a third of his life in God's service if his crown was restored. When it was restored he then used candles that burned for eight hours. This is supposed to be the origin of the normal working rhythm of eight hours for sleep, eight hours for work and eight hours for what-you-will. The Venerable Bede used candle clocks marked with 24 equal *horae*, 1/5 *horae* called: *puncta* and 1/12 *puncta* called: *ostenta* or *minuta*. The Latin word: *puncta* is the origin of the English word: punctuality.

Charles V (1500-1558 AD) succeeded his grandfather Maximillian I to become the Habsburg ruler, Holy Roman Emperor and, as the heir to the joint rulers: Ferdinand and Isabella, he also became the King of Spain. He practically held the Pope prisoner and controlled spiritual England through Cardinal Wolsey (1472-1530 AD) but refused to let Henry VIII (1491-1597 AD) divorce his aunt: Catherine of Aragon, and that led to the dissolution of the monasteries and the start of the Anglican faith. Charles V's rivalry with Francis I of France led to a war, he crushed a peasant revolt in 1525 AD and after a long struggle with the Lutherans in Germany, finally settled in 1555 AD, he then retired to a monastery. He used candles to divide his day into four equal parts and this rhythm continued in hot countries long after mechanical clocks were invented. The use of IIII instead of IV on clock dials is attributed to Charles V.

Our obsession with changing night to day slaughtered millions of whales, which were then rendered down to make wax for candles and lamp oil. Oil lamps with graduated glass containers were used as combustion clocks during the eighteenth century AD, so they had a dual purpose. The petroleum industry grew rapidly on the sale of lamp oil during the latter half of the nineteenth century AD and in the twentieth century AD. The inventions of Otto and Diesel turned an industry into a bonanza. Artificial light helped people to extend the length of their working day. This change to working habits started with candles and oil lamps, was greatly accelerated by gaslight and has been completed by electricity. However, Our body-clocks still tell Us to only work during daylight. Our so-called: daylight saving measures do not save any daylight at all. We waste a great deal of expensive energy trying to turn night into day.

Astrolabe Clocks

The Greeks were the first to use astrolabes (αστρωλαβου) and they were developed by the Arabs for orientation, astronomy and timekeeping. They work on the principle of stereographic projection, which allows the three-dimensional celestial sphere, representing the Sky, to be engraved upon a silver, bronze or brass disc marked with a grid of curved lines. By using Sun or Moon sights the user could find the time of day or night. If date and time were known, the user could find a position or bearing. Texts from Baghdad and Damascus indicate that astrolabes were widely used by the 8th century AD and then became databanks or computers. Islam developed astronomy, trigonometry, algebra, algorithms, alchemy. The caliph Abdallah al-Mamun built observatories in the 9th century AD. He drew a map of the World, measured the inclination of the ecliptic to be 23⁰ 33' and he estimated the girth of the Earth to be 20,400 miles. Astrolabes were used by Muslims to find the *qibla* (direction of Mecca). Some Islamic prayer mats have magnetic compasses woven into them. Instead of using a rose or 360 degrees some of them used 400 gradians. A right angle could be divided into 100 gradians rather than 90 degrees.

The Moors occupied Iberia for 700 years and built palaces, mosques, libraries and universities before they were expelled by Roman-Catholics. The Spanish Inquisition razed their mosques and burned all their books. However, some advanced Moorish technology found its way to Europe. Their fine architecture has survived in Granada, Seville and Cordoba. This often incorporates verses from the *Koran* carved into its structure. Astrolabes were introduced into France by a scholar named Fulbert who taught at Chartres Cathedral from 990 to 1028 AD and became bishop. Both the Arab and Latin astronomers in the Middle Ages called it their mathematical jewel and Chaucer described one in the 14th century AD. They were reintroduced to Europe when Constantinople fell to the Turks.

Astrolabes developed into circular calculators or logarithmic slide-rules. A circular calculator, called an equatorium, for predicting Lunar or Solar eclipses was made in 1600 AD and is now in the Liverpool Museum. Its databank and calibration ominously ran out in the year 2000 AD. Logarithms and decimal points were invented by John Napier in 1614 AD. Slide-rules were invented by Robert Bissaker in 1654 AD but others, including James Watt and Matthew Boulton, who invented steam engines from about 1779 AD, developed them and some engineers still use them. Muslims once used astrolabes, maps and compasses to find the direction of Mecca but they can now use an instrument known as a Mecca-meter. It computes the direction of Mecca and it is also a calendar and clock. Digital pocket calculators are descendents of the arithmetic machine devised by Blaise Pascal in 1642 AD and were sold in about 1975 AD. Pocket calculators could incorporate the age, date and time if they were globalized, digitized, decimalized as part of a **Worldwide Time System**.

Sextant Clocks

A cross-staff was a crude device for measuring angles between objects. Using trigonometry it could measure the heights of buildings or Stars. It was just accurate enough for determining latitude but not longitude. These evolved into circles, semicircles, quadrants, sextants and octants. A Portuguese mathematician/cosmologist Pedro Nunez (1502-1578 AD) invented the *nonius* which enabled fractions of degrees to be measured. The French military engineer Pierre Vernier (1584-1638 AD) devised a scale reading improvement which lead to more accurate measurements. John Hadley (1682-1744 AD) vice-president of the Royal Society, devised a swinging arm reflector so that both objects appeared in the viewfinder.

The telescope was not only useful during the day for finding sea marks but also at night for using the moons of Jupiter like a celestial clock. Whilst Galileo Galiei was credited with its invention four centuries ago, and was said to be the first to see Jupiter's moons and Saturn's ring, it was predicted by friar Roger Bacon who made lenses in about 1370 AD. The first microscope was probably made by the Dutch father and son Hans & Zacharies Janssen and the first telescope was probably made by the English father and son Leonard & Thomas Digges in about 1590 AD. The third Astronomer-Royal James Bradley (1693-1762) installed an eight-foot telescope, made by John Bird, at the Greenwich Observatory. He discovered the aberration of light, a periodic change in the apparent position of a Star caused by the movement of the Earth around the Sun. He used this phenomenon to make a close estimate of the speed of light. He found that the Earth wobbles on its axis due to the pull of the Moon. When the French and the British embarked on their great joint project to measure the exact distance between their Royal Observatories they used Bradley's Prime Meridian and this is still used by the Ordnance Survey.

By measuring the angle between the Sun and the Moon and knowing the date and the approximate time it is possible to calculate one's longitude. This was the only way of doing so before chronometers were developed. To save time and error, tables were published and these were still used long after accurate marine chronometers became generally available. To determine longitude to an accuracy of about one degree by the Lunar distance method required an accuracy of at least two minutes of arc. Astronomical navigation tables are still printed in nautical almanacs. Sextants are still used as a backup to electronic navigation equipment but this is now so accurate and reliable that they are very rarely needed.

The Navel of Our Planet Earth currently lies at **000N 000S 000E 000W.** This chart plot is not a landmark because it lies in the Atlantic Ocean. It is defined by four groups of three digits but each group of 360 degrees were divided by 60 arc-minutes and 60 arc-seconds - not by decimals. However, *Google Earth* and *Satnav* are based upon decimals of a degree.

Geared Clocks

Gears were probably invented by Archimedes of Syracuse (287 - 212 BC).
He may have designed the first geared clock and analogue computer.
A mechanism with thirty bronze gearwheels was found by sponge divers
in a Roman wreck near the Greek island of Antikythera in 1901 AD.
It incorporated the Greek Corinthian calendar and the Moon's phases,
the movement of the Sun, Moon and five Planets through the zodiac
and it also incorporated the Metonic ratio of 19 years to 235 moonths.
It allowed Solar and Lunar eclipses to be predicted with great accuracy.
And it also indicated the four year cycle of the Panhellenic Games.
The Tower of the Winds in the agora of Athens was erected in 50 BC.
It was designed and built by Andronicus of Kyrrhos and still stands.
The octagonal tower had eight sun-clocks, a vane pointing to eight winds
plus a water powered and geared astronomical clock, which simulated the
presumed motions of the *Seven Heavenly Bodies* around the Earth.

The Muslims developed water powered geared clocks with automatons
in about 900 AD and this, eventually, led to the striker and the bell.
Charlemagne owned one, which dropped a ball into a bowl every hour.
A treatise by Yazari in 1206 AD shows a geared water clock which had a
dial showing signs of the zodiac, figures which successively appeared,
lamps which successively illuminated, golden balls which dropped into
brazen cups held by brazen falcons and an automation orchestra with
five instruments showing that music and rhythm is related to time.
Whilst Islam, in recent years, seemed to turn against all progress the
Muslim school of science, at Haran, was centuries ahead of the West.
Albatanius calculated the distance to the Moon and Jabir bin Hayyan
suggested that if an atom could be split it would release great energy.
Much of their advanced technology was destroyed by the Crusaders.

The Chinese astronomers were probably the first to use decimal time.
Their astronomical days were divided into 96 then 100 units called *k'e*.
However, for other purposes they also used a duodecimal time system.
The Emperor wanted to keep a record of the very moment of conception,
for astrological reasons, when consorting with his wives and concubines.
Chinese Buddhists made water clocks with escapement mechanisms,
which were invented by I-Hsing together with Liang Ling-Tsan in 723 AD.
A great astronomical clock was erected by the mandarin, Su Sung at the
Imperial Palace in Khaifeng and this was used from 1088 to 1092 AD.
A great water wheel rotated a celestial globe and an armillary sphere.
It also operated a series of 96 jacks which indicated the time of the day.
12 *shi* (double-hours) x 8 = 96 *k'e* which were later divided into 60 *fen*.
Su Sung's clock did not lead to the development of others and was
forgotten until it was rediscovered by British historians in 1950 AD.
Mechanical clocks were re-introduced to China from the West by the
Jesuit missionary Father Matteo Ricci during the 17th century AD.

Astronomical Clocks

Attempts to build models of the Solar System probably began with a water powered clock with a dial, made by Archimedes in about 210 BC. The 24-hour dial revolved like a wheel but the hand remained fixed. The Romans had very little interest in either astronomy or timekeeping. However, the idea persisted in Arabia and the Muslims probably taught Spanish monks about their astronomical clocks and timekeepers.

Astronomical clocks developed into working models of the Solar System. They were fairly well developed by the 14th century AD and many embodied 24-hour or double 12-hour dials, zodiacs and Lunar phases. They were called *horologiums* and one is still working at Hampton Court. However, they were incorrectly based upon Ptolemy's geocentric views. An accurate planetarium could not be constructed until Galileo proved, four centuries ago, that the Sun was at the centre of the Solar System. A range of devices were then constructed including: orreries (Planetary machines) Lunaria (Moon) Jovilabes (Jupiter) Saturilabes (Saturn) Telluria (modelling the motion of the Earth and Moon about the Sun) cometaria (comets) volvelles (tides) and armilliary spheres (everything).

In the early hours of Sunday 8 May 1774 AD, Mercury, Venus, Mars and Jupiter appeared together with the Moon under the sign of Aries. This inspired Eise Eisinga to build a remarkable planetarium in his house in Telinga, Holland and his planetary system is mounted on the ceiling of his living-room - so his house is both a computer and a clock.

One of the most complex astronomical clocks is in Strasbourg Cathedral. This is a planetarium, clock, calendar, chronograph and an ephemeris. Completed in 1842 AD, it displays Solar, mean Solar and Sidereal times, the times of Sunset and Sunrise and the position and phase of the Moon. It takes into account leap years and the 400 year Gregorian correction. It shows the date of Easter, all movable feasts, fixed feasts, the names of the saints associated with each day and the Dominical Letter of the year. It predicts Solar and Lunar eclipses and allows for equinox precession. A procession of Pagan Sky-gods represent the seven days of the week. The twelve apostles appear at noon, because Time and *God* are related. Astronomical clocks attract many tourists as they chime at every hour in Venice, Vienna, Prague, Dubrovnik, Berne, Saltsburg and other cities.

The modern day equivalent of an astronomical clock is a planetarium. The London Planetarium, built in 1958 AD, attracted about 600,000 visitors a year and is owned by the Pearson Group whose old head office has an *horologium*, with the face of Sir Winston Churchill in the centre, mounted above the entrance, which is opposite St. Paul's Cathedral. Another planetarium has been built at the Greenwich Observatory, now a museum dedicated to the measurement of Time and Space.

Monastery Clocks

Western temporal organization can be traced back to the fifth century AD. Time was considered to be sacrosanct and so should never be wasted. Everything the monks did was regulated by the Rule of St. Benedict who founded a great monastery/fortress at Monte Cassino and eleven others. At the sound of a bell the monks would all do something different. Working became an hourly, daily, weekly, monthly and yearly ritual:

All things must be done at designated hours... Idleness is the enemy of the soul...
From Easter to October the brothers shall labour from prime to the fourth hour...
From the fourth hour until the sixth hour the brothers should read...
From Easter to Pentecost they shall dine at the sixth hour and sup at night...
From Pentecost they should fast until the ninth hour on Wednesdays and Fridays...
From September 14th until Lent dinner will be at the ninth hour....
After dinner the brothers should rest in silence and prayer...
Upon hearing the signal for the Divine Office all work must cease.

Gravity clocks were introduced to monasteries by the Catholic Church. The first gravity powered clocks were developed in Spain in 1278 AD. The first English gravity clock was used in Dunstable Priory in 1283 AD. The seven daily prayer ritual was changed and the variable hours fixed:

4 bells at first light		Matins or Lauds
3 at Sunrise	moved to daylight hour 1	Hora Prima
2 at mid-morning	moved to daylight hour 3	Hora Tertia
1 at noon	moved to daylight hour 6	Hora Sexta or Meridies
2 at mid-afternoon	moved to daylight hour 9	Hora Nona
3 at Sunset	moved to daylight hour 11	Vespers or Hora Vesperalis
4 at nightfall		Complene or Hora Completorium

The word: noon is derived from *nona* which was set back by three hours after dials were invented by Jacopo de Dondi of Chioggia in 1344 AD. He built many clocks and was the first person to be called an horologist. His dials were usually twenty-four hour full-day ones, with no chimes. It was more logical to move the start of the day to midday so that the highest point of the Sun corresponded with the highest point on the dial. Some people still believe that noon and midday are the same thing. We still use the Latin terms: *anti-meridian* or *post-meridian* (a.m. or p.m.) If a clock does not ring a bell or chime it is, strictly speaking, a timepiece.

Monasteries were once responsible for temporal and spiritual education. In England they owned one third of the land and much of the wealth. The monks and nuns ate very well; whilst the peasants were starving. When Pope Clement VII refused to grant King Henry VIII a divorce he dissolved the monasteries and founded Anglican universities at Oxford and Cambridge, based upon similar temporal and spiritual principles. They continued to teach Latin and used Roman numerals for arithmetic. Yet, they did not admit Catholics nor, later on, Quakers and Methodists. Protestant education became based on fixed hourly lessons and lectures. However, in some monasteries remaining in Roman-Catholic countries, the variable canonical hours were used until the nineteenth century AD.

Cathedral Clocks

The Book of Hours had many forms throughout medieval Europe and illustrated the work that should be done during each month and hour. From being a strict monastic discipline, time became a fad of the people. Until then the Sun's calendar and clock and the Moon's phases and tides had ruled their lives but now a Man-made device gradually took over. Cathedrals were the focal points of the burgeoning cities as industry and commerce developed, in addition to traditional agriculture and fishing. They represented the finest architecture, arts and crafts of their era.

Roger Stoke built a tower clock for Norwich Cathedral in about 1320 AD. Richard of Wallingford, an astronomical clock for St Albans in 1330 AD. The oldest surviving gravity clock in the World, dating from 1386 AD, still stands in Salisbury Cathedral and it was made by Johannes Lietuijt, a Dutchman, who was invited to England by King Edward III in 1368 AD. The Salisbury clock struck a bell and it worked for about five centuries. Its iron framework was held together, like a wooden one, without bolts. The vital innovation was its verge escapement, which kept it regular. When this was completed, Ralph Erghum was the Bishop of Salisbury. He moved to Bath and Wells, where the second oldest clock survives. The Wells Cathedral clock was made by John Lietuyt of Delft in 1392 AD. It has a double-XII-hour dial inside and a simple XII-hour dial outside. It shows the day of the month plus the phase and position of the Moon. It was modified many times as the technology of clock making advanced. By the end of the 15th century AD it was also striking the quarter hours. It has two jacks that strike a bell and knights that joust every quarter. A sixty minute dial and hand were added in the late 16th century AD. It is still working but an electric winding motor was added in 2010 AD.

Cardinal Wolsey's clock at Hampton Court had a double-XII hour dial, a calendar and a zodiac because it was used for astronomical purposes. It also showed, and still shows, the Moon's phases and tides in London. Hampton Court and its great clock was confiscated by King Henry VIII. He preferred the XII-hour dial and it became the norm in Protestant England whilst the double-XII hour dial continued in Catholic Europe. At the start of King Henry VIII's reign most clockmakers came from other parts of Europe but by the end of the Tudor dynasty both London and Geneva had become great centres of horology and they remain so today. This was due to greater freedom to trade that came with Protestantism. Protestants preferred Arabic numbers; Catholics used Roman numerals.

The 12-hour half-day clock eventually won the battle - but not the war - for the 24-hour full-day clock is back again - but only in digital form. The clock still rules Our lives with exactly the same divisions of time that were devised by the Greek astronomers over two millennia ago. Very few people have dared to question the divisions of *God's* own time.

Church Clocks

Churches were built in every village, town and city, their bells could be heard for many miles and they were believed to keep evil spirits away. In fact, they were a very effective method for calling the faithful to prayer. The ritual of bell-ringing developed into the art/science of campanology. A tower of 3 to 12 bells are rung in a non-repetitive sequence or method. A peal is a complete sequence, which can take three hours to complete. It is used for special occasions such as a royal wedding or a coronation.

The hourly ringing of the church bell was the responsibility of the verger but he was gradually replaced by the clock with its verge escapement. The Church was largely responsible for the development of clockwork and the keeping of good time for the spiritual and temporal community. As well as a visible indication of the time, they gave an audible one too. They rang an hour bell the appropriate number of times, usually rang the quarters and sometimes played a tune at noon or at every hour. The XII-hour clock with its falling weight, swinging pendulum, moving hands and ringing bells made everyone conscious of the passage of time. A XXIV-hour chime would have been very noisy and difficult to count.

The oldest church clock in England is at the Cinque Port of Rye, Sussex. Presented by Queen Elizabeth I it has a XII-hour half-day dial, two jacks that strike bells and a long pendulum, which swings across the nave. This was fitted later and made the church clocks much more accurate. The pendulum was invented by Galileo in 1583 AD and the first clocks to be fitted with them were developed by Christiaan Huygens in 1657 AD. Most English churches have XII-hour clocks on their towers or spires and they have gradually become an integral part of church architecture. Until they became more accurate and reliable, clocks needed to be reset every day at noon so that their hands pointed to the Sun at its zenith. Many believe in this ritual, although it was superseded by time zones. Since these were introduced, noon and midday are no longer the same.

The desire for regularity and punctuality was an act of faith in *God*. The Church was in control of every day, every hour and every minute. Attendance at church services on Sundays was sometimes compulsory and those who did not attend were ostracized or they were branded as heretics. The trade union movement was organized into chapels and members were expected to work to fixed hours and to attend a church on Sundays. British working time was remunerated at normal rates during weekdays, time-and-a-half for overtime and on Saturdays, double-time on Sundays.

The Christian World is governed by chronologies, calendars and clocks. However, various sects use different systems and this causes conflicts. Indeed, every religion still has its own age, date, time and maybe zone. If everyone used the same Time, Our World would be a much happier place.

Town Clocks

As industrialization developed, timekeeping became more important and so it was necessary for there to be more clocks than those on churches. A battle ensued between church and state about the ownership of time. A cacophony of bells were regularly heard as different hours were rung. A great deal of parliamentary time was, and still is, wasted on this issue. Lords spiritual and temporal passed laws on the measurement of time. Each city or town council became responsible for purchasing and setting the clocks in its borough and passing by-laws about working hours. Town Halls usually had large gilt clocks built into their architecture. Clockmakers had to be mobile in order to install their timepieces in different towns, until they were able to standardize their designs, open permanent workshops and have them installed by travelling specialists. The method of manufacture changed from a blacksmith's craft to an industry using mostly brass and precision machines for making parts.

The driving force behind the Industrial Revolution was the mechanical clock, which gradually became more accurate and reliable and most industries became centered on towns with public transport systems. Each town, punctiliously, kept to its own time, based upon a sundial and so noon time varied throughout the land from the East to the West. A new national law had to be passed following a famous test case in Dorchester where the plaintiff turned-up late, according to the judge's London time pocket watch, but on time, according to the town clock. So Greenwich Mean Time was legalized throughout Britain in 1880 AD.

Most states decided to institute national time based on their capital city. This was imperative because of increasing mobility due to the railways and instantaneous communications provided by the electric telegraphs. Indeed, telegraphs were the means by which clocks were synchronized. This was still an expensive manual operation, so subject to human error. Therefore various means were developed to synchronize many clocks. As the automatic synchronization of town clocks became more important the Swiss clockmakers were at the cutting edge of this new technology. There are now many ways of synchronizing clocks and it is perfectly feasible to adjust every clock on Earth to read exactly the same time.

Some people still argue that midday and 12 o'clock or noon should be the same because they say that Sundials are more accurate than clocks. Yet, imagine the chaos that would ensue if they were still used today. A few people still cling on to ancient systems in this postmodern World. Oxford and Cambridge Universities are still steeped in ancient traditions. Christ Church College, 50 miles west of Greenwich, still sets its clocks to five minutes two seconds behind GMT and this is known as Oxford time. At the Millennium, Ramsgate set its clock six minutes ahead of London and claimed that it was the first town in England to celebrate MM.

Public Clocks

As timekeeping became important, clocks were erected in public places and became architectural features on town halls, banks and post offices. As soon as there were enough public clocks, the banks began to work to stricter hours and this was soon followed by offices and shops. Laws were passed limiting the opening hours of all shops, public houses and wine merchants and it became the norm for offices to work from 9:00 AM to 5:00 PM and for factories to work from 8:00 AM to 5:00 PM. Each town passed its own by-laws about early closing on one week-day. Up to 1950 AD all shops closed on Saturday afternoons and on Sundays. Many women now work, so can only shop at weekends or in the evenings and so many by-laws on shop opening times are gradually being relaxed. Some banks now open on Saturdays to compete with building societies.

As the demand increased, clockmakers began to divide their labour into specialist gear makers, pendulum makers, dial makers, case makers or hole drillers, whilst their machinery became faster and more accurate. Because clocks were often dismantled, machine screws were developed and this idea had a huge impact on the development of engineering. The Clerkenwell district of London became a hive of small workshops, some specializing in making one type of part for several clockmakers. The Clockmakers Guild was formed in 1631 AD to create a monopoly and keep out foreign competition, which helped the industry to expand during its formative years and many patents were filed to protect ideas. A five shilling duty on clocks, imposed by Act of Parliament, introduced by William Pitt the Younger in 1797 AD, almost killed the clock industry. He was the prime minister who rejected the French Metric System.

It was a problem to ensure that all public clocks showed the same time. Mains electricity and the synchronous motor enabled public clocks to be installed and forgotten, until there was a power cut or they wore out. A number of public clocks are now digital and some show seconds. They might show for example: 21:54.36 which is an incorrect use of the decimal point because the clock only counts up to 59 - not up to 99.

Now that most people wear watches, carry mobile phones and laptops or have clocks in their cars, the public clocks are gradually dying out. Banks are now open-all-hours, because they all have cash dispensers. Many goods can now be dispensed by machine at any time of the day. On-line shopping and banking can take place at any time on any day. The motor car has had a great effect on retailing so most service stations open every day and many of the larger ones are open round-the-clock. They sell many kinds of goods as well as those related to motoring. Hypermarkets often have service stations that are open round-the-clock. Pubs and clubs can apply for a license to open-all-hours on any day. So opening and closing times do not need to be regulated any more.

Monumental Clocks

The Palace of Westminster stood for a millennium by the river Thames, and it always had a tower with a Sun-dial and/or a mechanical clock, but in 1834 AD it burnt down, with its standard weights and measures. A new building was designed by Sir Charles Barry and Augustus Pugin, who regarded all Gothic architecture as Christian; all Classic as Pagan. Pugin decended into madness and death after completing the design. They worked under the direction of Prince Albert of Saxe-Coburg-Gotha, who was the prince-consort of the empress, Queen Victoria of Hanover. Its monumental clock tower, with four faces, is surmounted by a cross, and so it is a symbol that Great Britain and its Empire are Christian. Its illuminated faces with Roman numerals can be read from a mile away. Edmund Denison, a barrister who later became the Baron Grimthorpe, appointed Edward Dent to design its extremely accurate mechanism. Big Ben, its hourly bell, rings twelve times when the Sun is overhead and its quarterly and hourly chimes were based upon Handel's *Messiah*. Since 1859 AD it has displayed Greenwich Mean Time, then Coordinated Universal Time or British Summer Time to within one second per day. Until 1913 AD it took about thirty man-hours every week to wind the mechanism but this is now achieved with the aid of an electric motor. This 315ft tall structure, now renamed: The Queen Elizabeth Tower, is leaning, the clock has stopped and Parliament will soon be closed. It could be replaced by a circular forum and a **decimal time** clocktower.

Muslims pray in the direction of the *Kaaba* in Mecca five times every day. This ancient monument is almost cubic and is faced with black granite. It is covered by black silk drapes and houses a sacred black meteorite in one corner, which is ritually kissed to bring the supplicant good luck. Up to five million pilgrims visit it, during the holy moonth of Dhul-Hijjah, when they circumambulate it, seven times, in an anticlockwise direction. Poor pilgrims live in tents but rich ones stay in air-conditioned hotels. The Abraj Al-Bait Towers, known as the Mecca Royal Clock Tower Hotel, overlooks the *Kaaba* and is now the second tallest building in the World. It is 591m high, its total floor area is 1,500m², it can accommodate up to 100,000 people and its prayer room can hold up to 10,000 worshippers. The hotel complex has seven towers, 800 seven-star suites, two helipads, a shopping mall and a garage capable of parking up to 1,000 vehicles. The clock tower is surmounted by a spire with a golden crescent Moon. Its four illuminated clock faces are six times the diameter of Big Ben's. They have no numbers nor numerals and can be read from 10 Km away. Prayer times were once based upon the position or shadow of the Sun, which varied according to the latitude and longitude of the supplicant. Then they were broadcast from atop a minaret by the local muezzin. However, they are now based upon the hands of this monumental clock, which point upwards when the Sun is overhead and so Saudi Arabian or Sunni Muslim Time is not based upon GMT, BST nor UCT.

Domestic Clocks

Domestic clocks were first used in Royal Palaces and Stately Homes. Hampton Court, Windsor Castle and Nonsuch Palace used them first. Buckingham Palace currently has a collection of three hundred clocks. They need two servants to wind and adjust them and changing the hour from Greenwich Mean Time to Summer Time must take them all week. We are all now ruled by the incessant tick-tock of the omnipotent clock.

Christiaan Huygens, working with The Royal Society, designed and built the very first pendulum clocks, which measured seconds accurately and repeatability in 1657 AD but they could not be used in ships nor vehicles. So Huygens developed portable spring-driven clocks in the Netherlands. They were also developed by Robert Hooke (1635-1703 AD) in England. Hooke was a founder and curator of experiments at the Royal Society. The French were the first to reduce mechanical clocks to mantle size. The elite of the 17th century AD were very fond of their Rococo clocks. Pendulums were often decorated with the face of *Apollo* - god of Sunlight. The French clock-making industry was restricted by guilds and the state, so the quantity of clocks and watches they produced was quite small. Clock-making in London, Augsberg, Paris and Geneva continued to grow. In 1786 AD the Clockmaker's Company reported to the Board of Trade that they were exporting about 80,000 clocks and watches every year. The industrial revolution made clocks essential in every household. Long-case grandfather or grandmother clocks were popular in England. They would run for eight days, timed by the bell of the local church. The Sunday wind-up ritual was the basis of the Protestant work ethic, which is considered to be stronger than the Roman-Catholic one.

Electricity overcame the need to regularly wind and synchronize clocks. The first electric clocks were invented by Alexander Bain in 1840 AD. In Britain they were synchronized by a frequency of 50 cycles/second. Frequent power cuts made it essential to own a mechanical clock too. The electronic revolution has brought clocks down to a commonplace position so that everyone in industrialized countries can afford several. Bell's invention of the telephone allowed all clocks to be synchronized. Marconi's invention of radio led to the global synchronization of time. The first signal was transmitted from the Eiffel Tower on 1 July 1913 AD. The global six-pip time signal, based upon Big Ben, began in 1924 AD. Radio and TV brought accurate and reliable timekeeping to every home. We can now buy inexpensive clocks and watches that are regularly adjusted by radio and changed to and from Summer Time remotely. The dominant position of Swiss and British clock and watch makers was lost after the electronic revolution and the dropping of trade barriers. The majority of clocks and watches sold today are battery powered. Yet, mobile phones, tablets, laptops and desktops all now incorporate the age, date and time, so the need to own a clock or a watch is fading.

Portable Clocks

In about 1500 AD Peter Henlein, a German locksmith, began to make small, spring-powered clocks, which were the first portable timepieces. Carriage clocks, that were capable of being jolted and roughly handled, were adjusted to run faster or slower as they travelled East or West. In 1800 AD it took eight hours to travel from London to Portsmouth. However, there was also a much quicker relay of semaphore signals and pigeon post was another way of sending messages over long distances.

Napoleon Bonaparte understood the importance of precise timing in his military campaigns and so he used carriage clocks as effective weapons. The Iron Duke of Wellington (1768-1852 AD) finally defeated Bonaparte, after he had escaped from Elba, at the battle of Waterloo in 1815 AD. Public stagecoaches were the fastest way of travelling, unless you were very rich and owned your own fleet of carriages, like the Rothschilds. They doubled their money after the battle of Waterloo by dispatching a false message to the London Stock Exchange that Wellington had lost. They bought shares as they plummeted and then sold as they soared. Waterloo station was named after the great battle that stopped Europe from becoming united and adopting the digital-decimal Metric System.

Brunel's Great Western Railway ran to Greenwich Time and the clock in the Bristol Corn Exchange still has two hands set eleven minutes apart. Greater mobility due to the railways and better communications by electric telegraph made national time not only possible but also necessary. Steam railways and ferries became more and more reliable until it was possible to publish and display regular timetables for a year in advance. The cartographer George Bradshaw (1801-1853 AD) published his first timetable in 1839 AD and this was followed by 150 annual editions. These, eventually, covered the entire globe and also included ferries. The 1893 AD edition mentions that a traveller could theoretically travel around the globe by steam-ship and steam-train in about eighty days. It inspired *Around the World in 80 days* by Jules Verne (1825-1905 AD). His intrepid globetrotter Phineas Fogg wagered that he could achieve this but thought he had lost until he remembered that he had gained a day by crossing the International Date Line in the Pacific Ocean.

Circumnavigating the globe in less than 80 days became a challenge. In 1889 AD Nellie Bligh was the first person to establish this new record. In 1993 AD the French catamaran *Commodore Explorer* sailed around the World in under 80 days to win the Jules Verne Challenge Trophy. In 1998 AD the UK designed and built powerboat *Cable and Wireless* named after its sponsor, motored around the World in under 80 days. In 1999 AD the UK designed and built helium balloon *Breitling Orbiter 3* named after its sponsor, floated around the World in under 20 days. The International Space Station now orbits the globe every 90 minutes.

Sea Clocks

Despite using charts, pilots, compasses, logs, sandglasses and sextants, navigation was dangerous and so seriously inhibited the growth of trade. Latitude was measured from the elevation of the Pole Star or the Sun. Longitude was much more difficult because there was no reference point. After the restoration of the monarchy King Charles II established the Royal Society who appointed John Flamsteed (1646-1719 AD), a priest with a keen interest in astronomy, as the very first Astronomer Royal. A new observatory, designed by Sir Christopher Wren (1632-1723 AD), also an amateur astronomer, was built, under royal warrant, upon a hill overlooking the river Thames, within the grounds of Greenwich Palace. Flamsteed was not given the funding to buy instruments so had to give lectures to earn enough to purchase clocks, quadrants and telescopes. After many years of observation he compiled tables, using the Greenwich Meridian as a reference point, which allowed longitude to be calculated from observations of the angle between the Moon and certain Stars. Sir Isaac Newton, President of the Royal Society, put pressure on him to publish but, although 400 were printed, Flamsteed bought 300 back and burnt them, because he was not convinced that they were accurate.

It came to a head when Admiral Sir Clowdisley Shovell (1650-1707 AD) the Commander-in-Chief of the British Fleet, was lost with his ship *Association* off the Isles of Scilly due to inaccurate navigation in fog. The whole squadron struck rocks and 2,000 crewmen were drowned. On 8 July 1714 AD Queen Anne gave her royal assent to a bill for: Providing a Public Reward for Such Person as Shall Discover Longitude. Most of the experts thought that this was impossible with timepieces. They favoured positional tables for the Sun, Moon, Planets and Stars. However, due to the government's encouragement, portable clocks were gradually developed into accurate, robust and seaworthy chronometers.

The £20,000 Parliament prize at the request of The Board of Longitude was claimed by John Harrison in 1773 AD, after 50 years of hard work. Not only on his five chronometers but also in proving that they worked and in persuading the government to keep to their side of the bargain. The establishment of university professors, including Sir Isaac Newton, looked down on the northern cabinet maker and self-taught clockmaker. Indeed, his first very accurate timepieces were made entirely from wood. By perseverance and inventiveness he eventually solved each problem. His most widespread innovation was the bi-metal strip thermometer. Harrison won the coveted Copley Medal of the Royal Society in 1749 AD. He eventually had to enlist the help of King George III to claim his prize. His chronometers are now on show at the Royal Observatory Greenwich. They were restored to working order by Rupert Gould (1890-1948 AD) in the 20s and 30s and he wrote a book about marine chronometers. A memorial to Harrison was unveiled at Westminster Abbey in 2006 AD.

Sea Clocks

John Harrison's first brass chronometer H1 was the size of a large clock but his last development H5 resembled a very large gold pocket watch. Captain James Cook embarked on a voyage in 1761 AD to observe the transit of Venus past the Sun from Tahiti and drew accurate charts, which are still in use today, then claimed new territories for the Empire. He used Neville Maskelyne's, (5th Astronomer Royal), *Nautical Almanac* to find longitude by the Lunar-distance method, however, on his second voyage Cook used a replica Harrison H4 chronometer to find longitude. On his third global voyage he was killed by hostile natives in Hawaii. Captain William Bligh used one in 1787 AD on his expedition to Tahiti in *The Bounty* but this was stolen by the mutineer Fletcher Christian. Robert Fitzroy (1805-1865 AD) used chronometers and kept records of their accuracy on his voyages with Charles Darwin (1809-1882 AD). During voyages in *The Beagle* Fitzroy made charts of South America and measured the air pressure, which led to the new science of meteorology. Fitzroy established a meteorological office in London and his forecasts saved many lives but when the Admiralty closed it he committed suicide. Although the Dutch were leaders in the art and science of cartography during the 17th century, based upon a zero meridian in mid-Atlantic, the Greenwich one was officially recognized for navigation in 1883 AD. A year later it also became the World Standard reference for timekeeping. One degree of longitude was now equivalent to four minutes of GMT. Navigation at sea was also improved by using lighthouses and buoys, now unified by the International Association of Lighthouse Authorities. The International Maritime Organization is part of the United Nations and is based in London, not far from Greenwich and the Prime Meridian.

It was Pierre Le Roy in Paris and rival British watchmakers John Arnold and Thomas Earnshaw who improved upon the principles established by Harrison and eventually put chronometers into production by 1800 AD. The Royal Navy took many years to, grudgingly, adopt them and many other captains could not afford them until they became much cheaper. The Swiss capitalized on this invention, which changed the World, and they became the World's leading, high quality, clock and watch makers. *Omega* made the first chronometer small enough to wear on the wrist. It was accurate enough for astronauts on the Moon but chronometers are now obsolete due to atomic clocks and electronic navigation aids. The US Global Positioning System, used since geo-stationary satellites were deployed in 1972 and 1984 AD, has become increasingly accurate. A special licence is needed to operate the differential GPS system which is used to guide missiles into bunkers in Iraq and caves in Afghanistan. The Russians have their own *GLONASS* system, which is less accurate. The European Union has its own *Galileo* system, which is more accurate. The Chinese have also built their own *Beidou* global satellite system. So the Americans can no longer take a dominating position on the globe.

Scientific Clocks

Although portable, spring-powered clocks became ever more accurate, gravity was still a force to be reckoned with and fixed pendulum clocks were used for scientific purposes until electronic clocks overtook them. Special pendulums were made which were unaffected by temperature. Gears and bearings rapidly became more accurate, anchor escapements were devised and much better alloys, including *invar,* were developed. By comparing a clock pendulum with a free swinging one Henry Kater measured geographical variations in the force of gravity after 1818 AD. George Airey, the seventh Astronomer Royal, measured gravity by this means at the top and bottom of a coal mine in Yorkshire in 1854 AD. He was then able to make an estimate of the mass of Our Planet Earth. This measurement was the beginning of the new science of geophysics.

The Scottish physicist James Clerk Maxwell came up with this radical new solution in his *Treatise on Electricity and Magnetism* in 1873 AD: "A more universal unit of time might be found by taking the periodic time of vibration of the particular kind of light whose wave length is the unit of length." It took a century before the Atomic second could be fixed in 1972 AD by the International Bureaux of Weights & Measures at Sevres in Paris. The Atomic second was then exactly the same size as the Cosmic second. Since 1987 AD leap seconds have been added to the mean Solar year by the International Earth Rotation Service at Frankfurt in Germany. However, the difference does not change in a regular or predictable way. Since 1983 AD the metre has been redefined by the wavelength of light rather than a metal bar kept in Paris and related to the Paris Meridian.

Electric clocks were invented in 1840 AD but did not come into common use until William Shortt produced the free pendulum clock in 1922 AD. A quartz clock in 1927 AD was accurate to a hundredth of a second/day. An Atomic clock in 1955 AD was accurate to one second in 300 years. An optical laser clock in 2008 AD, to one second in 2,000,000,000 years. These proved that Einstein's General Theory of Relativity was right. The Universe contains very mysterious dark energy and dark matter. Space-Time can be curved by large masses, causing gravitation waves. Extremely accurate clocks are needed to observe the Universe and the many elemental particles or energy waves, which make-up all matter.

Atomic clocks are part of the Global Positioning System, which uses geostationary satellites to aid navigation on land, at sea or in the air. Although navigators still use Kilometres, miles or nautical miles, most GPS or *Satnav* receivers now indicate latitude and longitude in decimals of a degree rather than the traditional degrees, minutes and seconds. In the **Worldwide System** one millionth of the arc subtended by a degree of longitude at the Equator is defined as one *han* and this distance could be expressed as a fixed number of wavelengths of light.

Precision Clocks

There has always been a rivalry between the English and the French. Especially in their very precise measurements of both Time and Space. The church of Saint Sulpicius on the Left Bank in Paris was built in the Merovingian era on the site of a temple to the Egyptian Sky-goddess *Isis*. A statue of *Isis* and *Horus* was used as the Virgin Mary and Christ Child. The church was rebuilt several times but in 1646 AD had a Sun-clock with a shaft of light falling on an obelisk and a brass line along the nave. This Rose Line was superseded by the Paris Observatory in 1672 AD. The French considered this to be the Prime Meridian on Planet Earth. The metre was based upon a faulty survey of part of the Paris Meridian. However, the nautical mile was based upon the length of the Equator. Latitude was based upon the distance from the Equator to either pole. Longitude was based upon the distance from the Greenwich Meridian. This became the Prime Meridian in 1884 AD when the Greenwich Royal Observatory took control of Time and Space throughout Planet Earth. Greenwich Mean Time was controlled by the Shepherd Clock, which has a twenty-four hour dial with Roman numerals - but 0 instead of XXIV. Its pulses were transmitted around the globe via the General Post Office electric telegraph so that many slave clocks kept exactly the same time.

The metre is still about the same size but is now defined as the distance that light travels in a decimal of a second and this is now defined as a number of Atomic vibrations rather than a vulgar fraction of a Solar day. The length of the mean Solar day varies because Earth is slowing down. So master Cosmic clocks are constantly adjusted due to astronomical variations based on photographs of the night Sky, which are carefully measured between the vernal equinoxes along the Greenwich Meridian. The corrected variation tables are properly known as Ephemeris Time. The tables were once printed by the Royal Observatory at Greenwich, which moved to Herstmonceux Castle, Sussex and then to Cambridge. The tables were then printed by *Le Bureau International de l'Heur* Paris. However, the Americans have now taken over control of Time and Space. They decide when a leap second should be added to Universal Time.

Precision clocks are at the heart of modern satellite navigation systems, which are accurate to about 10m, but yttrium clocks, developed at the National Physical Laboratory in Teddington, are accurate to about 1mm. Some made at the US National Institute of Standards and Technology, Boulder, Colorado are accurate to 0.000000000000001 second per day. However, the metre and the second are not the ultimate measurements. Time and Space must be based on the age, orbit, spin and girth of Earth. Then all land, sea and air navigation can be based on the same system. **The Worldwide System** is based upon decimals of a mean Solar day, which varies from year to year, however, for very small units of time, it is also based upon the *tik*, which was fixed when this system began.

International Clocks

The burgeoning railways in Britain made one national time essential. However, the problem was much worse throughout the vast expanse of North America because each railroad company had its own timetable. So in 1883 AD it was decided that there should be national time zones. The idea that there should be 24 global time zones was promulgated by Charles Dowd, a schoolmaster from Saratoga Springs, New York State. Yet, Sandford Fleming, a Scottish engineer on the Canadian Railways, suggested that there should be just one time used throughout the globe. Global standard time zones were first established in 1884 AD by the International Meridian Conference in Washington DC, but this was only attended by 41 delegates, with plenipotential powers, from 25 countries. They chose the Greenwich Meridian because it was used by most ships. The standard mean Solar day would be based upon midnight measured on the cross-wires of the principal transit instrument at Greenwich. Longitude would be measured to 180^0 East and West of Greenwich. Dividing the 360^0 of longitude by these 24 zones gives 15^0 increments. The 0^0 meridian passes through the centre of the first zone and so on. Every 15^0 time changes by one hour at sea, but on land Natural and Man-made boundaries made the time zone chart far more complicated.

There are now some forty different land time zones throughout the globe. Some of these are based upon the half-hour or even the quarter-hour. Ocean Liners have four clocks reading say: London time, New York time, Greenwich time and the ship's time based upon the local sea time zone. This creates much confusion, especially when the Date Line is crossed. Western Samoa decided it would rather be Eastern Samoa in 2012 AD. The International Meridian Conference could not anticipate air travel. It has now become necessary to use 24-hour digital clocks at airports. The airlines and airports say that time zones cause missed connections. This problem is exacerbated by the so-called daylight saving measures. International communications allowed all clocks to be synchronized. Personal computers, tablets and phones now show international times. Some watches now have a dual-time function based upon major cities. How much better it would be if clock time was the same everywhere. The crew of the International Space Station use Greenwich Mean Time. When We look at Planet Earth as a whole, We begin to realize that there can only be one age, one date, one time and one zone on each Planet.

The delegates at the International Meridian Conference concluded:

The Conference expresses the hope that technical studies designed to regulate and extend the application of the decimal system to the division of Space & Time shall be resumed, to permit the extension of this application to all cases in which it presents real advantages.

However, this subject has never been raised again - until now!.

Variable Clocks

The Japanese continued to use six daylight 'hours' and six night 'hours' until long after they started to use the new mechanical clocks that were introduced by Jesuit priests and Dutch traders in the 17th century AD. At first the Japanese adjusted these clocks daily but they later devised movable plates so that the divisions could be altered every fortnight. Instead of using circular clock dials they often used linear time scales. In summer, their daylight 'hour' was 2 1/3 the size of their night 'hour'. Some circular clock dials had two different sets of gearwheels and they automatically switched from one set to the other at Sunrise and Sunset. Their numbering system counted down but numbers 1, 2 and 3 were sacred and for religious use only, so the dials or the linear scales showed 9, 8, 7, 6, 5, 4 repeated, with 9 at the midday and midnight positions.

Nine midday was shown by a horse and midnight by a rat.
Eight in the morning by an ox and in the evening by a sheep.
Seven in the morning by a tiger and in the evening by a monkey.
Six in the morning by a hare and in the evening by a cock.
Five in the morning by a dragon and in the evening by a dog.
Four in the morning by a snake and in the evening by a boar.

They only changed to the twelve fixed-hour, half-day system in 1873 AD. The Japanese now make the most advanced digital watches in the World. Nevertheless, many Japanese still work from Sunrise to Sunset.

Many early clockmakers lost fortunes or went mad trying to devise a system that could do precisely what *Mother Nature* does for nothing. Variable electronic clocks or watches would now be easier to devise. They could show fixed hours and variable positions of dawn and dusk. Thus allowing the maximum use to be made of daylight all-year-round. It is also now possible to show how the length of the Solar day varies throughout the year - a phenomenon known as the Equation of Time. The Japanese were quite right in trying to maintain a variable working day that made the most of free Sunlight instead of expensive electricity. They have never accepted the nonsense about daylight saving measures. We waste £billions on trying to ignore what *Mother Nature* gave Us.

If We used full-day analogue dials they could incorporate segments showing light and dark areas indicating when to start and stop work. This would save a great deal of expensive energy and also a great deal of wear and tear or stress and strain in the Land of the Rising Sun. Indeed, the Japanese economy might recover from its current slump if they were to make such watches and sell them to the rest of the World. The rest of the World might then adopt a similar working pattern. However, a 24-hour dial is rather congested and not very easy to read at a glance and so it would be clearer and more logical to divide it into ten. This is the basis for the **analogue decimal time system**.

Works Clocks

When the Industrial Revolution began very few workers owned clocks. They were woken by town clocks, church clocks or knockers-up so that they arrived at their workplaces before a bell told them to start work. However, workers often destroyed factory clocks, seeing them as proof that the factory owners had taken control of their lives and their time. Works clocks punched or stamped the time on a card and this allowed workers to be paid by the hour, rather than by the day, week or month. The bell was replaced by a siren at mills and factories so that everyone started and stopped work at the same time: usually 8 am to 5 pm for factory workers and 9 am to 5 pm for office, bank and shop workers. This working pattern became so ingrained in the minds of workers that it was easier to move the clocks forward an hour for summer and back an hour for winter, rather than to start work an hour earlier or later, when it was realized that a great deal of free daylight was being wasted. Overtime was usually paid at a higher rate than normal working time.

As electricity gradually enlightened every corner of the industrial globe it replaced many other forms of light and power and is now in most homes. When alternating current replaced direct current its cycles could be used to regulate and synchronize clocks but there were frequent power cuts. Large factories, offices, hospitals and schools used synchronous master and slave clocks so that every clock in the establishment read the same.

Work Study or Time and Motion Study, is a vital part of production. Each operation is carefully timed to minimize the cost of manufacture. Stopwatches used for this sometimes display hundredths of a minute. Many manufacturers are nowadays using a system called: Just-in-Time, which penalizes suppliers if they deliver goods too early or too late. This system minimizes storage space and the capital tied-up in stock.

Clocking-on is slowly being phased out as factory workers become staff. Yet, many office workers now clock-on and clock-off using swipe cards because they are allowed to vary working times to avoid travel peaks. Some use a system called annualized hours to cope with working peaks. In America and Japan it is normal to work much longer than the official working hours, even though there may be little worthwhile work to do. Many British office and factory workers are working much longer hours than they are officially paid for, in order to keep their precious jobs. This is causing marriages to break-up as workers lose control of Time. Over half of all time-losing illness is due to undue stress and strain. If people stuck strictly to their contracts they would not get promotion. Productivity can be increased in any factory or office by working in shifts or sharing jobs and treating all days and hours as exactly the same. If workers had more rest, recreation, adult education and training they would be able to do more work and make fewer mistakes.

Clockwork

The automatons built into some medieval clocks attracted large crowds.
So the aristocracy commissioned clockwork automatons for amusement.
The public paid large sums to see them and some are now in museums.
Automatons became more and more sophisticated using stacks of cams.
Their designers began to think that they could simulate living beings.
This led on to the development of automated machines, such as looms,
which made many skilled artisans redundant and mill owners very rich.
Clockwork became extremely useful throughout industry and despite
being superseded by electric motors it still has important applications.
Automatons have been developed into much more sophisticated robots,
which have now taken over many of the repetitive jobs in industry.
Their hands are steadier than Ours and they do not suffer from fatigue.
Some even do brain and keyhole surgery or they can replace body parts.
Millions of robots, automatic machines and computers work tirelessly,
making more and more robots, automatic machines and computers.

Clockwork toys were popular but battery powered ones are more so.
The clockwork in musical boxes developed gradually into gramophones,
record players, tape recorders, walkmen, CD players, i-pods and i-pads.
Battery powered radios have progressively become smaller and cheaper,
whilst clockwork powered radios are now being used in remote places.
Radio led to the development of television in black & white then colour.
Our streets were guarded by ugly clockwork sentinels that ate coins.
These were superseded by electronic meters that accept magnetic cards.
They can take your photo and fine you automatically if you go over time.
Public telephones used to work by clockwork but have been superseded
by mobile phones that usually incorporate the age, date and time.

Charles Babbage (1791-1871 AD) designed the first computing machine.
However, he failed to make it work until one was completed in 1991 AD.
This difference engine can now be seen in the London Science Museum.
Electronic computers were developed for code-breaking in wartime.
They have made many simple, routine and repetitive jobs redundant.
Many workers have been thrown out of work by the great advances of
science and technology and do not seem to fit into society any more.
However, the younger generation now have computing in their blood.
They regard all days and hours as the same, so easily accept new ideas.
Each generation of computers is more complex and yet simpler to use.
They have become less expensive and can now be found in many homes.
Laptops, tablets and smart phones can now be found in the remotest
parts of the globe and they are rapidly reuniting Our Human Race.
The next step is for all of them to show the same age, date and time.
This would cost nothing but the very last step will be more expensive.
It will be to replace all of the obsolete software, designed and developed
by the ancients and moderns, with the post-modern **Worldwide System**.

Pocket Clocks

The English word 'watch' came from keeping watch on land and at sea. The first historical reference to a watch was when Henry VIII gave a 'gold pomander wherein is a clocke' to Catherine Howard in 1540 AD. Nevertheless, watch-making was not established in England until later. There is no record of an English made pocket watch until 1580 AD. Those made in the next 20 years were copies of French or German ones. The invention of pocket watches is credited to Peter Henlein of Augsberg. The Thirty Years War (1618 - 1648 AD) dispersed the watchmakers and clockmakers from Augsberg and Nuremberg to many parts of Europe. Most were half-day 12-hour Protestants who escaped persecution by the full-day 24-hour Catholics by moving their temporal skills elsewhere.

It was a Giant Leap forward when spring driven clockwork could be miniaturized sufficiently to become pocketable, for then the time could be determined anywhere and so it became a private and personal matter. Watches were expensive, until manufactured in the eighteenth century. It became very fashionable for the rich to own a pocket watch, preferably in gold, with jewelled bearings and with a matching chain and fob. A chiming watch was a prized possession, even though it may be wrong. A top pocket and a button hole in the lapel of a coat or a pair of pockets in a waistcoat were practical ways for a gentleman to carry his watch. During the eighteenth century the French clock and watch industry was severely restricted by high taxes and limits on apprenticeship, whilst the British workshops flourished and their products were sold Worldwide. Coventry was the watch-making centre but declined by the end of the nineteenth century as Americans and Swiss developed production lines. Coventry turned to producing many other things, including motor cars.

The time became increasingly important during the Industrial Revolution although not many workers in the new factories could afford a watch. So the foreman and various levels of higher management gained power and status by having one and when the time came to retire the usual gift to reward their service and loyalty was a pocket watch or a clock. Missionaries were given a pocket watch for their evangelistic journeys. So *God* and time continued to be thought of as inextricably entwined. At war the pocket watch became a crucial part of maneuvers and they were issued to sergeants and above in the Boer and Crimean wars. Many of the lower ranks could not tell the time and there were several major disasters due to troops being in the wrong place at the right time. The clock and watch industry grew in France, Switzerland and America and their ticking products found their way to every corner of the globe. French and Swiss produced quality but the Americans produced quantity. These timepieces were largely responsible for opening up global trade. Globalization continued to expand the market for clocks and watches. Although time zones still divide Our Human Race with invisible barriers.

Wrist Clocks

By further miniaturization, clocks became independent of clothing and could be strapped to the wrist and so pocket watches were superseded. The wealthy Brazilian innovator Alberto Santos-Dumont, who developed early airships and aircraft, suggested wrist watches to Louis Cartier, during the *Belle Epoch,* and he sold the first ones in Paris in 1904 AD. They were considered to be effeminate until they were issued in WW1. At first they were issued to the German troops and later to the Allies. So regiments of pals died simultaneously when they went over the top.

Ladies watches were even smaller and soon became items of jewellery. Taking the pulse is a vital part of nursing and some nurses still prefer a pendant because they frequently need to wash their hands and wrists. Some showed the day name, month name, month-day number and year. Innovations included shock-proof movements and water-proof cases. Gold was used and then stainless steel but many cases are now plastic. Telling the time at night was always a problem, throughout the ages. This problem was partially solved by using luminous dials and hands, until it was realized that the radioactive material was causing cancer. Self-winding was the ultimate mechanical refinement in wrist watches.

Electronics have now very largely replaced mechanisms because they are cheaper and more reliable, although they may not last quite as long. The biggest advantage is that battery powered watches continue to function whether they are worn or not and over the last thirty years watches have escaped from the jeweller's shop and have become so cheap that they are usually disposed of when their battery expires. Batteries are continuously being improved and some now last ten years. Some are now powered by photovoltaic cells, so never need a battery. They have become so accurate that most could be used as chronometers. At the heart of these modern marvels are quartz crystals that resonate at a constant rate and these are counted by transistors on silicon chips.

Some people now wear different wristwatches for different purposes. They have also become fashion accessories with a different colour or style to suit the dress or the occasion - so punctuality became a fetish. Most people in developed countries now own at least one wristwatch. There are still a few in undeveloped countries who have never seen one. Expensive watches often had alarms, chimes, Lunar phases and stop functions but these are now fitted to many cheap electronic timepieces. Many still use traditional analogue dials, that can also be illuminated but others use digital displays that can have more optional features. The battle continues to be waged between analogue and digital displays. The Swiss prefer the traditional analogue watch dial whilst the Japanese prefer the digital display but each type is best for particular applications. However, some watches now have both analogue and digital displays.

Decimal Clocks

The first decimal timepieces were made during the French revolution. The revolutionaries questioned the logic of their XII-hour half-day dials and so they introduced full-day dials displaying ten revolutionary-hours, a hundred revolutionary-minutes and a hundred revolutionary-seconds. Most of these also showed the Roman-Catholic time on a XXIV-hour dial. Roman numerals were used for time; Arabic numbers for decimal time. They sometimes had an extra hand showing the day in the digital week. Some of their analogue-decimal clock and watch dials were illustrated with images of *Liberte* wearing a red cap of freedom, as worn by the Magi. Charles Dickens wrote: "It was the best of times and the worst of times."

An ancient Egyptian obelisk now stands in the *Place de la Concorde*, at the geometric centre of Paris, where the bloody guillotine once stood. The revolutionaries wanted it to be the global centre of Time and Space. They invaded Egypt and then carried off many of its ancient artifacts, which they exhibited in the Louvre museum, formerly a royal palace. They attempted to globalize, digitize and decimalize Space and Time. They measured an arc of the Paris quarter Meridian to fix their metre. They adopted the ancient Egyptian Civic calendar with its ten-day week and the ancient Egyptian division of the day into 100,000 heartbeats. However, the global metre, the digital week and the decimal day were not very popular and most people continued to use their ancient system. Napoleon I reverted to Roman-Catholicism and to traditional measures. Napoleon III reintroduced the inaccurate Metric System in 1840 AD. But he omitted to reintroduce the digital week and the decimal day.

In 1862 AD Parliament voted in favour of adopting the Metric System. A decimal timekeeper was then made by Richard and Thomas Statter. This is now owned by the Worshipful Company of Clockmakers and it is kept and displayed at the Guildhall Museum in the City of London. It has midday on top, midnight at the bottom and rotates anti-clockwise. This is because Earth rotates anticlockwise when viewed from the North. An inscription reads: "The true basis of a Universal Decimal System." Since Nelson and Wellington beat Napoleon at Trafalgar and Waterloo the British have always looked down on the French and their systems. Yet, the British were the first to suggest a global-digital-decimal system.

The Russian revolution of 1905 AD is said to have started when print workers demanded equal pay for setting numbers and decimal points. The Soviets temporarily used a five-day week to increase productivity. The industrial revolution thrived on the mass-production of timepieces. Henry Ford (1863-1947 AD) could envisage making about half a million clocks and watches every year but he could not imagine selling them. They have been made to Metric sizes since the French revolution but the International Metric System has still not been adopted by everyone.

Digital Clocks

Mechanical digital clocks were first made at the start of the 20th century. Electrical ones then appeared at airports, seaports and railway stations. The first digital watches used light emitting diodes, which were read by pressing a button, but most now use continuous liquid crystal displays. Electronic watches can now incorporate many optional features such as: year, month, month-day, week-day, alarms, stopwatches, tides or zones. Computers, phones, mobiles, pagers, radios, TVs, cameras, faxes, videos, cookers, microwaves and cars now have them built-in but most have to be altered twice a year because of so-called daylight saving measures. However, many clocks and watches are now controlled by radio signals, which automatically make changes to or from summer time.

Electronic movements have now almost made mechanical ones obsolete. Clocks and watches can have either analogue dials or digital displays. Analogue dials are the same as the traditional mechanical timepieces. Consequently, they only show 12 hours, 60 minutes and 60 seconds. Digital displays can show 24 or 12 hours, 60 minutes and 60 seconds. Some adults were so familiar with analogue 12-hour half-day ones that they found digital 24-hour ones confusing and more difficult to read. So they insisted that digital ones should have 12-hour half-day displays. However, many children are unable to read traditional analogue dials. Converting between base 12 and base 24 necessitates mental arithmetic. This may be simple but well-educated people frequently make mistakes. So some clocks and watches now show both analogue and digital time.

The development of mechanical clocks led on to mechanical engineering and the development of electric clocks led on to electronic engineering. The British inventor and entrepreneur Sir Clive Sinclair was the first to sell cheap digital watches, pocket calculators and personal computers. Yet, he was unable to find the venture capital needed to capitalize on his revolutionary ideas, which are now considered to be ahead of their time. Perhaps an innovative electronics industry making global-digital-decimal clocks and watches in round-the-clock factories employing thousands of workers on **full-time-job-sharing-as-the-norm** would improve Our World. However, there is now little need to own any personal clock or watch; because digital time is now incorporated into so many electronic gizmos.

Digital computers incorporate age, date and time systems and they can be programmed to convert any ancient or modern system to any other. Most show the ancient Roman-Catholic chronology, calendar and clock. Some incorporate all of the land and sea time zones around the globe. They may show which parts of the globe are in darkness or daylight. They could have **global age, digital date & decimal time** as an option. This might be programmed into the computer's own operating system, it could be viewed online or it could be downloaded from the Internet.

Global Clocks

Chronologies, calendars and clocks are still governed by Mystic beliefs. Most clocks and watches show the Mystic Benedictine hours, some have Mystic Gregorian calendars and a few show the Mystic *Anno Domini* year. Many also display the day in the Mystic Jewish-Christian-Muslim week. The Royal Observatory and The National Physical Laboratory are sticking to this Mystic Time system, which they call: Greenwich Electronic Time. They hold that this twenty-four hour, sixty minute, sixty second system is still based upon ancient Babylonian traditions and it always will be. **The Worldwide Time System** is based on ancient Egyptian traditions. If adopted as the global standard it should take less than one year for everyone on Earth to purchase a new global-digital-decimal timepiece. They could be made automatically and would then be so cheap that they could be given away in advertising promotions - like calendars are now. It would take a little longer for **Worldwide Time** to be built into all the cars, boats, aircraft, cookers, computers, radios, televisions, phones... Nevertheless, most gadgets are worn-out or obsolete in a decade or so.

The Internet is an international network with no regard for the seasons, night and day nor any religious, social, economic or political dogmas. The entrepreneur Nicolas Hayak (1928-2010 AD) CEO of *Swatch* and 'savior of the Swiss watch making industry', suggested that Internet time should be based upon *beats* (thousandths of a day) with no time zones. His system, based upon Biel in Switzerland, started at the Millennium. He used digital displays instead of analogue dials like his other brands. These were the first digital watches ever to be made in Switzerland and were intended to steal the watch market back from the Japanese. However, these watches were not very popular and were soon withdrawn. They were difficult to read because they also showed conventional time. They had two watch movements in one case, so were twice as expensive as conventional ones and they were very large, heavy and cumbersome. *Ericsson* incorporated this *Swatchbeat* system into their mobile phones and some Internet games were also based on it - yet it failed to catch-on.

The long and fascinating history of timekeeping is not yet complete. The final step is analogue or digital **decimal time in** clocks and watches. Analogue ones could show day and night segments as well as the time. Some clocks could be made like a rotating globe, with no time zones. A tilting hemisphere could show which half of the globe is in darkness. Digital ones could show the **global age**, **digital date and decimal time**, either displayed as a row of nine digits or as a square of nine digits or more simply as three large digits showing only the **decimal time**. There are no global-digital-decimal nor global-analogue-decimal clocks or watches made anywhere today and so there is a huge potential market waiting to be exploited by somebody with drive, foresight and vision. This is further discussed and explained in parts five and six of this book.

THE WORLDWIDE SYSTEM

Part Five

Discussion

Choices and Compromises

"Little minds are interested in the extraordinary;
great minds in the commonplace."

Elbert Hubbard (1856-1915 AD)

Choices

From the very moment of Our conception We are faced with many choices. Some decisions are made by Our genes; others are made by Our brains. Sometimes, during Our hazardous climb in Life, the choice is clear to go in one direction or the other but We may occasionally take a middle way. Once in a while We decide to go one way but later change Our minds. Usually, however, We blindly and faithfully follow the person in front. So never think about the hazardous route to the top of Mount Progress. Nor about that challenging pathway into the middle of the Moral Maze. Every decision, throughout Our lives, can be reduced to a very simple and rational form, however, We cannot always take one step at a time. The complex game of chess is often won by thinking many moves ahead.

It is a clear choice about whether We drive on the left or on the right. However, when it comes to religion and politics, We have a wider choice. Our parents give Us names that indicate which religion they believed in, they also choose Our schools but We do not have to follow their example. There should be some school, college and university time devoted to theological, philosophical, ethical and political history but dogma should be kept inside the church, chapel, synagogue, mosque, temple or shrine. Christianity had a shaky start and needed the *Old Testament* of the Jews as well as the *New Testament* of St. Paul and others in order to survive. Constantine the Great merged the Roman years, months and days with seven-day weeks but Christianity was blamed for the fall of the empire. Christianity could well have disappeared with other religions and sects. Saint Augustine of Hippo saved the day by asserting in his great tome: *City of God* that *He* created the holy trinity of Time, Space and Life. Christianity has grown to be the greatest religion upon Our Planet Earth but some are questioning the very foundations of Time, Space and Life. Every religion has a unique way of determining its age, date and time. This makes Us seem different when We are all part of One Human Race. Humanists are at liberty to start again at square zero and choose their own secular names, as well as their own secular ages, dates and times.

All scholars now learn about computers, which think logically and teach Us to think logically too, because they use algorithms to make decisions. These are simple choices of 0 or 1, yes or no, because every decision is reduced to two choices, but in the real World there are often more. It is hard to put them into correct order and not leave out a vital step. Many choices made by Our ancestors have not been considered for ages. The Millennium provided an ideal moment to reconsider these choices. You choose your partner, your vocation, your home, your car, your boat, your pet, your food, your beverage so why not choose your own Time? The answer to this is that a self-sufficient man or woman can choose his or her working days and hours but most of Us depend upon others. So why not reconsider Our age, date and time on a global basis?

Compromises

The Brits are masters of compromise but must not do so on every issue.
Lord Orr-Ewing, the man who introduced the metre to Britain, told of a
cricket match he once played on the former British protectorate of Corfu.
He measured the pitch, which should be one Imperial chain or four rods.
However, it was neither 22 yards nor 22 metres but half-way in between.
Now Britain is metricated a pitch should not be 22 yards but 20 metres.
Yet, most people ignore the law and carry on as if nothing had changed.
The mile, furlong, yard, foot and inch varied from place to place because
they were based upon non-standard anatomy and so were a compromise.
Yet, the International System has also ended-up by being a compromise.

Most of the World uses *Anno Domini* chronology but this is inaccurate,
illogical and backward thinking so it is certainly not used by everyone.
Most of the World uses Roman calendars but their months are illogical
compromises and a leap-day after the second month is an anachronism.
Most of the World uses seven-day weeks that do not fit Lunar moonths.
Three ten-day weeks are closer than four seven-day weeks to a moonth.
Some use XII-hour half-day clocks but others use full-day 24-hour ones
and fixed working hours are a compromise during the seasonal year.
The crooked lines that differentiate land time zones are all compromises.
So are so-called daylight saving measures, which make no sense at all.
Time is not a matter for compromise, the most coherent system must be
chosen by means of logic and this must be for Our greatest convenience.

The Red Cross organization, which has no connections with Christianity,
was forced to change its emblem to a Red Crescent in Islamic countries,
but neither was suitable for the Jews, so they now use a Red Crystal.
The cross is linked with the rays of the Sun, the crescent with the Moon
and the crystal with Venus but Planet Earth is the emblem of the UN.
Most of the conflict around Our World today is due to ancient religious
beliefs about the Sun and the Moon, which can never be compromised.
Yet, their cycles are totally incompatible with one another and so they are
driving many learned professors and stupid computers into apoplexy.
They are trying to write one program that will convert any chronology,
calendar and clock to any other but are finding this to be impossible.
Computers use several measurement systems but they only need one.
Imperial, American, International and Navigation rules are compromises.

Many well-educated people now seem to be in an intellectual dilemma.
They are much freer, far wealthier and better informed than ever before
but the more they have learned the more confused they have become.
As We grow older, many of the black and white issues, which seemed so
clear to Us in the flush of Our youth, become greyer and greyer.
The Worldwide Measurement System goes back to the flush of my youth.
It gradually became clearer and clearer, so must never be compromised.

Linear or Circular?

The ancient belief in rebirth and the transmigration of the soul stems from the assumption that Time is circular and that history repeats itself. However, most rational, post-modern thinkers believe that Time is linear, history does not repeat itself and We are in control of Our own destiny.

The Sumerians divided their circles into 360 degrees and they divided their years into 360 days, which they then sub-divided into 6-day weeks. The Babylonians also used 360 degrees but they preferred a Lunar/Solar calendar because it combined the Lunar moonths with the Solar years. The Egyptians originally had 360 days in their calendar year, then they added five epagomenal days and, eventually, a leap-day every four years. They divided the 360 days into 36 ten-day weeks and daylight into ten hours plus two hours for twilight and twelve hours during the night. The Greeks used 360 degrees but divided days in 24 equal hours and divided each degree and hour into sixty firsts and then sixty seconds. When the Romans invaded Greece they adopted these linear Egyptian and circular Babylonian systems and also developed their own numerals. We still use this mixture of linear and circular measurement systems.

When the French adopted the Metric System, using the ancient Egyptian method of counting and dividing most things in 10s, 100s and 1,000s, they tried to divide circles into 1,000 but found that this was too fine. They divided circles into 400 *grads* so that right-angles had 100 *grads*. Nevertheless, their clock dial only needed to be divided into 10 or 100. Some clocks or watches now have digital counters, not analogue dials. These always show numbers that start at zero and count-up to nine. Linear measure is now divided into 1,000 parts but circular measure is still divided into 360 degrees, 60 arc-minutes and 60 arc-seconds. Nevertheless, it is also divided into 2π radians, which are decimalized. The year cannot be divided by 1,000 but 360 days plus a remainder is satisfactory since it is divisible by: 2,3,4,5,6,8,9,10 or 12 but not 7 or 11. The seven-day week does not fit the 360 day year nor the 365/6 day one. It is mathematically incompatible with any logical calendrical system. Yet, quite illogically, it is now used throughout this circular Planet.

The symbol for Time from ancient East to ancient West was a snake. The Hindu snake was usually shown as a circle swallowing its own tail. The Mayan snake had a head at each end to represent birth and death or the past and the future - for the present only lasts for an instant. We must not be in two minds about Time, the future is more important than the past, so We must get it out of Our heads that it is circular. We are not born again, history does not repeat itself, Time is a linear continuum - like snakes in a straight line swallowing each other's tails. **The Worldwide Measurement System** has linear scales, based upon tens, and circular scales, based on the round number three-hundred-and-sixty.

Forwards or Backwards?

The Greeks and other civilizations believed that the Universe was eternal. The Sumerians believed that their *sar* of 3600 years was significant. Jewish chronology was based upon the Creation in the year 3761 BC. They expected a Messiah to be born in year 3600 but he did not arrive. The Essenes thought he did, so called him the Teacher of Righteousness. Essenism was the prototype for Christianity and it began in 161 BC. This year also coincided with the dawn of the zodiac Age of Pisces, thought to coincide with the Age of Christianity, also linked with fish. Some Humanists believe that We are at the dawn of the Age of Aquarius.

Scythian monk Dionysus Exiguus got *Anno Domini* (Year of Our Lord) chronology wrong in 525 AD when he calculated, for Pope John I, the birth year of Jesus Christ as being 754 AUB (*Ab Urbe Condita*) using Varronian chronology, based upon the foundation of Rome. The contemporary chronicles of Flavius Josephus record that King Herod died near a Lunar eclipse, which occurred during the autumn of 4 BC. Some say that Jesus must have been born before 6 BC because the *New Testament* says Herod killed all innocents below the age of two. *Anno Domini* was used by the Venerable Bede in the 8th century AD. It was used by Holy Roman Emperor Charlemagne (742-814 AD). It was adopted by the Council of Chelsea in 816 AD, however it was not generally accepted for Civic use until the end of the 17th century AD. In 1681 AD Bishop Jacques-Benigne Boussuet, who was renowned for his sermons, suggested counting years before Christ as *Ante Christum*. Oddly, *Ante Christum* became BC but *Anno Domini* did not become AC.

There are several other Christian sects, each with different chronologies. The Orthodox Church based its age on the year of The Flood in 5509 BC. The Ethiopic Church (closely related to the Egyptian Coptic Church, the successor to the first Gnostic Church) believe Jesus was born in 7 AD at the heliacal rising of Sirius, now on the Gregorian 11 September. Sirius was linked with *Isis* who became linked with the Virgin Mary. Coptic chronology was based upon the terrible year 284 AD when the Roman-Pagan emperor Diocletian slayed many of the Gnostic Christians. Armenian chronology was based upon the year 551 AD when the head of its Church wiped the old slate clean and declared a New Christian Era. Every religion and sect has its own way of numbering its years.

The logical way to commemorate the second *Anno Domini* Millennium was to restart Our chronologies, tear-up Our calendars and scrap Our clocks. We now know that Earth slowly formed some 4,550,000,000 years ago. Most secular states currently use BCE and CE instead of BC and AD. So We could say that the year 2000 is really the year 4,550,002,000. Since civilization had its beginnings some twelve thousand years ago, why not begin again at: 4,550,012,000 **WT** or simply: 000y for short.

Names or Numbers?

We are all named by Our parents, according to their religious beliefs. Many still believe they are Christian because they have Christian names. Very few of Us change Our forenames to signify Our theism or atheism. Surnames once indicated one's trade or profession but few now follow their father and very few change their surnames to suit their occupation. Nowadays, We frequently use secret code numbers to identify Ourselves.

English speakers use Pagan names for the week-days and some months. Others are named after the Caesars or they are numbered incorrectly. Latins name their Pagan week-days after the Sun, Moon and five Planets. Quakers, however, number the days in the week and months of the year. There are now *Ten Heavenly Bodies*, so ten week-days could be named: Sun, Mercury, Venus, Earth, Mars, Jupiter, Saturn, Neptune, Uranus, ??? . Our Planet's Moon and all of the other moons could then be ignored. However, it is better to number these ten days from *zeroday* to *nineday*.

The ancient Egyptians and French revolutionaries had similar calendars. The Egyptians numbered all of the days in their 12 thirty-day months. The revolutionaries tried to erase Christian saints' days and festivals. However, they made the fundamental mistake of using French words for the names of their thirty-day months and for every day in their year. Their months were named after the seasonal activities of rural France. English poet George Ellis lampooned their calendar, calling the months: Snowy, Flowy, Blowy, Showery, Flowery, Bowery, Hoppy, Croppy, Droppy, Breezy, Sneezy, Freezy. Remainder days were named: virtue, talent, labour, opinion and rewards. Leap days were formally dedicated to: freedom, equality and friendship. They restarted their chronology at day one in the year of the revolution and numbered the ten days of their week and the ten hours of their day. However, they should have started at zero year, zero day and zero hour. It is impossible to remember 365 hieroglyphs, saints, heroes, foods, tools but very easy for most of Us to count to this number in any language.

Worldwide Time consists of **global age, digital date** and **decimal time**, which can all be displayed as a row of nine numbers e.g. 012:345.678. However, the new units need new names and these all have three letters. The 360-day work cycle is a *yer*, this is divided into twelve 30-day *mons* or into nine 40-day *anks* or into thirty-six 10-day *weks* plus 5 or 6 days. They are multiplied or divided in the same way as the International System. This system was mostly based upon the ancient Greek or Latin prefixes. And so there are: *Gigayers, Megayers, Kiloyers, Hectoyers* and *Decayers* as well as *decidays, centidays* and *millidays*, using standard SI notation. **Worldwide Space** uses this SI notation and some of its measurements. The metre, litre and gram are replaced with the *han, can* and *wan*, which are based upon one 360 millionth of the length of the Equator, the cube of this unit and the weight of water contained by this volume.

Remember or Forget?

We are the result of the steady process of evolution, punctuated by irregular mass extinctions due to catastrophic environmental changes. We are here by chance and may be the only creatures in the Universe who can study Our past, consider Our present and plan for Our future. Our own species has probably stopped evolving Naturally and We are wiping-out many others, which may soon be nothing but a fond memory. Some are asking why We need to save the tiger when We have captured its image on film and its genetic fingerprint in computer memories. They are asking whether We can modify other species to suit Our needs, or whether We may modify Our own species to prevent genetic disorders. We have modified Our environment so much that most of Our Planet bears the scars of Our species and there are already far too many of Us. We are now running out of water, fossil fuels and many raw materials. We now need to modify Our Time and Our Space to suit Our new needs. If We share Our Time and Space We can save Our Planet and Ourselves.

The ancient tree of knowledge is perpetually growing and flowering but its roots and branches need chopping and pruning from time to time. All holy books such as the *Torah, Bible and Koran* are well out-of-date. Each of their religions has a different chronology, calendar and clock. However, each remembers the commandment to keep the Sabbath holy. Although this now falls on a different day in their Mystic seven-day week. We now need to forget this commandment and rethink all of the others. Our World is completely different from the one that holy Moses knew. Our libraries are full of books that are out-of-date as soon as printed. Nevertheless, a careful study of the past can help Us see into the future. The Internet can be kept up-to-date and its electronic memory erased. Although the fundamental reasoning behind this book has not changed for many years; it has been necessary to update it on an annual basis. The author intends to continue this process for as long as he is able.

Chronologies, calendars and clocks remind Us of the past, they keep Us in touch with the present and they nudge Us to do things in the future. However, We have now arrived at a point in **Time** when We all need to wipe the slate of old scores clean and start again with a new hard disc. The Millennium was an ideal point in **Time** to reconsider **Time** itself. A new age, date, time and zone might pull Our Human Race together. Nevertheless, most of the media only looked backwards; not forwards. We must remember the past, nevertheless, We must try not to live in it. We remember 5 November 1605 AD for gunpowder, treason and plot when Roman-Catholics, led by Guy Fawkes, tried to blow-up Parliament. On 5 November 2001 AD some bonfires burnt an effigy of a guy with a long black beard and a white turban who disrupted the Western World. Both of these guys were religious fanatics, who would stop at nothing. We should have started at nothing or, more precisely, at: **000:000.000.**

Sun or Moon?

Natural light comes from the Sun, the Moon, the Planets and the Stars. Although some 90% of the matter in the Universe is thought to be invisible. Our Planet Earth's Moon is the largest satellite in the entire Solar System. The daily Sun and nightly Moon both appear to be roughly the same size. Sometimes they are in unison but at other times they are in opposition. Their gravitational attraction causes the tides in the sea, land and air. The Sun is a ball of hot gas and the Moon is a lump of cold rock. We are still living in their shadow and yet most of Us now use some form of artificial light, which helps Us to ignore their influence upon Our lives.

Most civilizations worshipped the Sun and the Moon as Time's deities. The Egyptians worshipped many gods, mostly associated with the Sky. The left eye of invisible *Amun* was the Moon; his right eye was the Sun. The Sun-god *Ra* became more dominant and was merged as *Amun-Ra*. The Moon-god *Thoth* invented the Lunar and Solar calendars and clocks. The omnipotent Sun-god *Aten* tried, but failed, to replace all the others. The Babylonians worshipped the Sun-god *Apsu* and the Moon-god *Sin*. The Greeks worshipped the Sun-god *Helios* and Moon-goddess *Selene*. The Persians worshipped the Sky-god *Mithras,* lord of the Sun and Moon. The Hebrew *Yahweh* is a composite of four gods of the Sun and Moon. The Jews originally worshipped *Yahweh (God)* and *Asherah (Goddess)*. The Muslim *Allah* is linked with the Moon by Sunnis; the Sun by Shiites. The Hindus make offerings to Sun-god *Surya* and Moon-goddess *Soma*. The Buddhist special days are based upon the Moon's quarter phases. The Taoists believe that the Sun and Moon change places in importance. The Shinto goddess *Amaritsu* is a deity in The Land of the Rising Sun. The Mayan Sun-god *Kinichahau* or Aztec *Tonatiah* liked human blood. The Inca Sun-god *Inti* and Moon-goddess *Mama-Kilya* lived in the Andes. The Christian *God* is **Time**, the Sun is Christ's halo, the Moon is Mary's.

Some of Us are enlightened about many things but others still worship the gods and goddesses, which are still linked with the Sun and Moon. Some believe there is a *God* and a *Goddess* or that they are one deity. The male Church has suppressed equality as heresy for two millennia. The Essenes and the Gnostics seem to have treated women as equals. The Essenes used a Solar calendar and a discontinuous seven-day week. The Gnostics used a Solar calendar and a discontinuous ten-day week. Some say that Jesus married Mary Magdalene and they were trying to introduce the Gnostic religion with 30-day months and 10-day weeks. Others say that Jesus married Mary Magdalene and they were trying to introduce the Essene religion with 30/31-day months and 7-day weeks. Some say that Jesus survived the crucifixion and had several children. They say that their bloodline continued through the kingdom of France. Symbols for the Sun ⊕ and Moon) are used to mean 40 and 30 days, in the **digital date calendar**.

Stars or Planets?

The ancient astronomers, throughout this Planet, spent a great deal of their time tracking the Stars, Constellations, Planets and Comets. And counting the days between each appearance and/or disappearance. Ancient astronomy, inevitably, led to astrology, superstition and religion. The Sky became a perpetual soap opera with many celestial characters. The Sky-gods and the battles between them are shown on Sumerian, Akkadian and Assyrian seals and are described in their *Enuma Elish.*

The Egyptians worshipped the Milky Way-goddess *Nut* and her children: Mummy-Constellation-Orion-god-*Osiris*,   Queen-Star-Sirius-goddess-*Isis*, Foe-Planet-Venus-*Seth*,   Wife-Stars-Pleides-*Nephys*,   Son-Comet-*Anubis*. The living pharaoh was Mars-*Horus* or Jupiter-*Horus* or Saturn-*Horus*. They also worshipped the Sun-god *Ra* and his twelve daughters-*Hours*. Plus the Mercury-god or Moon-god *Thoth* who designed their calendar. He divided the Stars into 36 *Decans* and the year into ten-day *decades*. The five remainder days were named *Osiris, Isis, Seth, Nephys, Horus*. The New Year began when *Ra* and *Isis* came over the horizon together. The four sons of *Horus* represented the North, South, East and West.

The Greeks and Romans borrowed their gods from earlier civilizations:

Shamash became the Greek god **Helios** and then **Solis** the Roman god of the Sun.

Sin became the Greek god **Selene** and then **Lunae** the Roman god of the Moon.

Nergal became the Greek god **Ares** and then **Martis** the Roman god of war.

Nabu became the Greek god **Hermes** then **Mercurius** the Roman messenger god.

Marduk became the Greek god **Zeus** then **Jovis** the Roman king of the gods.

Ishtar became the Greek goddess **Aphrodite** then **Veneris** the Roman goddess of love.

Ninurta became the Greek god **Kronus** then **Saturnus** the Roman god of seasons.

Thoth became associated with **Hermes Trismegistus** the founder of philosophy.

Osiris who was reincarnated as **Horus** eventually became personified as Jesus.

Isis the wife of **Osiris** and mother of **Horus** eventually became personified as Mary.

The Greek Time-god Kronus became the Roman Time-god Chronos who became God.

The seven Sabaean Sky-gods in the city of Haran in Mesopotamia, which were worshipped in seven temples during their continuous seven-day week, were:

Shamash = Sun, Sin = Moon, Nergal = Mars, Nabu = Mercury,
Marduk = Jupiter, Ishtar = Venus, Ninurta = Saturn.

Judaism, Christianity, Islam and the seven-day week had Pagan origins, based upon the ancient belief that there were *Seven Heavenly Bodies*. There are now *Ten Heavenly Bodies*: the Sun and nine major Planets. So there is now a celestial reason to use the **digital date calendar**.

Solar or Lunar?

Life is very simple in places where most people cannot read nor write. They do not have calendars nor clocks but rely on the Sun and Moon. Yet, some people may not see the Sun nor the Moon for weeks on end. The Icelanders used continuous seven-day weeks with no moonths at all. Artificial street lighting makes it difficult to see the Stars and Planets, which are so clear in the desert or at sea and there is much to commend the Lunar phases but they do not fit into the tropical or seasonal year. The Hindus used Solar calendars in some areas; Lunar ones in others. The Buddhists did not use weeks nor months but observed the phases of the Moon to determine their Buddha days at 7 or 8 day intervals. The Chinese used a Lunar/Solar calendar and the emperor decided when to add another moonth to keep their New Year near the vernal equinox. The Jews use a Lunar/Solar calendar, which simple folk cannot fathom. Judaism remains static, except in Jerusalem where Orthodox Jews are trying to outbreed Christians and Muslims to reinforce their Sabbath.

The ancient Egyptians originally used a Lunar calendar, and continued to do so for religious festivals, but they also devised a Solar calendar for Civic use and also a Stellar calendar for their astronomical observations. They knew that the 365 day Civic calendar year was moving through the seasonal year so they had another secret Stellar or Sidereal calendar for astronomical use with an extra intercalary day every four years or so. This became the Civic calendar during the Roman period and formed the basis of the Roman Civic *kalendar* after Julius Caesar visited Egypt. The change, by the Copts, from 10-day to 7-day weeks made this simple system into a more complex one, which then needed to be written down. The Copts, with a complex Solar calendar, are being pushed out of Egypt by Sunni Islam, with its simple Lunar calendar that can be memorized. Sunni Muslims use Lunar calendars but Shiite Muslims use Solar ones. The perpetual war in Afghanistan is between Sunni and Shiite Muslims. Lunatic Talebans banned the Solar New Year on the vernal equinox.

Islam is the fastest growing religion but Christianity is still twice as big. Some say that Christianity is growing as We pass the second Millennium but if their Messiah does not call again soon many will be disappointed. We are still suffering the complexities of the Roman-Catholic *kalendar*. The lengths of its higgledy-piggledy months are difficult to remember. The Flemish mathematician Simon Stevin wrote this chant in 1555 AD:

Thirty days hath September, April, June and November.
All the rest have thirty-one.
Except February alone, and that has twenty-eight days clear
and twenty-nine days in each leap year.

It was Stevin who suggested that the base of ten should be used in all calculations. The base-ten **digital date calendar** would be very much easier to remember.

Light or Dark?

The Enlightenment led the French to a ten-day week and a ten-hour day. Their revolution abolished their monarchy, aristocracy and theocracy. However, millions still starved with more liberty, equality and fraternity. The restoration of the monarchy returned the millions to the workhouse. The second revolution freed the miserable population from more tyranny. France has remained a republic but still uses the Mystic seven-day week. Most shops are now shut from midday Saturday until midday Monday. Commercial vehicles are not permitted to use the roads at the weekends. No wonder their economy is still in a mess and there are many riots. They could achieve liberty, equality, fraternity, perfect work/life balance and much less confusion if they used a ten-day week and a ten-hour day.

Twelve variable hours of daylight and twelve variable hours of darkness became twenty-four fixed hours when mechanical clocks were invented. Fixed working hours in the temperate zones do not make the maximum use of daylight and so the length of the working day should be varied, throughout the four seasons, as it was before clocks were invented. At the Equator there are about twelve hours of daylight and darkness. Some tropical countries set their clocks to read twelve at dawn and dusk. The government of The Gambia recently decided to work a ten-hour day from Monday to Thursday and make Friday part of a three-day weekend.

There is ten times more Natural light at a full-Moon than at a new-Moon. Several calendars divided the phases of the Moon into light and dark fortnights, which were about fourteen days long in order to make the most use of Moonlight for hunting, fishing, gathering crops or feasts. The harvest Moon was an important feature of the agricultural year. A blue Moon is when there are two full-Moons in one calendar month. There are two tides/Lunar day in most places but one or none in others. Tides, predicted in nautical almanacs, are the highest after full and new Moons and at solstices and equinoxes, so are also affected by the Sun. Special clocks have indicated the Lunar phases for hundreds of years. If We need to know about them We can buy a watch which shows them. They are printed in most diaries and are shown on many calendars.

Mankind would take a great leap forward if it only used one calendar for everything and the simplest system is to number the days in the year. They would drop into 10–day *weks* and 30-day *mons* or 40-day *anks*. Businesses would find the 40-day *ank* more useful than the 30-day *mon*. A 30-day *mon* is an approximation to a 29.6 Solar day Lunar moonth. From one *mon* to the next the full-Moon will fall upon the same day, but over a year it will fall behind, so the **digital date calendar** is much better for predicting the next new-Moon or full-Moon than the Gregorian. The perpetual **digital date calendar** can be printed onto a single sheet, or as twelve *mon* sheets, or as nine *ank* sheets, plus a remainder sheet.

Solstice or Equinox?

A Solar year should begin at a solstice or an equinox - but which one?
Western and Eastern zodiacs started at vernal and autumnal equinoxes.
The Babylonian year began at the new Moon before the vernal equinox.
Ra was conceived at the vernal equinox and born at the winter solstice.
Therefore the Egyptian astronomical year started at the vernal equinox.
It was subsequently changed to begin with the heliacal rising of Sirius.
The Coptic and Ethiopic years still start at the heliacal rising of Sirius.
The Jewish spiritual and temporal years started at both the equinoxes.
The Greeks regarded the vernal equinox as the start of the Solar year.
The Roman year began on the vernal equinox but this was changed to
the winter solstice, during the Republic, when the consuls took office.
The Shiite, Kurdish, Saka and Badi years begin on the vernal equinox.

Mithraism and Christianity had many spiritual and temporal similarities.
Mithras and Jesus were immaculately conceived on the vernal equinox.
They were both born exactly nine months later near the winter solstice.
Easter superseded the Mithraist Eostra festival of the vernal equinox.
Christ's Mass was chosen to coincide with the Mithraist Yuletide feast.
From 325 AD the Orthodox Julian year was reckoned from I September.
The Roman-Catholic year usually started on I January but before the
Gregorian reforms were introduced it began on I April (All Fools Day).
The vernal equinox fell on Julian 25 March when the Roman-Catholic
liturgical year was founded but it now falls on Gregorian 20 or 21 March.
In Venice, the year began on I March until the Republic fell in 1797 AD.

In England, the beginning of the calendar year has moved several times.
Two millennia ago New Year fell on Celtic *Samhain*, the second full-Moon
after the autumnal equinox, and the day before this was *Samhain Eve*.
One millennium ago Celtic *Samhain* became Allsaints or Allhallowes Day,
on the Julian 1 November, and the night before this became Halloween.
From the 7th to the 11th centuries AD, the Catholic New Year began on
25 December but it was moved to 25 March in the 12th century AD.
It was moved again to 1 May to obliterate the Pagan fertility festival.
It finally moved to 1 January in 1752 AD and has stayed there ever since.
The British Tax Year starts on 5 April because it was based on Julian 25
March but did not change when the Gregorian calendar was adopted.

The **digital date calendar** starts on day 000 and this could be on the
Catholic New Year's Eve, because SI year-day 001 is on New Year's Day.
The remainder days at the end of this proposed global calendar are
intended for global elections, so an equinox is probably the best option,
because the weather is neither too hot nor too cold anywhere on Earth.
Atomic Time and the zodiac are both based upon the vernal equinox.
The vernal equinox in the year 2000 AD also coincided with a full-Moon.
The most auspicious moment to start using: **The Worldwide System.**

Continuity or Discontinuity?

Some ancient weeks were continuous; whilst others were discontinuous.
The Egyptians had continuous ten-day weeks until they added dog days.
The Greeks divided Lunar moonths into three parts of ten or nine days.
The Etruscans used continuous eight-day weeks for their market days.
The Romans divided their *kalendar* months into *kalends, ides and nones*.
The Essene week was discontinuous so each year started on Wednesday.
The Celtic discontinuous senight and fortnight cycle began at *Samhain*.
The Chinese have used the continuous ten-day *xun* for three millennia.
The Babylonian seven-day week began again at every new Lunar moonth.
The Persian seven-day week began again at every new calendar month.
The Wicca seven-day week and 28-day sunth began again every year.
The Sabaean seven-day week became the Judeo/Christian/Islamic one.

There are four reasons for weeks: rest, recreation, retail and religion.
Our World mostly uses the Gregorian calendar with the seven-day week.
This makes Us discard Our calendars, diaries and planners every year.
Although We could reuse them every 28 years, when the cycle repeats.
By inserting a break at the end of each year, We would not only save a
great deal of money and trees but might also stop conflicting traditions.
Christmas and New Year's Day fall upon a different week-day every year.
These religious and secular festivals have practically become merged.
The Pagan/Christian feast of Yule/Christmas is now celebrated in many
secular, non-Pagan and non-Christian countries, including Little Britain.

Whilst some people who live far away from civilization may prefer to use
the Sun, the Moon and the Stars as indicators of the age, date and time,
the rest of Us can now afford a computerized chronology/ calendar/clock.
Now that We have several independent global communication systems,
We can all restart Our calendars and clocks, simultaneously, every year.
If We numbered the days in the year they would drop into groups of ten.
A ten-day week can be halved into two five-day work-sharing periods.
We are used to working five-day spans and so this is the best pattern.
If three digits indicated the year-day number, the first two digits would
indicate the week number and the last digit the week-day number.
Some astronomers already use the Modified Julian Time system with a
continuous day count and decimals of a day but this is not suitable for
everyone, because it does not incorporate the Solar year of the seasons.

We are remunerated hourly, daily, weekly, sunthly, monthly or yearly.
This difference not only divides Us but causes a great deal of confusion.
We could all be paid every ten days during 360 days in every year.
We should only be paid for work that We do; not for travelling to work;
not for coffee, lunch or tea breaks; not for holidays; nor for sick days.
We should not be paid during the remaining 5 or 6 days in the year.
They should be for local, regional, national and international elections.

First or Last?

Whilst it may seem obvious that the new-Moon should be at the start of a moonth, some ancient civilizations thought it began at the full-Moon. Persian good days were on the 1st, 8th, 15th and 22nd of every month. Babylonian bad days on the 7th, 14th, 21st and 28th of every moonth. This explains why Jews regard the 7th day of the week as sacrosanct; whilst Christians believe that the 1st day of the week is the holy one. There is no astronomical alignment with the continuous seven-day week, but some people still contend that this is a perpetual link with the past. It was broken when the Jews were dispersed by the Romans in 70 AD. So Sunday may really be Saturday or Saturday may really be Sunday. If the seven-day week is a cycle based upon the *Seven Heavenly Bodies*, it is obvious that it should start on Sunday, for the Sun is the greatest. The Christians grabbed the pole position on the weekly starting grid. Yet Christianity is based on the Essene sect which had its own calendar. The Essene week began on Wednesday, the most important day for the Jews is Saturday and the Muslims chose Friday - just to be different. In most diaries and calendars the first day of the week is now Monday.

The three greatest Western religions: Judaism, Christianity and Islam, all honour the seven-day week but they take different days off work. This causes a great deal of conflict where these three religions overlap. The Badis divide their Solar year into 19 'months' of 19 days plus 4 or 5. Most of the Eastern religions have no special day in the week for prayer. Whilst the EU wants to extend the unproductive weekend to include Friday, Saturday and Sunday this will make European goods expensive. Europe would have to close its borders and to charge higher duties to protect its economic system; but a ten-day week would allow Us to work harder **and** take more days off work - it would also encourage equality. If We were all to use a ten-day week and to number its days from zero to nine they would all be exactly equal - and We would all be equal too.

Does it matter which is the first day of the week, the month or the year? Is it not better for the year, the month and the week to start together? As an alternative to the date being shown as months and month-days; it can now legally be expressed as year-days, beginning with day 001. So New Year's Eve in 1999 AD could be expressed as: year 000 day 000, because the age, date and time are scalar and all scales begin at zero. Nevertheless, **full-time-job-sharing-as-the-norm** in a ten-day work week could begin immediately by numbering its days from day one to day ten. Eventually, it would be far better for the year, month and week to start simultaneously on the vernal equinox, where many ancient years began. If We had a ten-day week Our 'months' could be 20, 30, 40 or 50 days. For several commercial reasons: 9 x 40 + 5 or 6 days, would be best. However, for other reasons some may prefer: 12 x 30 + 5 or 6 days. This is purely a matter of convenience and so **digital date** has both.

Dawn or Dusk?

When each Solar day should begin was always a very difficult decision and so ancient civilizations arrived at different solutions to this problem. The Egyptian day began at dawn; the Babylonian day began at dusk; Greeks and Romans at midnight; Saxons at dawn; Normans at noon. The Jews, Muslims and most Christian sects begin their day at dusk. However, Protestants decided that their days should start at midnight. So that twelve o'clock and noon occurred at exactly the same moment. When the Sun was at its zenith a clock's hands were pointing upwards. However, when time zones were established this rule was abandoned. Most of Us now synchronize Our clocks and change to or from summer time according to the radio, television, telephone or internet.

Although the exact moment of dawn could not be measured, this did not matter because the morning crow of a cockerel was an adequate *alarum*. The few that are left out in the open are totally confused by street lights. Clocks replaced cocks and so they changed the start of the working day. Some tribes in Equatorial Africa still start their day at dawn and divide both daylight and darkness by twelve, so that midday is at six o'clock. On Mount Athos, where women and female animals are still banished, there are twenty Orthodox monasteries, which all use different calendars. In 19 of these the day starts at dusk but in the 20th it starts at dawn.

The solution proposed in this book has never been considered before. Days would start everywhere around the globe when the Prime Meridian passes through midnight, which is half a day before mid-light or noon. The time would no longer be a local, national or international measure but a global one, which can now be communicated by electronic means. The syndrome of working from 9 a.m. to 5 p.m. would become obsolete. It is probably impossible to calculate how much lost time and wasted energy have been caused by all the time zones and fixed working hours. My guess is that Our World would become at least 10% more efficient if it discarded them and well over 30% more efficient if it introduced a ten-day working week with **full-time-job-sharing-as-the-norm**.

The British Institute of Management say that: 90% of Britain's largest organizations have restructured and in 86% of them it led to job losses. The vast majority of organizations already use **flextime** and 75% expect flexible working hours, job-sharing and part-time working to increase. Some 25% of employees and contract staff are now working from home. The offices in many organizations are no longer assigned to one person because employees carry their mobile offices with them wherever they go. Virtual conferences lead to faster decisions and reduce the need to travel. The Institute of Employment Studies say the nine-to-five working day and the five-day working week are now the exception; not the norm. So changing over to **flexdate** and **flextime** should be a simple matter.

Odd or Even?

The Creator is supposed to have given Us odd years, months and weeks, because *He* is perfect, whilst We mortals cannot make even calendars. The Solar year is better than the Lunar year, which is held to be twelve moonths because that is the nearest approximation to the Solar year. The seven-day week is a close fit to the 365.24 day mean Solar year but 52 of them equal 364 days, so the Gregorian calendar is not perpetual. The seven-day week is a close fit to the 29.53 day Lunar moonth but three ten-day weeks are even closer and they have the great advantage that, being even numbers, they can, very conveniently, be divided by two. There are other even numbers such as: 8, 12 or 14 which could be used. Some jobsharers now use an 8-day cycle whilst others use a 14-day one. But neither of these cycles is the optimum for workdays and freedays. If a calendar year of 365 or 366 days is used then there are several different ways in which months and weeks can be fitted into it:

Minoan	12 alternate months of 30 or 31 days	- 31 days/40 years
Sosigenes	11 alternate months of 30 or 31 days	+ 29 or 30 days
Augustus	11 random months of 30 or 31 days	+ 28 or 29 days
Shiite	6 months of 31, 5 months of 30 days	+ 29 or 30 days
Essene	4 quarters of 30+30+31 day months	= 364 + 1 or 2 days
Essene	4 quarters of 13 seven-day weeks	= 364 + 1 or 2 days
Teutonic	13 sunths of 28 days	
Badi	19 months of 19 days	

It is more convenient to use a shorter year of 360 days plus a 5 or 6 day remainder, because it can be divided in many different ways:

Megalithic	twelve 30-day months	= 60 six-day weeks
Etruscan	ten 36-day months	= 45 eight-day weeks
Phoenician	nine 40-day months	= 40 nine-day weeks
Egyptian	twelve 30-day months	= 36 ten-day *decades*
Mayan	eighteen 20-day *uinals* (or thirteen *uinals* = 260 days)	
Worldwide	nine 40-day *anks* = twelve 30-day *mons* = 36 ten-day *weks*	

The **digital date calendar** *yer* of 360 days can be divided into four equal quarters but its ten-day *wek* does not approximate to one Lunar phase. A ten-day *wek* can be divided into two five-day periods, for those who cannot share their jobs, and one day-off in five is about the same as one and a half days-off in seven which is still the norm in many countries. The market week, which was shorter in hot places, has been superseded by shops that open every day and the various means of preserving food. The Mystic seven-day week is now used throughout the globe but it is no longer justifiable when it causes one billion people to be out of work. The Roman/Catholic years, months and weeks are difficult to program into a watch, mobile phone or computer and this causes many problems. **Worldwide Time** is the most computer friendly system yet devised.

Left or Right?

This text reads from left to right but the Arabs write from right to left. The Hindu numbers, zeros and decimals all read from left to right. The ancient Egyptian hieroglyphs could be written from left to right, from right to left or from top to bottom - like Chinese and Japanese. Since more people are right-handed than left-handed it is much more democratically and ergonomically correct to write from left to right. Which side of the road We drive along should have been resolved by an international convention a century ago, but may never be standardized. There are still 35 left-handed countries but 145 now drive on the right. The Chinese drive on the right and have done so since the Qin dynasty. Yet, in the former British colony of Hong Kong they still drive on the left. Nobody in Europe took the initiative to make Britain, Ireland, Gibraltar, Malta and Cyprus conform but this anomaly still causes many accidents. If Boney, Bill or Adolph had won We would all be driving on the right. The longer any problem is protracted, the more difficult it is to solve. It may be too late to change roads so that We all drive on the same side; yet changing Our chronologies, calendars and clocks would be easier.

The **global chronology** is best shown as a series of zeros and numbers, in groups of three, reading from left to right, as in all digital displays. The **digital calendar** is simply three digits from 000 to 364 or 365. The first two digits are the *wek* number, the last is the *wekday* number. This can be shown on a sheet of paper with each *wek* on a separate line. The first five days are *leftdays* and the last five days are *rightdays*. Thus, full-time-job-sharers would work on either *leftdays* or *rightdays*. There is absolutely no advantage to working on either side of the page. The **decimal clock or watch** could rotate clockwise or anticlockwise. However, most people would probably prefer to use a digital one anyway. The reason that Thomas Statter gave for his anticlockwise watch was that if it is viewed from the North Pole the Earth rotates anticlockwise. He had ten o'clock at the bottom of his dial and five o'clock at the top, so that the *deciday* hand was pointing up whilst the Sun was overhead. However, many people now reside in the southern hemisphere and this Sun-dial argument becomes irrelevant if all the time zones are scrapped. If a ten *deciday* clock dial also indicated the ten days in a *wek* it could rotate anticlockwise so that *leftdays* were on the left side of the dial. On the one hand We have five digits; on the other We have five digits. Consequently a digital week and a decimal day are evenhanded matters.

Wings are political terms: the left wing believe that We are all equal; the right wing believe that some of Us are more equal than others. It is becoming increasingly difficult to position British political parties. **Full-time-job-sharing-as-the-norm** could lead to a new kind of politics where left and right shake hands and then form a coalition government. But, at present, the left hand doesn't know what the right hand is doing.

Decimal or Duodecimal?

We have ten fingers and ten toes but twelve or twenty-four finger joints.
The debate about whether to use a base-ten digital and decimal system
or a base-twelve dozenial or duodecimal system has raged for millennia.
Most people now take the base-ten or digital-decimal system for granted.
Our children today do not memorize eleven or twelve times tables but
they all have pocket calculators, which are based upon the number ten.
They find it incomprehensible to use other bases when measuring time.
Yet some scholars consider that everything should be counted in twelves.
Because twelve can be divided integrally into halves, quarters or thirds.
They consider that We need two more numerals to construct a complete
duodecimal system for counting, multiplying and dividing everything.
Those who believe in this system do not advocate a 12-day week and
6+6 job-sharing but if they did it would fit into a 360-day working *yer*.

The Chinese used both of the decimal and duodecimal systems in their
zodiacs, chronologies, calendars, clocks and rules for several millennia.
The Babylonians counted in tens and twelves but also divided by sixties.
The Egyptians counted in fives, tens, hundreds, thousands and millions.
Nevertheless, they divided by 2, 4, 8, 16, 32 or 64 in a halving system.
The Etruscans counted in eights and used the eight-note musical scale.
The Greeks used to count most things in sixes, twelves and twenty-fours.
The Hellenes started to count everything in fives, tens and hundreds.
The Romans followed with Vs, Xs and Cs but used base-twelve fractions.
The British divided by four, eight, ten, twelve, fourteen, sixteen, twenty.
The Hindus and then the Muslims used zeros, numbers and decimals.
The French revolutionaries introduced the digital-decimal Metric System.
This system is currently used for measuring most physical quantities.
However, it is not used for counting and measuring every part of Time.
We count years in decades, centuries and millennia but days in sevens,
hours in twelves or twenty-fours, then minutes and seconds in sixties.
However, seconds are now decimalized - because fractions are pointless.

Give those digital-decimal Eurocrats an inch and they will take a metre.
They have even made it mandatory to pack hen's eggs in boxes of ten.
They would like every European to use the same digital-decimal euro.
However, they have never introduced a digital week nor a decimal day.
Because this would offend those who cling to the belief in a Sabbath day
and those who believe in the monastic ritual of praying at certain hours.
Europe is now divided into those who insist upon these ancient beliefs,
so they pass international laws protecting the Sabbath or the weekend,
and those who consider that all days and hours are now equal in value,
so they are prepared to work on any day at the same hourly rate of pay.
Few Europeans have considered using a digital week and a decimal day,
because most people take everything for granted, from cradle to grave,
but there is an increasing movement to digitize or decimalize everything.

Analogue or Digital?

Traditional 12-hour analogue clocks and watches are under attack from progressive 24-hour digital timepieces, that can be much more complex. Smart watches can now incorporate calculators, compasses, coordinates, cameras, pagers, telephones, radios, televisions or computer terminals. However, the analogue army have fought back, using electronics, so that they do not need winding and keep good time but have traditional dials. Most adults find that analogue dials are easier to read without specs. Yet, many children are now unable to read analogue clocks and watches. Analogue watches need simple mental arithmetic to convert from the 12-hour to the 24-hour system, which leads to mistakes at airports. Quite apart from watches, the digital v analogue battle still rages on in other kinds of instruments and many people consider that analogue ones are much easier to read on a car dashboard or an aircraft control panel. However, another revolution is now taking place on instrument panels. In place of dials, pilots and navigators have computers with monitors showing the information that they require in the clearest graphical way. If 12-hour and 24-hour timepieces were replaced with 10-*deciday* ones, then both analogue and digital displays would be easier to read.

An analogue electronic clock or watch could become very much smarter, in the technological sense of the word, if it had night and day sectors. This feature is not possible with the traditional half-day 12-hour dial; but this could easily be incorporated into a 24-hour or 10-*deciday* one. Clocks in the form of terrestrial spheres could indicate the **decimal time** and they could also indicate which parts of Our Planet were in darkness. Clocks could have celestial spheres showing the Stars and Constellations or even electronic planetariums, showing the positions of all the Planets. The ten points on a **decimal time** analogue dial could also indicate the ten days in the *wek* if the calendar and the clock both started at zero.

A digital watch would only need three windows to show **decimal time** but could use nine to show **global age, digital date** and **decimal time**. A **Worldwide Time** chronograph/calendar/clock could show: 012:345.678. A **Time** chronograph/calendar/clock shows: 14:32 MON 31 AUG 1995. This needs sixteen windows, which display both numbers and letters. Liquid crystal letter windows are more expensive than number ones. The windows and circuits in **Worldwide Time** clocks or watches would therefore be much less expensive than those now used in **Time** ones. Any digital calculator, phone or radio can incorporate **Worldwide Time**. It is no longer necessary to wear a watch if you use one of these gizmos. Nevertheless, the global sales of clocks and watches increase every year. **Worldwide Time** could open markets for analogue or digital timepieces. If they were mass-produced, everyone could afford to own at least one and the build-up of stocks before change-over need only take a few *yers*. It is only a matter of Time.

North or South?

This hypothesis assumes that **Worldwide Time and Worldwide Space** would be based upon Greenwich, because it marks the Prime Meridian. However, this line crosses the Equator at sea, so this is not a landmark. If We could start again where would We position Earth's Origin or Navel?

The Chinese used their Temple Of Heaven in Bejing as Earth's navel. The Babylonians used the Tower of Babel as the navel of their World. The Egyptians used the Great Pyramid as the centre of their World. The Greeks used the Omphalos at Delphi as the origin of their World. The Romans based their measurements on an outcrop of rock in Rome, where the Vatican City now stands and so all roads still lead to Rome. Roman-Catholics say St. Peter's obelisk is the centre of Christendom. Orthodox Christians use the Dikilitas obelisk in Istanbul which sits on rock at the hub of the Byzantine Empire, where Europe meets Asia. However, the *Mappa Mundi* shows Jerusalem as the centre of the World. Jews would indubitably choose the Rock in Jerusalem as their navel. Muslims would choose the *Kaabah* in Mecca and the clock that the has recently built there is now the tallest clock and obelisk in the World. Hindus would choose the temple of Bakeng, which has nine steps and 108 tower shrines or the pyramid-shaped Mount Kailas in the Himalayas. Buddhists would choose their greatest Borobudur temple mandala near the Equator in Java, which has seven steps and 72 Buddha stupas. The Amerindians used a totem pole atop their huge pyramid at Cahokia. The Inca capital Cuzco was the centre of their great mountain empire. The Mayan capital Tikal had the highest monument in the Americas. The Aztecs thought Tenochtitlan was at the very centre of the Universe. Easter Island was once called *Rapa Nui* meaning: The Navel of the World. The Washington Monument, still the largest stone obelisk, was almost complete when the Meridian Conference was held there in 1884 AD. The Americans wanted it to be the Center of the World and they are now in control of Time and Space through their *Satnav* and *Google Earth*.

The Sphinx and Great Pyramid are approximately 030 degrees north of the Equator near the point where the Nile fans out to become the Delta. They are said to mark the very centroid of all Our Planet's land masses. The Amazon flows due eastwards and follows the Equator to the sea. The Nile flows due northwards from its sources on the Equator itself. It is already visible from Space as a line of trees across the desert. There is now a small village on the Equator in Kenya called: Equator. A drop of rainwater falling upon this spot might flow northwards via Lakes Rudolph and Tana to the Blue Nile; another drop of rainwater might flow westwards into Lake Victoria and thence via the Victoria Falls into Lake Albert, which forms the great header tank of the White Nile. Since the origins of Mankind come from this part of the globe, perhaps **Worldwide Time and Worldwide Space** should be based there too.

East or West?

Our Human Race is still divided over different ways of measuring Time.
Bloody battles are still raging in Eastern Europe about whether to use
the Eastern Orthodox Julian or Western Catholic Gregorian calendar.
They are both ancient relics from the division of the Roman Empire.
Similarly, Sunnis and Shiites are raging over Lunar or Solar calendars.
It is incredible how different day-counting systems, attached to different
religions or sects make people hate, fight, maim and kill each other.
The simple answer is to tear them all up and start again at square zero.
All maps and charts had to be torn up when the Greenwich Meridian
divided the East from the West and were then based upon 000⁰E, 000⁰W.

If you were an alien approaching Earth from Outer Space, where would
you choose to be beamed down and what coordinates would you use?
You would to see the white poles and so work-out where the Equator is
but find it very difficult to discover the position of the Prime Meridian.
The British have planted a line of trees along it, visible from Outer Space.
The French have planted another line of trees along their Paris Meridian.
The Royal Observatory at Greenwich now has a laser beam showing the
Prime Meridian and this lies just to the West of the Millennium Dome.
The Dome is the World's largest structure and is just visible from Space.
It could have been a glass pyramid but that was considered to be Pagan.
The French built several glass pyramids near the entrance to the Louvre,
which now houses an important collection of ancient Egyptian artifacts.
The Millennium Dome was supposed to be based upon Time and Space.
It is 365 metres in diameter, the same number as the days in the year.
It has twelve yellow masts, which represent the hours on a clock dial.
This message was lost and very few visitors realized that it celebrated the
day when the French Metric System finally became adopted by Britain.
Yet, the metre was based on an inaccurate survey of the Paris Meridian.

Our Planet Earth is not a perfect sphere but it is a lumpy oblate one.
Each Meridian is different, so the nautical mile is based on the Equator.
The length of the Equator or girth of the Earth has now been surveyed
very accurately and so the nautical mile is a globally agreed distance.
Yet, this is based on an arc-minute of longitude instead of on decimals.
Nevertheless, this is now sub-divided by decimals instead of arc-seconds.
We now use a mixture of Babylonian fractions and Egyptian decimals.
Egyptians did not measure angles but sides of right-angled triangles.
Babylonians divided circles into 360 degrees, 60 minutes, 60 seconds.
The round number 360 is used to divide a circle, because 1000 is too fine
and 100 is too coarse, but this should then by divided by 1,000,000.
This new unit, the *han,* is approximately the width of the average hand.
It is the standard length or distance in **Worldwide Space** and is squared,
cubed and filled with water for the standard area, volume and weight.
These standard weights in gold could be the basis of a global currency.

Plus or Minus?

The time used for navigation at sea was standardized during 1884 AD.
A ship's time is altered in one hour steps at fifteen degree increments.
The time zones on land usually change in one hour increments based on
political or geographic boundaries but some change in halves or quarters.
It is up the government of each state to determine its own time zone.
So there are now some forty different land time zones around the globe.
USA, Canada and the former USSR are so big that they need several.
Chairman Mao said five time zones were divisive, so China only has one.
Hitler insisted that the German war machine should fight to Berlin Time.
The British war machine fights in 24-hour Zulu time (Universal Time).
Some say that time should be the same across Europe, North and South
America, Africa or Australia - why not throughout this entire Planet?

Time zones were set-up because of faster international communications.
Before then there was chaos because every state had its own time.
Before then there was total chaos because every town had its own time.
Before then there was absolute chaos but few clocks and no watches.
Natural Sundial time is now different from artificial clock time but many
people still seem to think that noon and midday are the same moment.
Time is wasted during international phone calls in checking local time.
Many trains, planes, appointments and programmes are missed because
travellers forget to change their watches when they cross time zones.
The zigzag International Date Line also causes many misconnections.
The standard time zone chart has to be to be redrawn, reprinted and
reissued, Worldwide, whenever there are any national border changes.
What a waste of time, effort and paper and what a source of confusion.
Those who lived in the Horse Age could not imagine the Railway Age.
Those who lived in the Railway Age could not imagine the Aircraft Age.
The airlines all work to Zulu time and then convert this to local time.
We should all use exactly the same time, everywhere on Planet Earth.

Worldwide Time would be the same, everywhere, but We would still
work, play, rest and sleep at different times in various parts of the globe.
Global age would change on the vernal equinox at Greenwich midnight.
Digital date would change, globally, at noon along the 180^0 Meridian.
Decimal time would be 000md when the 000^0 Meridian is at midnight.
Flextime would minimize the effects of the morning or evening rush.
Flexdate would allow Us to work longer in summer than in winter.
Worldwide Space would be based on latitude and longitude in degrees.
Terrestrial globes could be divided into ten 36^0 segments, like an orange.
Each segment would be big enough to encompass a complete continent.
However, employers and employees would be free to set working times.
Organizations would show working times and dates on their letterheads,
visiting cards, answer-phones, faxes, texts, e-mails, tweets and websites.
Electronic communications allow Us to forget about divisive time zones.

Today or Tomorrow?

The International Meridian Conference in 1884 AD agreed that the day should start at midnight along the Meridian in every standard time zone. There were supposed to be 24 standard sea time zones but, since the International Date Line zigzags across the Pacific, there are actually 25. Every state then decided which standard time zone it wanted to be in. Saudi Arabia and Israel, which were created later, have never signed this agreement and they still start their days at Sunset instead of midnight. Saudi Arabia wants to keep its five daily prayer times based upon Mecca. Israel wants to keep its seven daily prayer times, based upon Jerusalem. The standard time zone chart, issued by the Hydrographer to the Navy, can be consulted in most diaries, telephone directories and computers but it has to be altered whenever there is an international border change or whenever any state wants to change its time zone or its summer time. The cost of doing this must be huge and it is completely unnecessary. How much simpler Life on Earth would be if We only had one time zone. This aspect of **Worldwide Time** is known as the **single zone.**

When the standard time zones were established it is was not envisaged that it would one day be possible to fly right around the globe in a day. The airlines and their passengers have great difficulty in coping with all the different chronologies, calendars, clocks and zones around the globe. Our circadian biorhythms or body clocks, governed by the pineal glands in Our brains, are confused by this and take days to recover from jet-lag. Aircrews never really get used to this and it effects their metabolisms. Those who regularly switch shifts also experience some biological effects to their temperature, heart rate and other bodily functions, so that they cannot stay alert and often develop ailments that keep them off work. The fire, police and ambulance services have been found to develop high rates of mental and physical sickness and above average absenteeism. They now work a two-days-on/two-nights-on/four-days-off shift pattern. A five-days-on/five-days-off/five-nights-on/five-days-off shift pattern may be less stressful for shift workers, yet a **single zone** will not stop jet-lag.

We still have a very long way to go before We have created One World. The first step is to set all of our clocks and watches to the same time. Those involved in international commerce, such as buying and selling shares, realize that time zones are anachronisms, so it was announced at the Millennium that the Internet should be based on Greenwich Time. It will be known as: Greenwich Electronic Time, or by the initials: GeT. Internet age, date and time should be globalized, digitized, decimalized and all new computers should have this system installed as an option. The terms: yesterday, today and tomorrow, are all based upon daylight; not on the date, which would change at midday along the 180⁰ Meridian. Some critics of **single zone** find this concept difficult to comprehend. Nevertheless, the International Date Line is a chronographical clock-up.

Summer or Winter?

There are usually four seasons but in some places there are more or less. In Sudan there are two, in Egypt three, in Australia five, in India six, the Innuits of the Arctic Circle recognize nine, the Chinese twenty-four. When Sun-dials were used, daylight was divided into twelve variable hours but when mechanical clocks were invented, they became fixed. The length of the working day became fixed and by-laws were passed on shop and bar opening and closing times and on fixed working hours. This was all based upon the outdated idea that clock-time and Sun-time should coincide at twelve o'clock when the Sun was at its highest point. A great deal of cheap daylight was then wasted throughout the summer. A great deal of expensive energy was then wasted throughout the winter.

In 1784 AD Benjamin Franklin mooted shifting midday during summer. In 1907 AD William Willett suggested moving clocks forward for summer. Germany was the first country to introduce summer time in 1916 AD. Britain followed suit by putting all of its clocks forward by one hour. In WW2 UK had double (+2h) summertime and single (+1h) wintertime. In 1968, 1969 and 1970 AD UK had summertime all through the winter. Some southern states of the USA do not accept daylight saving measures and there has been civil unrest in Mexico, which recently adopted them. Only 20% of Us now use them and only 32% of countries now use them. Changing all of the timepieces to and from British Summer Time now wastes about 7M man-hours every year and 3M people regularly forget. We could have left the clocks alone and started work an hour earlier. Or, better still, varied the length of the working day throughout the year.

Part of the debate about whether Britain should be in Europe revolves around the question of making it into one time zone, based upon Rome. The English say that Greenwich was agreed to be the point from which all Time and Space should be measured; the Scots say that it will not get light until 10:00 in the winter and that this will cause many accidents. If they were one hour behind Scotland would soon want to return to being a separate state and another political time zone would be created. Northern Ireland might also be in a different time zone to the Republic. Portugal is still one hour different from the rest of continental Europe. Iceland works quite happily on Greenwich Mean Time all-the-year-round.

Midsummer's Day usually comes before the summer solstice and is at the midpoint of summer time, which runs from Saturday to Saturday. In 1995 AD summer time ended a week earlier, since the EU deemed that European summer time must end on the fourth Sunday in October. It had taken the Eurocrats over 17 years to negotiate this small change. In 2007 AD the USA adjusted its daylight saving time, to save energy. However, this needed expensive modifications to all computer programs. We should all use exactly the same time throughout summer and winter.

Rigid or Flexible?

Our future lies in a more flexible attitude to working practices but there are still many people in control of Our Time who think far more rigidly. It is multifarious ancient religious dogmas about the working week and the working day that are now holding back the progress of Mankind. Yet, work-sharing and wealth-sharing were the bases for most religions.

The nine-to-five syndrome has become a serious problem with increasing mobility using public or private transport but with a poor infrastructure. Many firms staggered working hours or gave employees the freedom to adjust their working times to their best advantage, so long as their total hours in the day or the week were met and this was known as: **flextime**. Their workers then had to clock-in and clock-out or log-on and log-off. Some construction firms and ship repair yards adopted an annualized hours scheme so that their staff could take a break between contracts. A Work Foundation survey showed that seventy percent of those who worked **flextime** were achieving more than their colleagues on fixed time. A Department of Trade and Industry survey showed that about seventy percent of workers would like to work more flexibly and about fifty percent would be prepared to change their jobs to gain more flexibility. However, The Equal Opportunities Commission reported that workers who reduced their hours had damaged their chances of promotion.

The largest employer in bonny Scotland is the national postal service. The posties recently went on strike for shorter working hours in winter. However, the General Post Office insisted that all its workers throughout Britain must work to the same hours, they must make two deliveries on week-days but none on Sundays, when there are now no collections. In Norway and Sweden the postal service is exactly the same every day but it is reduced in winter - no wonder the Scots wanted devolution.

Although We have artificial light this is not bright enough to convince Our body clocks that it is daylight and We waste a great deal of energy. Those who always work in artificial light develop stress related illness. There are more road accidents at night, many of them are due to the Sun's dazzle at Sun-rise and Sun-set or poor visibility during twilight. Many are due to ice, which is hard to see but melts soon after dawn. Farm workers still have to adjust their working hours to suit the season. Some form of seasonal adjustment to our working habits is needed the further we get from the Equator, whilst in the tropics there is no problem with working to the same routine or pattern all-year-round. The solution is to work for longer hours in summer than in winter. Or better still to divide the year into four and work for say: seven hours in spring and autumn, six hours in winter and eight hours in summer. Or say: 30 *centidays* in spring or autumn 25 in winter and 35 in summer. This flexible part of **The Worldwide System** is called: **flexdate.**

Yours or Mine?

An Englishman's home is his castle and no one may enter unless invited.
Any desk, workbench, machine or computer can be just as sacrosanct.
Psychologists call the invisible barrier around each of Us a comfort zone.
Inside every comfort zone, at home or at work, sits a clock, a calendar,
a diary and a timetable; therefore to change them would be to trespass,
even though it could give Us extra space, greater freedom and more pay.
Job-sharing is like a marriage of convenience or a special relationship.
It has proven to be more efficient than the conventional way of working.
And yet workers rarely meet the person with whom they share their job
and the multifarious gizmos, gadgets and widgets that accompany it.
Filofaxes, personal organizers, laptops, tablets or mobile phones became
symbols of one-up-man-ship, but not necessarily of greater efficiency.
And so the **digital date calendar** could be a symbol of two-up-man-ship.
Once they understand all the advantages, all the yuppies will want one.

Politicians and bureaucrats love to put up artificial barriers of all kinds.
Their time zones are not only artificial but they are usually invisible.
Time zones at sea can only be found by making careful measurements.
Time zones on land are marked by a Natural or imaginary boundary.
Every traveller has a tale about how he missed a bus, a train or a plane
or a ferry because he forgot to alter his watch when changing zones.
Those who cross the International Date Line, which is warped around
groups of islands, often arrive a day late or a day early for meetings.
Christians on the Pacific island of Vanuatu went to church on the wrong
day for over sixty years until they were told about this warped dateline.
Tonga tried to cash in on being the first to see the new Millennium but
the renamed island of Millennium in the Kiribati group usurped this
dubious honor by altering its time zone in every atlas of the globe.
Thousands flocked to this outpost to see the dawn of the Millennium.
Nevertheless, the Antarctic Circle was the first to see the new dawn and
those who live at the South Pole can choose any time zone they desire.
However, this is now a US base and so they use Eastern Standard Time.

Although Lowestoft is the most easterly town in Britain, Broadstairs saw
the new Millennium dawn first, because of the tilt of the Earth's axis.
Millions celebrated in the streets in London but many of those who had
bought tickets to the Millennium Dome Circus did not get them in time.
Gigabucks were wasted on fireworks, caviar and champagne throughout
the *Anno Domini* lands but most citizens of the World stayed at home.
The Millennium only had relevance to Christians but most realized that
the year, day and hour had nothing to do with the birth of Jesus Christ.
Many £millions of taxpayers' money were wasted on Millennium projects,
which were either faulty, several years too late or they soon went bust.
Nevertheless, the second *Anno Domini* Millennium was certainly the most
expensive, longest, dazzling, greatest televisual extravaganza of all **Time**.

Theirs or Ours?

Political geography has invariably been an extremely hit or miss affair. Arbitrary lines drawn on maps become walls of barbed wire or concrete, which divide Us and force Us to move, because of Our different beliefs. We should be tearing them down, like the Berlin wall, but opposing social, economic, political and religious dogmas are keeping them up. The sea belongs to everyone so We are as free as the wind when We sail. Our ultimate freedom is to wander at will around the globe as freely as the fish, the birds, the insects, the mammals and Our own ancestors. Yet, Our freedom to enter foreign waters, territories and airspace now depends on where We were born, who Our parents were, how old We are, what faith We believe in, if We are healthy and whether We are wealthy. We must tear down the artificial barriers which divide Our Human Race. Or else We will keep putting up more until We have a maze with no exit. Time zones are artificial barriers that can all be demolished at a stroke.

The British Isles are still not one United Kingdom after all these years. The British Empire was the greatest in the World but has now vanished. The British drew lines in the sand to keep the warring Arab tribes apart, after encouraging them to revolt against the despotic Ottoman Empire. The UN gave Israel to the Jews after WW2 but the Palestinians then had no territory of their own and the same thing happened to the Kurds. They are still fighting for their own territory in Iraq, Iran and Turkey. Romanies and Gypsies have had no territories for hundreds of years. They still travel around Europe in their caravans with no fixed abode. Lake Chad supported small communities living on floating reed islands. Their addresses changed with the wind, from Nigeria to Niger to Chad. The Lapps herd reindeer between Norway, Sweden, Finland and Russia. They have not recognized any artificial borders for thousands of years. They found America, via the top of the World, long before Leif Ericsson, St. Brendan, The Knights Templar, Zheng He, Columbus or Cabot. Will Canada, USA and Mexico always be separated by imaginary lines? Do native Americans, Africans, Australians and New Zealanders own the mineral rights or do they belong to vast international conglomerates? The UN drew lines across Antarctica - why not give all of it to the UN?

The Worldwide System would allow geographical, cultural, sociological, economical, philosophical and political barriers to be razed to the ground. Yet, who is responsible for chronologies, calendars, clocks and zones? Are Time and Space the responsibility of one man, every man or no man? Is Our Human Race now living in a Timeless Space called: Nomansland? Or could The International Meridian Conference be reconvened by the United Nations Organization to take account of the many changes that have happened in Our World since it met in Washington DC in 1884 AD? The fundamental aim of the UN is summed up in the slogan: One World. This book can be summarized as: **One Time + One Space = One World.**

Magic or Logic?

All of the miracles described in *The Bible* can now be explained logically. Ancient astronomer-priests captured the attention of their followers with magic tricks such as: burning bushes, sticks to snakes or water to wine. Science can now answer many of the questions posed by the ancients. Yet, blind faith in science is just as bad as blind faith in the scriptures. There are still a few people in remote locations who have never seen a watch, radio, TV, phone, laptop, tablet or global positioning system. These commonplace electronic gizmos must seem like magic to them.

The word: magic, is derived from the Persian word: *magi,* for: wise men. The *magi* predicted coincidences of events in the Sky and on the Earth. A conjunction or an eclipse was thought to be auspicious or ominous, especially if it occurred near a solstice, an equinox or a full or new Moon. They thought that atmospheric, volcanic, seismic and messianic events on Earth coincided with one or more of these events in the Heavens. *The Bible* says that *magi* brought gold, frankincense and myrrh to baby Jesus to show that he was destined to become the next 'King of the Jews'. It does not say that there were three of them nor that they were kings. We do not know what, where or when was their 'Star of Bethlehem'. The early Christians are thought to have used magic mushrooms, myrrh frankincense, cannabis, opium and other hallucinogens to talk to *God.* The Christian altar is a relic of Pagan ritual sacrifices and fertility rites. The cannibalistic act of holy communion is a prehistoric magical ritual. Stone Henge was thought to have been magically constructed by Merlin.

It is now time to break the magic spell of the Mystic seven-day week. We can be sure that *God* did not speak to Moses on top of Mount Sinai. There is no such mountain nor volcano in the land of the Moon-god *Sin.* Nevertheless, millions of pilgrims go there every year in search of *God.* There is no evidence that Moses or *The Ten Commandments* existed. The eruption that led to the Exodus was probably Thera in the Aegean. This event caused the destruction of the Minoan or Atlantis civilization and it may have driven the Children of Israel or Israelites out of Egypt. They probably thought that the 'ten plagues' were divine retribution. However, the Earth sciences can probably provide a logical explanation. The gravitational pull of the Sun and the Moon causes all the tides. They also pull on all of the tectonic plates and on the atmosphere. Similarly, the pull of all the Planets on the Sun causes spots and flares, which can also effect the climate and the weather here on Planet Earth. Our global weather and economy are both extremely complex systems, which are enormously difficult to simulate in powerful computer models. However, they are beginning to make accurate predictions of changes. We may be able to predict floods, droughts, earthquakes and eruptions. We may even be able to predict rises and falls in global stock markets. Or the effect of a ten-day week and **full-time-job-sharing-as-the-norm.**

Myths or Maths?

We should base all Our measurements upon maths; rather than myths. The bases 8, 12, 14 and 16 were used in the fractional Imperial System. The base 10 is the only one used in the digital-decimal Metric System. However, this inaccurate system only applies to Space but not to Time. Children find it very hard to understand why We still divide the day by twenty-fours and sixties when their pocket calculators divide by tens. They much prefer using digital clocks and watches to analogue ones. Whereas most adults prefer to use analogue timepieces and instruments. Some say that calculators and computers make children lazy and they can no longer do mental arithmetic; yet others say that these electronic gizmos free their minds to cope with much more important problems. Learned professors have difficulty in writing computer programs that can translate the Solar, Lunar, Lunar/Solar, Stellar and Planar calendars.

The prime number seven is used by the Jews, Christians and Muslims as the basis of their week but is not fundamental to the other religions. It is based upon the legend of the *Ten Commandments* contained in the Ark of the Covenant, which has now been lost - or was this all a myth? Egyptologists are sceptical that the events in the *Old Testament* really happened since there is no archaeological evidence that the Israelites were ever enslaved in Egypt and no record of someone called Moses. However, the author believes that the catastrophic eruption of Thera was triggered by the Solar eclipse near the vernal equinox in 1456 BC. Its tsunami and ash-cloud inundated Egypt and blotted-out the Sun. He believes this occurred during the reign of Akhenaten and Nefertiti who worshipped one Sun-god, the *Aten*, and used a seven-day week. He thinks that this was the origin of the 'pillar of fire' and 'ten plagues' and it led to a mass migration and the end of their heretical reign. The Egyptians rebelled and returned to their ten-day week and old gods. Carbon dating, dendrochronology and ice cores might pinpoint the date of the Theran eruption and correct Minoan and Egyptian chronologies. There may be more evidence of this theory in Tut-ankh-amun's tomb.

Worldwide Time is the best way to make years, months and weeks fit. We need a global chronology based upon the age of Our Planet, the age of Our civilization and some astronomical coincidences in 2000 AD. If a vague year has 360 days, a month has 30 days, a week has 10 days, it is then mathematically correct to have a remainder of 5 or 6 days. A digital week would encourage most jobs to be shared and this could benefit most businesses as well as many aspects of Our society today. A decimal day would avoid the confusion caused by 12 or 24 hours and the incompatibility of the hexadecimal system with pocket calculators. **Worldwide Space** would be the new yard-stick, foot-stick or hand-stick with which to measure the length, area, volume and weight of anything. What could be simpler than this **Worldwide Time and Space System**?

Imperial or Metric?

The Romans and Roman-Catholics developed an Imperial Time System,
which the Caesars and the Popes tried to spread throughout Our Planet.
Their *Anno Domini* chronology, Gregorian calendar and Benedictine clock
are now used by most of Us; but they are certainly not used by Us all.
The Imperial Space System was based upon anatomy, although We are
all different sizes, and each of its fractional units had a different base.
It was standardized throughout the Roman Empire, however, when it fell
each state devised its own distances, dimensions, weights and measures.
The British imposed their own Imperial System throughout their empire.
The Americans changed some of their measurements, just to be different.
This led to confusion and corruption until the Age of Enlightenment.
The Metric System was intended to be based upon the size of Our Planet.
The metre was based on the Paris Meridian from Dunkirk to Barcelona
but, although it took seven years to measure this distance, it was wrong.
The metre should have been based upon the girth of the Earth and then
land and sea distances could have been measured by the same system.
The metre is now an arbitrary size based on the second, which was once
an eighty-six-thousand-four-hundredth part of a mean Solar day but it
is now an arbitrary number of vibrations of a minute atom of caesium.
Caesar still rules Our chronology, Our calendar, Our clock and Our rule.

Our search for the perfect system of measurements has taken Us some
twelve thousand years and yet We still do not use a coordinated system.
The Imperial System was originally based on anatomical measurements
but these were divided by vulgar fractions and each had a different base.
The International System was intended to be global, digital and decimal
but it has many faults and has taken over two centuries to be adopted.
The Navigation System was based on the equatorial girth of Planet Earth
but this was divided by 360 degrees then by 60 minutes and 60 seconds.
The Worldwide System is based upon Earth's age, orbit, spin and girth.
It is also based on the linear number ten and the circular number 360.
This new global-digital-decimal system should be adopted by everyone.

This is an urgent matter for the International Standards Organization,
which already regulates all the other measurements that most of Us use.
It is also a matter for the International Bureau of Weights and Measures,
which is responsible for the accuracy of all the measurements We use.
The International Hydrographic Bureau is responsible for all sea charts.
These are based upon the Navigational System and the Metric System.
All land maps will, eventually, conform to The World Geodetic System.
Yet, there is no mechanism for land and sea distances to be integrated.
We now need a **Worldwide Standards Organization** to replace them all.
This should come under the wing of the United Nations Organization.
Digital notes and decimal coins took centuries to be adopted by everyone.
Old habits die hard - so it may take many years for the penny to drop.

Part Six

Recommendation

The Worldwide System

"The Time is out of joint: O cursed spite.
That ever I was born to set it right."

William Shakespeare (1564 – 1616 AD) *Hamlet*

Worldwide Talk

Our many dissimilar languages and dialects make Us seem different; when We all have the exactly the same origins - in the depths of Africa. It would be a tremendous achievement if We could all use the same language and script and all of Our measurements could be standardized. Skeptics claim that this is impossible to achieve and that the failure of Esperanto proves that We will never have a global script and language. The English language was based on many other tongues but is now the global diplomatic, commercial, scientific, aviation, marine and sport talk. Time is the most common word in English - yet few of Us understand it. The British Empire was once the greatest of all, throughout the globe. Britain is now the most secular territory in the English speaking World. So it could be the first to adopt a simple, secular measurement system. The Internet and Worldwide Web were originally based upon English. Nevertheless, they now incorporate many other languages and scripts. Although numbers are named and spoken differently in every language, they are written in approximately the same way everywhere on Earth. Handwriting is no longer taught in the USA, however, they still teach the *Anno Domini* chronology, Gregorian calendar and Benedictine clock.

The Imperial System had many different bases, so it was difficult to use in pocket calculators and it has now been replaced by the Metric System. The American System was based upon the Imperial System but it has several different units and is not being replaced by the Metric System. The Navigation System is based on 360 degrees, 60 minutes and decimals for finding position in latitude and longitude and for compass directions, yet distance is in nautical miles, altitude in feet and depth in metres. The International Metric System is used in the sporting, scientific and technological World, however, it is based upon a vulgar fraction of a day. It embodies Latin prefixes and the Roman-Catholic age, date and time. Latin was meant to be a global language and its script is still used as the basis for all of the European languages but few cardinals speak it now.

This Worldwide Measurement System can be summarized as: global age, digital date, decimal time with a single time zone; plus global-digital-decimal angle, length, area, volume, mass, substance, electrical current, light intensity and temperature; plus navigational direction, distance, latitude and longitude.

All of the new base names, which are needed for all of the new units, have three letters and all of the new primary units have three digits. Three letter words can be substituted for three digit numbers in digital timepieces and they also form the basis of a single syllable vocabulary. It can be pronounced and learned at any age, in any tongue, Worldwide. **The Worldwide System** could be the beginning of **Worldwide Talk**.

Worldwide Time

Worldwide Time is based on the age, orbit and spin of Our Planet Earth. A new age, date and time system should start at an astronomical event. The most convenient year was 2000 AD for several reasons including: the change of the zodiac age and the grouping of the five visible Planets. The most convenient day was on the vernal or northern spring equinox. This very auspicious day also coincided with a full-Moon in 2000 AD. The most convenient time was midnight along the Greenwich Meridian.

Computer software usually indicates the time, date and age, based upon a two-digit system e.g. 07:07:07 on 07-07-07 however this caused serious problems at the Millennium when many computers were liable to go haywire and the cost of putting them right was $1,000,000,000,000. **Worldwide Time** is based on the much more logical three-digit system, which can be incorporated into all computer software as an option.

The age of Our Planet is now estimated to be about 4,550,000,000 years. The age of Our civilization is now estimated to be about 12,000 years. The age used in Our chronology could therefore be 4,550,012,000 years. Only the last three digits are usually needed to show the **global age**.

Three variable periods can be used to measure the date and the time: day: the Time Our Planet takes to spin or revolve relative to the Sun; year: the Time Our Planet takes to orbit around the Sun. = 365.242 days; moonth: the Time Our Moon takes for its cycle of phases. = 29.531 days. The mean Solar year can be divided in many different ways but trying to fit any kind of Lunar moonth into any kind of Solar year is impossible. It is better to think of the year as being 360 working days plus a bit. These 360 working days can be divided into 36 ten-day working weeks. The bit is five democratic days plus a leap day every four years or so. Only these ordinal three digits are needed to show the **digital date**.

The diurnal cycle of one day can be divided-up in many different ways but is now divided, on most clock dials, into two equal twelve-hour parts. Sixty minutes and sixty seconds were convenient ways of dividing up the same dial but it is very confusing to incorporate two revolutions of the hour hand per day and it is very much simpler to use decimals of a day. Only the first three digits are usually needed to show the **decimal time.**

There are no time zones nor daylight saving measures with this system. The convention of starting the day at midnight should continue along the Greenwich Meridian but, since there are no time zones, this means that daylight and darkness will occur at different times in different places. Only nine digits are needed to show the age, date and time, everywhere.

Worldwide Time = global age + digital date + decimal time + single zone.

Worldwide Time Units

This hypothesis focuses upon ten completely different kinds of **Time: Cosmic Time** based on Astronomy, **Atomic Time** based on Physics, **Geotic Time** based on Planet Earth, **Bionic Time** based on Nature. **Humanic Time** based on Mankind, **Mystic Time** based on Religion. **Organic Time** based on Working, **Civic Time** based on Law and Order, **Olympic Time** based on Sport and **Music Time** based on Recreation.

In **Cosmic Worldwide Time** the mean Solar year and mean Solar day remain the basic units but they are divided in a completely different way. The new word: *yer* is used instead of the old word: year, because it has three letters and to indicate that a different measuring system is used. The *yer* has 360 days plus a 5 or 6 day remainder used for democracy. The old words: decade and century now become: *Decayer* and *Hectoyer*. Millennium is replaced by: *Kiloyer* and there are: *Megayer* and *Gigayer*. These longer words can more simply be abbreviated to: *Kil, Meg* and *Gig*. Their standard symbols can be respectively: *y, Dy, Hy, Ky, My* and *Gy*. Capital letters denote that the multiple unit is larger than its base. The mean Solar day is divided into *decidays, centidays, millidays...* which can be abbreviated to: *dec, cen, mil...* or in symbols: *dd, cd, md...*

In **Atomic Worldwide Time** the basic fixed unit is known as a *tik*. This new unit with the standard symbol *t* replaces the atomic second s. There were exactly one million *tiks* per day at the Metric Millennium.

In **Geotic Worldwide Time** there are now over one million *tiks* per day.

In **Bionic Worldwide Time** there are no changes to Natural timescales.

In **Humanic Worldwide Time** there are about 100,000 heartbeats a day and about ten menstrual periods to one gestation period.

There is no **Mystic Worldwide Time** as this is a simple secular system.

In **Organic Worldwide Time** a digitalized *wek* and decimalized day allow most jobs to be shared and working times to be much more flexible.

In **Civic Worldwide Time** the smallest unit is a variable *milliday* or *mil*. It is preferable to use primary units and so to only count in thousands. There are also secondary units: the *centiday* or *cen*, the *deciday* or *dec* and the *Decaday* or *wek*, which replace the quarter, hour and week. And tertiary units: *mon* a period of thirty days that replaces the month, or: *ank* a period of forty days, which can be used as an alternative. These new units are given the symbols: *md, cd, dd, w,*) and ⊕.

In **Olympic Worldwide Time** all speeds are in *hans* or *Kilohans* per *tik*.

In **Music Worldwide Time** the musical scale would have ten notes, volume would continue to be based upon the logarithmic decibel scale and all vibrations would be measured in cycles per *tik*.

Worldwide Time Digits

Anno Domini **age** started with the year 1 or 01 or 001; not with year 000. There were no zero years between BC and AD and so many people have questioned whether the Millennium was really at the end of 1999 AD. The zero was unknown to Romans so the Millennium was at their MM. Gregorian **date** starts at 01 months and 01 monthdays or 001 yeardays. This is why digital calculators and computers are confused by **Time**. The **time** can be measured using an analogue or a digital timepiece. These are based on the 12-hour half-day or 24-hour full-day systems. The first hour of the former is 12 but the first hour of the latter is 00. Digital **time** starts at 00 hours 00 minutes 00 seconds and this 24-hour system should have superseded the 12-hour system over a century ago. The French revolution introduced a new chronology, calendar and clock based upon the year of the revolution, a digital week and a decimal day. But French revolutionary Time had no zero year, zero day nor zero hour. They did not understand the difference between counting and measuring.

With **Worldwide Time** there are primary, secondary and tertiary units. The primary units of age, date and time are measured by three digits. Years in thousands, millions and billions; days from 000 to 364 or 365; days are divided into tens, hundreds and thousands in the decimal way. The secondary units of date and time: the *cen, dec* and *wek* are based upon the first, or the first and second, digits in the three-digit groups. The tertiary units apply to divisions of the 360-day part of the year. There is an option of using either a tertiary unit *mon* meaning: 30 days, or a tertiary unit *ank* meaning: 40 days, these are marked, respectively, with Roman numerals and English letters, rather than using numbers.

When using digital counters **global age, digital date** and **decimal time** all start at 000 and the system counts-up in a series of three digits. The largest unit is always on the left and the smallest on the right. These can be identified by primary unit symbols, shown after each unit. When using analogue dials it is impracticable to divide them into 1,000. So they are divided into 100 and can then display several different units. A dial can represent a complete day and it may show dawn and dusk. It can also show the 10 days in the *wek* or larger groups of 100 days. The size and shape of each hand indicate which unit it is measuring.

When marking Time or using other scalar measurements fingers should be numbered: left: **01234** right: **56789**. Number **9** is the **10**th finger. The number **10** has two digits and so this would need two fingers. The *Anno Domini* year **900** was considered to be in the **10**th century and **1900** in the **20**th despite the absence of the years **0** AD or **0** BC. When counting separate objects such as coins, instead of using scales, one must then omit the zero and count: **1, 2, 3, 4, 5, 6, 7, 8, 9, 10.** Decimal coinage is now used Worldwide - try explaining £.s.d to a child.

Global Age and Digital Date

The **global age** is the chronological part of the **Worldwide Time System**. Planet Earth coalesced, very slowly, about 4,550,000,000 years ago. Civilization began, soon after the last Ice Age, about 12,000 years ago. So, the year 2000 AD converts to *yer* 4,550,012,000 **WT** or 000 for short. This is not re-writing history but it puts today into proper perspective. Most states now use *Anno Domini* chronology, which was inaccurately based upon what was estimated to be the birth year of Jesus Christ. Therefore **global age** does not favor Christianity, nor any other religion. 2000 AD was the most convenient year to change to a new chronology, calendar and clock, although no countries adopted them in that year. The day for the changeover to occur does not have to be on 1 January. It is better to realign the Solar calendar year with Astronomical Time and the tropical zodiac, which both start on the Solar vernal equinox. The end of the old system was at midnight along the Prime Meridian on the vernal equinox, which occurred on 19/20 March in 2000 AD. The old year 2000 AD overlapped with the new *yer* 000 **WT** so that the first year in this millennium coincided with the first *yer* in this *Kiloyer*. The twenty-first century AD could now be renamed: *Hectoyer Zero* **WT**. The three-digit abbreviation of the *yer*, which would be used for most everyday purposes, would be better than the two-digit abbreviation used now because more people are living past the age of one hundred. The two-digit abbreviation would have caused many computers to go haywire at the Millennium if they had not been expensively tweaked. The *yer* should always be written before the day, rather than after it.

The **digital date** is the calendrical part of the **Worldwide Time System**. It is similar to the ancient Egyptian and French revolutionary calendars. The only inconsistency is that there are not a thousand days in a year. A *yer* would be 360 days long, plus a *yerend* remainder of 5 or 6 days. The days in the *yer* would also be measured in a three-digit system. Thus 000d means during the first day in the calendar *yer* and 364d means during the last day: except in a leap *yer* when it would be 365d. The first two digits give the *wek*: 00*w* is the first *wek*, 35*w* the last. Each working *wek* is divided equally into 5 *leftdays* and 5 *rightdays*. The 360 days can be divided by 2,3,4,6,9,10,12 or18 for various reasons. Nine 40-day *anks* are the most useful and they are lettered from A to I. Alternatively, twelve 30-day *mons* are Roman numbered from I to XII. The ten days in the *wek* are all named by numbers: *zeroday, oneday, twoday, threeday, fourday, fiveday, sixday, sevenday, eightday, nineday*. A timetable, diary, chronograph, calendar, clock or watch needs no names. Just three little digits replace the whole of the Roman-Catholic calendar. There are presently many different ways of expressing the same date. The common chronic confusion, due to some people writing the day number before the month number and some after it, would be avoided. Thus months and weeks would be replaced by *mons* or *anks* and *weks*.

Digital Calendar

⊕ ank	wek left-days					wek right-days					) mon
A	000	001	002	003	004	005	006	007	008	009	
	010	011	012	013	014	015	016	017	018	019	I
	020	021	022	023	024	025	026	027	028	029	
	030	031	032	033	034	035	036	037	038	039	
B	040	041	042	043	044	045	046	047	048	049	II
	050	051	052	053	054	055	056	057	058	059	
	060	061	062	063	064	065	066	067	068	069	
	070	071	072	073	074	075	076	077	078	079	III
C	080	081	082	083	084	085	086	087	088	089	
	090	091	092	093	094	095	096	097	098	099	
	100	101	102	103	104	105	106	107	108	109	IV
	110	111	112	113	114	115	116	117	118	119	
D	120	121	122	123	124	125	126	127	128	129	
	130	131	132	133	134	135	136	137	138	139	V
	140	141	142	143	144	145	146	147	148	149	
	150	151	152	153	154	155	156	157	158	159	
E	160	161	162	163	164	165	166	167	168	169	VI
	170	171	172	173	174	175	176	177	178	179	
	180	181	182	183	184	185	186	187	188	189	
	190	191	192	193	194	195	196	197	198	199	VII
F	200	201	202	203	204	205	206	207	208	209	
	210	211	212	213	214	215	216	217	218	219	
	220	221	222	223	224	225	226	227	228	229	VIII
	230	231	232	233	234	235	236	237	238	239	
G	240	241	242	243	244	245	246	247	248	249	
	250	251	252	253	254	255	256	257	258	259	IX
	260	261	262	263	264	265	266	267	268	269	
	270	271	272	273	274	275	276	277	278	279	
H	280	281	282	283	284	285	286	287	288	289	X
	290	291	292	293	294	295	296	297	298	299	
	300	301	302	303	304	305	306	307	308	309	
	310	311	312	313	314	315	316	317	318	319	XI
I	320	321	322	323	324	325	326	327	328	329	
	330	331	332	333	334	335	336	337	338	339	
	340	341	342	343	344	345	346	347	348	349	XII
	350	351	352	353	354	355	356	357	358	359	
	360	361	362	363	364	365	<	leap-day			

Decimal Time and Single Zone

The **decimal time** is the horological part of the **Worldwide Time System**. **Worldwide Civic decimal time** is based on **Worldwide Cosmic decimal time**. **Civic** time is the sub-division of the day and there are a total of 86,400 **Civic** seconds per day but if the day is divided into 1,000,000 new units, numbered 000,000 to 999,999, each unit is equal to 0.0864 of a second. We thus have two further groups of three digits for different purposes. The larger *mil* group is all that is needed for most **Civic** requirements. One *mil* is equivalent to 1.44 minutes and this unit is as small as is needed for setting timetables, writing diaries and arranging meetings. The smaller *mic* group can be used in a stopwatch but it is not **Atomic**. A fixed **Atomic** *tik* = a variable **Cosmic** or **Civic** *mic* at a Millennium. A *Megatik* would only then be exactly equivalent to a mean Solar day.

The simplest way to display **decimal time** on a digital clock or watch is in *mils* on a three digit array and this unit can be thought of as either: 1 day = 1,000 *mil* = 100 *cen* = 10 *dec* or 1 *dec* = 100 *mil* or 1 *cen* = 10 *mil*. A digital chronograph/calendar/clock could show *yers*, days and *mils*. A digital calendar/watch need only show the three digit unit selected. A calculator/clock/watch can show all this information as a single row. Pocket computers could show midnight, midlight, Sunrise and Sunset at any location chosen and could also be set to show tides or Lunar phases.

Analogue dials cannot have 1,000 divisions, unless they are very large. A 100 division analogue clock or watch could have a short, fat hand showing: 10 *days* and 10 *dec* and a long, thin hand showing: 100 *mil*. It could have another hand showing the *yerday* number, up to 100 days, then 200 days, then 300 days, it is then reset to zero after day 364 or 5. It might also have shaded segments showing nighttime and daytime. These would be very useful for determining the flexible working times. The confusion often caused by the simultaneous use of the 12 and 24 hour clocks would be eliminated and time lapse calculations would become very much easier, because the base of ten is used throughout.

A **single zone** is the geographical part of the **Worldwide Time System**. The **decimal time** would be exactly the same everywhere on Earth. There would no longer be any necessity for an International Date Line. There would no longer be any necessity for daylight saving measures. There is no longer any reason for clocks to be set by the Sun at noon. Most clocks would be set by radio signals based upon midnight along the Prime Meridian, which would probably still be based on Greenwich. The Greenwich Meridian is the origin of Time and Space and has been since the International Meridian Conference met in Washington DC and recommended, in 1884 AD, that Time and Space should be decimalized. Although the second of time and the minute of latitude and longitude are now decimalized, the rest of Time and Space are still fractionalized.

Comparisons

World Time				Ratio	Time			
Sign	Unit	Origin	Numbering		Sign	Unit	Origin	Numbering
Primary Units								
Gy	Gigayer	yer x 10^9	000-999	=	-	aeons	year x 10^9	1-1,000
My	Megayer	yer x 10^6	000-999	=	-	millions	year x 10^6	1-1,000
Ky	Kiloyer	yer x 10^3	000-999	=	-	millenia	year x 10^3	1-1,000
y	yer	Earth orbit	000-999	=	y	year	Earth orbit	1-1,000
d	day	Earth spin	000-359*	=	d	day	Earth spin	1-365/6*
md	mil	day x 10^{-3}	000-999	1:1.44	min	minute	Hour/60	1-60
t	tik	day x 10^{-6}	000-999	1:0.0864	s	Second ****		
Secondary Units								
Hy	Hectoyer	yer x10^2	0-9	=	c	century	year x 102	1st, 2nd..
Dy	Decayer	yer c 10	0-9	=	-	decade	year x 10	1st, 2nd...
w	wek	day x 10	00-35*	10.7	w	week	day x 7	1-52***
dd	dec	day x 10^{-1}	0-9	10.24	h	hour	day/24	(1-12) x 2
cd	cen	day x 10^{-2}	0-99	100:96	-	quarter	day/96	1/4,1/2, 3/4
Tertiary Units								
⊕	ank	day x 40	A-I	-	-	-	-	-
)	mon	day x 30	I-XII	-	-	month	lunations	1-12
-	-	day x 20		20:40	-	fortnight	day x 14	

There is little point in having a 20 day unit but if needed it could use Greek symbols. The fortnight is falling into disuse in Britain and is unknown in the USA.

* plus 5 or 6 day remainder
** year-days, month-days, week-days
*** 1 or 2 days less than a year
**** A *tik* is exactly 0.0864 of an Atomic second.

Digital Watches

Digital **Worldwide Time** is counted in 1000s or three digit groups. A timepiece could show the *yer, day* and *mil* together, or simply *mil*. The *tik* or the *microday* could be used in a stopwatch.

Chronograph/calendar/watch/stopwatch.
The left button operates the stopwatch function.
The right button operates the *YER/DAY/MIL/TIK* function.
Touch the right button and it shows the unit being displayed.
Press the right button and it changes to the next unit.

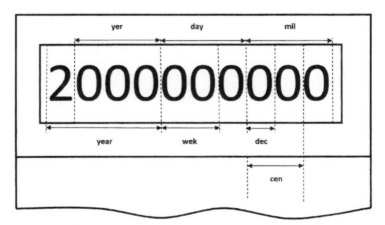

Combined calculator, chronograph, calendar and clock.
This would cost very little more than the calculator alone.

Analogue Clocks

If an analogue dial has 100 divisions the **digital date and decimal time**
It can also show the *wek* and either count to 100 or be reset after 36.
Light or dark segments show day or night and indicate working times.

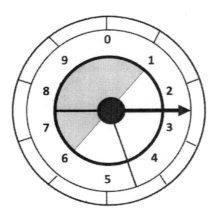

Calendar/clock or watch
The pointed hand shows *wek*.
The thick hand shows *day* and *dec*.
The thin hand shows *cen* and *mil*.
It is 247 *day* the time is 544 *mil*.
Dawn was at 100 *mil* and dusk will be at 600 *mil*.

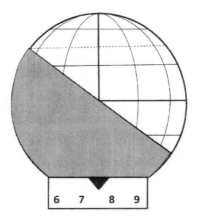

Global clock
Globe rotates daily and prime meridian pointer moves round the scale.
Dark hemisphere tilts with the seasons.

Digital Diaries

Diaries are a schedule of future events and a record of past ones. Since **digital date** is perpetual, a diary would be the same every *yer*. So stationery shops would not run out of stock or have to scrap surplus. Most Gregorian diaries now give the year, the month name or number, the year-day number, month-day number, week number and day name. They usually, nowadays, have a page per week beginning on a Monday. Most computers have Gregorian calendars and diaries in their memory. Some show year, year-day, month, month-day, week, week-day numbers. The **global age, digital date, decimal time and single zone** could be built in as another option so that computers could then be easily converted whenever it is decided to adopt this more logical system. Many organizations now insist that employees use electronic diaries so that everyone knows where everyone else is so they can arrange meetings. Nevertheless, most people still prefer traditional pocket or desk diaries. This is what your paper or electronic **digital date diary** might look like:

		left-days			right-days
210	250	train to London	**215**	325	dentist
	400	meet Bob at his office			shopping
	500	lunch with Colin			gardening
	550	progress meeting			service car
210	250	working on report	**216**	300	church
					lunch at club
				550	cricket
				550	phone Neil
		Dinner with family			
212	250	plane to Paris	**217**	400	French classes
	350	meeting with Jules		450	bank
	450	meeting with Oscar		500	music classes
	650	return via Chunnel			
213	250	drive to York	**218**		Sue's birthday
				400	meeting with Geoff
		Lunch with family			
	600	arrive home			
	700	Pool with Denis at club			decorate kitchen
214	250	Work at office	**219**		
	500	Lunch with Chris			charity work
	500	handover notes for Alan			
	600	complete report			art group

Decimal Timetables

Being at the right place at the right time has become more and more important to everyone, everywhere and We would all be lost without maps, compasses, calendars, clocks, watches, diaries and timetables. The first timetables were used by monks and nuns, who gathered seven times per day to say prayers, and they became important in schools, colleges and universities, which still revolve around the sound of a bell. Industry, business, defence, leisure and transport all have timetables. However, these are usually printed in such small type that they are impossible to read by older people who often need to wear spectacles. Think how much simpler train, bus, ferry and airline timetables would be if they were the same every day and they were printed in larger type.

Worldwide Timetables for all forms of transport and other kinds of activity could be exactly the same every day and so much easier to read. However, it would be much better if they changed with the seasons to make the best use of daylight and avoid accidents at dawn and dusk. Variable work times are **flextime** so variable work days are **flexdate**. This would be very easy to incorporate if 360 days were the same but extremely hard to build into Our existing timetables in which there are usually different schedules for Saturdays, Sundays and Bank Holidays. Higgledy-piggledy months and wasteful weeks make Our lives complex. **Digital date** would help Us to lead simpler lives and would save energy.

All school and college timetables are extremely difficult to organize and there are often two classes fighting for one room at the start of a term. Half hour lessons and one hour lectures are the norm but some are experimenting with different systems based upon the attention span of 80 minutes (50 *mil*) which has been found to give much better results. The British lunch hour is considered to be too long but the French think that it is too short and hot countries have a *siesta* of up to four hours. It has been shown that much less work is done after lunch, everywhere.

Railway timetables highlighted the apparent necessity to change times in zones throughout large countries like China, Russia, Canada or USA. Canada and USA now have railway time zones but the Russian railways all use Moscow time everywhere and China has no time zones at all. Airline timetables are based upon *Anno Domini*, the Gregorian calendar and the 24-hour clock but they are very confusing when summer time is incorporated and, in consequence, many people miss their connections. The Australian States and Territories all have different summer times because their politicians still cannot concur about this simple matter. The solution is to use Greenwich Time or **Worldwide Time** everywhere. Internet surfers are realizing that cyber-time is independent of daylight. These simple, logical, temporal ideas have never been considered before but it is now time to place them firmly on the Time table.

Zeroday

Worldwide Time is, simply, a non-religious, temporal or secular system. It may help to eliminate perpetual religious arguments and conflicts, which are frequently caused by different ages, dates, times and zones. A Giant Leap of 80 days (2 *ank*) is needed to replace *Anno Domini* age, Gregorian date, 12 or 24 hour time and multifarious crazy time zones. Historians have had to cope with Giant Leaps before - but never again. It may take a century for Us to count **Worldwide Time** on Our hands. Yet, this is a very small increment in the history of Our Human Race.

At 00:00 GMT on Monday 20 March (Gregorian) in the year 2000 AD

Worldwide Time was: **4Gy550My012Ky000y000d000md** everywhere.

Or, using commas, colons and decimal points instead of these symbols:

Worldwide Time was: **4,550,012,000:000.000**

Or, more simply, by ignoring the first seven digits:

global age was: **000y**
digital date was: **000d**
decimal time was: **000md**
Worldwide Time was: **000y000d000md** or: **000:000.000**

Organic Worldwide Time need not go smaller than the variable *milliday*. The **Cosmic** second is a variable unit of **Cosmic Time** but the **Atomic** second is now a fixed unit of **Atomic Time** and this is decimalized. An **Atomic** *tik* could be defined as one millionth of a mean Solar day at the moment **Cosmic Worldwide Time** began, but would then be fixed. The *tik* with its symbol **t** could be sub-divided using SI notation thus:

004Gy550My012Ky000y000d000md000t000mt000μt000nt000pt000ft000at

Or, substituting commas, a colon, a decimal point and a semicolon:

4,550,012,000:000.000;000,000,000,000,000,000,000

The International Metric System took two centuries to catch on and is still not a global standard but the **Worldwide Time System** is more logical and it could become a global standard as quickly as the Internet and Worldwide Web became essential systems in Our postmodern World. Global electronic mail is instantaneous and should be postmarked with the age, date and time it is sent but time zones make this impossible. Many Internet surfers already use **decimal time** with no time zones. Some already use three digits for the year and three digits for the day. Nevertheless the **Worldwide Time System** as a whole, must be adopted, or at very least recommended, by some influential global organizations. Regrettably, We have not formed a **Worldwide Standards Organization.**

Worldwide Time Conversions

Multiples

This is the International prefix system (with suggested alternatives):

Multiple	Prefix	Symbol	Multiple	Prefix	Symbol	
10^{-1}	deci	d	10	deca	da	(D)
10^{-2}	centi	c	10^2	hecto	h	(H)
10^{-3}	milli	m	10^3	kilo	k	(K)
10^{-6}	micro	µ	10^6	mega	M	
10^{-9}	nano	n	10^9	giga	G	
10^{-12}	pico	p	10^{12}	tera	T	
10^{-15}	femto	f	10^{15}	peta	P	
10^{-18}	atto	a	10^{18}	exa	E	

Note that 10^{-21} second, the smallest unit of **time**, is called a chronon. All units that are larger than their base should have a capital letter. This could cause confusion with K the SI unit for absolute temperature. However, Celsius is used in **The Worldwide System**.

Global age

000Gy000My000Ky000y WT = 4550010000 BC
004Gy550My012Ky000y WT = 2000 AD

Digital date

Ordinal year-day numbers are printed in many diaries and are based upon 1 January (Gregorian) = 001. Digital date = ordinal date - 80 days.

Decimal time

Any twelve-hour analogue clock or watch can quickly be converted to **decimal time** by fixing a sticker to the glass or the dial, the hour hand then shows 5 *dec* and the minute hand shows approx. 1 *cen* /quarter.

		1 *mil*	= 1.44	minutes	= 86.4	seconds
1 *cen*	=	10 *mil*	= 14.4	minutes	< 1/4	hour
2 *cen*	=	20 *mil*	= 28.8	minutes	< 1/2	hour
3 *cen*	=	30 *mil*	= 43.2	minutes	< 3/4	hour
4 *cen*	=	40 *mil*	= 57.6	minutes	< 1	hour
5 *cen*	=	50 *mil*	= 72	minutes	= 1.2	hours
1 *dec*	=	100 *mil*	= 144	minutes	= 2.4	hours
1 **day**	=	1000 *mil*	= 1440	minutes	= 24	hours

Single zone

Worldwide ages, dates and times would be the same as at Greenwich and there would be no so-called daylight saving measures.

Worldwide Space

The search for a simple system for measuring all lengths or distances, angles or directions, areas, volumes or capacities and weights or masses has taken thousands of years and We still have not found the solution. Most civilizations had a system based upon non-standard anatomy but some of the earliest seem to have been based upon the size of the Earth. As international trade developed, so did the need for only one system. Most of Us now use the International Metric System, which was meant to be based upon the surveyed girth of the Earth but this was incorrect. It is now the distance light travels in an arbitrary decimal of a second and this is now an arbitrary number of vibrations of a caesium atom. So both **Time** and **Space** are now based upon these arbitrary numbers. Although Our bodies grow in all shapes and sizes it is still useful to relate distances and dimensions to Our Human anatomy in some way. **The Worldwide Space System** is based on the arc of a millionth of one degree of longitude at the Equator - about the width of an average hand.

A nautical mile is the arc subtended by an angular minute of longitude at the Equator, so the Earth's girth is 360 x 60 = 21,600 nautical miles. The International Hydrographic Bureau now equates one nautical mile with exactly 1852 metres and one cable is one tenth of a nautical mile. It is confusing to use angular minutes and seconds as well as time ones, so these are often referred to as arc-minutes and arc-seconds but it is still confusing to use base sixty when most measures are based on ten. However, latitude and longitude are now measured using 360 degrees, 60 arc-minutes and then decimals; rather than using 60 arc-seconds. It would have been less confusing to have used decimals of a degree. These are used in *Global Earth* and most global positioning systems. Navigators used fathoms (six feet) for depths but they now use metres. Aviators use latitude and longitude but they still use feet for altitude and they usually measure their speed in knots (nautical miles per hour). Some motorists use road maps with the scale of one inch to one mile. Others use maps with the scale of one centimetre to one kilometre. Most countries have road signs in kilometres, whilst some still use miles. So there is no global standard system for distances on land, sea and air. The **Worldwide Space System** can be used anywhere on Planet Earth.

The International Metric System has gradually been adopted in Britain (except for the mile and the pint) and so it has to be used by all trades. Some tradesmen were so defiant that they were prepared to go to jail. The building trade still use some old Imperial sizes, converted to Metric. A sheet of plywood is still the same old size of eight feet by four feet but timber, bricks, paving, glass and cement are now sold in Metric sizes. The **Worldwide Time and Space** systems are separate but compatible. A few more fundamental global-digital-decimal measurements complete **The Worldwide Measurement System,** which might be used for ever.

Worldwide Dimensions and Distances

Most ancient measuring systems had no relationship between the units used for the dimensions of things such as chairs, chariots or boats and the sizes of fields or the distances between places on land and at sea. The International Metric System was meant to unify all measurements. Although the metre was based upon an inaccurate measurement, from the Equator to the Poles, kilometres are better than miles (1,000 paces), metres are better than yards (from the King's nose to his finger tips), feet (length of an average foot) and inches (a finger width) because they are not based upon anatomy but are a global-digital-decimal standard. The metre was originally a platinum bar, which had to be maintained under controlled conditions, in one location, for comparative purposes. It is now based upon the, presumed constant, Universal speed of light. So Space is related to Time although the metre and second are arbitrary.

When the metre was devised it was assumed that Earth was a sphere. Any great circle through the Poles is slightly smaller due to centrifugal forces that expanded the Equator and stopped Our Planet from toppling. Instead of basing the metre on the distance from a Pole to the Equator, it could have been based on Earth's diameter, radius or circumference. However, this was not possible when the Metric System was devised. The Paris Meridian was used to measure the metre but the Greenwich Meridian was used to measure latitude, longitude, age, date and time. We can now measure the Earth's circumference extremely accurately. The Atlantic Ocean is getting wider; the Pacific Ocean is getting smaller. Consequently the girth of the Earth always remains much the same size. The metre was based upon the distance between the North Pole and the Equator being 10,000 km, however, the actual distance is 10,013 km. Since Earth is an oblate sphere, the length of the Equator is 40,075 km.

We can divide Earth's circumference at the Equator, or girth, in four ways:

a.	If We divide it by	4×10^7	We get just over 1 metre.
b.	If We divide it by	10^{10}	We get just over 400 mm.
c.	If We divide it by	400×10^6	We get just over 100 mm.
d.	If We divide it by	360×10^6	We get just over 111 mm.

With any of these options the land and sea distances could be the same. Option d is roughly the same size as the ancient Arabic palm or hand. This 4 inch unit is still used for measuring the sizes of horses or camels. The *han* is the unit of length/distance in the **Worldwide Space System**. It can be multiplied or divided in the usual global-digital-decimal way. This could become the basis for all land, sea and air maps and charts. It is already built-in as an option on most global positioning systems. It is a handy size that will fit into your pocket and can be marked along the base of a protractor or multiplied when used on a tape measure.

Worldwide Angles and Directions

The cardinal directions divide the compass rose into four right angles but further subdivisions can be inscribed in several different ways. The French revolutionaries argued that angles should be decimalized. Dividing a circle into 100 units is too coarse and 1,000 is too fine so they experimented with decimal angles, navigation instruments and charts, based upon 400 angular units called: gradians, which worked very well. Each gradian was subdivided *ad infinitum* in the normal decimal way. By using this system land and sea distances could have been unified. However, they could not measure Earth's girth very accurately.

We can measure Earth's equatorial circumference, at average sea level, very accurately and We now know that Earth is not a perfect sphere. If We keep 360 degrees, divided into 60 minutes then decimals, We will not need the expense of changing maps, charts, compasses, sextants etc. Our Planet Earth rotates at the rate of 360 degrees per mean Solar day. A *deciday* would be the equivalent of 36 degrees of longitude anywhere on Earth and this would be equal to 2,160 nautical miles at the Equator. But if We keep 360 degrees then divide them in the decimal, rather than the hexadecimal, way all land and sea distances could then be unified. We would have to change all charts, maps and instruments to this new standard but they all have to be updated on a regular basis anyway.

The International System unit of plane angle is the radian and this is used for scientific and engineering purposes - but not for navigation. Nevertheless, most engineers prefer to work in degrees then convert to radians, which are mostly used for rotational speeds and accelerations. The International Standard unit of a spherical angle is the steradian. A circle of 360 degrees = 2π radians. A complete sphere = 4π steradians. The man or woman in the street may never need to know this and so the **Worldwide Space System** uses angular degrees, shortened to *ang*.

Both **Worldwide Time and Space** are based upon 360 as well as ten. Some critics of **decimal time** have said that a chronometer showing hours, minutes and seconds is essential in order to establish a position. This has been the main objection to changing to **decimal time** but this objection is no longer valid because decimals of a degree can now be selected on global positioning systems with electronic maps and charts. So position and direction are now decimalized whilst distances are still in nautical miles, statute miles or kilometers rather than *Kilohans*.

The second is now defined in terms of an arbitrary number of Atomic vibrations and the metre is currently defined as an arbitrary number of wavelengths of light - which means absolutely nothing to most of Us. For accuracy, the *tik* and the *han* could be defined in the same way. Yet, fundamentally, We would have both Time and Space on Our hands.

Worldwide Weights & Measures

There are no Natural weights nor measures so each civilization, nation or city developed its own system, enforced by its local laws and by-laws, until it became necessary for there to be some form of standardization. However, in most cases there was no mathematical relationship between weights and volumetric measures, which had each evolved separately. In both the Imperial and Metric systems volume and weight are related. Water is found everywhere on Our Planet and so it is used to equate volume with weight and is also used to define Centigrade temperature. One gallon (4 quarts or 8 pints) of fresh water weighs ten pounds. One litre (1,000 cubic centimetres) of fresh water weighs one kilogram. Strictly speaking one should use the term: mass, rather than: weight, because everything has the same mass wherever it is and yet its weight varies according to the gravitational attraction at its particular location.

The Imperial and Metric Systems incorporate both volume and capacity. **The Worldwide Space System** only has one volumetric measurement. The standard unit of volume or capacity could be one cubic *han*. The standard unit of mass or weight could be one cubic *han* of water. New three-letter names would be needed for both of these new units. The unit of volume could be one *can*, and the unit of weight one *wan*. The standard unit of wealth could be one *wan* of gold, called: a *gan*.

We now have a complete new system for measuring Time and Space. It can be called **The Worldwide Time and Space System** but there are several other basic measurements that are not related to Time or Space. They are substance, electric current, luminous intensity and temperature. All of these units are already globalized, digitized and decimalized.

Temperature was once measured in degrees Fahrenheit but it is now measured in degrees Celsius or Centigrade and this scale is based on the freezing and boiling points of water at normal atmospheric pressure. The International System specifies the Kelvin temperature scale which extrapolates the Celsius scale down to absolute zero (-273.15 C) but, although this is used by scientists and engineers, most people would choose to use the Celsius or Centigrade scale for everyday purposes. Scientists have now managed to measure temperatures as low as two billionths of a degree above absolute zero and as high as 200,000,000 C. The degree symbol: 0 has been discarded for both angle and temperature.

There seems to be no reason to change from mols, amps or candelas. So they are included, as they are, in the list of ten basic measurements. The complete ensemble is called: **The Worldwide Measurement System.** It has taken two centuries for many different measures to be replaced, in most nations, by: The International Metric System, with all its faults. It may take another century to replace this with **The Worldwide System**.

Worldwide Space Conversions

	Worldwide	International	Imperial	Navigational
Linear	1 han	111.32 mm	4.38 inches	
	1 Khan	111.32 m	365 feet	
	1 Mhan	111.32 Km	69.17 miles	1 degree longitude
	9 mhan	**1 mm**	0.04 inch	
	9 han	**1 m**	3.29 feet	
	9 Khan	**1 Km**	0.62 mile	
	228 mhan	25.40 mm	**1 inch**	
	2.74 han	0.31 m	**1 foot**	
	8.21 han	0.91 m	**1 yard**	
	14.46 Khan	1.77 Km	**1 mile**	
	16.65 Mhan	1.852 Km	1.15 mile	**1 nautical mile**
Area	1 han²	0.012 m²	19.21 inches²	
	1 Khan²	12392 m²	14820 yard²	
	80.70 han²	**1 m²**	1.20 yard²	
	0.807 Khan²	**1 hectare**	2.47 acres	
	80.70 Khan²	**1 Km²**	0.39 mile²	
	52062 mhan²	6.46 cm²	**1 inch²**	
	7.50 han²	892 cm²	**1 foot²**	
	67.47 han²	0.80 m²	**1 yard²**	
	0.327 Khan²	0.41 hectare	**1 acre**	
	209 Khan²	259 hectares	**1 mile²**	
Volume	1 han³	0.0014 m³	0.049 feet³	
	729 han³	**1 m³**	1.31 yard³	
	0.012 han³	16.39 cm³	**1 inch³**	
	20.53 han³	0.028 m³	**1 foot³**	
	558 han³	0.77 m³	**1 yard³**	
Capacity	1 can	1.38 litres	2.43 pints	
	0.72 can	**1 litre**	1.76 pints	
	0.41 can	0.57 litre	**1 pint**	
	3.30 can	4.55 litres	**1 gallon**	
Mass	1 wan	1.38 Kg	3.04 pounds	
	0.72 wan	**1 Kg**	2.21 pounds	
	725 wan	**1 tonne (Mg)**	0.98 ton	
	0.33 wan	0.45 Kg	**1 pound**	
	4.60 wan	6.35 Kg	**1 stone**	
	36.83 wan	50.80 Kg	**1 cwt**	
	737 wan	1.02 tonnes	**1 ton**	

Worldwide Measurement System

Worldwide Measurement System = Worldwide Time + Worldwide Space
plus several other basic units, which are not strictly Time nor Space.
It would supersede the Imperial, American, Navigation and International
systems but some of the SI units and most SI notation would continue.

Measurement	International System		Worldwide System	
Physical Quantity	Unit	Symbol	Unit	Symbol
atomic time	second	s	*tik*	*t*
cosmic time	day	d	*day*	*d*
distance or length	métre	m	*han*	*h*
cubic capacity	litre	l	*can*	*c*
mass	kilogram	kg	*wan*	*w*
plane angle	radian	rad	*ang*	*a*
solid angle	steradian	sr	*ste*	*s*
substance	mole	mol	*mol*	*m*
electric current	amp	A	*amp*	A
luminous intensity	candela	cd	*lum*	*l*
temperature	Kelvin	K	*cel*	C

Constants
All of the physical constants, such as the acceleration due to gravity (g)
would need to be changed by a conversion factor but would soon
become accepted by scientists and technologists.

Derivatives
There are many standard derived units that incorporate SI base units.
Some of these units have special names and symbols but others do not.
The modified symbols could be the same as the original but in *italic*.
Example: the Newton, the SI derived unit of force, meaning kgm/s2
now has the symbol N and this would then become *N* meaning: *wh/t* 2.
Once this system is in general use this *italic* notation could be omitted.

Names and Symbols
All of the new base units and the new derived units have three letters
(so Newton becomes *New*) and all of the new symbols are single letters.
It is better to state units in three figures, even if the last two are zeros.
It is better to use primary units rather than secondary or tertiary ones.
However, the *deciday* or *dec* and the *centiday* or *cen* are very useful.
Instead of *wek* we could use: *Decaday*, like the ancient Egyptian or
French revolution word *decade* but in English this means: ten years.
Some are confused by the prefix: milli, which means one thousandth,
and the term: million, but the International System has the term: Mega.
A millennium is a thousand years but a Millennium is its start or finish.
These could become *kiloyer* and *Kiloyer* then *megayer* and *Megayer*.
The term: *Gigayer* is probably better than either: aeon, or: billion *yers*.
The American Space Program has so far cost about a trillion dollars.
It was estimated that the Millennium bugs cost Us a trillion dollars.
However, they have not been cured but only postponed, because it was
assumed that a better system would soon be devised - and this is it!

The Worldwide System

The Worldwide System is not only a measurement system but it is also a management system and a government system, so it affects everything. If it were to be adopted, throughout the globe, it would have a huge impact on science, technology, ecology, sociology, economy and polity.

Science and technology are increasingly based on the metre and second. Some might argue that the second is now a global-digital-decimal unit, because it is part of the Imperial, American, Navigation and International systems, but it was based upon an eighty-six-thousand-four-hundredth part of a mean Solar day, so it is neither global nor digital nor decimal.

Society would gain immensely from **full-time-job-sharing-as-the-norm**. If everyone adopted a five-day-on/five-day-off working cycle there would be advantages in every field of endeavor because no one would ever be overworked or underemployed and everyone would reach their vocation. Moreover, everyone would be able to make more use of their free-time.

Ecology would be under far less pressure if all buildings and transport systems were used evenly and fully on every working day in the *yer*.

Economy would benefit from full employment and zero inflation if the whole of industry and commerce were working to maximum efficiency. There may be more danger of over-production and over-consumption but more people would share cars, boats, planes and many other things.

Polity would benefit from the five democratic days at the end of the *yer* when most people would stop work for elections and/or referendums. Election of local, regional, national and international governments would take place during the five remainder days for a fixed term of four *yers*. The sixth remainder day could be used for presidential elections.

You are now midway through this book and the remainder deals with the improvements that **The Worldwide System** would make to all Our lives. Part Seven - Motivation - considers what it is that makes Us Humans tick and how We, as individuals, would benefit from this logical system. Part Eight - Organization - analyses many different kinds of organization and explains how **full-time-job-sharing-as-the-norm** could benefit them. Part Nine - Civilization - discusses the numerous options and opposites, which face leaders and politicians when they try to govern Our lives. Part Ten - Religion - reveals how astronomer-priests used mysticism to control chronologies, calendars, clocks, zones and thereby the masses. Part Eleven - Legislation - explains how **The Worldwide System** can become the basis for a Global Constitution and a New World Order. Part Twelve - Conclusion - underlines important parts of this hypothesis and emphasizes how We can put Our World right - in one easy lesson.

Part Seven

Motivation

Changing Our Minds

"Think about a problem for long enough
and you will find a solution."

Albert Einstein (1879-1955 AD)

Ideas

Ideas that change Our World may occur to anyone, anywhere, anytime. Yet, it may take many years of development before an idea is turned into a system, a product or a process and others are convinced of its value. This small book is about a Very Big Idea that is just bursting to get a hearing but those holding onto power seem to have gone deaf or blind. Earlier editions have been sent to many World leaders for over a decade. Few of them have ever replied, so one frequently ponders upon how any new ideas can ever reach those who have the power to implement them. Our World is in a terrible mess but nobody else seems to be able to see the wood for the trees, because they are all hidebound by old dogmas. A logical solution, based on the ethos of sharing wealth by sharing work, could override many social, economical, political and theological dogmas.

Ideas that affect everyone have had a very rough ride throughout history. Socrates had many advanced ideas about the Universe but was charged with corrupting the young so was made to poison himself with hemlock. Galileo was put under house arrest by the papal inquisition because of his progressive but heretical ideas about Earth's age, orbit and spin. Newton was born in the year that Galileo died and was able to discover and then to evaluate several of the Universal Laws of Time and Space. Harrison was ostracized by Newton and by The Royal Society until he proved, conclusively, that his new chronometer could navigate the globe. Laplace was a proponent of the Metric System but it took a revolution before this idea could be introduced and it is still not used by all of Us. Darwin worked on his theories of evolution for many years before he became bold enough to challenge the Church's dogmas about Creation. However, the Church still preaches that Our World was created by *God* in six days followed by one day of rest, so We must use a seven-day week.

The Worldwide System is just like any new system, product or process. A need has been identified, however, this may not be generally realized. This system meets all the criteria and so the next step will be to start the marketing process because there will be no problem with production. It would be easy to manufacture billions of **decimal clocks and watches**. It would be possible to print billions of **digital calendars and diaries**. All computers can work to **global age, digital date and decimal time**. They can all be programmed to incorporate **global-digital-decimal rules**. However, there is bound to be a great deal of initial market resistance, even after extensive market research, global advertising and publicity. Alan Turing, Bill Gates, Steve Jobs and Tim Berners-Lee felt that there was a market for their ideas, if only they could convince their backers. They all had that gut feeling that their ideas could change Our World. Sometimes an idea can be like the spark that ignites a huge explosion. The Internet is a powerful means of communication and information. The Worldwide Web can be used to promote **The Worldwide System.**

Ideals

We seem to be spending so much Time watching others discuss global issues on the TV or listening to them on the radio that We do not spend enough Time discussing them Ourselves and forming Our own opinions. There are very few public meetings before elections and so opinions are formed by the media, who seem to think that Time and Space are taboo. Most of the political parties seem to be influenced by religious dogmas. So Britain clings to its Roman-Catholic chronology, calendar and clock, without any debate about the most logical age, date and time system. The Metric System was introduced surreptitiously, without any debate, because most politicians did not understand its whys and wherefores. So Britain has ended-up with this faulty, arbitrary measurement system. The author has written hundreds of letters to the local or national press but very few of them have ever been acknowledged, let alone published. The author has been interviewed on a few radio and TV programmes but has never been permitted to explain his rational but radical ideals. The author has attended many public meetings where ideas and ideals are discussed or debated but has not been allowed to explain his system.

Contraception was once a taboo subject but this is now a global issue, because the global population has doubled during the last four decades and it is also predicted to double again during the next four decades. Half of Our World is now hungry; the other half is overproducing food. Our Planet will not be able to sustain Us unless We take action soon. The UN brought the World's political and religious leaders together in Cairo in September 1994 AD to discuss Worldwide population control. The argument is overwhelming: We know what happens when there are too many people and not enough food, energy, work, Space and Time. As the result of this conference the Holy See changed their minds about birth control and no longer tell their followers to go forth and multiply. Many of the Islamic states have also agreed to encourage contraception, because most of them cannot sustain their burgeoning populations. The Chinese already had a one child policy and this helped them to stabilize their population but the Indians are still 'breeding like rabbits' a phrase used by Pope Francis on his visit to the Philippines in 2015 AD.

The United Nations Organization has convened World Conferences on: Human Rights, Economic and Social Development, Population Control, Cities, Women, Bio-diversity, Pollution, Global Warming and Race. There are still disagreements about many problems around the globe but it is time that We all reached an agreement about Time and Space. The ideal of using the same measurement system throughout the globe can be achieved if politicians had a World Conference on this subject. Yet, this seems as taboo as contraception and abortion a generation ago. The Catholic Church clings onto its belief that some days are special. Perhaps the Holy See will see sense - if they ever read this epistle.

Inspiration

What is it that inspires and stimulates Us - is it sticks, carrots or both?
Some are motivated by the fear of *God* and others by the love of *God*.
Some are driven on by the desire to discover all the laws of the Universe.
Some are obsessed by an urge to explore the far corners of Our Planet.
Some by the urge to create and then the urge to create something better.
Some by the acquisition of money, property, goods, wives or territory.
Some by the need to conform to the system or by the urge to be better.
Some are hooked on sex, drugs, drink; others on power, influence, fame.
Some are driven on by the relentless nagging of the calendar and clock.

It is said that those who have little education are motivated by money;
but those who are educated are motivated by the quest for knowledge.
What will motivate Us when We all have enough money, We know all that
We are capable of knowing and We have lost Our love or fear of *God*.
We will need a new stimulus and sharing jobs could help to provide it.
This could prove to be the love/hate relationship that encourages Our
competitive instincts, yet, allows Us to share the rewards of joint efforts.
We may need a financial incentive to achieve this new working pattern.

The survival of the fittest has been so much a part of Our evolutionary
motivation that We are all said to be born with an aggressive gene.
We will have to train it but it is difficult to hide Our Natural aggression.
This can take many different forms: on the road, at work and at play.
Competitive sport is intended to channel Our aggressive tendencies.
Nevertheless, it often seems to release Our very worst tribal instincts.
These instincts seem to be related to a cooperative gene that is found in
many species, which help each other, or even other species, to survive.
If We don't protect endangered species We may be endangered Ourselves.
We can save Our Planet and Our Species if We share Time and Space.

Our World is changing and some of Us are managing to survive without
always fighting for Our existence, but We have now lost Our motivation.
The Welfare State has turned Us into a bunch of spineless hangers-on.
If We lose Our jobs We no longer get on Our bikes to search for another
but make straight for a Social Security Office and then live off the state.
The younger generation's motivation to get-up-and-go; got-up-and-went.
The British Psychological Society report that clinical depression is now
five times more prevalent in twenty-five year olds than fifty years ago.
They also report that executives who shunned a nine-to-five day for more
flexible or shorter working hours are now outperforming their colleagues.
The British Institute for Employment Studies report that those who share
their jobs are far more motivated than their more traditional colleagues.
The current taxation and benefit system is undermining the work ethic.
The Centre for Social Justice is now trying to ensure that work pays but
has not considered the benefits of **full-time-job-sharing-as-the-norm**.

Innovation

The Worldwide System may be the final step in a sequence of temporal and spatial innovations from notches on sticks and piles of pebbles to laser clocks, laser rulers, laser printers, laser recorders, laser cutters... The laser beam was first demonstrated by Theodore Maiman in 1960 AD. Lasers can now measure the distance to the Moon extremely accurately. A laser beam marks the Prime Meridian at the Greenwich Observatory. Laser powered atomic fusion may help to solve the global energy crisis.

All innovations need champions and backers as well as inventors before they can succeed but these three people rarely come together in Britain. Thomas Jefferson and Benjamin Franklin once championed and backed complete decimalization but they did not obtain the support of Congress. Congress is still thinking about the Metric System - two centuries later. Like so many other important innovations, it was marketed and sold before it was perfected and so another system will eventually replace it. Millennium bugs show how important it is to get Our priorities right, pay attention to the smallest detail and never take anything for granted. Innovators can become very rich in the USA and the richest man in the World is now Bill Gates, who made his fortune from computer software. His latest *Windows* system has various options for the way in which the age, date and time are expressed and it also has several different rulers.

British inventors are invariably regarded as crackpots, very few of them become rich and the only reward that the best receive is a knighthood. Sir John Thornycroft (1843-1928 AD) invented an amphibious hovercraft. He made a working model but this was forgotten in the turmoil of WW1. Sir Frank Whittle (1907-1996 AD) invented jet engines but found no backing in Britain, so went to the USA and turned his ideas into dollars. Sir Christopher Cockerell (1910-1999 AD) filed patents on radio, radar, electronic watches, hovercraft and wave power but was not a rich man. Sir Clive Sinclair (1940-AD) invented cheap digital watches, calculators, computers and electric vehicles but he was never adequately financed. Sir Tim Berners-Lee (1955-AD) proposed the Worldwide Web in 1989 AD but had to go to USA before it was launched on the Internet in 1991 AD.

I have been privileged, through my work on hovercraft, to meet some of Britain's most successful inventors and have filed a few patents myself. I know how difficult it is to persuade others, who are set in their ways, to accept new ideas that could change their miserable lives for the better. I take nothing for granted and so I am constantly thinking of new ideas. Some think that I am eccentric; I think that everyone else is eccentric. This book needed to be marketed by one of the leading publishers but none of them seem to believe that any book could put Our World right. So I decided to publish it online and to market it through the Internet. Nevertheless, it still desperately needs a champion and a backer.

Priority

Getting one's priorities right is the essence of running any country, industry or household, however, most organizations get them all wrong. We all need to believe in the same philosophy, speak the same language, and use the same measurements, including the age, the date and the time. This cannot be achieved by force but it may be achieved by cooperation and willingness to start again at square zero with a clean sheet of paper. The revolutionary regimes in France, USA, USSR, China and the UK all started-off with a completely new Time and Space measurement system at the top of their agendas and yet they all got their priorities wrong. One of the first priorities of the UN was to introduce a global calendar, yet this was vetoed by the USA who wanted to retain the Gregorian one and to keep the continuous seven-day week with a two-day weekend. The UN needs to go back to basics, if it still wants to create One World.

One of the first priorities of the EU was to standardize the kilometre, litre and euro but Britain refused to give up its mile, pint and pound. It wanted Britain to use the same time zone and the same summer time. It even tried to standardize all working, driving and shopping hours. All that Britain wanted was to trade freely thoughout the continent but the EU insisted that this entailed the free movement of workers. Britain has now decided to leave the EU, so its priorities are changing and its parties are changing from left or right to forwards or backwards. It cannot go backwards to the British Empire with the Imperial System. It must go forwards to a New World Order with **The Worldwide System**. Britons voted to leave the EU because of the huge cost of membership. They considered this should be spent on security, education and health.

Security must be the top priority of any organization, whatever the cost. The Tories top priortity was to renew the independent nuclear deterrent, because it cannot rely on the EU or USA to come to its aid any more. However, this measure does not stop acts of vandalism or terrorism. It does not stop the huge number of migrants from entering the country. Nor the increasing amount of cyber crime that is ruining the economy.

Education is a priority and can be greatly improved from cradle to grave by a two-team, four-term, ten-day routine with **flextime** and **flexdate**. Book learning is now being replaced by interactive computer programs. **The Worldwide System** is easier to learn than either Imperial or Metric. If this system works well in Britain it could soon be adopted Worldwide.

Health is a priority but the NHS always seems to be short of staff. It has the buildings, the equipment, the medicines and the knowledge, yet, some 1M patients are waiting to go into hospital for an operation whilst the expensive operating theatres are empty for 2/7 of the Time. With **full-time-job-sharing-as-the-norm** it can catch-up on its backlog.

Expediency

Successive British governments just muddled on and moved from one expediency to another, without any idea of where they were heading. Britain is run on a crisis management basis with no overall plan for economic recovery and no attempt to help the companies developing new products that could stop it from sinking further into the mire. Although the government created Enterprise Zones and Science Parks, there are not enough new ideas coming up to take advantage of them. There are several government run competitions for small enterprises but the faceless stick-in-the-muds who select the winners usually seem to be incapable of understanding the potential of most new ideas. Other ideas are ill-conceived but somehow they get government support because they would rather lend money to large inefficient organizations than small efficient ones with good ideas but no previous track records. Many British industries have now vanished or they are in foreign hands.

The Labour government's *National Research Development Corporation* and *National Enterprize Board* became *The British Technology Group*. They financed the early development of hovercraft and held the patents. However, they did not understand their markets and gave licences to aircraft and ship manufacturers, rather than starting from scratch. Although these were all very large companies, they inevitably failed. Royalties on patents more than covered the government's investment; not the high costs of running their posh offices and expense accounts. Most are now built by small companies with appropriate technology. They now have a small niche market but this could grow rapidly as soon as they meet an increasing need to rapidly go almost anywhere, anytime. *The British Technology Group* was privatized by the Tories but they then only financed the development of pharmaceuticals and electronics.

The computer industry began in Britain and grew extremely rapidly. However, it soon became dominated by large American corporations. To save a few bits of memory, programmers used two digits for the age. Experts warned that computers would go haywire at the Millennium but most organizations and governments ignored their advice and ended up making expedient fixes instead of solving the problem once and for all. Instead of using a rational chronological system most secular states took the expedient solution of using BCE and ACE instead of BC and AD. Nevertheless they still use the same Roman-Catholic calendar and clock. The second and the metre are now completely arbitrary measurements, chosen by politicians as an expedient solution to a scientific problem. Most scientists and engineers would have gone back to first principles and may well have arrived at exactly the same solution as the author. Most working practices and patterns are based on expedient solutions. **The Worldwide System** is not an expedient nor a half-clock solution. It has been very carefully designed and it is based upon first principles.

Inertia

Our Planet Earth keeps on turning but We have not yet learned how to base most of Our measurements upon its age, orbit, spin and girth. Newton's First Universal Law states that: every body continues in a state of rest or uniform motion unless it is acted upon by an external force. This book has been written in order to point out to global leaders in particular and everyone in general that Planet Earth is way off-course. Yet, like ocean liners, the bigger they are the harder they are to turn.

The Americans accept innovation more readily than any other society. Yet, they will be the last nation to fully adopt the International System. Even in once-great Britain there is still considerable resistance to any kind of change and this is probably due to their fear of the unknown. They ridiculed the decimal Metric System and took too long to adopt it. They think in ^0F, pounds, pints, gallons, inches, feet, yards and miles. They were the very last nation on this Planet to adopt decimal coinage. They will probably be the last European nation to adopt decimal euros. They continue to use 12-hour half-day dials or 24-hour digital displays, odd seven-day weeks, higgledy-piggledy months and disorientated years. This is due to their inability to count on the digits in front of their faces.

All Human Beings need a sense of purpose - and other critters as well. We all need to feel that We are playing a constructive role in society. We have now arrived at the point in history where, in Britain and many other industrial countries, We only need to work for half of the year. However, We are not sharing this work equally throughout Our World. Communism had this aim but failed, due to too much central control and because much of the work was not constructive but destructive. Capitalism is also failing because there is too much disparity, not only in incomes but also in Our sense of fulfillment - for shares must be shared. If We could all work together, at something really constructive, then Our religious, political, cultural, tribal and racial differences would vanish.

The prophets lived away from civilization and by observing it from the outside they could sometimes suggest important changes of direction. Mahatma Gandhi (1869-1948 AD) studied in Britain, worked in Africa but helped his native India by living and working with his own people. He claimed to be a Hindu, a Sikh, a Buddhist, a Muslim and a Christian. However, he failed to prevent conflicts between these different beliefs. Today it is difficult to understand the complexities of socio-economics. The gurus and pundits are stumped for a simple answer to the problems of inflation, population, pollution, unemployment and many outbreaks of violence and lawlessness, which occur in all kinds of society, Worldwide. They can all see the World's problems but they cannot see any solution. This is because they have not, or they will not, read this revealing book. If they did it might help to turn Our Planet Earth in a new direction.

Power

The pyramids and obelisks were both Sun-clocks and symbols of power. Successive pharaohs, kings, emperors, popes, bishops, rabbis or sheiks built greater and greater monuments as symbols of their great power. Our tallest building is the Burj Khalifa, which has a mosque at the top to be nearer to *Allah*, but cost a fortune to build, maintain and operate. This is not a symbol of power; but decadence, extravagance and folly. The Saudis are now metricated and so they plan to build a 1Km tower. Yet, there is an oil glut, its price has dropped, so they cannot afford it.

The British Empire was built by the power of steam, the force of arms, the nerve of navigators and the accuracy and reliability of clockmakers. Steam driven factories made more goods and these were distributed by steam trains and steam ships, which were guarded by steam gunboats. The steam engines in factories were gradually superseded by internal combustion engines and these were then replaced by electric motors. Many factories, trains, boats and cars are now driven by electricity. Electrical power has become the greatest symbol of Human progress. It has reached the furthest corners of Our Planet, the demand for it is always rising but varies considerably, so that We need many more expensive power stations and ugly pylons than if it were evenly spread. Power stations and railway stations replaced temples and cathedrals as symbols of power but Bankside power station and Orsay railway station have been converted into temples of modern art in London and Paris. Nuclear power stations are nowadays considered to be temples of doom. Yet, the French generate eighty percent of their power by this means. Britain's dependent nuclear deterrent cost it dearly and We will never know whether it would have worked or if the money was well spent. It has not deterred many other states from building nuclear weapons. Mankind now has the power to destroy itself at the push of a button. The same nuclear fuel could have powered Our World for a century.

Our World's largest stone obelisk stands at the centre of Washington DC. It was completed in the same year that delegates from all over the globe gathered there and decided that the Prime Meridian should pass through Greenwich and that Our Time and Our Space should be decimalized. As the result of that meeting, latitude and longitude are now measured in 360 degrees and based upon the Equator and Greenwich Meridian. However, degrees were not decimalized and the mean Solar day is still divided by 24 hours, 60 minutes, 60 seconds and into 40 time zones. The Americans now have the global power to decimalize Time and Space. They have not adopted the International System and so they could go straight to decimals of a degree as part of the Global Positioning System. *Google Earth* incorporates decimals of a degree in its basic program. The Worldwide Web incorporates decimal time and a single time zone. The final political, social and economic solution lies in the power of ten.

Force

Invisible forces in Space control the motions of the *Heavenly Bodies* and they are responsible for the tides, earthquakes, eruptions and storms, which were once believed to be under the direct control of the Sky-gods. Although these have merged into one deity, called *Yahweh, God or Allah, He* does not protect Our Human Race from the forces of *Mother Nature*. Our Planet Earth and its many Life forms may be Universally unique. Yet, We are destroying many species and may soon destroy Our own. We must now use all of Our Natural and Man-made resources to the full, without destroying them in the process, by sharing Our Time and Space.

Newton taught Us that every force has an equal and opposite reaction. The British are very good at producing an equal and opposite argument, so that very little ever gets done and everything stays exactly the same. It was like that with hovercraft - no sooner had a completely new form of transport been invented than many officials adopted a negative attitude. Although amphibious hovercraft could go almost anywhere on Earth; they were restricted by laws and regulations to a few designated areas. Confusion reigns about this strange beast, which is neither fish nor fowl. Americans class them as boats, Canadians class them as aircraft whilst they both describe them as vehicles and although they would be ideal as ferries across the Great Lakes their bureaucrats have kept them away. We shall only have a free World when We have the freedom to trade all goods, services and ideas across all Natural and Man-made boundaries.

When a society needs to use force, to maintain the *status quo,* it is sick. This is the case in most countries in Our World today - even in Britain. The police are frequently out in force due to peaceful demonstrations, as well as political, sectarian or racial riots and vandalism or looting. The jails and prisons are not only full, they are bursting at the seams. However, most of their inmates are victims of the socio-economic system. The basis of this system is the religious dogma of the seven-day week. Most of Us take it for granted and do not realize that it could be changed. We now have free education, free speech and apparently free media, however, they are doing their best to keep superstition and religion alive. It cannot be suppressed by force but it can be replaced by philosophy, logical argument and common sense, if these are included in education. All of the political parties agree that they need to make radical changes. Yet, none of them have any notion about what those changes should be. The burgeoning army of bureaucrats want to keep everything the same. The fundamental problem, throughout the globe, is unemployment and it is no good creating more and more bureaucratic jobs in the public sector and stopping anyone from working whenever they need to earn a living. **Full-time-job-sharing-as-the–norm** may be the ultimate socio-economic system but this should not be imposed by force but by permitting people to work, shop, rest, play and even pray whenever they want to.

Pressure

Our World is under increasing pressure from its burgeoning population. However, by choosing pressure points it may be possible to change it. The greatest pressure group of all is the press yet they seem to be very wary of my newfangled way of sharing work, wealth and Our World. Perhaps they fear the changes that would follow in their own industry. There would be no more Sunday papers just left-day and right-day ones. They have often debated Imperial versus Metric but never a third way. They talk about a third way in politics but nobody knows what it means. There are signs all over the globe that neither socialism nor capitalism are working so this either leads to anarchy or religious fundamentalism. Democracy should only be moved by the pressure of logical argument. Yet, the Megabucks do all the talking, even if they have no new ideas. The USA is under pressure because their precious oil is running out. So the oil barons put pressure on politicians to capture more of the stuff. That is the real reason for most of the recent wars in the Middle East.

Fear of change is the equal and opposite pressure that holds-up progress. It can only be overcome by education and discussion but there is very little opportunity for the average citizen to think about socio-economics. The educational establishment seems to be against all radical new ideas. People in England and most of Britain have mostly lost their fear of gods, they have lost their fear of hunger, they are losing their fear of war, they all fear illness but know that they are generally in good hands. They all fear unemployment, no matter what or who they know or how young or old they are and the only way to dispel this is to share work. The most efficient and fairest way to do this is to share a ten-day week. Yet, We must not assume that there will be an answer to every problem. We will probably return to using beasts of burden more rapidly than We left them - provided We have not eaten them all in the meantime.

Pressure of work stops politicians from reading letters, articles or books and discussing important new issues and so it seems that they are only prepared to listen to large organizations who pay large sums of money to professional lobbyists; rather than to individuals with progressive ideas. There are currently several environmental pressure groups including: *The Green Party, Friends of the Earth, Earthwatch Institute, Greenpeace* and *The Real World Coalition* and they seem to be influencing politicians. Yet they have had very little effect in achieving sustainable development, despite the huge sums that have been donated to them over the years. So they have become self-perpetuating autocracies who do not listen to novel and radical ideas, which could help them to achieve their aims. **The Worldwide Campaign for Temporal and Spatial Reform** is a global pressure group and its email is: wwctsr@hotmail.co.uk. Membership is free to every member of Our Human Race and it works on an opt-out basis - so there are now over 7G members, Worldwide.

Stress & Strain

In engineering terms: stress is a condition caused by pressure or force and strain is the effect of it; then the material usually returns to normal. In Human terms: We suffer from much the same stresses and strains. To restore Our own systems to normal We need to take regular rests. One day of rest per week used to be quite enough but now a two-day weekend seems too short for Us to recover before the next week begins. The nine-to-five day has been abandoned in Britain, which has become a seven-day week, twenty-four-hour day society during the last decades. Many now work so hard that they are burnt-out by their middle age. Yet, 1 in 20 suffer from debilitating depression caused by unemployment. Over one million Britons are unable to work due to stress and strain, which now accounts for about half of all illnesses and many deaths.

Repetitive Strain Injury is due to Human Beings behaving like robots. Our bodies were not designed to sit or stand in the same position all day. Time Sickness is a phobia which makes some people feel hemmed in by the passage of Time - so they become incapable of achieving anything. Seasonal Affective Disorder is depression that only occurs in winter. Icelanders, Norwegians, Swedes, Finns, Canadians and Russians are most affected and they have been known to commit suicide because of it. The solution is to work a longer day in the summer than in the winter. The annual total of work completed would be the same or even more. Commuting leads to stress and many yearn to return to the days of the agricultural community, when the pace of living was very much slower. Yet, farmers and farm hands now have the highest suicide rate of all. They used to slow down or stop during the winter but modern methods, mechanization, demands and subsidies keep them going all-year-round.

Research shows that more people have heart attacks or strokes at the weekends or on the bank holidays than during normal working days. It has also been proven that those who regularly work for 11-12 hours are more likely to suffer heart attacks than those who work 7-8 hours. So it is better for non-stop industries to work for three shifts per day. The New Deal was F. D. Roosevelt's solution to The Great Depression. He made it mandatory for many factories to work for four shifts per day. Recent research by Melbourne University shows that to reduce stress and strain the over-forties should work part-time for three days a week. A part-time job keeps the brain stimulated, even beyond retirement age. Hobbies and voluntary work keep many people active in their old age.

We need just as many days for rest and recreation as We do for work. Five days of work followed by five days of rest may be the best rhythm. **Full-time-job-sharing-as-the-norm** in a ten-day week would eliminate black Mondays and Fridays and all of the syndromes that go with them. The stress-less week-end would be equal to the stress-full work-end.

Wear & Tear

We have always been obsessed by the measurement of Time and Space. Before the dawn of civilization, whilst We were hunting and gathering, We noticed the movements of the Stars, the solstices and equinoxes of the Sun and the phases of the Moon then related these to the seasons. When We eventually settled down, grew crops and bred animals it was crucial to construct chronologies, calendars, clocks and rules in stone. These became temples for annual, quarterly or monthly gatherings with great festivals, when We celebrated by making them bigger and better. These massive monuments still stand but have lost their meaning as they became worn by the ravages of Time and torn by the need for Space. The progressive development of timepieces over the millennia lead to the present day when the age, date and time is shown on electronic gizmos.

Mechanical clocks or watches need lubrication so that they do not wear. Electronic ones never need rewinding, resetting nor any maintenance. Paper calendars, planners and diaries still need to be torn-up annually. Electronic ones record the past, remind the present and plan the future. Wheels, bearings and lubricants have gradually been developed to the point where they now last the life of a car and never need renewing. Tyres are lasting longer too and might, eventually, last as long as a car. Wear and tear on hovercraft skirts was a big problem at first but now they are lasting as long as a set of tyres and can cheaply be replaced.

Our Life expectancy is constantly being extended by medical science. Transplants, bypasses and joint replacements are routine operations. Doctors are starting to understand the aging process and may be able to prolong Life, so We may be prescribed an elixir on the National Health. The average British baby born today may live to be over one hundred. So the two-digit abbreviation of a birth year will no longer be adequate. There are now more old people than ever before but I suspect that my own generation will not last as long as the Queen Mother's because they are considered to be over-the-hill at fifty, so are not worth employing. Unemployment for oldsters and youngsters is currently much too high. Yet, the official retirement age for men is being raised from 65 to 66, and in France there are riots because it is being raised from 60 to 62. The average retirement age in the USA is currently approaching 70. No state can afford to pay more money in pensions than it is collecting. The solution is job-sharing with a reduced workload for the elderly.

The *Anno Domini* chronology, Gregorian calendar and Benedictine clock have had a long run but have served their Time so must be retired and time zones are worn-out anachronisms that must be torn down. The **global age** chronology and **digital date** calendar are perpetual, the **decimal time** clock will *tik-tik-tik* forever throughout a **single zone** and the **global-digital-decimal rule** will always measure Our World.

Balance

The Egyptians invented balances and could then weigh goods and gold.
The weighing of the heart ceremony was their ritual of final judgment.

The Balance of Power
Since there is only one superpower this phrase now has less meaning.
The need to make Europe into another superpower is no longer obvious.
China is rapidly becoming a superpower, but it is short of oil and gas.
India is also becoming a superpower, so the East is catching the West.
Finding the balance between opposites is part of Eastern philosophies.
Libra, the balance, is a zodiac symbol that is used throughout the West.

The Balance of Supply and Demand
Some say the price of goods or services controls supply and demand.
However, when price of petrol doubled this did not halve consumption.
Oil and gas are found in increasingly inaccessible and unstable places.
Proven reserves of oil and gas are decreasing and coal mines are closing.
If pits worked every day the price of coal would be more competitive.
Renewable forms of energy are not given enough fiscal encouragement,
nor the electrification of railways, rapid transit systems and vehicles.

The Balance of Payments
Whilst some trade barriers are now falling, others are still being erected.
Governments should not allow goods to be imported that have been
subsidized by other states because this suppresses their own industries.
No government should subsidize its industries to keep out competition,
because this encourages inefficiency, but new ideas must be supported.
Every government must encourage **full-time-job-sharing-as-the-norm**.

Balanced Diets
Half Our World is hungry or starving; the other half is over-producing.
Consequently, We either need to move the food or move the consumers.
Food is the most important ingredient in a perfectly balanced diet.
However, water could soon become more important than oil and gas.
Those who weigh themselves in stones are still living in the Stone Age.

The Balance of Nature
We know that Nature tends to balance itself and that Our interference
can cause disaster as well as benefits but soon it will no longer be a case
of seeing the wood for the trees - there may not be any of either left.

The Balance of Time and Life
Scales are a symbol for justice, and there are two ways to balance them.
The loads can be adjusted or the fulcrum moved - this is often forgotten.
When work-days = free-days Time and Life will finally become balanced.
This is often referred to by social/economists as: the work/life balance.

258

Precision

The Greeks measured everything with greater and greater precision but they could not determine the age, orbit, spin or girth of Planet Earth. During the Age of Reason there were great advances in measurements. Yet, despite a seven-year survey, using the best instruments, it was not possible to measure the length of the Paris quarter-Meridian accurately. It would have been better to base the standard linear measurement upon Earth's circumference but that would have been quite impossible then.

During WW2 it was realized that Imperial and American inches were slightly different and so some high precision aircraft parts did not fit. It was one of the reasons for the International Standards Organization and this led to the Metric inch being defined as precisely 25.4 mm. However, the USA has still not officially adopted the SI Metric System. As clocks developed it became possible to determine Earth's orbit and spin more precisely but its age has only been known since 1956 AD. The circumference of Earth can now be accurately measured using GPS. **The Worldwide System** is based upon Earth's age, orbit, spin and girth.

I gave a talk on **Worldwide Time** at the British Horological Institute. The theme of their conference was: timekeeping in the next millennium. I was the only speaker who proposed changing the timekeeping system. A man who had made elaborate and expensive clocks for most of his life admitted that he had never asked: Why the hour hand goes round twice? And: why the dial has twelve hours, sixty minutes and sixty seconds? It had never occurred to him that time could and should be decimalized. Most scientists and technologists are so intent upon achieving precision that they never ever think about the size of the units they use.

We now know that there are billions of other galaxies and solar systems. We do not know if Life is evolving on other Planets, in different forms. We cannot write an equation that describes every force in the Universe. We still need to know more about the Very Big and the very small. We still have some puzzling questions about the invisible dark matter. We can closely estimate the age of Our Sun, Our Planet and Our Moon. We can make close estimates about the lengths of their Natural cycles. These are not quite constant so We need to use the vibrations of atoms, under controlled conditions, as the fundamental unit of Time and Space. The second is now based upon a fixed number of vibrations of an atom. The metre is now based upon the distance light travels in an instant. The fundamental units of **Civic and Atomic Worldwide Time** could both be defined by the length of a mean Solar day, at a Millennium. The basic unit of **Worldwide Space** could be the measured length of the Equator divided by 360 degrees and then by a million, at a Millennium. **The Worldwide System** is the logical solution to a perpetual problem, however, it would not be suitable for use on any other Planet.

Tolerance

In engineering terms: tolerance is the fit of one component into another. This can machined to be a loose fit, a tight fit or an interference fit.

In educational terms: the British system creates too many square pegs and then tries to fit them into round holes.

In spiritual terms: religious intolerance is rapidly becoming intolerable. Human Beings have fought with each other for millennia over the many different ways in which they counted days, weeks, months and years. If We used the same age, date and time We might be more tolerant.

In temporal terms: Our chronologies, calendars and clocks are a miss-fit. Our odd weeks do not fit Our unequal months nor Our misaligned years. Our 12-hour and 24-hour clocks are in eternal conflict with each other. Our time zones and warped date line do not fit the shape of Our Planet.

In spatial terms: Our dimensions and distances are a miss-fit because the metre was based upon the Paris Meridian instead of the Equator. We use kilometres, statute miles or nautical miles instead of one system. Our weights and measures are still not based upon one logical system.

In economic terms: on the one hand Britain was losing £1G per week but on the other it was urged by the EU not to work for three days in it. It could not provide more goods and services and so it redressed the balance of payments by selling all of its precious family gold and silver. It now imports most of the ships, trains, trucks, buses, trams, vans, cars, motorbikes and bikes upon which its fragile economy depends. It is no longer self-sufficient in food because of the EU set-aside policy. It is no longer self-sufficient in energy because its coal, oil and gas are running out, it has abandoned nuclear power and has few alternatives. Britain is trying to be friends with Europe and America but they both drive on the opposite side of the road and they use different measures. It does not use either monetary system, so it may be left out in the cold.

In political terms: Britain is now being polarized into the extremes of left and right, rich and poor yet again, which could lead to intolerance. Britons are leaving their birthplace in droves because they no longer fit. Whilst millions of legal and illegal immigrants are now taking their place. Every political party believes it has a system that fits the economy a little better but none of them have thought about sharing most jobs. Different Ministers are in charge of different parts of age, date and time. The Prime Minister should be in charge of Time but hasn't enough of it.

If We Humans were all to use: **The Worldwide Time and Space System**, which fits Our Planet very well, We might fit into it a little better too.

Perfection

Timekeeping was of great importance in all religions - the more perfect We were in this life, the greater Our chance of reaching the next one. However, each religion came up with a different solution to the problem. And this difference is still causing a great deal of strife on Our Planet. The Almighty was considered to be perfect but mortal sinners were not and that is why days, weeks and moonths do not fit perfectly into years. Jews consider their Lunar/Solar calendar is more perfect than others; although it is so complicated that only the rabbis fully understand it. Christians used to believe that the Earth was a perfect sphere and that the Sun, the Moon, the Planets and the Stars all revolved around it. Those who disagreed were liable to be executed or excommunicated. Muslims consider that their great clock in Mecca is the most perfect and so everyone on Earth should set their clocks and watches to Mecca time. The Universe is imperfect, there are no gods and it is quite impossible to discover any intermeshing gear ratios within its celestial clockwork. Mathematics is a perfect science, however it never quite reflects Nature. It does permit the use of a remainder if the numbers do not quite fit, such as: the number of days in a Lunar moonth or a Solar year.

The French revolutionaries thought that the Earth was a perfect sphere and that if they measured the Paris Meridian from Dunkirk to Barcelona and the latitudes of these places they could calculate the distance from the Equator to the Pole and the metre would be 0.00001 of this distance. However, the Earth is not a perfect sphere nor even a perfect oblate one. The metre should have been based on the circumference of the Equator, then land, sea and air distances could have been the same, but it was impossible to measure this distance accurately some two centuries ago. It is now possible to measure the length of the Equator very accurately. This is the basis of longitude and global positioning systems can give an accurate position but are based on arc-degrees, minutes then decimals. Nevertheless, *Google Earth* is now based upon arc-degrees then decimals.

John Harrison was the perfectionist who cracked the serious problem of finding longitude at sea by means of a robust and accurate chronometer. I now wonder if he ever thought about making a decimal chronometer. Or if chronographers ever wonder whether We need any time zones at all. Or if publishers of diaries, calendars and planners have ever considered the possibility of printing perpetual ones, which can be used every year. Or whether the manufacturers of rulers, tapes, measures or scales have ever thought about their lengths, distances, capacities or weights.

I am a perfectionist because every sentence and essay fits every page. Every page prompted me to write another but one day it will be finished. However, after it has reached bookshops and libraries I shall probably be running from one to the next, altering it with my stumpy blue pencil.

Punctuality

The Talmud, The Bible, The Koran, Dead Sea Scrolls, The Book of Kells, Old Moore's Almanac, Whitaker's Almanack, Reed's Nautical Almanac, P&O's Timetable, British Airways Flight Schedule, British Rail's Timetable and London Transport's Omnibus Timetable were all full of predictions. However, some of the predicted events were more punctual than others. The Jews have waited for nearly six millennia for their Messiah to come. The Christians believe that their Messiah came and He will come again. The Muslims believe that Moses, Jesus and Mohammed were prophets. There have been many missed connections.

Leonardo da Vinci (1452 - 1519 AD) invented the very first alarm clock. Most of Us now use them and they have almost taken over Our lives. Benjamin Franklin (1706 -1790 AD) invented some mechanical clocks. Yet, punctuality was not listed by this great scientist and statesman as one of the virtues by which a man or woman could become more perfect. When the Gregorian reforms were finally adopted in the USA he wrote:

> What an indulgence is here, for those who love the pillow to lie down in peace on the 2nd of this month and not, perhaps, awake till the morning of the 14th.

By the end of the 18th century punctuality appeared in dictionaries. By the middle of the 19th century many people owned a pocket watch. They became status symbols - like mobile phones and tablets are now. Punctuality was a new fetish described by Lewis Carroll (1832-1898 AD). We are still behaving like his White Rabbit, who was invariably late, or his Mad Hatter and March Hare, who thought it was always tea time. But as a reverend and a mathematician he was perplexed by clock times in different places and he could not decide when the day should begin. We have got it fixed into Our minds that We must always get up at the same clock time every day and have lunch at midday, so when Summer Time was introduced many people objected to it on religious grounds. Changing all of Our numerous clocks and watches twice a year is quite ridiculous when all We need to do is change the alarm on one of them.

The measurement-management-government of Our Time is fundamental. We are told that Cosmic Time is relative and Space-Time can be warped, because the Universe is still expanding at the constant speed of light. However, Atomic Time is fixed and should stay exactly the same forever. Clocks are now so accurate that they can measure light slowing down. The management of Organic Time is now considered to be good business. Some are so punctilious that they time everything; others go with the flow. The government of Civic Time is the foundation of each and every state. Politicians try to make their time zone different from the one next door. Much international phone time is lost by folk asking each other the time. **Global age, digital date, decimal time and single zone** can solve this; but what will We do with all of the **Worldwide Time** that We have saved?

Regularity

Every religion and/or sect has its own chronology, calendar and clock. We regularly celebrate New Year on different ages, dates and times. The continuous seven-day week was considered to be more regular and better than one that restarted at the beginning of a year or a month. Regular visits to church on Sundays were supposed to make one virtuous. The fixed 24-hour Benedictine clock was revered as *God's* Own Time and so was considered to be better than *Mother Nature's* variable hours. However, *She* made Man to work in the daylight and to sleep at night. Higher rates of illness, divorce and death are found in night workers. Fatigue causes many accidents and is responsible for major disasters. Physiological research has looked into variations of working patterns during the day and the week but its length is considered to be invariable.

Regularly starting work at nine a.m. and stopping at five p.m. became a discipline, a dogma and a syndrome: it became the norm in most offices Worldwide and worked quite well when people lived near to their work. However, it caused a great deal of congestion when We started living further from work and travelling by car, bus, train, ferry and plane. The rush hours are a nightmare: 90% of traffic moves in 10% of the time. **Flextime** helps to ease the problem and the regularity dogma has now been relaxed by many employers who accept that office workers may now vary their travelling and meal times in order to minimize congestion. This is more difficult for factory workers, nevertheless, if three people share their shift work it does not really matter when they change-over; so long as their work is done and there is constant coverage on the job. With a ten-day week: the norm for round-the-clock shift workers would become six people sharing one job, with maybe a spare in case of illness.

Congestion is always worst in the winter when most people have to travel in the dark in order to keep up the regular pattern that is demanded by their calendar, their clock, their zone and their very regular employers. The working day always has a fixed number of hours all-year-round but it has been proven that We can work harder for longer in the summer. So We should vary Our working times to suit the season in the same way that hunters, gatherers and agricultural workers did for many millennia. Some may argue that the bills still drop through the letterbox regularly and that heat and light costs more in the winter, however, most oil, gas and electricity companies now allow their bills to be spread throughout the year and most building societies are now flexible about repayments. Tax and National Insurance is proportional to pay and so lower pay in winter would have lower deductions, thus Our annual total income and expenditure would be about the same but Our fatigue would be less. The posties wanted seasonal hours like this but management disagreed. Devolution allows the Scots to work for different hours than the English. Yet, this is not a national nor an international matter but a global one.

Independence

We are all dependent upon other people to a greater or lesser extent but We are becoming increasingly independent and thinking for Ourselves. Fewer people are getting married as they prefer to remain independent. Cohabitation is no longer considered immoral and has no social stigma. There are now numerous financial advantages to not getting married. The cost of housing has risen so much that many children cannot afford to leave home and get married and so they depend upon their parents. The electronic revolution allows many of Us to return to an independent way of life, which most of Us enjoyed before the industrial revolution. Many are doing their own thing, such as writing and publishing their own books, playing their own music or selling their own arts and crafts.

Britain steamed ahead of the rest of Europe because it permitted most shops to open on Sundays and abandoned the tradition of double-time. Whereas most of Europe still shuts down for at least two days in seven and it pays through the nose if workers have to work 'unsocial hours'. Some Eurocrats want to extend the unproductive weekend to three days. France is already working to a maximum of 35 hours per 7-day week. This is crippling its economy and causing riots by jobless immigrants. Although they ratified the Maastricht Treaty the Tories avoided signing the Social Chapter, which would have controlled British working hours. But as soon as they came to power New Labour ratified this part as well. Britain was bound to working a maximum 48 hours per 7-day week. Yet, many organizations ignored this rule and it was never enforced. Britain consequently became the fifth largest economy in Our World; whilst many other states in the EU were struggling to make ends meet.

Britain has recently voted by referendum to leave the European Union. The United Kingdom is now on the verge of breaking-up because Scotland wants to stay in the EU, Northern Ireland may want to join the Republic, whilst the majority in England and Wales now want to leave the EU. The older generation voted to leave; the younger generation voted to stay. However, many of the younger generation did not even bother to vote. Since WW2 most former colonies have achieved their independence. Britain still has a few dependent territories - but of their own free will. The Falklands would rather remain British than become Argentinian. Gibraltar would rather remain British than become a part of Spain. The EU is on the verge of breaking-up because several other members are fed-up with the high costs and the faceless bureaucrats in Brussels. Many member states are fed-up with mass economic and political migrations within the EU and from many other parts of the globe. Some now want England to pull-up the drawbridge and go-it-alone. It should now be able to make up its own mind about many matters and it may even decide to use **The Worldwide System** and show the rest of the World the advantages of using **full-time-job-sharing-as-the-norm**.

Security

An Englishman's home was his castle, yet, nobody is secure any more.
Very few have a job-for-life and many lose their jobs before they retire.
Britain reached a peak of security in the sixties but is now in decline.
Its pioneering social security system is overloaded and breaking down.
One in three households now receives some form of social security.
It is impossible for any state to sustain this level of financial support.
When the long-term jobless run out of benefits they often turn to crime.
It is impossible to get insurance on some kinds of property because of
the ever increasing number of burglaries, robberies and break-ins.
Social security was intended for the very few who are unable to work,
however, it fails when two thirds are paying the other third not to work.

Having been an employee of a multinational corporation for a decade as
well as an employer myself for a decade I can see both sides of the coin.
When I joined *Esso* in 1958 AD there were 16K employees in the UK,
when I left in 1972 AD there were 8K but in 2000 AD there were 3K.
All of their fleets of ships and vehicles have been sold to sub-contractors.
All of their maintenance is now done by contractors and sub-contractors.
Much of the office work is done by consultants because the hatchet men
have decimated the teams who used to run the core of the company.
The distribution of products is shared amongst all of the oil companies.
However, none of them seem to be making any profit here in Britain
and it is said that most of their money is now made on the high seas.
There are several multinational companies who pay no tax in Britain.
I gave up a secure job with *Esso* to become an insecure entrepreneur.
As an employer you are responsible for your employees and families.
Many of my former employees were then and still are my firm friends;
others were swinging the lead but it was very difficult to get rid of them.
Several times I had to go without paying myself in order to pay them.
As soon as I trained them they would leave, so my efforts were wasted.
Their wives would not let them go abroad or were constantly phoning.
They stole my tools, my materials, my products, my ideas and my time.
I would now rather sub-contract all of the manufacturing to specialists.
If sub-contractors do not deliver on time or they make a mistake you do
not have to pay them and you also know exactly what everything costs.
Many multinationals realized this and they did their best to shed jobs.
Others could not reduce their payroll and so they went to the wall.

We are now living through a period of great social and economic change.
Men and women are gradually being replaced by machines but some are
now working their socks off whilst others are sitting at home on the dole.
If most jobs were shared there would be little need for social security.
National insurance would decrease, however, pensions might increase.
We are all living longer and so Our age of retirement must increase,
although We should all gradually work a shorter day as We grow older.

Enjoyment

We have been conditioned to think that enjoyment must cost money. Yet, the most enjoyable things in Life are completely and utterly free. Many people in Calcutta have nothing, yet it is known as: The City of Joy. The Hindu religion teaches sharing - the poor often give to the poorer. However, there comes a point where there are too many people for the land to support and this Planet can no longer sustain its population. Children bring joy but also much hardship, big families are the norm in many developing countries, although girls are less welcome than boys. Prosperity breeds smaller families so the best way to spread birth control is to spread prosperity, not by handouts but by freedom of information. The problem with having children today is that they cannot find jobs and so they never leave home and then become a burden to their parents. Many are so well educated and trained that they cannot do simple jobs.

The industrial revolution promised greater prosperity and enjoyment. However, millions gave-up clean rural lifestyles for filthy urban drudgery. Instead of working in daylight they worked by the hands on a clock. Saturday afternoons became free for the enjoyment of sport but now a large part of the population are more interested in sport than in work. Sundays are no longer devoted to religion but are now devoted to sport. However, many sports have become avaricious, dangerous or corrupt. The electronic revolution may lead to another socio-economic revolution. Many more of Us could share Our jobs and then enjoy more free-time. We could all take part in sports instead of watching others participate. Social networks can lead to the weekend becoming as big as the workend. They have already led to the downfall of despotic and tyrannical regimes.

Successive British governments have all failed to cure unemployment. They all fudge the figures instead of getting to the root of the problem. Millions are unemployed but not drawing benefits, millions are drawing sickness benefits whilst fit, millions are drawing benefits whilst working and millions are working but not paying national insurance nor taxes. When these millions retire they will not have any pensions or savings. Millions who paid into pension funds all their lives will not get a penny. Millions of Britons left because they could no longer afford to live here. Millions of legal and illegal immigrants have now taken over their jobs. Millions are working illegally at well below the minimum living wage. Millions are only working part-time or working on zero-hours contracts. Millions are self-employed, so they are not earning a wage nor a salary. Millions depend upon food banks because otherwise they would starve. If We are not careful, Workfare could be another name for Workhouse. New Labour's Welfare to Work and the Lib-Cons Work Programme could result in more youngsters getting jobs but more oldsters losing theirs. The Tory Universal Credit Scheme failed to simplify taxes and benefits. It is now time for **full-time-job-sharing-as-the-norm or Workshare**.

Happiness

Happiness is an elusive state of mind that is almost impossible to define. It cannot be bought, has to be won, is more important than money and is the ultimate measure of the success of a person, family or civilization. The European aristocracy purchased artistic calendars and ornate clocks but they were not really happy because they needed many poor servants. The people who lived and sailed in the South Pacific had no Time-gods, no chronologies, calendars nor clocks, yet they were supremely happy.

In a recent survey the happiest people in Our World were found to live in Bangladesh, one of the very poorest nations, because everyone has a job. Most of the European countries came in the middle of the list but some of the richest countries, with high unemployment, were near the bottom. The Danes are at the top of the European happiness league whilst the Italians are at the bottom and this could be due to several differences. The Danes are mostly middle class with low unemployment, they balance work with leisure, trust their politicians and they are mostly Humanists. The Italians are rich or poor with high unemployment, do not balance work and leisure, do not trust politicians and most are Roman-Catholics. One in four Americans is under psychiatric care for clinical depression. Some of these patients are overworked whilst the rest are unemployed. **Full-time-job-sharing-as-the-norm** would be a happy medium between the stress and strain of overwork and the boredom of unemployment.

Science and technology expanded so rapidly during the last turbulent century that We tended to forget what life was like before they began. Religion filled a large part of everyone's life, from the cradle to the grave. One could not die happy without belief in the supernatural and afterlife. Religion used to be the inspiration for many artists, sculptors, writers, musicians, architects and engineers but most now find ideas elsewhere. Many people are now finding that the quest for knowledge can fill their entire lives and that they can die very happy without religious belief. We all need to feel that We are contributing to the well-being of Us all. The Welfare State has not been the answer to the problems of Our World. The sociologists and economists have yet to consider the socio-economic advantages of **full-time-job-sharing-as-the-norm** in a ten-day work week.

Religion often provided the motivation needed for many of Us in the past. Humanism may provide the motivation needed by all of Us in the future. Greek Humanists believed in the *trivium* of grammar, rhetoric and logic. To discover complete and everlasting happiness We must first achieve: the five Tao goals : harmony, simplicity, symmetry, stability and quality; the three aims of the French revolution: liberty, equality and fraternity; the three fundamental virtues of Christianity: faith, hope and charity; the four ideals of Humanism: trust, fairness, serenity and democracy. These great maxims are the themes of the next series of essays.

Harmony

There are many examples of civilizations achieving great advances once they found a common purpose and then worked together in harmony. Once they had devised one temporal and spatial measurement system and one working pattern, they built monuments that still stand today.

The Chinese emperors believed, for five millennia, that their task was to keep Human society in balance with the eternal order of the Universe. If they achieved harmony they would receive the mandate of Heaven. They would then be blessed by their ancestors, who they venerated. Taoist harmony between *yang* and *yin* means perfect balance between: male and female, man and machine, manager and worker, left and right, black and white, rich and poor, big and small, long and short, hard and soft, loud and quiet, love and hate, sweet and sour, fast and slow. None of these opposites is ever likely to dominate the other, so they must all work together with the common aim of achieving perfect harmony. Confucius believed that a ten-day week was the perfect working pattern. The bells and gongs, rung in temples to indicate the times for prayers, were related to their standardized dimensions, weights and measures.

Pythagoras of Samos, (c 582-500 BC) the founder of Western philosophy, believed that the Universe expressed a divine mathematical harmony. His discovery that whole numbers govern musical harmonies convinced him that harmony and planning lay behind the complex Universe and that everything should be based upon anatomy and the size of the Earth. The Athenian foot was based upon the girth of the Earth at that latitude. The Roman foot was based upon the girth of the Earth at that latitude. The **Worldwide** *han* is based upon the girth of the Earth at the Equator.

The Greeks thought that they had *Her* measure with their geometry. Newton thought that he understood *Her* but his sums did not add up. He could not find the measure of Time, so ascribed the difference to *God*. Laplace was able to correct Newton's work with his: *System of the World* and yet he championed the Metric System, which had numerous faults. Einstein boggled Our minds, relatively speaking, when he told Us that Space and Time are not separate dimensions but Space-Time which can be warped and that energy and matter are completely interchangeable. His theory that gravity travels at the speed of light is proven to be true. The physics of the very large and the very small are very different. The laws of gravity and quantum mechanics appear to be incompatible. So they still cannot be expressed by the same Equation of Everything. There is still much to discover about the Harmony of the Spheres.

We can all achieve global harmony if We forget about all gods and idols and then pay homage to Our Human Race and to Our Planet Earth. We can find harmony with the global-digital-decimal **Worldwide System**.

Simplicity

Simplicity is the essence of architecture, engineering, art and design. It may take many attempts before We arrive at the simplest solution. The Victorians were extremely prone to over-elaboration in all things. Our Neo-Elizabethan solutions have usually been much more simple. Religious buildings were simple but gradually became more complex. Christianity started by being a simple religion with a simple message. Some of its simple oratories are still standing in the west of Ireland. They developed into complex basilicas, monasteries, abbeys, priories, cathedrals and churches, embodying a much embroidered message. Civilization and complexity go together but many yearn for a simple life. Life could be very much simpler in civilizations like Ours if We were able to switch-off and return to Our roots on a more regular basis. This would only be possible if most of Us were able to share Our jobs. If We discarded months and weeks and numbered the days in the year most of Us could share Our jobs on a five day-on/five day-off basis.

The calendar used by the Copts was very simple because it was based upon an ancient Egyptian one but the Orthodox and Catholic ones are extremely complex and they are festooned with numerous saints' days. The Cathars were simple Christians but the Catholics annihilated them. Methodists use simpler buildings and services but the same calendar. Quakers use numbers for the days in the week and days in the month; but not for the days in the year, which drop into handy groups of ten. The 24-hour clock face was too complicated to read very quickly and so We now have a simpler 12-hour one, which only works for half a day. A whole-day 12-hour dial would be better, like Chinese double-hours, but their later clock face with 100 *k'e* per day was much simpler still. What a pity Jacopo de Dondi was not encouraged by Pope Clement VI to continue with his development programme and simplify his dial further. If he had started with a clean sheet of paper he would perhaps have designed an X-hour dial and We would all be using **decimal time** now. Mercator's globe would have been simpler if 360 degrees of latitude and longitude were decimalized and there were no divisive time zones.

Counting everything in tens is not as simple as possible because the binary system is much simpler and is used within digital computers. However, We would very soon become bored with using it Ourselves. Ten gives the optimum digital system for counting simply everything. Complex theory is a new branch of mathematics that can predict the spread of diseases, the migration of birds or the gridlock of road traffic. It can be used to study Human social, economical and political systems using computer models and the effect of small changes can be studied. Perhaps it could be used to study the effect on Our post-modern society of a change from a uni-cycle seven-day week to a bi-cycle ten-day one. A unicycle is much simpler to make but a bicycle is much easier to ride.

Symmetry

Symmetry is a sign of perfection: you can tell at a glance when all is well. It is the essence of science, engineering, design, philosophy and religion. It is the basis of architecture from Classic temples to Gothic cathedrals from Islamic mosques to Jewish synagogues, from Buddhist shrines to Hindu temples and from Stone Age henges to the Egyptian pyramids. The great temple at Karnak had a matched pair of obelisks at its portal. They are very important symbols in Freemasonry and they hark back to the temples of ancient Egypt and to the temples of Solomon and Herod. The Freemasons are thought to be the successors to the Knights Templar who brought stonemasonry back to medieval Europe from the Holy Land. Freemasons transported 'Cleopatra's Needles' to London and New York. The twin towers of the World Trade Center were symbols of symmetry.

The Taoist *kua* symbol and the trigrams and hexigrams of *yin* and *yang* are totally symmetrical and based upon the equal balance of opposites. The first watches to be exported to China from the West were ordered in pairs with their decorations in a perfect mirror image of each other.

Buddha taught that symmetry and balance are the route to harmony. Buddhists worship Time and they turn prayer wheels to make it pass. Their pass-time is to use coloured sand to make symmetrical patterns. Their shrines are symmetrical mandalas representing the Universe.

The Universe is made of atoms or compounds, which are as symmetrical as can be and every particle or wave has an equal and opposite one. It is thought that all positive matter and forces are cancelled out by an equal and opposite number of negative ones, like those in a magnet. Stick them together and you would have absolutely nothing - no matter.

All animal life is symmetrical and so are most vegetables and leaves. The Human body is symmetrical on the outside and most of the inside. We start life as twins, We have two of almost everything and are able to 'run on one cylinder' but the two sides of Our brains do different things. On the one hand We have 5 digits; on the other hand We have 5 digits.

The leaves in every book are equally left and right or odd and even but most calendars, planners, diaries and timetables are not symmetrical. The 7-day week does not fit a pair of pages and this causes disharmony. The 10-day *wek* is perfectly symmetrical and therefore it is harmonious. The **digital date** calendar is as symmetrical as it is possible to devise, providing that the variable length of the *yerend* is used quite separately. The compass is symmetrical about its north-south and east-west axes. A XII-hour clock is more symmetrical than an analogue **decimal time** one, so some say that everything should be measured or counted in twelves. However, this does not apply to digital **decimal time** clocks or watches.

Stability

A pyramid is a very stable structure, provided it has firm foundations. The Egyptian pyramids were built by many competing teams of ten men, who quarried, transported, placed and shaped millions of stone blocks. It was an honour to be chosen to build them in the inundation season, when the Nile flooded and it was no longer possible to work on the land. They worked during ten hours for nine days, then took the tenth day off. The pharaohs used a measurement, management and government system, based on the digital number ten, in their lifelong quest for immortality. Their early mud-brick pyramids soon collapsed but their later stone ones have lasted for millennia, as a monument to their leaders and builders. Society is like a pyramid, with the rich at the top; the poor at the bottom, but it may have shaky foundations that cause its structure to collapse. They must be replaced with a new base, not shored-up or underpinned. Our global civilization is crumbling, because there are more and more bricks who do not fit into its structure, so they are likely to undermine it. If not it will soon collapse, under its own weight, and have to be rebuilt.

The modern state of Egypt was apparently stable until a great uprising in 2011 AD destroyed the structure created by the pharaoh Mubarak. Egypt cannot support its own population and has much unemployment, so it now needs **full-time-job-sharing-as-the-norm** in a ten-day week, and a more democratic system for choosing and sacking its leaders. The rebels were coordinated through social networks on the Internet. So the electronic revolution is now helping to build a New World Order. Many other states with despotic rulers have also succumbed to anarchy, because there is no social, economic and political blueprint to work from. The transition from the old to the new is a painful and bloody business, which needs more guidance from the very top of their global pyramid. Britain was considered to one of the most stable countries in the World but the riots in 2011 AD show that it also has socio-economic problems.

There is always a better way of doing anything, from making mousetraps to constructing more stable buildings and building lasting civilizations. The first step is to realize that there is a problem and then to define it. The next step is to start at first principles and then build a new system. The last step is to ensure that everyone understands the new solution. **Worldwide Time** as a complete system, involving the age, date and time, could not have been proposed by anyone else over the last millennium, until the age of this Planet was finally determined some fifty years ago. **Worldwide Space** as a complete system, involving distance, direction, angle, length, area, volume or capacity, weight or mass and wealth, could not have been proposed by anyone else over the last millennium, until the girth of this Planet was finally determined some fifty years ago. Our World has changed a very great deal during these last fifty years; yet its measurement, management and government systems have not.

Quality

The Americans demonstrated that they could mass-produce watches and clocks of high quality at low cost by using selective assembly techniques. They taught the Japanese how to utilize these techniques after WW2. The Japanese showed the World that they could improve every product by a continuous process of development in its design and manufacture. The quality of their electronic products became the envy of the World. As the result the quality of everyone's lives have improved a great deal. But now the Japanese need a new incentive to improve all their lives. They lost much of their motivation when they lost their jobs-for-life. Job-sharing-as-the-norm may be a better way of organizing themselves. They have already started to share their jobs, to ease unemployment.

Quality assurance has become a vital part of every kind of organization. Continuous improvement and assessment is a vital management tool. We should and We must criticize every one of Our management systems. To begin with We need to reassess the way We count Our Solar years. Counting backwards and forwards from any arbitrary date is nonsense. We must count forwards from the year zero via the Metric Millennium. Next, We need to reassess the day on which the Solar year commences. The most logical day is the first one where the day and night are equal. Then We need to divide-up the year into convenient groups of days. The most convenient size of working week is the digital ten-day one. For this would allow most jobs to be shared and this would encourage healthy competition as well as the best use of all capital equipment. The most convenient way of dividing a day is to use the decimal system. For that is the way We now divide everything else that We measure. If We are prepared to do this We might as well scrap all time zones. For they divide-up Our Planet in a most confusing and inefficient way. This global-digital-decimal system is compatible with every computer. Similarly, the girth of Earth should also be divided-up in a decimal way.

The Internet can only work properly if We all use the same software. Whilst We already have one math; We do not yet have one science. Astronomers, physicists, chemists and biologists study the same matter. Nevertheless, they are often at loggerheads about many other matters. We are living in a technological age but do not yet have one technology. The many different technological institutions are trying to get closer together but do not speak the same jargon or use the same measures. Pilots and navigators at sea, over land or in the air use different systems for measuring their positions, directions, heights, depths and speeds. Architects, engineers, builders and decorators use different dimensions. As well as the same measurements We also need the same language. The United Nations should be encouraging one word and One World. Yet, UNESCO is spending a fortune on keeping dead languages alive. **Worldwide Time** and **Worldwide Space** could lead to **Worldwide Talk.**

Liberty

The Egyptians did not take any slaves: their pyramids were constructed by paid workers, who built the foundations of the very first nation-state. However, the Mesopotamians, Greeks and Romans all used slave labour. Slavery was thought by the Greek philosophers to be a necessary part of civilization and it helped to build many empires - including the British. A freed slave, say from Phrygia, would then be obliged to wear a red cap. The French revolutionaries adopted this as their symbol of freedom. This was often used on their digital calendars and their decimal clocks. Some 9M slaves died during transportation during the 18th century AD before William Wilberforce (1759-1833 AD) did something about this. Long after that poor men, women and children were regarded as slaves. This sadly impoverished underclass is now rapidly returning everywhere. In Europe: legal and illegal immigrants work below the minimum wage. In USA: there is no minimum wage and migrant workers earn very little. In the rest of the globe: unemployment is now far worse than slavery. Millions of people, who used to be self-sufficient, migrated to city slums. Very, very few of the millions of slum-dogs will ever become millionaires.

Many socio-economic barriers are falling but others are still being built. Even in Britain, where there appears to be freedom of expression and many other freedoms there are some that have not yet been granted. For example: the freedom to work, shop, play or pray any-time, any-day. It may well prove to be just as important to abolish this middle-class inequality as those at the extreme left or the extreme right of politics. Religion should be completely separate from politics but many politicians now believe in the dogmas associated with the Mystic seven-day week. Britain seems to have free media but radical new ideas are edited out. Radio, TV and the press are organized on a seven-day week basis and so they cannot envisage a ten-day week in which all days are the same. Two billion of Us now have computers and two billion now have mobile phones all with access to social networks such as *Facebook* or *Twitter,* so new and radical ideas can now spread around the globe in an instant.

We are not compelled to think how Our parents thought, nor must We do as they did, so We cannot expect Our children to think as We do now. If We want to make progress, in all its forms, We must re-examine all of Our assumptions, attitudes, beliefs, ideas, traditions, commandments, commands, customs, habits, regulations, laws, standards, conventions. Change must be fast, so that We can reap its benefits in Our lifetimes. Many innovations were unsuccessful because the World was not ready for them or the technology they needed was not sufficiently advanced. Yet, many old ideas became outmoded as new ones took their place. In order to hit all Our targets We need hindsight as well as foresight. Many forgotten or obliterated ideas like the Egyptian digital calendar and the Chinese decimal clock can be reinvented - like the wheel.

Equality

We all have different ethnic backgrounds, yet We all came out of Africa.
Some of Us are born with greater abilities and some have greater drive.
Some are males, some are females and some are somewhere in between.
Some have different religious beliefs; whilst others have no beliefs at all.
We must be given equal chances to seize the opportunities We are given.
How high We rise up the ladder must depend on Our individual merit.
Equality of income is impossible since no one would take responsibility.
Yet, there is an increasing disparity between highest and lowest incomes.
If you are born to rich or poor family you are likely to stay rich or poor.
Although there is greater equality of opportunity in some societies.

The English revolution did not create equality but greater democracy.
The French revolution allowed many rational, secular ideas to blossom.
The American revolution freed all of the slaves and promised equality.
Yet, Native-, African-, Hispanic-, Asian– and East European-Americans
were considered to be inferior by Anglo-Americans who held onto power.
The American Constitution stipulates that all days should be the same.
Yet, Sunday is still considered to be a weekly day for rest and religion.
Inequality is still the greatest problem in this so-called land of the free.

Searching questions are continually being asked about the future of
the polity, the theocracy, the aristocracy and the monarchy in Britain.
Because all of these socio-economic traditions are based upon inequality.
In the Thatcher-Major Era the fat cats grew fatter; the thin ones thinner.
In the Blair-Brown Era fat cats grew even fatter; thin ones stayed thin.
Many fat cats have now exploded; leaving many thin cats out in the cold.
Neither capitalists nor socialists have any solution to this great problem.
Gender equality in Britain has advanced since the suffragettes and yet
the age of retirement is different and women still earn less than men.
Nevertheless, there are now far more women than men in employment.
Yet, since more women have gone out to work, unemployment has risen.
Little Britain has a female monarch, its second female Prime Minister,
a female Speaker and Leader of the Opposition but no female archbishop.
The Church has been largely responsible for the inequality of women and
now looks like having a schism over the ordination of women and gays.
Pope Benedict XVI even attacked New Labour's proposed equality law.

With the **Worldwide System** We would all be able to use the same tools.
Every satchel would contain the same timetable, protractor and ruler.
Every year would start at an equinox, when day and night are equal.
Every day would start when Earth's Prime Meridian passes midnight.
The outward expression of an advanced society is a calendar that allows
work-days or free-days to be equal, so job-sharing can become the norm.
People who share jobs should have equal qualifications and experience
but they may have different backgrounds, ethnicity, beliefs, or genders.

Fraternity

Fraternity develops from common interests, which may be in business, science, technology, politics, religion, culture, sport, leisure or tourism. The British Commonwealth is a fraternity of 51 members of the former British Empire who speak the same language and have similar interests. They all used to use the same Imperial System of weights and measures as well as the same chronology, calendar and clock but different zones. Taken together they won most medals in the 2012 AD Olympic Games, which was an excellent example of fraternity between many nations. International sport, and the media coverage of it, is helping to break down barriers and to highlight the cultural differences and similarities. Tourism helps understanding and more people are now globetrotting but there is very little opportunity for visitors to talk to their hosts, because different languages, religions and systems are barriers to fraternity.

There are many ways in which friendship is growing between nations; but also many cases in which old animosities are coming into the open. The European Union aspires to closer relationships between members. This is essentially a trading fraternity and there are similar groups in the Middle and Far East, Eastern Europe, Africa, South America and now Canada, USA and Mexico have torn down many of their trade barriers. Yet, the USA is talking about building a wall to keep the wetbacks out. As the UK entered Europe barriers were built between it and the World. The General Agreement on Trade and Tariffs broke down as soon as Britain agreed to the Maastricht Treaty and the USA elected Clinton. However, this GATT agreement was signed by 115 countries in 1993 AD. This treaty has now been superseded by the World Trade Agreement, signed by 157 countries in 1995 AD, but there are still many barriers to free trade and some are bitterly opposed the very idea of globalization.

The United Nations Organization is the greatest fraternity of all Time. It now has more influence than ever before and is the only forum where Worldwide matters can be discussed in a friendly fashion and then changed by democratic means; however, it is not a World Government and so it has no powers to enforce any of its humanitarian decisions. Its attempts to form a multilateral peacekeeping force have often failed. Nevertheless, Our faith in this great organization can only be upheld if We allow it to make some worthwhile global changes from time to time. The United Nations Association is a non-government organization and is supposed to be a forum for new ideas to be put forward by anyone. However, membership is declining and is dying out with its founders so members with new ideas are not given the opportunity to debate them. In theory, any NGO can present new ideas for better systems to the UN. In practice, the author failed to persuade any NGO to discuss this idea: We would all think of Ourselves as One Human Race living in One World if We all used the same chronology, calendar, clock, compass and rule.

Faith

Faith can certainly move mountains but it can also destroy skyscrapers.
A man from Afghanistan was recently granted asylum in Britain because
he had lost faith in *Allah* and would have been executed for this at home.
Several African countries persecute atheists, agnostics and Humanists.
Thousands are seeking asylum in Britain but their cases may take years
to be heard and they may be unable to prove they have been persecuted.
It was not too long ago that Catholicism was compulsory in Europe and
the Inquisition would torture or execute the Jews, Muslims or heretics.
The Inquisition still exists and its leader Joseph Ratzinger became Pope.
Benedict XVI was a member of the Hitler Youth and so had to resign.
Britain persecuted Catholics and then banned them from universities
but it now welcomes students with all faiths from all over the globe.
The USA is supposed to be a secular federation, however, the CIA works
with the Vatican to combat Communism and other religions or sects.

Many of Us still have faith in some form of idol, icon, god or religion.
The Americans worship the almighty dollar but they all live on credit.
They believe that everything can be reduced to bucks and all problems
can be overcome by spending; but need to learn that Our future depends
on saving and sharing, for We must all learn to live within Our means.
The greatest act of faith in science and technology that We have ever
seen is that historic moment when Neil Armstrong stepped on the Moon.
Some believe that science and technology will always come to Our aid.
Regrettably, blind faith in science is just as futile as blind faith in gods.

The Rotary and Humanist movements are said to have been responsible
for the formation of the United Nations which recently staged some of
history's most ambitious Earth Summits in order to put Our World right.
Rotary, formed by Paul Harris over a century ago, has over a million
members in over 150 countries and they sponsor humanitarian projects.
Working with the UN they have almost eradicated polio and they provide
shelter, water, food, sanitation and hygiene to the developing countries.
The British Humanist Association evolved out of the 19th century AD
Ethical Societies and Sir Julian Huxley was its founder and president.
They use reason and experience to establish their code of conduct.
They have faith in themselves and aim to improve their quality of Life.
They support all measures to create a global family of Human Beings.
The National Secular Society campaigns against religious bias in the
press, radio and TV, in the education system and in laws and by-laws.
However, Little Britain is still considered to be a Protestant Kingdom.
Prince Charles hopes to be: Defender of Faith, rather than: The Faith.
He hoped that the Millennium would mark a spiritual renaissance and
erected an obelisk or column at Highgrove with a golden phoenix on top.
This harks back to the ancient Egyptian worship at the Benben stone
and to their use of ten-year decades, ten-day weeks and ten-hour days.

Hope

A new chronology, calendar and clock could lead to a new kind of hope. A single time zone would demolish the invisible barriers that divide Us. A new global ruler could lead to a global ruler who puts Our World right. The French, Russian and Chinese revolutionaries may have used similar words when they, collectively, hoped that their atheist and Communist ages, dates, times, zones and rules would improve their wretched lives. Whilst their alternative ways of living did not last for very long and all hope was again lost, this does not mean that there will never be a better way of organizing Our Time, Our Space, Our Planet and Ourselves.

I was recently made aware of despair and hope on my own doorstep. A Russian couple exchanged their flat in Moscow for a leaky sailing boat with a faulty engine in which they had sailed to the village where I live. All they had were some worthless rubles, a tatty chart, an outdated almanac, very little equipment, food or clothing but a great deal of hope. Britain was in deep recession, they had no visa and so they were told to leave as soon as their boat was repaired - but they said that they would rather die than go back to Russia - which is now a capitalist state. Many hopes are dashed in former and present Communist countries as comrades try to escape the system but are sent back by capitalist states. The fundamental problem is that Our Planet is already overpopulated and this will only get worse unless We share Our Time and Our Space.

Britain is sending back many illegal immigrants and it now has over 70,000 stateless citizens of Our World locked-up in its detention centres. Expansion of the European Union to include former Communist states has led to mass migrations and many people have come to Little Britain. Many of them then depend on social security or they do menial jobs. The Home Office reluctantly admits that it has lost count and lost track of all the legal and illegal immigrants who now live and work in Britain. Many Britons used to emigrate to Canada, Australia or New Zealand but now they have little hope of a new life anywhere outside of Europe. Nevertheless, more Britons than ever are evacuating their sinking ship.

Social security does not come from a bottomless barrel, pensions are being eroded by inflation and many people living in capitalist countries, with or without welfare systems, may spend their lives without a job. Most of Britain's gold and silver has now been sold to foreign investors. Its Natural resources and its manufacturing or service industries are now owned, wholly or partially, by conglomerates from outside of Britain. Will this end in all of the true Brits being expelled from Little Britain? Or is there still hope in another chronology, calendar, clock and rule that We can all share whether We are Communists, Socialists, Nationalists, Liberals or Capitalists; whether We are atheists or followers of one of the many religions; whether We are black, brown, yellow or pink.

Charity

I am pleased to report that our Russian friends were treated very well by my local sailing club, their boat was patched up, they were given an engine, clothes, food, charts, a chronometer and plenty of friendship. Charity begins at home but they were not permitted to stay in Britain. They sailed to Australia but they were not allowed to stay there either. They may be forced to live on charity and sail around the globe forever. There are many millions of stateless people living throughout the globe. Yet, they are all members of Our Human Race and citizens of Our World.

Fortunately, they did not need to be rescued by the Royal National Lifeboat Institution, which is wholly financed by charity, unlike most other rescue boat services, which are normally run by the state. Every year the RNLI raises its funds by selling calendars, diaries etc. then has to pay £Ms in VAT - what a waste of money, time and paper. I am pleased to report that the RNLI are now using small hovercraft. So they can reach the parts of the coastline where the others cannot and they can be rapidly launched across a beach, over mud and shallows. Yet, it has taken the RNLI over fifty years to understand this advantage. Now that the RNLI are using them and saving lives, many other rescue organizations are beginning to take them seriously, around the globe.

Rotary International is a global organization with over a million members. This voluntary organization is helping to eradicate polio and providing shelter for the homeless as well as many other humanitarian charities. International aid via the Red Cross, Crescent and Diamond or through the UN has been a great benefit but there is never enough funding. There are probably too many of these non-government organizations now and they often seem to be fighting each other for vital charitable funding. International air and sea travel has now become, relatively, too cheap; whilst national road and rail travel has become ridiculously expensive. The reason for this is, of course, excessive taxation but no government has the legal right to tax travel over international waters or airspace. What is now needed is a global charity tax on marine and aviation fuel. This kind of tax would be relatively easy to collect via the oil companies.

Industrialists such as Henry Ford, Andrew Carnegie and Bill Gates have done a great deal to save Our Planet, through charitable foundations. Charities such as Oxfam, Save the Children Fund and Band Aid have done a great deal to save Our Species and they are continuing to do so. Yet, there are many humanitarian projects that never seem to get done. Whilst many people now have the time to help others; they do not get around to it because they are preoccupied with their own misfortunes. **Full-time-job-sharing-as-the-norm** would encourage voluntary work in free-time, say collecting funds for charity or doing something useful. We can save Our Species and Our Planet if We share Time and Space.

Trust

Trust can take a lifetime to construct but only one moment to destroy.
We used to trust MPs but they were found to be fiddling their expenses.
We used to trust Lords but they were demanding cash for questions.
We used to trust newspapers but they were hacking into Our phones.
We used to trust bankers but these fat cats have licked Our cream.
We used to trust priests and nuns but many have abused Our children.
We used to trust police but they have lied and altered Our statements.
We used to trust judges and lawyers but they were only after Our fees.
We used to trust doctors and dentists but they do not work at weekends.
We used to trust grocers and butchers but they sold horsemeat as beef.
We used to trust each other but a handshake is no longer a contract.

Our leaders are no longer trustworthy, many have their hands in the till.
Boris Yetsin used secret funds to annihilate Muslim fundamentalism.
Kohl and Mitterand used slush funds to finance their political parties.
George Bush promised that he would not raise any taxes but he did.
Bill Clinton, was impeached whilst he quadrupled the annual deficit.
George W. Bush lowered taxes but also increased the annual deficit.
Margaret Thatcher used kickbacks from contracts to raise party funds.
John Major gambled with the £ sterling and so lost much of its value.
Tony Blair, allegedly, raised party funds by giving honours for donations.
Gordon Brown raided pension funds to pay his million tax collectors.
Maybe We would be able to trust Our leaders if they shared their jobs.

Loyalty was a great motivator, when most people had their jobs-for-life.
Employers, invariably, respected their employees' loyalty and *vice-versa*.
However, American hire-and-fire methods destroyed this mutual respect.
Employers are now realizing that employee loyalty is worth a great deal.
They now have to spend a great deal on job-training and team-building.
Some have already discovered that job-sharing is very good for the soul.
Job-sharers have to acquire complete trust in each other, even though
they rarely see one another, and so they eventually become soul-mates.
All organizations, of any kind or size, could maximize their integrity
if they adopted **full-time-job-sharing-as-the-norm** and a ten-day week.

Whereas Europeans dominated Our World during the last millennium,
and all races are gradually becoming integrated in Europe and America,
there is still a great deal of mutual mistrust between all of the faiths.
Communism was supposed to wipe-out these fundamental differences,
but newfound comrades found that they could not trust their leaders.
Capitalism is based on the dogmatic, dog-eared doggerel of dog-eat-dog,
so political, racial, tribal and spiritual wars are erupting all over again.
Humanism was always based upon sharing work in some way or other.
This is the fairest way of organizing any company, country or continent.
Full-time-job-sharing-as-the-norm can help to unite Our Human Race.

Fairness

Fairness is a buzzword amongst politicians as they try to decide which taxes must be increased; which benefits and public services must be cut. Their efforts to stimulate the global economy, by bailing-out the biggest banks, insurance companies and businesses, made many matters worse. Many small companies went-to-the-wall and global unemployment rose. Deficits were written-off by printing money, free trade was restricted by erecting artificial barriers and aid was cut to many developing countries. No politicians have realized that most jobs could and should be shared. The work ethic is fundamental to the success of every kind of civilization. Our problem is the dogma that some time is worth more than other time. Prejudice and tradition are still the causes of many humanitarian issues. The fundamental causes of ethnic or religious prejudice are not really the colour of Our skin, the cut of Our hair nor the style of Our clothes but all of the different age, date, time and zone systems, which divide Us. Civilizations have clashed for many reasons but their greatest difference was their chronologies, calendars, clocks, rules, weights and measures.

The only way to overcome prejudice and tradition is to demonstrate that a new idea, system or widget really works, but this may take many years. Most people would rather reject an innovation, which could save them Time and Space, rather than try it, for no one wants to be the first. Yet, when their neighbour has a shiny new widget, they want one too. The older generation always cling to systems they were brought up with; the younger generation are always ready to accept new working practices. This generation gap is now greater than ever as information technology and social networking become the norm, yet job-sharing has yet to do so. Computers will be a great help in spreading this new idea and helping to implement it by logging completed tasks and those yet-to-be-done.

Britain is proud of it welfare state but it has undermined the work ethic. This system is widely abused and benefit fraud costs many £Billions. Some are earning more on the dole than they could if they were at work. Many of those currently out of work have more merit than those in work. We cannot create a meritocracy if Our graduates go straight on the dole, or they start their careers owing for their tuition fees and student loans. Education is a key to the future and must be based on merit at all levels. We must do everything in Our power to achieve equality of opportunity. There is no reason why any university could not adopt a ten-day week and **full-time-job-sharing** today and set an example for others to follow. They are supposed to be autonomous and independent of every state but most have long vacations when their very expensive facilities lie unused. Britain needs a complete overhaul of its taxation and benefit system to encourage managements to adopt **full-time-job-sharing** and unions to accept this as the normal way of working in most kinds of organization. **Full-time-job-sharing** is the fairest way to run any company or country.

Serenity

The Dead Sea Scrolls reveal, clearly, that the schisms which separated Sadducees and Pharisees from Essenes and then Christians from Jews were due to conflicts over the use of chronologies, calendars and clocks. These schisms are still causing conflict throughout this disparate Planet two millennia after the predicted Messiah was believed to have arrived. Religious leaders have already made some attempts to get together and see eye to eye but there is still a long way to go before they have one code of morals and ethics and one chronology, calendar, clock and time zone. The fundamental difference between Jews, Christians and Muslims is their special days in the week but they will probably never agree upon the same day, so why not scrap the 7-day week and adopt a 10-day one? The fundamental difference between the Hindus, Buddhists and Taoists is their special days in the Lunar moonth, so why not scrap the moonth? Moonlight is no longer important when We now have electric lamplight. Calendar months are only useful as the start of a new sheet of paper. The fundamental difference between all faiths is the date upon which New Year is celebrated, so why not begin again with a new Solar year?

Religion is the fundamental cause of all the conflicts around the globe. The foundation of every religion was a chronology, calendar and clock. They still cause a great deal of conflict throughout this disparate Planet. The Time is ripe to build on Our similarities and forget Our differences. We are all Human Beings and so We should all become Humanists. We must rebuild Our Time and Our Space with firmer foundations, so that Our Civilization and Our Global Village can last a little longer. The Internet is a one-eyed idol that is worshipped throughout Our Planet. It is rapidly becoming a post-modern guru who can answer all questions. The Worldwide Web could lead to a global-digital-decimal measurement, management and government system and then on to global serenity.

We all need to work for peace because idle hands always lead to conflict. Work is good for the soul but there is no point in working for nothing. The gap between the rich and the poor has become much too large. Some claim that unemployment benefits are more than they could earn. However, many are still earning less than the minimum living wage. Many illegal immigrants are working like slaves in the black economy. Too many jobs have been created just to minimize the jobless statistics. Too many jobs have been destroyed by management and by the unions. We must forget the dogmas associated with the Mystic seven-day week. A ten-day week would encourage Us to share Our Time and Our Space. All the days were created equal and 360 of them should still be so. All 360 equal days and all parts of days should be paid at a flat rate. This would encourage Us to share Our worktime and Our freetime. The most positive advice that can be given to any community is: **Share the work and you will share the wealth and live in peace.**

Democracy

Democracy was instituted in Greece during the era of Socrates and Plato but suppressed by the Roman emperors and the Holy Roman emperors. The State and the Church have been at loggerheads for a millennium. In Britain the monarch is both Head of State and Head of the Church. Parliament is divided into two Houses: the Lords and the Commoners. The Commoners are democratically elected but the Lords are selected. The House of Lords is divided into Lords Spiritual and Lords Temporal. The Lords Spiritual still have a great influence on temporal and spatial matters such as: what chronology, calendar, clock, zone and rule to use. They have recently called for double time to be mandatory on Sundays.

Big Ben is a symbol of democracy, in the same way that the Eiffel Tower is a symbol of revolution and both have been used to broadcast the time. Twelve chimes of Big Ben ring out at midnight in Greenwich Mean Time to *BBC* listeners Worldwide and they mean the same in every language. However, the chimes are now silent and their future seems uncertain. And the future of the *BBC World Service* also seems to be uncertain. Both Houses of Parliament now need to be replaced instead of restored. A circular forum is better than the government and opposition benches. Instead of party politics each candidate should be chosen on merit. We no longer need monumental clocks as We have digital radio and TV.

$$\begin{array}{ccc} 4 & 9 & 2 \\ 3 & 5 & 7 \\ 8 & 1 & 6 \end{array}$$

Nevertheless, this is how a global-digital-decimal clock-face might look. It may seem superfluous to show the age and the date as well as the time but this magic square of numbers shows **Worldwide Time** which could be broadcast, around the globe, with every *BBC World Service* online bulletin.

The **digital date calendar** sets aside the five or six democratic days, at the end of the year, when We could vote without leaving home. Most homes in Britain now have televisions, telephones and computers linked to the Internet and many now vote for their favorite pop group. It is now technically feasible for votes to be cast on specific issues; rather than for a particular candidate or for a political party with a basket of policies that may, or may not, be mentioned in its manifesto. Every major issue could be the subject of a referendum or a free vote. This would be true democracy or people power and it is what makes **The Worldwide System** so different from all the party political systems.

Part Eight

Organization

Changing Our Jobs

"Work is the cure for all the maladies that ever beset Mankind."

Thomas Carlyle (1795-1881 AD)

Sharing Time

This book describes a new recipe for a larger and tastier pie, which We can all make and then share, it gives new measures for old ingredients, which have not been changed for ages, and then adds some new ones. Theologians argue that We must cling to the hallowed recipes of the past. Politicians argue about ingredients, stir things up then cook the books. Civil servants, lawyers, accountants, sociologists, economists, financiers and many other non-productive hangers-on all take a slice of the pie. The poor worker at the end of the line is lucky to get a few crumbs. They have all forgotten, lost or hidden that essential basic ingredient, whose measure has not been changed for ages: the fragrant herb thyme.

We must find better ways of sharing, not wasting, all of Our resources. The more work that is shared; the more jobs there will be for everyone. The more positions that are filled; the more wealth will be created. The more wealth that is created; the more there will be for all to share. The more homes that are shared; the fewer new homes will be needed. The more journeys that are shared; the less will be the waste of fuel. The more responsibility that is shared; the better will be the decisions. The more power that is shared; the less will be the chance of corruption. The more recreation that is shared; the more it can be enjoyed by all. Sharing is good for the soul and it can help to save Our Planet Earth.

If you are alone in the wilderness, a self-sufficient hunter/gatherer will invariably share his last crust of bread or his last cup of water with you. Stand by the road and anyone will give you a lift, yet not want payment. Stand by the road all day in New York and no one will give you a lift. Lie in the gutter and no one will come to your aid, but you will not go hungry because the trash cans are full of half-eaten burgers and pizzas. The USA is depleting its resources and gobbling up much of Our World. Whenever it runs out of almighty dollars it simply prints more and more. Many of its banks, industries and businesses have had to be bailed-out.

Schools, colleges and universities are all costing more to build and run, because of the expensive buildings, equipment and energy now needed. Their overhead costs could be halved if they were used by two teams. Hospitals have to be open every day but routine operations are not performed at weekends and local surgeries are all closed on Sundays. Many factories already work every hour of every day with several teams. Most offices have one team and are closed at weekends and on holidays. Shops could be run by two teams if they were allowed to open every day. Time-share apartments have a bad reputation but it makes no sense for expensive holiday accommodation to be left empty for most of the year. Most leisure facilities can be shared and their running costs reduced. The utilization of, very expensive, religious buildings is the lowest of all. They could be shared by all of the religions during a ten-day work week.

Sharing Space

As global trade develops it is imperative to use the same measurements. Britain is in the throes of changing to the International Metric System, which is now used throughout every industry, but old habits die hard. So most people still weigh themselves in stones, measure themselves in feet and inches and take their own temperatures in degrees Fahrenheit. British companies mostly changed to Metric packaging in the seventies. The rest, apart from dairies and breweries, changed at the Millennium. However, this International Metric System has numerous disadvantages. **Worldwide Space** is better than the International System because it is based upon anatomy and better than both of the Imperial and American systems because it is based upon the global-digital-decimal number ten. It is better than the Navigation system because it is based upon the girth of Planet Earth in arc-degrees and then subdivided in the decimal way; rather than the hexadecimal way, which can cause navigational errors.

Worldwide Space is better than fractional Imperial or decimal Metric, because it is based upon the approximate width of an average hand. A *han* is a very handy size because it can be inscribed on a protractor. A *Khan* is a very handy size that is approximately equivalent to 365 feet. A *Mhan* is a very handy size that is equivalent to one degree of longitude. A brick was 4 1/2 inches x 9 inches but would measure 1 *han* x 2 *han*. A sheet of plywood was 4 feet x 8 feet but would measure 10 *han* x 20 *han*.

Worldwide Space is better than the Imperial, American or Metric areas. The square *Kilohan* would replace both the acre and the hectare.

Worldwide Space is much better than the Imperial, American or Metric, which each have different measurement units for volume or capacity: the cubic foot, cubic yard or cubic metre and the pint, gallon or litre. A cubic foot of water contains 6.23 gallons, which weigh 10 pounds. A cubic metre of water contains 1,000 litres, which weigh one Kilogram. A cubic *han* of water contains one *can*, which weighs one *wan*. A cubic *han* or *can* is a more convenient unit for volume and capacity. 0.1 *can* is just under a quarter-pint wine glass. 0.2 *can* is just under a half-pint milk tumbler. 0.4 *can* is just under a pint beer tankard. 0.7 *can* is just under a litre wine bottle. 1.0 *can* is just under a 2.5 pint or 1.5 litre milk container. 1.0 *Dcan* is just under a 3 UK gallon or 3.65 US gallon fuel container. 1.0 *Hcan* is just under a 35 UK gallon or 42 US gallon barrel of oil. 1.0 *Kcan* is just under 47 cubic feet, 1.75 cubic yards, 1.33 cubic metres.

Worldwide Space is better than the Imperial and the American systems, which each have irrational fractional measurement units for weights. The *wan* is better than the Kilogram because a gram was the base unit.

Sharing Work

Most Britons now work for 5 days out of 7 and for 7 hours per day. They take 20 days paid holiday per annum (mandatory under EU law). Many are given 25 days paid holiday and some take more unpaid leave. There are 9 days of public holidays (most EU states now have 3 more) plus 104 days off at weekends (some EU states want a 3 day weekend) and an average of 8 sick days, making a total of 146 days not worked. Hence, most people now work for: (365-146) x 7 = 1533 hours/year. If they were to do the same amount of work during half of the working days in the *yer* (assuming that remainder days are used for elections) they would work for about: 1533/180 = 8.5 hours/day or 35 *cen*/day. However, if all work was shared with the unemployed, trainees and early retired and if sick days were made up later, this figure could be reduced to around 7 hours/day or 3 *dec*/day, which is about the same as now. They would work for 30 to 35% of the day on 50% of the days in the *yer*. They could also work a shorter day in the winter than in the summer

If paid at the same rate, incomes for the employed would be reduced, but so would their state pension and national insurance contributions. Net incomes could be further increased by lower taxation as the result of increased productivity, lower inflation and less public expenditure. By using **full-time-job-sharing-as-the-norm**, with half the population working for five days whilst the other half were resting and *vice versa*, all factory or office buildings and capital equipment would be utilized fully and the need to construct or purchase more would be delayed. Many organizations would then be able to increase their output without increased capital investment, or to significantly reduce their overheads. Profits would rise, prices would fall and so the economy would deflate.

Payment would be for the actual time worked during a 5-day period, in arrears, and the terms: 'wages' and 'salary' dropped in favour of 'pay'. This change would help to eliminate the divisive 'them and us' syndrome. There would be no holiday or sick pay, but if someone wanted to take 10 or 15 days off for a vacation he or she would arrange to do so with his or her pair who would then cover for him or her and *vice versa*. Sick days would be treated similarly with the pair covering for the sick person if possible and the sick person making up for lost time later. Or a locum could be employed, which is now normal medical practice. Insurance would only be drawn in severe cases of illness or injury.

Most jobs can be shared and this is more productive and less stressful. Very few jobs are so responsible or creative that they cannot be shared. The time worked during the day should be as flexible as possible, to cope with daylight, supply and demand changes and travel peaks. Those who are not working would Naturally avoid travel in peak times. So Britain (or anywhere else) would be more efficient and less congested.

Sharing Pay

Unemployment is, officially, only 10% of the British working population. The true level of unemployment is well over 20% since the long-term unemployed do not receive any benefits and are encouraged to go sick, whilst many school leavers and graduates are unable to find any work. The Socialist Welfare State has eroded the British workforce's motivation. The Capitalist Poll Tax drove well over two million people 'underground'. The black economy is growing fast - especially in car boots on Sundays. The TUC reckon that unemployment costs Britain £25 billion per year. Various government schemes are ineffective because they are hiding some of the symptoms of the disease but are not treating the causes. A radical remedy is needed and **full-time-job-sharing** is the only cure. The same medicine would work well anywhere in the developed World. This does not involve over-manning or increased public expenditure. It could lead to much higher productivity and much lower taxation. Anyone could work to an older age if they were willing and able to do so. However, they would probably work part-time or on a consultancy basis. It makes no sense for workers to retire earlier when they are living longer.

Pay-scales would be set so that all time would be paid at the same rate with no higher rates for overtime or working so-called unsocial hours. There would be no pay for no work, so sick pay would come to an end. We would be responsible for Our own sickness and accident insurance. It would be in Our own interest to remain fit and healthy all the time. Promotion would be more rapid since there would be two chains of command, with joint responsibility for policy but otherwise autonomous. Leaders of large organizations may prefer to overlap both *leftday* and *rightday* periods and perhaps work on six shorter days every *wek*. Part-time-job-sharing is catching on, **full-time-job-sharing** is used by some organizations with encouraging results but they are hampered because 7 is not exactly divisible by 2 and by the dogma of overtime. **Full-time-job-sharing** could become the norm if it were to be organized on a 5-workday + 5-freeday basis throughout 36 ten-day weeks per year. Even with full employment it would be worthwhile for jobs to be shared.

Exactly the same solution would work well in every part of the globe. Especially in towns and cities that have overgrown their infrastructure. But also rural areas that are suffering from the population explosion. All transport systems are grossly overloaded and extremely congested. Yet, it is often much quicker and cheaper to drive and park at weekends. If 360 days were all equal, congestion would be reduced considerably. Imagine the chaos if all of the jobless were to travel in the rush hour. Job-sharing is based on the principle that everyone is entitled to earn their living for as long as they are able but too many people are being denied this fundamental Human right and many prophets of doom are predicting widespread unrest if more positive action is not taken soon.

Sharing Production

Whether the product was a stone axe, bronze arrow-head or iron nail, it paid to standardize its design and to productionize its manufacture. This was usually achieved by the division of the work into simple tasks. Each task was performed by workers who specialized in one operation. The industrial revolution was based upon working from dawn to dusk. The development of artificial light led to shift-working-around-the-clock. Nevertheless, most factories closed down for the holy days and holidays. Many production lines are now fully automated and work continuously. This is the fastest way for industries to get a return on their investment. And the fastest way for a new product to reach its full market potential. Most markets are globalized and extremely competitive these days as trade barriers are demolished and transportation costs are slashed.

The improved design, manufacture and marketing of clocks and watches led to the development of cars, computers and other electronic gizmos. Henry Ford started life as a farmer but then he became a clockmaker and eventually a successful car, truck, tractor and plane manufacturer. Ford taught Us a great deal about increasing productivity and profits. He succeeded in making transport and food cheaper for all Mankind. Yet, the *Ford Motor Company* does not build vehicles in Britain anymore, because labour costs are less and the unions are less militant elsewhere. His home town of Detroit is a depressed area with much unemployment. The pioneering British car industry is no longer owned by the British. The Japanese vehicle manufacturers like *Toyota* were more successful because they could start again with new factories and new agreements. They were not hidebound by the dogma that some hours and days were worth more than others and most of their production lines work 24/7.

Most people are still hidebound by the traditional seven-day week and many still think that some hours and days are worth more than others. These are known as unsocial hours but there would be none if the whole of society was based upon a ten-day week and most jobs were shared. The laws and bylaws making Sunday special are slowly being repealed and the week-end is becoming the same as the work-end for many of Us. Many new positions are now filled by part-time or self-employed workers, who do not qualify for pensions, sickness benefits or redundancies. Some 20% of Britons now do shift-work in all kinds of occupations and this trend is rapidly increasing but can play havoc with Our body clocks. The science of chronobiology is still in its infancy but it already tells Us when We should be awake, when We should be asleep and when to eat. Regular night workers are prone to heart attacks and strokes but Our body clocks can be fooled by artificial light into being more productive. Chickens can be fooled into laying more eggs by this time-shifting ruse. Scientists may be able to prove by experiments that **full-time-job-sharing** and shift-work in a ten-day week is less stressful and more productive.

Sharing Processing

Process industries such as oil refineries, chemical plants, power stations, gasworks, waterworks and sewage farms need to be constantly manned. Some kind of **full-time-job-sharing** with shift-work is already the norm. Some companies use double 12-hour shifts for 4 days then 4 nights followed by a few days off; others use triple 8-hour shifts with 4 teams. Oil drilling and production rigs often work a week on/week off system. They forget about months and simply number the 52 weeks in the year. Working for 12-hours at a stretch is very tiring and disorientating and it can cause serious mistakes as well as many health and social problems. Yet, it is often argued that two handovers per day are better than three, because most mistakes seem to occur during these overlapping shifts. The use of computers to monitor and control processes and roster the teams who watch their dials has had a huge effect on these industries.

A new working pattern, based upon a digital week and a decimal day could not only transform this industry but also the lives of its workers. Regrettably, they would also have to work during the 5 or 6 remainder days when most other workers would be resting, canvassing or voting. Perhaps it will be the oil, gas and other kinds of process industries that will set the example for all others to follow by simply numbering the days in the year and forgetting all about odd weeks and odd months. They could start straight away, without waiting for the rest to catch up. Most process industries are multi-national, so if 5+5 job-sharing was proven to work well in one state it could soon be adopted Worldwide.

It is not only process industries that need to operate on a continuous basis for fire brigades, ambulances and police forces need to do so too. Many essential services already use a 4 day-on/4 day-off work pattern. So there should be no problem for them to adopt a 5-on/5-off rhythm. However, there are public services like grass cutting, park keeping, road sweeping and refuse collection, which only operate five days in seven. If they were to operate every day in the year, or for 360 days per annum, their overheads would be reduced and so local taxes could be lowered.

During the Great Depression four 6 hour shifts per day became the norm. Roosevelt's New Deal increased productivity and reduced unemployment. However, his policy of increased state spending, protectionism and the abandonment of the gold standard then led to inflation and devaluation. We are now in another Great Depression or Global Economic Meltdown. This needs radical new economic thinking by all the pundits and gurus. However, they all seem to be hidebound by the old calendar and clock. The author approached a number of universities about further study of his proposals but they could not get their heads around the problem. Similarly, all of the existing think-tanks seem to cling to the *status quo*. Perhaps there needs to be a completely new team starting at square zero.

Sharing Construction

Construction is different from the production and process industries.
It is not very repetitive and so it needs different management skills.
Personal and portable computers and organizers can help considerably
with the planning, organizing and monitoring of all construction projects.
It is very important that everything needed arrives on site just-in-time.
If it were to arrive too early it could get in the way or may be stolen;
but if it were to arrive too late it could hold-up the complete project.
It is easier to hand-over to another team if a schedule is kept up-to-date,
so that they know what has already been done and what is still to do.
Containerization and modularization is keeping construction costs down.
Now that larger and heavier loads are allowed on most of the roads,
mobile homes, ships cabins, apartments, hotels, bathrooms, offices,
workshops, classrooms and prisons can be produced in factories and
then installed on site more economically and rapidly than if built in-situ.

The discovery of oil and gas led to the burgeoning of Our Human Race,
due to increased mobility, more efficient heating, lighting and cooling,
petrochemicals, fertilizers, pharmaceuticals and many other byproducts.
Yet, it also led to the production of better explosives and other weapons.
The manufacture of cement to build concrete jungles accounts for 5%
of greenhouse gases and the destruction of the forests accounts for 10%.
As the oil runs out, during this twelfth millennium of civilization, there
will be less bitumen for roads and less fuel for vehicles that use them.

Most construction projects are closed-down for weekends and holidays.
This is because overtime is usually paid at a higher rate and because
some projects are very noisy and so they are shut-down on Sundays.
However, very few construction workers refuse to work on the Sabbath.
All projects could be completed more quickly if **full-time-job-sharing**
was to become the norm and if **flextime** and **flexdate** were adopted.
Costs would be lowered because of the quicker return on investment.
Yet, with better and more even utilization of infrastructure, the need for
more buildings, roads and other construction projects would be reduced.

In the olden days, village people used to get together to construct barns.
If We had five days off in every ten We would have more time to embark
upon community projects again, like building halls, museums, galleries,
occupation centres for the elderly and recreation facilities for the young.
Unemployed people are not motivated to do voluntary work but if you
know you have earned your crust you are more willing to help others.
The main obstacle to all of this happening now is the seven-day week.
The weekend is too short and many complain that they work too hard
and never have enough time for leisure pursuits or community work.
So a ten-day week and **full-time-job-sharing-as-the-norm** would have a
beneficial effect upon all of the infrastructure and society as-a-whole.

Sharing Energy

Our World's fossil fuels were deposited in some of the most inaccessible and politically awkward places and they are rapidly becoming depleted. Whilst new reserves are continually being found and cheaper ways are being developed to extract them, the next generation may well run out of fossil fuels and then have to resort to more renewable forms of energy. Fracking may provide a short-term solution; but a long-term disaster. Electricity generated by wind, wave or tide is becoming cheaper than coal, oil or gas but it can only supply a small proportion of the total. Nuclear energy has still failed to live up to its promise and its apparent cheapness was based upon enormous subsidies and false accounting, which did not include the huge costs of waste treatment and demolition. In some parts of the globe Solar power is the cheapest form of energy. This is helping people in remote areas to stay alive and keep in touch. Yet, most forms of renewable energy require fossil fuels to make them. So they may not be economical, viable or sustainable in the longer term. Electric vehicles are neither cheap nor clean due to dirty power stations and only seem to be cheap because electricity is taxed at a lower rate.

Britain was self-sufficient but is now a net importer of coal, oil and gas. It also imports electricity from France, which is mostly nuclear powered. The Conservative government has pledged to phase out coal in a decade, because it emits more pollution, causing acid rain and global warming. Renewable forms of energy are better because they emit no pollution but are more expensive at present because the price of oil has dropped. It is incongruous that some forms of energy are taxed whilst others are not and organizations can claim back VAT on fuel when people cannot. If this was abandoned it would increase the prices of many goods and services but would simplify accounts, especially in the grey area between business and pleasure mileage, which is subject to fiddles and perennial arguments about whether a journey to or from work is part of a job. Petrol and diesel has not had value added because it has been burned. A global tax on marine and aviation fuels should go directly to the UN. It could then become financially and politically independent of all states.

Some experts from the oil and gas industry predict that We will start to run out of energy, in all of its forms, throughout the globe, by 2050 AD. If **full-time-job-sharing** was the norm and overtime rates were abolished, most power stations would experience lower peaks and higher troughs. So fewer of them would be needed and they could be more efficient. If public and private buildings were used every day they could be built to a higher standard with better insulation and lower energy consumption. Fewer buildings would be needed and there would be less congestion. **Flextime** and **flexdate** working can save a lot of congestion and energy because daylight is free whilst energy is becoming much more expensive. **The Worldwide System** could help to minimize the global energy crisis.

Sharing Mining

The 'Iron Lady' undermined iron, steel, coal, gas and power industries. Coal and iron ore mining was the foundation of the industrial revolution. Yet, they only represent a very small part of the British economy now. The days of the pick and shovel are over and it is now a much more capital intensive industry, where almost everything is done by machine. However, the miners still use restrictive practices to hold-up progress.

The coalminers' strike in 1973 AD brought the Heath government down. The Thatcher government was adamant this should not happen again. So they privatized steel, gas and electricity and then encouraged them to find alternative sources of supply and to build-up large stocks of coal. Thatcher changed the laws so that the miners' strike in 1984 AD failed. The fundamental differences between the Heath and Thatcher eras were the huge increase of unemployment from 1 to 3M and North Sea gas. Heavy industry was decimated, the demand for coal dropped, most of Britain's mines were closed and are full of water so cannot be reopened. There were 250K unemployed miners but they did not appear in the jobless statistics because they were encouraged to go on the sick list. What was left was highly mechanized and largely open cast, it was then privatized, for a fraction of its real value but it is still making a loss. Some 20% of UK electricity is generated from coal but half is imported. Some power stations now burn wood chips but these are imported too.

Had Arthur Scargill not stuck in his heels about Sunday working it might already be the norm and many more miners would have jobs. By working the mines every day with **full-time-job-sharing** British coal could be competitive again, provided imported coal is not subsidized. More mines would still be open and the cost of energy would be lower. Neither Old Tories nor New Labour got to the bottom of the pit problem. Yet, Britain still has enormous reserves of coal that it cannot utilize. Although coal and steel are now privatized they are still not competitive. The unions still insist on their restrictive practices and overtime rates. British coal is now American owned and British steel is Thai or Indian. There is very little iron or steel manufactured in Little Britain today. Much of its coal now comes from open cast mines in South America. Much of its steel is now imported from China, Russia or North America. The labour costs are lower but the transportation costs are higher. Although mechanical handling and larger ships have lowered the cost of importing many raw materials, there is no import duty or tax on fuel.

In Brazil 1M men mine gold, with their hands, every day of the week. They chop down the rainforest and then wash away the precious soil. They amalgamate gold with mercury and drive it off with open flames, thereby poisoning themselves and the mighty Amazon river forever. The Swiss bank vaults are filled to the brim with the filthy stuff.

Sharing Farming and Fishing

About two thirds of Us are engaged in some kind of farming or fishing. Yet, farmhands and fishermen are the poorest people on Planet Earth. Life on land depends upon the season and the weather, not the week. Life at sea depends on winds and tides rather than calendars and clocks. Science and technology allow the agricultural year and the working day to be stretched so that farm hands now work harder than ever before. Tractors allow fields to be ploughed when they are baked or frozen. Fertilizers, pesticides and herbicides greatly increase the crop yields. Electricity and engines allow land to be cultivated, drained or irrigated. Veterinary science allows much more livestock to survive and thrive. Lights trick hens into laying more eggs but cows need milking every day. Nevertheless, half of all the food produced in Our World is now wasted.

In Britain only 3% of the workforce now toil in the soil or fish in the sea. Many of these low-paid manual workers are legal or illegal immigrants. The farms are producing more but hands are suffering from overwork. Most farms are now subsidized by the EU Common Agricultural Policy, intended to minimize competition from many other parts of the globe. Some are paid to set-aside land; whilst millions are starving elsewhere. The cost of fertilizers, pesticides and herbicides is becoming prohibitive. Diseases have decimated livestock and so many farmers have given up. Very few youngsters are prepared to follow in their father's footsteps.

Britain has the longest coastline in Europe but does not catch the most. EU quotas have had a disastrous influence upon UK's fishing industry. Ports, jetties and harbours and the internal combustion engine have helped to extend fishing times and grounds, electronic navigation and fish finding equipment have greatly increased efficiency to the point where fishing now has to be restricted in order to maintain the stocks. Nevertheless, many fish that have to be thrown back are already dead. Fish farming is more efficient but this encourages diseases to spread. Job-sharing is already the norm for many fishermen whilst others only work when the season, the tide, the weather and the fish allow them to.

If We all enjoyed the same standard of living as the average American this lifestyle would need the produce of three Planet Earths to sustain it. Although science and technology are increasing the efficiency of farming and fishing, We are using up Our Natural resources at an alarming rate. Subsistence farmers and fishers produce enough for their own survival but the same land and sea can produce far more, if properly managed. Yet, there are many parts of Our World where nationalization and bad management have reduced the yield for home consumption and export. Job-sharing-as-the-norm could not only spread the work and the wealth within any size of community, from a small village to a conurbation, but it could also help it to become a more competitive exporter.

Sharing Transport and Communications

Job-sharing-as-the-norm would have a beneficial effect on transport and communications and thus on the overhead costs of most organizations. All physical communications or transportation systems would be shared evenly and there may be no need to widen roads, build more car-parks or restrict access to cities, since many more cars would be shared. Buses, trams, tubes and trains would be less crowded, more regular and more profitable and their timetables would be seasonal and perpetual. Most airports, seaports and hoverports would be much less congested because the peaks and troughs of demand would be evened out.

Postal services would operate daily and thus be improved considerably. Correspondence would be headed with the working times of the sender e.g. L 45cd-75cd meaning: "I work *leftdays* between 45 and 75 *centidays*." Thus you would know when others were likely to be working, anywhere. Answerphones, websites and directories could provide this information. Telephones would have few peaks so may be charged at a standard rate. Mobile phones with ten digit numbers would have enough permutations and combinations for the global population and could be used as a calculator or for displaying **global age, digital date** and **decimal time**. Electronic communications such as telex, faxes, e-mail and websites are already having a big effect on where people work and when they travel. **Flextime** and **flexdate** work well with modern communication systems. If we were to adopt **digital date** there would be little need for those working on *leftdays* to communicate with those working on *rightdays*.

We need to take a regular rest day but this does not have to be Sunday. Only a century ago horses were the main form of transport and they needed to have a day of rest every week but modern forms of transport can work every day, although they do need to be regularly maintained. Many ferries stopped and most petrol stations were shut on Sundays. Parking and congestion charges are still free on Sundays in most towns. The laws and by-laws enforcing the Sabbath day protected workers from overwork and exploitation as well as giving more power to the Church. All British days are becoming the same again as restrictive laws making Sunday special are repealed, in some states this has already happened but Friday, Saturday or Sunday are still very special days in other states. The Sabbatarians do not seem to realize that their dogmas are causing so much conflict, inefficiency and hardship in Our post-modern World.

All the above assumes that **full-time-job-sharing-as-the-norm** would be adopted multilaterally, throughout the entire industrialized World. If Britain, or any state, were to break-step and to adopt it unilaterally then international communications should be able to cope for a while. There would be a few problems with correspondence and telecoms might become more difficult if the week and the *wek* were used in parallel.

Sharing Environs

The British environment and the health of its population have improved considerably since enforcing the Clean Air Acts of 1956, '68 and '93 AD. These Acts also coincided with the burning of oil and gas instead of coal. The government now wants to scrap all its coal-fired power stations. The use of tetraethyl lead to increase the octane of petrol was a serious pollutant until it was banned and some cities now want to ban diesel. The electrification of the railways has saved a great deal of air pollution. However, the total consumption of carbon fuels has continued to rise, despite the rapid increase of various renewable sources of electricity. The traffic on motorways has doubled over the past decade and it could double again during the next, despite fluctuations in the price of fuel. Desperately needed road improvements are invariably twenty years late. Our roads would be perfectly adequate if We shared Our jobs and cars. The British government claims that it has taken appropriate action to minimize global warming but it has destroyed its manufacturing industry and now has to import the same goods from states with more pollution.

The environment of the USA has deteriorated over the last two centuries. Their railroad system united the states but their timetables disagreed. There were many missed connections and numerous serious accidents. This led to the establishment of national and international time zones. Yet, no one considered one time zone throughout the USA or the globe. Their big cars and highways changed the face of the continent yet again. The Energy Crisis in 1973 AD led to lower speed limits on their roads. However, this led to many more people commuting and polluting by air. LA is a great big freeway and has the worst air pollution in the USA. Electric cars will help but most electricity comes from the burning of fossil fuels and most batteries use poisonous lead and dangerous acid.

There is little doubt that the terrestrial climate is changing due to Us. Nevertheless, it may also be changing due to extraterrestrial causes. The UN Kyoto protocol in 1997 AD resolved to limit greenhouse gases. The UN Copenhagen Summit in 2009 AD made Us think about the issue. The UN Durban Summit in 2011 AD did reach a tentative agreement. The UN New York Summit in 2014 AD resolved to reduce global warming. The UN Paris Summit in 2015 AD agreed that urgent action was needed to minimize all pollution, waste, global warming and climate change. This agreement was signed by every member of the United Nations. Whether this has any effect on the weather or not remains to be seen. One way of minimizing all kinds of pollution and waste is to make industry and commerce more efficient by sharing Our Time and Space. By using Our infrastructure equally every day We would minimize the disruption to Our environment caused by the growth of Our population. Our carbon footprint and its effects on Our climate would be drastically reduced in this way and further reduced by mostly working in daylight.

Sharing Offices

Perhaps it is the idea of sharing your desk, chair, computer, phone, pen, pencil and rubber that is the least palatable aspect of job-sharing. Nevertheless, many already do so and this trend is rapidly increasing. Job-sharers do not have to share an office for they can work at home. Many people now carry their offices with them in the form of a laptop and smart phones are making all forms of business travel less urgent. Computers now do much of Our writing, drawing, recording, planning, reminding, calculating, communicating, filing and handing-over for Us. Filing cabinets are disappearing but there is still too much paper about, which takes up valuable office space, as well as being a fire hazard.

There are now far too many office blocks - because the banks could not think of anything better to do with their customers' money and they did not anticipate how many office jobs would be shed due to computers. If job-sharing was the norm there might be twice as many as needed. Many dwellings were turned into offices but could be converted back. Many more offices could be used as temporary homes for the homeless. This could have a big influence on the spiraling cost of living and the difficulty many young couples have of getting onto the property ladder.

Many blue collar workers share their jobs but few white collar workers do. Most office workers are parasites because they cannot exist on their own. They do very little to create real wealth and they usually gobble it up. Service industries depend upon manufacturing for their existence but they seem to have grown much larger than their clients - like cuckoos. Solicitors and accountants are finding it much easier to enter into joint practices, so there should be no problem with them sharing their jobs. They would only have to deal with business clients who were working on the same days and with private clients during their rest days.

Cabinet Ministers rarely seem to alter the course of history but spend most of their days in office covering-up the mistakes of their forebears. Civil Servants always seem to be having days off but they should all have the same holiday entitlement as everyone else, with no privileges. The Tories promised to cut down the Civil Service and yet it grew larger. They cut-out Labour's quangos so that market forces could take over but then formed more of their own with no feel for the pulse of industry. New Labour created many jobs for the civil servants and politicians. There were 250,000 more tax inspectors after they came into power. The Lib/Con government said that they would not increase income tax. Nevertheless, they undemocratically increased value added tax instead. Now that VAT is increased to 20% many other taxes could be abolished. However, every government seems to make taxation far more complex. An increase of VAT to 25% would reduce the number of tax inspectors and job-sharing would reduce the number of offices that they occupy.

Sharing Shops

Over the last fifty years or so there has been a revolution in retailing. Hypermarkets account for 65% of the business with only 40% of the staff, due to better use of space, bulk purchases and mechanical handling. This trend has reduced shopping time and cut down the cost of living because most shoppers now own cars and there is plenty of free parking. Parking meters and fines have driven shoppers away from the high street. Some 20% of purchases are now made online and delivered out-of-hours. Local convenience stores are expanding but many local shops are shut. Most of the small towns and villages now have no bank or post office. Some 20% of small shops are currently vacant or used by the charities. Several of the large city centre chain-stores have now gone to the wall. Many inner cities will become deprived areas, unless something is done.

Most shop workers already share their jobs in some way, because most shops are open six days per week and many are now open on Sundays. Large shops may open for six hours but small shops may open all day. Convenience stores often have two six hour shifts every day of the week. With **full-time-job-sharing** shopping could be spread evenly on every day. There would be less need for supermarkets and convenience stores to open late at night because most people would go shopping on free days. Shops could open between peak times to reduce traffic and give staff a less tiring day, since most are women with families to look after as well. Working mothers would be able to take their children to and from school. This working pattern may help to stop child neglect, abuse or abduction and could minimize juvenile delinquency, solvent abuse or drug taking. **Full-time-job-sharing-as-the-norm** could soon enhance family values.

Scrapping the Sunday trade laws, the seven-day week and Sunday itself could prove to be a huge benefit to society as well as to the retail trade. The vast majority of shop assistants and delivery drivers have no moral, ethical, social, political nor religious objections to working on Sundays. If they are rostered to work on Sundays they take another weekday off. The old trade union dogma of time-and-a-half or double-time is gone. Yet, there are several pressure groups who want to turn the clock back. They stand in the way of progress and interfere with Our Human rights. In trying to do good they are actually doing harm to Our new society. The vast majority of shoppers want free trade every day but some of the politicians who represent them are reluctant to give them this freedom. Parliament is undemocratic if it does not reflect the will of the people. Most Britons now own personal computers and frequently shop online. Shelves are now stacked, orders picked and deliveries made out-of-hours. The busiest online shopping days are now at Christmas and Easter. So the Anglican Church has lost its battle to keep control of shopping. The priests often preach that *Mammon* is now taking over from *God*. **Full-time-job-sharing-as-the-norm** would allow them to coexist.

Sharing Care

The British National Health Service is terminally sick and overworked. Routine operations are only performed on weekdays and so expensive operating theatres and other facilities lay dormant at the weekends. There is a 16% higher risk of dying if you are taken ill at a weekend. Many are dying at home waiting for the doctor or paramedic to call. Others wait for hours in ambulances queuing outside of the hospitals. One hundred babies die every year because they are born out-of-hours. Surgeries are closed at weekends, bank holidays and in the evenings. So workers have to take time-off if they need to consult their doctor. Some doctors are now being paid triple-time for working at weekends. Others are moving to Australasia where the work/life balance is better. Doctors and dentists are closing their lists because they are overloaded and so their patients have no option but to pay for private treatment. There are not enough British doctors, nurses and general staff and so foreigners with dubious qualifications are taken on and make mistakes. Medical science is advancing rapidly but there is not enough money to put it into practice, so it is considered more cost effective to treat many patients with minor complaints than a few patients with major ones. Mental illness is on the increase and many patients commit suicide.

Full-time 5+5 job-sharing should reduce the waiting lists considerably. Every practice would have twice as many doctors or dentists if they shared their surgeries and the pharmacies would be open every day. With more recreation and less stress & strain Our general health should improve and thus the pressure on the Health Service could be eased. There should be fewer accidents because of the better utilization of all transport systems and, if there was less road congestion, ambulances would be able to serve a larger area and allow smaller hospitals to close. Mental health would improve with less stress and strain on workaholics and the clinically depressed unemployed, at opposite ends of the scale.

The average working mother pays a quarter of her income on child care. One in ten mothers and one in a hundred fathers stay at home to look after the family, although they usually take maternity or paternity leave. A quarter of mothers are bringing up their family on their own and this has led to many cases where children need to be taken into state care. One single mother has ten children and receives £16K p.a. and a home. One single father had thirty children by ten mothers, whilst on the dole. If job-sharing was the norm children could be better cared for at home, even with single parents who could then look after each other's children. Yet, two single policewomen, who shared their job and their children, were taken to court by the social services for not taking care of them. More elderly people could be looked after by their relatives at home; instead of having to pay huge fees at rest homes and nursing homes. Whilst **Time** is a great healer; **Worldwide Time** could be the best cure.

Sharing Education

The Worldwide System is simpler than Imperial, American or Metric. So teaching: age, date, time and other measurements, would be quicker and mathematics would be greatly simplified at every level of education. This would lead to a much higher level of numeracy at an earlier age, leaving more time to study ten core subjects and numerous optional ones. The ten core subjects could be: English, History, Geography, Humanity, Literature, Mathematics, Science, Technology, Economics, Computing. This list does not include optional subjects, which could be studied in different establishments during the five freedays in every ten-day *wek*. Many textbooks and instruments would need to be replaced but they are all expendable and if planned ahead the cost need only be nominal. Primary Education would be financed and organized at the local level, Secondary at regional, Tertiary at national and Higher at international.

If education could be organized with **full-time-job-sharing-as-the-norm**, the overhead costs of all levels of education would effectively be halved. Parents would not have to pay for compulsory education at any level. However, some of the voluntary subjects such as sport would be free and run by volunteers whilst others such as music would be either fee paying and run by experts or sponsored by bursaries according to proficiency. All classes would be on a 5 work-days/5 free-days system with pupils or students working during the same period as the family breadwinner. Timetables would be very much easier to organize and to computerize. The academic *yer* would exactly coincide with the 360 day calendar *yer*. There could be four equal terms of two *ank* or eighty days, each with a different length of day, plus a summer holiday of one *ank* or forty days. The 5 or 6 days at the end of the *yer* would be the only public holidays.

All schools would be secular but religion could be studied on free-days. Language classes could be held for mixed age students during free-days. Physical education would be organized on a completely separate basis. Vocational and skill training centres could begin at a much earlier age. More people would take higher degrees or courses during their free-time. Some people could, eventually, attain twenty GCSE's and ten A levels. Others may be awarded several first and second degrees or doctorates. Exactly the same academic standards would apply throughout the globe. Many people would continue with adult education throughout their lives. Or undertake specialized training courses for a better or different job. Adult Education in daylight would be much better than evening classes. Research and development would be more rapid and new ideas would be in greater demand due to increased manufacturing capacity, higher productivity, greater competitiveness and much better buying power. There could be much closer cooperation between universities, industries, financial institutions and government departments with less duplication of effort and waste of Time, Space, Life and other valuable resources.

Sharing Defence

Sir Francis Drake (1540-1596 AD) was reputed to be playing bowls on Plymouth Hoe when the Armada was sighted - yet he finished his game. Britain often seems to be undefended on Wednesday afternoons, when the Navy go sailing, the Army play football and the Airforce play darts. It also seems to be defenceless at weekends and on public holidays. A ten-day week would allow half of the services to defend their country whilst the other half were training, playing sport or at home on leave.

Europe has yet to coordinate its forces into one effective fighting unit, because it still has too many leaders, languages and defence systems. Britain has only recently started to use the same Metric ammunition. NATO was a way of sharing American and European defence systems. But Europe expects America to resolve problems on its own doorstep. The American solution is usually to drop more and more bombs or fire more and more missiles without leaving the safety of their own base. Now that the Cold War is over, Britain does not need a big defence force. Nevertheless, there have been over 150 wars since WW2 and Britain has been drawn into many foreign conflicts, leaving its home base at risk. The best solution is probably to give the UN more power and allow them to collect their own funds from the international transportation systems. However, the UN has done very little to prevent the genocide in Africa and it could do far more to use its defence forces for rescue missions.

The electronic revolution has had a great impact on defence or offence. Radio was first used (by my father in the Battle of the Somme) in WW1. Radar, RDF and computers were developed and first used during WW2. Soldiers are now more used to pushing buttons than pulling triggers. Yet, Britain was defenceless when the Millennium Bug hit spy satellites. Many £billions have been wasted on sophisticated systems that failed; whilst investment upon simpler systems has been withheld.

It was decided by the British government, many years ago, that the Army, Navy, Marines and Airforce should share all of their resources. Nevertheless, this logical directive has never been put into practice. They all use very similar aircraft, boats, vehicles, missiles and bullets but each service is still extremely inefficient and hidebound by tradition. Those who fight behind their desks far outnumber those behind guns. Many of the ships, vehicles and aircraft are obsolete or out-of-service. There is not enough basic equipment like flak jackets or even boots. Whether you take the view that selling arms stops wars breaking out or the opposite, 1M people are employed in the British defence equipment industry, which increasingly relies on its, very profitable, export trade. Yet, Britain has difficulty in deciding who are its friends and its foes. If peace were suddenly to break-out there would be longer dole queues. Unless it adopted a ten-day week and **full-time-job-sharing-as-the-norm**.

Sharing Arts and Crafts

All self-employed people would benefit from the ten-day *wek* because shops, restaurants, bars, banks, post offices would be open every day. Every day in the *yer* would be exactly the same and so self-employed people would be able to choose the working pattern that suits them best. Most artists and craftspeople are self-employed and work on their own. Some employees and students do freelance jobs in their spare time. Many people who work outside, such as: gardeners, house painters and window cleaners work alone and are very dependent upon the weather. So they could perform their service at any time on any day in the *yer*. Many plumbers, decorators, carpet-layers and electricians work alone indoors and they would also find that the *wek* would suit them better. They would probably choose either leftdays or rightdays and advertise their services accordingly, perhaps in *Yellow Pages*, with someone else who chooses to work in the same trade but on the other half of the *wek*. Many self-employed taxi drivers share their cabs with somebody else.

Self-employment is now on the increase whilst employment is in decline. The flexible workforce in many enterprizes is now mostly self-employed. So they can expand or contract with the economy and their order book. Zero hours contracts avoid legislation about the minimum living wage. Many young people are now being encouraged to become entrepreneurs. This is part of the education system and is taught as a separate subject. A large proportion of those who have retired early or have been made redundant are later taken back as consultants or as part-time workers. If they work from home and pay their own insurance their cost is lower and they do not have to conform with any particular working pattern. Most of the great businesses, industries and institutions were built by individuals who had nothing more than a bright idea to begin with. Many people turn their favorite hobby or sport into their profession. So it is sometimes extremely difficult to distinguish work from leisure.

Writing any plays, books, papers and articles can be shared and some authors employ researchers to do much of the donkey-work for them. Artists cannot, usually, share a painting but they could share a studio. Old masters employed apprentices to prepare their paints and canvases. Composers usually work alone but songwriters sometimes share their vocation when one composes the score whilst the other writes the lyrics. Actors, entertainers and those who work behind the scenes are mostly freelance and they may well have a second or third string to their bow. Indeed, anyone who is creative can usually work better on their own. Researching and writing this book has been a very solitary experience. It has taken me over thirty years to complete this in my own spare time. I have not worked on it in any regular way nor on any particular day. So I do not practice what I preach and my rewards will be in royalties. My motivation has only been to put Our World right, in one easy lesson.

Sharing Shares

The success of large enterprises is measured by the value of its shares, which are always quoted in decimals at stock markets around the globe. Most worked from 9 to 5, but closed on weekends and bank holidays, which made it very difficult for international share trading to take place, because of many different time zones, weekends and bank holidays. It has now been realized that stock markets could work continuously. However, many traders now work very long hours and may burn out. Fortunes can be made or lost automatically by computers, in an instant. The answer must be **full-time-job-sharing-as-the-norm**.

Banking with auto-teller and deposit machines is now a 24/7 business. Yet, if you need to discuss your bank account with your local manager, you will find that he/she does not work on weekends nor bank holidays, so you may have to take time-off to discuss your financial arrangements. Banks are money shops and so they should open when shops are open. The governor of the Bank of England was governor of the Bank of Canada. Canadian banks are open from 8 AM to 8 PM on every day of the week. So the staff need to share their jobs and are very reliable and efficient. Perhaps he will institute a similar system in the British banking sector.

Most shares are now owned by investment companies or pension funds. Many people invest in a package of shares through unit trusts or banks. The individual investor has little sway in the running of big business. The British banking sector has made enormous investment mistakes. Most of its shares are now owned by the taxpayer after it collapsed. They earn no interest whilst the bosses earn huge salaries and bonuses. They put their trust in rogue traders, who bankrupted several banks. If most people shared their jobs they would have more time to look after their financial affairs and stop the big cats from drinking all the cream.

The Post Office was privatized by the Lib/Con government in 2014 AD. The taxpayers lost £1G due to the government undervaluing its shares. Many local post offices are now open all day on every day of the week, whilst others have been closed, especially in the remote rural areas. The post men and women still do not collect or deliver mail on Sundays and this puts snail mail at a disadvantage with email and text messages. Nevertheless paper documents have still not been completely eliminated and it is still necessary to use traditional cheques for some transactions.

Many enterprises have found that by giving shares to their employees, or selling them at a discount, motivates them to work harder and longer. The *John Lewis* shops are run by a partnership who share their shares. This has proven to be very successful and could be adopted by any firm. If they were permitted, they could increase their profits and dividends by opening their shops every day of the *wek* and sharing most jobs.

Sharing Responsibility

An example of shared responsibility is the chain of command on a ship, with one captain and two or three crews sharing watches during the day. Some captains work for six months and then have six months on leave, others work for one or two weeks then take one or two weeks leave, but there always has to be one man or one woman at the very top. Almost any organization can be managed with this shared responsibility. Delegation, within the aims stated by its constitution and the constraints set by top management, is the key to running a successful organization. However, bad management is the root cause of many business failures. It is said that most managers rise to their highest level of incompetence.

Full-time-job-sharing could solve these perennial personnel problems. If lefts worked on left-days and rights worked on right-days there might never be any need for lefts to talk to rights whilst they were at work. They could switch sides to suit their firm, their families or themselves. It would make no difference on which side of the calendar single people, those with a spouse at home or those with young children worked. Their greater flexibility compared with couples who both work or those who have older children would help managers to fill all available posts. Everyone's performance or productivity could be more easily monitored, so that promotion would be based on education, experience and ability. Reorganization is necessary in most organizations from time to time. This allows the most effective or productive employees to rise to the top. The British Psychological Society say that seventy percent of executives who share their jobs achieve thirty percent more than those who do not.

My father worked for *Esso* for forty years and relocated fourteen times. His first job was ordering hay for the horses that delivered petrol in cans. His last job was Joint Managing Director of *Esso* in the UK and Eire. They introduced revolutionary working practices in the *Esso Blue Book*. This applied to all the trades working in their refineries and terminals. The agreement with the unions treated all days and hours as the same. Tea breaks were flexible, mates were upgraded and demarcation relaxed. This increased productivity so, consequently, the workforce earned more. *Esso* outsourced many of its routine operations to other organizations. It no longer owns its own ships, vehicles, railway tankers or pipelines. *Esso* became *Exxon* which has merged with *Mobil* and is now globalized. The largest oil refinery in Europe is at Fawley which currently works a 12-hour shift for four days, then four nights, then a rest for few days. It is now timely for *Exxon-Mobil* to take another look at its organization. This could lead to a ten-day job-sharing week and a three-shift day. This working pattern could be adopted by businesses in the same area. The local community could then adopt the same working pattern. If it can be demonstrated that this working pattern works well in one industrial area, it could soon spread, like a virus, throughout the globe.

Sharing Power

History shows that power corrupts; absolute power corrupts absolutely. The Greeks invented democracy and they passed it on to the Romans. The republican consuls shared their job on a month by month basis. However, one became stronger than the other and so became a dictator. He was succeeded by the emperors and some of them shared the empire until the Western empire fell and the Eastern empire became Byzantium. The Eastern Church still uses a different calendar from the Western one.

We will only achieve full democracy when We have regular referendums. The electronic revolution has already had a great deal of influence on the democratic process, due to radio, television and information technology. Further innovations could allow much greater improvements to be made. Electronic banking has proven to be secure and free from impersonation. Electronic voting will soon be viable from almost any home in Britain. Votes can be counted and analyzed instantly - this is true people power. We could control Our own destiny - if only the politicians would let Us. The party system has many faults, fundraising comes close to bribery, manifestos are a joke and when you vote for a party you have to choose a basket-full of policies, although some of these may be unacceptable. It would be better to separate education from health, defence, transport, trade, industry... and to vote for specialists as well as generalists. Thus party politics would soon be replaced by coalition and consensus. Every political proposition might, eventually, be voted upon separately. Each issue could be subjected to a referendum at the end of the *yer*. Candidates for ministerial posts would present their cases on the net. If they won, they would have four *yers* to implement their proposals. This assumes that the electorate is widely educated and experienced, so that they can understand the full range of issues presented to them.

A 360 day *yer* with 5 or 6 remainder days would enhance democracy and make Us feel that We can contribute to decisions which affect Our lives. Half of the population would have the previous 5 days-off and the other half the following 5 days, so everyone would have a 10 or 11 day break. It would be a free period when nearly everyone would be at home, except for the essential services, and public transport would stop. As well as being a time for free thinking and talking about democracy, it would be a fraternal time amongst friends, neighbours and relations. The 5 or 6 day *yerend* would supersede New Year's Eve in all calendars. Variable election dates always cause long periods of indecision and the period between an outgoing and an incoming government is too long. By restricting hustings to a fixed timetable, everyone would have the chance to listen properly to speeches and join-in on the local debates. The four *yer* cycle of local, regional, national and international elections, if used in each country concurrently, would mean that all leaders would change simultaneously and this seems preferable to the current system.

Sharing Government

A fixed-term election round for four levels of responsibility in a four-year voting cycle would lead to equal opportunity for all candidates and a chance for politicians to advance progressively throughout their careers. The fifth and highest level should only deal with global matters.

GLOBAL GOVERNMENT
The United Nations is not a global government but it should be given the powers to govern all global measurements and intercontinental matters. Its role as the global police and rescue force should be reinforced.

INTERNATIONAL GOVERNMENT
Each continent has established a free trade area and a political union. The European Parliament in Brussels imposed many international laws. Nevertheless, many of these were unacceptable to its member states. Although Britain was part of the European Union few knew their MEP's. It still used its own currency, its own time zone, drove on the left, used the mile and the pint and did not sign the Schengen agreement. However, English became the language spoken in the corridors of power.

NATIONAL GOVERNMENT
Electoral reform is now overdue and should take account of job-sharing. If MP's shared their jobs, one member could stay in a larger constituency whilst the other was away at a smaller parliament, thus eliminating the need for one MP to have two dwellings, two cars and travel expenses. The Houses of Parliament could be replaced by a single Round House. This might be used alternately by upper and lower tiers of government. The upper tier could be elected by proportional representation and the lower tier by first-past-the-post - provided there were political parties. However, the party system is becoming discredited and it would appear to be far better for the lower house to become a coalition of independent representatives and the upper house to be a coalition of elder statesmen.

REGIONAL GOVERNMENT
Separate laws are being passed in Scotland, Wales and Northern Ireland. Northern Ireland will, sooner or later, become part of the Irish Republic. Devolution is needed for matters which are not of national interest. Such as: police, fire, ambulance, hospital, doctor, dentist and education. Regional assemblies in Scotland, Wales and eight parts of England could replace the County Councils, which are elected voluntary organizations.

LOCAL GOVERNMENT
Representatives have other occupations so job-sharing could work well. Many local matters, such as planning permission, could be speeded-up. Capital equipment would be used more intensively and at lower cost. The Sunday trading laws have wasted too much local government Time.

Sharing Leisure

The arguments for sharing leisure are just as strong as those for work. Spare time can be used for many purposes such as shopping, gardening, house maintenance, cooking, exercise, hobbies, reading, writing, talking, listening, learning, viewing, touring, entertaining, praying and resting. Britons now spend over £100G/y on leisure and it has become a major industry employing some 3M people, who are much busier at weekends. They usually take some week-days off and sometimes they share jobs.

Now that many wives are working there is less time for them to do their shopping so they should be free to do this at any convenient moment. There was recently a very fierce argument raging about shopping on a Sunday and many large retail outlets were apparently breaking the law. Some said that Sunday should be kept as a special day but others said that the laws are ridiculous and unenforceable and should be abolished. No pressure group has asserted that Britain should abolish seven-day weeks but Sunday has now become almost the same as Saturday. If all of the Sunday laws were abolished, the way would be clear for a five-day-on/five-day-off *wek,* which would equalize the work/life balance.

Many people get trapped in a treadmill and never have time to learn about new technology and methods, which could help them in their job. Courses in their spare time would help them to improve their skills. Many would find time to attend courses that are unconnected with their jobs as well as reading, writing, viewing and discussing their problems. One should always have another career in mind, for none of Us have a job-for-life anymore and many of Us have several, quite different, careers. Hobbies sometimes lead to new businesses and even to new industries.

We would have more freedom to take a five-day break away from home when we wanted and not dependent on school, works or office holidays. This would help tourism which would have less seasonal variations. Most people would be willing to work for 10 or 15 days in a row whilst their pair was on leave in order to take a longer holiday themselves. A mid-career break of up to a year can give one a wider perspective. In some cases it may be possible to pay for the hire of a locum to mind one's job whilst one was away, as often occurs in the medical profession.

Many people would enjoy their leisure more if they were able to share equipment such as cars, caravans, tents, boats, planes and homes. Hotels, bars and restaurants would be utilized evenly and so could make better profits or lower their prices - so fun would be more affordable. Clubs would be able to take more members and lower their overheads. We are in danger of becoming too reclusive, especially now that many people are working at home, We need to mix more with our fellows and with five days free every *wek* We should be able to find the time to do so.

Sharing Sport

Is it the fair way for golfers to spend more time waiting than playing?
Do game birds hide and have fish learned not to take bait at weekends?
Is weekend skiing going downhill? Is booking courts becoming a racket?
You are absolutely snookered if you always have to queue for a cue.
It is not cricket if you wait for more than an innings to go in to bat.
In order to enjoy football more We need to move the goalposts a little.
We need a level playing field so that We can all have an equal chance.

Eric Liddell refused to run on Sundays and became a missionary but the
Church is less zealous today and most sports can take place on any day.
Motor Racing Grand Prix are now always held on a Sunday, Worldwide.
Horse Racing was prohibited on the Sabbath in Britain for 200 years.
Sunday betting is now permitted - all days are the same to a horse.
However, working horses also need a regular rest day or they drop dead.

Sport and exercise take up a large amount of the education timetable
but they could be entirely separated from the academic curriculum.
Many schools have sold their playing fields or built on them and so there
are now many more obese kids and Britain has lost its competitive edge.
Students or pupils would be encouraged to use some free-days for sport.
Many people give up sport and all forms of exercise when they leave
school but would be more likely to continue it in their spare time if they
had become accustomed to this routine during their formative years.

Many sports are becoming expensive and it is just as important that the
equipment involved be as fully utilized as that in factories or offices.
Sports grounds would be utilized more evenly, ball game stadiums could
be shared between two clubs and every sport could have two leagues.
Inevitably, amateurism would improve; professionalism would decline.
Some minority pursuits might become more difficult to organize but,
on the whole, all kinds of sports would benefit from a ten-day week.
People would participate in sporting and recreational activities to a
much greater extent and, inevitably, become healthier as the result.
Watching sport is very unhealthy for people stand in the cold and wet
breathing in germs or sit at home by the TV and become couch potatoes.
We now seem to forget that sport was intended to make us fitter.
Professional sportsmen often seem to get killed or injured then need
medical attention and many suffer from arthritis when they get older.

Sport was invented by the Greeks, after they stopped fighting each other.
Their Olympic Games continue but staging them became ridiculously
expensive and the real point of holding them has now been forgotten.
Some athletes resort to cheating by using performance-enhancing drugs.
Olympic Time is now based upon the International Metric System but all
sporting records would have to be updated to the **Worldwide System**.

Sharing Things

Sharing possessions in monastic communities is part of many religions. It is also part of many Utopian concepts, which have rarely been tested. Sir Thomas More penned *Utopia* but he dared not publish it in England. He lost his head when he objected to the divorce of King Henry VIII. His Utopian ideas were adopted in part of Mexico and worked very well. However, the establishment of the Roman-Catholic Church objected to it. The kibbutz system, in Israel, consists of all the participating families sharing all of their property and all of the profits from the enterprise. This works very well in all kinds of businesses from farms to hotels; until someone wants to leave and then there can be serious problems. The Communist system, where the state owned everything and took all the profit, did not work because the people had little incentive to work. Nevertheless, the Capitalist system is very wasteful and some sort of middle path must be the final solution to most socio-economic problems.

Most people are not in the habit of sharing any of their possessions. However, many people already cooperate and share things in some way. If you live in a flat or apartment you probably share a lift and a garden and you may also share a car park, a laundry, a lounge and a caretaker. Some flats and housing complexes share swimming pools, tennis courts, squash courts, moorings, workshops and many more recreation facilities. Quite a large proportion of private cars, boats and aircraft are shared. Renting, chartering, and hiring is a form of sharing which is widely used but a third party makes a profit and so this is much more expensive. Timeshare apartments are attractive because there is no middleman. Many farms are in cooperatives where they share expensive equipment that is not in constant use such as: ploughs or combine harvesters. Many small businesses find it cheaper to share accounting, computing, communications, reception, conference, printing and secretarial services. Many people are now sharing things through information technology. This is: the sharing economy, peer-to-peer or collaborative consumption.

If 360 days were the same they would drop into ten-day weeks or *weks*. If two people or families knew that they were working on opposite ends of the *wek* they could easily share possessions with a neighbour or friend. Some job-sharers may also decide to share their accommodation but this may well be provided for them as part of their job by their employer. Many second homes could be shared far away from work as a retreat. Quarter shares would make very good sense and give each shareholder five days use in every twenty, which is more than most owners enjoy now. In the USA, many share minibuses, which have free parking in cities. This must save them a great deal of money and congestion but with a ten-day *wek* they could be used every day and the proportion of tax, depreciation and maintenance costs paid by each user could be halved. We must tear-up Our old calendars and share new **digital date** ones.

Sharing Wealth

Sharing Our World's wealth out fairly amongst its population may seem impossible but it is a problem that each generation must try to solve. There is no easy solution and the problem is greatly worsened by the extremely high population growth in many of the developing countries. Poverty breeds poverty, however, wealth has quite the opposite effect. This is not just an economic fact but also a medical one for very rich lifestyles make it impossible to conceive, so wealthy bloodlines die out. The law of supply and demand has a great deal to do with costs, prices and with the flow of systems, materials and goods about Our World. Industrialized countries can help developing ones by increasing trade. They can also help in many other ways such as with education, medicine and disaster relief, which is not a free handout but an act of compassion.

Many of the richest countries in Our World have very little industry. Oil wealth does not create much employment in the Gulf states and so it is a problem for the hierarchy to share it out amongst their population. They have little agriculture or industry to finance or subsidize and so they give their people nominal jobs, whilst migrants do most of the work. However, a great deal of the wealth that was generated from oil has now been invested in the industrialized countries and especially in Britain.

Many of the poorest countries in Our World have very little industry. Handing out cash, medicine or food has, all too often, lead to corruption. Many beggars in the streets of Calcutta are said to be in organized gangs. However, lower labour costs throughout India have meant that many service industries, such as airline seat bookings, are now based there. The Indians can now sell goods and services to the rest of the World, in 'English', via cheap satellite telephones and other electronic gizmos.

Whilst Our World's mineral resources are frequently found in the most inhospitable places, there are some that are more conveniently situated. The North Sea oil bonanza helped Britain and Norway to survive the recession but they took different attitudes to helping new industries. Britain has paid about 6M people, every year, to do absolutely nothing. It poured £billions into established industries, which should have been self-financing, yet let many new industries, like hovercraft, fade away. Norway used its windfall to protect jobs and encourage new industries to develop, so was able to minimize unemployment, deficit and inflation. Norway now supplies Britain, by pipeline, with some of its oil and gas. If unemployment, deficit and inflation could all be reduced in Britain by adopting a ten-day *wek* and **full-time-job-sharing-as-the-norm** then its goods would become cheaper and it would be able to export more. This would help the developing countries that supply raw materials and should help to provide their workers with better working conditions. They may also discover that full-time-job-sharing is the best way to work.

Sharing Prayer

Britain is said to be a Christian country, yet less than 1M go to church and it has become a multi-cultural, multi-ethnic, multi-religious society. The British are still very fond of their queen, the constitutional monarch without any written constitution, whether she has a divine right or not. Morning prayers are still said before work at the Palace of Westminster, but they are no longer required at the regional or local government levels and there is a strong movement to ban them at most of the state schools. The Archbishop of Canterbury has admitted that only 2M attend Church. Yet, independent estimates currently put this figure at less than 1M. The British born population of Greater London is now less than 50% and much of urban and suburban Britain is no longer British born. Prince Charles has said that when he succeeds the Queen he wants to be known as: The Defender of Faith rather than: The Defender of the Faith.

There was no form of religious census in Britain nor Northern Ireland. However, in 2001 AD this was included in the census for the first time. Since England, Wales, Scotland and Northern Ireland are now devolved, separate results should have been published for each one, as well as for Britain as a whole and yet England and Wales were lumped together. Some 72% declared that they were Christians but 14% were Humanists. In 2011 AD 55% were Christians 40% had no religion, 5% other faiths. Age had a big influence, with only 38% of 18-34s being Christian and 53% having no faith but for the over 55s the figures were 70% and 26%. The Welsh attend church and chapel more regularly than the English and so it is probable that England is no longer a Christian country. By the next census in 2021 AD the whole of Britain may well be secular. So it should no longer use any Christian age, date and time system. The last census asked more searching questions: 79% agreed but 11% disagreed that religion is the cause of much misery in Our World today.

There is no proof that group or individual prayer has any effect at all. However, it still affects many Billions of supplicants around the globe. Weekly holy days became crucial to the three great monotheist religions. As they fall on different days it causes problems in mixed communities. Some say that a three-day weekend would solve this Sabbatical problem. Many people already need to work at weekends and on the Sabbath day, and so the Sabbath and the Mystic seven-day week are now fading away. **Full-time-job-sharing-as-the-norm** in a ten-day week could help to pull communities together, as religion still does in many parts of the globe. There could even be two semi-Sabbaths with Jews, Christians, Muslims, Hindus and Buddhists using the same building but on different days. However, a better solution would be for all religious buildings to be made into secular community centres for education, recreation and debate. We shall only be free to make up Our own minds about anything when politics are separated from religion and 360 days are equal once more.

Sharing Life

Whilst it is becoming overcrowded; this can still be a very lonely Planet. Marriage is a life-time commitment to share life and bring up a family. Written between the lines of the ancient marriage rites was, until very recently, also a commitment to jointly own property and to pay taxes. Many working couples found that it was cheaper not to get married. Whilst most people now have more free-time, family life has deteriorated. There are more divorces, broken families, single parents and truants. Families do not share their time and do things together as they used to. Now that most mothers are working, their children get less attention. Television has provided many benefits but this also has its downside. One channel pulled families together; many channels now divide them. It may be a challenge for children to win a video game or to enjoy the wonders of virtual reality but the real challenges are in the real World.

Full-time-job-sharing can have a beneficial influence upon family values. If the mother and the father were both working and their children were below school age they could go out to work on alternate free-day periods. If all the children were at school, the entire family could go to work or attend school during the same period, so no one would be at home alone. Therefore many of the problems of working parents would be avoided. Families would share many more leisure pursuits and may also find more time for worshipping or attending philosophical meetings together. More elderly relatives would also be cared for by their own families. Too many people are ending their lives in solitude at expensive nursing and rest homes; when they could be cared for by their own families. Single parents could look after each other's children when not at work. Sharing life in one's own accommodation is far better than living alone. Yet, many of the flats and houses built today are for single occupants. Living alone, at any age, frequently induces mental health problems. More people are consulting analysts and therapists than ever before. The best therapy is having a purpose in life, especially a worthwhile job.

The Keep Sunday Special Campaign wants to return to an old **Time**. A **Time** when one religion dominated the whole of civilized society. A **Time** when there was no sport, no betting, no drinking on Sundays. A **Time** when one went to church, had lunch and rested in the afternoon. A **Time** when all the shops were shut and even the service stations. The Lord's Day Observance Society admit that only a few go to church. Most people only go there today for baptisms, weddings and funerals. Some used to find solace by talking to a priest and in serving a god. It can be much harder to find any meaning to Life without a religion. However, Humanists do take a positive view and hold regular meetings. The New Age of Aquarius, associated with Humanism, has now begun. The Old Age of Pisces, associated with Christianity, is now fading away. **Worldwide Time** could generate a new philosophy for this New Age.

Sharing Earth

The Natural and artificial barriers that divide Us are gradually falling. Nevertheless, We need to demolish all those invisible, divisive time zones. If We use all of Our resources efficiently We can minimize waste and pollution and perhaps survive the looming calamity upon the horizon. For it has been calculated that, if We all had the same standard of living as North Americans, We would need about three Earths to sustain Us. If We carry on the same way that We are going We will destroy Ourselves. However, there may be a solution through science, technology and logic. Science is discovering ways to preserve Our lives and provide more food. Technology is discovering ways to provide more homes, vehicles and fuel. Logic is obscured by traditions that are standing in the way of progress. **Full-time-job-sharing-as-the-norm** is the basis for a better way of Life. We could utilize all Our existing buildings and infrastructure more fully. However, if everyone who is now unemployed were to find a job the environmental crisis would be accelerated - so We must ration work. By rationing and reorganizing Our work We can redistribute Our wealth. The Worldwide Web has encouraged Us all to share Our information. **The Worldwide System** could encourage Us all to share Our Planet.

There are estimated to be some 1G unemployed citizens on Planet Earth. The only logical solution is to adopt **full-time-job-sharing-as-the-norm.** This simple system could be organized with any equal roster such as: 3+3, 4+4, 5+5, 6+6 or 7+7 but five workdays in a row is what We are now used to and We can make much better use of five free-days in a row. Many people already share their jobs but this is far from being the norm. If We were all permitted to work at any time on any day, then everyone and every organization would be free to work whenever it suited them. However, complete freedom from law and order could soon cause chaos. So it would be better for every one of Us to work to the same rhythm. Laws may be needed to prevent workers from doing two full-time jobs. Yet, some of Our extra free-time should be utilized for voluntary work. All laws and bylaws making some days special should now be scrapped. It is not against any law to write or print year-day numbers in diaries, calendars and planners or to use them in letters, emails and texts. Multinational organizations can help to spread the use of ten-day *weks*. The *wek* might slowly replace the week as **full-time-job-sharing** grows. Yet, the change from one to the other should be as rapid as possible. We can only achieve One World if We have one age, date, time and rule. This could soon be achieved through the United Nations Organization.

The Worldwide Time System must be proven by socio-economic experiment before it replaces all Our chronologies, calendars, clocks and computers. **The Worldwide Space System** must be tried and tested before it replaces all of the Imperial, American, International and Navigational systems. **The Worldwide System** could help to save Our Planet and Our Species.

Part Nine

Civilization

Changing Our States

"Time rules everything."

Inscription under the clock face of Big Ben

Options

Civilization is based upon cooperation, specialization and standardization. If We can put Our ages, dates, times and zones right, as well as Our lengths, areas, volumes and weights, We can put Our World right too. We now have many global forms of cheap and efficient communication. We now have many global media with the power to influence opinions. We now have many global organizations with the power to change things. Logic will ultimately prevail and all Man-made systems can be changed.

Nevertheless, the proceedings of the International Meridian Conference in Washington DC during 1884 AD make one despair that We shall ever achieve a global-digital-decimal system for measuring Time and Space. This summit took 12 years to convene but only 25 delegates turned-up. The Greenwich Meridian was unpopular with the French who considered the obelisk standing in the middle of Paris to be the Navel of the Earth. They agreed to Greenwich, on the understanding that Time and Space would be decimalized as soon as possible, but abstained from the vote. They continued to use Paris Time as their standard until 1911 AD and even then referred to GMT as: Paris Mean Time retarded by 9 min 21 sec. The USA said that the Washington Monument should be Earth's Navel. It was just being completed and was the largest obelisk in Our World. There was still much disagreement about where their time zones should be drawn, even though they had called the conference in the first place. Some states are still debating time zones and daylight saving measures. As late as 1905 AD Portugal, The Netherlands, Greece, Turkey, Russia, Ireland and most of South America still refused to recognize Greenwich. The free state of Liberia was the very last to come into line in 1972 AD.

It took the EU 17 years to agree upon one date for summer time to end. They wanted to introduce a constitution including: the Roman-Catholic age, date and time; the Mystic seven-day week; a three-day weekend and one time zone based upon the ancient Egyptian obelisk at the Vatican. This was rejected by several states and so it was rehashed as a treaty. The Lisbon Treaty may lead to the recreation of the Holy Roman Empire; instead of the secular federation of European states in a free trade zone. Britain would rather remain free to trade with any state in Our World.

The following essays attempt to explain why **Worldwide Time and Space** could solve many temporal and spatial problems in Our World today. These are not being solved by other means, despite what politicians say. They do not ask the right questions, so they do not get the right answers. They never get their priorities right but go over the same old ground in search of a simple solution and, invariably, opt for the most complex. What a small cost it would be and what a huge return on investment if by: restarting Our chronologies, tearing-up Our calendars, replacing Our clocks and watches, merging Our zones and breaking Our rules, We could build one **Worldwide** civilization that might last forever.

Opposites

There are many controversies in Our daily lives and We can express at least two opposite viewpoints on most subjects from trivial matters like brown or white, sliced or unsliced to important matters of Life or Death. Just like singular issues such as One World, one language, one currency or one philosophy, these plural ones are highly relevant to the way that We measure, manage and govern Our Time, Our Space and Our World.

Men and women are of opposite sexes but they somehow manage to live and work together, even sharing their jobs, without too many quarrels. Life is full of opposites, within Ourselves and throughout the Universe: matter and antimatter, positive and negative, night and day, up and down, in and out, North and South, East and West, left and right, right and wrong, good and bad, love and hate, war and peace, Life and Death...

The Greeks believed in dualism, stating that everything has an opposite: good v bad, love v hate, right v wrong, light v dark, black v white. There are often many shades of grey in the real World that We live in. The Romans adopted many Greek ideas, which came down to Us via Catholicism and the legal system but some of them proved to be wrong. It may take years, decades, centuries or millennia to put them all right.

The *I Ching* belief considers that opposites are *yin* & *yang* principles. Such as: light & dark, hot & cold, hard & soft, left & right, good & bad, chaos & order, Sun & Moon, male & female, competition & cooperation. Together they manifest the *Tao*, a secret law, which rules the Cosmos. The male *yang* dragon represents the creative force in the Universe with Space and Time as its field and 2000 AD was the year of the dragon.

Democracy is based upon strong opposition but much of the debate, in Mother Parliament, Daughter Congress and other off-springs, is simply: contrariness - because both sides often want to go in the same direction. Democracy is extremely wasteful of manpower, brainpower and Time. Autocracy is held to be worse but is the essence of private enterprise. We are often told that a country, a county, a town, a village or a club should be run like a private company, with as much private enterprise, and so as little democracy, as possible - yet private enterprise often fails. There are an increasing number of failed states throughout the globe.

Even if We are of different races, different sexes and different faiths, We are all in the same Human Race but We are told that opposition is healthy, so Our class at school is divided into teams and We proceed to wage tribal warfare over the possession of a leather or plastic ball. Yet, teamwork is essential for any kind of enterprise to win any prizes. We must strive to use all Our Natural and Human resources to the full. This ideal can only be achieved with **full-time-job-sharing-as-the-norm**.

Cause or Effect?

It is difficult to separate the cause of a chronic disease from a symptom. Yesterday's remedies will not work on today's patients because they are becoming immune and the monetary virus is changing its spots. Inflation is the sign of an unhealthy society and an inefficient economy. Nevertheless, lowering inflation pressure by reducing taxes, increasing interest rates and reducing public expenditure has killed many patients. On the other hand, the totally opposite remedy with low interest rates, high taxes and high public expenditure it has also killed many patients. Successive Chancellors of the Exchequer have done all the wrong things to the British economy, whilst they were trying to make the right noises. The only way to help an economy to thrive is to encourage development of new and better products and services, greater efficiency, less waste and to give the people confidence that it will all come right in the end. Low or no inflation, low taxes, fair interest rates and full employment, can all be achieved by sharing most jobs in a ten-day working week. This is both capitalism and socialism - so it is the middle or third way.

The industrial revolution caused many people to give up their rural lives and then move to be near their chosen industries in smoky cities. It led to the development of better transport systems so that most people could live where they pleased and then commute to their place of work. However, most people now have longer journeys, there are too many cars and traffic congestion would be very much worse if everyone had a job. The electronic revolution has reversed this trend, so that there is less need for offices to be in cities and many more people can work at home. Laptops, tablets, portable printers and smart mobile phones enable some people to carry their offices with them, wherever they are in Our World. Automatic machinery and computers are now reducing the amount of manual and clerical work needed in every field of endeavor but the work that is left is not being shared out fairly amongst the workforce. The rewards for greater productivity should be more pay and more play. Although both have already occurred, the balance has been upset by dogmatic thinking and so some are now richer; whilst others are poorer. Many organizations are now having to work 24/7 to stay in business. They could easily change to a more balanced 10/10 working routine.

Full-time-job-sharing-as-the-norm would help Us to redress the balance. This has never been proposed by any of the political parties nor by any of the pressure groups, financial consultants, sociological think tanks, learned societies, university academicians, international conferences nor any of the pundits and gurus, who earn fortunes by writing and talking, because of all the dogmas associated with the Mystic seven-day week. If it was scrapped then many of the dogmas, which cause so much strife in Our World, would be scrapped with it and We might be able to coexist. Despite being one of the *Ten Commandments*, it is not carved in stone.

Prevention or Cure?

Our Planet is sick. Violence is rife. Drugs are abused. Sex is perverted. The USA is dominated by Christianity but also by guns, drugs and porn. Many Islamic states have strict laws, sensor their media and ban alcohol but they are ruled by the gun and some of them proliferate narcotics. Israel is dominated by the strict laws of the Torah and yet it is ruled by the gun and supported by the USA, whose media is dominated by Jews. We seem to be heading for an Apocalypse, because it was predicted in an ancient book, which is still believed by Jews, Christians and Muslims. Politicians always seem to let matters become critical before they bother to do anything about them and always use old remedies to cure new ills.

Prevention is better than cure and the key to the future lies in education. The National Curriculum is concentrating upon all of the core subjects; whilst many children have little opportunity to study any other matters. They spend many hours on their own whilst their parents are at work. No wonder they play hooky and experiment with solvents and drugs. No wonder they smoke, drink and have sex before they reach maturity. No wonder their elders and betters abuse them and treat them so badly. A survey shows that one million British children are abused every year. We all mourned for the schoolchildren who were shot in the Dunblane school massacre and the London headmaster knifed by a schoolboy. At the same time many schoolchildren were causing disruption in class at their free schools and their teachers were threatening to go on strike. They may no longer administer punishment nor even touch their pupils. The government is trying to do something about the sale of weapons but the use of guns and knives is increasing and all of the prisons are full. They talk about moral values and turn to religion for help but the cause is that society is sick and, no matter how many cures are administered, it is the way that work is organized that is the root cause of the problem.

Full-time-job-sharing-as-the-norm could lead to full employment and a sense of belonging to a global civilization, which knows where it is going. If both parents worked they could do so on alternate five-day periods. So that there was always somebody at home for their younger children. In later life the family could go to work or to school on the same days. If schools were staffed by two teams working alternate five-day periods they could concentrate on the core subjects whilst other establishments could concentrate on many of the other matters for students of all ages. This simple remedy would allow all of Us to reach Our full potential. It would permit Us to change course several times during Our lifetimes. The National Curriculum should include religion and philosophy but not any particular one and it should include the history of Time and Space. It should also include lessons on how Our bodies function and how tobacco, alcohol, solvents, drugs and unprotected sex can ruin Our lives. By this simple means many of society's ills could be cured - at a stroke.

Man or Woman?

There was a Queen of Sheba, Queen Hatshepsut ruled Egypt and there were seven Cleopatras, not forgetting Queen Boudicca who ruled England. Etruscans treated women as equals; Romans treated them as chattels. There are many female Rabbis, conscripted Israeli women fight beside men and Golda Mier became the Prime Minister of Israel in 1969 AD. The Church treated women as equals but St. Augustine demoted them. The Roman-Catholic Church still downgrades women as inferior to men. The Church of England ordains men and women as vicars and bishops. The British Methodist Church now regards *God* as both male and female. Females did not work, vote nor take holy orders in the Muslim World. Women were first given the right to vote in New Zealand in 1893 AD, in USA in 1920 AD, in England in 1928 AD and in France in 1945 AD. The British Commonwealth want the firstborn to be their King or Queen.

British universities did not accept any women until the 19th century AD, when many of them slaved as domestic servants with little or no income. A major change to working practices in British industry and commerce, during the past century, has been the increasing equality of women. There are now more women than men employed throughout Britain. About 60% of British women have become bread-winners but they only earn 80% as much as men and they officially retire at 60 instead of 65. Some 50% of men retire by 60 but they get no pension until they are 65. The Old Tory government promised pension equality by the Millennium. The New Labour government wanted to gradually raise the retirement age for men and women to 68 because people are living longer, the state pension scheme is running out of funds and it is not enough to live on. The Lib-Con coalition wanted to abandon all compulsory retirement. Britain's largest employer: *Tesco*, has increased its retirement age to 67.

Little Britain is ruled by a queen and has had a female prime minister, opposition leader, speaker and leaders of both Houses of Parliament. Nevertheless, the vast majority of Members of Parliament are still male. There is some way to go before men and women are equal but changes to the working laws have already had a major affect upon the family. The downside of equality is that many children are left alone at home. This leads to anti-social behavior, drug abuse, promiscuity and crime. Kids are also suffering from the breakdown of marriages or partnerships and this is often due to a conflict between mother's and father's careers. It is usually a mother's responsibility to do the cooking and shopping but if she is working this has to be done in the evenings or at weekends. If women shared their jobs they could cook and shop on their free-days. Traditional family values could soon be restored if both the parents spent more time with their children by sharing their jobs and their lives. **Full-time-job-sharing-as-the-norm** would help to equalize both genders and it would allow whole families to spend more quality time together.

Man or Machine?

Life, for those who read this book, has become dominated by machines. It was so since clocks were invented and their influence is increasing. The early clockmakers needed accurate lathes, drills and mills to cut gears, spindles and bearings and this lead to bigger and better ones. Yet, modern machines are not controlled by men but by computers. Men are needed to design products but use computers to help them. The same computer that allows a part to be designed can also control the machines that make it and the robots that can load or unload it. Men are no longer needed to inspect the work for robots can do this too. One computer can learn from another and has limitless concentration. All products are improved by making some, using them and then going back again later to produce the next generation in the light of experience. If the Sun-clock was a Mark 1, the clocks We use today are Mark 9s. We now need a Mark 10: a new chronology, calendar and clock based upon the age, orbit and spin of Our Planet Earth coupled with the global-digital-decimal number ten and the circular, round number 360.

Futurologist Rohit Talwar predicts that in the next five years some 20% of existing jobs will be automated away, in ten years this could be 50% and in twenty years some 80% of existing jobs will disappear altogether. Talwar predicts that by 2020 AD 70% of chief executive jobs will go. Many low-tech companies will vanish, to be replaced by high-tech ones. He says that the advance of artificial intelligence will eradicate the need for millions of office staff and knowledge workers, including doctors. Artificial intelligence is accelerated by sharing data via the Internet. The millennial generation were born into a global-digital-decimal World. They believe that every issue can be solved by getting data, managing it, applying the right algorithms and then underpinning it with technology. In his book: *The Future of Business*, 60 contributors from 21 countries agree that technology will soon eliminate half of all the existing jobs.

Machines have taken over mines, factories, offices, farms and homes. They have replaced much of the manual power of the working classes and they are gradually replacing the brain power of the middle classes but the upper or so-called ruling classes have very little power any more. The class system was developed by almost every civilization and it was very difficult for a slave to become a ruler, especially in ancient Rome. There were 175 free days *per annum* for Roman citizens, two millennia ago. There are 175 free days *per annum* for Roman citizens, two millennia later. Their chariots and slaves have now been replaced by *FIATs* and *Zenussis*. However, the scourge of unemployment in Rome is now extremely high. A new master and slave society is developing throughout Our World, as millions are having to accept part-time jobs at below the living wage. The answer to this predicament is **full-time-job-sharing-as-the-norm**. The Romans would have 180 work days and 180 free days *per annum*.

Home or Office?

Working at home, in a car or with a smart briefcase is on the increase. This not only saves expense but also a great deal of stress and strain. Electronics are already having a big effect upon the congestion in cities. Job-sharing does not have to be in an office but can be done at home. Incoming calls can automatically be switched from one place to another. International communication systems are now so fast and inexpensive that some businesses can be run from almost anywhere in Our World. A *Datamonitor* survey showed that 25% of Britons worked from home, whereas only 20% of Americans and 15% of Europeans did so in 2000 AD.

Many Britons now commute long distances because it is too expensive to move home when they change jobs and the largest cost is stamp duty. It also stops upsizing and downsizing as families expand and contract. If it was abolished there would be less congestion and homelessness. The Ministry of Transport predict that traffic volumes will double over the next twenty years and they are taking steps to widen motorways. They want to regulate the number of vehicles allowed into cities and may charge motorists for using motorways, that they have already paid for. Some cities ban cars with one occupant or all cars when there is smog. Lagos banned all cars with even number plates on even dates and all odd ones on odd dates, however many rich people bought a second car. Singapore has a licensing system for the city but full cars get in free. New York gets complete gridlock during week-days but the Teamsters Union demands double-time for deliveries made at night or week-ends. The combined effects of job-sharing and more working at home could save much expense and a great deal of frustration for the commuter.

It has become the norm for university students to study away from home and this certainly gives them some independence and mixes them up. Yet, the grants have not kept pace with inflation and it is much cheaper for them to stay at home, even though they then receive lower grants. Alternating between studying and a job, during a ten-day week, could halt a crisis of rising costs and falling finances for students of all ages. The Student Loan Scheme now means that most graduates start their careers in debt and about half of them never repay their loans.

Many mothers combine home working with bringing up their family. They are often able to combine outwork or bookwork with housework. Fathers are less able to combine their two responsibilities in this way. Yet, many have proved that it is not only possible but also preferable. For many single parent families, home work is the only solution but with 5+5 job-sharing and 5+5 child-care, where two families are minded by one parent, they should be able to lead a far more outgoing life. With homes occupied in daytime the number of break-ins should fall. Yet, the local authorities stop some from running a business at home.

Home or Away?

A grand tour of the capitals of Europe was the education of the idle rich. The poor never went away from home but the new habit of going away on holiday grew with the railways and with the industrial revolution. Seaside towns with stations flourished and sea bathing became popular. Sunbathing grew when Coco Chanel decreed that a tan was fashionable. This fashion is dying out as We realize that the Sun causes skin cancer and that this is more likely now that there are holes in the ozone layer. The statutory one week holiday with pay has grown to four or five weeks and some work on bank holidays then add this to their annual vacation.

Whilst factories often shut for works holidays, offices and shops usually stay open and temporary staff are employed to cover for those absent. Either they need to be specially trained, which takes up valuable time, or they struggle on without knowing anyone or where anything is. Output drops and mistakes are made, but if temporary staff are not employed then those who are still on duty are put under extra pressure. Employment and enjoyment could be better if everyone shared their jobs with someone who could cover for them when they were away or sick.

High speed road, rail and sea travel now makes it possible to do and see much more in spare time and it has become comparatively inexpensive. Anyone can now fly half-way around the globe in less than one day. The return airfare from Britain to Australia is less than a month's pay. A generation ago the journey took three months and the cost was higher. Many Australians of second or third generation still think of Britain, Greece, Italy or Ireland as their home and they are allowed, by law, to take a sabbatical every few years to visit home - so why not reciprocate? A long holiday every ten years or so is far better than early retirement. Many students take a gap year before or after university to see the World. These trends are all helping to reduce the unemployment statistics.

Many people now stay at home and do some decorating or gardening. This is not only a matter of cost but also of getting fed-up with being herded about and ripped-off, especially during annual school holidays. To have five days off in every ten would allow anyone to take a break at home or away whenever they wanted and so avoid the holiday peaks. A five-day visit to most cities is usually enough to see the main sights. By swapping with a pair one would be able to take 10 or 15-day trips. With a caravan or a boat you can go away when the weather permits. We might even discover a little more about Our own delightful country, wherever it is, and thus save a great deal of fuel and foreign exchange. However, one in ten Britons has now moved overseas, because they could no longer afford to live here and they may never be able to return. The stress of modern living is taking its toll of all kinds of workers. **Full-time-job-sharing-as-the-norm** can give more rest at home or away.

Urban or Rural?

The global trend is for workers and their families to migrate to cities. This mass migration was originally due to the industrial revolution. Over 50% of Us live in cities and about 90% of Britons now live there. However, 40% of households in London are on supplementary benefits. Over 50% of London homes are now occupied by economic immigrants. Similar statistics apply to all the great conurbations throughout Britain. Yet, the very rich have a house in town and a home in the country. Many are living outside of green belts and so commuting long distances.

Consider the effects of **full-time-job-sharing-as-the-norm** on building. If houses were built by two separate teams, they would be completed much more quickly, therefore more cheaply and so the cost of housing, the largest part of the cost of living, would be considerably reduced. If they had five days off in ten more people would improve their homes. It is the best investment in the future, because homes do not depreciate. Many people are now commuting long distances, because they cannot sell their homes, although they would prefer to live nearer to their work. Cheaper housing would allow an up-size or a down-size, when needed. More people would be able to rent or own two homes, like the Danes. Many more would rent, buy or share a *peid-a-terre* near their work in cities and have their main home much further away in the country. People in depressed areas would find it easier to work away from home.

Most businesses would make better profits and expand more rapidly. All construction including factories, warehouses, offices, shops, schools, hospitals, sewers, tunnels, bridges, railways or roads would be cheaper. Projects would speed-up and provide a quicker return on investment. As the state's overall efficiency is increased, its wealth and balance of payments should improve and it should then be able to increase its expenditure on capital projects, which would improve its infrastructure. There would be less pressure from building development due to growth; more pressure to renew or maintain the existing building infrastructure. There would be less peak travel, peak energy consumption and peaks in recreation but more Time for community help and for the protection of flora and fauna, so the green belts around cities would be maintained.

There would be very little change in the outdoor agricultural and fishing industries, which are dependent upon the seasons, tides and weather. Except that there would be more efficient marketing and distribution. Mechanization has changed this sector from labour intensive to capital intensive anyway, often requiring round-the-clock, everyday operation. Crops and weeds depend upon the seasons and still grow at weekends. Cows and goats usually give milk and hens often lay eggs on Sundays. **Full-time-job-sharing-as-the-norm** would have a beneficial effect on the environment, so it should be advocated by the environmental lobby.

Urban or Suburban?

Only the very rich and the very poor live in London, the rest moved out. A larger proportion live in the suburbs rather than in the city centres. However, the transportation systems have not kept pace with this trend, so now many people are moving back into flats, which were once offices. Parking meters were intended to keep cars from jamming the streets and to give people the chance to stop for a short time but they have become regarded by city councils as a source of revenue and by motorists as a source of aggravation, although they are free when the shops are shut. Gridlock in central London has been reduced by the congestion charge, which relies on electronic cameras that read number plates and powerful computers but does not operate at weekends when the streets are clearer. Trains, tubes and buses have become even more overloaded and now that they are privatized most of their fares have become very expensive. If 360 days were the same there would much less congestion everywhere.

Many shopping streets, throughout the globe, are dying as supermarkets, hypermarkets and shopping malls, with free car parks, take their trade. Some of this trend could be slowed down or perhaps stopped if town centre shops were open every day and if town centre car parks were free. So many of Us now have motor cars that they have become a necessity, rather than a luxury, and We are now far more mobile than ever before. **Full-time-job-sharing-as-the-norm** would tend to favour larger shops. The trend for smaller ones to be operated by families would continue. The latest trend is for shopping to be done from home via catalogues and the net, which reduces traffic and parking problems and lowers prices. Another new trend is cut-price warehouse clubs, which are out-of-town. This new system would also help pubs, bars, clubs, cafes or restaurants. It is often difficult to find an empty table on a Friday or Saturday night, whilst on other days of the week the bars and restaurants are empty. Most of these would be open all day, every day and so experience far fewer peaks and troughs, floods and droughts or feasts and famines.

It is not only shops that are moving out of town but also many offices, warehouses and factories because most employees now drive motor cars. Most manufacturing is still organized on a single shift five-day basis. Everyday operation would lead to lower overheads, quicker deliveries, less work-in-progress, less machine downtime, far greater productivity, higher profitability, more job satisfaction and better career development. Increased production would allow rationalization, modernization and expansion and the use of morning and afternoon shifts together with **full-time-job-sharing** would allow production capacity to be redoubled. Night shifts are essential in some industries but they should be avoided. Companies that are already operating on a continuous basis would not notice very much change, except that their employees would benefit from longer breaks with their families and hence be far healthier and happier.

Right or Wrong?

The Persian beliefs that there were forces of enlightenment and darkness or good and bad influences evolved into the belief in Heaven and Hell, with angels and demons, and then into the belief in right and wrong. Wrongdoing needed atonement, like spending 40 days in the wilderness. Jewish Law still uses atonement and the Israeli government recently banished 400 Palestinians to Nomansland for 40 days and 40 nights.

Jesus may have been the one referred to in the Dead Sea Scrolls as the Teacher of Righteousness, he was soon regarded as the long predicted Messiah by his followers and some Sadducees, if not by the Pharisees. He taught love not hate, prayers not curses, evangelism not exclusivity. The 7-day week was regarded by the Pharisees as good, right and holy. To observe the Sabbath was to be righteous and this entitled the faithful to enter the Kingdom of Heaven when their Day of Judgment arrived. Yet, the Romans used an eight-day week with *kalends, ides and nones.* Sacrificial animals were bought in Jewish shekels, not Roman denari. Jesus overturned the moneychangers' tables and so he exposed a racket. There was much disagreement, amongst the Jews, about whether it was right or wrong for the Romans to be allowed to enter the sacred Temple and whether or not they were allowed to make Pagan sacrifices there. This was Nationalism and lead to the schism that separated Christians from Jews as well as to the Jewish revolt against Rome in 66-70 AD.

The first Christians in Egypt were hermits and monks who continued to use their ancient calendar with its ten-day weeks and thirty-day months. The Coptic Church in Egypt still uses these ancient calendar months. The Roman Empire adopted Christianity during the fourth century AD. Only the Pope, the father of the Church, was permitted to alter Time. He changed the week to seven days and moved the Sabbath to Sunday. He changed the 12 hours of dark and 12 of light to 24 equal ones. He moved the very start of every day from dawn to dusk to midnight. He misaligned the Roman-Catholic calendar with the mean Solar year. His years, months, weeks, hours, minutes and seconds became sacred. The various dates for Easter caused great schisms within Christianity. Other religious leaders decreed completely different systems and this is the fundamental reason why there is so much strife in Our World today.

The best system for measuring, managing and governing Time and Space is the one that fits Our World and Our socio-economic needs at present. The present needs of the industrialized World are completely different from those of countries that are still as they were in biblical times. Our World needs two different calendars to suit both sets of conditions. **Digital date** is two calendars in one: because it offers the opportunity for the developing World to use a five-day week with one rest day and the developed World to use a ten-day week in which most jobs are shared.

Good or Bad?

The strange idea that some dates on the calendar are more auspicious than others goes back to the very beginnings of superstition and religion. The Babylonian idea that every 7th day was a bad one became linked with the Seventh Heavenly Body: Saturn, and then with *Satan,* the devil. The Egyptian gods, *Osiris, Isis, Seth, Nephthys, Horus* all had good or bad days. The Persian religion was based upon opposite forces of good and bad. The Canaanite god *Baal,* was the lord of thunderstorms and disasters. The Chinese zodiacs, calendars and clocks were used to find auspicious ages, dates and times for performing various rituals or rites of passage. Good and bad days became part of Jewish, Christian, Muslim dogmas. They were a fundamental part of the Inca, Maya and Aztec calendars. The Solar solstices and equinoxes, Lunar phases, Lunar or Solar eclipses are still regarded by the Pagans as good or bad dates for their festivals.

The Children of Israel regarded themselves as *Yahweh's* chosen people. So long as they all obeyed the written law they would keep away dark influences, such as drought, disease or war, from the nation as a whole. The law had to be obeyed by everyone or else they would be punished. Deciding which duties were essential on the Sabbath was the cause of much controversy and this may have been one of the causes of the splinter group which formed the modern religion called: Christianity. The Christians used the Jewish week but moved the Sabbath to Sunday. The Muslims also used the Jewish week but went to mosque on Friday. The Eastern religions have no seven-day week and no Sabbath day. The sabbatical aspect of **Time** is still the cause of much disagreement and led to bloody arguments at the beginning of the American Civil War, because their constitution stated that it should be a secular federation.

The dogma that working on the Sabbath is against the divine laws has almost died out in Britain, yet shopping hours are different on Sundays. The dogma that some days are more valuable than others has also gone. The only laws about Sunday work relate to shops in England and Wales. Scotland used to be stricter but now many shops are open every day. Surveys show that only 2% of shop workers refuse to work on Sundays. St. Paul's Cathedral staff work every day and are paid at the same rate. Many Jewish shops are now open on Saturdays but closed on Sundays. Hindu shops are open-all-hours, so the Sunday laws are unenforceable.

There are no good days nor bad days - they are all exactly the same. There are no divine influences on Us - all laws and lores are Man-made. We must make up Our own minds about all rational things and not allow others to control Our lives by their superstitions and religions. **The Worldwide Time and Space System** is much more rational than the *Anno Domini* chronology, Gregorian calendar, Benedictine clock and International Metric System but good news travels slowly these days.

Love or Hate?

Sigmund Freud (1856-1939 AD) wrote about love-hate relationships.
He was a Jew who escaped the Nazis and fled from Vienna to London.
Freud pioneered psychoanalysis and often diagnosed split personalities.
Many politicians seem to be in two minds about how to run Our World.
However, two brains are often better than one in solving any issue.
Job-sharing for example: two share the same office, bench or computer,
however, they rarely see each other and only one will get promotion.
They are rivals with the same interests, which is healthy competition.
This can increase efficiency and productivity in any organisation.

The philosophy: love thy neighbour as thyself, started two millennia ago.
However, the philosophy of romantic love is merely one millennium old.
It came with the troubadours - before then women were merely chattels.
The troubadours sang ballads, which are an important source of history.
The famous legend about Robin Hood was told entirely by these ballads.
One is about a pinder from Wakefield who beat him with a quarter staff.
The pinder was appointed to impound lost animals and trained them to
perform tricks for the annual fair that was held on the pinder's field.
Pinderfield's Hospital in Wakefield is now one of the largest in Britain.
Pinder's Circus, which began in Wakefield, is one of the largest in Europe.
The author's family came from Wakefield and were travelling showmen.
The author's father loved caravanning and travelled throughout Europe.
He eventually became the president of: *The British Caravanners Club*.

We are all different, yet We are all members of the same Human Race.
Differences in style of hair or dress make similar people look different.
In many cases these differences are ethnic, tribal or religious in origin.
They can make similar looking people hate and even kill each other.
One of the differences between one religion and another is its calendar.
Special days for feasts, fasts and prayers highlight social dissimilarity.
The Jews were *God's* chosen people and so their religion was exclusive.
Christianity is supposed to be much more evangelistic and submissive.
Islam was spread by the sword and it still seems to promulgate hate.
Hinduism and Buddhism preach love and have few warlike tendencies.
Confucianism and Taoism teach all about harmony between opposites.
Most religions have similar ethics whilst they appear to be very different.
Communism suppressed religion, nationalism and tribalism by forcing
people to think the same, look the same and all use the same system.
Atheism is a negative belief which can cause hatred of all the religions.
Contrarily, atheists are hated by many believers and can be outlawed.
Humanism is more positive and helps everyone of Us to love each other.
We must break-down the physical and invisible barriers that divide Us.
We must use one chronology, calendar, clock, rule, weight and measure.
We must use one language and script - whilst preserving old cultures.
This will help Us to build One World.

Hard or Soft?

Some of Us are having a hard time; whilst others are having a soft time. If We are having a soft time now; We may soon be having a hard time. Britain seemed to be thriving, whilst it lost its industry and resources because it was living on its reserves and windfalls, until they all ran out. The politicians sold the gold and silver and are having to cut welfare. This is bringing hardship to many who thought that they had a career, as well as those groveling at the base of the socio-economic pyramid.

None of the political parties seemed to dig to the root of the problem. The problem is that there are now far more old people than there are young ones to support them and the post-war bulge will soon stop work. Whilst this may lead to shortages of skilled workers in some industries, so that older people may be in greater demand, the global population is still growing fast and the need for highly skilled workers is diminishing. Nevertheless, it is still very hard to find a good plumber or electrician. Some 10% of Britons have left because they could not find a proper job. They have been replaced by immigrants who will work for less money. They do most of the menial jobs for much less than the minimum wage.

The problem of unemployment is exacerbated by demographic changes. This has led to a major break-down of family values and marriage vows. Many youngsters are now destined to live alone throughout their lives. The demand for single occupancy accommodation far outstrips supply. Some put a higher priority on acquiring a laptop than finding a spouse or putting something aside for the hard times ahead and their old age. Who can blame them when both state and private pension schemes are mismanaged and they are promised £millions on the state-run lottery. The other main cause of the problem is computers themselves, for they have already made many jobs redundant and will continue to do so. This problem has already started a great debate on the future of work. It is far better to redistribute work than to redistribute wealth for the latter only leads to inefficiency, jealousy, corruption and hopelessness.

Work is fundamental to Our Human Race for without it We degenerate. Nevertheless, there is no point in making work, just for the sake of it. Workers must try to produce more in less time by being more productive. Productivity is usually measured for a single person; whereas it is the total productivity of the team or the whole firm that is most important. **Full-time-job-sharing-as-the-norm** could increase global productivity. A ten-day week, would allow most jobs to be shared and this would allow buildings, machines, transport and infrastructure to be fully utilized. Many would continue their education and training in their own time, without disrupting their work and so skill shortages would be minimized. If the sacred seven-day week has to be scrapped in order to save jobs, then so be it, because profits are more important than prophets today.

High or Low?

Morality is not, fundamentally, a matter of religious nor political belief. The rich and powerful are just as liable to be immoral as the poor, but inequality does tend to increase social, economical and political ills. We all need to feel that We are cogs in the gear-train of Life on Earth. Civilization can run like clockwork if everyone is gainfully employed. Religious and political leaders take a position on the moral high ground; but their morals are often as low as their congregations or constituents.

The Archbishop of Canterbury said that his Church should do everything that it can to help the unemployed - yet it is against Sunday working. His Anglican Church has just gone through a period of great change. The ordination of women caused 100 priests to change to Catholicism. Homosexuality is no longer a sin and many vicars admit they are gay. All the Churches are now finding it difficult to recruit new ministers. Northern Ireland is still dominated by two opposing Christian sects. Yet, Ulster probably has more Roman-Catholics than Protestants now. There are probably more in Britain as a whole and yet it has recently become a multi-faith society with far more non-believers than believers. All of the big cities have synagogues, mosques, temples, pagodas and shrines as well as chapels, churches and cathedrals: all in juxtaposition. In the main, all faiths, sects and non-faiths live in perfect harmony.

However, in other parts of the globe religious intolerance causes wars. The ultimate solution is to make every state a secular one, to make all days and hours the same and to share all the work and the wealth. The USA was supposed to be a secular federation but most Americans go to church, the leaders thump the *Bible* and preach high moral values. Nevertheless, it is a very unequal society and its moral values are low. It has one of the highest rates of infidelity, divorce and venereal disease. The UK was supposed to be a Christian state but only 1% go to church and one-in-four children have only one parent to give them moral values. Yet, couples who live 'in sin' are often more moral than married ones. The Scandinavian countries, with sexual, social and economic equality, have low unemployment and low crime rates, yet most are non-believers. Humanists do not take anything for granted, they use their experience and knowledge to solve many social, economical and political problems.

Education is supposed to provide everyone with a kit of tools for life; yet very few schools warn about crime, promiscuity and drug abuse. The solution to the moral dilemma will not be found by teaching religion. Humanity is best taught by good example, such as helping the aged. Far too many leave school, college or university with no job to go to. Unemployment is the root cause of crime, promiscuity and drug abuse. The answer is to make 360 days and all parts of days worth the same. **Full-time-job-sharing-as-the-norm** could be the best moral solution.

Them or Us?

Business schools teach managers how to avoid 'them and us' situations. They teach about cooperation and teamwork beating the competition. Teamwork and job-sharing go together to create a more efficient team, even in organizations with no competitors, such as the Civil Service. Competition is healthy but too many firms are chasing too few orders. It is not always the fittest who survive; whole industries are vanishing. Britain is losing its industrial base but it might be more competitive if it used its resources more efficiently - especially its calendar and clock.

The 'them and us' syndrome is encouraged and perpetuated by rough or dangerous sports and games, which sometimes lead to tribal warfare. However, the Olympic Games was instituted to stop the Greek city-states from fighting each other and it then welded them into one fighting force. The Greek chronology became based upon the four-year Olympiad cycle. The Olympic Games has become so expensive that it bankrupts nations. Greece has become one of the poorest states in the European Union. Some states are so keen to win that they tell their athletes to take dope. Doping seems to be undermining the fairness in many kinds of sport. Competitive sport does not have to involve one person, one pair or one team beating another for We can all attempt to beat the clock.

If We all used the same measurement system, We might think the same. There would be one less fundamental issue to debate or even fight over. The Americans say that their own measurement system shows that they are independent and yet it was based upon the British Imperial System. In the American Civil War many brothers and cousins fought each other without fully understanding the fundamental issues that were at stake. In the Bosnian Civil and Religious War there were many people in mixed marriages who did not know which of the three sides they should be on. Bosnia is now a failed state and there are riots due to unemployment. Wars are often fought about religion, ideology and imaginary dogmas. It may seem trivial to fight to the death over different calendars but it is, fundamentally, what separates all of the Jews, Christians and Muslims. The seven-day week and twenty-four-hour day may now be the global standard but they are the cause of a great deal of conflict and confusion. Standard time zones are invisible barriers that divide us from them. It is high time they were demolished to create one time and One World.

The *Star Wars* movies make Us consider intergalactic Time and Space. Many futuristic thinkers are now describing their own religion as: Jedi, because they realize that different religious beliefs cause most wars. If Planet Earth were to be attacked by aliens We would all pull together. Our Human Race is being attacked by alien ages, dates, times and rules. What could be more logical than a measurement system based upon the Earth's age, orbit, spin and girth, the number ten and the number 360?

In or Out?

Now that all travel is so cheap and easy We are touring and migrating all over the globe, which spreads ideas but causes a great deal of conflict. Millions are migrating from poor countries to rich ones in search of work. However, rich countries are having to restrict the number of immigrants. We are, little by little, being churned-up in that great big melting pot. Yet, ethnic cleansing is now on the increase in many parts of the globe. People of different ethnic, cultural or religious origins tend to congregate when they start to live in another country, because of their similarities. Yet, the reason for moving was to start a completely new way of Life. It has so far proved impossible to build any truly multi-cultural societies. Nevertheless, it may, eventually, be possible to build a uni-cultural one. USA would not exist if Zheng He, Columbus, Cabot, the Pilgrim Fathers, other immigrants or slaves, from all over the globe, had stayed at home. Although the USA is currently supposed to be freeing both its northern and southern borders; it is generally tightening its immigration policy. Many walls have been demolished but many others are still being built.

Britain has always been a multi-ethnic society, which makes it difficult to understand those who talk about breeding as though We were horses. During my lifetime the population of Britain increased from 50M to 60M. This is partially due to a greater life expectancy but families are smaller, so much of this increase is due to more immigration than emigration. Britain has 70K asylum seekers locked up for years in detention centres. Some are sent home but there are many legal and illegal immigrants. Many of these are now doing menial jobs at below the minimum wage or drawing benefits when they have not contributed to the welfare state. The Home Office has lost track of the situation and there are now very few customs and immigration checks at British seaports and airports. Since the EU formed 3M Britons have moved to other parts of Europe; whilst another 3M Europeans have moved in and taken over their jobs. When they retire many Britons buy a boat, a caravan or a timeshare and spend their holidays globetrotting on expensive cruises to exotic places. Those who live in these exotic places cannot afford to travel and if they try to migrate to another country they are usually interned or sent home.

Britain has recently decided, by referendum, not to remain in the EU. It trades in £s, drives on the left, travels in miles and drinks in pints. It was not part of the Schengen agreement to permit mass migration. Millions of refugees are now fleeing from the many war zones around the globe but the UN is doing very little to assist or control migration. It seems to be losing its motivation to become the global police force and appears to have forgotten its fundamental aim of creating global unity. We need a unified global society using one age, date, time, zone and rule, one language and one script, although this may take many generations. We can only build One World when We adopt **One Worldwide System**.

Privilege or Merit?

It is easy to build a society based on privilege but hard to do so on merit. To construct a meritocracy, everybody needs to be educated to a basic minimum standard and this must be achieved for several generations. A large selection of the population must be educated to a higher level, then a smaller group to the highest, so that there is a choice of leaders. The main qualities required of candidates for political leadership include: education, experience, diplomacy, presentation, conviction but not dogma. No one ever reached the top by reiterating the beliefs of someone else. Our education begins at birth and then continues throughout Our lives. So children of educated parents are likely to reach a higher standard. Yet, some of the most educated people came from a humble background. Good qualifications are very important but many leaders in commerce and industry rose to the top by clear thinking, hard work and good luck. Some say: advancement is based on who you know; not what you know. Yet, it is usually a matter of being in the right place at the right time. We are now, unfortunately, in the wrong place, with the wrong **Time**.

The privileged and underprivileged are fading away in classless Britain. Britain was led by a man with five GCE's who wanted a classless society. John Major did not climb to the very top of his profession by privilege but the education, grading and selection system is still steeped in it. Tony Blair came from a humble family but had an Oxford education. He said he believed in state schools but his kids went to private ones. Gordon Brown had a humble beginning, however he was never elected. He is now campaigning for everyone on Earth to have a basic education. Both David Cameron and Nick Clegg went to public schools and Oxford. And so the Lib-Con coalition was based on privilege rather than merit. Theresa May attended a comprehensive school before passing to Oxford and has progressed to the top job by sheer hard work.

Our knowledge is tested by examinations at every level of education. The number of GCSE and A level GCE passes are now the highest ever. Yet, whilst these measures of merit are rising; the standards are falling. The universities are unable to select candidates with the highest merit. The standards in some UK universities are getting so low that advanced industrial countries, such as Singapore, will not accept UK graduates. Students who cannot find a place are usually regarded as failures. Those with highest merit sometimes drop-out of the education system and those with the highest qualifications are sometimes unemployable. The Open University was founded by Michael Young (1915-2002 AD). Lord Young was the author of: *The Rise of the Meritocracy*, and was the first to suggest **full-time-job-sharing-as-the-norm** in a ten-day week. This would allow the cost of all education to be drastically reduced. It would provide much better career opportunities for everyone and the chance for further study towards career development at any age.

Role or Dole?

We all need a role in society but far too many of Us end up on the dole.
An underlying cause of this imbalance is the dogma of the Sabbath day.
In the Roman-Catholic countries some 50% unemployment is common,
in the Protestant countries this is lower and in secular states lower still.
In Communist states everyone had a job, even if they had no work to do.

In wartime: everyone had a job, throughout The Great British Empire.
In peacetime: many became jobless and on the dole, in Little Britain.
The Welfare State ensured the jobless did not starve when on the dole.
However, many became used to benefits and so lost their will to work.
Lord Beveridge's report defined full employment as 3% unemployment.
All of the political parties assert that full employment is still possible.
The Tories' so-called: Business Start-up Scheme paid the unemployed,
who had stopped receiving the dole, the same as the dole for six months.
New Labour's so-called: Welfare to Work scheme, did not create any jobs.
As soon as the 1M trainees finished training they went back on the dole.
The Lib-Con so-called: Work Programme fell short of its targets and cost
far more than the unemployment and disability benefits that it saved.
The Conservative government now claim that unemployment is only 5%.
The true level is very much higher than this ridiculous propaganda.
It is now around eight million or about 20% of the working population,
another 30% are working part-time and only 50% have a full-time job.
Well over 4M oldsters, over the age of 50, are currently unemployed.
Well over 1M youngsters, aged between 15 and 24, may never find a job.
Well over 1M able workers are now receiving disablement benefits.
Well over 3M able workers have given-up hope and moved overseas.
Well over 1M are working to zero hours contracts - not steady jobs.
Nevertheless, an increasing number of workers are now self-employed.
These and casual or immigrant workers do not appear in the statistics.

Much greater equality and far greater wealth can both be achieved soon.
Not through taxation and handouts, which destroy incentive and distort
supply and demand, but through spreading work by sharing most jobs.
Many people would rather work for shorter hours, even if paid less, so
that they could enjoy Life more, but they do not want to give their boss
the impression that they are not ambitious, and so they plod on and on.
Unemployment is a social evil, caused by the dogmatic seven-day week.
It leads to homelessness, poverty, crime, illness and family breakdown.
Despite all of this hardship many politicians still seem to believe that
Sunday is so special that it is worth more than other days of their week.
It is 'their' week because they have the elected power to change things.
It is no longer a case of 'getting on your bike' for We need a new cycle.
A ten-day working bicycle could solve unemployment problems for ever.
The unions are fighting for more flexibility in working hours but have
not considered all the advantages of **full-time-job-sharing-as-the-norm**.

Jail or Bail?

Ever since they were invented, clocks and watches have been a prize for highwaymen, robbers, thieves, burglars, muggers and pickpockets. If you want to know the time ask a policeman - for it forms a crucial part of all court cases and has done so since the era of water clocks. The time of the offence is critical to both prosecution and defence. It is impossible for anyone be in two different places at the same time. Yet, if you do not appear in court on time you will have lost your case.

Thatcher's 'return to Victorian values' produced the worst crime figures for many years and there are now far more on bail or in jail than ever. Blair's tough approach to 'crime and the causes of crime' was no better. There are well over 80K Human beings in jail - and more are being built. Nevertheless, this is not enough and so sentences are being reduced. Every year 20K people go to jail because they cannot pay their fines. They are not crooks but victims of circumstance, prisoners of the system. There have been many prison riots but these are not due to overcrowding and bad conditions, for modern prisons are as good as a one-star hotel, they are complaining about 'the system' in the only way that they know. Some 70% of crime is now linked with unemployment and with poverty. Although being poor or unemployed does not turn one into a criminal. There will always have to be some form of punishment but so many are in prison now that it is not the inmates who are wrong but 'the system'. There have been far too many miscarriages of justice in recent years. This is partly because the judges, juries, barristers and magistrates are overworked and often out of touch with the complexities of modern life. The system is failing when it takes a year for a case to come to court. There is very little compensation for those who are found not guilty. In the USA there are now a staggering 3M people in jail - with no votes. Instead of reforming their inmates they become universities of crime.

Full-time-job-sharing-as-the-norm would lead to more jobs, less crime. The courts could minimize their ever increasing backlog with a two-team judiciary for they could then be used every day and minor crimes could be punished by the loss of free-time so that careers would not be ruined. Employers would not be penalized for the crimes of their employees. Families would not be penalized for the petty crimes of one parent. Doing Time in prison would be only used for the very serious offenders. Juries could be those on rest days so their work would not be disrupted. More lawyers, solicitors and barristers would enter into joint practices. People would be able to consult their lawyers and other advisers during their free-time, so they would not need to take valuable time off-work. Criminals do not rest on a Sabbath, so the police have to work-all-hours. A rhythm of five days-on and then five days-off should suit them better than the rhythm of four days-on then four days-off that they work now. However, many of them now have to do other jobs to make ends meet.

Busy or Lazy?

A government is awfully lazy if it cannot organize its calendar and clock in such a way as to share-out all the work and keep everybody buzy. Many politicians and civil servants in secure full-time jobs think that people without jobs are lazy but they should try being unemployed. Searching for another worthwhile job can become extremely hard work. The Old Tories were doing other jobs and making money on expenses, when they should have been earning their living and running the country. The New Labour created a million civil servants but a quarter of these were tax inspectors, who soak-up most of the revenue that they collect. The New Tories say they want to make savings but are still borrowing. Their Universal Credit Scheme failed to reorganize taxes and benefits. The European Union has created millions of eurocrats and migrants but unemployment is higher than ever and some of its states are failing. Unemployment is a global issue and so it needs a **Worldwide** solution.

The Roman Empire was run by a handful of officials for a millennium. Everyone paid their taxes because the tax collectors had more power. There was a Roman welfare system with plenty of slaves and beggers. The British welfare system cannot tell who is deserving or undeserving. The taxation and benefit system has created skivers instead of strivers. Some are earning more in benefits than they could on a minimum wage. We should not be making more work to do but more time to do things. The more food that is grown; the more waste and obesity it causes. The more things that are manufactured; the more pollution it causes. The fiscal solution is to raise VAT and cut-out most of the other taxes. Taxing expenditure rather than income would encourage more saving. The **Worldwide** solution is scrap all chronologies, calendars and clocks and to start again with a global year, a digital week and a decimal day.

Every religion and sect has a different chronology, calendar and clock. Their annual, monthly, weekly and daily rituals keep believers busy. Yet, this is based on myths or legends, so they are wasting their Time. The Orthodox Jews work hard at being lazy for they are not supposed to lift any loads nor to walk more than 1,000 cubits on their Sabbath. The Orthodox Christians are extremely strict about Sunday observance, the Catholics are not so strict and the Protestants are not strict at all. The Orthodox Muslims use the cycles of the Sun and Moon as well as the week but they do not regard their holy day of Friday as their Sabbath. The Eastern religions do not have any Mystic weeks in their rituals so they usually keep busy during daylight and take a rest when it is dark. The Buddhists ritually waste time when they turn their prayer wheels. They do not need more food and stuff but often depend upon charity. Humanists have no chronology, no calendar, no clock but if they were to adopt a ten-day working week and **full-time-job-sharing-as-the-norm** they could spend half their lives being busy and the other half being lazy.

Public or Private?

Ever since Sir Thomas More published *Utopia* in 1516 AD a battle has raged about the merits of public or private ownership in an ideal World. The Utopians shared all their property and only worked a six-hour day. These radical ideas were tried out in Mexico and they worked very well. However, the Catholic Church trashed this socio-economic experiment. The twentieth century AD saw several attempts to build utopian societies but they ended in Stalin's labour camps and Mao's cultural revolution. So utopianists are now regarded as deluded dreamers and most secular states are under the dystopian rule of autocracy, pragmatism and spin.

The Tories encouraged people to buy their own homes by selling their council houses and they allowed more homes to be built but then raised interest so much that many new property owners became homeless. New Labour lowered interest rates so much that the only investment worth owning was bricks and mortar, so prices went through the roof. Millions of Britons found that they could sell their houses and go to live abroad, at much lower cost, without even having to work for a living. Millions of others found that they could never hope to own their home. Homelessness is now higher than before the start of the Welfare State. The North Sea oil windfall and the revenue from the sale of nationalized industries have all been squandered on paying workers to do nothing. It made good sense to privatize steel, coal, oil and gas production and electricity generation but all of the networks including water, sewage, gas, power, phones, rail and roads should be kept in the public sector. It made sense to privatize the car, bus, truck, ship, aircraft and railway rolling stock industries and truck, ship, aircraft and hovercraft operating companies but the rail, tube, bus and road networks are another matter. The issuing of franchises for the bus, railway, ferry or airline routes and the public utilities became a fiasco when civil servants made mistakes. In the past there has been a considerable amount of over-manning and bad management in the public utilities and services as well as in the nationalized industries, because there is usually no direct competition. With **full-time-job-sharing** there could be competition in monopolies.

The Tories privatized almost everything and said it was more efficient. Old Labour planned to renationalize every large enterprise in the land. New Labour compromised with public-private partnerships for networks e.g. The London Underground, but this turned into a City gravy train. The banks went bust and many of them had to bailed-out by the public. In 2010 AD 40% of jobs and 50% of new jobs were in the public sector. The electorate saw that this was ruining the economy so voted for change. The Lib-Con coalition planned to axe 25% of public sector jobs as well as many quangos, although these changes would increase unemployment. They could have cut working hours and introduced **full-time-job-sharing**. This could be the ultimate step towards a public and private Utopia.

Borrow or Lend?

Banking gradually developed from money-lending and money-changing. This was one of the causes of conflicts between Rome and Jerusalem. The Jews became Europe's money-lenders, because the Pope forbade it. During the Middle Ages the Knights Templar were the principal bankers. They became rivals to the Roman-Catholic Church, so were exterminated. The Medici banking family used their great wealth to finance Europe. Their banking system was based upon trust and lines of credit were extended without bullion having to be transported from place to place.

Bankers still make a great deal of profit by speculating with Our money. They control everything but they make huge mistakes such as lending: £billions to rogue traders who lost it all and bankrupted their banks; £billions to developing countries, who will probably never pay it back; £billions to grandiose construction projects, which never make a profit; £billions to property speculators, who always use creative accounting; £billions to American mortgage companies without enough collateral. The International Monetary Fund and The World Bank can now make or break any nation but they are under the thumb of the United States. The United States is now deeply indebted to China and Japan because they have both, traditionally, saved most of their capital for a rainy day. The average American is deep in debt and although the USA has the largest economy it also has the largest deficit in the whole of Our World. "Remember that time is money" advised Benjamin Franklin in 1748 AD. He realized that it was more efficient and productive to work in daylight.

British Chancellors of the Exchequer played with the bank rate without understanding the long term damage that they were causing to industry. The high value of the £ at the end of the '90's caused many large and small manufacturers to fold-up and many service companies to cut-back. Interest rates are now too low so there is no point in saving or investing. Britain is now living on credit and the total is now well over £1 Trillion. The British government is also overdrawn and now owes over £1 Trillion. The answer is not to borrow more but to put everyone back to work. The fiscal solution could prove to be **full-time-job-sharing-as-the-norm**.

Computers turned banking into a round-the-clock service so job-sharing and shift-work became the norm and bank holidays are no longer needed. A ten-day week would allow bank workers to share their responsibility. Global stock markets should operate every day and around-the-clock. Worldwide banking, accountancy and book-keeping would be greatly simplified with a 360-day financial *yer* a 40-day *ank* and a 10-day *wek*. The bankers already use **digital date calendars** for calculating interest, so they should find it simpler to share their jobs and their shares. We are all living on borrowed money and borrowed time and may soon need to return to a **Worldwide Gold Standard** measured in *gans*.

Inflate or Deflate?

We have come to accept the idea that if We run out of cash We can then borrow or print some more and this credit is the main cause of inflation. Runaway inflation ravaged Germany, Argentina, Russia and Zimbabwe. This could occur in Little Britain too - unless most jobs are shared. Britain lost 1M jobs in manufacturing whilst it gained 1M civil servants who did not add anything to the income of the country as a whole. The USA recently devalued its currency thrice by printing several $T, to make it more competitive - they called this fudge: quantitative easing.

Inflation is measured by the prices of mortgages, goods and services. These have increased by more than 1,000% during the last fifty years. The mortgage system has not only led to inflation but also to people becoming much too rooted to the spot so that they cannot change jobs. A large and increasing proportion of any price is due to overheads. Overheads are largely made up of rents and rates for buildings and the depreciation of capital equipment such as tools, vehicles and computers. If most jobs were shared and most offices, shops and factories worked every day the major part of overhead cost could be spread more evenly. If one major manufacturer adopted **full-time-job-sharing-as-the-norm**, all of the others would have to follow suit in order to remain competitive. Pretty soon the cost of all the manufactured goods would be reduced. The cost of energy and raw materials could also be reduced in this way. Transport is part of the cost of goods and if there were less congestion and no overtime at higher rates of pay this would also reflect in prices. If government offices also used the same system, then the cost of their administration would be reduced and taxation could also be lowered.

Take for example: *Daimler-Benz*, the oldest car maker in the World, who recently laid off 25,000 workers and put the rest onto a four-day week. Suppose they decided to institute **full-time-job-sharing-as-the-norm**, to work 360 days per year and so reduce their overhead costs by 30%. This would probably result in a cut in their retail prices of about 10%. Demand would increase and people would buy a *Merc* instead of a *Ford*. Every car manufacturer seems to be subsidized by its own government. *General Motors* and *Crysler* were bailed-out by massive loans from USA. They have now renegotiated agreements with the trade unions and are able to value all days and hours as the same and to share many jobs. *Rover* was bailed-out by successive governments but it still went bust. British governments have thrown many babies out with the bathwater, because they could not distinguish between lame ducks and fledglings. They have given huge handouts and subsidies to established industries; whilst ignoring new enterprises which could, eventually, replace them. Inflation can be beaten without raising interest rates or taxes, without pay freezes, without unemployment, without cutting public expenditure but by changing the way We measure, manage and govern Our Time.

More or Less?

Our Human Race quadrupled from 1.5G to 6G in the 20th century AD.
It has already grown to 7G in the first decade of the 21st century AD.
And is predicted to grow to 10G before the end of the 21st century AD.
Our Planet cannot support this population explosion and so We must
minimize the size of Our families, maximize the yield of Our agriculture
and fisheries and optimize the efficiency of Our industry and commerce.
Economic growth is still considered to be a necessity for every country.
Yet, this usually means more pollution and so more global warming.
The emphasis should be on sustainable development rather than growth.
This ideal can only be achieved with **full-time-job-sharing-as-the-norm**.

The European Union subsidized some industries that then grew too big.
The Common Agricultural Policy created mountains of food that were
often destroyed, to keep the price high, rather than given to the needy,
but many farmers are now finding that they cannot make ends meet.
Many kinds of raw materials and manufactured goods are tending to
stockpile because the emphasis has been to help the largest industries,
which have the most voters and give the largest donations to the party,
whilst many small innovative companies are struggling to get going.
Britain used to supply a large part of the globe with iron and steel.
Then the Iron and Steel Community built mountains of iron and steel.
So Britain lost much of its heavy industry - and the pollution it caused.
The politicians then claimed the credit for reducing its carbon footprint.
British manufacturing industry halved its employees over twenty years.
Their special skills cannot be replaced and are probably lost forever.
One of Britain's fastest growing export industries is now scrap metal.
The USA has minimized all of its imports by using trading restrictions
and maximized its exports by subsidizing its manufacturing industries.
Their solution to their unemployment problem was to increase spending
and print more money, rather than share the work amongst the workers.
This will inevitably lead to another recession, depression and slump.
The reason for the phenomenal economic growth in India and China over
recent decades is that they use all of their Human resources to the full
and they are not encumbered by the dogmas of overtime and holy days.
China limited population growth by only permitting one child per family
but the burgeoning population of India will soon overtake that of China.

Every industrial nation should use **full-time-job-sharing-as-the-norm,**
because this makes the most efficient use of any nation's infrastructure
and it gives every member of their communities a reason to be living.
More free-time would mean more time in which to develop new ideas
as well as more time for other diversions from the routines of working.
If less manpower is required, due to greater automation, then all of the
remaining work should be shared out evenly, whether it be in a family,
a farm, a firm, a company, a corporation, a state or an entire Planet.

Trade or Aid?

The ancient civilizations developed a market economy based upon trade.
Flint or obsidian tools and weapons were traded with furs or foodstuffs.
Eventually, the invention of a money economy made the World go around.
Nevertheless, politicians are forever making it rotate in fits and starts.
Market forces must always be allowed to prevail in a democratic society.
We will only have a global economy when We all use the same currency,
We all use the same system of weights & measures and the same Time.
Yet, the law of supply and demand is often distorted by protectionism.
And economic aid money often finds its way into the wrong pockets.

There are many trade deals between different parts of the globe but it
may take many years before We achieve free trade across Our World.
The French tried to use GATT to hold-up trade, throughout Our World.
This was to protect their, heavily subsidized, food and drink industries.
They stopped British beef from crossing the Channel and their militant
truck drivers blocked their roads and ports then sabotaged the Chunnel.
They allowed Britain to sell them lamb but did not prevent their farmers
from attacking British trucks and they permitted Britain to sell them fish
but they did nothing to stop their fishermen from blocking their ports.
They blocked the import of electrical goods by having different standards.
The European Common Agricultural Policy subsidizes its farms and this
makes it very difficult for developing countries to sell produce to Europe.
Little Britain is now subsidizing all kinds of electrical power generation.
This distorts the balance of nuclear or fossil fuels and renewable energy.
The USA is supposed to encourage trade but is restricting many imports.
They also subsidize farming and fishing to keep out foreign competition.
They prohibit the importation of iron, steel and many other commodities.
They prohibit all foreign built passenger vessels, including hovercraft.
The World Trade Conference was disrupted by American anarchists who
wanted to restrict global trade in order to protect their high rates of pay.
The World Trade Center was destroyed because it was in the USA.

It is incredible that a country such as Sierra Leone, which is so rich in
diamonds, can become so desperately poor and so totally disorganized.
Europe plundered Africa without teaching it how to be self-sufficient.
Africa currently imports well over 80% of the food that it consumes.
China is buying huge parts of Africa and South America to feed itself.
The British Raj helped the Indian sub-continent, with the power of steam,
to become one industrialized nation but religion has pulled it apart.
India buys industries in Britain whilst millions of Indians go hungry.
Many farmers commit suicide because they cannot make ends meet.
Once a country has achieved self-sufficiency it can then start to trade.
We have a moral obligation to help poor countries to reach this stage.
Full-time-job-sharing-as-the-norm can help to develop their economies
and to give them the chance to build a self-sufficient community.

Little or Large?

Large oak trees grow from little acorns but they need to be nurtured and only a very small proportion of the animal or vegetable seeds ever survive. Many British firms grew rapidly but then fell, like a great tree in a storm. The word: *British*, in their title seems to be at the root of their downfall. *British Coal, British Steel, British Shipbuilding. British Railways, British Motors, British Aerospace* and *British Home Stores* rose and then fell. *British Airways, British Gas* and *British Petroleum* are no longer British. So they have all been reduced to renaming themselves: *BA, BG* or *BP*. The hovercraft industry was supported by Labour but not by Conservatives. *British Hovercraft Corporation* grew rapidly as part of *Westland Helicopters.* Yet, when they inevitably ran into turbulence, *BHC* had to be jettisoned, despite the promise of Margaret Thatcher to help the hovercraft industry and the efforts of Michael Heseltine to save *Westland* from being taken over. *BHC* had grown from a model to six Cross-Channel ferries in a decade. These fast ferries ran profitably for over three decades carrying vehicles and passengers but were scuppered by Thatcher's loss-making Channel Tunnel. Isle of Wight passenger hovercraft have made profits for over five decades. The latest ones are derived from those that I pioneered three decades ago.

Pindair, my small hovercraft company, was born in my garage and despite the three-day week it grew rapidly by reinvesting profits into development. I exported hundreds of my *Skima* inflatable hovercraft around the globe. They were packed into small boxes, so could be cheaply shipped anywhere. *The British Technology Group* were supposed to be helping small companies. They held Cockerell's hovercraft patents but did little to help my company. I was forced to put *Pindair* into liquidation during the global recession. My local MP did little to help but was interested in feathered amphibians. He was later sacked when he claimed for a duck house on his expenses. All that I needed was a little financial help from *BTG* or one of the banks. Nevertheless, many of my ideas were adopted by other British companies. They are still finding it hard to keep going in today's economic climate. A new company on the Isle of Wight would like to build updated versions of my proven hovercraft designs but are finding it impossible to raise funds. I collected over fifty hovercraft of all sizes for *The Hovercraft Museum Trust* but they are also finding it very hard to find funding and may close down. So another great British industry may soon be nothing but a fond memory.

It now seems that the European Union is about to suffer the same malady. Britain voted by referendum to leave and other members may also do so. The former United Kingdom seems to be disintegrating into smaller units. New Labour increased the size of the Civil Service to reduce unemployment. The Tories are now trying to reduce the size of the Civil Service to cut costs. This may all seem to be inevitable but there may be a way out of the mire. **Full-time-job-sharing-as-the-norm** would increase competition, efficiency and productivity within all organizations of any size and keep them afloat.

Long or Short?

Politicians are interested in short-term tactics; not long-term strategy. This is short sight: because they can only see as far as the next election. They are continually mucking about with time zones and playing with daylight saving measures, without understanding what they are doing. This is now considered to be a non-political issue, subject to a free vote. However, the European Union would like all of its member states to be in the same time zone and to use the same daylight saving measures.

The last Tory Government commissioned The Policy Studies Institute to write a report on whether Britain should adopt Central European Time. This became a private members bill sponsored by John Butterfill MP. It was a waste of time - there were not enough MPs to vote in 1996 AD. New Labour's John Prescott, who represented Britain at the UN climate negotiations at The Hague in 2000 AD, convinced himself that if Britain moved its clocks an hour forward it would cut its CO2 emissions by 23%. The Conservative Tim Yeo, Chairman of the Environmental Audit Select Committee proposed a bill to introduce summer time during winter. He claimed that this time change would cut the evening peak in energy consumption, save 104 road deaths and 450 serious injuries every year, reduce crime and give more chance for outdoor activities and sports. The daylight saving debate rekindled at the vernal equinox in 2010 AD. Lord Tanlaw, crossbencher, claimed that the cost of a new nuclear power station could be saved by keeping summer time throughout the winter. However, the power generation industry retorted that this was nonsense. Ben Bradshaw, the New Labour Culture Minister, supported a study by the Daylight Forum Discussion Group at Exeter University which called for double summer time to be included in the New Labour manifesto. They lost the general election, so this ball was kicked into the long grass. Rebecca Harris, Conservative, tried to adopt CET with a private members bill but, after another protracted debate, it ran out of time in 2012 AD. Lord Deben, chairman of the Conservative Committee on Climate Change, said that Britain should put its clocks forward by two hours in 2015 AD. Cambridge said this would cut annual CO2 emissions by 450 Ktonnes.

We do not need any time zones nor so-called daylight saving measures. It would cost nothing to alter all Our clocks & watches to the same time. We could easily go back to Our old custom of working mostly in daylight. This should be a personal matter between any employer and employee. **Full-time-job-sharing-as-the-norm** coupled with **flextime and flexdate** would save a great deal of energy and would minimize carbon emissions, deaths or injuries due to road accidents would be dramatically reduced, there would be less crime, more time for outdoor activities and sports. Little Britain still sits astride the Greenwich Meridian of Time and Space. So it should be the first to suggest any fundamental changes to the way in which they are measured, managed and governed in the future.

Boom or Gloom?

Ever since the beginning of the industrial revolution there have been boomy periods of economic growth followed by gloomy periods of decline. Economics is an academic subject but there are still conflicting theories, whilst the boom and gloom cycle has grown from a local to a global one. Adam Smith (1723 –1790 AD) suggested in his *Wealth of Nations* that the fiscal policy of every nation should be likened to any family business. However, today's politicians have forgotten this good advice, so they are spending instead of saving and are not sharing all the work out evenly. John Meynard Keynes (1883-1946 AD) suggested spending rather than saving in the Great Depression and his *General Theory of Employment, Interest and Money* influenced economic thought throughout the globe. However, his economic theory did not prevent the recent cycle of global recessions and there could soon be another Great Worldwide Depression. Frederic Hayak (1899-1992 AD) believed in free market economics and warned against all governmental intervention in *The Road to Serfdom*. Yet, the fiscal controls now administered by the banks, stock exchanges and politicians are insufficient to prevent calamitous economic failures. We now need a radical fiscal solution and that is explained in this book.

The electronic revolution booted-up to a false start because of old **Time.** Correcting all of the Millennium bugs created a mini employment boom, amongst the nerds, but many firms are now very wary of computers. Successive British governments wasted £Gs upon failed IT systems and most of their public projects cost far more than was originally estimated. We ended the second millennium AD with a period of gloom as the tiger economies of Japan, South Korea, Thailand, Philippines, Malaysia and Indonesia were hit by recession, which lead to the global depression. Europe, America and Russia have also experienced this domino effect. Great changes in exchange rates caused conglomerates to move their manufacturing to another part of the globe or to close-down completely. China has now taken over the manufacture of many consumer goods, which can now be shipped around the globe very cheaply in containers. India has taken over service industries with its cheap communications and it now owns much of Britain's iron, steel and vehicle industries. The global banking industry has failed and many manufacturing and service industries have either been decimated or have gone to the wall. The, apparently stable, socio-economic pyramid fell like a house of cards.

We will only be able to begin this third millennium AD on a sounder footing if the very foundations of Our global civilization are replaced. We can create a new economic pyramid if the four cornerstones of Time: age, date, time and zone are replaced and if We share the same Space. **Full-time-job-sharing-as-the-norm** in a ten-day working week is a simple way of increasing Our productivity and enlightening Our gloomy Planet. If We do not achieve this change, gloom could very easily lead to doom.

Gloom or Doom?

As We pass the second Millennium AD there seem to be more Natural catastrophes and Man-made calamities afflicting Our only, lonely Planet. A feeling of gloom and impending doom has descended upon all of Us. Wars have broken-out in the very region where two global wars began in the last century and these are still due the same religious dogmas. These have all broken-out because Our land will not support all of Us. And We are using-up all of Our Natural resources at an alarming rate. Despite all the casualties during all the conflicts, epidemics and Natural catastrophes of the twentieth century AD Our population has exploded. This was despite all of Our efforts to limit the size of Our families. Our life expectancy has increased due to medication and sanitation. There are now over seven Billion of Us and there will soon be ten Billion.

We seem to be in a perpetual battle with the forces of *Mother Nature*. During the last thirty years We have destroyed a third of *Her* resources, as *She* destroyed many of Our lives and livelihoods around the globe. Bangladesh and Pakistan were both submerged by extensive flooding. The Yangtse and Mississippi burst their banks making millions homeless. Forest fires raged in North and South America, Australia and S-E Asia. Volcanoes, which had long been dormant, started to erupt once again. Earthquakes shook Kyoto, Istanbul, San Francisco and Christchurch. Tsunamis wiped-out many thousands who lived near the Indian Ocean. These catastrophes are all due to the movement of the tectonic plates and this is mostly due to the gravitational pull of the Sun and the Moon. Hurricanes, tornadoes, typhoons or cyclones destroyed many buildings. They are caused by Sun-spots or Solar flares due to the pull of Planets. The new holes in the ozone layer at both Poles grew larger and larger. And so it was no longer protecting Us from those harmful Cosmic rays. This phenomena was Man-made but it is now being gradually solved. Global warming is causing great ice-shelves and glaciers to melt-down. The sea has risen by sixty metres since the last Ice Age and it would rise by another forty metres if all the ice in Our World was to melt. Many cities of history and prehistory are now at the bottom of the sea. There is nothing to prevent other low-lying cities from joining them.

We must not blame Ourselves for all of these disasters because some of them are due to cycles and coincidences within Our Solar System. Nevertheless, Our burgeoning population and insatiable desire for more and more energy, food, drink, goods and services is killing Our Planet. Our infrastructure and transport systems are overloaded on week-days. Our shopping and leisure facilities are all overloaded at the week-ends. None of the remedies now being proposed and imposed by governments will have much effect on the global predicament that they have created. It is only by sharing Our Time and Our Space that We will be able to look forward to a millennium of peace, health, wealth and enlightenment.

Rich or Poor?

The rich are becoming far too rich; the poor are becoming much too poor. The richest 62 people have as much wealth as the poorest half of the globe. Time starts to run-out when the dispossessed demonstrate that they have had enough and so riots break-out in cities throughout the globe. This is happening more often today in the supposedly affluent societies. Our World's richest people speak English, French, German or Japanese. Our World's poorest people speak Italian, Spanish, Portuguese or Chinese. Some Chinese are sharing their jobs and so they make the most of their infrastructure and can produce the same goods at much lower prices. They used to have a continuous ten-day week and took baths in rotation. They have no rest, recreation nor prayer days when no work is done. In the USA there are currently over 34M people living in abject poverty. Politicians rarely mention this and say that it is an intractable problem. Capitalism is failing when such a high percentage cannot find any job. Communism is failing when the comrades have a job but no work to do. There has to be a middle way and that is the main theme of this book.

The rich frequently say that the poor do not want to work but most of them come from a working class that has simply fallen upon hard times. About 10% of British children are underprivileged whilst in the USA this figure is about 20% and yet wealth is not a completely monetary matter. Some 90% of British children are considered to be literate and numerate by the time that they leave school but in the USA this figure is only 50%. It is far more difficult today to become rich without a proper education. Some British politicians say that 50% of children should reach a higher education standard and the school leaving age must be increased to 18. However, this is also their way of reducing the unemployment statistics. Little Britain now has over 4M people living in the inner city ghettos. Over 1M depend on food banks, established by charitable organizations. Whilst house prices continue to rise and many more are worth over £1M. Taxing the rich to give to the poor is not the most equitable solution. We now need a new way of sharing Our wealth by sharing Our work.

When the United Nations Organization was established one of its aims was to try to minimize the disparity between the rich and the poor. Yet, the gap widened and 1% now earn more than the 99% remainder. Some earn more in a day than others earn in a year and the ratio of the highest to lowest paid workers in many organizations now exceeds 20:1. Some 20% of Our Human Race are homeless and live in abject poverty. Millions are migrating from poor countries to rich ones when the best solution would be for them to stay at home and find more work to do. It is far better that poor people get themselves out of trouble by making and/or selling something rather than by receiving welfare or charity. What a great miracle it would be if an extremely simple idea such as **full-time-job-sharing-as-the-norm** could start to redress the balance.

Strong or Weak?

In the past, the strong countries dominated the weak and ideas such as: BC/AD years, Gregorian months, seven-day weeks, twenty-four hour days and divisive time zones were all superimposed upon the weaker ones. England was an outpost of the Roman Empire and Holy Roman Empire. Both of them fell and yet their age, date and time system has continued. England, the cradle of democracy, became the centre of an empire and used its strength to introduce its own temporal and spatial systems. The Imperial System was spread around the globe but was full of flaws. The British Empire became the greatest and Britannia ruled the waves, but nearly became a part of Napoleon's, Kaiser Bill's or Hitler's Empires. Britain was the geographical, political and economical centre of the globe and the Prime Meridian of Space and Time passes through Greenwich. However, the Imperial System is being eclipsed by the Metric System. London is the nearest city to the Prime Meridian and is a major hub in air transport but it is no longer the main seaport of Europe, due to historical, geographical, political, social, economic, strategic and tactical reasons. London is losing its importance as the banking, financial and insurance centre of the World as Little Britain becomes separated from Europe. The British Commonwealth has almost gone and its special relationship with USA is fading as they see Britain as a land where Time stands still. They even tried to invade Canada and add it to their Empire in 1912 AD.

Britain enjoyed a special position in the Old World due to its inventions: the chronometer, the steam engine, the bicycle, the telephone, the radio, the television, the computer, the internet and, of course, the hovercraft. Britain is now teetering on the brink of a closer relationship with many former foes in Western Europe, it represents a central position in the New World Order between the extremes of Communism and Capitalism. British goods used to be regarded as the best in the World but lack of investment in new industries and too much in old ones has opened the door to foreign companies making products designed outside of Britain. Much of Britain's industry is owned by the banks or foreign investors. Not only has the level of unemployment risen dramatically in Britain during the last decade but this lead to an unprecedented crime wave, many family breakdowns and a feeling of malaise throughout the land. No one seems to have any go in them anymore, the rate of business failures is the highest ever and the small businesses that are being helped by the government to start-up are often men with boxes of tools, women with bags of curlers or freelance insurance salespersons.

Large, wealthy, strong countries dominate smaller, poorer, weaker ones. However, in the UN General Assembly, Cuba, Monaco and Nepal have the same voting power on general matters as USA, Russia and China. The UN is committed to creating One World but few member states seem to be committed to creating **One Worldwide Measurement System**.

War or Peace?

The fundamental reason why very devout people of every religion or sect, want to maim or kill each other is their different ages, dates and times. The very devout still observe the Sabbath on different days of the week, which was based upon the Sun, the Moon and the five visible Planets. The very devout still observe the ancient Sun-clock prayer times and insist that all clocks should point upwards when the Sun is overhead. The very devout still observe the phases of the Moon as their calendars and insist that their Lunar moonths are much better than Solar months. The very devout still observe the positions of the Stars and the Planets and regularly consult astrologers and horoscopes about their future. The very devout are much more prone to mental illness than atheists.

There are examples, throughout history, of wars about Time and Space. The Crusaders captured Jerusalem whilst the Muslims were at prayer. They stayed for over two centuries before Saladin recaptured it for Islam. Seven sects now pray at the Church of the Holy Sepulcher in Jerusalem. They all use different ages, dates and times, so are all jostling for Space. The Muslims tried to take Jerusalem during the Yom Kippur holy day. The Sunni and Shiite sects of the Muslim religion use different Lunar or Solar calendars and so they are forever fighting holy wars about dates. During the First Gulf War the Allies agreed they would not fight during the holy moonth of Ramadan but the intelligence services miscalculated, with disastrous religious and political consequences around the globe. Muslim fundamentalists threatened to destroy the Millennium Dome and LAX airport at the Roman-Catholic Millennium, so caused pandemonium. They destroyed the World Trade Center on the Coptic New Year's Day. The Second Gulf War was scheduled to start on the Shiite New Year's Day, but started a day earlier when the Crusaders bombed Saddam's bunker. Muslim terrorists retaliated by massacring civilians in Crusader capitals on significant dates: London, Madrid, Paris, Brussels...

Differences of opinion in business and industry are invariably solved by fully researching and redefining the problem and then having a meeting. If changes are appropriate then everyone agrees to implement them. We can resolve all disputes with this systematic approach to problems. It may seem idealistic and unattainable but if it works in business and industry it should work in politics and perhaps even in religion as well. Some say that it is impossible to change ages, dates and times because We could never agree on the same system and it would be too expensive. It would cost nothing to adopt **global age** and **digital date** everywhere. It would cost nothing to alter all watches and clocks to the same time. It would cost very little to replace all Our timepieces with **decimal time**. It would cost more to adopt **Worldwide Space** but it would be forever. If We were all to adopt **The Worldwide System** We might suddenly find, to Our great surprise, that peace breaks out everywhere.

Life or Death?

The ancient belief in Life after Death led to the demise of millions of Us. Many Jews, Christians and Muslims believe that this Life is unimportant and so they are prepared to throw it away to fulfill their sacred beliefs. During the Crusades millions of Jews, Muslims and Orthodox Christians were brutally put to death in the name of the Roman-Catholic Church. During the Papal Inquisition many millions of witches and heretics were sadistically put to death because they did not go to church on Sundays. During the Conquest of the New World millions of native Americans were put to death if they would not adopt the Christian beliefs and dogmas. During WW2 millions of Jews, Gypsies and 'substandard' people were ethnically cleansed, whilst the Catholic Church said absolutely nothing. At the second Millennium AD Pope John Paul II finally apologized for the Crusades, the Inquisition and the Conquest - but not the Holocaust.

Fundamentalism in any religion, sect or cult is a very dangerous trend. In 1978 AD, 900 People's Templars committed mass suicide in Guyana. In 1993 AD, 86 Branch Davidians committed mass suicide in Texas. In 1994 AD, 48 Solar Templars committed mass suicide in Switzerland. In 1997 AD, 39 Heaven's Gaters committed mass suicide in California. In 2000 AD 1,000 Roman-Catholics committed mass suicide in Uganda. In 2001 AD 3,000 Citizens of Our World were slaughtered by lunatic Muslim fundamentalists at the World Trade Center and at the Pentagon. Christian fundamentalists from the so-called Bible Belt of the USA retaliated by waging holy warfare upon all Muslim fundamentalists. Many of their leaders still believed in: The Rapture - when Christ will swoop down to Earth and transport them to Heaven at a Millennium. Some of them may even be members of the Christian Ku Klux Klan. Fundamentalists still have their digits on the atomic doomsday button. They have Our World in their hands - but may drop it in terror or error.

Atomic weapons do not deter terrorists from bombing and shooting. Time bombs are still ticking away throughout this sanctimonious Planet. We can learn to defuse them if We all use the same Time and Space. Many schools still pump religious myths, legends and dogmas into kids; whilst omitting to instruct them about good manners, ethics and morals. Every school timetable is based upon a chronology, calendar and clock. Every curriculum is designed around different holy days and holidays. Children are taught to fear *God;* when they are supposed to love *Him.* *The Samaritans* were established after a 14-year old schoolgirl committed suicide in her first period because she thought *God* was punishing her. The simplest way to solve this problem is to scrap the Mystic seven-day week and to make 360 days in every year exactly the same once again. All religious ages, dates, times and zones would be replaced by secular ones and so every school slate would be wiped clean of its chalky past. We have all been brainwashed by the dogmas of politics and religion.

Politics or Religion?

Every nation has a different mixture of political and religious opinion. In some the country is run on a strictly political basis, in others it is religion which dominates, yet in most there is an awkward compromise. Those who are not religious, but in a minority, are obliged to observe the laws of the religious majority; whilst those who are religious in a secular state are obliged to observe the law, which may oppress all religion.

Politics and religion have been intertwined in England, since Elizabeth I became established as Head of the Church as well as Head of the State. The Monarch is still crowned by the Church but has not been in control of the State since Oliver Cromwell (1599-1658 AD) was Lord Protector. Between 1688 and 1828 AD all Englishmen had to become fully paid-up members of the Church of England in order to become full citizens. Before then there were separate taxes to the State and to the Church. There is an increasing debate about the disestablishment of the Church. These fundamental issues came to a head at the Millennium because of: questions over the divine rights of the Monarchy in a secular society; royal marital problems affecting the succession and suitability of the heir to be head of an organization that upholds the sanctity of marriage; internal problems in the Anglican Church due to the fall in attendance, the shortage of clergy, the ordination of women and shortage of funds; the troubles between the Catholics and Protestants in Northern Ireland; the urgent need to reform the two-tier government and electoral systems.

Every parliamentary day begins with an Anglican service in the House. England still has many laws about working or not working on Sundays, on the Christian feast of Christmas and on the Christian fast of Easter. Lord Balfour was the last Prime Minister to admit that he was an atheist. John Major, the last Tory Prime Minister, was an atheist but became a Christian before the Mayday election in 1997 AD - which he then lost. Tony Blair wanted New Labour to become a Christian Democratic Party. Gordon Brown, unelected Prime Minister, believed in Presbyterian values. David Cameron was raised in the Anglican and Conservative traditions. Nick Clegg does not believe in *God* and he is in favour of Liberal reforms. It is probable that over fifty percent of English voters feel the same way. Yet, over fifty percent of English voters cannot, do not or will not vote. Voting at all levels should be made compulsory, as in Australia.

I suggested **full-time-job-sharing** in a ten-day week to my local MP but he said: "We must use a seven-day week because it is in *The Bible.*" Many states claim to be secular, yet they still use the Roman-Catholic chronology, calendar and clock instead of starting again at square zero. **Full-time-job-sharing** would allow politics and religion to be separated. Either half of the ten-day week would be used entirely for working; the other half would be free for other uses, including politics and religion.

Politics or Science?

Queen Elizabeth I was the first English monarch to encourage science.
She installed clocks in churches and some used the first pendulums.
Oliver Cromwell drove science underground but Charles II restored it.
His Royal Society encouraged the development of many new sciences.
They took nothing for granted, so even suggested a global-digital-decimal
measurement system, based upon the length of a one second pendulum.
The Academy of Sciences was its rival and developed the Metric System,
based on an extrapolation of the surveyed length of the Paris Meridian.
Great Britain did not adopt their Metric System for over two centuries
but proposed the Navigation System, based on the Greenwich Meridian.
Politicians never take the time to understand science and technology.
It may take another century before they adopt **The Worldwide System**.

The Space Race spurred on technological advances in USA and USSR.
After the race to the Moon was won, much of the political impetus to
advance science was lost, yet many spin-offs are still being developed.
Your electronic wristwatch can be traced back to J.F.K's bold Democratic
decision to go for it, and Tricky Dicky's Republican one to stay with it.
Your laptop computer is more powerful than the one used in *Apollo 11*.
Your *Satnav* and *Google Earth* will take you to any part of the globe.
However, there are some fundamental faults in their operating systems.
Hardware and software designers realized for at least two decades that
their products would crash at the Millennium but did nothing about it.
Computer users warned the politicians that a huge problem was looming
but they took no notice and probably hoped that it would fade away.
When it arrived everyone blamed everyone else for the $Trillion bug.
In the meantime Bill Gates banked and then gave away his first $Trillion.

Hovercraft were a completely novel form of fast amphibious transport.
They were developed by Sir Christopher Cockerell FRS (1910-1999 AD).
There were several earlier attempts to use air for lubricating boats but
it was not until Wilson's Labour government decided to back his ideas
and to build a man-carrying prototype that progress was finally made.
The first public demonstration of the *SRN1* was on 11 June 1959 AD.
On 25th July *SRN1* crossed the Channel, fifty years after Bleriot's flight.
Within a decade, six *Westland SRN4* hovercraft were crisscrossing the
English Channel carrying millions of passengers and their vehicles.
Three decades later, these hovercraft were still the fastest way across.
Yet, when the Tories got back in they axed all hovercraft development.
The British hovercraft industry almost vanished and progress stopped.
Hovercraft were not even mentioned during the *Westland* crisis, which
nearly brought the Tories down, nor during the Channel Tunnel debate.
The loss-making Chunnel inevitably put the hovercraft out of business.
The USA, Russia, China and India now build many types of hovercraft.
The same thing has happened with many other great British inventions.

Science or Religion?

To a scientist the truth is something which best fits the observations.
To a believer the truth is *God*-given and so it can never be changed.
Nevertheless, many scientific advances were made by religious people.

The Venerable Bede (8th century AD) and several other monks, realized
that the Roman-Catholic calendar was slipping behind the Solar year.
Yet, successive popes did nothing to correct it for over eight centuries.
Hindu and Muslim scholars developed zeros, numbers and decimals.
However, when Pope Sylvester II wanted to adopt these in 999 AD,
instead of Roman numerals, he was bumped-off for being a heretic.
The Roman-Catholic Church still numbers years and popes in this way.
Nicolaus Copernicus (1473-1543 AD) trying to devise a better calendar,
deduced that the Earth orbits the Sun and the Moon orbits the Earth.
Yet, he dared not publish this hypothesis until he was on his deathbed.
Galileo Galilei (1564-1642 AD) used his telescope to prove that the Earth
orbits the Sun but was confined to house arrest because of his heresy.
Gerard Mercator (1512-1594 AD) used the information brought back by
global explorers to construct his cylindrical projection map of the globe.
This heresy contradicted the *Mappa Mundi* with Jerusalem at its centre.
In 1600 AD Giordano Bruno, an Italian monk, was burnt at the stake for
suggesting that the Sun is a Star and Planets revolve around other Stars.
Evangelista Toricelli (1608-1647 AD) inventor of the mercury barometer,
was called a heretic for showing that nothing could exist in a vacuum.
Charles Darwin (1800-1882) was destined for a career in the Church;
before he discovered Natural Selection and the survival of the fittest.
He was lambasted by the Church after he dared to publish his work.
The genetic law of heredity, discovered by cross-breeding coloured peas,
was published in 1866 AD by Austrian biologist-priest Gregor Mendel.
However, the Church suppressed this important thesis until 1900 AD.
The origins of the Big Bang theory were developed by Henri Le Maitre,
a Belgian astronomer and priest, between 1927 and 1933 AD.

Gabriel Mouton, vicar of St. Paul's Church in Lyon, proposed in 1670 AD
that a new standard measure should be based on the arc of one degree
of longitude at the Equator, which would be divided in the decimal way.
However, it took over a century before his ideas could be implemented.
In the Age of Enlightenment scientific proof overcame religious dogma.
This led to the fall of the French monarchy, aristocracy and theocracy.
It also led to a revolutionary new chronology, calendar, clock and rule.
The Roman-Catholic Church fought back and so France restored the
monarchy, aristocracy, theocracy, chronology, calendar, clock and rule.
The next French republic reinstated the faulty decimal Metric System,
whilst it retained the Roman-Catholic chronology, calendar and clock.
Most of Our World is still using religious Time and scientific Space.
It is now time to return to square zero and use **The Worldwide System**.

Science or Art?

There is no doubt that some of Us are more artistic and some are more scientific but most of Us specialize far too early during Our education so that We cannot understand each other nor find Our true vocation in Life. With a ten-day work week secondary pupils could spend five school-days on ten compulsory subjects: English, History, Geography, Philosophy, Mathematics, Physics, Chemistry, Biology, Economics and Technology and then five free-days, according to ability, on ten optional subjects: Arts, Crafts, Music, Dance, Stage, Languages, Sport, Life, Politics, Faith. Although We must specialize during Our tertiary education this should not be less than five core subjects plus five optional or general ones. When We take a degree We should specialize in one or two subjects but also continue to study as many other general subjects as possible. Graduates in the arts or sciences usually base their careers on the same subject but some vocations such as architecture combine both cultures. Many scientists and engineers are competent artists in their spare time. Many artists are using science and technology to create stunning effects.

Multi-national organizations are ensuring that We do mix Our cultures. They are far more powerful than states and will create a global village. This may only take one generation, throughout the developed World. They insist upon the use of one language and one computer language. The next step is to insist upon the use of one global-digital-decimal measurement system throughout all of their globalized subsidiaries. Computers are opening many windows but also closing many doors. Magnetic and optical discs are displacing books and so saving trees. Most daily newspapers can now be scanned and read on the Internet. The next step was multi-media - the ability to select a book or a video through a phone line direct to a VDU and to pay for it automatically. This could soon kill education and be the route to an electronic culture. Home study is completely independent of the calendar or the clock and the search engines seem to have all the answers to all the questions. Yet, they all seem to assume that the seven-day week was written upon tablets of stone and the twenty-four hour day has come to stay.

A ten-day week could have a big effect upon the formats of the media. All magazines and newspapers would be edited by two separate teams. The traditional Sunday and week-day newspapers would merge together. Many programmes would be transmitted twice during the ten-day *wek*. More free-time would encourage more sporting and artistic activities. Theatres could have two productions, two casts and two performances. Concerts would have regular attendances and performers more work. The theme parks, visitor centres, stately homes, galleries and museums would attract equal numbers of visitors every day and so break-even. **Full-time-job-sharing-as-the-norm** would lead to a unicultural society and there is no reason for having more than one age, date, time or rule.

Capitalism or Socialism?

The industrial revolution started a new dichotomy because lord v serf became: landlord v tenant, owner v worker or management v unions. Machines were meant to give more freedom and wealth to the people; yet ground them into the dust to feed the greed of the mill owners. Many factory owners today were once shop floor workers themselves; but there is still a great deal of mistrust for bosses with any background. Most bosses are capitalists, on negotiable monthly salaries with bonuses. Most workers are socialists, on fixed-rate weekly wages with overtime. Britain's political party system is based upon those old divisions and it is still dominated by the Conservative Capitalists and Labour Socialists. Most Liberal-Democrats and the other parties come from other vocations. Yet, the proportion of voters is not the same as the number of seats. Many voters have become totally disillusioned with the same old political dogmas, which come from opposite sides in both of the ancient houses. They no longer have faith in any political parties nor the parliamentary system but a few can remember how they all pulled together in wartime.

Perhaps this wartime spirit and system could be recreated in peacetime. Dogmas were forgotten and the best person was chosen for every job. We could build a completely new meritocracy, based on power sharing, and so avoid the extremes and the corruptions of the current 'system'. There must be a middle way and this is through job and profit sharing. Some form of mixed economy will inevitably prove to be the best way. Many other parliaments have circular forums that rule by consensus. The Houses of Parliament are crumbling away and so are their parties. We are now living in the electronic revolution and it is quite feasible for the whole population to vote on any issue by electronic referendums; rather than for a traditional political party with a basket full of policies.

Communism, proposed by Marx and implemented by Lenin, Mao, Castro and other revolutionary regimes is the most extreme form of Socialism. Many Capitalists were overjoyed when the Soviet Union finally collapsed. This was not only because the military threat was over but also because they thought there would be a chance of more business in the East. However, the lack of an Iron Curtain has, unfortunately, meant that many more immigrants have now poured into the prosperous West and there are now fewer business opportunities in the poverty-stricken East. China is different from Russia, because they are far more industrious, but, once their floodgates open, the flow is likely to be in one direction. Capitalism is the basis of the USA Democratic and Republican parties, which both rely on enormous donations from big business but neither wants to upset the vested interests of the established Church leaders. There is a middle way through the socio-economic and political jungle. **Full-time-job-sharing-as-the-norm** could lead to a new philosophy and a government system that is both/neither Capitalist and/or Socialist.

Management or Unions?

The British conflict between management and unions began soon after the French revolution and at the beginning of the industrial revolution. A naval mutiny led to the passing of the Unlawful Oaths Act in 1797 AD. The trades union movement began when six agricultural workers from Tolpuddle were deported to Australia for breaking this law in 1834 AD. They became popular heroes and this led to the formation of the unions in various trades with the power of striking and collective bargaining. They won a one week holiday and Saturday afternoons off in 1850 AD. This was in exchange for various holy days dotted throughout the year. The General Strike was by workers who demanded a forty-hour week, time-and-a-half for overtime and double-time on Sundays in 1926 AD. The Labour government caved-in and this became the industrial norm. The workers were given a one week paid holiday every year in 1938 AD. This led to them being paid whilst having their lunch and tea breaks. The working week shrank from five-and-a-half to five days in 1950 AD. However, the trade unions brought in many restrictive practices such as: demarcation, closed shops, working–to-rule, wildcat strikes, flying pickets, which made many industries so inefficient that they went to the wall.

Industrial relations appeared to have improved in recent years under the Tory government because there were fewer strikes, lockouts or disputes. However, the real reason was that everyone was afraid to lose their jobs. New Labour claimed to have reduced unemployment, yet they created bureaucratic jobs in the public sector, whilst manufacturing declined and most new jobs in the private sector were in the service industries. The European Union now has laws giving workers four weeks holiday with pay every year, their official working week is now only 35 hours and they may pass laws extending the unproductive weekend to three days. Yet, many British employees work for over ten hours of unpaid overtime.

The British Institute of Directors, The Confederation of British Industry, The British Institute of Management, The Institute of Fiscal Studies and especially The Chartered Institute of Personnel and Development have found that higher productivity is possible if most jobs are shared, if all time is worth the same and if the maximum use is made of daylight. All the political parties agree that there should be more flexible working but they do not seem to have thought about working mostly in daylight. The Trades Union Congress represents about half of all British workers. They are now trying to add three more bank holidays to the Gregorian calendar in order to bring Britain into line with the rest of Europe. If management and unions carefully studied the proposals in this book they might agree to equate the benefits of full employment, more leisure, lower taxes, lower national insurance and much better career prospects with flat-rate pay, no pay for no work, sexual equality, mandatory profit or loss sharing, **flextime, flexdate** and **full-time-job-sharing-as-the-norm**.

Majority or Minority?

Plato (429-347 BC) wrote that democracy soon passes into despotism. There are still many examples of this occurring, throughout the globe, especially in poorer states with little education and bad communications, but also in richer states where the electorate have become apathetic. Democracy, with everyone having one vote, is the best system We have; but it is far from being the best system that We could possibly have. We could earn the right to more than one vote as We become wiser. Our education should include the study of all the political issues. Anyone should be capable of reaching the top and running the country.

Britain has the mother of all parliaments, yet is hidebound by tradition. Antique buildings encourage traditional thinking rather than progress. The first-past-the-post system favours the *status quo* and it leads to government by a minority rather than management by consensus of all. The alternative vote system is used in some countries, however it has very little effect on the final outcome, unless voting is made compulsory. Proportional representation means that party politics must dominate, because the party selects the lists of its candidates and its policies. The ruling Conservative party currently has only 150,000 members. Few independent candidates are elected to parliament, none to power. Yet, in an ideal World, all of Our representatives should be independent. Another way, which is technologically feasible, is to have a government based upon electronic elections, on democratic days, for every minister and referendums on single issues that may have more than two options. Some 50% hate the Imperial System, 50% hate the International System but 100% may prefer to use: **The Worldwide System**.

If democracy is to work at all there must be change, from time to time. The ballot box is not the only way to accurately measure public opinion. If the majority were against Sunday trading they would all refrain from purchasing things on that day: no papers, no petrol, no diesel, no gas, no electricity, no TV, no radio, no tickets, no food, no booze - no way. Somehow, the vocal minority are elected and pass inhumane laws that are against the will of the silent majority, who do not or will not vote. The silent majority are not religious and do not trust any politicians. They think that they are hypocrites who say one thing and do the other. They believe in consensus, not conflict and that they could make a better job of running the town, the region, the country or the World. World issues must all be faced democratically or We will never, ever be able to achieve Our common goal, which must be, of course, One World. Perhaps the majority of people in Our World believe that all days should be the same but how do We organize a ballot on this global issue? There has to be a proposal which can be read, understood, discussed, debated, perhaps modified, then put to a vote before being implemented. You have it: **The Worldwide System** - in and on Your hands.

Temporal or Spiritual?

Temporal is a Latin root-word denoting all matters concerned with Time.
It means: worldly or secular matters; rather than spiritual or clerical ones.
Charles I polarized public opinion in England, Scotland and Ireland into
High Church Royalist Cavaliers or Puritan Parliamentarian Roundheads.
He dissolved parliament three times and this soon led to the Civil Wars.
He was beheaded by Oliver Cromwell, the Lord Protector, in 1649 AD.
He also dissolved parliament and abolished all the holy days in 1653 AD.
Nevertheless, most holy days were restored by Charles II in 1660 AD.
He encouraged the arts and sciences and he also reformed parliament.
Parliament urgently needs to be reformed yet again - from top to bottom.

The monarch has no authority and Parliament is meant to be in control.
Yet, Britain was devolved and was increasingly controlled by the EU.
The elected House of Commons is controlled by the political parties,
who select 650 yes-men and yes-women, but few independent thinkers.
The selected House of Lords is also controlled by the political parties,
who select over 800 yes-men and yes-women, who then become life peers.
The Scottish Nationalists now sit in the Commons but not in the Lords.
Most hereditary peers have now been expelled but a few of them remain.
So there are now very few lords without political or religious affiliations.
The Prime Minister appoints bishops, so the State still runs the Church.
Yet, the Church still runs the State because the 26 Lords Spiritual insist
that every English school must hold regular acts of Anglican worship.
They also stipulate that Christmas and Easter are public holy days and
that most people stop work for rest, recreation and religion on Sundays.
All the political parties support the Church of England and *vice-versa*.
The Church spends £Ms on trying to infiltrate and influence Parliament.
It threatened to sell its considerable shareholdings in shop, supermarket
and hypermarket chains if they continued to trade on the holy Sabbath.
However, Sunday is now the most popular shopping day, after Saturday.

The oldest universities are still very closely interlinked with the Church
and together they own and control much of the real estate in England.
So they have no interest in making higher education more cost effective
and completely independent of all the political and religious influences.
Oxbridge dominates the establishment including the press, radio and TV.
Most attempts to challenge the *status quo* are surreptitiously edited out.
Most secular states ban the teaching of religion but it is still encouraged
in Britain and New Labour wanted to increase the number of schools
with a religious bias, when this is clearly responsible for global conflicts.
The theory of religion and philosophy should be taught in all schools.
The practice of religion must be kept out of educational establishments.
The Lib-Con coalition pledged to totally reform the House of Lords,
by ejecting all the Lords Spiritual and electing all the Lords Temporal.
Both Houses of Parliament are now falling into disrepair and despair.

Kingship or Kinship?

Rome was a kingdom, a republic, a dictatorship then an empire, that fell. Some of its rulers shared their jobs but others became megalomaniacs. Its history can be traced through its chronologies, calendars and clocks. Roman chronology was originally based upon the birthday of Romulus, it was later changed to the birth of *Mithras,* then to the birth of Jesus. British chronology was based upon the year of the sovereign's succession but in the seventeenth century AD it changed to the 'Year of Our Lord'. Chronology should not be based upon monarchy, presidency, autocracy, aristocracy, plutocracy or theocracy but geology - the age of Our Planet.

The English Monarch, as Head of State and Head of the Church, would need to approve the temporal, spiritual and spatial changes in this book. A Church of England canon recently asked whether it's unconstitutional monarch should be chosen from outside of the European royal families, because many of its inbred kings were considered to be raving lunatics. To suggest that the head be changed could lead to one losing one's own. Nevertheless, William of Orange and Mary Stuart shared the Kingdom.

Should a president be independent of all party politics, like a monarch or an emperor, or should he or she be more like the President of the United States of America or the Commonwealth of Independent States? If Bush and Putin are taken as examples the answer may be neither. USA is not a democracy because $Ms are needed to run for the White House and the electoral college system has been shown to be flawed. Russia is not a democracy either because it always under the control of the Communists, the Secret Service, the Orthodox Church or the Mafia. Australia held a referendum on this subject but the motion was lost because the politicians wanted to choose the president; not the people. Austria democratically voted for Nazis Kurt Waldhiem and Jorg Haider but the Eurocrats wanted to maintain a so-called Christian Democracy. Poland was recently run by identical twins who shared the two top jobs.

Would Britain vote for Anne and Charles Windsor to be joint Presidents? As the Defender(s) of the Faith(s) and Head(s) of the Church of England, the Monarch(s) would need to approve of the abolishment of Sunday. Perhaps a dead heat should result in both candidates sharing the job. The USA voted for Al Gore and George W. Bush to be joint Presidents. The USA Senate was comprised of fifty Democrats and fifty Republicans. The Catholic Church seems to control American politics in both parties. The USA uses Roman-Catholic chronology, calendar, clock and zones. The New World should have had a new age, date and time but no zones.

The **digital date calendar** is part of a system for full democratic rule. Its remainder days should be reserved for elections and referendums. Its leap days should be reserved for electing presidents every four *yers.*

Conformity or Diversity?

There are people in all organizations who believe that if they conform to the rules and do not put a step wrong they will eventually reach the top. Yet, it is very often the non-conformist, who is able to see a better way of doing things, who gets there first and reaps the rewards of diversity.

Civilization seems to, inexorably, rise and fall as a new way of working or fighting becomes the norm and is later superseded by a better one. It is still evolving, in fits and starts, just as it did in ancient Greece. Each city-state had a different style of working, fighting, recreation, dressing, art, architecture, pottery, cooking, government and calendar. They were prepared to change if they found a better system but they usually stuck with tradition and so were overtaken by another state. Alexander was young enough to learn from his tutor with experience on the battlefield and he was prepared to learn from other civilizations. He decided that the Egyptian system of tens, hundreds and thousands was better than the Babylonian sixes, twelves, sixties and twenty-fours. He realized that he could not force all of his new empire to conform with all his ideas and that it takes a generation for new ones to be accepted. He established the great library in his new city of Alexandria in Egypt.

Some say that Caesar destroyed Alexander's library, to erase the past. His alternate 30 or 31-day calendar was based on the Egyptian one but, after he was stabbed in the back, it was soon corrupted by his nephew and adopted son Octavian, who later became the first emperor Augustus. The Roman Empire standardized its chronology, calendar and clock as well as its weights and measures but there were still many religions. Constantine gathered together elements of many religions to create a united Roman Empire based upon the idea of one *God* and one Messiah. The Roman Church did its best to destroy all traces of former gods and other prophets, so the great library in Alexandria was again destroyed. The Catholic Church insisted upon conformity and murdered heretics, including millions of Christians who did not believe in their theocracy. Most of Us now use its BC/AD years, twelve higgledy-piggledy months, 52 seven-day weeks, 24 hours, 60 minutes, 60 seconds in 40 time-zones.

The International Standards Organization controls Our Time and Space. However, their Metric System has many faults and their feeble attempts to standardize the Roman-Catholic age, date and time are unreasonable. What is needed is a World Standards Organization that starts again from square zero and comes under the jurisdiction of the United Nations. The UN, through UNESCO, helped to build a new library in Alexandria. This will help future generations to study the past, present and future. They may agree that a new measurement system is needed and that this must be based upon tens, hundreds, thousands, millions and billions. This global-digital-decimal system is called: **The Worldwide System**.

Optimism or Pessimism?

As We pass the Millennium: some are optimistic; others are pessimistic. Science and technology improved the lives of everyone on Planet Earth; yet there are predictions of a Natural catastrophe or Man-made calamity. We cannot prevent catastrophes but We may be able to predict them. We can probably prevent calamities if We reorganize Ourselves properly. It is clear that if We keep going in the way that We have in the last few decades there could well be a complete social and economic breakdown. Yet, the sociologists, economists and politicians have no idea what to do. Planet Earth is now full and cannot sustain Our burgeoning population. We have squandered Our oil, gas, coal and the other Natural resources. Their emissions have probably caused global warming or climate change. The sensible thing to do is to share Our work, Our wealth and Our week.

There is now a misanthropic backlash against Humans and Humanism. Humanism is now blamed for socio-economical and political breakdowns and some clerics believe that Humanists have lost their spirits or souls. One source of this pessimism lies in chronologies, calendars and clocks, together with the religious ages, dates and times embodied within them. Every religion has its own system but Humanism does not yet have one. Humanists use the secular term: Common Era instead of: *Anno Domini* but this is a backward and forward chronology based upon Jesus Christ. This system is no longer viable, because We know the age of Our Planet. Humanist chronology should now be based upon this very large number. Yet, We only need to use the last three digits for most everyday purposes. Most Humanists use the Gregorian calendar and the Benedictine clock. Their Roman-Catholic months, weeks, days, hours, minutes and seconds are no longer rational when everything else is now measured in tens. Humanists should simply count and divide their days on their ten digits. Our Human Race must not be divided by invisible, irrational time zones. We can create One World with One Time and One Space.

Militant Muslims believed that *Allah* had told them to fight Christians. George W. Bush and Tony Blair believed they were leading a crusade. They killed Saddam Hussein but destroyed secular Iraq in the process. Barack Obama killed Osama bin Laden but Afghanistan is still a mess. Despotic rulers were overthrown throughout Arabia, Africa and Asia, by the power of the people, with the help of electronic social networks, but this rational system of measurement, management and government may take many years before it eventually becomes the global norm. Unemployment, poverty, homelessness, family breakdown and crime can all be eliminated at-a-stroke by adopting this simpler, secular system. Many states claim to be secular, yet, use religious ages, dates and times. They are reluctant to use logic and reason; rather than ancient dogmas. **Full-time-job-sharing-as-the-norm** in a ten-day week would encourage everyone to have a soul-mate with whom they solve numerous problems.

Steps or Leaps?

Reaching the Moon was the greatest challenge Mankind has ever had.
A man had taken a small step and Mankind had taken a Giant Leap.
It filled Us all with hope and Our World would never be the same again.
What a pity Jack Kennedy did not live to see the result of his decision.
Our children compare these events with programmes like *Doctor Who*,
which began on the day after President Jack Kennedy was assassinated.
We have sent unmanned spacecraft to the edge of Our Solar System
and they have now visited all of the other Planets and their moons.
Yet, We still use different systems for measuring land, sea and air Space.

Each of the changes to Time and Space have been made by different
people in different places on different dates, so We do not have a system.
Time has been neglected for so long that it all now needs to be changed.
Chronologies, calendars, clocks and zones could be changed separately
but it would be better if they were changed simultaneously, Worldwide.
We know the age of Our Planet and the age of Our Civilization and so
We should abandon all of Our many different chronologies, at-a-stroke.
New Year should align with the vernal equinox and the tropical zodiac.
We should use a Solar calendar and forget the phases of the Moon.
The week could easily be changed without changing the months and
vice versa but it would be very much better to change them together.
We can share jobs on a 7-on/7-off basis but 5-on/5-off is the optimum.
Our chronology and calendar need only have three-digit ages and dates.
Our clocks and watches need only have three digits, making nine in all.
Time zones are usually changed two at a time but must all be scrapped.
Daylight saving measures are a waste of time and do not save daylight.
Why not change Space as well, so that We have a complete system,
based upon the age, orbit, spin and girth of Our Planet Earth?

Christopher Wren suggested decimal coinage over three centuries ago.
Each of the many changes to the British coinage and banknote system
was made by different people on different dates, however, UK now has a
digital-decimal currency system, which may last for a few years until:
inflation makes it obsolete, Charles, William or George becomes King,
the former United Kingdom elects a president or changes to using euros.

It was a bold step for me, an innovative engineer, to write this big book.
I have no right to change chronologies, calendars, clocks, zones or rules.
My only qualifications and authority are that I am a lifelong member of
Our Human Race and citizen of Our World, I studied at six universities
and have a wide range of experience in different kinds of organization.
I do not believe in gods but I do not want to stop anyone else believing
whatever they like in their own Time, so long as it does not affect me.
Keeping Sunday special does affect me, it marks the start of the week.
I want the 7-day week to end - it is holding-up the progress of Mankind.

Brolly or Folly?

Did the Great Millennium Dome at Greenwich mark the very pinnacle of British achievement at the end of the second millennium of Christianity and the progress of all Mankind - or was it just a big top and a big flop?

The Festival of Britain in 1951 AD revitalized the population after WW2. The 365ft Dome of Discovery inspired me to study science & technology. However, the 365m Millennium Dome was an enormous white elephant. When it was announced by the Tory Tarzan its theme was to be: Time. When New Labour took over this theme was soon lost and became: Spin. Tony and Mandy used £1G of lottery money and taxes to create the World's largest structure, yet, it was only open for one calendar year. If it had stayed open for two years it might even have broken-even. Built with foreign labour and materials, it was not a British achievement. Its American outer skin was ordered in metres but then delivered in feet. Its public transportation systems were slow, unreliable and unfinished. Its access and parking for the private motorist were almost impossible. Its British managing director was sacked and replaced by a French one. Its Central Theme was an aerial pageant with no discernible message. Its Play Zone was a children's' playground using gigantic clockwork. Its Space Zone was an extremely expensive fairground roundabout. Its Body Zone was the product of queer people with twisted minds. Its Spirit Zone was a Catholic calendar filled with other feasts and fasts. Its Mind Zone was merely a hackneyed collection of optical illusions. Its Learning Zone was a bookcase, which became a tree of knowledge. Its Work Zone was only placards that could have been in a pamphlet. Its Journey Zone omitted that great British invention - the hovercraft. Its Future Zone was only a film based upon *Blackadder* and *Doctor Who*. There was nothing about a future Time and Space measurement system.

The Great Pyramid is greater in volume and has lasted for 4,500 years. The Great Coliseum marked the very pinnacle of public entertainment. The Great Hall of Westminster was the largest meeting place in Europe. The Great Exhibition marked the very pinnacle of the British Empire. The Great Millennium Dome lies very near to the Greenwich Meridian. From this and the Equator latitude and longitude were measured using the old Babylonian system of 360 degrees, 60 minutes and 60 seconds. From this time was measured in 24 hours, 60 minutes and 60 seconds. The Dome has twelve masts, like a clock-face, its diameter is 365 metres, like the number of days in a year, and it also marked the year 2000 AD. So it is a Roman-Catholic chronology, calendar, clock and time zones. At the stroke of midnight most Imperial measures became illegal and so it marked the Metric Millennium and the end of the British Empire. We will look back upon the Great Dome and the Metric Millennium as two of Our greatest follies, because the only logical Time and Space system is based upon the age, orbit, spin and girth of Our Planet Earth.

Part Ten

Religion

Changing Our Beliefs

"All argument is against it; but all belief is for it."

Dr. Samuel Johnson (1709-1784 AD)

Mystery

Every kind of religion and sect could be defined as: a system of Human norms and values that is founded on a belief in a superhuman order. Chronologies, calendars, clocks, compasses, rules, weights and measures were the foundations of every religion and sect - so became sacrosanct. Judaism, Christianity and Islam were built upon Pagan superstitions and many synagogues, churches and mosques were built on Pagan sites. Taoist, Hindu, Buddhist, Sikh, Jain, Shinto, Maya, Aztec, Inca, Nazca and many other sacred temples incorporated Mystic Time and Space. Once any belief has been carved in stone it is extremely difficult to erase.

The greatest mystery of all Time is the origin of the seven-day week. It is observed throughout the globe; yet few know where it came from. Most people believe that it was one of *The Ten Commandments* or that it was based upon The Creation in seven days, however it was originally a convenient market interval based upon the *Seven Heavenly Bodies*. The idea that one day in every seven should be reserved for prayer is causing Our Human Race to destroy itself, because different religions chose different prayer days and so there is conflict wherever they meet.

There now seem to be more weird sects in the USA than anywhere else. William Miller (1782-1849 AD) predicted that Jesus Christ would be born again upon the vernal equinox in 1843 AD - however he did not come. Ellen White (1877-1915 AD) who was brain damaged at the age of nine, immersed herself in *The Bible* and then began to have hallucinations. She wrote down all her experiences and married a Christian minister. He believed that Jesus Christ would return to Earth at a Millennium. They founded the Seventh Day Adventist movement - which holds that Saturday is the true Sabbath - and it still has over one million followers.

As We enter the third millennium AD there is increasing curiosity in the mysteries of the Universe and unexplained phenomena here on Earth. Monsters, ghosts, unidentified flying objects are Natural phenomena or overactive imaginations and mystic crop circles are an elaborate hoax. There may be a modicum of truth in phrenology and palmistry but Our destiny is in Our brains and on Our digits rather than skulls and palms. In New Age Britain many are now looking eastwards to *tai'chi* or *yoga*. Others are turning to Buddhism or Paganism in the search for the truth. There were many Mystic beliefs two millennia ago and these included: Kabbalism - sacred geometry that involves 10 numbers and 22 letters. Eshatology - the belief in death and the after-life at The End of Days. Millenarianism - the belief that a Millennium will bring global changes: e.g. Armageddon, The Apocalypse, The Last Judgment or The Rapture. Many people, especially in the USA, still believe in these esoteric ideas. The terminal term: The End of Time, can have many different meanings: It could mean the end of **Time** and the beginning of **Worldwide Time.**

History

The age, date and time of Our birth, marriage and death are not only records of Our being here but also vital historical and legal documents. Our chronologies age different historical, mythical or theological events. Our calendars date many different feasts, fasts, holy days and holidays. Our clocks time travelling, learning, working, resting, playing, praying. The passage of Time is not only measured with chronologies, calendars and clocks but also in the way that We perceive it in Our own Life-times. The older We are, the faster the years, weeks and days seem to slip by. We also mark the passage of Time with generations, lifetimes, birthdays and anniversaries as well as with many jubilees, ages, eras and epochs. These are the themes of some of the essays in this part of the book.

History is confined to written records, which go back to about 5,000 BC. Yet, We now know that ancient civilizations go back to about 10,000 BC. The Garden of Eden may lay at the source of the Tigris and Euphrates. This was in the former land of Kurdistan and the Kurds still worship the angels who watch over them and guard the seven days of their week. The Sabaeans of Haran worshipped seven gods during their seven-day week and the Mandaeans continued this ritual in the marshes of Iraq. The Essenes seem to have practiced the basics of Christianity in 160 BC. They believed in the sanctity of baptism, marriage and burial rites. The Gnostics thought that Jesus was a prophet but not a messiah. They treated women as equals and believed in knowledge, not myths. *The Bible* is a Roman compilation of many Pagan myths and legends. The Romans and Catholics deliberately destroyed or concealed the past then fabricated new myths and legends, designed to control the masses. Instead of a sharing and caring society they imposed a cruel hierarchy. Instead of a Church of simple poverty; they imposed a complex richness. Anyone who challenged their dogmas was branded a witch or a heretic.

Turning points in prehistory and history were caused by catastrophes. The Flood may have been due to a collision with an asteroid or a comet. The Old Kingdom in Egypt ended with a famine of biblical proportions. This may have been caused by an asteroid or by a meteorite shower. The Exodus may have been due to a volcanic eruption and a tsunami. The Fall of the Roman Empire may have been due to a volcanic eruption. The French revolution was sparked-off by a famine caused by a volcano. The recent global recession was also sparked-off by a volcanic eruption. Mount St. Helens caused widespread crop failures throughout the USA. The Great Storm that felled Ms of trees on Friday 16 October 1987 AD was followed by the stock market crash on Black Monday 19 October. The second Millennium AD will be remembered for Natural droughts, floods, eruptions, earthquakes, hurricanes, cyclones, typhoons, tornadoes, plagues and pestilence as well as for Man-made fires, floods, ozone holes, computer bugs, terrorism and sharp falls in the global stock markets.

Astronomy

The ancient astronomers were a priestly class who used their privilege and knowledge to control the ignorant masses and to persuade their rulers to build observatories that would withstand Natural cataclysms. These acts of *God* were then thought to coincide with Cosmic events. Early civilization was wiped-out by a Great Flood some 12,000 years ago. Civilization began again and rapidly expanded due to fertility festivals at many stone observatories, which were built to warn of Cosmic events. Another Great Flood destroyed most of them some 6,000 years ago. Again the astronomer-priests rebuilt them in the form of stone pyramids, circles and temples, which were so massive that they still stand today. Plato described the fall of the city-state of Atlantis in his book *Timaeus*. This was probably the collapse of the Minoan civilization in the Aegean due to the eruption of Thera near to an equinox and eclipse in 1456 BC.

A zodiac is a stellar calendar, which astronomers used to find their way around the Sky, but it has taken on mystical meaning and may be found in many churches and cathedrals linked with an image of Jesus Christ. His birth and death are both based upon annual astronomical events. The Church did its best to bury or destroy many ancient monuments. During the Middle Ages it was even forbidden to visit these Pagan sites. The faithful believed that they would be turned to stone by witchcraft. If you visit Avebury today, which contains a crossroads, village and pub, you may notice that next to the great Pagan ring lies a Norman church. The museum at Avebury describes a hilltop observatory as a sanctuary. This is an example of how Christian perspectives distort the facts and sometimes make it very difficult to discover the truth about Our roots.

Mystic Time was based upon astronomy but different civilizations and religions had many different ways of calculating the age, date and time. In most cases the age was based upon a count of Solar years subdivided by dynasties but in some cases a Lunar year of twelve moonths was used. We now know the age of this Planet, so this is the basis of **global age**. It has always been difficult to decide when the New Year should start. The first point of Aries in the zodiac regresses through the tropical year. The Sidereal year of the Stars started with the heliacal rising of Sirius. However, this has to be observed from one particular place on Earth. So the Stars are not suitable for starting a perpetual seasonal calendar. The twelve-moonth Lunar year moves through the Solar year and it has no obvious starting point so it is no use for planting and sowing crops. The Solar year of the Sun could start at any of the solstices or equinoxes. The vernal equinox is the same everywhere, it was used as the start of many ancient Solar calendars and so it is used to start **digital date**. Astronomers now use a continuous day-count with decimals of a day. This is unsuitable for everyday use, because it does not incorporate years, but their decimals of a day are exactly the same as in **decimal time.**

Astrology

Astrology and divination are still the foundations of the Hindu religion. Some Hindu festivals are believed to be some five thousand years old. The Maha Kumbh Mela is an astrological festival, which brings salvation. Holy men and women bathe at the confluence of the Ganges, Yamuna and mythical Sarawati rivers near Allahabad at planetary conjunctions. These occur every 12 years when Jupiter completes its orbit of the Sun. A Solar or Lunar eclipse during this big festival is especially auspicious. In the auspicious year 2013 AD it attracted a hundred million pilgrims. This was the largest religious festival, of any kind, anywhere on Earth. Judaism, Christianity and Islam also celebrate auspicious days, weeks, moonths and years, which were based upon Pagan astrological beliefs. Millions of supplicants annually converge on Jerusalem, Rome or Mecca on very auspicious days in their Lunar/Solar, Solar or Lunar calendars.

A horoscope is a snapshot of the Sky at a particular age, date and time. Some royal tombs in Mesopotamia have a row of statues representing the Stars, Constellations and Planets visible at the moment of birth or death. Each of the twelve tribes of Israel was ascribed a different zodiac sign. Bethlehem was a town in the province belonging to the tribe of Judah. Jerusalem was a town in the province belonging to the tribe of Benjamin. The reference in *Revelations* to the 'Lion in the tribe of Judah' refers to the heliacal rising of Sirius coinciding with the Regulus Star in Leo. The prophet Isaiah must have based his predictions upon this horoscope. The birthday of the Messiah was predicted to be on 25 December 7 BC. The Bright Star was probably a rare conjunction of Venus with Mercury. This conjunction, called a *Shekinah* in the teachings of the *Kabbalah*, occurs every 480 years and is supposed to confirm the presence of *God*. The nativity story told by Matthew is based upon horoscopic astrology developed in Persia and spread around the ancient World by the Magi. They consulted the Sky to cast a horoscope and could calculate when certain conjunctions of the Sun, Moon, Stars and Planets would occur. Their religion was Zorastrianism and Jupiter was their god *Ohrmazd*. They expected to find the Messiah somewhere in the town of Bethlehem. Matthew does not mention how many wise men visited baby Jesus but only says that they bore gifts of gold, frankincense and myrrh. The Adoration by the Magi, depicted on many icons in the Middle Ages, is actually a secret, coded or esoteric message based upon astrology. However, there is no historical evidence that a Messiah was ever born.

Various magazines, newspapers and websites still publish horoscopes. Some people still believe that their destiny is governed by the Stars. Adolph Hitler consulted astrologers and so did Sir Winston Churchill. The revelation that Nancy Reagan controlled Ronald's diary by astrology and that Boris Yeltsin consulted astrologers, like the Tsar and Rasputin, demonstrate that neither politics nor religion help Us to think ahead.

Archaeoastronomy

Archaeoastronomy is the study of architecture related to Time and Space. Henges, pyramids, temples, synagogues, churches and mosques embody dimensional systems, dimensionless ratios and astronomical alignments. The Great Pyramid was accurately aligned with the cardinal directions. Its sides were 440 cubits long; although some say 365 'sacred' cubits. Many Egyptian temples were aligned and dedicated to the Sun-god *Ra*. The temple at Karnak was aligned to the Sun-rise on the winter solstice. The temple at Abu Simbel to 60 days before and after the winter solstice. Many Greek temples, which housed statues of their gods, incorporated the proportions of π and φ which can only be expressed as decimals. Many Roman temples were aligned with the rising or setting of the Sun. The Pantheon in Rome has a hole in its roof that cast a Sun-beam on the emperor appearing in the entrance at midday on the vernal equinox. Caesars were thus linked with *Apollo* at the beginning of their Solar year. Most churches and cathedrals were aligned on an East-West Solar axis. Many architects have incorporated round numbers, the age or the length of the year in their designs and they are still trying to reach for the Sky.

In 10000 BC the first Solar Temple was built at Gobekli Tepe in Turkey.
In 4000 BC Avebury's tilted henge was a 1:36524 scale model of Earth.
In 2500 BC Stonehenge's sarsen ring was a 1:100,000 model of Earth.
In 1800 BC Abraham's Kaaba in Mecca measured 1,000 cubic cubits.
In 1200 BC the Temple of *Amen*, Karnak, was about 1,000 cubits long.
In 1000 BC Solomon's Temple, Jerusalem, was 20 cubits wide, 60 long.
In 500 BC the Temple of *Artemis*, Ephesus, was about 365 feet long.
In 400 BC the Parthenon Temple of *Athena*, Athens, was 100 feet wide.
In 20 BC Herod's Temple Mount, Jerusalem was 1,000 x 1,500 feet.
In 128 AD Hadrian's Pantheon Dome, Rome, was 150 feet high & diam.
In 500 AD Justinian's Hagia Sophia, Constantinople, was 365 feet round.
In 800 AD the Mayan rattlesnake temple, Chichen Itza, had 365 steps.
In 1250 AD Chartres Cathedral had spires of 354 feet and 365 feet high.
In 1550 AD Michelangelo's Dome of St. Peter's, Rome, was 365 feet high.
In 1700 AD Wren's Dome of St. Paul's, City of London, was 365 feet high.
In 1821 AD Louis XIV's Dome over Napoleon's Tomb was 100 metres high.
In 1851 AD Paxton's Great Exhibition Crystal Palace was 1851 feet long.
In 1861 AD Thornton's Capitol Dome, Washington DC, was 365 feet high.
In 1889 AD Eiffel's revolutionary Tower, Paris, was 300 metres high.
In 1931 AD Johnson's Empire State Building, NY, was 1453 feet high.
In 1951 AD Roberts's Festival Dome of Discovery was 365 feet diam.
In 1958 AD Waterkeyn's Atomium in Brussels was 100 metres high.
In 2000 AD Rogers's Millennium Dome in London was 365 metres diam.
In 2010 AD Baker's Burj Khalifa in Dubai is 828 metres or 2716 feet high.
In 2012 AD Piano's Shard in London was meant to be 365 metres high.
In 2013 AD Libskind's New World Trade Center, NY, was 1776 feet high.
Will those independent Americans always measure everything in feet?

Geomancy

Geomancy is the esoteric or occult belief about the Natural landscape. Unusual rocks, hills, mountains and caves were thought to be sacred. Uluru or Ayer's Rock is still considered by the Aboriginals to be sacred. Mount Kailas in the Himalayas is honoured by Hindus and Buddhists. Mount Fuji in Japan is still considered to be the sacred Shinto volcano. The Temple of the Sun in Cuzco was the centroid of the Inca empire. The Temple of the Sun in Tikal was the centroid of the Mayan empire. The Temple of the Sun in Mexico was the centroid of the Aztec empire. The Temple Mount in Jerusalem is the cause of much bloodshed today.

The archangel *Michael* was said to have spoken to Moses on the Mount. The originator of the seven-day week was guardian of the Sabbath day. Many mountains, hills, mounds or rocks were named after *St. Michael*. He was the only one of the archangels to be considered to be a saint. An immense Man-made mound built near Carnac in around 4500 BC was usurped by the Roman-Catholic Church, who built a chapel on it. This Pagan tomb or tumulus is now known as: *Tumulus Saint Michel*. *Mont St. Michel* Normandy now has a Romanesque/Gothic abbey on the very spot where a Pagan menhir once stood and where Bishop Aubert of Avrances saw *Saint Michel*, in a suit of shining armour, during a dream. *St. Michael's Mount* in Cornwall has a similar abbey upon its summit. The Pagan Tor of Glastonbury is surmounted by *St. Michael's* chapel. The foot of this hill is said to be the site of England's oldest church. This eventually became a great abbey, which was razed by Henry VIII. According to Bishop Laurentius in 493 AD *Michael*, in shining armour, appeared in a cave in Sicily and commanded that it become a shrine. Now called *Monte Sant' Angelo* it has become one of the greatest shrines in all Europe and is visited by Jews, Christians and Muslims of all sects. *Sacra di San Michelle* in Val di Susa, Italy has Europe's oldest zodiac. *Michaelsberg* near Germany's Moselle valley is where he also appeared. *St. Michel* is a district of Paris where there is huge statue of him, clad in shining armour, standing on an outcrop of rock, slaying the devil. He inspired a maid from Orleans to lead the Dauphin's army into battle. She was captured by the English and burnt at the stake as a witch. *St. Micheal's Cave* under the Rock of Gibraltar was a hospital in WW2. He is often shown slaying the Dragon of Time, which sometimes has seven heads, as described by John the Devine in the book of *Revelations*. This may be linked with Greek legend of Hercules slaying a hydra and is probably the basis of the Roman legend of St. George slaying a dragon. St. George was a Roman soldier who became patron saint of England. Saint Andrew and Saint David have greater claims to be the patrons of Scotland and Wales but their special days are not taken as holidays. If the former United Kingdom becomes several, separate, secular states, their holy crosses, emblazoned upon the union flag, will fly no more. How did the author's namesake: *Michael*, become an angel and a saint?

Mythology

Many of the myths from all over the globe were based upon Sky-gods. Most of these mythical Sky-gods were closely linked with Time or Space.

Egyptian mythology was based upon their view of the day and night Sky. The Sun-god *Amen/Ra* and his wife *Mut* begat the Moon-god *Khonsu*. The Milky Way-goddess *Nut* and the Earth-god *Geb* had four children: *Osiris*, the first mummy, was the great god of death and reincarnation. Whenever he died he was reincarnated as the Constellation of Orion. At her death his sister/wife *Isis* became the brightest Dog-Star Sirius. Their brother *Seth* = Venus, killed Osiris and cut him up into 15 Stars. *Isis* found all of these parts but his phallus, raised him from the dead, impregnated herself and then begat *Horus* = Mars or Jupiter or Saturn. *Horus* begat four sons who represented the four cardinal directions. *Seth's* sister/wife *Nephthys* = Pleiades, gave birth to *Anubis* = Comets. *Anubis* came and went but always officiated at the funeral ceremony. *Osiris* was the dead Pharaoh, *Horus* the living Pharaoh, who fought *Seth*. Much of their knowledge is attributed to the Time Lord *Thoth* = Mercury. *Thoth's* Civic calendar embodied five dog days for honouring these gods. This ancient myth was translated into Greek after Alexander's invasion. *Thoth* became merged with the Greek *Hermes* or the Roman *Mercury*. *Osiris* became merged with the bull-god *Apis* to become the god *Serapis*. After the Roman invasions by Julius Caesar and Octavian or Augustus *Serapis* became their healing-god and *Isis* became their fertility-goddess.

The Romans usurped many Sky-gods to create their own Pagan religion. Nevertheless, other religions with their ages, dates and times persisted. The legions worshipped the Persian Sky-god *Mithras* every seven days. The Pagan Sky-gods were eventually replaced by the one *God* of Time. He may have been based upon the Egyptian creator-god *Amun* or *Amen*. The Sun and the Moon were the eyes of this invisible, omnipotent god. Christianity was based upon many myths taken from other religions. The outer Planets: Mars, Jupiter or Saturn represented *Horus* or Jesus, the Bright Star Sirius was *Isis* or Mary and Orion was *Osiris* or Joseph. Mary was linked with the Greek Moon-goddess *Artemis* or the Roman Moon-goddess Diana, who was associated with virginity and chastity. Christianity became the state religion after Constantine's mother Helena adopted it and built many churches over sacred sites in the Holy Land. The image of Christ was taken from the ivory statue of *Zeus* at Olympia. The image of The Madonna and Child was taken from *Isis* and *Horus*. The Roman-Catholic calendar was based upon the old Roman *kalendar,* together with the Mystic Sabaean, Jewish or Mithraist seven-day week. The Catholic clock was based upon the Egyptian belief in twelve *Hours* and the Babylonian Mystic belief in the importance of the number sixty. There is still no historical proof that Jesus the Christ ever existed but if he did it is now almost impossible to separate history from mystery.

Theology

Theologians try to understand polytheist, monotheist and atheist beliefs. Most religions feared Sky-gods who could unleash global catastrophes. It is probable that Heavenly Concordances do cause global catastrophes; although astronomers, seismologists and volcanologists often deny this. Concrete evidence linking many astronomical alignments or coincidences with global catastrophes is kept secret or ridiculed by many Christians, who believe that *God* is on Our side and prayer will solve all problems. Yet, Our Human Race has no divine right to inhabit this Planet Earth.

The French revolution was sparked-off by a series of volcanic eruptions in Iceland, which sent up clouds of ash and sulphur, that ruined crops throughout Europe and caused a great famine and civil disobedience. Napoleon took advantage of this Natural catastrophe to invade Egypt. His savants discovered numerous artifacts from its ancient civilization. After the revolutionaries adopted a digital Solar calendar, similar to that used in ancient Egypt, some people started to return to Pagan beliefs. However, Napoleon's *concordat* with Pope Pius VI led to the restoration of Roman-Catholicism and its Gregorian calendar throughout Europe.

Astrologers divided Western chronology into twelve Ages of the zodiac. The difference between Arian Judaism and Piscean Christianity is the change in belief from the fear of *Jehovah*, who would bring retribution if his law was broken, to the love of *God*, who would forgive all sins. This great astrological change in belief is symbolized by the resurrection. The Church has always stuck rigidly to the words written in *The Bible;* but theologians question many of the statements that do not ring true. The Christian perspective has coloured Our thinking and still, to some extent, lies behind the editing of all books, newspapers and programmes. However, there are now a few books which examine Christianity and all of the other religions and some even compare the merits of each one. Their ideals, morals and ethics are practically the same but their clothes, clerics, temples, chronologies, calendars and clocks are all different.

Moses' religion of an eye for an eye and a tooth for a tooth is vanishing. Jesus' religion is also fading and there may never be another pope. Mohammed's religion was spread by the sword and it is still spreading. Yet, many people are beginning to question the validity of all religions. Some now turn to astrology which disgraces newspapers and magazines. There are more astrologers in France and Italy than there are priests. This is not the solution to all of Our spiritual and temporal problems. Perhaps a new chronology, calendar, clock and rule based upon Earth's age, orbit, spin and girth would convince Us that it belongs to all of Us. If We were to share Our jobs We could share its wealth more equitably. We are now faced with a global catastrophe, caused by global warming. We must fight it together by minimizing Our so-called: carbon footprint.

Numerology

Numerology is defined as the study of the occult significance of numbers. Some of the many superstitions about numbers come from *The Bible*. The *Book of Numbers* is based upon the census taken of the Israelites as they wandered, without a leader, through the Sinai Desert for forty years. Many biblical ideas such as One *God*, The Creation and The Apocalypse were taken from the *Avesta:* the holy book of Zoroastrianism in Persia. The prophet Daniel lived during the reigns of Darius and Cyrus of Persia. He predicted the End of Time but salvation for those who believed in *God*. The *Old Testament* book of *Daniel* was written some four centuries after some of his 'predictions' became historical facts, so it is an ancient hoax. *Revelations,* the final book in the *New Testament,* repeats some of these eschatological predictions and then adds a few more, for good measure. Its author: John the Divine, a Christian hermit, hid from the Romans. It is because of his warnings that many people believed that there would be an Apocalypse at this Millennium or the Messiah would come again.

One thousand years is now expressed as a one followed by three zeros. The zero and one make a binary code that is used in digital computers. This binary system is the very foundation of the electronic revolution. Yet, many people are confused about whether to start with zero or one. In some places lifts or elevators are numbered from the ground as zero. In other places lifts or elevators are numbered with the ground as one. The Japanese considered that numbers: one, two, three were so sacred that they were not permitted to be used on their calendars and clocks. Some Japanese lift manufacturers still perpetuate this ancient tradition. The Korean word for: four, is similar to: death, so they try not to use it. Korean hotel lifts usually have a space for floor four in the same way that some European hotels have no rooms or floors numbered thirteen. To solve this numerical confusion some are now marked alphabetically. Nevertheless, there are still many different alphabets around the globe as well as many different ways of writing the numbers one to nine. The French way of writing one is similar to the British way of writing seven and the French way of writing seven can look like the British four. The letter: O is often confused with the number: 0 and this can cause problems in computer operating systems and their program languages. We now have the advantage of several global communication systems, so that revolutionary new ideas can be introduced much more rapidly. Nevertheless, most people seem to be unable to understand why the measurement of Time and Space is so fundamental to every civilization. Or why one measurement system is vital for the creation of One World.

Over the next few pages the most important numbers in the measuring of Time and Space are considered and their religious significance noted. Superstitions about different numbers still persist in different cultures and this might delay the introduction of: **The Worldwide System**.

Noughts

The Sumerian bean counters or tallymen used spaces to denote nothing.
Alexander the Great captured this idea in Babylon and took it to India.
The Hindus developed it as part of their astronomy and mathematics.
Their science and technology were more advanced than anywhere else.
Their religion encouraged them to discover more about the Universe.
The symbol meaning: zero, nothing, nought, nil or zilch is a magic circle.
Magic circles and numbers were built into the Hindu temple mandelas.
The Hindu zero was brought to Europe a millennium ago by the Muslim
mathematicians but was not used by Christians until the Renaissance.
The concept was thought to be heretical for over five hundred years.
God had created everything, so how could *He* possibly create nothing?
We were *God's* chosen people and Earth was the centre of the Universe.
So how could there be other worlds out there and perhaps other people?
There was no void until Evangelista Torricelli (1608-1647 AD) proved it.
A pupil of Galileo, he invented the barometer and improved the telescope.

Mayan mathematicians discovered the zero a millennium ago and they
used it as a number at the beginning of their various calendar rounds.
The Mayans and Aztecs adorned their pyramids, tombs and temples
with glyphs from their various astrological chronologies and calendars.

The French revolutionaries omitted zeros in their chronology, calendar
and clock, so their new system was not global, nor digital, nor decimal.
Napoleon Bonaparte reverted to the ancient measurement system when
he restored the Roman-Catholic monarchy, aristocracy and theocracy.
The French still use the Roman-Catholic chronology, calendar & clock,
although most of them are now agnostics, atheists or Humanists.

The Roman numerals are still used for counting years, popes and kings.
The Roman-Catholic MM was used to mark the Metric Millennium.
This coincided with the Protestant 2000 AD or the Humanist 2000 ACE.
The Millenium Dome contained a Faith Zone sponsored by the Hinduja
brothers, who were alleged to have done so to gain British passports.
Inside the Faith Zone was a circular space where one could contemplate
the Almighty One but instead of *God* there was absolutely nothing.

Mathematicians found that the zero was essential when drawing graphs
and they then found that it was useful to imagine negative numbers.
There is still some debate about whether the zero is a number or not,
because it behaves differently from the other numbers and it is used
before or after numbers to lower or raise their value by the power of ten.
The ubiquitous zero has become an essential part of everyday living.
We now use it daily when Our smart watches pass 00:00:00 at midnight.
Yet, Our stupid calendars still start each year, month or week with one.
This may seem to be much ado about nothing but zeros really are vital.

Ones

The number one was the basis for all numbering and counting systems.
A single stroke was the simple symbol used to tally all commodities.
In some cases there were also special symbols meaning: five and ten.
This developed into the Roman numeral system, still used by Catholics.
The Catholic clock was numbered from I to XXIV but now from I to XII.
The Protestant analogue clock has always been numbered from 1 to 12.
The secular digital clock is now numbered from 00:00:00 to 23:59:59.
The *Anno Domini* chronology age and the Gregorian calendar date are
now sometimes abbreviated to a single row of two digits: YY/MM/DD
The Times noted the year/month/monthday/time: 01/01/01/01:01:01
The Sunday Times published an article by the author suggesting that
Worldwide Time should have begun at: 0,000,000,000:000.000...

Cosmologists call the cluster of matter before the Big Bang a singularity.
At that moment all the laws of science and mathematics were invalid.
Some cosmologists believe that before the Universe there was nothing.
Other cosmologists believe that there have been several other universes.
Some theologians say that *God* created the Universe, then left it alone.
Other theologians say that *He* still watches over each and every one of Us.
Some theologians say that there are still a great pantheon of other gods.
Other theologians say that there is only the one god: The Almighty One.
When Pharaoh Akhenaten and Queen Nefertiti deified one god: *Aten*,
in a new central temple, all the priests of the old temples revolted.
The same kind of violent reaction to change still happens today when
Humanists try to create One World without any gods, temples or priests.
We will only achieve One World when We have one age, date and time.

The original digital system was, of course, using Our fingers to count on.
However, We do not have a global sign language, let alone a verbal one.
The British count the index finger as one but the French use the thumb.
This still causes a great deal of confusion amongst French wine waiters.
The French use the thumb and index finger to signal: two, whereas the
British use two fingers, which also means victory or something rude.
The rude gesture goes back to the battle of Agincourt where the British
archers signalled to the French that they could still pull their bowstrings.
It was then common practice to amputate a captured bowman's digits.
Winston Churchill was famous during WW2 for his digital victory sign.
I remember, as a boy aged ten, being taken to Paris in my father's V8
car and all the children giving us a Churchillian gesture as we drove by.
The British and French have been friends and enemies for centuries.
The Paris Meridian was the basis for the International Metric System.
The Greenwich Meridian is the basis for the Global Navigational System.
The Equator is the basis for a global-digital-decimal **Worldwide System**.
**One global age:digital date.decimal time+global-digital-decimal rule
could help Us to forget about Our differences and create One World.**

Twos

A straight line can be drawn by using a taut string between two points. This was how Egyptian mathematicians, masons and astronomer-priests assisted Pharaoh to lay-out the foundations of temples and pyramids. A pair of obelisks were erected at the entrance to many of the temples. During the night a pair of astronomer-priests sat back to back on the top of each temple to measure the hours by twelve *Decans* in the dark Sky. During daylight another pair tended the Sun-clocks and water-clocks. Sharing these temporal jobs was considered to be a spiritual experience. Geometry allowed the fields to be measured out fairly after each flood. Chronometry divided the Solar year and day into work, rest and play. By using these scientific and mathematical methods their civilization lasted for thousands of years, until catastrophes finally destroyed it. Egypt fell to Rome when Octavian defeated Antony and Cleopatra VII. We are saddled with the illogical Roman chronology, calendar and clock. If the Egyptian fleet had beaten Octavian's fleet at the battle of Actium, We might be using a **digital date calendar** and a **decimal time clock**.

The primary socio-economic reason for using the **digital date calendar** is that it is split right down the middle into two equal 180-day halves. The ten-day bicycle week can also be divided into two five-day halves. A five-day week with one rest day is the same as a seven-day week with one and a half rest days, which is the norm in developing countries. The basis for job-sharing-as-the-norm is that most jobs can be shared. Provided that the people sharing the job can agree about common policy. Two people should always be able to come to a logical conclusion but if one of them cannot or will not think logically, arguments become rows. My long-suffering wife and I have been together for over fifty years. She often claims that she is not perfect but I always argue that she is. I am convinced that job-sharing will become as common as marriage. However, I am not so sure that marriage will last for very much longer.

Mother Nature gave Us all two hands, two feet, two eyes, two ears, two nostrils and two of almost everything else but We only have one brain. Our brains and bodies are more intelligent and versatile than computers and robots will ever be, however, they need a rest from time to time. Unfortunately, many people are working to death whilst many others are unemployed and this is leading to a break-down of modern civilization. Robots can work continuously until they break-down or are superseded. Computers have created many jobs but they have destroyed many more. The binary system reduces numbers down to zeros and ones so that billions of transistors on silicon chips can process vast amounts of data. Computers have more than doubled their memories every couple of years. The electronic or information revolution is accelerating so much that in a couple of years the Worldwide Web has captured most airline bookings. In the same way **full-time-job-sharing** could rapidly become the norm.

373

Threes

The number three had a great influence upon geometry and geography. A triangle is the simplest geometrical shape and setting up a right-angle by means of a length of string divided into three, four and five parts became the basis of trigonometry, surveying, masonry and architecture. The Egyptians knew that: the square on the hypotenuse of a right-angled triangle was equal to the sum of the squares on the other two sides, for a millennium before Pythagoras promulgated his famous theorem.

Pythagoras came from the Greek island of Samos, off the coast of Turkey. He believed that he was the reincarnation of Euphorbus, the Trojan hero. He learned about right-angles, triangles and squares from the Egyptians. He learned about circles, cylinders and spheres from the Babylonians. He thought the relationship between shapes and numbers was mystical. He revered whole numbers and believed that the three/four/five triangle and fifty, the sum of its squares, were inspired by the Greek Sky-gods. He established a school in southern Italy where his number-philosophy became a secret, sacred cult whose followers were called: Pythagoreans. Students flocked to him because they wanted to learn from the master. They ate raw vegetables, drank only water and did not wear any wool. They thought that sex with women should only take place in the winter. Any student who revealed any of the secrets was violently put to death. Pythagoras and his clan were murdered because of their strange ideas. We are still extremely suspicious about all kinds of exclusive societies.

The Holy Trinity is a strange idea that is thought to have derived from the Egyptian concept that Pharaoh was *Horus* the reincarnation of *Osiris*. This idea became *God* the father, *God* the son and *God* the holy ghost. Reincarnation is still a part of the fundamental creed of Christianity. The virgin birth and the resurrection were not in the original versions of the four gospels but were added later by the scribes in the monasteries. The strange idea that bread and wine represent the flesh and the blood of the Messiah, seems ghoulish and cannibalistic to most Humanists.

Humanism goes back to the Greek philosophers, it was revived at the end of the Middle Ages and it has grown since the industrial revolution. Today the idea that people can live an honest meaningful life without following a formal religious creed of some kind does not seem shocking. Yet, fifty years ago the BBC was censored for broadcasting this doctrine. Today well over fifty percent of Britons are considered to be Humanists. They consider personality to be only the product of Nature and nurture. Humanists do not want to create any kind of exclusive or closed society. Man should show respect to man irrespective of class, race or creed. Women are equal to men in all respects except, of course, having babies. *God* is sometimes depicted holding a globe, a clock, a compass or a ruler. Humanists believe that Man is the measurer of all things.

Fours

Every square or rectangle has four sides and corners with right-angles.
Architecture progressed when circular constructions of wattle and daub;
were replaced by the rectangular buildings of brick, stone and mortar.
Most of the greatest cities were laid out upon rectangular street plans.
There are usually four seasons in the year which vary with the weather.
There were originally four ancient elements: earth, air, fire and water.
There are now over a hundred elements and one property is valency.
Every organic compound contains carbon, which has a valency of four.
Organic chemistry is the basic building block of every living organism.
Most mammals have four limbs and most vehicles have four wheels.
The square number four is the very foundation of Time, Space and Life.

Rectangular temples and square pyramids became centres of religion.
Most religious buildings and burials were aligned with cardinal points.
They divide the globe and are a great help to navigation on land or sea.
There are four solstices and equinoxes, which equally divide up the year.
They marked religious festivals at Pagan temples throughout the globe.
These four Pagan festivals have largely been obliterated by the Church.
Christianity is identified by the four-limbed symbol of a cross or crucifix.
Now a symbol for Death, they adorn the flags of many Christian states.
This was probably developed from the ancient Egyptian *ankh* symbol,
which was their symbol for Life and it is still used by the Coptic church.

The number four is part of: **The Worldwide Time and Space System.**
The circle of 360 degrees can be divided into four equal right-angles.
The 360 working days in the **digital calendar** can be divided into four
equal terms, which start at the vernal equinox and then fall just before
the summer solstice, the autumnal equinox and the winter solstice in the
northern hemisphere, which roughly correspond with the four seasons.
These four ninety-day periods could be used for accounting purposes,
as quarter days or rent days and so make book-keeping much simpler.
They could be used as four semesters throughout the academic year.
The academic calendar is in an unholy mess, mostly caused by Easter.
Maybe schools, colleges and universities could have a break of ten days
between each of their semesters of eighty days, *two anks* or eight *weks*.
But for most other organizations every term would consist of nine *weks*.
Terms could replace legal sessions: Hilary, Easter, Trinity & Michaelmas.
And may help the magistrates and judges to catch up with their backlog.
Parliament might adopt the same sessions and so put the World right.
Terms might even be used to divide the football and the cricket seasons.
All trades and professions would be singing from the same hymn-sheet
and perhaps society would begin to see itself as a working organism.
If We continue to sing from many different hymn-sheets in the form of:
chronologies, calendars, diaries, planners, timetables and time zones,
We could soon meet the four horsemen of the Apocalypse.

Fives

The symbol of the Pythogoran cult was a five-pointed star or pentagram. Inside this star was a pentagon and inside that was another pentagram, and so on and so on - like fleas upon fleas upon fleas - *ad infinitum*. Pentagrams and pentagons are still important symbols in Freemasonry. Most of the streets of Washington DC were laid-out in pentagrams. The Pentagon is its largest building and the Washington Monument is its highest stone structure at 555 feet high and 55 feet square at its base.

In ancient Egypt the number five had very great religious significance. The five dog-days at the end of each year were particularly auspicious. They were named after Star-gods: *Osiris, Isis, Seth, Nephys* and *Horus*. Originally, the Constellation of Orion, representing the Star-god *Osiris*, rose in the night and the dog-Star Sirius, representing Star-goddess *Isis*, rose as the Sun-god *Ra* turned night into day and the river Nile flooded. *Seth* (Venus) and his sister/wife *Nephys* (Pliades) were enemies of *Osiris*. *Horus* fought *Seth* and was represented by Mars or Jupiter or Saturn. On Earth: *Horus* represented Pharaoh, leader in peacetime and wartime. *Seth* represented the deserts whilst *Osiris* represented the fertile land. The *Sed* festival was an annual renewal of Pharaoh's authority to rule. He was double-crowned, King of Upper and Lower Egypt, at Memphis. So for almost three millennia Egypt had a pharaoh and five special days. The Greeks failed to add the leap-day but the Romans finally did so. Although Augustus imposed the Julian calendar throughout the whole of his new empire he regarded Egypt as his personal property so he let the ancient Civic calendar continue, but with the addition of the leap-day. These months continue in the Coptic, Ethiopic and Armenian calendars.

The French revolutionaries adopted the Egyptian calendar as a whole. Their remainder days were: Virtue, Talent, Labour, Opinion and Rewards. Their leap day was to be dedicated to sports like the Olympic Games. The egalitarians wore trousers instead of breeches on these days in the same way that blue jeans became a symbol of equality during the sixties. Some Communist regimes also tried to create dress equality in this way and a five-pointed star became the symbol of Communism.

How should We utilize the five days at the end of a **digital calendar?** They could become Our global festival of freedom, democracy and unity. There would no rents, rates, taxes, wages or salaries paid on those days. There would be no public transportation and all shops would be closed. So almost everyone would stay at home or in their local community. In a democratic society it is fitting that they should be used to renew all the governments in a local, regional, national and international cycle. The sixth day in leap years could be used to appoint secretary-generals. It would then be known as the United Nations Day and the leap year could coincide with the Olympic Games and other global festivities.

Sixes

Back in 3600 BC the Sumerians used a *sar* of 3,600 years which was the ultimate expression of the number six, used throughout their arithmetic. Six squared times ten was 360, the number of days in their vague year. They divided all by 60 and we still have 60 minutes and 60 seconds. The number 60 is the smallest number divisible by both 10 and 12. A cycle of 60 days was used by Chinese with a 10 and 12 day count. The Chinese and Japanese divided day or night into six double-hours, and so the length of these divisions of time varied throughout the year.

Every snowflake is quite different and yet they all have six branches. Six-sided hexagons are found in honeycombs made by six-legged bees. The hexagon is also used throughout engineering for nuts and bolts. The ancient Greeks developed mathematics based upon the number six. A die or dice is a six-sided cube that is spot-numbered from one to six and there are 28 dominoes numbered from double-zero to double-six. In cricket an over consists of six balls and the maximum score is six. Six is a perfect number because it is the sum of its divisors: 1+2+3=6.

The Star of David has six points and is made of two equilateral triangles. It was named after King David and is technically known as a hexagram. It was placed upon Solomon's Temple in Jerusalem and all synagogues. It is the symbol of the Zionist movement and is now on the Israeli flag.

The belief that the World was created in 6 days followed by one of rest not only led to the use of the 7-day week but also the belief in a World Week of 6,000 years and this would be followed by a day of reckoning. Bishop Usshar arrived at the age of only 4004 BC for The Creation. Allowing for missing 0 BC and 0 AD, he put the end of **Time** at 1998 AD. A dreadful feeling of anxiety spread throughout the Christian World. This was compounded by another belief that the end of the Age of Pisces and the start of the Age of Aquarius would mark the end of Christianity. It is declining rapidly in most parts of Europe but expanding elsewhere. Most of Us stopped following in the footsteps of the Creator years ago. The Sabbath has now grown to be the weekend, most of Us take many more days off work and so, if this work/life balancing trend continues, We will soon only be working on about half of the days in the calendar. **Full-time-job-sharing-as-the-norm** can be organized on a six-on/six-off basis and this would fit into a 360 day working year but five-on/five off is probably the optimum rhythm, based upon the digits on Our hands.

Superstition about certain numbers is reflected by their popularity in the National Lottery but even the Civil Service believes in bad omens. Number 666 is the sign of the Beast or the Antichrist, so is never issued for car number plates and some drivers dread the moment when their odometer reaches 666 Km or miles - so would they dread 666 *millidays*?

Sevens

The Mystic number seven was venerated throughout history:

The 7 Days of Creation	The 7 *Heavenly Bodies*
The 7 Virtues and 7 Deadly Sins	The 7 Heavens
The 7 Branched Tree of Knowledge	The 7 Gates to Eden
The 7 Branched Candlestick	The 7 Stepped Ziggurats
The 7 Hills of Rome and Byzantium	The 7 Daily Prayers
The 7 Wonders of the Ancient World	The 7 Guardian Angels
The 7 Good Years and 7 Bad Years	The 7 Ages of Man
The 7 Colours of the Rainbow	The 7 Seas

Many believe 7 to be a lucky number, so car registration 777 is valuable. The lucky number 777 always brings the jackpot in a one armed bandit. However, the Gregorian date 7/7 was unlucky for London in 2005 AD when seven Muslim fundamentalists bombed the tubes and the buses.

The Sumerians wrote of 7 gates between the Overworld and Underworld. The Babylonian Kings rested every 7 days during their Lunar moonths. The Sabaeans worshipped gods of the *Seven Heavenly Bodies* in rotation. The Elimites believed that the Universe was Created by *El* in 7 days. The Jews believed that *Yahweh* commanded them to use a 7-day week. The Greeks worshipped *Apollo* on the 7th day in every Lunar moonth. The Hindus believe in the 7 *yoga chakras,* their bodily centres of energy. The Buddhists honour their founder on 7x7 Lunar days every Solar year. The Muslims must circumambulate 7 times around the *Kaaba in Mecca.* The Inuit tribes worshipped the 7 Stars of the Great Bear Constellation.

Joshua marched the Ark of the Covenant 7 times around Jericho and the walls came tumbling down. [We now know that it never had walls]. In the third century BC the Babylonian astronomer Berossus described a Great Year in which the Universe is repeatedly destroyed and recreated. He taught that when all the *Seven Heavenly Bodies* appear together in Cancer there is a Great Winter and Great Flood but when they appear in Capricorn there is a Great Summer and the Universe is consumed by fire. Jews turned this into a Great Week, which was absorbed by the classics. The Christians also divided Human history into a Great Week of 7 Ages. The Seventh Day Adventists dominate Christianity throughout the USA. They say that Saturday is the true Sabbath and 7 angels guard the week. Some expect the Messiah to come again to begin the final Age very soon.

The 7-day week, with one rest day, has become regarded as sacrosanct, because it has been used for so long by Jews, Christians and Muslims. Missionaries spread it and the 2 x 12 hour clock throughout the globe. They became so habitual that many people believed they were *God*-given. However, many conflicts would soon be solved if they were replaced with a decimal day and a digital week in which most jobs were shared.

Eights

The Etruscans developed an eight-day week, an eight-note Musical scale
and counted everything in eights, upon their fingers with their thumbs.
The flute was played with only eight fingers and We still use octaves.
Pythagoras saw the Universe as not only harmonious but also harmonic:
philosophy, religion, music and maths were all aspects of a single idea.
He developed a theory of music, based on halving the lengths of strings.
The violin, bass and most stringed instruments have only four strings.
However, the harp, harpsichord and piano are played with all ten digits.
Europeans tune pianos to A = 440 cycles per second; Russians use 444.
A decimal musical scale could be based upon A = 40 cycles per *tik*.
There would be ten notes in this new scale with J = 400 cycles per *tik*.

The art of architecture is all about geometry, proportions and numbers.
Most religious buildings incorporate sacred directions and dimensions.
Many pleasing and structurally sound buildings are built upon octagons:
the Tower of the Winds in Athens with its Sundials and water clocks,
the Hagia Sophia in Constantinople with its dome on an octagonal base.
Charlemagne's great chapel in Aachen also embodies this sacred shape
and so does the layout of the famous Knights Templar chapel of Rosslyn.
Leonardo da Vinci used octagons in many of his architectural designs.
The baptisteries in Florence and other Italian cities were all octagonal.
Many mosques, including the Dome of the Rock, have octagonal bases.
This has become the Muslim plan form with a Lunar crescent on the top.
Roman-Catholic cathedrals and churches are usually built in the shape
of a cross, with a cross on the top, although this still has eight corners.

The first global currency was a Spanish silver coin called: pieces-of-eight,
because they could be divided into eight segments known as: *reales*.
This coin became the basis of the Mexican peso and the American dollar.
The British pound was divided into four crowns and eight half-crowns.
Most of the British coinage was originally minted from Sterling silver
however, all coins have now been debased with much cheaper metals.
They are now divided by decimals and have become smaller and smaller.
All currencies have been debased and devalued with paper and plastic.
We may soon have to return to the gold standard - based upon the *gan*.

Stonemasons prefer to use vulgar fractions rather than decent decimals.
Carpenters prefer halves, quarters, eighths, sixteenths, thirty-seconds.
Metalworkers prefer tenths, hundredths and thousandths of an inch.
Many old people still prefer to use the old units of the Imperial System.
There used to be 8 pints to a gallon, 8 furlongs to a mile and 8 stones to
a hundredweight but 16 ounces to a pound and 14 pounds to a stone.
Some weigh themselves in stones but they are living in the Stone Age.
It may take generations before a new idea becomes the accepted norm,
even if it is perfectly rational - like the **Worldwide System**.

Nines

Whilst decimal currency is now used in every country, the last to adopt it was Burma whose president liked nines, so they issued a nine *byat* note. The mystical symbol of the new Baha'i religion is a nine-pointed star. Nine also reminds us of those ancient and modern games and pastimes: Ninemen's Morris, Ninepin Bowling, Noughts & Crosses, Rubik's Cube. On that dreaded ninth day of the ninth month in the year 1999 AD a number of digital computer programs ceased to function properly. However, each window in a digital counter is numbered from 0 to 9. Eggs are now packed in boxes of nine as well as in sixes and twelves.

Chinese mathematics is explained in a volume called: *The Nine Chapters*. The ancient Chinese *Su Doku* is a mathematical matrix of nine squares, where all the columns, rows and diagonals add up to the same number. The Nine Roads of the Moon is the forward motion of the Moon's orbit. These nine roads were traditionally assigned different symbolic colours. In ancient Egyptian religion there was a Great Ennead of nine Sky-gods. The ancient Egyptians venerated domestic cats, which they mummified because they believed that they had nine lives - some still believe this. The Greeks believed there were nine daughters of *Zeus* called *Muses*: *Calliope, Clio, Euterpe, Terpichore, Erato, Melpomene, Thalia, Polyhymnia* and *Urania* ruled the arts and the sciences, now studied in museums. The Greek astronomers believed that the Earth was surrounded by nine crystal spheres to which the Sun, Moon, Planets and Stars were fixed. This incredible idea became the Christian doctrine (each sphere was the domain of a different order of angels) until the end of the seventeenth century AD when Tyco Brahe proved that they are suspended in Space.

The Phoenicians from Byblos used a Solar calendar with nine forty-day periods or forty nine-day weeks in a 360-day year plus five or six days. Forty days appear many times in *The Torah, The Bible* and *The Koran*. The early Christian liturgical cycle was based upon nine *quadrigesima*. The Roman-Pagan New Year of I March fell upon the vernal equinox. The Roman-Catholic New Year of I January falls eighty days before it. The 40-day fast of Lent marks the start of the liturgical cycle of movable feasts and fasts including Ascension, when Christ ascended to Heaven. Many country folk tales continue to confuse superstition with religion. If it rains on Saint Swithan's Day it will rain for forty days thereafter.

Worldwide Time in its simplest, abbreviated, form consists of 9 digits. There are nine 40-day *anks* in a 360-day *yer* plus 5 or 6 remainder days. An *ank* would be a useful period for accounting purposes and it is very much better than the twelve higgledy-piggledy Roman-Catholic months. The number 360 divided by four is three *mons* or nine ten-day *weks*. This fits into a zodiac with twelve signs and with the four seasons, provided that there is a remainder of five days, or six in every leap year.

Tens

Ten is a Natural number because We all have ten digits, there are ten *Heavenly Bodies* in Our Solar System and ten occurs throughout maths. There are ten fundamental units of measurement, including wealth. There are ten Human menstruation periods to one gestation period. Some cosmologists believe that there will prove to be ten dimensions. Base ten is in The International System and **The Worldwide System,** not the base twelve nor the base twenty, and so We should forget the words: eleven, twelve, thirteen... and use: one-one, one-two, one-three... This numbering system has been proven to be much clearer and quicker. We often say: one-two-three, instead of: one hundred and twenty-three.

Whilst ten is a temporal number it also has many spiritual connotations. The Egyptians measured everything - it was part of their sacred beliefs. They revered the sum 1+2+3+4=10 and so ten was a very holy number. They usually counted things in tens, hundreds, thousands and millions. The Romans learned from the Egyptians and Greeks to count in tens. They counted and numbered years in decades, centuries and millennia. However, it took many centuries before the century became established. Only a few astronomers and priests celebrated the first Millennium AD. Over one billion Roman-Catholics celebrated the second Millennium AD. The citizens of Jericho celebrated its tenth Millennium on 10/10/2010. They were using the Gregorian calendar and *Anno Domini* chronology. The Christians believed in *The Ten Commandments* or *The Decalogue.* The Jews believe there are many more *Torah* which govern everything that they do including: brewing tea, using phones and switching lights. If they disobey the *Torah* they will be condemned to eternal damnation.

Daniel described a dream about the mythical beasts of the four winds: The fourth, which had ten horns and iron teeth, came before the Ancient of Days. A thousand-thousand ministered to Him; ten thousand times ten stood before Him. The beast was slain but another horn with eyes and a mouth spake pompous words. He that shall speak pompous words against the Most High and shall intend to change the Time and the Law, then the saints shall be given into his hand for a time and times and half a time... And they shall take away his dominion.

When the French revolutionaries adopted a discontinuous ten-day week, Jews, Christians and Muslims accused them of adoring the Antichrist. Their dread of the number ten may go back to the fundamental dispute between the ancient Mesopotamians and Egyptians about whether to use the continuous seven-day week or the discontinuous ten-day week. The Jews say that their continuous week was commanded by *Yahweh.* The Muslims say that their continuous moonth was commanded by *Allah.* The Christians say that their continuous year was commanded by *God.* They all say that their ages, dates and times link them with the past. Nevertheless, Our Human Race urgently needs a link with the future.

Elevens

Every year at the 11th hour of the 11th day of the 11th month those who use the Gregorian calendar and the Benedictine clock stop work for two minutes silence to remember those who fell in both of the World Wars, many that have raged since then and others that are still raging today. Whilst We must always remember those who fought for Our freedom; perhaps that freedom should allow Us to reconsider all of Our systems.

Every year We will remember 11 September 2001 AD when We saw the American Airways flight 11 fly into the 111 story World Trade Center. Then, a few minutes later, We saw exactly the same thing happen again. This event marked the start of the Worldwide War Against Terrorism and a decade later a great democratic uprising throughout the Arab World. Was it because Islam wanted to have the tallest buildings in the World? Was it because the Sunni Muslims wanted to be the closest to *Allah*? Was it because the twin towers looked exactly like the number eleven? Were they connected with the symbolic twin obelisks of ancient Egypt? Why did Osama bin Laden choose this date in the Catholic calendar? Was it because this is One Tut or New Year's Day in the Coptic calendar? Was it because 911 is the emergency telephone number in America? Why did he try to blow-up Los Angeles airport on 1 January 2000 AD? Why did he try to blow-up the Millennium Dome on 1 January 2000 AD? Why did George W. Bush invade Iraq on Friday 21 March 2003 AD? Was this because the vernal equinox is the Shiite or Kurdish New Year? Was it because Friday is the day when Muslims should go to a mosque? Why did bin Laden blow-up Madrid's railways on 11 March 2004 AD? Why did bin Laden blow-up London's underground on 7/7 2005 AD? Why did bin Laden plot to blow up 11 transatlantic airliners in 2006 AD? Why was bin Laden finally assassinated in Pakistan on 1 May 2011 AD? Why was the city of New York on high alert on 11 September 2011 AD? Why was the city of London on high alert on 11 November 2011 AD? Why do the Americans write the date 9/11 whilst the British write 11/9? Why are the fundamentalists obsessed by numerology and calendrology?

The New Years, feasts and fasts in the calendars of one religion may be very special to one fundamentalist; completely meaningless to another. There are many examples, throughout history, of attacks and invasions or ceasefires and armistices on certain auspicious or suspicious dates. Alexander captured Jerusalem whilst the Jews prayed on the Sabbath. The Crusaders captured Jerusalem whilst the Muslims prayed on Friday. The Yom Kippur War almost caught the Israelis napping on holiday. The Catholics and Protestants of Ulster agreed to peace on Good Friday. The Hindus, Sikhs, Buddhists, Jains and Parsees all use different dates. However, the Roman-Catholic calendar is used as the Indian Civic date. India will not become one nation and Earth will not become One World until We all use the same chronology, calendar and clock.

Twelves

Twelve is linked with twelve tribes, twelve disciples, twelve zodiac signs, twelve months, twelve hours of day or night, twelve days of Christmas. The latter are probably the difference between the Lunar and Solar years. The foot was divided by twelve inches, which were divided by twelfths. Some say that all measurements should be based upon number twelve and this is better than ten because it can be divided into four quarters. Astronomers use the twelve zodiac signs as an approximate Sky-chart, whilst they use degrees and decimals to pinpoint the location of Stars. Astrologers use the twelve zodiac signs, although the position of the Stars and Planets can have no effect on Us at Our age, date and time of birth.

A bas relief in the ceiling of an observatory atop the Ptolemaic-Roman temple of *Hathor*, the fertility cow-god, at Dendera shows the Babylonian, Egyptian, Greek and Roman gods or Constellations of the Stellar zodiac. They include twelve gods of the zodiac plus the Roman god *Ophiuchus*. Around the perimeter are the 36 *Decans,* identified by groups of Stars. There are gods of the circumpolar constellations plus Orion and Sirius. This temple was aligned with the dawn rising of the Dog-Star Sirius, which marked the beginning of the year and the inundation of the Nile. It also marked the very end of the ancient Egyptian civilization when the last of the pharaohs: Cleopatra VII and her lover: Mark Anthony finally succumbed to the legions of the first Roman emperor Octavian/Augustus. Cleopatra is depicted on a bas relief paying homage to *Hathor* or *Isis*. However, the ancient Siriac calendar continued and it is still used by the Coptic Church, which had its origins in the Pagan temple at Dendera. The zodiac stone is now in *la Louvre* where it was taken with other booty after Napoleon invaded Egypt in 1798 AD, however, many other artifacts were captured by the British or they went the bottom of the sea when Bonaparte was defeated by Nelson during the Battle of the Nile.

Worldwide Time is a Solar system with no links with the Moon or Stars. It is based on the number ten but could equally well be based on twelve. Its chronology counts in billions, millions, thousands, hundreds, tens. Its calendar is similar to the ones used by the ancient Egyptians and the French revolutionaries, but I knew nothing of them when I devised it. My philosophy of dividing the ten-day *wek* into two halves and sharing most jobs is probably original, because no one else has ever claimed it. My **digital date** has either twelve 30-day *mons* or nine 40-day *anks*. It could have twelve **digital zodiac** signs of 30 days plus 5 or 6 days. If this system started on the vernal equinox in 2000 AD or 000 **WT** the signs would align with the *mons* but they would then slowly regress. The Constellation of Ophiuchus, which might represent the 5 or 6 days, lies on the ecliptic between Sagittarius and Scorpio, but this point in Time will not coincide with the vernal equinox for another six millennia. Will it take this long for **Worldwide Time** to be adopted Worldwide?

Thirteens

A thirteenth Constellation from the stellar zodiac: Ophiuchus, which is a Latinized version of the Greek man-god *Asklepios,* usually shown with a snake coiling around his staff, was used in the Greek tropical zodiac. The snake is the Constellation of Serpens, which lies across Ophiuchus. In Egypt, the 3rd dynasty vizier Imhotep was linked with this Greek god. *Asklepios,* whose parents were *Apollo* and the mortal Coronis, had the power to cure all ills and so the sick were taken to *asklepions* (hospitals). He met his death at the hand of *Zeus* for presuming to raise the dead. His sanctuaries were built at Epidaurus, Delos, Pergamom and Kos. Those who went to be cured saw comedies and tragedies at a theatre. He was worshipped from 800 BC up to the Christian Era of 400 AD. The physicians on Kos formed a guild where Hippocrates (460-370 BC) wrote the Hippocratic Oath, which is still sworn by medical graduates. The staff and snake are in the logos of the British Medical Association and the World Health Organization and are like the double-helix of DNA. The *Asklepios* myth is similar to parts of the legend of Jesus Christ. Constantine laid down the Creed at the Council of Nicaea in 325 AD. He used many myths and legends to construct a composite new religion. His mother founded the Church of the Holy Sepulchre in Jerusalem. It was thought to be on the site of Calvary and the tomb of Gethsemene. Christianity held-up the development of medicine for over a millennium.

Sun-spots take a sunth of about 28 days to rotate relative to the Earth and there are approximately 13 of these sunths to one mean Solar year. These cycles seem to be linked with Human menstruation and gestation. The menstruation period is one sunth and gestation takes ten sunths. It is now thought that positive or negative Solar winds might affect Our personality through Our genes and that it may also affect Our fertility. However, the science of astrogenetics has nothing to do with astrology. Sun-spots seem to be affected by the orbits of Jupiter and lesser Planets. They occur in 11-12 year cycles, affect air, sea and land temperatures and they reached their peak during the year of the Metric Millennium.

The Mayan *tzolkin* calendar was based upon thirteen as well as twenty. And they identified thirteen different Constellations with zodiac glyphs. These thirteen zodiac glyphs may have been linked to thirteen sunths. Four seven-day weeks = one sunth, and thirteen sunths = 364 days. The Teutons added a day to their 13 sunth calendar to make 365 days. Half a sunth was a fortnight and a quarter of a sunth was a senight. It is still said to be used by the witches who meet upon Black Sabbaths. These can coincide with any day of the Judeo-Christian-Muslim week. A coven of witches consists of twelve men or women together with *Satan.* The superstition about thirteen at dinner is linked with the Last Supper. Number 13 is thought to be unlucky and Friday the 13th very unlucky. On Friday 13th November 2015 AD Muslim extremists terrorized Paris.

Umpteens

Every religion postulated a different estimate for the age of this Planet. In the Roman-Catholic Church this guess became the undeniable truth. Anyone who challenged this fundamental truth was branded a heretic. So scholars did little work in this area, until the Age of Enlightenment. Nevertheless, many of them had suspicions that the Earth was far older than six millennia computed by Bishop Usshar and printed in the *Bible*. Geologists realized that Earth was much older than had been supposed but it was Charles Darwin who really set the cat amongst the pigeons. He believed in the Creator and was set for a career in the Church when he went for a trip on the *Beagle* and came back with a bee in his bonnet. On the Galapagos Islands he observed how different finches had evolved. He then realized that evolution must have taken many millions of years. He took many years before publishing his book: *The Origin of Species*. The Church exploded with anger and refers to Humanists as Darwinists.

Hindu astronomers and mathematicians went to extraordinary lengths to calculate the celestial alignments and conjunctions for their festivals. They built huge permanent observatories and took precise astronomical sightings, from several different viewpoints, at exactly the same time. They all came from the priestly *Brahmin* caste who were well versed in sacred knowledge but they had no social contact with the lower castes. Their heavenly observations were continued through many generations. Mathematicians used both the hexadecimal and digital-decimal systems. Their zero-number-decimal system is now used throughout mathematics. Hindu chronology was based on the life of their great Sky-god *Brahma*. The life of *Brahma* is 100 *Brahma* years and each has 360 *Brahma* days. A *kalpa* is a day in the life of *Brahma* and it lasts 4,320,000,000 years. This happens to be an extremely close estimate of the age of Our Planet. They used a calendar of 360 days divided into 12 months of 30 days or three ten-day weeks and they then intercalated from this ideal system. A Solar day was divided into 60 *ghatikas,* then 60 *palas*, then 60 *vipalas*. The Hindu Space system is embodied in the dimensions, orientations and proportions of the sacred temple mandalas, built throughout India. The Hindu caste system continues and is still used by Indian Christians. It has been argued that equality of opportunity is a very wasteful idea and that Britain and USA are supported by a caste of illegal immigrants.

The biggest number in the **Worldwide System** is the age of this Planet. The estimate of 4.55 Gy made fifty years ago has never been challenged. One day it may have to be revised and in this event the chronological part of the **Worldwide System** would have to changed in accordance. In the meantime it is much better than any other system yet devised. Most of Us will only need to use the last three digits in the **global age**. These would continue to align with the *Anno Domini* system, except that the *yer* starts at the global astronomical marker of the vernal equinox.

Generations

Time was counted in generations and *The Bible* tells who begat whom.
Abraham became a father at the age of 99 and lived to be 175 years old.
There is still no archaeological proof that he ever existed but rocks near
Jerusalem and Mecca are said to be where he offered his sons up to *God*.
The family *Bible* was, traditionally, where We could look-up Our roots.
However very few of the younger generation ever read the scriptures now.
In 2013 AD Dr. George Carey, the former Archbishop of Canterbury,
warned that the Church of England could die out in another generation.
During the last generation the tradition of following in father's footsteps
has died-out in Britain and many other ancient beliefs died-out with it.
Many traditional vocations have now been overtaken by Big Business.
Big companies are no longer paternal, so nobody can expect a job for life.
We have to be prepared to change course several times during Our lives.
There are millions of highly qualified young people who cannot find a job.
They are victims of the system and are referred to as the lost generation.
Nevertheless, those born after 1980 AD, called the millennial generation,
are not hidebound by tradition, so they are thinking outside of the box.
They are finding new ways to work with the Internet and Worldwide Web.

As We grow older We gain more experience but We need to slow down.
However, the pace of living always seems to be getting faster and faster.
My great-grandfather saw the coming of the railway train, which moved
faster than a galloping horse but depended upon a fixed steel track-way.
My grandfather saw the coming of the automobile, which needed no rails
and could be driven almost anywhere but depended upon smooth roads.
My father saw the coming of the aircraft, which could fly anywhere but
was restricted by severe weather conditions and needed flat runways.
I saw the coming of the hovercraft which can reach many of the parts
where aircraft, powerboats and automobiles cannot go and could cross
over the English Channel faster than a train could cross under it.
My son saw the coming of the spacecraft, which took men to the Moon.
His son may see men and women living and breeding on another Planet.

Many generations of skilled clockmakers gradually improved the clock.
Yet, very few of them ever thought about the time they were measuring.
Their jobs have now been taken over by fully automated machines.
Computers have passed through many generations during Our lifetimes.
They soon became smaller, faster, cheaper, friendlier and more versatile.
Hovercraft are in their fourth generation and it is interesting that there
are now several sons following their fathers into the hovercraft industry.
Hovercraft suffered because bankers, accountants and politicians did not
understand that the first and second generations were not the ultimate.
Yet, the designers knew that they could make significant improvements,
if only they could be allowed to start again with a clean sheet of paper.
This was the starting point of the logic behind the **Worldwide System.**

Lifetimes

The idea that there is a Heaven and a Hell goes back to Zoroastrianism. This belief, eventually, became part of Judaism, Christianity and Islam. If We are good We will go to Heaven; if We are bad We will go to Hell. We only have one lifetime here on Earth and there is no Heaven nor Hell. However, many still believe that they will have other lives and some are prepared to die for their cause, because they will then go to Heaven. Conversely, it is proven that those who have a just cause will live longer. Humanists have a just cause and they may live longer than *God* fearers.

We are all living longer but should work a shorter day as We grow older. The advances of medical science are having a big effect upon mortality. Yet, some are never ill because they keep fit and have a healthy lifestyle. Statistics show that some people live longer in certain parts of the globe. It is certainly due to living in a state of peace and never going to war. It may be due a diet of fruit, vegetables, whole grains, nuts, cheese, fish, olive oil and red wine or to not smoking, drinking and eating junk food. It may be due to living in a warm climate with a minimum of pollution. It may be due to having an active family or social life and sharing work. **Full-time-job-sharing-as-the-norm** could prove to be very good for Us.

Our electro-mechanical goods seem to have shorter and shorter lifetimes. Every generation of personal computers is much better than the last. This hypothesis has taken me thirty years and ten computers to write. Computer images can now be converted directly into three dimensional shapes and this greatly speeds up tool-making and prototyping so that new generations of many products can quickly be put into production. Crafts like drawing, modelling and tool-making could soon be obsolete. Many crafts were preserved by handing over from father to son but some organizations grew too big for this, so continuity was no longer possible. Bad mistakes were frequently made due to these hire-and-fire methods. Computers help to maintain continuity and they should now ensure that **full-time-job-sharing-as-the-norm** will work as efficiently as possible.

Gold watches were treasured possessions, which often lasted a lifetime. Mass-production made clocks and watches cheaper and more accurate. There are few gold watches sold in the shops today and it is no longer traditional to present one to an employee after a lifetime of service. We are so used to throwing things away after a few years that a new generation of **decimal time** clocks and watches would soon be accepted. It is so easy to design and tool-up for a new product today that clock and watch manufactures would soon be able to cope with the demand. However, calendar, planner and diary manufacturers could soon go bust, because their **digital date** products would be exactly the same every *yer*. It took well over two hundred years to replace the foot with the metre but it may only take a decade to replace the metre with the *han*.

Birthdays

During Our first year of life Our age is zero - We keep on growing and
learning until We are about thirty and then We start to physically and
mentally decline, whilst We are still gaining very valuable experience.
It is important to cram in as much as possible during Our formative
years and it is proven that Time spent in kindergartens is worthwhile.
It is vital that outdated ideas are weeded out, so by counting everything
in tens We would be able to save a great deal of Time and learn more.
We share the same physical aging processes but can reach the peak of
mental performance at any age, so great ideas occur to anyone, anytime.
Exceptional men can sometimes write symphonies at nine and ninety.
Exceptional women have been known to give birth from six to sixty.
We all remember the date of Our birthdays in one particular calendar.
So changing to another calendar could be a very disruptive procedure.
Yet, anyone who moves to another part of the globe has this problem.
Our given names reveal the nationality and religion of Our parents.
Many migrants adopt new names as they settle down in another state.

Britain became a socio-economic welfare state after the end of WW2.
Its laws prohibit discrimination against race and gender but not age.
The official retirement age is now 65 for men and 60 for women but
many people have been retiring earlier as computers take over their jobs.
Company pensions were originally meant to be untaxed perks but they
are now causing redundancies because they cost too much to service.
The funds, which grew rapidly in boom years, were used to shed jobs.
Many of the jobless are using-up their savings before they can retire.
The older generation are living longer but, despite better conditions and
medical progress, mine may not, for it is proven that retirement kills.
During my own working lifetime the ratio of pensioners to workers has
increased from two to four and this is causing a geriatric time-bomb.
Successive governments have failed to tackle this enormous problem.
As soon as New Labour got in they plundered private pension funds.
The Tories promised to equalize the retirement age at 60 by 2000 AD.
But there were not enough state pension funds to honour this promise.
So the current Lib-Con coalition has abandoned compulsory retirement.
We must keep going but Our workload must taper-off as We grow older.

Many states have tried to prevent bankruptcy by printing more money.
This was Franklin D. Roosevelt's quick solution to the Great Depression.
Other Presidents followed suit, so the USA has its biggest deficit ever.
New York went bankrupt because it paid its cops 2/3 of their salary on
retirement after 20 years of service; they might live for another 40 years
and so could receive more for doing nothing than for doing something.
An overwhelming financial and demographic crisis is looming throughout
Our World and it has all been brought about by the ravages of **Time**.
Worldwide Time would allow all the work to be shared by all of the ages.

Anniversaries

Counting years in tens, hundreds and thousands, since a birth, a death or another historic event always seems to have some special importance. Silver and gold are now given on 25 and 50 year wedding anniversaries. Some say that it was Mrs. Beeton, who started this expensive tradition. We commemorate the start or finish of wars with special years or days; although each side may have used a different chronology and calendar. We commemorate the birth or death of famous politicians, economists, philosophers, scientists, engineers, inventors, artists, artistes or authors. We commemorated the steamship, horseless carriage, flying machine with a centenary and will do so for the aircushion vehicle and spaceship, in the same way that most of the various religions commemorate their founders, prophets, gurus or saints by red letter years, days and hours.

Every religion or sect is based upon a chronology, calendar and clock linked with the birth or death of its founder or another historic event. Nevertheless, in most cases, the exact age, date and time were unknown. In several cases the calendar year started on the vernal equinox when day and night are equal but the start of a day varied from dawn to dusk or from midday to midnight and these times vary from place to place. The mechanical clock allowed time to be unified throughout each state. The electronic watch allowed time to be unified throughout the globe. The telegraph, telephone, television, Internet and global position system allow the age, date and time to be unified everywhere on Planet Earth. Mankind's inventiveness could soon supersede many religious dogmas. Whether this progress will lead to the end of religion remains to be seen.

Jewish *Anno Mundi* chronology is based on the Creation on Monday 7th October 3761 BC but some say this was the age and date of the Flood. The year and day of the birth and death of Moses and of the Exodus are unknown but the festival of Passover is a Lunar and Solar anniversary. The second Millennium since the birth of Christ was very special and holy to all Christians, although the year, day and time were not known. So its sects celebrate with different chronologies, calendars and clocks. The age and date of the Crucifixion and Resurrection are also unknown. Yet, these movable feasts and fasts were linked to the Jewish Passover. The year and day of the birth of Mohammed are unknown, however, the year and day that he fled from Mecca to Medina is the basis for both the Lunar chronology of the Sunnis and the Solar chronology of the Shiites. The Badi chronology and calendar are based upon the vernal equinox in 1844 AD when their religion was founded and their day starts at Sunset. However, they have nineteen 'months' of nineteen days plus 4 or 5 days. Humanists borrowed the Roman-Catholic chronology, calendar and clock as they have no year, date or time when their secular movement began. They could use the chronology, calendar and clock explained in this book, which is based upon the age, orbit and spin of Our Planet Earth.

Jubilees

Pharaoh's coronation was celebrated at the great *Sed* or jubilee festival, after thirty years of his reign, and followed by others every three years. Jubilees were also a time of great rejoicing throughout ancient Greece. The Sadducees represented the Hellenistic influence in the Holy Land and they were responsible for keeping the *Book of Jubilees* up-to-date. This was a perpetual diary in which they recorded every major event for posterity, so that it could later be celebrated on the appropriate day. The fiftieth anniversary of important events such as the end of a war, the birth of a leader or the start of a reign were especially important. We now think of jubilees as being special occasions reserved for royalty. British queens are far more likely to celebrate their jubilees than kings.

Queen Elizabeth I sat on the throne of England and Ireland in 1558 AD. She ruled alone for 45 years but she did not reach her Golden Jubilee. She established Protestantism as the state religion and then witnessed a flowering of culture, especially in the arts, crafts, theatre and literature. William Shakespeare made numerous references to the passage of Time. She presented chiming clocks to churches to call the faithful to prayer. She resisted pressure from the Pope to adopt the Gregorian calendar. Her Royal Navy used the measurement of Time and Space to build the British Empire and repelled the armada from Roman-Catholic Spain. Her last words were: "All of my possessions for a moment of time."

Queen Victoria succeeded the throne in 1837 AD and had the longest reign in British history: she lived through both the American and the industrial revolutions, then celebrated her Golden Jubilee in 1887 AD. During her reign Britain reached the summit of its power and prosperity. Charles Dickens highlighted the poverty that still remained in the land. Steam gave Great Britain its military, industrial and commercial power. During her 64 year reign calendars, clocks and watches were essential and the Imperial System was imposed throughout her British Empire. She celebrated her Diamond Jubilee and reviewed a great fleet in 1897 AD. Her last words were: "Oh that peace may come. Bertie."

Queen Elizabeth II succeeded the throne of Great Britain in 1952 AD. She reviewed the Royal Navy's great fleet off Portsmouth in 1953 AD. She celebrated her Silver Jubilee and reviewed a small fleet in 1977 AD. She celebrated the Golden Jubilee of her accession throughout 2002 AD. But her royal yacht had been retired so there was no review of the fleet. On the bicentenary of the victorious sea battle of Trafalgar in 2005 AD she reviewed an international fleet of ships but very few British ones. She is now the oldest monarch to ever sit upon the throne in Britain. She did not celebrate her Diamond Jubilee with a fleet review in 2012 AD. Instead there was a waterborne pageant along the Thames in London. There were one thousand vessels of all kinds - including one hovercraft.

Ages

Human development has been marked by many different Ages brought about by geological, scientific, technological, industrial and social change: The Geological Ages, The Ice Ages, The Stone Age, The Bronze Age, The Iron Age, The Zodiacal Ages, The Dark Ages, The Agricultural Age, The Printing Age, The Scientific Age, The Industrial Age, The Steam Age, The Coal Age, The Gas Age, The Oil Age, The Electric Age, The Nuclear Age, The Automobile Age, The Air Age, The Space Age, The Aircushion Age, The Radio Age, The Television Age, The Video Age, The Computer Age...

In ancient times the four seasons divided Our lifetimes into Four Ages: Spring=Childhood, Summer=Youth, Autumn=Maturity, Winter=Old Age. The Christian Solar calendar also marks this seasonal cycle of renewal. Yet, Christ's birth and death are not remembered in spring and winter. The Church fathers did not want to follow the Pagan Age precedence. The Christian way of looking at the Human life cycle is to divide it into: The Seven Ages of Man - probably based upon the Pagan seven-day week. The Sunni Muslim Lunar calendar is not linked with temperate seasons. The Shiite Muslim Solar calendar is linked with the temperate seasons.

Plato wrote about Golden, Silver, Brazen, Heroic and Iron [current] Ages. He described regular global catastrophes, which terminated each Age. The *Old Testament* book: *Daniel* and *New Testament* book: *Revelations* divided Time into millennia and they also warned of global catastrophes. It now seems that there have indeed been a series of global catastrophes. This has been proven by excavations and boreholes around the globe. *Anno Domini* was not widely used until the holy reign of Charlemagne (742-814 AD) when it was introduced to suppress chronologies that were fuelling apocalyptic predictions about the last days of Our Planet Earth. Abbot Joachim of Fiore (1135-1202 AD) popularized the idea of dividing history into Great Ages corresponding to members of the Holy Trinity. We are now in his Age of the Spirit, which inspired a godly society and led to the expectation that Jesus Christ would return at this Millennium. Korean Christians erected gigantic neon crosses to show him the way. We may have to wait several decades for him or her to come forward. However, on the other hand, We are now in the Age of Enlightenment. All religion may eventually be superseded by logic and common sense.

The Age of Our Planet is considered to be about 4,550,000,000 years. The Age of Our Civilization is considered to be about 12,000 years. These are incorporated in the chronological part of the **Worldwide Time**. This is called **global age** and was 4,550,012,000 at the last Millennium. It can be abbreviated to 000 and then counts-up at every vernal equinox. The Millennium gave Us all a chance to look backwards and forwards at Our great Human achievements and mistakes, which are called Eras, and at great Natural changes or phenomena, which are called Epochs.

Epochs

These are longer periods, for example: the Dinosaur or Human Epochs. Our Human Race could be wiped-out just as quickly as the dinosaurs. We could all meet Our end for exactly the same reason and the ancients have given Us plenty of warning if We care to read their messages to Us. Every civilization had a different myth about creation and destruction. These may have been based upon the experience of a global catastrophe. Indeed, Our Human Race nearly became extinct one million years ago. Many warnings have been sent to Us by people who could not write. Their graphic images seem to speak with the same eternal language:

A serpent symbol is etched upon rocks throughout the ancient World. Alongside there are often 'wheels' with four spokes indicating the four cardinal directions, the four seasons or the four solstices and equinoxes. Yet, they are usually out of alignment with the true cardinal directions.

The Chinese calculated that all of the Planets align every 138,240 years. And after a *chi* of 31,920 years everything returns to its original state. Their chronology, calendar and clock are based upon a mythical dragon.

The Hindus believe that there are four universal *yugas* in a great cycle. We are now in their dying fourth Universe, which they call the *kaliyuga*.

The Egyptians remembered and wrote about a First Time when their land emerged from a Great Flood, their Sky-gods were forever having battles and a serpent was mounted upon the two crowns of the pharaoh.

The Mesopotamians venerated a Great Year of 3600 years called a *sar*. In a Babylonian legend *Marduk* slayed the primordial dragon *Taimat*.

A Greek legend remembers a cataclysm which nearly wiped Us all out. *Phaethon* son of *Helios* crashed through the Solar System in his chariot causing the destruction of a Planet, [now the asteroid belt] orbital and revolutionary changes to other Planets or moons and Earth's axis to tilt.

The Mesoamericans believed in the feathered serpent-god *Quetzalcoatl*. Many Maya and Aztec temples have images of serpents built into them. Their calendar cycle is based upon five Great Years of over 5,000 years. The pyramids of the Sun and Moon in the ancient city of Teotihuacan in Mexico are out of alignment with the cardinal points by over 15 degrees.

The Aboriginals left signs on their rocks that this Planet was in turmoil, some 6,000 years ago, when a sea serpent arose to swallow their land.

The *Heavenly Bodies* were closer than for 6,000 years in 2000 AD. Did this event portend the extreme weather conditions that ensued?

Eras

Ideological periods are called Eras: the Egyptian Era, the Greek Era, the Roman Era, the Napoleonic Era, the Nazi Era or the Marxist Era. As we pass the 2nd Millennium of the Christian Era some say it will end; others believe that its license will be renewed and a recent survey showed that 100M Americans are expecting the second coming of Christ. Nevertheless, others are expecting the End of Time, which they take to mean the end of civilization as we know it or the end of Our World. Civilization seems to be falling apart when We watch with horror on TV the tragic result of apocalyptic bombs exploding from New York to Kabul. Religion is still the fundamental cause of millions of murders every year.

At the termination of the first millennium AD all was doom and gloom. Many believed that the World would soon end with the Apocalypse. Soon after this, in 1054 AD, the Great Schism occurred in the Christian religion when the Church leaders disagreed about the date of Easter. In 1095 AD Pope Urban II raised a rabble and the first Crusade began. Christians hated Jews for the death of their savior Jesus Christ: a Jew. Much of Jerusalem, holy city of the Jews, Christians and Muslims was destroyed, with its coexisting Jewish, Christian and Muslim inhabitants. Jews, Orthodox Christians and Muslims still hate Catholics for this orgy, which even gave absolution to those who committed cannibalism.

The 20th century AD began with a great surge of optimism but this soon proved to be short lived as the Old World Order crumbled and fell apart. Bismarck (1815-1898 AD) said a World War would start in the Balkans. He was right about WW1 and WW2 and he could be right about WW3. Hitler (1889-1945 AD) promised his 3rd Reich would last 1,000 years. Churchill (1874-1965 AD) said: If the British Empire and Commonwealth last for a thousand years men will still say: This was their finest hour. Pope Pius XII did nothing to stop 6M Jews being brutally slaughtered. Pope John Paul II did very little to stop ethnic cleansing in the Balkans. The Crusades are still being fought one thousand years after they began.

We are entering the third millennium AD without very much optimism. Great public and private enterprises are failing throughout the globe. The year 2000 AD could mark the top of a learning curve beyond which We cannot think of anything better; yet, many people feel that there should be a better way of organizing Ourselves, if only We could find it. It is up to Us: whether We then stop dead, begin Our descent to oblivion or stay on the plateau by very careful management of Our population, Our industry, Our commerce, Our economy and, especially, Our Time. This Millennium marks the end of the Piscean Age and the Modern Era. Will it mark the End of History? The End of *God* ? The End of **Time**? Humanists use BCE or ACE to mean: before or after the Common Era. Will We soon be using **WE** to mean: We are in the **Worldwide Era**?

Knowledge

The Book of the Dead (2500 BC) is the oldest religious text in the World. Written on the walls of the inner sanctum of several pyramids, it consists of a series of utterances about the death and rebirth of *Osiris* as *Horus*. This sacred knowledge told the rite of passage of one pharaoh to the next and the afterlife of the dead pharaohs as Constellations in the night Sky. Writing permitted Egypt to change from a Lunar calendar to a Solar one with 36 ten-day weeks plus a remainder of 5 days, and later a leap-day.

The *Dead Sea Scrolls* and *The Nag Hammadi Texts* were hidden from the Romans who used higgledy-piggledy calendar months and 8-day weeks. They expand Our knowledge of Essene and Gnostic sects, who converted some Jews and Egyptians to 'Christianity' well before the birth of Christ. Essenism had its origins when the Seleucid dynasty ruled Mesopotamia. The monastic Essene sect remembered their Teacher of Righteousness; not a miracle worker with a virgin birth and reappearances after death. They adopted a Solar calendar with a discontinuous seven-day week. Gnosticism, the possession of ancient knowledge, was kept by hermits in Egypt who used a Solar calendar with a discontinuous ten-day week. We have only discovered these calendrical facts during the past few years because the Romans tried to destroy all traces of previous civilizations. The Roman-Catholics also tried to destroy all traces of previous faiths.

Ptolemy's library at Alexandria was (accidentally?) burned to the ground by Julius Caesar but rebuilt by Antony and Cleopatra in the Serapeum. It contained many documents about the origins of the seven-day week, astronomical records and the foundations of science and mathematics. Early Christian texts were burned by Theophilius in the 4th century AD because they were considered by the new Roman Church to be heresies. When Muslim conqueror Amrb ibn al-As entered the library in 642 AD he asked the Caliph Omar what he should do with all of the books: 'If what is written agrees with the Book of *Allah* they are not required; if it disagrees with the Book they are not desired, destroy them therefore.' Those that were not destroyed are one of Our main links with the past.

UNESCO has recently built an enormous new library in Alexandria. Libraries are now free, so knowledge is no longer the property of an elite. The fibrous roots of the Tree of Knowledge have entered many homes and offices in the form of a glass filament the size of a Human hair. Computers can now memorize every book that has ever been written. It will soon be possible to search every library from your own home. Information Technology is now available to everyone and will encourage all of Us to use the same language, script and measurement system. Books and websites represent the accumulated sum of Our knowledge. Cosmologists are now discovering many hidden secrets of the Universe. Nevertheless, a few of them consider that some of them are unknowable.

Wisdom

Artists, sculptors and architects, throughout the ages, have incorporated esoteric wisdom into their one, two, three and four dimensional works. Religious drawings and paintings incorporate many hidden meanings. Sculptures embody myths about gods, goddesses, beasts and mortals. The designs, dimensions, proportions and orientations of many buildings reveal hidden wisdom about the measurement of both Time and Space. Stone henges and pyramids appear to be monuments, temples or tombs, but they were also observatories, chronologies, calendars and clocks. The observation of the Sky was the foundation of science and religion. The Sun, Moon, Planets and Stars controlled the ages, dates and times. They also became the Sky-gods who were worshipped with *Mother Earth*. We can now, after twelve millennia of civilization, use Our accumulated wisdom, knowledge, intelligence or common sense to build a new system.

The three great monotheistic religions of today have many Pagan origins, but these have been suppressed and are only now being rediscovered. They are all based spiritually, temporally and spatially upon Sky-gods. The orientation of many henges was towards a Sun-god and Moon-god. The orientation of the Egyptian temples was towards their Sky-gods. The orientation of the great temple in Jerusalem is towards the West. The orientation of the great cathedrals of Europe is towards the East. The orientation of the great mosques of Asia is towards holy Mecca. The major axis of the *Kaaba* in Mecca is oriented towards the heliacal rising of Canopus, the brightest Star in the southern Sky, and its minor axis is oriented towards midsummer Sun-rise and midwinter Sun-set. The Latin word: *sophia,* means: wisdom and Hagia Sophia, Constantinople, the greatest basilica in the Roman Empire, eventually became a mosque. Justinian the Great had it built to align with the four cardinal directions. The Muslim Ottoman sultans added minarets, the words of the prophet and an angled pulpit so that the imam could face the direction of Mecca. Praying towards Mecca is one of Mohammed's *Five Pillars of Wisdom.*

Great mounds and pyramids, built in ancient times all over the globe, have given-up some of their secrets but probably have many more to tell. They symbolize measurement, management, government of Space-Time. The pyramid symbol is used upon the great seal of the United States. It is reproduced on every dollar bill and also used by the Freemasons. They are linked with the Knights Templar who sought ancient wisdom. The Roman-Catholic Church decided they were too rich and powerful and so they were annihilated on Friday the 13th of October in 1307 AD. The Roman-Catholic Church is still very powerful and it works with the Central Intelligence Agency to overthrow regimes it does not agree with. Some 95% of Americans still believe in *God* and only 5% are Humanists, so they will probably be the last to discard the US measurement system, *Anno Domini* chronology, Gregorian calendar and Benedictine clock.

Intelligence

Astronomical intelligence sometimes helped to win battles and wars. Herodotus (485-425 BC) wrote that on May 28 in 585 BC the troops of Lydian King Alyattes defeated the Medes army at the battle of river Halys because they knew that there was going to be a Solar eclipse on that day. The Medes army fled from the battlefield as the midday Sky darkened, because they thought that the Sun-god was on the side of the Lydians. This event led to the Greeks leaving the land that now belongs to Turkey.

Conventional wisdom says that We are more intelligent than those who built Stonehenge or the Great Pyramid but they had fewer distractions. Whether they were built with the knowledge of the exact size of the Earth and the exact length of the year is open to question but their architects must have had very good reasons to build them with a particular size. Ctesias (416-476 BC) wrote that the walls of Babylon were exactly 360 furlongs in circumference, as many as there were days in their year. The number 360 was also used for Babylonian angles and directions. The Egyptian calendar year was originally 360 days long and was divided into twelve 30-day months or 36 ten-day *decades* without a remainder. The five remainder days were added later and, ultimately, a leap day too. The ancient Chinese zodiac appears to have had 360 days at some point. When it was extended to 365.25 days the circle was divided by this too. The Hindu Solar year consisted of 360 days or 12 months of 30 days. The Mayan or Aztec *tun* was 360 good days : five bad days were added plus an extra bad day every fourth year when everyone stopped work. The Inca calendar also had 360 days or twelve 30-day months plus five unlucky days and an extremely unlucky leap-day every fourth year. How much simpler Our World would be if there were 360 days in a year.

Scientific research now shows that the forces of gravity and magnetism, the motions of the winds and tides, and movements within Our Planet are gradually causing its spin to slow down and its orbit to get smaller. However, it may be wrong to assume that Earth's orbit, spin and tilt are changing gradually, for it may have had a close encounter with a rogue Planet since the most ancient of all the Stone Age monuments were erected and they have only survived because they were so massive. It is certain that the gravitational pull of the other Planets perturbs the orbit of Earth so that it either moves nearer to or further from the Sun. Similarly, the Sun is gravitationally pulled by the motions of the Planets. Global warming may be due to Solar forces as well as Our own stupidity. We are certainly using-up Our vital resources faster than ever before. Our greatest resources are not oil, gas, coal, water but Time and Space. We are wasting them because some still believe that the seven-day week and its Sabbath were designed by *God* but, if this is so, *He* is not green. Surveys show that very few of Us with a high IQ level believe in *God;* whilst most of Us with a low IQ tend to be extremely superstitious.

Truths

Beliefs that are repeated over and over again eventually become 'truths'.
In Egypt: the eyes of *Amen*, who knew the truth, were the Sun and Moon.
The measurements of Space and Time were considered to be sacred.
The vertical, horizontal and right-angle were venerated as the truth.
The Sun-dial is still said to be more accurate than the electronic clock.
The larger the pyramid, obelisk or temple the more accurate it became.
Monoliths became monuments to monarchs and yet they were originally
used to determine the length of the year and the divisions of the day.
Pharaoh regarded obelisks as the truth and used them to align temples.
Caesar prized Pharaoh's obelisks and erected classic columns or pillars.
The Pope usurped and consecrated several obelisks, columns or pillars.
War memorials all over the globe, usually in the shape of an obelisk,
are often inscribed with the dates of battles and the names of the dead.
The Freemasons honor two pillars of wisdom in King Solomon's Temple.
One represents a spiritual messiah; the other represents a temporal one.
Some say that Solomon was another name for Pharaoh Amen-hotep III.
Kings still erect obelisks to mark their reigns and their divine authority.
Presidents are sometimes commemorated in the same Time-honored way.
George Washington was a Freemason who secretly formed the USA elite.
The City of Washington was laid out using esoteric Masonic methods.
The Washington Monument is the greatest stone obelisk in the World.

The Great Pyramid and the El Giza plateau still contain many secrets.
A door at the end of the shaft pointing to Sirius, discovered in 1992 AD,
was pierced by a robot in 2002 AD but behind it there was another door.
What these small, secret doors were used for remains a great mystery.
It is the air shaft from the Queen's Chamber through which the *ka* of
the dead queen (identified with *Isis*) passed on its way up to Sirius.
A similar air shaft from the King's Chamber through which the *ka* of the
dead pharaoh (identified with *Osiris*) passed on its way up to Orion.
The myth of *Osiris, Isis* and *Horus* is similar to Joseph, Mary and Jesus.
Some scholars say that Jesus, who lived in Egypt, was the last pharaoh.
However, history tells Us that Cleopatra's suicide ended that dynasty.
Cleopatra's 'needles' symbolize the digital week and the decimal day.
They were moved and erected in London and New York by Freemasons.
The eye is used by the Freemasons and it is on the almighty dollar bill.
Some say that Freemasonry secretly controls both the USA and the UK.

The obelisk has become a symbol of power, permanence and greatness.
It was a development of the ben-ben or phoenix pillar and the pyramid.
Charles Windsor has decided that he does not want to be Charles III.
He would prefer to be known as Mountbatten-Windsor or George VII.
At the Metric Millennium he erected a classical column at Highgrove,
surmounted by a golden phoenix bird symbolizing: The Rebirth of Time.
Are We about to see the rebirth of the digital week and the decimal day?

Testaments

The Old Testament is a collection of many ancient myths and legends, written down in c500 BC and believed by Jews, Christians and Muslims. *The New Testament* is a collection of many modern myths and legends, written down in c300 AD and believed by many of the Christian sects. However, there is no historical proof that any of these events happened.

The Garden of Eden may lay near the source of the Tigris and Euphrates. The legend of Adam and Eve may mark the beginning of civilization. There is no archaeological proof that Noah and his ark ever existed. There were many legends of a Great Flood and one certainly occurred. We have no firm proof that Abraham, Ishmael and Isaac ever existed. These patriarchs may have been invented by the Jews and the Arabs. We have no firm proof that Israel, Jacob, Joseph, Moses or Joshua lived. There is some archeological evidence that the Israelites lived in Egypt, by choice, but not that they were led by someone called Moses, nor that they crossed the Red Sea, nor that they wandered in Sinai for 40 years. The evidence that Moses went to the top of Mount Sinai to talk to *God*: the Ark of the Covenant with *The Ten Commandments*, has been lost.

The Bible says that the treasures of The Temple were plundered by an unknown pharaoh called Shishak and some think he was Ramesses II. Some say that they were taken to Elephantine Isle on the Nile at Aswan, where a Jewish temple has been found dating back to when it was lost, it was taken up the Blue Nile to a monastery on an island in Lake Tana and it is now hidden inside a Christian sanctuary at Axum in Ethiopia. No one is allowed to see inside there, because it probably does not exist. Others say it was buried under The Temple, discovered by the Knights Templar and is now buried again under Rosslyn chapel near Edinburgh. No one is allowed to excavate this strange site and so it remains a secret. Tales of Solomon and Sheba, David and Goliath and the Promised Land were probably concocted during their captivity in Babylon in order to persuade the King to let the Hebrews, Israelites or Jews return home. The book of *Isaiah* foretells that a son from the house of King David would come, at a Great Year after the Flood, to save them from slavery, that he would be put to death and that he would later be resurrected. Whether their expected Messiah ever arrived is still open to question. Yet, billions still believe that he did and that he was Jesus the Christ.

We are now quite certain that Our World was not created in seven days. We can now explain creation, evolution, floods, tsunamis, earthquakes, volcanoes, Bright Stars, and everything about Us, which We previously thought to be mystical, magical or strange, in logical scientific terms. The miracles can now be explained as Natural phenomena or chicanery. There are no tablets of stone telling Us to use a Mystic seven-day week. We are totally free to choose any size of week that suits Us best today.

Gospels

There were many *God Spells* but four were selected for the *New Testament* by Bishop Athanasius of Alexandria (296-373AD) because most of the others did not conform with the belief that Jesus was the son of *God*. Most were destroyed but some were found at Nag Hammadi in 1945 AD. These *Gnostic Gospels* show that men and women were considered equal and that Christianity was based upon sharing work and sharing wealth. We do not know who the authors: Matthew, Mark, Luke and John were. Their gospels were probably written several generations after the event. Matthew lists 28 generations from David to Jesus but Luke lists 43. Mark probably wrote the *Acts of the Apostles* and it is likely that Paul, who never met Jesus, was the one who turned him into the Messiah. His ability to preach and write in both Greek and Latin spread the Word. If the Gnostics had had their way all Christians would now be using the ancient Egyptian calendar with its 30-day months and its 10-day weeks. The Copts still use 30-day months, however, they now use 7-day weeks.

The 7-day week was forgotten when Jerusalem was destroyed by Rome, causing the Jews and Christians to be scattered throughout the globe. It was restored three centuries later by Constantine the Great when he reunited the Roman Empire and ruled that the Julian calendar and the continuous 7-day week must be used by all of the new Roman-Catholics. However, he continued to worship the old Pagan gods until his deathbed. Subsequent emperors returned to Pagan beliefs and Christianity might have been forgotten, instead of becoming the greatest religion on Earth. By 321 AD, the 7-day week had been adopted by the Byzantine Empire and the Lord's day had been moved to the Mithraist Sun-god's day. It was regarded as the first day of the week and was also the week-day on which Jesus was believed by Christians to have arisen from the dead. However, the resurrection was not part of the gospel according to Mark and was probably added by scribes to make the religion more mystical. The gospels were ratified by Pope Innocent I in the early fifth century AD.

The Roman-Catholic Church often refers to Sunday as the eighth day. Judaea was a Roman province, with an 8-day week, by the era of Jesus, raised in Egypt with a 10-day week, then in Galilee with a 7-day week. Was he trying to clarify this temporal confusion, which included many other chronological, calendrical and horological options and opinions?

The Sabbath was made for Man and not Man for the Sabbath. (Mark 2:27)

In other words: the 7-day week and its one special day for rest was designed to suit Our own needs and if We want to change it to one of another size, to suit Our changed circumstances, it is alright with *God*. Our circumstances have changed radically since the gospels were written. Scribes have been replaced by word processors with desktop printers. We can all now achieve the ethos of sharing work and sharing wealth.

Scrolls

Many of *The Dead Sea Scrolls* were from around the lifetime of Jesus. They were hidden when Herod's Temple was razed by Titus in 70 AD. Most of them were found by Bedouin tribesmen in caves at Qumran soon after the state of Israel was created in 1948 AD but the caves were in Jordan before the West Bank was annexed during the Six-Day War. Many more Essene texts are thought to be hidden in bank vaults or still buried in caves, which have not yet been discovered or excavated. In 1991 AD it was revealed that the team of theologians who examined the *Scrolls*, in Jerusalem, had suppressed very important information. This information relates to the very period of the schism which divided the Christians from the Jews during the Roman occupation of Judaea. The ancient *Book of Enoch*, which describes the Great Flood, was left out of the *Old Testament* but fragments of it survived in the *Scrolls*.

The Teacher of Righteousness featured in several Scrolls of the Essene community who lived at Qumran, which is some 30 Km from Jerusalem. They indicate that their leader was trying to add to and clarify Moses' Laws of the Covenant rather than trying to start again with new ones. The Essenes used many proto-Christian ideas like baptism, communion, sharing possessions, money, bread and wine for 160 years before 1 BC. According to Jewish chronology this was a Sumerian *sar* of 3,600 years after Noah's Great Flood and so their Messiah was expected about then. The Essenes used their own Solar calendar rather than the traditional Judaic Lunar-Solar one, Greek Lunar-Solar one or Roman Solar one, which was imposed on the Roman Empire by Augustus Caesar in 7 BC.

Saul may have been an 'agent' for the Romans, since he was a Gentile. He came from Tarsus in the province of Syria, so had Roman citizenship. However, Tarsus was originally part of Alexander's former Greek empire. The Scrolls indicate that Saul's conversion to Christianity on the road to Damascus was really conversion to Essenism at the Qumran monastery. Many new religions were in competition in Rome at that time and so Saul or Paul embellished the story of Jesus, like any salesman tends to do. Jesus became the Messiah, the King of the Jews, the son of *God*, Christ. Many of the miracles, including the virgin birth and the resurrection, are thought to be the inventions of Paul, much to the chagrin of James the Just, the brother of Jesus and leader of the Essenes in Jerusalem. There is no evidence that Simon called Peter ever went to Rome. That story is probably an invention by the Roman-Catholic Church, to give the Romans more power when the *New Testament* was edited.

The four *Gospels* differ in many details, like the date of the Last Supper. The fifty *Gnostic Gospels* indicate that John the Baptist was the Messiah and that Jesus, a priest of the Nazorean cult, was one of his followers. They were discovered in a jar at Nag Hammadi in Egypt in 1945 AD.

Translations

There have been many translations, explanations and interpretations of *The Old & New Testaments, The Dead Sea Scrolls, The Gnostic Gospels.* There is still no historical proof that someone called Jesus ever existed. He may have been a mixture of ancient myths, legends and predictions. He may have been the rightful successor to the ancient kingdom of David. He may have been the rightful successor to the priesthood of the Temple. He may have been a freedom fighter against the iron rule of the Romans. He may have never claimed to be immortal, divine or the son of *God.* There are very few records of that period and they may have been edited. Josephus Flavius (38-100 AD) the author of *History of the Jewish War* was a Jewish Zealot who later defected to the Pagan Romans and so his record of the events during that period may be biased or tampered with. We know that Herod and Pilot existed but there is still no trace of Jesus.

There was an obvious need for one language, script and religion in the Roman Empire as well as one chronology, calendar, clock, rule and coin. Many different years, months, weeks, days and parts of days were used in Jerusalem during the era of Jesus and some of them still are today. Pharisees had continuous 7-day weeks, Sadducees had 3 weeks/moonth, Essenes had a discontinuous 7-day week, Romans had an 8-day week as well as their *kalends, ides* and *nones,* which counted backwards, and the Romano-Egyptians still had their discontinuous 10-day *decade.* These temporal differences were the root cause of many old disputes; and spatial differences, in the form of rules, weights, measures or coins, caused many heated disputes in the marketplace - and they still do today.

Christianity took a millennium to become the principal European religion, another millennium to spread around the globe, yet it is still not catholic. The Roman Empire then the Holy Roman Empire tried to ensure that Latin became the Universal language but only the priests understood it. The invention of the printing press by Johann Gutenberg of Strasbourg in 1440 AD broke the power of Latin clerics and scribes over the masses. The first English *Bible* was written by William Tyndale (1494-1536 AD). He was strangled and burnt at the stake for calling *God*: 'It' but many of his passages were later used in the King James I/VI authorized version. This was the very foundation of English language, literature and culture. English has now replaced Latin as the Universal language of Christianity.

Although the whole World now uses the same continuous 7-day week, Muslims go to mosque on Fridays, Jews go to synagogue on Saturdays, Christians go to church on Sundays, however, most of the other religions do not have a special day in the 7-day week for rest, recreation or prayer. The many different holy days and holidays still divide Our Human Race. We will only achieve One World when We share the same language, the same script, the same currency, the same Time and the same Space.

Creation

The first five books in *The Bible* were supposed to be written by Moses, but since they describe his birth and death, this seems to be unlikely. They were written by Ezra, the first rabbi, during his captivity in Babylon. This was about a millennium after the lifetime of someone called Moses. Many Jews, Christians and Muslims still believe that *Yahweh/God/Allah* created everything in six days and then took a rest on the seventh day. So they must do likewise, as written in Moses' *Ten Commandments,* which were placed in the Ark of the Covenant and kept in the Temple. However, the Ark of the Covenant and the *Ten Commandments* were lost. *God* has always been believed to be the measurer of the Cosmos and, although images of *Him* are forbidden in Moses' *Ten Commandments,* *He* is portrayed holding a pair of compasses or counting upon *His* digits. Michelangelo's painting in the Sistine Chapel shows *Him* creating Adam. On the contrary, We created *Him* in Our own image.

We have known about Darwin's theories of evolution for over a century. We can now be sure that Adam and Eve were not created but evolved. Some now believe in Intelligent Design, since nobody can yet deduce the full story of the origin and evolution of all the species on Planet Earth. This is currently causing conflict between scientists and theologians, especially in the Bible Belt of the USA, where George W. Bush grew up. He supports the idea of Intelligent Design and is backed by the Vatican. A global row is now brewing about what Our children should be taught. If taught evolution but not creation and freethinking but not dogma, they may even question their chronology, calendar, clock, zone and rule. We can create one measurement, management and government system. However, We must share all the work - as monks did in the monasteries. We must have regular days for rest, recreation and reflection but these do not have to be taken together and religion is no longer necessary. All men, women, days and parts of days were created equal in value.

Most cosmologists now agree that the Universe began with a Big Bang, some 13.82 Gy ago and that Our Solar System began some 4.55 Gy ago. Stephen Hawking now concludes that the Big Bang was the inevitable consequence of the laws of physics and that it is no longer necessary to invoke *God* to 'light the blue touch paper and set the Universe going'. In his book *The Grand Design* he sets out a comprehensive thesis that the scientific framework leaves no room for a deity and he deconstructs Isaac Newton's belief that the Universe could not have risen out of chaos, due to the mere Laws of Nature but must have been created by a deity. Stephen Hawking held the same prestigious post as Sir Isaac Newton: Lucasian Professor of Mathematics at the University of Cambridge. Some cosmologists believe that the Universe will end in a Big Crunch. However, it still expanding and some say that this is due to dark energy. This unknown force overcomes Newton's Universal pull of gravity.

Flood

The biblical legend of the Flood may be based upon a prehistoric event that was half-remembered and passed down through many generations. Some are still searching for Noah's Ark on the volcanic Mount Ararat. Noah was supposed to have saved the endangered species - two by two. We now realize the importance of saving them as well as Our own species.

The Earth sciences are helping Us understand Our past and Our future. There is geological evidence of Great Floods in many parts of the globe. Earth's tectonic plates, oceans and atmosphere are all effected by the pull of the Sun and Moon, causing quakes, tsunamis, eruptions and storms. Britain was once joined to Europe but the land bridge was washed away by a rise in sea level due to global warming and a tsunami in 6200 BC. Noah's Flood was probably caused by the rising sea levels that gouged through the Bosporus gorge in about 5500 BC to form the Black Sea. Remembered for millennia, this was the basis of Byzantine chronology. The Black Sea was originally a fresh water lake, fed by several rivers. A Flood in Mesopotamia in 3761 BC was the basis of Jewish chronology. This was in the epic of Gilgamesh, inscribed on clay tablets in 2000 BC, found in Nineveh in 1853 AD and deciphered by George Smith in 1880 AD. Thousands of clay tablets are still preserved by the British Museum. The flooding of the Tigris and Euphrates occurs near the vernal equinox and this annual event was the start of the Mesopotamian calendar year. The Nile flooded the Sahara but reached the Mediterranean in 10,000 BC. Its annual floods were 'the gift of the Nile' which created ancient Egypt. They occured near the heliacal rising of Sirius at the start of their year.

The gravitational pull of the Sun keeps all of the Solar Planets in orbit. Their equal and opposite pull causes the Sun-spots and the Solar flares. There were many Ice Ages, every 100,000 years or so, when Earth's icecaps became larger and the sea level dropped to some 60m below its present position, and Great Thaws, when it rose to some 40m above. These great climate changes were due to perturbations in Earth's orbit, and these were caused by the gravitational pull of all the other Planets. Solar winds have a 28-day sunth cycle and also a twelve-year *El Nino* cycle. There was a mini Ice Age during in 16th century when the Thames froze. This is thought to be when the Sun-spots and Solar flares were minimal. They hit maximum in the summer of 2000 AD when Britain experienced exceptional rainfall and icecaps and glaciers were found to be melting. Some say it is due to greenhouse gases but that is only part of the story. Ice cores in Antarctica show that this was once in a tropical region. Earth's centre of gravity is now moving and causing its axis to change. *NASA* say that the North Pole is slowly moving towards Little Britain. It now seems certain that many low-lying islands will soon disappear. Whilst We must all try to minimize the pollution of greenhouse gases, it would be prudent to build more arks or to move to higher ground.

Exodus

Sigmund Freud considered that Atenism and Judaism were interlinked because both religions were based upon the worship of only one god. He concluded that the legend of Moses and the Exodus must be true. Some say Moses was Thothmosis or Tutmosis, elder brother of Akhenaten.

The only evidence in Egypt of the Children of Israel is the 'Israel Stela'. This was erected in Thebes by Pharaoh Merneptah, son of Ramesses II, and mentions a decisive military victory over Israel in about 1215 BC. The Israelites are thought to have captured Canaan in about 1400 BC. Egyptologists estimated the reign of Akhenaten to be 1353 to 1336 BC. However, there are many anomalies in the king lists and other chronicles. He was not even mentioned in some king lists because he was a heretic. There are very few events during ancient civilizations that can pinpoint exact dates and so their chronologies could be up to a century wrong. There was a Solar eclipse very near to the vernal equinox in 1456 BC. This could have triggered the eruption of Thera and lead to the Exodus. It would have blotted-out the Sun and caused global climate changes. There are many examples of celestial-terrestrial coincidences in history. There have been numerous volcanic eruptions, earthquakes or tsunamis around Solar or Lunar eclipses, occurring near solstices or equinoxes, followed by famines, mass migrations and the belief in divine retribution.

The cataclysmic eruption of Thera decimated the Minoan civilization and its tsunamis wiped out many ancient settlements around the Aegean. They would have swamped the delta and travelled a long way up the Nile, causing much loss of life, destruction of crops and poisoning of the soil. The shepherds on higher ground would have survived but would have had to flee the subsequent plagues, which may have ended Akhenaten's reign. The remaining population would have blamed him and his new Sun-god. They would have wanted to return to ancient gods, priests and temples. Excavations at the village of Amarna show that Akhenaten's new capital Akhetaten with its Great *Aten* Temple was devastated by the tsunami. This washed away its hundreds of ritual mud-brick offering tables and when it was rebuilt, during the middle of Akhenaten's reign, the hundreds of stone offering tables were arranged in lines of seven and groups of 28. This indicates that Akhenaten and Nefertiti used 52 seven-day weeks and thirteen 28-day sunths; rather than the traditional 36 ten-day weeks and twelve 30-day months with 5 remainder days named after five Sky-gods. The next pharaoh Tut-ankh-aten changed his name to Tut-ankh-amen. He returned to the traditional gods, calendar, capital and architecture. Akhetaten was razed and all traces of the Sun-god *Aten* were removed. A cache of clay tablets found at Amarna shows that the Egyptians were corresponding and trading with the Minoans, Babylonians, Assyrians... It could even be that Akhenaten and/or Nefertiti were Semitic in origin and they brought their one god and their seven-day week with them.

Apocalypse

Aristotle believed that all global catastrophes were linked with the Sky. We now know that there were several apocalyptic phenomena including: impacts of asteroids, comets or meteorites; earthquakes and volcanoes; and catastrophic climate changes due to perturbations of Earth's orbit. These caused the demise of the dinosaurs plus many other species and the end of ancient civilizations, from the Stone, Bronze and Iron Ages to many of the great empires that rose and fell throughout prehistory. The Babylonians predicted catastrophes when all of the Planets aligned. They also feared solstices, equinoxes and both Solar and Lunar eclipses. The Persian Zoroaster said civilization would end after twelve millennia. The Hindu *Aryabhatiya says* We are at the end of the fourth Universe. This is called the *Kaliyuga* because *Kali* is the goddess of destruction. The Maya predicted the Sun would expire at the end of a calendar round. The Maya long count calendar round ended on 21 December 2012 AD. The Jewish *Talmud* predicted Time will end six millennia after it began. Jewish chronology began in the year 3761 BC; so it will end in 2239 AD. Their religious year starts at the month of *Nisan* on the vernal equinox. A total Solar eclipse is a warning to Gentiles and a sign of Judgement. If this occurs near a vernal equinox it is a very rare and ominous event.

According to the *Gospel of Luke,* it was a Roman census that sent Mary and Joseph to Bethlehem, where she gave virgin birth to Jesus Christ. Many still believe in the biblical Rapture when Jesus will be born again. The Christian *Book of Revelations* predicts an Apocalypse at a Millennium. After the first Millennium, Saxon Britain was invaded by the Normans. They built castles, monasteries, cathedrals, churches and took a census: *The Domesday Book* - and Britain still conducts a census every decade. After the second Millennium AD the census showed that Christianity was declining in Britain and that it was rapidly becoming a secular society. John Paul II said: the Antichrist is amongst Us and Doomsday is at hand. He foretold the end of Christianity unless Jesus the Christ comes again.

The Metric Millennium brought many Natural and Man-made disasters. The five visible Planets formed a very close group on May 4th 2000 AD. This was marked by extraordinary climatic conditions causing floods, droughts, wildfires and outbreaks of epidemics in livestock and in Us. It was also marked by outbreaks of suicide or genocide all over the globe. There is increasing evidence that the global climate is changing and that this may be partially due to the rapid growth of Our own population. We are rapidly running out of enough agricultural land to feed everyone and enough energy to power all of Our wonderful labour-saving devices. Despite all the many Natural catastrophes that could wipe Us all out; the greatest potential danger to Mankind is extreme religious beliefs. There are enough nuclear weapons to annihilate Our entire Human Race and some of those US generals believe in the Rapture at the End of Time.

Saturdays

As Abraham passed through Haran he would have encountered the gods of the *Seven Heavenly Bodies* and he may have used the seven-day week. *Yahweh* promised his followers [Jews or Arabs?] the holy land of Israel. The Israelites moved to Egypt, with its many gods and its ten-day week. However, the Semitic pharaoh Akhenaten worshipped one Sun-god *Aten.* He introduced a seven-day week, a 28-day sunth and a 13-sunth year. However, his reign and his calendar ended after a Natural catastrophe. His son Tutankhamun reverted to the ten-day week and the old religion. Moses lead the Children of Israel away from their bondage in Egypt, they passed over the Reed [not Red] Sea, which drowned the Egyptians, he climbed up to the summit of the volcano in Sinai [there are none], *Yahweh* taught him *Ten Commandments* through the archangel Michael, including the one about the seven-day week with only one day of rest. He brought down two tablets of stone on which these laws were written, they were broken, rewritten and then placed in the Ark of the Covenant. This was later kept inside Solomon's Temple, but lost in about 650 BC.

The Israelite leaders were enslaved by the Babylonians between about 597 and 538 BC and during this period they continued to use the seven day week and to strictly observe the law of the *Shabbat* to keep it holy. Ezra, the first Pharisee, wrote the *Torah,* which must be obeyed by all. Otherwise their one god *Jehovah* would bring them more misfortune. Babylon was invaded by the Persians, who used a 7-day week, in 539 BC. Their next misfortune was Alexander's invasion in 333 BC but the Greek Sadducees adopted 7-day weeks and so their sacred *Shabbat* survived. The Romans used an 8-day market week in a higgledy-piggledy calendar, which was totally incompatible with Sadducee and Pharisee traditions. The Jews revolted but, perhaps, the Essenes suggested a compromise. They used a discontinuous 7-day week, which began on a Wednesday. The Sabbath was the main cause of the revolt in Jerusalem, at the end of the tyrannical reign of Nero, because Jews refused to work on that day. They were annihilated throughout the Roman Empire, Herod's Temple was razed to the ground and the old city of Jerusalem was destroyed. One of the Jews, however, founded a new sect, now called: Christianity.

What would Jesus have to say about the continuous seven-day week? What would he think about the sacred Sabbath being moved to Sunday? What would he think of the backward and forward chronology, which is supposed to be based upon his birthday but is wrong by at least 4 years? What would he think about the Roman-Catholic Church and all of those who have been abused, tortured, maimed and killed by its priesthood? During the papal inquisition, millions of Jews, witches and heretics were tortured or executed for meeting on the *Shabbat*, Saturn or Satan's day. During the holocaust six million Jews were exterminated by Christians. However, Saturdays and Sundays have now become: the weekend.

Sundays

Abraham, Israel and Joseph; Mary, Joseph and Jesus all lived in Egypt, so would have used a 10-day week with one day of rest on a Sun-day. Akhenaten and Nefertiti scrapped the 10-day week and used a 7-day one. Tutankhamun scrapped the 7-day week and restored the 10-day one. The early Christians in Egypt continued to use the Siriac calendar with its 30-day months and its 10-day weeks until the first popes decreed the use of a 7-day week and moved the Christian Sabbath to Sunday. This was because of Mithraism in the legions, who used a 7-day week, venerated the Sun's day and they made animal sacrifices to it and on it. Christians say it was because Jesus arose from the dead on a Sunday but Jerusalem was using the 8-day Roman week in the first century AD. It was not until the Roman Empire became Christian and then organized the Church in the fourth century AD that Sunday had any importance. The Church still holds that the 7-day week and Sundays are sacrosanct.

The continuous seven-day week has no celestial reference point and so a Sunday may really be on a Friday or a Saturday, because the Jews lost track of it after they were expelled from Jerusalem by the Romans. Because of the International Dateline some Christians are praying on Sunday whilst others are praying on the day before or the day after. So much for the power of prayer when everyone thinks simultaneously. Going to church every Sunday has nothing to do with Jesus the Christ, nor with early Christianity and it has almost lost its meaning today. Only about 1% of Britons still worship, in empty churches, on Sundays; yet they restrict the remaining 99% from working and shopping all day. Sundays were the special days upon which the devout went to church. Sundays then became dead days when people stopped going to church. They had little to do because the sanctimonious were stopping progress by passing laws that were contrary to the Declaration of Human Rights. Sunday became the weekend and only five days remained for working. Much of industry and commerce ground to a halt for two days in seven. However, many churches are now closed and reused for secular purposes.

Whilst most of the Sunday laws have been repealed in Protestant Britain and its economy is now surging ahead; most of the south of Europe is still Catholic, so it upholds the Sunday laws and is now falling behind. Politicians will tell you that this is due to their excellent management of the economy but the reason is that all days are now almost the same. However, more Britons are now going to cinemas, theatres and clubs on Sunday nights so they start working on Mondays without having a rest. Absenteeism on Mondays is on the increase and could get out of control. The final step will be when the seven-day week is scrapped altogether. Yet, curiously enough, this could lead to more people going to church, because they could then return to the ten-day week, which Jesus used, but only go to church during either the five left-days or five right-days.

Special Days

Looking at Our Planet as a whole it is clear that those countries who still enforce special days for religion are now falling behind economically. In southern Europe, where the Roman-Catholic sect is still dominant, there is mass unemployment and over half the youngsters have no job. The northern Europe where there are more Protestants and Humanists the work ethic is stronger, the week is weaker and there are more jobs. West Europe is falling behind Asia because they have no Sabbath day. East Europe has abandoned Communism but it is still in recession. North America is falling behind Asia although they have fewer holidays. South America is now catching up, whilst it remains steeped in religion. Africa is losing its dependence on Europe and turning to Asia for help. Australia has no special days but New Zealand still observes some.

Both Houses of Parliament are still living in the nineteenth century AD. The Big Issue which nearly brought the Tories down in 1986 AD, during Margaret Thatcher's era, was Sunday trading - even though she wanted to return to Victorian values she saw that this was a basic Human right. John Major's Cabinet wanted to end the Sunday Trade Act of 1950 AD. On 29 November 1993 AD, 311 MPs voted to scrap it and 26 to keep it. Despite public support for freedom to trade on any day, the House of Commons voted against it on 8 December 1993 AD but allowed small shops to open every day and big stores to open for 6 hours on Sundays. The House of Lords debated the shopping issue on 8 March 1994 AD. Lord Boyd-Carpenter said the House of Commons should think again and vote for freedom to trade, treating shops like other economic activities. The Bishop of Liverpool said that those who voted for the total freedom to shop on any day were weakening the family and secularizing Sunday. Lord Jakobovits made a heartfelt plea for a return to observing the ancient Mosaic laws of the Sabbath for 'man does live by bread alone'. On 6 September 2001 AD Cardinal Murphy-O'Connor, the Catholic leader, admitted that: 'Christianity has almost been vanquished in Britain'. The Archbishop of Canterbury, Protestant Primate Dr. Carey concurred, saying, very sadly: 'Most Britons have no room in their lives for Christ.' All shops may open-all-day in Scotland, with higher wages on Sundays. Yet, Scottish MPs scuppered a Tory plan to permit local authorities in England and Wales to allow shops to open-all-day on Sundays in 2016 AD.

By making 360 days equal and encouraging, not enforcing, job-sharing any country can become much more efficient and have more free-time. Shops would be open every day but perhaps for a shorter period because most people would do their shopping inside the rush-hours on free-days. There would be more time for philosophy or religion, not less, because most people would work for five days in ten instead of five days in seven. There would be more holidays and no holy days throughout the year. The Mystic seven-day week has had its day and it may soon fade away.

Ordinary Days

Whilst there are several pressure groups like the Keep Sunday Special Campaign, the Lord's Day Observance Society and opposing them the Shopping Hours Reform Council, there is no 'Scrap Sunday Campaign'. Keeping Sunday special favours British Christians in this multi-ethnic, multi-cultural, multi-religious society, which is trying hard to integrate. Grabbing pole position in Our Human Race was a very selfish thing to do. However, there is no Jewish 'Keep Saturday Special' campaign in Britain. Muslims have no 'Keep Friday Special' campaign because they have always been permitted to shop and work on Fridays - if they need to. Hindus, Sikhs, Buddhists, Taoists, Shintoists, Animists and Humanists have no sabbatarian campaigns - because all days are the same to them.

The Queen gave approval to Parliament to make up their minds freely on this issue, even though she is the Head of the Church of England. Apart from the shopping laws there were also many sporting, betting, drinking, eating, singing and dancing laws which made Sunday special. Whilst most have now been repealed others are still in the Statute Book. Many people now work on Sundays and take other days off in the week. This is no longer a religious issue but has become a party political dogma. John Major wanted to scrap all laws making Saturday or Sunday special. The 1986 AD Shopping Hours Bill was supposed to be a free vote issue. However, a Welsh Labour whip was alleged to have brought pressure, using office allocations, to maintain the higher wage rates on Sundays. Although not in their manifesto, the Conservative Party tried to devolve the issue of Sunday shopping hours to the local councils in 2016 AD. If this had been a free vote or an English issue they might have won. However, a number of Tories defied their whip and the Labour Party, Scottish Nationalists, NI and Welsh MPs voted against the government. So this important socio-economic issue was 'kicked into the long grass'.

The European Union gave their approval for Britain to make up its own mind on the Sunday issue; although some of the rest of Europe now want to make three days of the week special and to only work on four. On 1 October 1998 AD Britain adopted the EU 48-hour working week. Yet, this is largely ignored and many people work much longer hours. The French started working a 35-hour week and wanted to introduce this throughout Europe but it is very inefficient because it meant that many small villages had to have two bakeries and many cafes, bars and restaurants were forced to close when they could have been very busy. The eurozone is now in a monetary mess and some states are failing. The European Union is now falling apart, due to immigration issues. Britons decided, by referendum, on 23 June 2016 AD, to go-it-alone. Some economists, sociologists and psychologists now envisage a 24/7 society, in which large shops are open for 24 hours on 7 days of the week. Many are already open online and deliveries may be made on any day.

Holy Days

The Sun and Moon still have Mystic influences over Roman-Catholicism.
The rising Sun illuminates the altar of St Peter's Rome at the equinoxes.
The Venerable Bede allotted days to saints and held that Easter should
fall upon the first Sunday after the full-Moon after the vernal equinox.
This was agreed at the Synod of Whitby in Saxon England during 664 AD.
However, this has been changed to read: '21 March' not: 'vernal equinox'.
The Roman-Catholic calendar is full of saints' days and Pope John Paul II
beatified more of them than any other pontiff throughout church history.
On 20 March 2000 AD the vernal equinox coincided with the full-Moon.
So John Paul II decided to follow in Christ's footsteps on 26 March.
He flew to Israel and visited many holy places mentioned in *The Bible*.
Nevertheless, Easter Sunday did not fall until St. Georges Day on 23 April.

The Roman-Catholics still celebrate holy days but the Protestants do not.
Thomas Cromwell (1485-1540 AD) chief minister to Henry VIII was put in
charge of the dissolution of monasteries and reformation of the Church.
Christmas and Easter were the only remaining Protestant holy days.
Catholic Charles I (1600-1649 AD) reinstated many of the saint's days.
After he was beheaded, lord protector Oliver Cromwell (1599-1658 AD)
banned all saint's days and holy days, including Christmas and Easter.
Protestant Charles II (1630-1685 AD) restored both of these holy days.
The British version of the Gregorian calendar still includes them both;
even though the majority are not Christian or they do not believe in *God*.

We have had bank holidays since 1871 AD when they were suggested by
John Lubbock, a politician and banker - who was knighted for this idea.
Good Friday is a Protestant holy day; Easter Monday is a bank holiday.
Christmas is a holy day; Boxing Day and New Year's Day are holidays.
The Labour Party stopped the bank holiday Monday after Whit Sunday
and replaced it with Mayday bank holiday to celebrate workers' solidarity.
The Conservative Party turned this into the Spring Bank Holiday in May.
Parliament is now debating whether this should be moved to autumn.
The victorious title: Trafalgar Day has been suggested but this would not
be popular with the former French and Spanish partners in the EU.
Most EU states have more holy days and/or bank holidays than the UK.
However, Portugal now wants to scrap its holy days and bank holidays,
since Catholicism is on the wane and it needs to become more efficient.

The secular **digital date calendar** has no holy days nor bank holidays,
although everyone would be entitled to 180 days off-work every *yer* plus
five democratic days at the *yerend,* which would be reserved for voting.
Leap days, every four *yers*, would be designated: United Nations Day.
During the 180 days off-work people would be free to do what they like.
If they were religious there would probably be certain days in the *wek*
for going to church, chapel, synagogue, mosque, temple - or all of them.

Holidays

Over the last 160 years British holiday entitlement has grown from one week to four and some take five or six weeks paid holidays every year. Nevertheless, most Americans still only take a two-week annual vacation. On the continent of Europe many firms close for a month in the summer. In France most small shops are closed on Saturday afternoons, Sundays, and Monday mornings as well as on the holy days and public holidays. Commercial vehicles are not permitted to use the roads at weekends. There are still a few parades through the streets on these holy days in Roman-Catholic countries but this old ritual is gradually fading away. Nevertheless, pilgrimage is booming as many tourists visit the holy sites. Many students now take a gap year before or after university and some workers are allowed to take a mid-career break or a sabbatical year to broaden their experience of the World and to 'recharge their batteries'. This practice is very common in Australia and New Zealand where many immigrants want to visit their parents' country to uncover their roots.

British holy days, bank holidays and vacations are in an unholy mess. The long school, college or university holiday in summer is a throwback to the old days when many pupils and students helped with the harvest. Britain has eight holy days and bank holidays but Italy has sixteen. The Fabian Society is calling for more bank holidays, in line with Europe but this would make Britain less competitive in international trading. The Centre for Economics and Business Research say that the average bank holiday costs Britain £2.3G and so they should all be scrapped. Britain is now a secular state, so why not scrap all the holy days and bank holidays and then simply add them to annual holiday entitlement? But why should anyone be paid when they are not doing useful work? We should only be paid for the time that We actually spend working. Europe has almost reached the point where only half the year is worked. Why not work for 180 days and take 180 days off during a 360 day *yer* and reserve the five or six remaining days for democratic elections?

The **digital date calendar** encourages **full-time-job-sharing-as-the-norm**. There are five free days in every ten and if a longer period off-work is needed this can easily be arranged by swapping days with one's pair. We would tend to take more short holiday breaks at home and away. Foreign holidays would be cheaper because the season would be spread. There would be fewer travel peaks due to school or works holidays. Many more people would be able to afford holidays and so take a break. The overall benefits to the country and its population would be huge. On a global basis, the total benefits of **digital date** would be gigantic. **Full-time-job-sharing-as-the-norm** is the main socioeconomic advantage but sharing holiday homes, cars, caravans, boats and planes is another. We do not need to own these things and this system would make hiring, renting or chartering much more economically and ecologically viable.

Feasts

Feasts are held, throughout the globe, to celebrate the passage of Time.
Time is the greatest force in civilization and food is the essence of Life.
Yet, it is Our different chronologies, calendars, clocks and zones which
divide Us and the peculiar diets of various religions that set Us apart.
The significance of any feast depends upon its rarity, so a millennium
is much more important than a century, decade, year, month or week.
As We all passed the second Millennium in *Anno Domini* chronology
We experienced the greatest festival and waste of money of all Time.
As the caviar was savoured and the champagne was swilled, very few
remembered the billions of hungry victims of the great *God* of Time.
His weekly feasts cause much of the misery in the World today for they
waste a great deal of productive time and stop work from being shared.

For most people today the weekly cycle has nothing to do with religion.
Because meat would not keep, animals were slaughtered for the village.
This weekly ritual became a religious feast and then the Sunday joint.
To women the highpoint of their week is shopping and Sunday lunch.
To men the highpoint of their week is a football match or a game of golf.
For the young it is Saturday when they socialize and let their hair down.
Refrigeration has replaced religion and Sunday has no ritual meaning.
It should be fairly easy for most people to adapt to a ten-day work cycle.
Perhaps the traditional lunch hour can be dispensed with on work days.
For it wastes productive time and reduces performance in the afternoon.
The *wek* could consist of five feast-days and five fast-days or *vici versa*.

Most people around-the-globe celebrated the second Millennium AD.
Some booked New Year vacations in Tonga to be the first to see it dawn;
then found that an island called: Millennium, was closer to the dateline.
Pagans said that the Millennium commenced a New Age of Mysticism.
The Giza pyramids were the setting for a *son et lumiere* extravaganza.
Jews said that the Millennium marked the beginning of Armageddon.
They held a Hell of a party on the site of their defeat at Mount Megiddo.
Christians said that it was 2000 years since the birth of Jesus Christ.
They ignored the evidence that he was probably born at an earlier date.
Muslims said a Solar Millennium meant nothing in their Lunar calendar.
They held bloody demonstrations in Beirut against Jews and Christians.
They threatened to blow-up the Metric Millennium Dome at midnight,
together with the Queen, the Prime Minister and the Mayor of London.
This disrupted the opening ceremony and thousands were unable to get
through the police barriers, whilst others did not get their tickets in time.
Humanists said that the Millennium marked the New Age of Reason.
They celebrated it with firework displays in every corner of the globe.
We should celebrate *New Yer* at the same age, date and time everywhere.
The moment when a global-digital-decimal chronology/calendar/clock
displays: **000:000.000** will only occur once every *Kiloyer*.

Fasts

Each religion incorporates fasts, which demonstrate its followers' piety.
Orthodox Jews have several annual fasts, they do not eat any pig meat,
their kosher meat must be killed by the rabbi by bleeding it to death
and they are not permitted to prepare any kind of food on the Sabbath.
Orthodox Christians observe the forty-day fast of Lent before Easter.
Roman-Catholics may not eat meat but they can eat fish on a Friday.
They may eat breakfast but must not eat lunch before midday or noon.
Protestants do not have any saints' days nor any dietary restrictions.
The Copts in Egypt and Ethiopia still fast on Wednesdays and Fridays.
The Cathars in France fasted on Mondays, Wednesdays and Fridays.
They were brutally annihilated for their heresy by the Roman-Catholics.
Sunni Muslims fast during daylight in their holy moonth of Ramadan,
they must not eat pork and their halal meat must be specially prepared.
Hindus, Buddhists, Jains and Sikhs are not allowed to eat any meat.
Some fast for long periods, which is supposed to be good for the soul.
Hundreds of elderly Jains fast to death every year, so commit suicide.
Orthodox Yazidis, in Iraq, worship peacocks and they do not eat lettuce.
They use a 366 day calendar, pray twice a day and rest on Wednesdays.
Orthodox Badis begin every 'month' with a feast and end it with a fast.

One Billion of Us are underweight but one Billion of Us are overweight.
Overeating is now said to cause as many global deaths as malnutrition.
We all have very different genes and so We come in all shapes and sizes.
This is *Mother Nature's* way of ensuring that Our Human Race survives.
During famines it is not the fittest, but the fattest, who usually endure.
Many Americans hoarded food in preparation for the Metric Millennium
when they expected computer bugs to start the predicted Apocalypse.
Advertising and the habits of modern living encourage many to over-eat
and over-drink - then feel guilty and harm their metabolism by fasting.
Obesity is far more common in the USA with its many fast food outlets.
Too much sugar or salt often leads to diabetes, strokes or heart attacks.
Slimming sometimes leads to eating disorders, which can prove fatal.
It has been proven that slimmers are dimmer and cannot concentrate.
Nevertheless, the slimming industry is still growing - like Topsy.

We have incisors, canines and molars, so are herbivores and carnivores.
Yet, many of Us would be vegetarians if We had to kill Our own meat.
We cannot expect the starving masses to save the endangered species.
We will certainly have to kill some sacred cows in order to survive.
The seven-day week is a sacred cow, so the superstitious fear to kill it.
A ten-day week and job-sharing-as-the-norm could help Us to produce
distribute and prepare enough food and drink for everyone on Earth.
It could help Us to regulate and vary Our diets, take regular exercise
and then We might all look like film stars, pop idols or sports heroes.
Nevertheless, some of Us may still look like couch potatoes.

Christmas

There is no archaeological or historical record of Mary, Joseph or Jesus. Most of the nativity story is a modern invention, based on ancient myths. A Bright Star, a virgin mother and babe, stable, manger and crib, angels, shepherds and wise men are found in many ancient tales and legends. Matthew's gospel is the only one to describe the birthday of the Messiah. This was expected at an astronomical event at the end of the Sumerian *sar* of 3600 years, when the messianic Essene sect formed in 160 BC. The wise men may have been visiting astronomers, astrologers or magi. The Bright Star may have been a conjunction, a comet or a supernova. Sirius rose with Venus, Jupiter, Mercury, Sun and Moon in 158 BC. Hipparchus, the Nicaean astronomer, observed a supernova in 125 BC. Chinese astronomers in the Han dynasty recorded a supernova in 5 BC. The same astronomers recorded a visit from Halley's Comet in 12 BC. There was a rare triple conjunction of Saturn with Jupiter during 7 BC. There was also a rare conjunction of Venus with Mercury during 7 BC. Other reasons to match historic facts with biblical accounts include the death of Herod the Great in 4 BC and Caesar Augustus' census in 6 AD.

The birthday of Christ was celebrated by the Gnostic Church during May and this was recorded by Clement of Alexandria in the 2nd century AD. The Ethiopic Church celebrates its New Year at the heliacal rising of Sirius on 11 September (Gregorian) and their chronology started in 7 AD. The Roman-Orthodox Church first celebrated Christ's Mass in 354 AD when it was decreed by Pope Julius I to fall on 25 December (Julian). It was formerly the midwinter feast marked by the Jewish *Hanukkah*, the Roman *Saturnalia* and *Brumalia*, the Saxon *Yule* and the birthday of the gods: *Ra, Horus, Attis, Tammuz, Baccus* or *Dionysus* and *Mithras*. The Mithraic Birthday of the Unconquered Sun was at the winter solstice. Both Jesus and *Mithras* were conceived and died on the vernal equinox.

Saint Nicholas, the bishop of Myra, lived on the Agean island of Gemile. He was imprisoned by Emperor Diocletian but released by Constantine. He was reputed to have saved several young girls from prostitution by throwing some coins through their window and he died in about 343 AD. His bones are now in the Basilica of Saint Nicholas at Bari in Italy. His eve is celebrated on 5 December in Holland where he is *Sinterklaas*. He changed his name to Santa Claus when he emigrated to New York. Father Christmas, was first named in an American poem in 1823 AD. He had a long white beard and he always wore green and white robes. The Lapps ate red and white fungi which gave an hallucination of flying. This lead to the legend of a flying sleigh, pulled by reindeer, driven by an old bearded fellow, clad in red and white robes, carrying lots of presents. The image of Santa Claus was created on a *Coca-Cola* advert in 1931 AD. Rudolph the red-nosed reindeer was created for *Sears* stores in 1939 AD. Christ's Mass became Christmas and Santa still rings his bell of **Time.**

Easter

The Crucifixion of Jesus Christ, on the eve of the Passover, marked the beginning of Christianity and the Jewish revolt against Imperial Rome. Jews and Christians have never agreed about the Lunar or Solar dates of these movable events, upon which many other religious festivals depend. The Jewish feast of the Passover marks the anniversary of the Exodus. It is based upon the complexities of the Jewish Lunar-Solar calendar. Pontius Pilate was the governor of Judea from 26 AD to 36 AD and it is said that Jesus was crucified in 33 AD and died during a Solar eclipse. Yet, there is no Roman record of Jesus nor a Jewish revolt in 33 AD. A revolt led to the expulsion of Jews from their promised land in 70 AD. A further revolt in 132 AD led to the deaths of about half a million Jews. There was a Solar eclipse in 33 AD but this was not visible in Jerusalem and it did not occur until 12 September (Gregorian).

The Christian fast of Easter is also based upon the Sun and the Moon. Yet, Christian sects mark the death of their founder on different dates. Good Friday commemorates Christ's death, Easter Sunday celebrates his resurrection on the third day but this may be based upon the Egyptian ritual that Pharaoh was born as *Horus* three days after he died as *Osiris.* This myth of resurrection was the means by which pharaonic dynasties prevailed and astronomer-priests maintained their privileged position. Christianity was torn apart by the use of very different Solar calendars. There was discord about the dates of the Messiah's birth and death. The Celtic, Saxon and Roman Churches each adopted different liturgies. Roman-Catholic Easter was agreed at the Synod of Whitby in 664 AD. However, there was still much debate amongst different Christian sects. The Eastern and Western Churches excommunicated each other during the Great Schism of 1054 AD, over this thorny issue, and grew further apart when the Roman-Catholic Church adopted the Gregorian calendar. Easter now falls on the first Sunday after the full-Moon after 21 March. The EU uses this calendar but Greece still observes the Orthodox Easter. In 1923 AD The League of Nations agreed and in 1928 AD the House of Commons ratified that Easter Day should fall upon the first Sunday after the second Saturday in April but this has never been put into practice. The World Council of Churches are talking about a fixed date for Easter.

Easter replaced the Anglo-Saxon festival for the goddess *Eostra* at the vernal equinox when eggs and hares were venerated in rites of spring. Eggs turned to chocolate, hares became bunnies, so it lost its meaning. Easter became a four-day holiday and commercial hype, like Christmas. Since it moves about it makes a great deal of unnecessary work for every organization that publishes a timetable and there are often mistakes. If We were to use **digital date** movable feasts and fasts could be fixed. There is no reason why any religion should not be able to fix its feasts and fasts to a perpetual, rational, secular, **digital date calendar**.

Catechisms

The continuous seven-day week was originally a Mystic Pagan tradition, based upon worship of gods associated with *The Seven Heavenly Bodies*. Then it became a Jewish, tradition, based upon *The Ten Commandments*. This was adopted by all of the Christians and then by all of the Muslims. The Gnostic Egyptians, the earliest Christians, were led by Saint Mark, who may have written at least one gospel, probably helped to establish Christianity in Rome and gave his name to the cathedral in Venice. The Coptic Christian age is based on the Gnostic martyrdom in 284 AD. Copts still use the 365/6 day Siriac years and 30-day months but they gave-up discontinuous ten-day *decades* for continuous seven-day weeks. The Sabbath day was the foundation of Judaism, Christianity and Islam. Although the founders of each religion chose a different day in the week: Jews on Saturdays, Christians on Sundays and Muslims on Fridays. *The Old Testament* forms the basis for all three monotheist religions.

The Third Commandment   Exodus 20:2-17

Remember the Sabbath day, to keep it holy.
Six days shalt thou labour and do all thy work.
But the seventh day is the Sabbath of the Lord thy *God*...
For in six days the Lord made Heaven and Earth... and rested on the seventh day.
Wherefore the Lord blessed the Sabbath day and hallowed it.

The first Catechism of the Roman-Catholic Church since Gregory XIII introduced his calendar, four centuries ago, was issued by the all-male Vatican Council in 1993 AD but not published in English until 1994 AD, due to bitter arguments about whether *God* created men and women. The Catechism describes hundreds of cardinal, venial and lesser sins. If non-attendance at church and Sunday working were to be no longer included in the 2865 paragraph list of sins, a cataclysm of Worldwide unemployment, poverty, crime and war might be avoided but the end of Sunday and the Mystic seven-day week would then be nigh:

2181 Those who deliberately fail to go to Church on Sundays commit a grave sin.

2187 Traditional activities (sports, restaurants etc.) and social necessities
     (public services etc.) require some people to work on Sundays.

At the full-Moon on the vernal equinox in the Millennium year 2000 AD Pope John Paul II apologized to the Jews for the anti-Semitic doctrine that Jews were expelled from the Holy Land as a punishment from *God* because they did not recognize Jesus Christ as the predicted Messiah. However, his explanation is not the real reason for the Jewish diaspora. The Romans expelled them because they refused to work on the Sabbath. Rome was still using the Julian *kalendar* with *kalends, ides* and *nones*. This was incompatible with Jewish calendar years, months and weeks. The Roman-Catholics eventually adopted the continuous seven-day week.

Encyclicals

Pope John Paul II's Encyclical: *The Splendour of Truth Shines,* addressed to all the bishops of the Catholic Church, was published in 1993 AD in order to coincide with the Vatican's first Catechism for four centuries. He discussed the last seven of the *Ten Commandments,* or *Decalogue,* however he did not mention the first three, nor the seven-day week. It would have been tactless to tell Catholics that they must work for six days in every seven when many millions of them were unemployed. It would have been equally tactless for the pontiff to pontificate upon Catholics resting on Sundays when many millions of them now need to work on that day to keep the wheels of industry and commerce rolling. He stressed that Human freedom and *God's* law are not in opposition. He might have said something about the freedom to file for divorce, the end of celibacy for the priesthood, the ordination of female priests, the freedom to use birth control, the unholy terrors of ethnic cleansing, the continuation of the crusades, the inquisition and the conquistadors. He might have said something about sharing work, wealth and things.

The Pope had second thoughts about working and resting on Sundays. In the summer of 1998 AD the Vatican issued an apostolic letter from John Paul II to all faithful Catholics entitled *Dies Domini* (Day of the Lord) in which he exhorted that Sunday is special and must not be worked, because *God* created the Universe in six days and then rested for one. If all Catholics follow this advice Our World will return to the Dark Ages. Taking a regular rest is important but there is no need to do it together. Simultaneous prayer would only be possible if there were no time zones.

Pope John Paul II was succeeded by Benedict XVI and then Francis I who pledged to reform the Vatican and to help the poor of all religions. He formally worked as a Jesuit priest with the poor people of Argentina. There is high unemployment in most of the Latin American countries. In the summer of 2015 AD Pope Francis published his own encyclical, calling for global action to combat climate change and global warming. Our Human Race became much faster and larger in the last century, due to faiths out-breeding each other and advances in medical science. Our Planet cannot sustain all of Us and migration is now a global issue. Millions of poor people are risking their lives to travel in search of work. The solution is not to build more fences and walls but to help the poor to stay at home and be more productive, without becoming more prolific. The way to achieve this is for most jobs to be shared in a ten-day week. This would ensure that Our infrastructure was used evenly every day. It would increase global productivity without increasing global pollution. At the beatification of Pope Paul VI in 2014 AD Pope Francis said:

God is not afraid of new things, that's why He is continually surprising Us, opening Our hearts and guiding Us in unexpected ways.

Spiritual Unity

Whether you are a Jew, a Christian, a Muslim or a Humanist, some of *The Bible* still has relevance, although We are living in a different World. A small Jewish sect grew to become the largest religion on Our Planet. Yet, there are fewer and fewer Christians living in the Holy Land now. Jews, Christians and Muslims cannot live, work and pray there in peace because they all use different chronologies, calendars, clocks and zones. The Eastern religions also have different ways of measuring the Time. The Badi religion tried to unite these spiritual and temporal differences with a new calendar based upon 19 'months' of 19 days - but it failed. Humanism could unite Us if it started again with a clean sheet of paper. Yet, some Humanists are against any changes to the *status quo*.

Pope John Paul II wanted everyone on Earth to use his Roman-Catholic chronology, calendar, clock and zones - but they will never be catholic. On 5 October 1995 AD, the fiftieth Anniversary of the United Nations, he stood before the General Assembly and told them that they should become a family of nations that fosters greater equality and mutual trust between its members and he also said that because of changing global conditions the UN should be primarily concerned with resolving conflicts. He warned about extreme nationalism and all religious fundamentalism leading to a fear of difference and a nightmare of violence and terror. Pope Francis I visited the USA in his *Fiat 500* during September 2015 AD. He visited the White House, spoke to both houses of Congress then stood before the General Assembly of the United Nations and preached about inequality, unemployment, homelessness and religious fundamentalism. When Barack Obama became president, with the help of black churches, it seemed that Martin Luther King's great dream might soon come true. However, there are still many racial and spiritual conflicts everywhere. Obama used drones, controlled from Arizona, to kill fundamentalists in Pakistan and Yemen, whilst the whole of the Middle East is in turmoil. Most Sunnis and Shiites distrust the USA, the UK, the EU and the UN. Each of these bodies has unity in its title but disunity within its ranks. Although the Roman-Catholics are still the largest faction in the USA, Humanism is the fastest growing ideology - without a global leader.

The Millennium was an artificial point in Time but it seemed to create mistrust, anxiety and disunity; rather than reuniting Our Human Race. Jews, Christians, Muslims, Hindus, Sikhs, Buddhists, Taoists, Animists will not see eye to eye until they use one chronology, calendar and clock. Our World is not the one that Adam, Noah, Abraham, Joseph, Moses, Jesus, Mohammed, Zoroaster, Krishna, Buddha, Lao or Confucius knew. Our Holy Grail, taken so long to discover, could be a complete system of measurements based upon the age, orbit, spin and girth of Planet Earth. Our Good Samaritan is the United Nations Organization and it could bring about Our salvation by advocating: **One Worldwide System**.

Temporal and Spatial Unity

We can create One World with one age, date, time, rule, measure and weight. However, fundamentalism, sectarianism and nationalism are pulling it apart. Unemployment, inflation, recession, poverty, disease, sleaze and crime are chronic problems, which can and must be solved on a global basis.

The government of The United Kingdom is now is in the state of disorder. Some wanted the UK to leave the EU; others wanted the UK to break-up. In Scotland there is now much more spiritual and temporal freedom. Scottish politicians say that their clocks should go back for one hour. In Northern Ireland the Sabbath day is still considered to be sacrosanct. Yet, Catholics and Protestants are singing from different hymn sheets. Regional matters are now dealt with by devolved national assemblies. However, the division of England into eight new regions was mishandled. The left wing is supported by the trade unions, who insist upon higher rates of pay for working at weekends and during 'the unsocial hours'. The right wing is supported by donations from industry and commerce who maintain that all days and hours should be paid at the same rate. There are now many different political parties, of almost every hue, but none of them seem to realize that the root cause of many problems is the measurement, management and government of Time and Space.

The European Union wants to control working hours and working days; free migration of its citizens but limited immigration from other states; free trade within its borders but limited importation from other states. If it really wants to encourage free trade it should allow all businesses to work at any time and all vehicles to use all of the roads on any date. It wants all of its states to use the same time, currency and systems. Yet, Little Britain has now left the EU so it can now do its own thing.

World leaders have yet to consider **full-time-job-sharing-as-the-norm**, at their regular summit meetings, as a solution to many global issues. Jacques Delors said that European unemployment was far too high and must be tackled by borrowing, spending and cutting the working week. Bill Clinton said that full employment was the key to solving many ills, and yet he could not prevent the post-Millennium economic slow-down. Boris Yeltsin said that organized and petty crime was his biggest problem, and yet he did nothing to alleviate the underlying cause of this issue. The root cause is the seven-day week and the twenty-four hour day.

Our Human Race can be reunited by the same temporal-spatial system. The United Nations was established to solve global problems of this kind. As a member of Our Human Race and a Citizen of the World I formally asked the UN Secretary-General to set-up a study group to look into this. I suggested **One Worldwide System** and sent him a copy of this book. I was informed that he had no control over temporal nor spatial matters.

Sacrilege

It was considered to be sacrilegious to work on holy days and in some religious states this is still considered to be a reason for punishment. It is not only different religions that cause wars but also different sects, who celebrate different holy days, because they use different calendars.

Britain is now considered to be a Protestant country because it does not celebrate saints' days, yet Christmas and Easter are still public holy days. Protestant William III arrived when Roman-Catholic James II abdicated. The Troubles in Ulster during recent decades were a continuation of the Battle of the Boyne between the Protestants and the Roman-Catholics. The Easter Uprising in 1916 AD soon resulted in the foundation of Eire. Most of Ireland became a republic but Ulster remained loyal to the King. In Ulster the Protestants were allowed to vote but the Catholics were not. This led to the bloody Troubles, which ended on Good Friday in 1998 AD. Northern Ireland is now a self-governing province of the United Kingdom. Nevertheless, it may take another generation before all of Our days are considered to be equal and the island of Ireland is one secular nation. Children who were born after the Troubles were over are fighting again. Bigotry is being passed on to the next generation through faith schools. Attempts to solve this by making them take a proportion of their pupils from other faiths is never going to work, because faith is all in the mind. The only rational solution is to start again with a clean calendar.

The recent wars in the Balkans were the continuation of the ancient Pagan animosities between the Western and Eastern Roman Empires. This became a conflict between the Roman-Catholic and Orthodox sects with a remnant of the Muslim Ottoman Empire sandwiched in between. The Balkans were part of the Roman-Catholic Austro-Hungarian Empire, which sided with Protestant Germany but broke-up after World War 1. Tito pulled the Balkan states together to fight the Axis in World War 2. He created one secular state, under Communism, called: Yugoslavia. However, Marx's Big Idea of a state run by the workers did not work. So when Tito died the ancient sectarian conflicts began all over again. Despite a UN arms embargo on all sides in the dispute, the CIA was secretly arming and training Croats, the KGB was secretly arming and training Serbs and Islam was secretly arming and training Muslims. As the Bosnian War ended, NATO took over as peace keeper from the UN. Both were dominated by USA so white armored cars were painted green. The Church claimed it was a political war and nothing to do with religion but everyone saw television footage of churches and mosques being razed.

Christmas and Easter are not holy days in USA because the Bill of Rights and First Amendment do not allow the celebration of religious festivals. However, the USA uses the Roman-Catholic age, date, time and zones. It also celebrates the Roman-Catholic New Year as a public holiday.

Sacrifice

The sacrifice of calves, lambs, goats, slaves and even their own children,
on certain days in the year, was the Pagan way of divining the future.
By appeasing their gods, in this way, they hoped to avoid catastrophes.
Abraham offered his sons up to *Yahweh, God* or *Allah* as a sacrifice.
The sacraments of bread and wine mean the flesh and blood of Christ.
The Jews made sacrifices to The Ark of the Covenant in The Temple.
The Muslims still sacrifice camels and goats in their holy city of Mecca.
The Christians still sacrifice their son of *God* on every bloody Sunday.
The Roman legions sacrificed their animals to their Imperial standards.
The Egyptians made sacrifices to obelisks, which represented the Sun-god.
The Phoenicians sacrificed their children to honour their fertility gods.
The Maya and Aztecs tore out the hearts of slaves to honour Sky-gods.
The Inca sacrificed their children to the gods of the Andes mountains.
The Minoans sacrificed bulls and boys to appease the god of the volcano.
The Hindus in Indonesia still make sacrifices to the gods of volcanoes.
The sacrifice of bulls is still a public entertainment in parts of Spain.
The burning of witches and heretics took the place of public sacrifice.
Public executions became a cruel form of entertainment for the masses.
Guy Fawkes Night on 5 November is an annual reminder of this practice.

The pocket watches issued to the British and German troops in WW1
ensured that they all died simultaneously when they went over the top.
Both sides moved the hands on their clocks forward by one hour in the
summer to make the most of daylight and to confuse their enemies.
They used the same calendar and even played football on Christmas day.
This did not stop them from fighting and killing each other on other days.

Kings often lead their armies into battle but presidents hide in bunkers,
playing on boards with warships, tanks and planes, like a game of chess.
Pawns are often sacrificed in order to gain a little Space or a little Time.
To win it is necessary to sacrifice knights, bishops, castles or queens.
Perhaps, to gain greater democracy, We now have to sacrifice kings too.
Chronologies, calendars and clocks are thought to be sacrosanct but if
We were to scrap them it could be the start of a whole new board game.

If We are prepared to sacrifice Ourselves and even Our children for
a hidden leader, a sacred god or a great ideal, why not sacrifice **Time**?
Worldwide Time can ensure that We would never make sacrifices again.
It is time to wipe the slate clean and start again with better standards.
To scrap all of Our calendars, diaries, timetables, clocks and watches,
at exactly the same moment, would be a high point in Human history.
It would be an act of solidarity which could reunite Our Human Race.
We would all give up something in order to create something better.
We would all carry with pride a new global-digital-decimal standard.
Every one of Us would be involved in this greatest sacrifice of all **Time**.

Schisms

The schisms which started new religions during the first millennium AD, those which occurred in these beliefs during the second millennium AD and those occurring in all these sects during the third millennium AD are still causing bloody conflicts in all the holy lands where they began. Christianity emerged after of a schism within the Orthodox Jewish faith, partially due to using different years, months, weeks, days and hours. The great schism which separated the Orthodox and Catholic Churches was due to a quarrel over the true date of Easter and this difference was increased when the Orthodox and Anglican Churches retained the Julian calendar after the Catholic Church adopted Pope Gregory XIII's reforms. The Anglican Church took two centuries to adopt the Gregorian calendar. The ten Eastern Orthodox Churches still adhere to the Julian months. The Coptic, Ethiopic and Armenian Churches still use the Siriac months. There are many other sects and calendars within the Christian faith. Similarly the Muslim faith is divided by Shiite Solar and Sunni Lunar calendars and by the feasts, fasts and other rituals that go with them. The Hindus still use a variety of chronologies, calendars and clocks. The Sikhs once used a Lunar calendar but they now use a Solar one. Buddhism uses its own chronology, calendar and clock to pass Time.

Ethnic cleansing has been used in the Balkan States for a millennium. Orthodox Serbs, Catholic Croats and Bosnian Muslims were born with empty brains which, as soon as they could learn, were filled with dogma. Many babes and infants were murdered before they could even begin to understand the cruel World about them, their killers did not understand why they did it and old friends or neighbours vowed to kill each other. Muslim girls were raped and forced to bear Serbian or Croatian children. Their genes are all very similar, it is only their dogmas that are different. Whilst Saddam Hussein was a brutal dictator he did turn Iraq into a secular state and it is hard to see how all the religious factions will ever learn how to live in peace, unless they use the same age, date and time. As soon as the Americans left they were at each other's throats again and exactly the same thing is happening throughout the Islamic World. Just when We thought the Catholics and the Protestants were making peace in Ulster they started to burn each other's churches and families. Their Troubles began when they started to observe different holy days.

Jews, Christians, Muslims, Hindus, Sikhs, Jains, Buddhists, Taoists and followers of other religions and sects all belong to Our Human Race. Whilst there are outward differences like dress, diet and hairstyle as well as inward differences in their beliefs, rites, dogmas and cultures, there are very few fundamental differences in their morals or ethics. It is their many different chronologies, calendars, clocks and time zones which, directly or indirectly, cause great conflicts everywhere on Earth. We will only be able to rebuild One World when We have One Time.

-isms

Religion was considered to be the cement that bonded society together. Yet, the World's great religions were separated by different Time systems. Judaism was divided by calendars into traditional Phariseeism, classical Sadduceeism, radical Esseneism, militant Zealotism, modern Zionism. The Christian Church was divided by calendars into many different sects: Coptism, Orthodoxism, Catholicism, Anglicism, Quakerism, Methodism. Mohammedism was divided by calendars into Shiitism and Sunniism. Hinduism, Sikhism, Jainism, Buddhism, Shintoism, Taoism, Bahaism use different chronologies and calendars based on the Sun and/or Moon. Holy days and holidays cause religious, political, social and ideological conflict but these different beliefs are all private and personal matters, which only become public affairs when politics come into the picture. Politicians have not yet realized that public holidays are anachronisms and that private holidays could be taken whenever it is most convenient.

No sooner had the religious wars stopped than the political ones started. Many of the wars in the developing World are the relics of colonialism. Those who drew the border lines across Africa, Asia and South America cut-off nations from the sea and, consequently, the rest of the World. Many of them were drawn along imaginary lines of latitude or longitude. Time zones divide Our Human Race with imaginary political barriers that could be instantly demolished if We decided to use the same time zone. We applauded the smashing of the Berlin Wall but there are now many more fences across the steppes where Genghis Khan once freely roamed. We should be pulling down all of the barriers but We keep erecting more. Totalitarianism is certainly not the answer to religious fundamentalism. Yet, freedom of thought, a liberal education and democracy may well be. Capitalism and Socialism could flourish together, in the central ground, if 360 days were the same, most jobs were shared in a ten-day week and the remaining 5 or 6 days were reserved for the democratic process. This ideal embraces antisabbatarianism and disestablishmentarianism - two of the longest words in the English language.

We cannot begin to share Our wealth until We learn to share Our work. Keynesism and monetarism could be used, simultaneously, to control the economy if there were no inflation, no unemployment and no deficit. Full employment would be the solution to racism, sexism and ageism. Only when We realize that We are all the same and that We all have the same aims in Life will We be able to live together in some kind of peace. Idealists dreamed up: Nationalism, Communism, Socialism, Liberalism, Capitalism, Fascism, Pragmatism, Materialism and, inevitably: Idealism. All idealists tend to be frowned upon by most of the political parties. However, they have completely lost sight of their own original ideals. They all confuse religion with sociology, economics, science and politics. The ideal society embraces a new kind of Humanism: **Twomanism**.

Revelations

It has taken Us millions of years to understand *Mother Nature's* secrets. Storms, floods, droughts, eruptions, earthquakes were ascribed to gods and are they still considered by insurance companies to be acts of *God*. The Pagan civilization who built numerous stone monuments throughout Europe worshipped *Mother Nature* or *Mother Earth* as the *Great Goddess*. The Mesopotamians and Egyptians invented gods to control everything. The Greeks and Romans adopted many of these gods, rules and ideas. Judaism, Christianity and Islam have one invisible deity but many tales in *The Talmud*, *The Bible* and *The Koran* hark back to earlier inspiration. Inevitably, the Sky and the bowels of the Earth became Heaven and Hell. The prophets enlarged upon verbal traditions to forecast the future but they often ascribed their revelations to the greater authority of angels. It is thought that this belief in bird-men goes back to a tribe of giant blue-eyed watchers called: *nephilim,* who wore cloaks made from feathers and lived in the mountains that are now in the region called: Kurdistan.

Abraham was guided by three angels, who were in the guise of mortals. Moses was visited by the archangel *Michaiel* on the top of Mount Sinai. *Michaiel* spoke to *Yahweh* who handed down *The Ten Commandments*. These are similar to the *Negative Confessions* in *The Book of the Dead*. The prophets predicted that the Messiah would arrive at a conjunction and that his miraculous birth to a virgin would be heralded by angels. This might hark back to the belief in the virgin birth of *Horus* to *Isis*. This myth may also have led to a belief in the virgin birth of *Mithras*. Or it may have its origins in the virgin birth of *Krishna or Krista* (Christ). John the Divine wrote about angels, demons, dragons, beasts and the Last Judgment at the End of Time when *Michaiel* will weigh Our souls before admitting Us to Heaven or Hell but this vision may hark back to the weighing of the heart ceremony described in *The Book of the Dead*. *Anubis* balanced the scales and *Thoth* recorded all the measurements. Saint John's revelations were numerical and linked with a Millennium. *Michael* slayed the 666 Beast, the 7-Headed Dragon and *Satan* himself. The prophet Mohammad dictated the *Koran* over a period of twenty years but he then ascribed his divine inspiration to the archangel *Gabriel*. According to Islamic belief: the archangel *Michaiel* will sound a trumpet to herald in the New Age when the power of **Time** is finally defeated.

Angels often appeared in hallucinations or dreams to religious fanatics. They even inspired architects, writers, sculptors, artists and musicians. Spiritual experiences can now be explained as malfunctions of the brain. As We pass the Millennium there is renewed interest in guardian angels. Many superstitious Christians still believe in supernatural happenings. Many Americans believe in angels and that some visited Los Angeles. *Superman* was inspired by many revelations about the guardian angels. *Batman* was inspired by many discoveries about science and technology.

Discoveries

Christianity is based on the myth that *God* created Time, Space and Life.
Its chronology is based on the myth of the virgin birth of the Messiah.
Its calendar is based on myths of 12 months and *Seven Heavenly Bodies*.
Its clock is based on myths about the 12 day-hours and 12 night-hours.
Its zones are based on the myth that clocks should point up at noon.
These fundamental Christian beliefs are all based upon unsubstantiated
revelations which are now entirely challenged by scientific discoveries.
Pope John Paul II encouraged the arts but he also stifled the sciences.
He even regarded scientific enlightenment to be the very root of all evil.
Yet, many important scientific discoveries were made by churchmen.
It is only since the French Revolution that real progress has been made.
He said this was the worst thing that happened to the Catholic Church.
In France today there are as many Humanists as there are Christians.
Humanists believe in Evolution whilst Christians believe in Creation.

We are still discovering the mysteries of Outer Space and Inner Space.
Our Outer Space probes have reached to the edge of Our Solar System.
They are also investigating the Sun-spots, Solar flares and Solar winds.
We have been to the Moon and seen the Planets, Asteroids and Comets.
Our Inner Space probes have reached to the very bottom of the oceans.
We now know that all the continents are moving on tectonic plates.
Our Planet's mantle is still being created and destroyed simultaneously.
We have seen earth emerging in ridges and disappearing in trenches.
Magma forms peaks and troughs which are magnetized when they cool.
They represent a continuous chronology of this Planet during its lifetime.
Every 200,000 years or so the magnetic polarity of this Planet reverses.
The Earth's solid iron inner core spins slightly faster than its mantle.
This vast dynamo probably causes the magnetic poles to vary and flip.
We know that the Sun and the Moon control the seasons and the tides.
They also affect the earthquakes and eruptions in the Earth's mantle.
More of these cataclysms occur near solstices, equinoxes and eclipses.
We now know that the force of gravity has frequently caused the Planets
and moons to change their orbits or spins throughout Our Solar System.

Science and technology may be able to answer many crucial questions.
Yet scientists and technologists in various fields rarely talk to each other.
The study of Time and Space is divided into many different disciplines.
Mathematicians are supposed to solve any problem by using numbers.
Computers can quickly solve many complex equations simultaneously.
However, the ages, dates and times used in computers are supernatural.
They are incompatible with mathematics and can give wrong answers.
Many of Our computers were predicted to go haywire at the Millennium
due to using only two digits to indicate the age since Christ was born.
The Metric Millennium arrived at exactly the right moment to put all of
Our chronologies, calendars, clocks, rules and measures right - forever.

Hindsight

Hindsight is normally 20/20 but the mists of Time often cloud the issue. It is becoming clear that many of the ancient tales, myths and legends, from around the globe, were warnings from past generations to Us today. Some of them seem to be based upon the arbitrary age of a Millennium. Yet, this Millennium is not an arbitrary age; it is a rare celestial event. It is marked in Heaven by extremely rare conjunctions and alignments. It is marked on Earth by twelve millennia of civilization, the end of the Christian Age of Pisces and the start of the Humanist Age of Aquarius. Perhaps, it is also marked by Our strange fascination with rows of zeros. If so, then 000:000.000 is far more fascinating than 00:00 on 01/01/01.

Many new theories about the Universe seem to get queerer and queerer. The further We gaze into Outer Space, the nearer We get to the Big Bang. Stephen Hawking said that the Universe was once the size of a pea and that it will keep expanding for ever but John Paul II warned him not to think about what happened before the Big Bang, for he might find *God*. Many clever physicists, chemists, biologists, astronomers and astronauts believe that everything in the Universe fits into some vast eternal plan and *God* wrote the laws of physics, chemistry, biology and astronomy. Conversely, Richard Dawkins contends that We are all here by chance, through Natural Selection and that the belief in *God* is just a delusion. Dawkins maintains that all *The Ten Commandments* are perfectly logical. Nevertheless, the Universe was not created in six days plus one of rest although many still believe that this was the origin of the Mystic week. The author suggested to Dawkins that the Mystic week has had its day. He contended that it is now part of Our culture, so it cannot be changed. Yet, all the days in the year are rapidly becoming the same once again.

Civilizations died out because they could not learn from past experience. We are learning about their mistakes; yet making them all over again. Religion has returned with a vengeance to former secular states, where it was forced underground, but this will inevitably end in more bloodshed. All religion is based upon fear, ignorance, misguidance and superstition. There is no deity watching over Us; We are all mortals and will all die. There is no life after death; We have no spirits, no souls and no ghosts. Yet, some still cling to these ancient beliefs, rather than logical thoughts, and these often lead to bloody conflicts where religious ideas overlap. Ancient conflicts were about the survival of the fittest men and ideas. Modern conflicts are the result of misunderstanding and misconception. The way to prevent them is to all use the same language and system. English is now spoken in all of the international corridors of power and this is also the language spoken by all the air and sea traffic controllers. All navigators now use latitude and longitude, based upon Greenwich. In another generation Our World might learn to speak English and use: **The Worldwide Measurement, Management and Government System.**

Foresight

The Victorians had foresight: they built great public and private buildings
as well as canals, railways, roads, bridges, tunnels, sewers and drains.
They created national and local parks and green belts around the cities.
They created a Great British Empire and Imperial Measurement System.
No one has any foresight today; everyone is scared to make a decision.
Most politicians would rather cling to ancient traditions than modernize.
The Houses of Parliament and their great clock tower are crumbling away.
The rational solution is not to renew them but to replace them with a
circular forum and electronic referendums, without any political parties.
We no longer need Lords Spitual, Lords Temporal nor a House of Lords.
We no longer need monumental clocks, since We all have electronic ones.
Margaret Thatcher wanted Little Britain to return to Victorian values.
Yet, it no longer has an Empire and it no longer uses the Imperial System.
It does not have to use the faulty Metric System and needs to start again
at square zero with the global-digital-decimal **Worldwide System**.

The Victorians who drew the Prime Meridian through Greenwich did not
have sufficient foresight to implement one global-digital-decimal system.
We now need to look again at those invisible lines around the globe.
We only need one time zone, yet We should only work during daylight.
We should also decimalize the 360 degrees of latitude and longitude.
And base all measurements upon a millionth of a degree of longitude.
We also need a secular, global-digital-decimal age, date and time system.
We are in the 21st century AD but this is a Roman-Catholic chronology.
Many secularists now use the same chronology but with Common Era.
However, there is no need now to count years backwards and forwards.
We know the age of Our Planet and the age of Our global civilization.
So Our new secular chronology should be based upon the year zero.
We need to forget the higgledy-piggledy Roman-Catholic calendar months
and all of the other ways of counting the days throughout the Solar year.
Our new Solar calendar should start at day zero on the vernal equinox.
If We number the days they will Naturally drop into handy groups of ten.
A ten-day week will encourage Us to share Our work and Our wealth.
We should no longer use Roman-Catholic hours, minutes and seconds.
Our new secular clock should start at zero, then show decimals of a day.
We no longer need monumental clocks, with bells on, to tell Us the time.
Zero is silent, so analogue **decimal time** clocks should have ten on top.

We need a vision of the future: Atlantis, Paradise, Utopia, Decadeciland.
Decadeciland is a place where everything is multiplied or divided by ten.
Everybody has a full-time job, which they share with somebody else.
Computers are now so intelligent that they might soon replace brains.
They are already taking over jobs but the remaining work is not shared.
The only way to share work efficiently and fairly is to divide weeks in half
so that the left and the right can share Our Planet - wherever it is.

Time, Space and Life on Earth

If God created Time, Space and Life:
If He created all of Us in His likeness:
Is the face of Man the very face of God?
Are the hands of Man the hands of God?
Did He intend Us to count on Our digits?

If God created Man here on Planet Earth:
Why do We need many different ages?
Why do We need many different dates?
Why do We need many different times?
Why do We need many different zones?

If God created the Sun and the Moon:
What is the number of days in a year?
What is the number of days in a moonth?
What is the number of moonths in a year?
How did He intend Us to make calendars?

If God created the Earth and the Moon:
When was the beginning of the Earth's age?
When was the beginning of the Earth's orbit?
When was the beginning of the Earth's spin?
When was the beginning of the Moon's phases?

If God created the Ten Heavenly Bodies
Did He command Us to use 1000-year millennia?
Did He command Us to use 100-year centuries?
Did He command Us to use 10-year decades?
Did He command Us to use 10-day weeks?

If God created the Heavenly Clockwork:
Did He intend Us to use a global age?
Did He intend Us to use a digital date?
Did He intend Us to use a decimal time?
Did He intend Us to use a single zone?

If God created Us and Our Planet Earth:
Did He intend Us to measure its girth?
Why is this so difficult to measure?
What size of measure should We use?
Did He intend Us to use a global rule?

If God created the Universe with a Big Bang,
And all the laws of science and technology:
Why are they so difficult for Us to discover?
Will We ever find all of His hidden secrets?
Or will He destroy all of Us before We can?

Part Eleven

Legislation

Changing Our Laws

"A stand can be made against the invasion of an army.
No stand can be made against the invasion of an idea."

Victor Hugo (1802-1885 AD)

Time Gods

Most ancient civilizations imagined then worshipped a pantheon of gods. The fear of catastrophes: fires, storms, floods, earthquakes or volcanoes, which coincided with astronomical events, led to the religion of Sky-gods. It also led to the superstition of astrology and the science of astronomy. Every civilization developed a different chronology, calendar and clock. Their different temples had different dimensions, different proportions, different alignments to celestial markers and venerated different gods. These gods were worshipped at different times on different days of the different weeks, different months and different years in different places. These temporal and spatial differences still divide Our Human Race.

Abraham, Moses, Jesus and Mohammed believed in one omnipotent god. Half of the inhabitants of Our Planet now believe in *Yahweh/God/Allah*. Yet, Jews, Christians and Muslims are still killing each other and razing each other's sacred temples, synagogues, chapels, churches or mosques. Other religions still worship many different gods in different temples. Different sects of the same religion are fighting and killing each other because they all use different chronologies, calendars, clocks and zones. There are other differences but rituals are the main cause of conflict. An attempt was made to devise one new religion with a new calendar. The Baha'i religion has 19 'months' of 19 days plus a 4-5 day remainder. However, this odd calendar has no working weeks and no Sabbath days.

Our Planet is divided by religion but some of Us are starting to question whether We still need gods and what kind of civilization can be created if We use the same measurement, management and government system. Most of Us now use the International System but this has many faults. The metre is based on the Atomic second, so Space is based upon Time. Nevertheless, a Cosmic second is an eighty-six-thousand-four-hundredth part of a mean Solar day and an Atomic second is almost the same size. So Metric Time and Space are neither global nor digital nor decimal. The Americans have not yet adopted this faulty system and so they could be the first to adopt a brand new system, then spread it around the globe. They have quickly adopted many electronic systems but seem reluctant to adopt any new measurement, management and government systems.

We are the youngest Humanoid species, yet We advanced the fastest. We *Homo sapiens* took a Giant Leap some 200,000 years ago when Our brains were suddenly enlarged by 50% and We took another Giant Leap some 12,000 years ago when We started to measure Time and Space. Our last Giant Leap was when Mankind landed upon Our Planet's Moon. Our next Giant Leap could be when We step on another Planet or Moon. Yet, it could occur when We realize that We are all the same species and so must use the same system of measurements throughout Our Planet. If We can find temporal and spatial unity We might find spiritual unity.

Time Lords

Chinese and Japanese emperors, Egyptian pharaohs, Babylonian kings, Persian shahs, Greek princes, Indian rajahs, Mayan lords and Inca chiefs relied on astronomer-priests to tell them the age, the date and the time. These Time Lords realized that religion was 'the opium of the people'. So, by linking Time with faith, they could keep control of the masses. Each religion or civilization had its own chronology, calendar and clock. This, fundamentally, set them apart from other religions or civilizations. They all had different distances, lengths, areas, volumes and weights. These differences divided Our Human Race, yet one system of measures, based upon the number of digits on Our hands, could soon reunite Us.

The Time and Space 'system' now used by Christians and atheists alike was devised by numerous astronomer-priests over several millennia. Popes said that annual, weekly and daily rituals were ordained by *God*. Rulers said that inches and feet should be measured with their rulers. The poor gradually realized that they were being duped by the rich. The Pope had no divine authority and abused the power he was given. There was no *God* so there was no divine chronology, calendar and clock. The ruler had no real power, so there were many inches, feet and yards. Yet, there was an obvious need for one global Time and Space system. The French revolutionaries saw the light, two centuries ago, and tried to put their age, date, time and rule right; but their system was wrong. Their Solar chronology was based upon the year of their revolution. Their Solar calendar months, weeks and days were named in French. Their Solar clock started at ten, not zero, when the Sun was overhead. The time in Paris was still different from the time in Lyons or London. They surveyed the Paris Meridian but did not measure the girth of Earth. Their prototype Metric Time and Space System still had many faults. Napoleon did not understand this faulty system and so he abolished it. It was far from being a perfect solution that could be used by all of Us. Yet, no one seems to have proposed a more rational system - until now.

Our problem today is that We have no Space-Time Lords; only impotent monarchs, corrupt clerics, sleazy politicians and faceless bureaucrats. Today's scientists, inventors and visionaries are either thought to be mad or trusted too much, because today's leaders do not understand them. The International Standards Organization controls the Metric System. It should also be unifying Our chronology, calendar, clock and zones. However, it still uses the Roman-Catholic age, date and time system. The World's only superpower has taken over the control of Space-Time. The USA regulates the Atomic second and therefore the metre or meter. It currently controls the Global Positioning System, the Internet and the Worldwide Web, so it can prevent the rest of Our World from using them. The science fiction writers suppose We might travel through Space-Time. What age, date, time and rule will We use in MMM, Y3K or 3000 AD?

Time Laws

Our Time on this Earth was once regulated by the Sun and the Moon. Then by gods linked with the Sun, the Moon, the Planets and the Stars. Then by leaders who imposed their chronologies, calendars and clocks. Then by officials who regulated working, shopping, eating and drinking. It is time to reconsider the measurement, management and government of Time and Space in England, Britain, Europe and the rest of Our World.

The International Metric System has now been adopted by most states. Little Britain stubbornly stuck to its traditional way of doing things. It clung to its fractional Imperial System although it had lost its empire. When it became part of the European Union it was dragged, kicking and screaming, into metrification and yet it still uses miles and pints. It was considered to be too expensive to engrave 250 ml or 500 ml lines on tankards, yet Tony Blair proposed larger ones with anti-spill lines. It was considered too expensive to change road signs to kilometres but every car has a speedometer calibrated in kilometres and miles per hour, although its odometer only reads in one unit of distance or the other. The ultimate answer is to scrap the mile, the kilometre and the hour, then start again with the global-digital-decimal **Worldwide System**.

Britain was a member of the European Union so had to abide by its laws. The Social Chapter in the Lisbon Treaty still makes Sundays special. The Working Time Directive imposes a maximum of 48 hours per week. Some Eurocrats are talking about reducing this to 35 hours per week and imposing a maximum of four working days in every seven-day week. France has already adopted this restrictive system and, although it now has the best infrastructure of any European state, it is almost bankrupt. Commercial vehicles are not permitted to use the roads at weekends. Many shops are closed from noon on Saturday to noon on Monday. These restrictive laws and bylaws are strangling the European economy. Britain is now out of Europe so it can pass new laws and scrap old ones. It must start again with a clean sheet of paper and a global-digital-decimal measurement, management and government system.

We have no global government but We subscribe to many multinational conventions and We have already agreed to the international time zones. This was a great mistake and We should have agreed to use the same clock time everywhere and to do most of Our work during daylight. We have yet to agree upon the same chronology, calendar and clock. Although We all use the 12 or 24-hour clock and the seven-day week, it is now time for these archaic, Man-made units of Time to change. The Metric System is not global, nor digital nor decimal but a disaster, perpetrated by lawyers and politicians; not by scientists and engineers. Since the Prime Meridian passes through Greenwich it is beholden upon the English to point out that both Time and Space are way out of kilter.

Time Wars

Wars broke out, throughout history, when civilizations, races, religions, philosophies, doctrines, dogmas or cultures clashed, instead of coexisted. The greatest difference was in their chronologies, calendars and clocks; their distances, directions, angles, dimensions, weights and measures; as well as their languages, scripts, numbers, currencies and standards.

An argument over time zones led to WW1 when Serbian dissidents shot Archduke Frans Ferdinand and so ended the Austro-Hungarian Empire. During WW1 Kaiser Wilhelm II introduced summer time to Germany. Britain followed suit, then the USA and, eventually, much of the World. During WW2 Adolf Hitler's war machine used Berlin time everywhere. Winston Churchill introduced double summer time throughout Britain. Franklin Roosevelt moved the USA's clocks forward after Pearl Harbour. The Japanese dawn attack on a Sunday sunk much of the Pacific Fleet. Joseph Stalin put all the USSR's clocks forward for summer in 1930 AD. He forgot to put them back again for winter - but nobody dared tell him. The Russians now realize that eleven time zones divide-up their nation. President Medevlev wanted to cut this to four but they should have one, like the Chinese, and simply go back to working, mostly, in daylight. At the Chinese New Year of the Dragon (Gregorian 23 January 2012 AD) some Tibetan activists were shot for refusing to recognize the calendar. Every European city was on alert at the Gregorian New Year in 2016 AD. We will not achieve global peace until We celebrate only one New Year.

The Battle of Britain during 1940 AD marked the turning point in WW2. The Spitfires and Hurricanes were only just superior to Messerschmitts but Britain had radar and its hidden factories were working double shifts for six days every week, whilst Germans were only working single shifts. The Brits were prepared to work unsocial hours - it was their finest hour. Yet, in peacetime, management and unions pulled industry apart again. Shift-working is a form of job-sharing and the management of time is crucial at times of national crisis, such as many nations are facing now.

The EU want Britain, Ireland and Portugal to use Central European time. This could be called Roman-Catholic time - based upon midday in Rome. The whole of the EU already uses the Roman-Catholic age and date. They decided to change to and from summer time on the same days. Nevertheless, the USA still starts its daylight saving time one week later. Turkey's President Erdogan postponed the end of daylight saving time until after the general election but many clocks changed automatically, causing confusion throughout the land, in the autumn of 2015 AD. Jewish time and Muslim time are still out-of-step with Christian time, because they are still based upon midday in Jerusalem and Mecca. The final solution is to abandon all the time zones and daylight saving measures and use the same age, date and time everywhere on Earth.

Commandments

The Ark of the Covenant, with its *Ten Commandments*, has been lost. Does it contain two tablets of stone, in what language were they written and do they command Us to always use the Mystic seven-day week? Must We keep taking those tablets; now that We have tablet computers?

Our World is different from the one Moses, Jesus and Mohammed knew. Yet, Jewish, Christian and Muslim priests still dominate their followers, from cradle to grave, with different chronologies, calendars and clocks. They all use exactly the same seven-day week but each of these religions has a different day for praying to and paying for *Yahweh, God* or *Allah*. We know for certain that the Universe was not created in seven days. There are *Ten Heavenly Bodies*: the Sun and its nine major Planets. So We can forget the dogmas associated with the Mystic seven-day week. We have now reached the point in history when those who live in the developed World only need to work on half of the days in the year and those in the developing World only need to work on four days in five. So it is now time to begin again and share most jobs in a ten-day week. A post-modern Decadecilogue might look something like this:

The Ten Worldwide Commandments

1 **All Members of Our Human Race or Citizens of Our World must use one language, one script and one measurement system.**

2 **You only have one life so make the most of your opportunities.**

3 **Share your work, wealth and possessions as much as possible.**

4 **Men and women are born equal, so must be given equal rights, irrespective of race, creed or age and equal opportunity to advance.**

5 **Obey your superiors but always question their judgment.**

6 **Do not do to others anything that you would not allow them to do to you and do not abuse your own body.**

7 **Do not increase Our population nor damage Our Planet.**

8 **Think, write or portray whatever you want but do not impose your beliefs upon others.**

9 **Do not give or take credit without funds, plant viruses, hack into phones or computers, divert pension funds, use creative accounting, destroy endangered species, waste resources...**

10 **Count everything in tens, hundreds, thousands, millions, billions...**

Commands

The pharaohs, kings, queens, emperors, dictators, presidents and popes all issued their commands about the measurement of Time and Space. In 586 BC King Nebuchadnezzar decreed one day of rest in every seven. In 878 AD King Alfred divided all working days into three equal parts. In 1100 AD King Henry I measured the length of his arm to make a yard. In 1215 AD King John's *Magna Carta* decreed that England should have only one bottle of wine, one measure of corn and one width of cloth. In 1303 AD the pound (*libre*) was standardized by merchants in London. In 1352 AD Edward III commanded that a stone must weigh 14 pounds. In 1532 AD Henry VIII decreed that a pound must divide into 16 ounces. In 1824 AD George IV's peers passed The Weights and Measures Act, which established the Imperial System with feet, pounds and seconds. In 1972 AD Britain handed-over its weights and measures to Europe. In 1995 AD all goods throughout Europe had to be sold in Metric sizes. In 2008 AD Europe permitted Britain to use Imperial alongside Metric.

Francis Bacon proposed a scientific society in *New Atlantis* in 1627 AD. His hypothesis influenced the Freemasons in England and New England. They were behind the establishment of scientific societies or institutions. The British beheaded their Roman-Catholic King Charles I in 1649 AD. Parliament then appointed a Protector, Oliver Cromwell (1599-1658 AD) who annihilated many of the Roman-Catholic theocracy and aristocracy. After the Monarchy was restored in 1660 AD, Charles II (1630-1685 AD) chartered The Royal Society and it soon became the driving force behind more accurate measurements and many other scientific advancements. Its first secretary: John Wilkins (1614-1672 AD) wed Cromwell's sister. He became the Warden of Wadham College Oxford, then Master of Trinity College Cambridge then, after the restoration, C of E Bishop of Chester. His main interest was to establish a global standard scientific language. At the suggestion of Christopher Wren (1632-1723 AD) he promulgated a measurement system based upon the length of a one second pendulum. This length of about 39.25 inches would be multiplied or divided by tens, squared for areas, cubed for volumes and filled with water for weights. This digital-decimal scale would be the basis for a new gold standard. His *Essay Towards a Real Character and Philosophical Language* was destroyed in the Great Fire of London in 1666 AD but was rewritten and published by The Royal Society in 1668 AD, pre-empting metrification. The Royal Society established the Royal Observatory at Greenwich and its Meridian as the one on which both Time and Space should be based.

The Metric System was proposed by Abbe Gabriel Mouton in 1670 AD. He suggested that it should be based upon the size of Our Planet Earth. The Academy of Sciences supported this and it was adopted in 1799 AD, after the monarchy, aristocracy and theocracy had all been guillotined. This system is now used by most of Us but it is far from being perfect.

Rules

Every civilization must have its own set of rules, which must be obeyed; but changing these rules is very much more difficult than it may seem. We searched in vain for any Natural units for measuring distances and directions or dimensions and angles and so We used Our own anatomy. This was not very satisfactory because We come in all shapes and sizes. And so different rulers decreed different standard rulers and protractors. Many men from Alexander to Hitler have attempted to rule Our World. We rule it now, through Our global membership of the United Nations. However, it seems impossible for any Citizen of Our World to put it right.

All of the ancient and modern monuments, built throughout the globe, are records of all the different dimensions used by different civilizations. The Jews believed that *Yahweh* had told them to use the sacred cubit. It was used to measure their Ark, their Tabernacle and their Temple. They were forbidden to walk more than 1,000 cubits on the Sabbath. If there was a *God* then *He, She* or *It* would solve all of Our problems. Including the perpetual problem of which measurement system to use.

Two centuries ago it became obvious that there should be a global set of standards, because global trade in manufactured goods was increasing. The Metric System was supposed to be the global standard but it was based upon an inaccurate survey of a Meridian, instead of the Equator. We now have three distances: statute mile, nautical mile and kilometre; four lengths: inch, foot, yard and metre; two angles: degree and radian. None of these distances and lengths are satisfactory but degrees are OK. Most compass roses are divided into 360 degrees and cardinal directions. If Our Planet is divided-up into 360 degrees of latitude and longitude and circles are divided into 360 degrees, then the length of the Equator should be divided by 360 million *hans* - the width of an average hand. This handy unit can be multiplied or divided in a digital-decimal way. It can be used for all distances, lengths, areas, volumes and weights. Replacing one measuring stick with another is not a big deal but I can already hear all the mechanics moaning: Not another set of spanners! The International Standards Organization screwed-up Our nuts and bolts.

Like billions, throughout the World, who grovelled to the Sun, the Moon, the Planets and the Stars, there are now billions grovelling to VDUs. The personal computer has now become an omnipotent New Age deity. Information **T**echnology has led to the global communications network. **IT** has certainly changed Our World but **IT** cannot think for **IT**self. **IT**'s age is still backwards and forwards, **IT**'s date is still out-of-date, **IT**'s time is way behind the times and **IT**'s zones are anachronisms. **IT** has several rulers at the top of **IT**'s page but they are all wrong. **IT** must lead Us to freedom in the future; not handcuff Us to the past. **IT** must incorporate **The Worldwide System**.

Weights & Measures

There is no Natural basis for weights nor measures and so there were different trading standards for each territory and this caused a great deal of confusion, corruption and conflict in every corner of the ancient globe. One of the greatest achievements of the former British Empire was to enforce the standard Imperial System throughout all of its conquests. This helped to encourage trade between each of the member territories. However, it was not at all logical because it had many different bases. When the USA broke away from the British Empire it devised its own weights and measures, although its system was not very logical either. The International Metric System was an attempt at a global standard but has not yet been adopted by the USA, Liberia or Myanmar (Burma). Will these mavericks eventually come into line with the rest of Our World or will the USA be the first to use the more logical **Worldwide System**?

The Imperial, American and International Systems have different units for capacity or volume but in the **Worldwide System** they are the same. The only unit that stays about the same, the *Hcan* is just under a barrel. The petroleum industry uses the standard barrel, throughout the World. This barrel of 35 UK gallons or 42 US gallons is the only common unit. In the International Metric System a barrel contains about 159 litres. Yet, a standard barrel of beer contains 36 UK gallons or 288 UK pints. The topic in every British pub and club at the Metric Millennium was whether their pint tankards should have been replaced by half-litre ones. It would have been a simple matter for weights & measures inspectors to engrave lower levels on glasses, so that less beer would be spilled. However, the politicians realized that this was such an emotive issue that they had better leave things as they were for the time being. So they said that beer must be sold in litres in shops but pints in bars and that milk should be sold in litres in shops but pints when delivered. Fortunately, four tenths of a *can* is just under one pint tankard of beer. So British pubs and clubs can keep their traditional glassware after all. Unfortunately, milk delivery is dying out because it is much cheaper at the supermarkets where it is sold in plastic containers not glass bottles.

In the British Imperial System one gallon of water weighs ten pounds. In the International Metric System one litre of water weighs one kilogram. However, the precise definition of this standard is far more complicated. In the **Worldwide System** a cubic *han* or *can* of water weighs one *wan*. Using water is a convenient way of relating capacity/volume with weight. The division or multiplication of weights by this digital-decimal system results in a convenient range of standard sizes for weighing anything. So the *milliwan* or *Kilowan* would be used for smaller or larger objects. However, the force of gravity varies slightly on the surface of the Earth or greatly throughout the Universe, so scientists and engineers use mass. The force of gravity would need to be converted to the **Worldwide System**.

Rites

Many of the ancient monuments were chronologies, calendars or clocks, used for worshipping gods of the Earth, Sun, Moon, Planets and Stars. The Pagans met at these places during solstices, equinoxes or eclipses. The Egyptians made ritual offerings on certain dates at certain times. The Babylonians made ritual offerings on other dates at other times. The Hindus still gather together at planetary conjunctions and eclipses. The Maya, Aztecs and Inca went to the extreme rite of Human sacrifice to appease their Sky-gods, rain-gods, volcano-gods and mountain-gods. Each religion had its own burial rites - archaeologists can tell which one. Today's cemeteries are becoming so full and land is so expensive that most Chinese are buried standing-up and most Britons are cremated.

The Catholic priests and armies who followed Christopher Columbus to the New World, 500 years ago, introduced baptism, marriage, burial and holy communion rites as well as horses, genocide, slavery and smallpox. At the same time as Catholics were discovering and then conquering the New World they were also pushing the Muslims and Jews out of Spain. The Christian-Pagan Nazis attempted to push the Jews out of existence. The Muslims are pushing the Hindus out of Pakistan, Kurds out of Iraq, Christians out of Egypt, Libya, Sudan, Syria, Taoists out of Indonesia, Buddhists out of Afghanistan and have pushed Christians out of Turkey. The Christians have pushed the Jews and the Muslims out of Ethiopia. The Buddhists are pushing the Hindu Tamil Tigers out of Sri Lanka and the Muslims out of Burma, when they are supposed to be peaceful. The Hindus are still pushing the Muslims out of India and Kashmir. The Catholic Croats, the Orthodox Serbs and the Ottoman Muslims tried to push each other out of Bosnia Herzegovina in the former Yugoslavia. The Orthodox Serbs tried to push the Albanian Muslims out of Kosovo. The Orthodox Russians are trying push the Muslims out of Chechyna. The Catholics are still trying to push the Protestants out of all Ireland. Even when completely new religions are devised, such as the Badi faith with its new chronology, new calendar and new rites of passage its new peace-loving followers are pushed about by all of the other believers.

All over the World, very religious people are still pushing each other about because their chronologies, calendars, clocks and zones are incompatible. Humanists still tolerate the ancient rites and rituals of all the religions. However, they do not have a chronology, calendar and clock of their own. So they do not have any yearly, monthly, weekly or daily rites of passage. The Sabaeans honoured the *Seven Heavenly Bodies* in seven temples. Their ritual seven-day week has gradually become a global institution. Humanists could honour the *Ten Heavenly Bodies* with a ten-day week, based upon the number of digits that We all have on Our two hands. We are all Life members of Our Human Race and citizens of One World. We should all use exactly the same **Worldwide System**.

Rights

The first declaration of Human Rights was inscribed on a cylinder seal, when Persia became the greatest empire throughout the ancient World. In England it was the *Magna Carta* agreed at Runnymede by King John and his barons, 800 years ago, that gave his citizens their Human Rights. John Locke (1632-1704 AD) had lived through the English Civil War, when the people and the crown fought over the right to run the state. He had also lived through the period when King James II had tried to impose Roman-Catholicism on Great Britain but was opposed by force. Consequentially, he argued that it was a basic Human Right to believe whatever one likes and not have any kind of religion thrust upon one. Thomas Paine (1737-1809 AD) emigrated from Britain to the United States. His public statement that they should be independent was based upon:

> Nothing more than simple facts, plain arguments and common sense.

This secular ideology led to the separation of the United States from the rule of mad King George III and to the Declaration of Human Rights. The Founding Fathers demanded that politics be separated from religion. The following sentence is taken from the United States of America's Declaration of Independence from Great Britain in 1776 AD:

> We hold these truths to be self-evident, that all men are equal,
> that they are endowed with certain inalienable rights,
> that among these are: life, liberty and the pursuit of happiness.

Yet, slavery continued until 1860 AD, women did not vote until 1920 AD, racial discrimination until 1960 AD, religious discrimination until today. The USA still interns suspected terrorists for many years without trial.

When the French revolution broke out in 1789 AD enlightened thinkers dreamed of an egalitarian society, where there would be no privileges, no state religion and no Catholic chronology, calendar and clock. Their Declaration of the Rights of Man and the Citizen began:

> The representatives of the people sitting in the National Assembly,
> considering that ignorance of, neglect of, and contempt for the rights of men,
> are the sole causes of public misfortune and the corruption of governments,
> have resolved to set out the natural, inalienable and sacred rights of man...

H.G.Wells's book: *The Rights of Man* appealed to everyone after WW1. It led to the formation of the League of Nations and the United Nations. The UN published its Universal Declaration of Human Rights in 1948 AD.
> Article 23: everyone has the right to work.
> Article 24: everyone has the right to rest and leisure.

Europe adopted them at the Treaty of Rome in 1950 AD, however the European Court of Human Rights has been very slow to come into effect. Britain has adopted them, in the form of the Human Rights Act 1998 AD. Yet, it now wants to issue its own Bill of Rights to restrict immigration. Migration is now the greatest Human Rights issue throughout the globe.

Customs

Most of Us follow customs or traditions without knowing their origins, or their fundamental significance in the establishment of their society. It is customary for Jews to take Saturdays off work, Christians to take Sundays off work and for Muslims to take Fridays off work for prayer. None of the other religions have a special day in the week for prayer. Our name plus Our age, date and time of birth registers Us as a follower of a particular religion but, when We grow up, We may have no faith. Hairstyles, clothes, cuisines and beverages all exhibit different customs. Fashions may change but it is harder to change Our Time or Our Space. Britain is becoming a multicultural society based upon Christian values. It could become a unicultural society based upon Humanist principles. Yet, firstly it needs a new secular Time and Space measurement system.

The USA is supposed to be secular and yet it is dominated by Christians. *The Ten Commandments* are prominently displayed in many law courts. *The Star Spangled Banner* has been superseded by: *God Bless America.* Every almighty dollar bill or coin is inscribed with: *IN GOD WE TRUST.* American Christians often give ten percent of their income to the Church. Polling booths are located in churches, so non-Christians do not vote. Dwight D. Eisenhower added the phrase: (under *God*) to the following:

I pledge allegiance to the flag of the United States of America and to the Republic for which it stands, one nation, (   ) indivisible, with liberty and justice for all.

Ronald Reagan had a hotline to the Vatican, who worked with the CIA to bring down communism in Eastern Europe and in the Soviet Union. George Bush Sr. claimed that *God* was on the side of the Republicans. Bill Clinton, however, claimed that *God* was on the side of the Democrats. George Bush Sr. attempted to disenfranchise all atheists and agnostics. George Bush Jr. talked about a crusade against terrorism and used the Roman-Catholic age and date of 11 September 2001 AD as his battle cry. Barack Obama involved the Black Church in his presidential campaign. He needed more than his faith in *God* to get out of the mess he inherited.

Tony Blair tried to shore-up Christianity and the Monarchy in Britain by manipulating the Millennium celebrations, which began the New Age. It was supposed to wipe the slate clean of ancient customs and beliefs. The Sunday Observance Act of 1780 AD has not been repealed, although it has been superseded by the modified Sunday Trading Act of 1950 AD. Many of its restrictions have now been relaxed by the local authorities. Yet, there are still many laws and by-laws about shopping on Sundays. Much has been said about preserving the traditional British Sunday, because this was the only day when families could do things together. However, no one has been permitted to present the case for scrapping it. If We were to scrap the odd seven-day week and replace it with an even ten-day week, families could have more time together; not less.

Disciplines

For over half of the year most schools, colleges and universities lie idle. Yet, their staff claim to be under much more pressure than ever before. Teachers are frustrated by fixed hours, fixed feasts and movable fasts. Lecturers are now using a two-semester system which is interrupted by the fixed feast of Christmas and New Year and the variable fast of Easter. The Local Government Association wants to replace the three-term year with six equal terms and a long summer holiday but no Easter break. Most educationalists claim that Britain is no longer a Christian country. The Archbishop of Canterbury agreed to consider a fixed date for Easter.

In Little Britain about 38% of young people now attend a university. The politicians want to see the number of university students doubled. They now want to raise the school leaving age from sixteen to eighteen. Regrettably, higher education has now become a convenient means of reducing the unemployment statistics and thereby winning more votes. Most courses are geared to what students want to do rather than what society needs, so thousands are training to be film and TV directors, whilst there are not enough scientists, engineers, doctors or nurses. The Government has decided that there are too few students going into engineering and so they are going to give a financial incentive to do so. The real problem is that engineers, who made Britain great, are given lower status than television directors, actors, footballers or pop singers.

Everyone works away in their own small stall, like horses with blinkers. Interdisciplinary study is not encouraged, not even at postgraduate level. Equal Time should be allocated to general studies as to the special ones. The key to the future is the study of the future and this will necessitate more interdisciplinary study and free-thinking about how to use science and technology for the benefit of Us all, as this hypothesis demonstrates. We spend years studying the past and then fail to apply this hard won knowledge to the study of the future, which is far more important to Us. Every discipline should include a short course, at graduate level, on the measurement, management and government of Time and Space.

My earliest memory of school is being brainwashed by morning prayers, then learning the Imperial System and the Gregorian calendar by rote. This led to my rejection of religion and then to **The Worldwide System**. The influence of **Worldwide Time** on education would be revolutionary. With **global age** the educational *yer* would begin at the vernal equinox. With **digital date** the educational *yer* would be four eighty-day terms, and four ten-day breaks or one forty-day break plus 5 or 6 *demodays*. The optimum length of lesson or lecture has been found to be 80 minutes. With **decimal time** this equates to approximately 50*md*, 5*cd* or 0.5*dd*. With **flexdate** school timetables would take into account the variable length of daylight, so that pupils would not have to travel in the dark.

Rhythms

The Roman galley slaves rowed much harder with a rhythmic drumbeat and factory workers produce more with some form of musical rhythm. Our bodies are internally governed by Natural circadian biorhythms. Small clusters of cells, deep in Our brains, regulate Our body clocks. They detect day or night when We should be working, resting or sleeping. It therefore takes a few days to adjust to long flights around the globe. Our hearts regulate Our bodies at approximately 100,000 beats per day. Hence, the *tik* is much more Natural unit of Time than the second, the *han* is a more Natural unit of Space than the foot, yard or metre. Our Natural biorhythms are important but how many of Us think about the supernatural seven-day week and how this rhythm affects Our lives, or how the hour, minute and second control Our work, rest and play?

The men's record for the 100 metres stands at less than 10 seconds. Nevertheless, the metre and the second are both quite arbitrary units. The 100 yard sprint was replaced by the 100 metre one and this could be replaced by the *Kilohan* sprint if 1 *Kilohan* = 111.123 m = 120 yds. The Human sprint target could then become 1 *Kilohan* in 100 *tiks*. We like to think in these round numbers or in measured distances. The Marathon of 25.4 miles or 40.8 Km could become 365 *Kilohans*. The the length of the stadium at Olympia became the Greek standard. The Olympic Games are now Metric but the Highland Games are still in Imperial measure - including the 32 pound shot and the 21 foot caber.

Full-time or part-time job-sharing is the exception rather than the rule. Nevertheless, it has recently been found to produce far better results. Some job-sharers now work for seven days and then take seven days off. Others work for three days in one week and then two days in the next. However, if 360 work days were considered to be exactly the same, then the best full-time rhythm would be 5-on then 5-off or *vice-versa*. Full-time workers should vary their working times with the seasons. Part-time workers could either work in the mornings or the afternoons. Shift workers sometimes work for half-days, rather than thirds, because this minimizes their travel time and reduces mistakes due to handovers. It is just as important to use Our Time-off as efficiently as Our Time-on. With five days-off in a row We can make better use of Our spare Time.

The Sabbath eventually became the weekend, when no work was done. France is governed by those who want Sundays to remain special; although over half of the French population are atheists or Humanists. Many French cities, towns and villages seem to have died on a Sunday. Most commercial vehicles are not allowed to use the roads at weekends. Many religious people think their chronology, calendar, clock and zone were all *God*-given and so they never dare to question their origins. Yet, as We enter a new millennium, others question *God* and so **Time.**

Routines

The alarm rings and We climb out of bed at the same time every day.
We usually perform daily, weekly and yearly routines, without thinking.
However, the further We live from the Equator, the nearer to the Poles,
the more We need to vary Our routines to make the most of daylight.
Two centuries ago this was the norm, when a cock's crow woke Us up.
We are now like battery hens, fooled by artificial light to lay more eggs.
Yet, free-range chickens and free-range eggs are much more healthy.
Cocks are now banned in some places but hens still lay eggs on Sundays.

Routines control all of the great organizations, throughout Our World.
They keep growing, like Topsy, until they collapse - due to their obesity.
Many jobs have been systematically reduced to routine operations so
that they can be performed with much less training and fewer mistakes.
Henry Ford demonstrated the advantages of automated assembly lines.
He reduced manufacturing to routine tasks, now performed by robots.
Computers have taken over boring paperwork and make it easy to hand
over a job to the next person - so all routine jobs can easily be shared.
The best way of achieving this freedom is to adopt a ten-day week.
However, most organizations still slavishly follow the seven-day week.
Very few managers have ever thought that the week could be changed.
As jobs become more and more routine, We will need to find other ways
of keeping Our brains busy such as reading, writing, games and travel.
When We jet about the globe We become disorientated, but if all clocks
showed the same time, We might feel more at home when We were away.
Yet, in many places in the East, with no traditional Sabbath or weekend,
some are working for twelve hours per day and seven days per week,
grafting and dying like slaves - making timesaving gadgets for the West.

The working week starts on Black Monday when workers are getting
over the week-end and it ends on POETS Friday when they are looking
forward to the next - so never buy a car built on a Monday or a Friday,
unless it was built by robots, who never tire nor have any hangovers.
The week-end has become just as much a routine as the working week.
In fact, it has become more important and so the tail is wagging the dog.
The week-end is controlled by the routines of culture, media and sport.
They have now taken the place of religion in many parts of the globe.
Yet, too many people watch sport and not enough people take part in it.
A five-day week-end would encourage everyone to take more exercise.
Many sports activities are highly repetitive and training consists mainly
of the same physical action repeated over and over and over again.
Repetitive strain injuries are now quite common at work and at play.
Professional athletes are often ridden with arthritis when they are older.
A successful lecturer, actor or entertainer is one who can do the same
thing night after night, yet not bore himself or his audience with it.
Life would be much less boring if We shared most of Our jobs.

Regulations

Calendars and clocks regulate Our working week and Our working day. They form the basis of regulations by management over their workforce. Management often exploited the workforce, until the unions were formed. Then they became too powerful, which drove many firms out of business. Collective bargaining was a step forward for management and unions but Britain was held up to ransom by strikes in all of its major industries. The longest industrial battle in British industry raged for eight years. Both sides in the *Keetons* dispute stuck to their guns but neither won. This was both a lockout and a strike and it was symptomatic of the malaise running throughout British industry in the 20th century AD. Many British employers are now using so-called zero hours contracts. They do not guarantee any work but they average 25 hours per week. These contracts stop them from earning money from other sources. The employees have had to accept this deal but have no job security. This change has been introduced during a period of high unemployment. The government turns a blind eye because it decreases jobless figures.

The unions tried to hold the oil industry and the country over a barrel; but there are very few industrial disputes in this vital supplier today. In the 60's a few industries and businesses made major changes to their working agreements and the *Esso Blue Book* was the most progressive. It disposed of tea-breaks, mates, demarcation and restrictive practices. Higher productivity was achieved at the cost of higher rates of pay. Nowadays, *Exxon-Mobil* out-sources as much work as possible because this minimizes its payroll, inventory, overheads and insurance liabilities. Oil rigs are usually operated on a 7 day-on/7 day-off fortnightly pattern and sometimes on a 28 day-on/28 day-off sunthly roster of job-sharing. Oil tankers are operated by two crews whilst another two are on leave. Refineries usually work on a 4 day-on/4 day-off pattern of job-sharing. Petroleum products are distributed by pipeline, road, rail, sea and air on every day of the week around-the-clock and the vast majority of service stations are open for 24 hours on every day of the 7-day week. Many hypermarkets now also sell petrol and diesel and open every day. Most of this fuel is already refined near its source before it is imported. All brands of fuel are now refined and sold to exactly the same standard.

Industrial Relations have changed for the better over the last decades. Restrictive practices, dating from the very beginning of trades, have gone. Companies must make their own regulations and unions must have the power of collective bargaining but government must never interfere. Most unions are now fighting for more time-off rather than more pay. The next round of collective bargaining should be to have half the working days in the *yer* off in exchange for the same rate of pay for normal time and overtime, no unsocial hours and no pay for no work. **Full-time-job-sharing-as-the-norm** can transform industrial relations.

Laws

British law was based upon Roman law, so Little Britain still uses the Roman-Catholic years, the Gregorian months and the Benedictine hours. It also uses the Mystic seven-day week decreed by Constantine the Great. In 1780 AD the British Sunday Observance Act kept one day special. In 1850 AD Britain legally adopted a week-end of one and a half days. In 1950 AD the week-end became all day on Saturdays and Sundays. In 2010 AD, at the Court of Appeal, Lord Justice John Laws ruled that: **Christian beliefs have no place in the law and no right to protection in the courts.** In 2012 AD Celistina Mba, a devout Christian and childcare worker, was sacked by Merton Council for refusing to go to work on a Sunday. At a subsequent employment tribunal Judge Heather Williams ruled that: **Keeping Sunday as a rest day is not a core component of Christianity.** This was upheld, at the Court of Appeal, by Lord Justice Maurice Kay. In 2015 AD the Conservative government attempted to devolve to local authorities the power to allow all shops to open-all-day on Sundays. However, this was defeated in a long debate in the House of Commons, although no one said that all days and hours were created equal.

British Law has its own calendar of Hilary, Easter, Trinity, Michaelmas. The quarter days, near solstices and equinoxes, were when rent was due. The age, date and time form part of legal documents, however there are several different ways of writing them, which can cause legal arguments. A period of, say, three months could have several different meanings and this sometimes causes legal arguments, especially over prison sentences. The Gregorian calendar months have 28, 29, 30 or 31 days but monthly payments are traditionally based upon one twelfth of an annual salary. Private occupational pensions are usually based upon the same system. However, state pensions are now paid on a sunthly basis, every 28 days. There are usually thirteen payments per annum but there can be fourteen if the first is at the start of the tax year and so income tax may be higher.

Each part of the UK has its own patron saint with his own holy day. England and Wales celebrate Christmas, whilst in Scotland it is Yuletide. The Scots have celebrated Hogmanay since 1600 AD, when the start of the year was moved to 1 January, but many laws in Scotland are still different from England and they are now considering their own time zone. Nevertheless, the European Union wants to create just one time zone. Some Eurocrats are talking about extending the week-end to three days, including: Muslim Fridays, Jewish Saturdays and Christian Sundays. Does devolution mean that England, Scotland, Wales and N. Ireland could all use different chronologies, calendars, clocks, zones and rules? Does integration mean that all of the members of the European Union must use exactly the same chronology, calendar, clock, zone and rule? Does unification mean that every member state of the United Nations must use exactly the same chronology, calendar, clock, zone and rule?

Standards

Roman Emperors had divine authority to impose their imperial standards. After the fall of the Roman Empire every country adopted its own system. This caused many problems until trading standards were reintroduced. The French persuaded most of Our World to use their decimal system. However, the USA have continued to use their own fractional system. The vehicle, aircraft and ship manufacturers are putting pressure on all governments, especially the USA, to adopt exactly the same standards. The North American Free Trade Area is also urging the USA to metricate. Both Canada and Mexico are already using Kilometers, meters and liters. In 1968 AD Congress called for a program of investigation, research and survey to determine the impact of increasing the use of the Metric System. The report in July 1971 AD said: This is a decision whose time has come. It recommended a ten-year change-over but this was never implemented. The EU imposes standards on everything from apples to working hours and it has imposed most of the International Metric System on Britain.

The International Standards Organization (ISO) is based in Switzerland. However, all of its standards are proposed by member organizations. In 1971 AD the British Standards Institution (BSI) ratified German (DIN) suggestions for a new age, date and time standard which they entitled: *Data elements and interchange formats: Representation of dates & times.* This has become ISO 8601:1988 or BS EN 28601:1992 [16 pp for £48]. It is based upon *Anno Domini* age, Gregorian date and Benedictine time. Monday has now become the first day of the week, the week-end is now at the end of the week and Sunday has now become the seventh day. The age, date and time can now be expressed in two alternative ways. The Gregorian date: 1 January can be: month 01, day 01 or : day 001. For example: 1995-01-31 **T** 23:55:23.345 or 1995-031 **T** 23:55:23.345 The central symbol **T** meaning **Time** separates **age** and **date** from **time**. The latter system replaces months and weeks with year-day numbers. These are now incorporated into many calendars, diaries and planners. But they cannot be incorporated into digital clocks nor watches because the **time** starts at 00:00:00.00 whilst the **date** starts at 01-01 or 001. Mechanical or electronic digital counters all start with a row of zeros. Time and Space are scalar quantities, so they should both start with zero.

I wrote to the ISO about this and suggested **The Worldwide System.** They referred me to the Consultative Committee for Time and Frequency (CCTF) of the *Bureau International des Poids et Mesures* (BIPM) Paris. I sent this book to the secretary, then visited him, but he shrugged and said that politicians never take any notice of their recommendations. I consider that there should be a **World Standards Organization (WSO)** reporting directly to the General Council of United Nations Organization. However, the UN is under the thumb of the USA, who have taken control of Time and Space, and they still use the Roman-Catholic Time System.

Conventions

The Geneva conventions on warfare were proposed by the International Red Cross between 1864 and 1949 AD, yet they are still being ignored. The International Meridian Convention in the USA in 1884 AD agreed that both Time and Space would be based upon the Greenwich Meridian. The International Standards Organization was established in Geneva in 1946 AD and their SI system was agreed by a convention in 1960 AD. The USA has still not adopted it but now controls Time and Space. The League of Nations was established in Geneva during the 1920's AD but it was ignored by the USA and was, eventually, disbanded in WW2. The United Nations was established in 1945 AD and has the membership of every nation and but it is increasingly under the thumb of the USA. The annual World Economic Forum at Davos in Switzerland is a very expensive junket where conventional wisdom is regurgitated by delegates from all over the globe but no one is allowed unconventional ideas.

There have been many World Summits, organized by the United Nations. The '92 World Summit in Rio on bio-diversity agreed to save the species that are endangered because of the rapid growth of Our own species. The '93 World Summit in Vienna on Human Rights has had little effect because much of the inhumanity in the World today is due to religion. The '94 World Summit in Cairo on population was a generation too late. Overpopulation is at the root of most of the problems around the globe. The '95 World Summit in Copenhagen on social development did not consider the many advantages of job-sharing becoming the global norm. The '95 World Summit in Bejing on women did not redress the balance. **Full-time-job-sharing** would allow men and women to share most jobs. The '96 World Summit in Istanbul on cities did not reduce congestion. A ten-day week plus **flextime** and **flexdate** would minimize congestion. The '97 World Summit in Kyoto on pollution did not stop global warming. The USA were the only nation not to agree to this global convention. The '00 World Summit in New York established eight Millennium Goals. The '08 World Summit in New York set-out plans for achieving them. Many of these are now being achieved but there is still a long way to go. The '09 World Summit in Copenhagen on global warming was attended by every nation but they could not agree on how to reduce emissions. The '11 World Summit in Durban finally agreed to reduce emissions but it is up to each nation to implement this agreement or face a penalty. The '15 World Summit in New York established a revised set of Goals; End Poverty, End Hunger, Ensure Health, Ensure Education, Gender Equality, Water & Sanitation, Ensure Energy, Promote Employment, Build Infrastructure, Promote Industry, Foster Innovation, Reduce Inequality, Make Cities Safe, Ensure Sustainability, Combat Climate Change, Conserve Seas & Oceans, Protect Ecosystems, Promote Peace & Justice, Strengthen Gobal Partnerships. What We need, right now, is another World Summit on Time and Space. All of these goals could soon be achieved with **The Worldwide System**.

Reforms

The League of Nations took calendar reform very seriously after WW1. They accepted the principle of reform in 1923 AD and after examining hundreds of proposals in 1927 AD they invited their members to report. This lead to the formation of numerous national calendar associations. The most influential was The World Calendar Association in the USA. This great calendar debate was still raging when WW2 intervened. The United Nations Organization was formed after WW2 in 1945 AD. It is committed to the ideal of One World and one of its main aims is to:

Achieve international co-operation in solving international problems of an economic, social, cultural or humanitarian character and promote or encourage respect for Human Rights and for fundamental freedoms for all without distinction as to race, sex, language or religion.

The UN started to consider a global calendar soon after it was formed. The delegates considered the World Calendar to be the best option but they did not think of it as part of one age, date, time and zone system. This minute shows what went wrong:

CONSIDERATION OF QUESTION OF WORLD CALENDAR REFORM

At the 18th session of the Economic and Social Council (June-August 1954), the Indian Government introduced a proposal for the reform of the Gregorian calendar. During discussions it was proposed that a study be made of World calendar reform and that the Secretary-General of the United Nations be requested to obtain the views of governments and to place them before the Council for consideration at a later session.

A resolution was adopted on 28 July 1954 requesting members and non-members of the United Nations to study the problem and furnish their views by early 1955. At its resumed 19th session (16-27 May 1955) the Economic and Social Council decided to defer consideration of the question of World calendar reform to the 21st session.

At the Council's 21st session in the spring of 1956, a number of delegations took the position that the time was not ripe for consideration of the question of calendar reform. A proposal was made that the Council should adjourn further discussion of the matter *sine die* and that those governments that were in favor of calendar reform could then continue to work on it and it could be put forward again at some future time if any major change in the climate of public opinion took place. This proposal was adopted on 20 April 1956.

To date, there has been no re-introduction of the matter of calendar reform into the agenda of the Economic and Social Council.

The Worldwide Measurement System could not have been proposed then because the age of Our Planet had only just been established and the girth of the Earth could not be measured as accurately as it is today. Nevertheless, *NASA* say that the Poles and the Equator are still moving.

Resolutions

The reason that the Economic and Social Council abandoned work on a rational global calendar was this memorandum dated 22 March 1955 from the administration of President Dwight D. Eisenhower:

The United States Government does not favor any action by the United Nations to revise the present calendar. This Government cannot in any way promote a change of this nature, which will intimately affect every inhabitant of this country, unless such a reform were favored by a substantial majority of the citizens of the United States acting through their representatives in the Congress of the United States. There is no evidence of such support in the United States for calendar reform. Large numbers of United States citizens oppose the plan for calendar reform, which is now before the Economic and Social Council.

Their opposition is based upon religious grounds, since the introduction of a 'blank day' at the end of each year would disrupt the sabbatical cycle.

Moreover, this Government holds that it would be inappropriate for the United Nations, which represents many different religious and social beliefs throughout the World, to sponsor any revision of the existing calendar that would conflict with the principles of important religious faiths.

This Government, furthermore, recommends that no further study of the subject should be undertaken. Such a study would require the use of manpower and funds which could be more usefully devoted to more vital and urgent tasks. In view of the current studies of the problem being made individually by governments in the course of preparing their views for the Secretary-General, as well as the previous study by the Secretary-General it is felt that additional study of the subject would serve no useful purpose.

The United Nations is under the control of the United States of America which, despite its claim to be secular, is under the control of the Roman Catholic Church, because it still uses its chronology, calendar and clock. However, the Vatican has recently agreed to changes:

If it could be shown that there was a general desire for reform, motivated by the requirements of the economic and social life of the peoples of the World.

If the USA was to honor its own Bill of Rights it would then consider all days to be equal and its citizens could then share most of their jobs. A unified Time and Space system has not been reconsidered since the International Meridian Conference was convened by the USA in 1884 AD. This established 24 sea time zones based upon the Greenwich Meridian. One global time zone has never been properly considered before but this could be the first step towards one global civilization or One World.

Different rituals, habits, rhythms, routines, regulations, rules, measures, laws, standards and conventions divide Us but they are all Man-made. If We reform those units involving Time and Space they could unite Us. We Humans must believe that it is possible to reconstruct One World. Every New Year is an age, date and time for making good resolutions. Unfortunately, every faith and every sect celebrate a different New Year.

Suggestions

The League of Nations and United Nations considered many suggestions but rejected some of these because the 7-day weeks were discontinuous. The World Calendar divided the year into four 91 day quarters plus a day. The International Fixed Calendar had thirteen 28-day sunths plus a day. The British benefits scheme currently pays pensions on a sunthly basis, but this is a continuous sunth linked with the continuous 7-day week. Stijepo Ferri (1880–1941 AD)(Kingdom of Serbs, Croats and Slovenes) suggested that year-days should be numbered from 001 to 365 or 366. Some calendars, diaries and planners now show year-day numbers and the days remaining until the end of the year, alongside Gregorian dates. These year-day numbers could be utilized as a kind of ten-day week. These weekdays could be numbered from one, not zero, but this would allow **full-time-job-sharing** to become the norm without any legislation.

India still has seventeen different religious chronologies and calendars. Although the Gregorian calendar is now the official one it is probably the worst of them all and so it will never be accepted by everyone. Most Hindus dislike Roman-Catholic years, months, weeks and hours. *The Independent* reported in 1991 AD that Indian 'metricologists' were lobbying their government about a digital calendar and a decimal clock. The day would have twenty 'hours' and the week would have ten days. This would solve bloody arguments about the dates of Hindu festivals. It would help the clock industry and stop smuggling of foreign watches. *The Times* reported in 2007 AD that Indian scholars were suggesting that Indian time be moved forwards by half an hour to save energy. Noon would occur when the Sun was over the ninety degree meridian. Artificial, invisible time zones now divide-up the Indian sub-continent. It could be reunited if it used the same age, date, time, zone and rule.

Different years, months, moonths and sunths still cause great conflicts. The continuous seven-day week is now used throughout the globe but Muslims pray on Fridays, Jews on Saturdays, Christians on Sundays and this is the root cause of much of the bloodshed in Our World today. It has so far proved impossible to build a multicultural society anywhere. A unicultural one is possible with one chronology, calendar and clock. This must be completely secular and not linked with any religious belief. However, this great issue is not being considered by the United Nations. The climate of public opinion on **Worldwide Time** has not yet been tested. However, parts of it have been used before, all over this disparate Planet. Egypt had a 10-day week and divided the day into 100,000 heartbeats. Greece had a 10-day week and the Greeks did share some of their jobs. China had a 10-day week, an 100-part day and still has one time zone. India had a 10-day week and originated the use of zeros and numbers. Incas had a 10-day week and worked together to build a great empire. At least half the World may already prefer to work with **Worldwide Time.**

Opinions

The Worldwide System and then **full-time-job-sharing-as-the-norm** were developed over many years but this book was started in 1984 AD when the author acquired a *BBC* micro computer for word processing. He is currently using his tenth personal computer with *Windows 10*.

In 1990 AD the *BBC Radio 4 Punters* programme asked listeners to phone-in with their opinions about the holy days and bank holidays. The author then explained **The Worldwide System** for the first time.

In 1993 AD *Channel 4* broadcast the *Opinions* series in which a number of public figures gave their views on: **How to put Our World right**. The President of Magdalan College, Oxford remarked that the author's contribution was the only original one in the entire series.

On 1 April 1995 *The Portsmouth News* wrote an article on the author. This was entitled: **One man who would give us a 10-day week**. He explained **global age, digital date, decimal time and single zone** as well as **flextime, flexdate** and some of their many advantages.

In March 1996 AD *New Scientist* published an article by the author. It had many letters of support, including one from Sir Arthur C. Clarke. He approved of scrapping all time zones and daylight saving measures.

In 1996 AD the author was interviewed by Clive Anderson on *Channel 4* about **The Worldwide System** and **full-time-job-sharing-as-the-norm.** Like many lawyers and barristers he tried to defend the *status quo*. At the end of the interview he declared: "You heard it here first folks."

On 13 February 2001 AD *The Daily Telegraph* published an article by Andrew Marr: **Coming soon to a clock near you - decimal time.** He quoted a website campaign by 'some scientific types' in America: 'Those of us who have grown-up in a decimal-using culture think in decimal. It's just perverse for us to be using the Babylonian base sixty for telling the time.' There are now hundreds of worldwidewebsites advocating **decimal time.** The author's own website: **www.worldwidesystem.co.uk** is the only one to advocate a complete global-digital-decimal system of measurements.

On 22 January 2012 AD *The Sunday Times* published the author's piece on **The Worldwide System** in: NEW IDEAS FOR THE 21st CENTURY. Their own headline was: **Work less, live better with the 10-day week**. On the very next day The British Weights and Measures Association, who wanted to retain the Imperial System, set up a website claiming that this was: 'bonkers stuff' and the author was: 'nutty as a fruitcake'. However, the UK Metric Association want to end the Imperial System. This would finally say: farewell and good riddance to the British Empire.

Comments

Timeless!
Tenacious!
Clock Wise!
Seconds Out!
World beating!
Ten Out of Ten!
A New Yardstick!
The Time is Ripe!
Ten Time Tabled!
Real Time is False!
A Sign of the Times!
Back to square zero!
Ten is more Tenable!
Here's to the next Time!
Time is not on Our side!
Defuses the Time Bomb!
A simple, secular system!
We'll soon be Decimated!
Wake up to Decimal Time!
The week has had its day!
Solves a weighty problem!
Decimals are not Decadent!
Chronology is in a chronic mess!
The second hand will be secondhand!
Week-ends are a complete waste of Time!
We'll put Our clocks forward for the last Time!
This book has arrived at the right Time!
We'll be counting on our digits!
We can do it in half the Time!
Next Time we'll get it right!
Breaking the Time Barrier!
Its rational to ration Time!
Greenwich Time is mean!
The pulse of the Planet!
Time Zones are warped!
Time is past its prime!
Time is running out!
Time to call it a day!
In the nick of Time!
The hour is struck!
At the last minute!
Updates our dates!
The Power of Ten!
Second thoughts!
Overtime is over!
Perfect Timing!
Just in Time!
Miles better!
Clock Work!
Watch Out!
Time's Up!

Part Twelve

Conclusion

Changing Our World

"A man who dares to waste one hour of time
has not discovered the value of Life."

Charles Darwin (1809-1882 AD)

Time Changes

Nobody likes change, even from worse to better, but there have been many changes to Our World in the last millennium, century and decade. We can reach the opposite side of the globe in a day and talk to anyone, anywhere on mobile phones with digital messages and decimal numbers; and yet We do not use a global-digital-decimal Time and Space system. Science and technology have partially eclipsed many religious dogmas, yet some are dogmatic about their different Time and Space systems. These are not only incomprehensible, incompatible and inconvenient, they also make Us seem different, so that We fight and kill one another.

We devised ten kinds of Time for various temporal and spiritual needs. These ten different systems were explained at the beginning of this book. They frequently cause chronic confusion, congestion, conflict and chaos. Chronologies have been used for ages; yet show many different ages. Calendars have been checked every day; yet show many different dates. Clocks have been around for a long time; yet show many different times. This book is not only about the 3c's but also about what makes Us tick. Its aim is to clearly explain why the entire system by which We count and measure the passage of Time should be changed to the base of ten. We all have ten digits and so We should use this global-digital-decimal number for counting, measuring, multiplying and dividing everything. In different places, throughout history, parts of Time have been counted in tens but it has never been globalized, digitalized and decimalized. **Worldwide Time** is a global-digital-decimal system for the measurement, management and government of Time, throughout Our Planet - forever.

This book is also about the 3d's: distances, directions and dimensions. Very different systems are currently used to measure position, elevation, depth, direction, speed and acceleration over land, at sea and in the air. There is no reason why the same system could not be used by all of Us. The Metric System is based on an arbitrary second and arbitrary metre. It is not now based upon anatomy nor geodesy and so it has no rational relationship with Our Human Race nor the Planet upon which We live. The *han* is based upon the width of Our hands and the girth of Earth. It measures: distances, directions, dimensions, areas, volumes, weights. **Worldwide Space** is a global-digital-decimal system for the measurement, management and government of Space, throughout Our Planet - forever.

Various proposals to rationalize, humanize or secularize Time and Space have been made before but this is different from all of the previous ones. No similar hypothesis has ever been written before, because it not only explains **The Worldwide Time and Space System** but also discusses its many benefits in relation to the World about Us today and tomorrow. Politicians are usually reactive instead of proactive, so do not like change. Yet, Labour and Conservatives both used this slogan: *Time for Change.*

Time Scales

Your Life is completely dominated by chronologies, calendars and clocks. Chronologies show: how old you are and the ageing World about you. Calendars show: which days are for working, shopping, playing, praying. Clocks show: when to get up, catch a bus, tram, train, plane or ferry, start work, have a meeting, take a break, make a phone call, stop work, park your car, cook a meal, switch on radio or TV and finally go to bed. You may be paid by the minute, hour, day, week, month or sunth. As you grow older and older the years seem to pass quicker and quicker because each one is a smaller and smaller fraction of your Life-span. Your own perception of Time depends upon who you are, what you are, where you are, what you believe in and when you think about it.

If you are a cosmologist you think in billions of years in the past.
If you are a geologist you think in millions of years in the past.
If you are an archaeologist you think in thousands of years in the past.
If you are an historian you think in hundreds of years in the past.
If you are an accountant you think about the past year.
If you are an economist you think about the next year.
If you are a farmer you think about the next season.
If you are a forester you think in decades ahead.
If you are a town planner you think in centuries ahead.
If you are a family planner you think in months ahead.
If you are a technologist you think in hours, minutes and seconds.
If you are a scientist you think in nanoseconds.
If you are a musician you think in octaves, rhythms and scales.
If you are a Muslim you think in moonths, weeks and Fridays.
If you are a Jew you think in years, moonths, weeks and Saturdays.
If you are a Christian you think in years, months, weeks and Sundays.
If you are a Hindu, Buddhist or Taoist the week has little importance.
If you are a Humanist you try to work everything out logically.

Yet, there is no reason why everyone could not use the same system, based upon the age, orbit, spin and girth of Earth and the number ten. The big and small ends of Our Time scale are already multiplied and divided by tens, hundreds, thousands and millions but the middle is not, because it is named and/or numbered in multifarious different ways. Time is a scalar quantity, like temperature, yet days are counted as units. The first hour in the twenty-four hour digital clock is the hour zero. The first day in the week, the month or the year should be the day zero. The Celsius scale is much more logical than the Fahrenheit one because it is based on zero, when water freezes, and one hundred, when it boils. The absolute Kelvin scale is not really suitable for everyday purposes. We shall only have a complete and coherent Time and Space system when all parts are measured, added, subtracted, multiplied and divided using the number of digits upon Our hands - including the number zero.

Time Frames

Unfortunately, the Great Architect of the Universe did not create a round number of days in the year with which to construct simple Time frames. However, We can divide it into 360 days plus a 5 or 6 day remainder. The 360 day *yer* divides into 12 *mons* or 9 *anks* or 36 ten-day *weks*. We already use 360 degrees for angles, including latitude and longitude. If We divide the Equator by 360 Million We have a handy unit, the *han*, for land or sea distances as well as lengths, areas, volumes and weights. We needed an astronomical marker for this new system to begin and the year 2000 AD was ideal because the *Heavenly Bodies* nearly coincided, Our journey around the Sun started at midnight on the vernal equinox along the Prime Meridian and this moment coincided with a full-Moon. It was the dawn of the Age of Aquarius and the dusk of the Age of Pisces. So it was an auspicious moment to start a new measurement system. Indeed, others had the same idea but they all chose the wrong system. Little Britain became fully metricated in the Millennium year 2000 AD. Except for the statute mile (1609.344 metres) and the pint (0.568 litre).

Little Britain has passed through the Metric Millennium - nevertheless: most people still think in inches, feet, yards, chains, furlongs and miles; most people still think in pounds, stones, hundredweights and tons; most people still drink draught beer and bottled milk in Imperial pints; most people still measure their own temperature in degrees Fahrenheit. The government have done a very poor job in explaining Metrication. The media still use the Imperial System and are reluctant to go Metric. Do they realize that these systems are faulty, because they incorporate fractional hours, minutes and seconds rather than decimals of a day? Do they realize that the metre is faulty because it was based upon an incorrect survey of the Paris Meridian instead of the girth of the Earth? Do they realize that the Navigation System is faulty because it is based upon fractions of a degree of equatorial longitude instead of decimals?

I suggested the **Worldwide System** over a decade before the Millennium. I wrote many letters to every organization involved with Time and Space. These included many politicians, government departments, agencies, committees, policy study groups, think tanks and learned professors. However, the well educated and highly paid experts who are in control of Our Time and Our Space did not seem to understand this simple logic. Very few of them acknowledged receipt of my letters and none replied. It took Little Britain two centuries to adopt the arbitrary Metric System and so the Civil Service do not want to contemplate any more changes. I wrote to the European Union but they admitted they were incompetent. I wrote to the United Nations but they claimed that they had no powers. The International Standards Organization and British Standards Institute were so involved with their arbitrary Metric System that they could not understand the common sense of the more logical **Worldwide System**

Time Slots

We used to check the time, in the old days, by the radio or television. Those who organized their programmes controlled Our work and leisure. They also influenced Our destiny by allocating time-slots to politicians; or denying them to those with bright ideas that could change Our World. Lord Reith (1889-1971 AD) forbade the *BBC* to compare the religions. So it could not compare one chronology, calendar or clock with another. Although the *BBC* broadcast *Measure for Measure* in 1993 AD, and the accompanying book considered that year-day numbers were a good idea, there was no programme to explain the Metric System at the Millennium. This would have been a good opportunity to discuss the pros and cons of scrapping the mile, the pint, the year, the month, the week and the hour. However, it might also have led to scrapping the metre and the second. I expected the Millennium to stimulate lots of programmes about Time. There were very few and I was only allowed one *mil* on **Worldwide Time.** The producer of *BBC*'s *Suspended in Time* read this book and then asked me to condense it so much that it was almost impossible to explain.

Our screens are full of houses, gardens, antiques, cooking, pets and DIY. We are bored with interminable re-runs of antediluvian comedy shows. Every football, rugby, cricket, tennis or golf match looks almost the same. Soaps are supposed to reflect Life, yet never get down to the real issues. The current affairs programmes are all about the mess that We are in. Yet, no one is allowed to explain a new way of getting out of that mess. There are a number of phone-in programmes but if anyone comes up with a new idea they are immediately cut-short or may even be cut-off. Prime Time is occupied with quizzes, which show how little We know. A contestant on *Who Wants to be a Millionaire* was asked whether the orbit of the Earth around the Sun was a day, a week, a month or a year. She did not know, so asked the audience - only half of them got it right. A contestant on *The Weakest Link* was asked to name a pre-decimal coin with the value of two shillings and sixpence but he forgot the half-crown. We soon learn to use new systems and then forget about the old ones.

We can now use electronics to time-shift television or radio programmes, so are no longer restricted by all the time-slots selected by the media. This means that We do not have to stay in any more and can even watch or listen to Our favorite programmes whilst We are travelling abroad. Most programmes are recorded and so they can be viewed at any time. Others, such as news, sport and weather, are live and can be viewed on dedicated channels at any time of the day or night, anywhere on Earth. There are now so many channels that We can live in a fantasy land. The electronic revolution has not only changed Our working practices but also Our leisure pursuits, so that the seven-day week is fading away. *The BBC World Service* always broadcasts in Greenwich Mean Time. When will it inform Our World about **The Worldwide System**?

Evolution

We have only discovered Our ancient origins during the last century,
but are now beginning to understand how all of the species evolved.
We can now read the genetic codebooks of DNA so can correct disorders
within Our own species and in many of the other creatures as well.
Yet, We are destroying many of them and degrading those that feed Us.
We are imprisoning the cattle, pigs, sheep and poultry, like convicts.
We are demolishing unique habitats in order to produce more crops;
without realising that they help to protect the essential ecosystems.
Some think that they can use the DNA of frozen woolly mammoths to
recreate them in surrogate elephants but We cannot bring back dodos.
By sharing most jobs We can reduce Our carbon footprint everywhere.
This can help to save endangered species and Our own species too.
Our species is now growing so fast that it is gobbling up Our Planet.
Many of those living in industrialized countries are now living to 80.
Whilst many of those living in other parts of the globe only live to 40.
In another century most *Homo Sapiens* may live for over a century.

We have all evolved left and right hands with ten digits to count upon.
We count years in millennia, centuries, decades; but days in sevens.
It would be very much simpler if all weekdays were counted in tens.
The Gregorian calendar gradually evolved over two millennia from the
logical one used by ancient Egyptians to the hotchpotch in use today.
Nobody else seems to care about this hideous mutation, in which odd
weeks do not fit into higgledy-piggledy months nor misaligned years.
Our cars, boats, trains, planes, phones or computers have all evolved
but chronologies, calendars, clocks and watches still use old systems.
The hardware has changed whilst the software has stayed the same.
Clocks evolved from Sun-dials into the electronic watches in use today
but they still use twenty-four hours, sixty minutes and sixty seconds.
Yet, seconds are now divided into tenths, hundredths, thousandths...

This book was written on a *BBC* computer, then several *Apple Macs*,
then a variety of PCs with different operating and software systems.
As soon as a new system is published there are some who corrupt it.
The author set up a website outlining his new system and its benefits,
which was very popular, but it was purloined by a hardcore porn outfit.
His current website: www.worldwidesystem.co.uk had thousands of hits
but its feedback system was clogged with adverts about sex or drugs.
Cyber crime is increasing so rapidly that the lawyers cannot keep pace.
$ Billions have been made or lost in seconds on the stock exchanges.
Jails and prisons may soon be full of geeks with high IQs but no jobs.
There are already far too many of Us locked away, all over the globe.
This is a signal that Our civilization is failing to keep everyone happy.
We must stop treating Our species in the way We treat other critters,
by sharing Our work and wealth with **full-time-job-sharing-as-the-norm**.

Revolution

Every major advance by Our Human Race was due to a revolution.
Each step from making fire to using steam was invented by someone.
Many of the technological revolutions in the past happened gradually.
Although they were bloodless, they led to great upheavals in society.
Many of the technological revolutions in the present are much faster.
These are also leading to great social upheavals, including joblessness.
However, many of the religious and political revolutions, in the past
and the present, have only been achieved by the spilling of blood.
Most people cling on to the customs, methods, routines and systems,
that they have been brought up with, without ever questioning them.
Some are prepared to kill or die for their belief in outdated systems.
Our chronologies, calendars, clocks and zones are outdated systems.
We could soon bring them up-to-date without spilling any more blood.

The Industrial Revolution began in Little Britain and its steam driven
pumps, railways and ships helped to build the Great British Empire.
We are witnessing another revolution due the advance in electronics.
You may now be reading this on a screen rather than a printed page.
The facts and figures in this book can now be checked on *Wikipedia*.
So there is no need to include any footnotes, references or appendices.
There is no need to print images that can easily be found on the net.
Our desktops, laptops, tablets, smart phones and smart televisions
now give instant news reports to everyone, even in remote locations.
We can now communicate with everybody using *Facebook* or *Twitter*.
Social media systems were used to overthrow the despotic regimes in
North Africa but they have not been used to propose better systems.
We need a new measurement, management and government system.
Full-time-job-sharing-as-the-norm could be the revolutionary new idea
that changes Our global civilization and solves many global problems.
No politician seems to have the power to change these things anymore.
We now have this people power in Our hands via The Worldwide Web.

We do not need another Alexander, Caesar, Napoleon, Hitler or Mao.
Each of these great leaders tried to rule their known World but failed to
introduce new measurement, management and government systems.
They had no way of communicating their ideas to the rest of Our World.
So they killed Millions in their attempts to change everything by force.
The French revolutionaries failed to introduce a digital calendar and a
decimal clock, however they did introduce a global-digital-decimal rule.
We are now able to measure everything on Earth far more accurately,
including the exact length of the Equator or the girth of the Earth.
Nevertheless, all of the scales that We use now need to be recalibrated.
Sometimes We need to go back to square zero, or even zero-zero-zero.
The Worldwide System could be the beginning of a global revolution,
literally, based upon the age, orbit, spin and girth of Our Planet Earth.

Deification

Different viewpoints of all the *Heavenly Bodies* by different civilizations lead to different beliefs about the gods of Time, Space and Life on Earth. The Egyptians, Mesopotamians and Persians had different viewpoints of the Heavens and their ideas led to Greek, Druidic and Roman Paganism. These religions subsequently led on to Judaism, Christianity and Islam. The Hindus, Buddhists, Jains and Sikhs had different views of the Sky and so they each developed different religions and different philosophies. Many Western ideas, ideals, values and beliefs came from the East. Whether We live in the East, the West, the North or the South, We are all becoming part of a global village, bound together by electronic circuitry and with a detached viewpoint of Heaven and Earth from Outer Space.

The Book of the Dead was the foundation of ancient Egyptian religion. *The Pyramid Texts* deified Time-gods, Space-gods, Life-gods, Death-gods. They were probably written by the scribe, architect and vizier Imhotep, who designed the first pyramids and was deified as the vizier-god *Thoth*. They were translated by Pythagoras, who spent twenty years in Egypt. He also visited Babylon and learned about their beliefs and systems. *Thoth/Nabu/Hermes* (Mercury) became known as *Hermes Trismegistus*. *The Hermetica* was the foundation of philosophy, science and technology. It formed part of the greatest archive of ancient wisdom in Alexandria. However, it was driven underground by the Roman-Catholic Church, which destroyed the library in Alexandria during the fourth century AD. Christians defaced the temples and slaughtered the astronomer-priests. And so scientists, technologists and philosophers formed secret societies. Hermeticism was preserved in the Dark Ages by the Sabaeans at Haran and later by the Knights Templar, who were annihilated by the Church. It re-emerged in Florence, in the Middle Ages, where Cosimo di Medici collected Pagan documents and employed scholars to translate them. Yet, they remained hidden by secret societies because of the Inquisition. Hermeticism influenced philosophers, artists and scientists including: Leonardo, Michelangelo, Botticelli, Copernicus, Bruno, Kepler, Milton, Blake, Johnson, Bacon, Donne, Newton, Hugo, Defoe, Shelly and Jung.

Thoth/Nabu/Hermes said that *Amen/Marduk/Zeus/God* is the Universe. The many different cycles in the Universe represent the mind of *God*. He/She/It created himself/herself/itself and wrote the Laws of Nature. Scientific discovery is consequently a fundamental religious experience. A university education should include a broad knowledge of all subjects. Enlightenment is the deep understanding of the properties of numbers. *Thoth* was credited with the invention of the Egyptian calendar with twelve 30-day months or 36 ten-day weeks plus 5 or 6 remainder days; observatories and Sky-clocks with 12 day-hours and 12 night-hours; standard distances, directions, lengths, areas, volumes and weights. His measurement system was carved in stone and lasted for millennia.

Realization

The Metric Millennium marked the moment when We replaced old ways of measuring Space, however, We still use old ways of measuring Time. We do not realize that a comprehensive way of measuring Space-Time could lead to the fundamentally new philosophy of sharing Our Planet.

Rene Descartes (1596-1650 AD) was the father of modern philosophy. He was also the father of analytical geometry and he developed algebra. He considered that mathematics was the logical approach to Our perfect understanding of the Universe and was the driving force of civilization. He was a man before his Time in considering that We should clear away the rubble of ancient systems and beliefs and start again at square zero.

Baruch Spinoza (1632-1677 AD), a Jewish lens grinder, thought that We should think of Ourselves as living in infinite Space and eternal Time. He was excommunicated for his view that *God* did not inspire *The Bible,* that it should be read bearing in mind the date when it was written and saying that Jesus should be regarded as preaching a religion of reason. He asserted that *God the Father and Son* are *Mother Nature* in disguise.

John Locke (1632-1704 AD) from England, said that We are born with empty minds and that every thought in there was first in Our senses. George Berkeley (1685-1753 AD) from Ireland, thought that We only exist in the mind of *God* and that We must all have a spirit and a soul. David Hume (1711-1776 AD) from Scotland, thought that We should forget about all ancient religion and philosophy and just use Our senses. They all advocated empirical methods for measuring everything that can be measured and this led to scientific methodology and metrification.

Immannuel Kant (1724-1804 AD) lived in Catholic Prussia, he became a professor of philosophy and was an expert on the history of the subject. He considered that Our reason and senses are influenced by intuition. Our perception of Space and Time changes, as We grow larger and older, Our World seems to shrink and the years seem to pass more quickly.

Karl Marx (1818-1883 AD) the German Communist, worked in England. He divided Time into that needed for sustaining and reproducing the Human Race and that used by Capitalists to exploit the working classes. He ranks as the most original and influential thinker of modern times. However, Communism has proven to be just as corrupt as Capitalism.

We now need a rational global-digital-decimal Time and Space system. **Full-time-job-sharing-as-the-norm** has never been proposed before. It could lead to a new philosophy combining Capitalism with Socialism. This hypothesis may eventually become a standard textbook for future philosophy, sociology, economics, politics and mathematics students.

Rationalization

Pythagoras thought that everything could be expressed in the form of rational numbers; but when he found that the square root of two could not be expressed as a vulgar fraction he tried to conceal this discovery. There is now a rational explanation for all of the miracles in *The Bible*. Most of its incredible tales were based upon ancient myths and legends, handed down by word of mouth and enhanced over many generations. However, many people would rather believe an irrational book, written around two millennia ago; than a rational book that is written today. It is only during the last five centuries that We have really begun to understand the Universe and Ourselves by the use of applied logic. Mathematics is the science of numbers and logic but it is amazing how long it took to discover the zero and the decimal point and how long it is taking Us to incorporate them into the measurement of Time and Space.

The French revolutionaries rejected all religious dogmas and supported the new ideas of more rational scientists, engineers and mathematicians. A new global chronology was based upon the year of the revolution, a digital calendar was adopted and a few decimal clocks and watches were made but politicians soon corrupted a perfectly rational suggestion. The Metric System was based upon an inaccurate survey of Our Planet and an eighty-six-thousand-four-hundredth part of the mean Solar day. Politicians have introduced this irrational system throughout the globe without really understanding or thinking about what they were doing. Very few rational thinkers dared to question the faulty Metric System, which is better than the Imperial System, and so it has become the law. Most people accept that it is a more rational system but few realize that there could be an even more rational one based upon the age, orbit, spin and girth of Our Planet Earth and the global-digital-decimal number ten. We are now enlightened about many things: the discovery of electricity and the invention of the electric light bulb changed Our World forever; radios, televisions, mobile phones and computers have also done this, yet many people believe that it is impossible to change Time or Space.

Futurology, the study of the future, is the nub of post-modern thought. It is recognized by a few universities but has yet to be properly funded. Multi-disciplined teams of researchers form themselves into think-tanks and ask themselves hypothetical questions that they then try to answer using statistical information, original research and analytical techniques. They are never permitted to use the argument that existing methods or systems must be the best, because they have stood the test of Time. The influential British think-tank *Demos* recently concluded that:

If the 20th century was all about money; the evidence from values, surveys, systems analysis, economics and psychology suggests that the 21st century will be all about Time and how to use it.

Secularization

An increasing number of Us are no longer religious but are Humanists, who use their own experience and logical arguments to solve problems. Eastern Humanism began with Confucius in China and Buddha in India. Many of their secular sayings are still relevant to post-modern society. Western Humanism began with Greek philosophers, who rejected gods. It was born again in the Renaissance but had to remain underground. It can be seen in the work of the great Florentine artists and sculptors. Leonardo da Vinci was a Humanist and was probably the last man to know everything there was to know about all of the arts and sciences. He was fascinated by the functions and proportions of the Human body. His famous diagram of Vitruvias' *homo quadratus* divides a man's height and arm span into four cubits, each divided by six palms of four digits. The total is 96 digits and so he almost reached the digital number 100.

Over the last five centuries We have become more enlightened through the arts and crafts as well as through the sciences and technologies. Nevertheless, We still have not rationalized Our Time nor Our Space. Many think that they are Christian because they have a Christian name and because they use a Christian chronology, calendar, clock and zone. Yet, they never pray, never go to church and they never read *The Bible*. They may send Christmas cards but 90% of these have secular images. Some Humanists use: Common Era, instead of: *Anno Domini*, but this is still a forward and backward chronology based upon an arbitrary year. Some Humanists use month, month-day, week and week-day numbers, instead of names; but their calendars are based on the higgledy-piggledy Roman-Catholic Gregorian months and on the Mystic seven-day weeks. Some Humanists use digital watches with no hands pointing up at noon; but they are still based upon Benedictine hours, minutes and seconds.

Little Britain is no longer a Christian country because other religions have become established by the increasing proportion of immigrants and the vast majority are now agnostics, atheists, secularists or Humanists. Britain has no constitution and the Head of State is Head of the Church. So Britain is not yet a secular state, although many states in the British Commonwealth have written constitutions with no religious preferences. The Office for National Statistics reported that in 2001 AD only 28% of Britons were not religious but by 2013 AD this had risen to 48%. The National Secular Society expects that this will now be over 50%. The British Humanist Association says that less than 12% are religious. The USA is a secular federation, although the majority are Christians. Yet, very few in the congregations who attend their huge Catholic masses and Evangelical rallies could articulate the gospels with any coherence. Many now consider Human Rights issues from a Humanist standpoint. Over 20% of Americans have no faith and Humanists are called Brights. What Our World needs now is a Bright Idea: **The Worldwide System**.

Modernization

Modernization is a buzzword used by politicians about working practices. Nationalization by the Labour party and privatization by the Tory party have not been the answer to running an efficient and competitive ship. Britain led the World in ship, boat, vehicle and aircraft manufacture but these industries vanished because they were no longer competitive. Many shipping, road or rail transportation and aviation industries have succumbed and now it is insurance, banking and all of the other service industries that are suffering from inefficiency and foreign competition. Many workers would be prepared to work shorter hours for less pay but are reluctant to suggest this because it may affect their career prospects. However, in Holland they have found that if they work for shorter hours they increase their productivity and this is now the highest in Europe. A six-hour working day is now being tested in Sweden and many are finding that they can do as much work, yet have more time for leisure. On the other hand, here is high absenteeism in the French Civil Service so the government is paying a bonus to those who turn up for work. The remaining British shipyards are working on four days in the week, on government contracts, because there is no competition.

Key workers have regularly tried to hold Little Britain up for ransom. The nationalized industries were particularly inefficient and overmanned. The nationalized railway workers were frequently going on strike but since the railways have been privatized there have been fewer disputes, although their fares are now some of the highest throughout the globe. Britain's fire, police and ambulance services already share their jobs, on a four days-on, four days-off, four nights-on, four days-off basis. Firemen have a dangerous job but most of the time it is pretty cushy. They are allowed to sleep on night duty, they have an excellent pension scheme and they usually retire on about half pay at the age of fifty. There are fewer fires, faster roads, better equipment and electronic aids, so it makes good sense to reorganize firefighting on a regional basis. New Labour built regional headquarters but they refused to modernize. Postal workers refused to deliver mail on Sundays and bank holidays. Many of them have already been made redundant by new technology. New Labour said they must accept modernization to compete with email. Lib/Cons privatized the Post Office but it still does not work on Sundays.

The solution to many of these industrial relations problems is to make 360 days the same, to share most jobs on a five day-on/five day-off basis and to vary the length of the working day throughout the four seasons. Those working left-days would compete with those working right-days, so that productivity could be measured in every kind of organization: from small businesses to national industries, public utilities or services. Regionalization must lead to greater efficiency in all the public services. This might even help Little Britain to become Great Britain once again.

Globalization

The dream of one global-digital-decimal Time and Space system began during the Age of Enlightenment but has now turned into a nightmare. The metre and second have been globalized, digitized and decimalized but they are quite arbitrary and not related to geodesy nor anatomy. Over the last two centuries many global issues, affecting all of Mankind, were resolved by International committees, conferences or conventions. It is now time for a Global Summit to consider **The Worldwide System**.

The International Metric Conference, convened in Paris during 1799 AD, concluded that Time and Space should be global, digital and decimal. The International Meridian Conference in Washington DC in 1884 AD decided that both Time and Space should be based upon Greenwich. There should be 24 sea time zones and the girth of Earth should be divided by 360 degrees, then by 60 arc-minutes and 60 arc-seconds. Each of the arc-minutes would then be equivalent to one nautical mile. The General Conference on Weights and Measures defined the metre as the length of a standard bar of platinum-iridium at zero degrees C in 1889 AD. The International Hydrographic Conference in Monte Carlo measured the girth of the Earth and said the nautical mile was 1,852 metres in 1929 AD. The International Committee for Weights and Measures defined the second as 9,192,631,770 cycles of the caesium 133 atom at zero degrees K in 1967 AD. The General Conference on Weights and Measures redefined the metre as the distance travelled by light in 1/299792458 of a second in 1983 AD. The International metre and the second are now completely arbitrary units. *Google Earth* is already based upon decimals of a degree, like the *han*. Cosmonauts and astronauts are now using decimals of a day, like the *mil*. The *han* and *mil* are the fundamental units of **The Worldwide System**.

We have yet to learn how We can live together in peace, how to share Our Planet's resources more evenly and how not to ruin or waste them. Organizations of any size can increase productivity without increasing capital investment by instituting **full-time-job-sharing-as-the-norm**. By adopting the ten-day week, industrial countries could produce more goods with the same investment or the same amount at a lower cost. Developing countries could afford to purchase more goods from them. The demand for their own labour, products, produce and raw materials would increase, allowing them to improve their balance of payments. By these simple means, Our Planet could benefit from the ten-day week without the need for more economic aid programmes or trade barriers. Some industrial and commercial corporations have become so large that they are no longer national, international nor multinational but global. Our World has benefited from this trend because costs and prices have been minimized; whilst profits for shareholders have been maximized. Some global industries are now much stronger than any state or religion. If they adopted **The Worldwide System** the rest would have to follow.

Digitalization

On the one hand We have 5 digits; on the other hand We have 5 digits. Almost every electronic device became digital over the last few decades. This either means: that they embody a binary series of zeros and ones; or: that they have a counting system based upon numbers zero to nine. Most of Us use digital calculators, many of Us have digital computers, but digital watches became *passe,* so most of Us now use analogue ones. This is mainly because two digits are used for the hour, two digits are used for the minute and, sometimes, two digits are used for the second. These are too small to be seen clearly without the use of spectacles, needed by about fifty percent of Us, yet a three-digit system, based upon decimals of a day, would be easier to read with the naked eye. Just nine digits can indicate the age, the date and the time, everywhere.

Digitalization became a dirty word when British commercial television companies thought they had cornered the market in football coverage. Experts predicted that everyone would clamour to buy a converter and subscribe to the new digital channels but so few people did this that it would have been cheaper for the companies to buy them the best seats. The television companies and football teams faced insolvency, whilst the sleazy politicians made a killing from licensing these new wavebands. This demonstrates that no one can foretell the future and that new ideas in both science and technology do not always catch-on straight away. Nevertheless, digital radio and television has now become the norm. Whilst politicians, the World over, are very slow in adopting new ideas; the general public know a good thing when they see one and my guess is that they will soon be using one age, date and time system based upon nine windows in their digital computers, calculators, phones and clocks. Most global positioning systems already incorporate decimals of a degree in latitude and longitude instead of 60 arc-minutes and 60 arc-seconds.

Zeros and numbers have been used for a millennium, yet some people, even learned professors, still do not know how to use them properly. Marcus du Sautoy, Oxford professor promoting science, says that there should be one zero between BC and AD but there should have been two. The International Bureaux of Weights and Measures (BIPM) still do not understand that the age, the date and the time should all start at zero, like their rulers, measures and scales, because time is a scalar quantity. Nicholas Negroponte, Head of the MIT Media Lab, co-founder of *Wired* and author of *Being Digital,* supports the idea that cyber time should be independent of location or night and day and it should be decimalized. Tim Berners-Lee invented the Worldwide Web, the biggest contribution to communications since the printing press, and this is a global system. Sir Tim is now working at MIT on the next version of the Worldwide Web. This system could incorporate **global age, digital date, decimal time and global-digital-decimal rule,** which can be built into every computer.

Decimalization

Britain has been very slow in realizing the advantages of decimalization. Decimal coinage was first proposed by Sir Christopher Wren in 1700 AD. He also proposed a decimal measurement system, based upon the second. The florin, introduced in 1849 AD, took until 1971 AD to become 10p. Some wanted to retain £.s.d. and disliked the idea of decimal coinage. Although they counted £ notes in tens, they moaned when the £ coin replaced the £ note and, contrarily, when the $ bill replaced the $ coin. Some hated the European Currency Unit without the sovereign's head. Yet, if you started off with £100 and changed it into every European currency in turn you would only have about £50 left in the end. The euro was launched on the Metric Millennium 1 January 2000 AD. The Eurozone notes and coins were introduced on 1 January 2002 AD. Nevertheless, Britain, Denmark and Sweden did not use common cents. Some predict that smart plastic cards will soon replace cash altogether.

It has been obvious for two centuries that the fractional Imperial System had many faults and that the decimal Metric System was much better. Parliament voted, unanimously, to adopt the Metric System in 1862 AD. Nevertheless, it took over a century for their legislation to be enacted. The CGS (centimetre/gram/second) system was taught in British schools from 1947 AD as well as the Imperial FPS (foot/pound/second) system. The MKS (metre/kilogram/second) system was introduced in 1952 AD. The SI system, or BS 5555 (1960) was introduced by Harold Wilson's Labour government in 1965 AD with the aim of full change by 1975 AD. After thirty years of procrastination, EU directive 89/617 finally made John Major's Conservative government enforce its Draconian measures. On 1 October 1995 AD traders were obliged to use Metric lengths, areas, volumes and weights for packed goods, whilst sizes were often the same. Unpacked goods were sold in Imperial measures until the Millennium. Yet, Brits still drink pub beer in Imperial pints and drive Imperial miles. The Metrication issue caused a great deal of debate and condemnation by the public and the press, who dubbed the protesters 'Metric Martyrs'. Everyone blamed John Major, so Tony Blair was elected and re-elected. The Tory party now appears to be in favour of complete decimalization.

Le Systeme Internationale d'Unites was given this name by the ISO in Geneva because it stems directly from the proposal of Gabriel Mouton. Since it is a French idea it is entitled to have a French name but the British are still wary of the French, who they last fought and beat soon after the revolutionary Metric Space and Time System was abandoned. Metric Space was reinstated in 1840 AD but Metric Time was forgotten. Both Time and Space have now been decimalized because the metre and second are arbitrarily defined by the frequency and wavelength of light. Half the Brits hate the Metric System; the other half hate the Imperial. Consequently, both halves may prefer to use: **The Worldwide System**.

Chronological Order

Little Dennis did not realize that zeros existed, so We cannot blame him for omitting to put the year 0 AD into his new *Anno Domini* chronology. The problem did not arise in 1000 AD because zero had only just arrived. It took another millennium for the zero to be accepted as a number. The Big Issue at the end of the 20th century AD was whether We should have celebrated the second Millennium at the end of 1999 or 2000 AD. The Ministry of National Heritage decreed that the Millennium should be celebrated at the end of 2000 AD but everyone pushed the boat out at a special public holiday on the day before MM: 31 December 1999 AD. The Home Office wanted to scrap *Anno Domini* in favour of Common Era. The Foreign Office and Department of Trade and Industry agreed that Britain was no longer Christian and so should use a secular chronology. The Anglican Church maintains that Britain is still a Christian country, although less than one million Britons are now practicing Anglicans. There are more practicing Roman-Catholics than practicing Protestants. The Vatican now holds that Time began when the Earth was created and admits that this was not in 4004 BC, but has not yet accepted evolution. Catholics believe that their Messiah will be born-again at a Millennium. Will He use this language and what Time & Space system will He prefer?

If We adopted the same age, date and time and lived in the same zone then many anachronisms, which cause chronic wars, would be over. Most other religious differences such as: playing different music, wearing different clothes and eating different dishes, make Life more colourful. You enjoyed your Gregorian turkey in 2000, your Julian turkey in 7508, your Coptic kebab turkey in 1715, your Jewish kosher turkey in 5759, your Shiite halal turkey in 1421, your Sunni halal turkey in 1466, your Hindu curried turkey in 1920, your Buddhist turkey ghee in 2543 and your Mandarin sweet and sour turkey in the year of the dragon. One of these years, all of you turkeys may decide to use the same age.

If We were to start at square zero and base Our global chronology upon the age of Our Planet, the age of Our species and the age of civilization, We would be able to put Our own Human evolution into perspective. Our **global age** at the Millennium would have been 4,550,012,000 WT. However, We do not need to use this big number for everyday purposes. Since most of Us already use *Anno Domini* chronology the year 2000 AD should be *yer* 000 because a two-digit abbreviation causes computers to go haywire and more of Us are now living past the age of one hundred. There is no reason for the mean Solar *yer* to start on the first of January. The vernal equinox is the best day on which to start the new Solar *yer*. The education year differs in many states but should be the same *yer*. The tax year could lose fifteen days to align with the start of the *yer*. The legal year has its own peculiar divisions and is a law unto itself. It is Time to start again at square zero or 0,000,000,000 WT.

Calendrical Order

The Sunday trading laws are much more important than they may seem.
For they are the only remaining laws about the seven-day working week.
At the 1992 AD Conservative Conference at Brighton, Peter Lloyd M.P.
Minister of State at the Home Office, admitted that Sunday trading was:
> A nettle too long un-grasped and must be resolved once and for all.

His shopping bill offered three options from total ban to total freedom.
This was the first time that Parliament had ever voted for three options.
The Consumers Association said that 2/3 of shoppers wanted the latter.
The Shopping Hours Reform Council said:
> It is a tremendous victory for shoppers who will soon have the
> freedom to shop whenever they want to, and for shop workers
> who will benefit from the protection that the government promised.

USDAW, the shop workers union, said:
> We want to ensure that most shops are closed on Sundays,
> that Sunday working is voluntary and paid at double-time.

The Keep Sunday Special Campaign said:
> More and more business sentiment is swinging our way and on a free
> vote in the Commons we believe that a 'type of shop approach' will win.

Despite strong public support for free trading on every day, the House of
Commons voted against it, however, they did agree that small shops
could open every day and big shops could open for 6 hours on Sundays.

Over half the shops, in England and Wales, are now open on Sundays.
In bonny Scotland there has been total deregulation for many years.
Sunday has now became the most popular shopping day, after Saturday.
There has been no noticeable deterioration in family morals or values.
Many service stations are open-all-hours and have convenience stores.
Whilst most hypermarkets have service stations with lower priced fuel.
Online trading makes a nonsense of the shopping laws because anything
can now be ordered online and delivered at any time on any day or night.
During the 2012 AD Olympic Games in Britain all kinds of shops were
permitted to open all day on Sundays, to boost the flagging economy.
The Institute of Directors called for this to become permanent but the
Lib/Con Government said that this would need a new Act of Parliament.
However, after the 2015 election, the Tory Chancellor of the Exchequer
announced that in future all Sunday trading laws would be devolved so
that local government would be empowered to set its own restrictions.
Nevertheless, the Scottish Nationalist MPs sided with the opposition
against changes to the Sunday shopping laws in England and Wales.
They wanted to preserve higher rates of pay for working on Sundays.
So the bill was put-on-hold and the old trade union dogma continues.
In other parts of the globe the shops are open for 7 days and 24 hours.
Shop workers are paid at the same rate for every hour and every day.
This is the case in most countries with a secular constitution, like USA.
The next step is **full-time-job-sharing-as-the-norm** in a ten-day week.

Horological Order

Some people still think of the Natural Sun-dial as indicating holy time. Yet, the artificial clock has now superseded it for all secular purposes. Some say: Britain should not adopt Central European Time because its Sun-dials would be wrong; on the other hand: if Europe were to adopt Coordinated Universal Time, the Vatican Sun-dial would then be wrong. The alternative is to use the same time everywhere and forget the idea that the hands on clocks should point up when the Sun is overhead. Setting hands to twelve o'clock when the Sun is at its zenith is a practice that has had its day, for We have better ways to synchronize Our time. Many people now use digital clocks and watches that have no hands.

Our body clocks inform Us that We should only work during daylight. Artificial light is extremely useful but this is not the complete solution to increasing productivity and it will gradually become more expensive. All days should be the same, yet they do not have the same daylight. We used to vary Our working day when We worked on the land and so We should go back to this Natural system which is much less stressful. Working days and hours are still considered to have varying values. Some trades unions still demand double-time for working on Sundays. However, the power of the churches and the unions is now declining. When working on Sundays costs twice as much as on weekdays there is no incentive to adopt it; but if all of time is paid at the same rate a different answer is found and many redundancies could be avoided. However, there is a valid case for being paid more for working at night.

Some argue that We now use one clock, so there is no need to change. Yet, We now use two: the 12-hour analogue clock was used for centuries before it was found to cause confusion for those who jet about the globe; the 24-hour digital clock was designed to take over from the 12-hour analogue one but it is most unlikely that it will ever take over all time. We now use both systems, so We need to convert times after midday. This needs mental arithmetic, so many uneducated people are confused. It is surprising that scientists and engineers have put up with hours, minutes and seconds for so long, but if the division of the day were to be decimalized it would save a lot of time wasted by mental arithmetic and time calculations could be made on calculators programmed in tens. **Worldwide decimal time** works well in either analogue or digital forms. Analogue decimal clocks and watches could show light and dark sectors. Digital decimal clocks and watches could show the age, date and time or simply show the decimal time as an easily-to-read three-digit display. Although *Swatch* tried and failed to introduce a version of **decimal time** at the Millennium this does not mean that the idea is a non-starter. Many inventions are sold before their time and without enough publicity. This book may help to educate those who make those timely decisions.

Geographical Order

The globe needs fixed points and imaginary lines so that We can find where We are, where We want to go and the age, the date and the time. The Prime Meridian bisects Greenwich and it probably always will do. However, there is no need to use the ancient divisions of 24, 60 and 60. Latitude and longitude should be measured in degrees, then decimals. A millionth of a degree of longitude at the Equator could equal one *han*. This is the geographical basis for **Worldwide Space System**.

Yesterday's solution to the global problem of efficient working patterns was to start when there was enough light and stop before it was dark. This is still the most Natural way for Us to behave and it saves energy. Artificial clocks and watches are not for getting up but for meetings. Meeting a person, a phone, a bus, a train, a plane, a ship or a hovercraft. Cockerels were used by the French as a symbol for Time and Liberty. Cockerels woke us up but are now confused by electric enlightenment. Cockerels are now banned in some places for making too much noise. Cockerell's invention was banned in some places for the same reason. However, the latest types are now very much quieter than many boats. Hovercraft are the fastest way to cross the English Channel/*La Manche*. In England they use statute miles per hour, at sea they use nautical miles per hour but in France they use kilometres per hour.

Dictators are forever changing their time zones for political reasons. Mao Zedong decreed that Communist China had only one time zone. This, with two languages and one script, helped it remain as one nation. Hugo Chavez changed the time zone in Venezuela, during 2007 AD, by half an hour, because he did not want to use the same zone as USA. Kim Jong-Un changed the time zone in North Korea, during 2015 AD, by half an hour, to celebrate its liberation from Japanese imperialism. The Eurocrats want all their member states to use the same time zone. It would be very much better for the entire Planet to use the same time.

The great walls of Hadrian, China and Berlin are now tourist attractions. Artificial borders made of barbed wire are gradually being taken down. Although walls of concrete have now been erected across the Holy Land. Passports are no longer needed as We sail, drive or fly across Europe. However there are now many stateless persons on this patchwork Planet. Barbed wire is appearing again between many of the European states. Asylum seekers are clogging European prisons and living off the state. Freedom is still a relative term for it depends on where you were born. As We become more educated and enlightened about the past and about Our options for the future, We realize how wrong Our leaders and their political, economic, sociological, scientific and religious advisers often are. Every year We have more orders, laws, treaties, rules and regulations. We need less.

British Order

The first Prime Minister: Robert Walpole (1676-1745 AD) was appointed by King George I of Hanover, because he could not speak any English. Walpole was given Number Ten Downing Street as his official residence. It has remained the Prime Minister's London home and office ever since. This book was written to point out, to all those residing at Number Ten, the huge benefits and tiny costs of basing everything on the number ten.

The author suggested **The Worldwide System** to six Prime Ministers. Margaret Thatcher, a Methodist, who liked to be at the centre of things, said: "Go Back to Basics" but she passed the buck to the Home Office. John Major, an atheist or agnostic who pretended to be a Protestant, had no new ideas of his own, so passed the buck to the Foreign Office. Both of these ministries replied with exactly the same words:

It is unlikely that we would commit ourselves to any review of the present system without overwhelming calls for reform and strong public support. Unilateral adoption of a new system would cause immense problems in the field of international business, transport and telecommunications.

Tony Blair, who posed as a Protestant but was really a Roman-Catholic, said that he listened to sensible ideas, believed in joined-up government, the need to have clear objectives and the importance of logical argument. However, he passed the buck to the Department of Trade and Industry, National Measurement System Directorate, who concluded:

The economic impact of making such changes would be enormous costs and virtually no benefits.

Gordon Brown, a Presbyterian, who liked to hark back to his school days, never questioned the faulty Time and Space system that he was taught. The author wrote to him but did not receive a reply.

David Cameron, a Protestant, and Nick Clegg, a Humanist, shared power. They failed to introduce proportional representation to the House of Commons and they also failed to introduce secular reforms to the House of Lords. The author wrote to them both but did not receive a reply.

David Cameron became the next Prime Minister, with a small majority, but resigned when Britain decided, by a small majority, to exit the EU. Theresa May, a Protestant, took over after 3 weeks of revolution, saying: "We will make Britain a country that works not for a privileged few but for everyone."

There is now a golden opportunity to go back to square zero, question the old systems and devise some better ones for this new millennium. All days are becoming equal and so the Mystic seven-day week is weaker. Little Britain could be Great Britain again with a secular ten-day week. Because this would encourage **full-time-job-sharing-as-the-norm**.

European Order

Rome was not built in a day but it's very foundations now need replacing.
Julius Caesar introduced a Solar calendar but was stabbed in the back.
His higgledy-piggledy months are still in use but *kalends, ides & nones*
were replaced by month-day numbers and continuous seven-day weeks.
Had Antony and Cleopatra won at Actium We might now be using the
ancient Egyptian Solar calendar with its XXX-day months and its X-day weeks.
Romans tried to obliterate Christians but became Christian themselves.
They changed their age from the founding of Rome to the birth of Christ.
Pope Gregory XIII had a golden opportunity to redesign Our chronology,
calendar and clock for all Time but he only made a small adjustment.
The French revolutionaries attempted to globalize, digitize and decimalize
Time and Space but Napoleon Bonaparte reverted to Roman-Catholicism.
The Roman-Catholic Church now wants to absorb the Anglican Church
and to become the only official religion within the European Union.

The EEC Treaty of Rome was signed by six states on 25 March 1957 AD.
The EU Treaty was signed by 25 states in Rome on 29 October 2004 AD.
The EU Reform Treaty, by 27 states in Lisbon on 13 December 2007 AD.
The EEA Treaty was ratified by all the states by 4 November 2009 AD.
Will Europeans still use the Roman-Catholic age, date, time and zone?
Will Europeans be forced to take three rest days in the seven-day week?
Will Europeans be forced to work a maximum of 35 hours per week?
Will Europeans be forced to use the faulty, arbitrary, Metric System?
Will Europeans be forced to use the same euro currency in every state?
Will Europeans be forced to drive on the same side of the Roman road?
Will Europe become an exclusive Roman-Catholic federation or empire?
Will Europe's Roman-Catholic President become its Holy Roman Emperor?

The EU tried to make Little Britain conform to its Sunday trading laws.
The Treaty of Rome (Article 30) was not judged by the European Court
to conflict with the British Shops Act of 1950 AD and so they referred
the matter back to the British Government on 16 December 1992 AD.
On April Fool's Day 1993 AD the House of Lords ruled that the foolish
British Sunday trading laws did not breach EU free market regulations.
This House of Lords ruling was overturned by the House of Commons.
So some shops may stay open on Sundays whilst others must be shut.
It is a very simple step to make 360 days, legally, the same everywhere.
Most jobs could be shared and most socio-economic ills could be cured.
The author wrote to the Secretary-General of the European Commission,
suggesting that **full-time-job-sharing-as-the-norm** could solve its problems.
His minion replied: 'This does not lie within the competences of the EU'.
On the *ides* of March in 1999 AD Jacques Santer and the whole of the
European Commission resigned when they were found to be incompetent.
The EU is still in a chronic mess and the only way of building a Eutopia
is to start again at square zero with a new global-digital-decimal system.

World Order

We still have many different ages, dates and times in use Worldwide.
Some say: it's impossible to change Our World so there's no point in trying.
Yet, others have changed Our World for the better in many other ways.
Some say: if it ain't broke and it still keeps turning, why try to fix it?
Yet, it is broke, in so many different ways, and so it does need fixing.
Some say: that calendars and clocks are too expensive for Us to discard.
Yet, We discard Our calendars every year and often replace Our clocks.
Most of Us have already changed Our rules, weights and measures.
However, the International Metric System still has numerous faults.
The most powerful argument for not making changes, is change itself.

Julius Caesar had the authority to change the date throughout his World
but he was stabbed in the back soon after, for assuming divine power.
Constantine the Great ensured that Roman-Catholic months and weeks
were used throughout Christendom, yet other states used other dates.
Pope Gregory XIII realigned the calendar with the year, in one great leap,
but there is no reason for the mean Solar year to begin on January 1.
The Metric System, based upon the size of the globe, was agreed by the
first International Conference in 1799 AD but it was not very accurate.
Napoleon I was the first great leader in Our World to understand it.
Yet, his *concordat* with Pope Pius VII ended a revolutionary new idea.
The Metric System was restored by Napoleon III in 1840 AD but it was
wrong and, although it has been modified many times, it is still wrong.
The International Meridian Conference in 1884 AD agreed that the Prime
Meridian should pass through Greenwich and that both Time and Space
should be decimalized but, although all maps and charts are based upon
its latitudes and longitudes and all times are now based upon its zones,
the decimalization of Time and Space has yet to be fully implemented.
The Worldwide System is not only a new global-digital-decimal system
of measurements but also a new system of management and government
which could transform business and industry as well as local, regional,
national and international politics, thus creating a New World Order.

No one seems to have the power to alter Time and Space today but We do
have instant communications and membership of global organizations,
who are looking for Big Ideas to help solve Our World's chronic problems.
This Big Issue should be raised at Global, World or Earth Summits,
The United Nations, Commonwealth Conferences, European Parliament,
International Standards Organization, International Hydrographic Bureau
International Astronomical Union, *Bureau International de l'Heure,
Conference International des Poids et Measures* and any other forum.
Nevertheless, most of these organizations try maintain the *status quo*
and radical ideas are usually dismissed as impractical or impossible.
Especially, if they can't be completely explained in a few chosen words.
So this great juggernaut: Earth, keeps rolling along towards the abyss.

Universal Order

The properties of numbers are manifestations of One Universal Order. There are many universal constants e.g. the speed of light in a vacuum. If these measurements were any different this Universe could not exist. Nevertheless, none of the units in the International System have scales that could be deduced by aliens before making contact with Earthlings. The term: Coordinated Universal Time is a misnomer for it is based upon an eighty-six-thousand-four-hundredth of a mean Solar day on Earth. It uses the 24-hour digital clock rather than the 12-hour analogue one. If We ever make contact with Life - but not as We know it - the simplest common denominator will be the binary system of zeros and ones. Carl Sagan (1934-1996 AD) suggested that: somewhere in the infinite number of decimal places of the ratio π there may be a binary message which proves that *God* created the Universe in six days then took a rest.

This Universe is stranger than anyone could have believed a generation ago and new discoveries are being made almost every day but the work of cosmologists is becoming increasingly incomprehensible to everyman. The Higgs boson or *God* particle is the smallest thing in the Universe. Black holes, wormholes, singularities, superstrings, wrinkles in Time are Cosmic concepts which stretch everyone's imagination to the very limits. It may even prove to be possible to travel faster than the speed of light. Whether We shall ever be able to travel outside the Solar System and explore the Milky Way is doubtful but the conquest of Space or the fear of alien objects and beings is starting to pull Our Human Race together. It is very probable that Life exists on many of the billions of other planets in this Universe and it could be that ET is far more intelligent than Us. A recent survey showed that more Britons believed in aliens than in *God*.

The Egyptians were excellent astronomers capable of making accurate measurements of the Sky and their religion was based upon Sky-gods. Napoleon's invasion of Egypt in the early years of the French revolution coincided with its use of a chronology, calendar and clock based on tens. Archaeology and Egyptology were based upon the pioneering work of Flinders Petrie (1853-1942 AD) who surveyed Stonehenge and the Pyramids. Some believe that they both have dimensions which indicate that their designers knew the exact size of this Planet and the length of its year. Others believe that these massive monuments, leylines and Nazca lines were built to communicate with alien civilizations on other planets.

We have yet to discover whether there is, or has been, Life on Mars. This could have been a single cell organism rather than a complex one. The recent *Spirit* landing on Mars played havoc with the body clocks of the NASA scientists controlling the mission, who used special watches based on the Mars 'day', which is 40 minutes longer than the Earth day. However, this was divided into 24 'hours' 60 'minutes' and 60 'seconds'.

The End of the Second

There is confusion amongst astronomers, physicists and technologists over the very, very small difference between the variable **Cosmic** second, which is an eighty-six-thousand-four-hundredth of a mean Solar day, and the fixed **Atomic** second, an arbitrary number of atomic vibrations. Astronomers prefer **Cosmic Time**; whilst physicists prefer **Atomic Time**. Technologists use a blend of the two called: Coordinated Universal Time. Astronomers from the International Earth Rotation Service use radio telescopes to pinpoint various quasars in distant parts of the Universe. This enables them to measure the mean Solar year and mean Solar day. The International Telecommunication Union utilizes all this information to compare mean Solar time with fifty caesium clocks around the globe. It then adds a leap second whenever the difference exceeds 0.9 seconds. Since it began in 1972 AD UTC has had 23 leap seconds added to it, because the Earth is gradually slowing down, but not in a regular way. In another millennium this difference will probably amount to one hour. The Naval Research Laboratory in Washington DC monitors this system. It then reports to: The Director of Time at the US Naval Observatory who is in charge of the Global Positioning System, known as GPS or *Satnav.*

This difference between **Cosmic Time** and **Atomic Time** results in leap seconds having to be added to Coordinated Universal Time, however this can cause glitches in clocks, computers and global positioning systems. Digital computers are liable to print-out the wrong information such as double interest rates or they omit invoices without this being noticed. When GPS started in 1980 AD it was synchronized with UTC but does not add leap seconds, so it is ahead of UTC and behind **Atomic Time**. The Russian *GLONASS* system shut down unexpectedly when a leap second was added in 1997 AD and the American GPS could do so too. The European Space Agency is now building its own *Galileo* system. This could be based upon the Prime Meridian and the girth of the Earth. Most GPS receivers can be switched from degrees, minutes and seconds to degrees, minutes then decimals or degrees then decimals of a degree. The US Coastguard use decimals of a degree for position and direction and electronic charts can fix a position by this system but distances are still measured in nautical miles and speeds in nautical miles per hour. The final step is **Worldwide** positions, directions, distances and speeds.

Most of Us are confused by **Cosmic Time** and **Atomic Time** differences. Changing over to decimals, rather than fractions, of a day would permit the system to be corrected and my suggestion is that **Civic World Time** should be based upon **Cosmic Time** as far as a thousandth of a day and then it should be based upon **Atomic Time** for all the smaller units. A variable millionth of a mean Solar day could be called a *microday* but for physical measurements a new fixed unit, called a *tik,* could be used. Every century the *tik* could be restarted to be the same as the *microday.*

The End of the Minute

If We abolish the second then We should also get rid of the minute. The minute should be replaced by the *milliday* or *mil* (1.44 minutes). The Babylonian hexadecimal or sexagesimal system is no longer sexy. We can count most things in tens, hundreds, thousands and millions. The number 360 is useful in Time and Space, so We should keep it for the days in the *yer*, for measuring compass directions and for angles. It seems logical to base land, sea and air distances upon one thousandth of a degree of longitude at the Equator, called a *Kilohan*, and all linear, area and cubic measures upon one millionth of a degree, called a *han*. This measurement happens to be about the width of the average hand. Squared *hans* are for areas and cubed *hans* are for volume or capacity. It also seems logical to base standard weights upon a cubic *han* of water. We now know the size and shape of Our Planet very accurately because electronic distance measuring systems have facilitated geodetic surveys. Satellite observations and international collaborations have led to the possibility of adjusting all existing primary geodetic and astronomical observations to a **Worldwide** datum and if this is based upon decimals of a degree then it is possible for grid references to be compatible with distance measurements and scales ranging from 1:1,000 to 1:1,000,000.

Although the Prime Meridian is based upon Greenwich, Britain is way behind the times and its armed services are still fighting the last war. The Royal Navy and the British Army are steeped in tradition and never seem to talk to the Royal Air Force and so they all use different systems. When the Hydrographer to the Royal Navy decided to scrap arc-seconds and to replace them with decimals, he omitted to scrap arc-minutes. He resisted attempts to replace the nautical mile with the kilometre; yet he replaced the fathom with the metre on new Admiralty charts. The Ordnance Survey, on the other hand, decided to adopt the kilometre for distances and the metre for heights, although they still sell maps with the scale of one inch to one mile as well as with various ratios. In Britain, the mile is still a legal measurement and yet the inch is not. Aviation charts are completely different because they use nautical miles and so airspeed is measured in knots but altitude is measured in feet. These differences still keep the British Navy, Army and Air Force apart. Various governments have failed to merge them into one fighting force. Maybe a European Defence Force would make all of them see sense. However, the EU would probably make them all use Metric measures. If NATO continues it will probably make them use American measures. However, the basic unit used for the *Google Earth* navigation system is a decimal of a degree so this is a step towards **The Worldwide System**.

A camel is said to be a horse designed by a committee and the same may be said for the Imperial, American, International and Navigation Systems. Committees are groups of people who keep minutes but waste hours.

The End of the Hour

The ancient Egyptians divided daylight into ten hours, then added an extra hour at each end for twilight, plus twelve hours during the night. Twelve variable hours of lightness and twelve variable hours of darkness continued throughout Christendom and monks were detailed to ring a bell every hour according to the Sun-clock, water-clock or sand-clock. The monastic ritual of changing duties at the sound of an hourly bell spread to the surrounding communities and has continued ever since. Illustrated *Books of Hours* were commissioned, by the gentry, detailing the duties to be performed during every hour in every day of the year. The Benedictine bell is still used in schools, colleges and universities but some lessons, seminars and lectures last for longer or shorter periods.

After mechanical clocks were invented the whole day was divided into twenty-four equal hours and, eventually, into ninety-six quarter hours. The Chinese were probably the first to develop geared water clocks and they originally divided all of their days into ninety-six equal parts. Nevertheless, they later divided their days into a hundred equal parts. The Japanese invented a variable-hour mechanism for mechanical clocks because these allowed them to continue working from dawn to dusk. The Japanese are not interested in so-called: daylight saving measures, because working to fixed hours wastes a great deal of time and energy. The dogma that some hours are worth more than others is disappearing. Millions are working in zero hours contracts with no fixed working times. Politicians claim that this practice has reduced unemployment statistics.

Hours are mostly used for tuning into radio or television programmes. These are mostly organized by the hour, half-hour and quarter-hour. If We digitally divided each mean Solar day into ten *decidays* (*decs*) or one hundred *centidays* (*cens*) or one thousand *millidays* (*mils*) We would release Ourselves from the slavery of working to fixed hours. A clock-face can be divided into a hundred units and if it has two hands then the short hand can show ten *wekdays*, divided into ten *decidays* and the long hand can show ten *centidays*, divided into ten *millidays*. A digital watch with only three number windows can indicate either the *yer*, the *yerday*, the *milliday* (or the *tik*) - at the touch of a button. A mobile phone, a pocket calculator or a global positioning monitor can show all of this information as a row of numbers at very little extra cost. The cost of replacing every timepiece in Our World would be much less than all of the many benefits - they only last for a few years anyway. Calendars, planners, diaries and timetables would become perpetual, instead of being discarded every year, saving time, paper and energy. Computers, calculators and telephones could easily incorporate these changes as an option, then be switched-over at the appropriate moment. There is much less reason now for Us to do everything simultaneously, because time can be shifted by using mail, email, voicemail and text.

The End of the Day

Mystic astronomer-priests controlled the masses with their knowledge that an eclipse would occur on a certain day, a river would flood when a Bright Star appeared at dawn or when day and night were equal. New gods of the Sun, the Moon, the Planets and the Stars took over from the old gods of the soil, the sea, the rivers, the winds and the rains. Celestial knowledge became power and led to the belief that everything that happened on Planet Earth was controlled by one deity in Heaven. Mystics still control the masses with their ages, dates, times and zones. We must try to break the hypnotic trance that they have cast over Us. They have turned Us into robots that obey commands without question. We must now, urgently, question everything that they ever taught Us. Because their beliefs are rapidly destroying Our Planet and Our Species.

We must now base Our Time and Our Space upon science not religion. The mean Solar day must remain the basis of **Cosmic** and **Civic Time** but it is a variable unit and its division into light and dark also varies. The exact moment when day becomes night or *vice versa* is difficult to predict exactly but for some people the day began at dawn, for others it ended at dusk whilst most eventually decided that midnight was best. Some still believe that the Sabbath starts at dusk on the day before. Midnight once moved around the globe on the opposite side to the Sun; now it jumps about, like a drunken frog, from one time zone to another. Different states start summer time and winter time on different dates. Now that We have several dependable global communication systems it would be quite simple to begin and end each day, everywhere upon this spinning Planet, when Britain's Prime Meridian passes through midnight. We would all think of Ourselves as members of the same Human Race.

This does not mean that We must start and stop work at the same time. It is best for most of Us to start work after dawn and stop before dusk, as everyone did before the artificial clocks and watches were invented. The imposition of artificial working days by the rigors of **Civic Time** has proven to cause many maladies such as Seasonal Affective Disorder. Stress & strain caused by timetables, calendars and clocks is no longer necessary when We use i-players, DVDs, texts, e-mail and voicemail to shift date and time rather than Ourselves from one place to another. **Civic Time** is making Us ill; instead of freeing Us from the drudgery of daily tasks that could be performed at a more convenient moment. This never happened before, when We rose at dawn and retired at dusk, because Our body clocks could cope with diurnal and seasonal changes. Some of the happiest people in the World have no calendars nor clocks but they have an inbuilt sense of **Bionic Time** and that is all they need. We should try to adopt **flexdate** as well as **flextime**, for Our own good. It would work wonderfully well with **full-time-job-sharing-as-the-norm**. Yet, tomorrow is another day.

The End of the Week

The seven-day week is getting weaker but this Judeo-Christian-Islamic tradition is now holding back progress throughout the Western World. Many states name its days after the gods of the *Seven Heavenly Bodies*. We now know that there are no gods and there are *Ten Heavenly Bodies*. Judaism initiated the idea of a Sabbath when no work was done at all. Jews may not use planes, boats or cars when they take Saturdays off. However, they may now e-mail their curses to be put in the Wailing Wall. Christianity has developed its own chronologies, calendars and clocks, which the secular World now programs into organizers and computers. Christians worship the Sun because they traditionally take Sundays off. Islam continued to make progress whilst Europe was in the Dark Ages. With concrete they build higher minarets, with amplifiers they reach a wider audience and with bright lights a mosque can be seen at night. Muslims still worship the Sun or the Moon and they take Fridays off. Each of these ancient Western religions now have different week-ends, which make international communication and commerce more difficult. None of the Eastern beliefs have a special weekday for prayer although most of them have holy days or holidays scattered throughout the year.

Humanists can make up their own minds and have probably become the majority in Britain, although many still claim that they are Christians. All political parties behave as though Britain is still a Christian country. So it still needs an unproductive week-end, holy days and bank holidays. All laws on Sunday shopping, betting, eating, drinking, singing, dancing and parking should be repealed, so that 360 days can be the same again.

Half of the French population believe in *God* but the rest are atheists. Most small shops are closed on Saturday PM, Sunday and Monday AM. French believers want to extend their week-end to three days of leisure. French atheists want the freedom to able to work whenever they want. France is in a deep economic crisis because it is relatively unproductive. President Hollande is now trying to put the French nation back to work. He should try **full-time-job-sharing-as-the-norm** in a ten-day week. He may then be able to achieve: Liberty, Equality and Fraternity.

Abraham, Moses and Jesus would have all used the ten-day *decade*, because, if their legends are true, all of them once lived in ancient Egypt. There is no reason why any spiritual, ethical, moral or philosophical belief cannot be adapted to fit a temporal, logical, digital, ten-day week. Our future happiness and prosperity now seem to depend upon whether *The Talmud, The Bible, The Koran* and many other holy texts are still interpreted as saying that the week must always be seven days long, whether there must always be one special day set aside for religious devotion or whether We may now choose to work on either *leftdays* or *rightdays* and rest, shop, play or pray on any *freeday* in a ten-day week.

The End of the Month

The Moon is waxing and waning in this Age of artificial enlightenment.
Yet, there are many places where moonlight is still as important as ever.
The holy moonth of Ramadan remains one of the Five Pillars of Wisdom.
Turkey lies in both Europe and Asia and so it has a mixture of cultures.
The Ottoman Empire, based upon Sunni Islamic beliefs, fell after WWI.
In 1926 AD Kemal Ataturk dissolved the sultanate and the caliphate.
He abolished the fez and the veil, adopted the Roman alphabet, made
Sunday the day of rest and adopted Roman-Catholic Gregorian months.
He laid the new foundations for a democratic, industrial, secular state.
Fundamentalists now want to pray on Friday, restore the veil and the fez,
the Lunar calendar and Ramadan, when no one may eat during daylight.
Yet, most politicians and industrialists would like Turkey to join the EU.
Pope Benedict XVI said Europe should be a Roman-Catholic federation.
However, an increasing number of Europeans are becoming Humanists.
On the other side of the Mediterranean most people are Sunni Muslims.
In 1994 AD Muammar Gadaffi decreed Libya's return to a Lunar calendar.
He denounced the Roman chronology and calendar for being imperial.
He has now been deposed by rebels who may revert to a Solar calendar.
Nevertheless, the Shiite Muslims in Iran use a different Solar calendar,
which causes a great deal of friction with the Lunatic fringe.

The Sun and the Moon still control Our lives to a greater or lesser extent.
The Pagans worshipped them both and they will always control the tides.
They still have as much pulling power but they have lost their mysticism.
Some digital watches now incorporate the Lunar phases and the tides.
No religious calendar is suitable for secular use - especially the Gregorian.
It was devised when the Pagan Romans still worshipped their Sun-god.
It is used as a Solar calendar by most of the World, but still has many
Roman-Catholic connotations, so it is not suitable for use by Humanists.
Its higgledy-piggledy months and irrational month names defy all logic.
Most European states now number the months instead of naming them.
They now have little meaning, except as the start of a new sheet of paper.

Digital date is only based upon common sense and simple arithmetic.
It does not need months at all, for it is based upon an annual day-count.
Yet, this perpetual calendar, planner, diary or timetable can incorporate
12 x 30-day *mons* or 9 x 40-day *anks* as well as 36 x 10-day *weks*.
It could show Lunar phases but would have to be discarded every *yer*.
It should also be compatible with all the computer operating systems.
Computers can incorporate almost any language and any script, but
their operating systems and handbooks are invariably written in English.
English is spoken in the corridors of power, it is rapidly becoming the
global commercial language and it is the main language of the Internet.
However, all of the new three-letter names in **The Worldwide System**
are meant to be used in any, and every, language on Our Planet Earth.

The End of the Year

Here in Little Britain or the former United Kingdom there are still many different laws and bye-laws based upon different holy days and holidays. The Scots do not celebrate Christmas but the New Year or Hogmanay. This small temporal difference may end with them leaving the union. There are few temporal differences between the Welsh and the English, but temperance was one of them and all pubs had to close on Sundays. The Welsh Nationalists now agree that all pubs may open on Sundays. Ulster has now became an economic, sociological, political and religious anachronism because the majority of British people are now atheists. There are many Jews, Muslims, Hindus, Sikhs, Taoists and Buddhists living here and there are probably more Catholics than Protestants now.

All of Catholic Ireland was once under the control of Protestant England. During 1798 AD Father John Murphy, a Catholic priest from Wexford, decided that freedom was a good idea so, to show his solidarity with the new ideas coming from France, he started to use their digital calendar. A million moms followed his example, throughout the island of Ireland. When the English heard about this heresy and treachery they sent in the army and, during the following bloodbath, many more lives were lost than during the terrible days following the storming of the Bastille. The Wexford Rebellion is now commemorated by ballads and a museum.

The zodiac is a Stellar calendar that precesses through the equinoxes. So most astrologers consult their horoscopes under the wrong Star sign. The Age of Pisces is now ending and the Age of Aquarius has begun. The Christian Age is fading away and the Humanist Age is emerging. The mean Solar year is celebrated at all of the solstices and equinoxes by the Old Age druids and by the New Age travellers at Stonehenge. The winter solstice was marked by the Pagan feast of Yule when nothing much was happening on the land and so the community held a feast. The meanings of Yule, Christmas and New Year have all been forgotten. Yet, it is still the occasion when many friends and families are reunited. *Mammon* has taken-over from *God* as Britain's greatest festive deity. Chocolate Easter eggs are now being sold in the shops before Christmas. Frozen hot cross buns are now sold, in packs of ten, all-the-year-round.

At the end of every year it is usual to look back at Our achievements and look forward by making some resolutions about the year to come. During the past calendar year there have been many wars and a few peace agreements which divide, rather than integrate, Our Human Race. There are many different Natural and Man-made divisions in the way that We measure everything, yet We all have ten digits to count upon. Most people have forgotten the Pagan origins of the calendar they use. We must not return to Paganism; We must advance to Humanism. A *New Yer* would help Us to achieve this aim, throughout Our Planet.

The End of the Century

We have just passed the end of the most tempestuous century in history. More of Us lived and died in that century than all the others put together. It has been a century of scientific, technological and industrial advances. It has also been a century of ideological, political and social retreats. Our leaders, their advisers and opposition are still lurching from one major crisis to the next with absolutely no idea of where they are going. Most governments are still swinging from left to right and back again, with no rhyme nor reason, for they have yet to discover the middle way.

The United Nations was established by Humanists after WW2, to make sure there would never be a WW3 and to bring about peaceful change. However, there have been many wars since the UN charter was signed. Many idealists who staffed its first secretariat were forced out of office by J. Edgar Hoover and Joe McCarthy, who branded them as Communists. Hoover was a pervert, linked with the Mafia, who had a secret hold over the first UN Secretary-General: Trygve Lie, and several USA presidents. McCarthy conducted a witch-hunt against many prominent politicians, saying that they were spies, yet was unable to substantiate his claims. The UN is still dependent upon the direct political control of the USA, who starved it of funds by not paying their share of its immense costs. It was a mistake to locate the UNHQ in New York but it is hard to find a completely neutral territory with no political or religious influences. It was a great mistake to give the veto to so few countries and yet it was also a nonsense to give little states the same voting power as big ones. The UN has succeeded in preventing more religious conflict in Cyprus but it has failed to intervene in the break-up of the former Yugoslavia or the tribal genocide throughout Africa and there is still no solution to the conflict between Palestine and Israel, which was created by the UN. It has become a self-perpetuating bureaucracy without any real power. Its Earth Summits became politicians' junkets, which achieve very little. In 2005 AD an Earth Summit considered various organizational reforms. However, they failed to consider **full-time-job-sharing-as-the-norm**.

We cannot turn back Our clocks but We can review the last century. What may or may not have occurred had **One Worldwide System** been used? Would Archduke Franz Ferdinand have been assassinated in Sarajevo? Would Kaiser Wilhelm II still have yearned to expand his fatherland? Would there still have been a Great Depression, Recession or Slump? Would We still be on the gold standard and now have zero inflation? Would anyone have listened to Franco, Hitler, Mussolini or Hirohito? Would anyone have listened to Marx, Lenin, Stalin, Mao or Castro? Would anyone have developed guided missiles and nuclear weapons? Would We have resolved the fundamental causes of religious conflicts? Would We be able to travel and trade freely all around Our Own Planet? Would We have a United Nations Organization that lived up to its name?

The End of the Millennium

A Millennium is a good moment to reflect upon the past thousand years.
And then make some fundamental changes for the next thousand years.
At the first Millennium AD there was a sad feeling of impending doom.
Many Christians expected: The Apocalypse, or: The Day of Judgment.
Many others expected that the Messiah would be born or born again.
When it was over, many great cathedrals were built throughout Europe.
We have now passed the second Millennium AD and there was again a
sad feeling of impending doom and this was due to a glitch in Time.
Some $1T was spent at the Millennium on eradicating computer bugs.
Nevertheless, the fundamental cause of the problem remains unsolved.
What is needed is a global-digital-decimal chronology, calendar and clock.
Our World's stock markets peaked at the Millennium, then plummeted.
The third millennium AD started very badly as the forces of the Sun and
the Moon pulled at Planet Earth and caused many global catastrophes.
Pope John-Paul II sent out this warning: "The Antichrist is amongst Us."

The British government have lately encouraged what devout Christians,
only decades ago, would have denounced as a sin: The National Lottery.
Some of the funds raised from greed were put into a Millennium Fund.
A great deal of this money went up in smoke at the stroke of midnight.
Greenwich was to host a £1G Great Exhibition with the theme of: Time.
The largest dome in the whole World celebrated the Metric Millennium.
Opened at the stroke of midnight at the beginning of 2000 AD, it is 365
metres in diameter - like a calendar and has twelve masts - like a clock.
The master plan to incorporate twelve time zones was soon abandoned.
Instead there was a hotchpotch including a queer statue but no message.
The Dome lay unused and empty for seven years but, now renamed O₂,
it is one of London's busiest venues for exhibitions, concerts and sports.
The London Eye was to take one hour to turn and to have 60 capsules.
It was three months late, takes half-an-hour and there are 32 capsules.
The Millennium Bridge developed a wobble, so was not opened on Time.
Most of the MM projects were too late, over budget or soon went bust.

We have known about numbers for a millennium
yet
We are still using numerals.

We have known about zeros for a millennium
yet
We have learned nothing.

We have known about decimals for a millennium
yet
We have missed the point.

The End of Time

The measurement, management and government of Time and Space is the cement that holds a community, civilization or religion together. However, many different systems are pulling Our Human Race apart. All of the existing systems are faulty and must be replaced with one. This means that every one of Us will have to make fundamental changes. It is an urgent matter, so it must be implemented by the establishment.

Our Planet is now under threat from the expansion of Our Human Race. Our Species is now in the grip of the worst economic crisis ever known. The fundamental reason for this slump is too much credit everywhere. The fundamental reason for global warming is Our own inefficiency. The fundamental reason for so many global wars is religious fanaticism. The fundamental solution is simply: **full-time-job-sharing-as-the-norm**. Some of Us have already started to share Our jobs but this has never been considered for an entire community, let alone a global civilization. We can work together in this way to save Our Planet and Our Species. But if We do not abandon Our old systems, ideas, dogmas and gods, then the end of Time, Space and Life here on Earth is, indubitably, nigh.

The Persian: Zoroaster, taught about The Creation and The End of Time. His monotheistic ideas were adopted and adapted by the Western World. Many ancient Time-gods gradually merged into the one *God* of Time. Yet, the Egyptian Time-god *Heh,* alias the Babylonian Time-god *Anu,* alias the Persian Time-god *Zurvan,* alias the Parthian Time-god *Mithras,* alias the Greek Time-god *Kronus,* alias the Roman Time-god *Chronos,* alias *The Angel of Death*, alias *The Grim Reaper*, alias *Old Father Time* will be reaped by his own scythe when the sands of Time run out.

R.I.P.

**Old Father Time
passed away
in Greenwich
at midnight
19/20 March
2000 AD
or
000:000.000 WT**

The End of the Book

Writing this book took far more **ten**acity than I originally anticipated.
First, I needed to research the **3c's**: **c**hronologies, **c**alendars and **c**locks.
Next, I needed to research the **3d's**: **d**istances, **d**irections and **d**imensions.
Then, I needed to know more about many different academic subjects:
from the **3r's** taught at school to many ending in **y** taught at universit**y**.
I began by asking a simple question but now I want to change the World.
Ideas have done this before and they will do so again - so why not mine?
They are not really my ideas, of course, but those of many others, which
I reassembled into a more logical order and then discovered the holy grail
of chronolog**y**, calendrolog**y**, horolog**y**, metrolog**y** and even philosoph**y**.

I now have a feeling that this book was written through me; not by me.
The opinions expressed are my own but I have borrowed many of the
ideas and ideals from other thinkers and doers, who are mostly dead.
I have found that very few people disagree with my radical proposals,
once they have taken the time to think about them logically and freely.
Yet, We do not live in a free-thinking World and there are very few of Us
who can find the time to consider Time or the space to consider Space.
Many spend their lives without considering Life and how it has evolved.
Charles Darwin's great book: *The Origin of Species* changed Our World.
He challenged the idea that, six thousand years ago, *Yahweh/God/Allah*
created everything in six days then rested - yet many still believe this.
That is why We still use a seven-day week with, at least, one day of rest.

This book can be downloaded onto a desktop, laptop, tablet or phone.
It can be printed and bound as a single volume or in many millions.
Some say that paper is obsolete and the days of the book are numbered.
I say that chronologies, calendars, clocks, zones and rules are obsolete.
If all of the days of the year were numbered, starting with the day 000,
they would drop into tens and soon make the seven-day week obsolete.
If We shared work in a ten-day week We would all have a role to play.
This could be the final step in the reorganization of Our Human Race.

The best-selling novels of all Time are the *Harry Potter* series, so maybe I
should have written a novel along the lines of *The Emperor's New Clothes*.
There are still several standards for the sizes of clothes, shoes and hats.
We have all been duped by a bunch of confidence tricksters who have
persuaded Our leaders to impose their different measurement systems.
The fractional Imperial System was used throughout the British Empire.
The decimal International System was based upon the fractional second.
The global-digital-decimal **Worldwide System** includes Time and Space.
This is the only really comprehensive measurement system ever devised.
Megalomaniacs have tried to rule Our World with top-down governance.
We can rule Our World with a global-digital-decimal bottom-up system.
The Worldwide System could help Us to build One Wide World.

Appreciation

Firstly, I must thank my wife, my children, our relatives and friends who have put-up with my single-mindedness and absent-mindedness for years. Secondly, I must thank all those who have developed word processers and personal computers, which have been a tremendous help in writing this. Thirdly, Sir Tim Berners-Lee and all those who posted information on his Worldwide Web, which has proved invaluable in searching for hard facts. Lastly, all the organizations whose artifacts, books and records helped me to understand the past, present and future, including the following:

The United Nations Organization
The International Standards Organization
The International Bureau of Weights and Measures
The National Physical Laboratory
The Hydrographer to the Navy
The Ordnance Survey
The Royal Society
The Royal Institution
The Royal Observatory
The Royal Astronomical Society
The British Astronomical Association
The British Association for the Advancement of Science
The British Horological Institute
The Antiquarian Horological Society
The Clock and Watch Makers Guild
The British Library
The British Museum
The Science Museum
The Guildhall Museum
The Victoria and Albert Museum
The Ashmolian Museum, Oxford
The Museum of the History of Science, Oxford
The Museum of the History of Science, Cambridge
The Fitzwilliam Museum, Cambridge
The National Museum, Edinburgh
The Kelvingrove Museum, Glasgow
The Directorate of Time, Washington DC
The Smithsonian Institution, Washington DC
The Library of Congress, Washington DC
Musee du Louvre, Paris
Musee Carnavalet, Paris
Bibliotheque Nationale, Paris
Musee D'Horologerie, La Chaux de Fonds, Suisse
Die Staatliches Museum für Volkerkunde, Müchen
Die Deutches Museum, Müchen
Die Uhrenmuseum, Wien
Biblioteca de la Universidad, Valencia
Museo Nacional de Antropologia e Historia, Mexico
The *Te Pua Museum,* Wellington NZ
The Museum of Egyptian Civilization, Cairo
The Archealogical Museum, Athens
The Vatican Museum, Rome

Authorization

Eur. Ing. Michael Pinder BSc (hons). CEng. FIMechE.

The author is a member of Our Human Race and a citizen of Our World. Consequently, he was authorized, by every one of Us, to write this big book.

Born in Wimbledon in 1940 AD he was sent to a private preparatory school, then opted to attend a secondary school and passed into a technical school. He studied advanced maths, physics and chemistry at a technical college, then became a student-apprentice and has since studied at six universities: London, The City, Southampton, Solent, Portsmouth and Bournemouth. He worked in the petroleum, marine, aviation and aircushion industries. He has been a technologist, inventor, entrepreneur, manager and director. He has also worked as a senior lecturer, museum curator and navigator. He is still working as an author, historian, philosopher and futurologist. He has travelled to over ninety countries where he has given many lectures. He not only devised: **The Worldwide System** but was also the founder of:

The Worldwide Campaign for Temporal and Spatial Reform.

If you have read this book and would like to make any comments, or keep in touch with further developments, please contact:

wwctsr@hotmail.co.uk

Lightning Source UK Ltd.
Milton Keynes UK
UKOW02f0618030916

282075UK00002B/146/P